CCi
CORINTHIAN
COLLEGES, INC.

The Paralegal Professional

Custom Edition

Henry R. Cheeseman
Thomas F. Goldman

Taken from
The Paralegal Professional
by Henry R. Cheeseman, JD, LLM, and Thomas F. Goldman, JD

PEARSON
Custom
Publishing

PEARSON
Prentice
Hall

D1399734

PEARSON CUSTOM PUBLISHING
75 Arlington Street, Suite 300, Boston, MA 02116
A Pearson Education Company

DEDICATION

Dedicated to the memory of my parents,
Morris and Ethel Goldman,
who guided me through life,
encouraged me to pursue an education,
and delighted in my becoming a teacher.

—THOMAS GOLDMAN

In memory of
Henry B. and Florence Cheeseman

A grain of sand
has been
ten thousand mountains.

Who are we
to hold it?

—HENRY CHEESEMAN

CONTENTS *in Brief*

CONTENTS

CHAPTER 3
Careers in the Paralegal Profession   54

CHAPTER 4
Paralegal Workplace Skills   90

PART II
THE AMERICAN LEGAL SYSTEM   117

CHAPTER 5
The Constitution and Sources of American Law   118

CHAPTER 6
Judicial and Alternative Dispute Resolution   148

CHAPTER 13

Property and the Environment   360

CHAPTER 14

Agency and Employment Law   394

CHAPTER 15

Business Organizations   426

CHAPTER 21

The Internet, the Computer, and the Paralegal   616

APPENDIX A

How to Brief a Case   641

APPENDIX B

Professional Rules of Conduct   655

APPENDIX C

Effective Learning: How to Study   675

APPENDIX D

The Constitution of the United States of America   679

APPENDIX E

Internet Resources   689

APPENDIX F

Glossary of Spanish Equivalents for Important Legal Terms   691

When we were asked to write this text for Pearson Prentice Hall, we welcomed the opportunity to create a text that would present essential information for paralegal students in a memorable way, using a format that is easy to read and enjoyable to use. We worked with an award-winning design and production group who thought outside the box and understood the need to present information for traditional and returning students in a unique format. What we have produced is, we hope, the best combination of paralegal career and skill information and substantive law concepts.

For the student, we have tried to present the material in a visual format that has been referred to as a *textbook magazine*. Topics are broken down and presented in a variety of formats, including traditional text, brief sidebar items, and contemporary perspective and ethical issues boxes.

Because many legal assistant students today work in law offices, we have tried to provide a number of practical checklists, sample documents, tips, and resources for use in the working environment. Beginning students of paralegal studies are provided with a series of checklists to stimulate their thinking and help guide their educational pursuits. With these materials they can start the process of employment planning by preparing resumes and refining the art of interviewing.

We have incorporated exercises and material focused on skill development and knowledge acquisition as recommended in a report approved and adopted by the Board of Directors of the American Association for Paralegal Education that states

> . . . a person must not only possess a common core of legal knowledge, but also must have acquired vital critical thinking, organizational, communication, and interpersonal skills.

We have tried to address in one text the varying needs of instructors teaching Introduction to Law classes and Introduction to Legal Assistant Studies classes. In this book, planned variety in presentation gives students the best opportunity to excel. Each chapter contains an assortment of real-world cases.

The importance of ethics in business and in the American legal system has become clear in the post–Enron era. Our text emphasizes business and legal ethics, and numerous questions and review problems challenge readers to consider various forms of ethical responsibility borne by paralegals, lawyers, and businesspersons. In solving the exercises, using citations to actual cases and references to related websites, readers develop critical thinking skills while enhancing their research and communication skills.

No one today can be properly prepared to work in the modern legal environment without knowledge of technology. In this text we provide students with a foundation in the use of computers in the law office and in conducting legal research, and students get ample opportunity for technology practice by completing the *Working the Web* exercises.

In-class discussions are encouraged by the feature *Cases for Discussion*. These cases, variable in length, present students with opportunities to develop verbal communications skills and public speaking opportunities and to think critically about issues.

It is our wish that our commitment to these goals shines through in this labor of love. We hope you have as much pleasure using this text as we have had in creating it for you.

Henry Cheeseman
Thomas Goldman

PREFACE

Written by an award-winning author team, *The Paralegal Professional* combines a solid introduction to the paralegal profession with a thorough introduction to law. The two-books-in-one format prepares students with the substantive and procedural legal knowledge and real-world skills they need to succeed. The fully up-to-date and extensive coverage of technology in the law office, legal and business ethics, international perspectives, and diversity prepares students for today's work environment.

CAREER GUIDANCE + THE LAW

The Paralegal Professional provides a critical combination of topics designed to enhance the course teaching structure in any environment. Paralegal programs differ widely in the nature of the student body, the academic environment in which they are grounded, the business environment in which the school resides, and the talent available for driving the program. Each program emphasizes the areas of law and the skills students need to succeed in the world around them.

Paralegal students come from various backgrounds and have a variety of learning skills and styles and differing professional interests. *The Paralegal Professional* was created for every kind of learner, whether they already possess a 4-year degree or are working on their first 2-year degree; whether they are employed in law offices or returning to the workforce; whether they are enhancing their careers or exploring a career change.

Chapter Outlines, Chapter Objectives, and *Chapter Summaries* guide students through the logic of the course. *Boldface terms* in text, chapter-end *Legal Terminology* lists, and the text *Glossary* work hand-in-hand to introduce a new vocabulary and reinforce its proper use. Colorful *exhibits* guide visual learners through the material. These basic features are enhanced with:

- Full chapters on each area of *substantive law*
- Numerous examples of both *brief and full cases*
- Integrated coverage of *diversity*
- *Ethics* guidelines for action
- Legal applications for *technology tools* in the law office
- Sample *documents*

PROFESSIONALISM

The paralegal profession is one of the fastest growing occupations in the United States today. By understanding the role paralegals play, students gain a respect and perspective appropriate for their chosen field.

ETHICS: ANALYSIS AND DISCUSSION

- In each chapter, *Ethics Questions for Analysis and Discussion* provide readers the opportunity to strengthen ethical reasoning. In addition, on-going discussion of both *legal* and *business ethics* demonstrates the connection between the two worlds.

CONTEMPORARY PERSPECTIVE

- *Contemporary Perspective* boxes include *articles, interviews,* and *essays* about the critical issues that impact careers.

Meet THE COURTHOUSE TEAM

- Numerous *Meet the Courthouse Team* boxes describe the roles of personnel paralegals are likely to encounter.

CASE FOR BRIEFING

- Each chapter's *Case for Briefing* walks students through one of the most important tasks they will perform as professionals; the briefing task is reinforced with *legal reasoning, legal writing, legal research,* and *ethics research* questions.

CRITICAL LEGAL THINKING AND WRITING

- *Critical Legal Thinking and Writing* questions provide practice for practitioners in all areas of the law.

INTERNATIONAL PERSPECTIVE

- *International Perspective* features explore global legal and economic issues.

INFORMATION TECHNOLOGY

- *Information Technology* boxes highlight digital advancements and legislation relevant to legal personnel.

SIDEBAR

- *Sidebars* emphasize facts and issues relevant to the surrounding discussions.

PRACTICE

In addition to the *Cases for Briefing*, chapter-end features encourage review through such features as *Working the Web*, *Cases for Discussion*, and others.

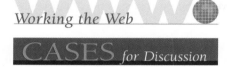

QUICK REFERENCE

Every feature of the book is designed to be a quick reference for professionals and a study review for new learners. Features include:

- Marginal references to *related websites*.

- *Checklists* for career guidance and for paralegal procedures.
- *Appendices* on the U.S. Constitution, English/Spanish Legal Terminology, Internet Resources, Case Briefing, and Professional Rules of Conduct
- Guide on *pronunciation of Latin terms*

SUPPLEMENTS

The Paralegal Professional is backed by digital and print *course supplements* that support distance learning and lifelong skills. These include a complete *Online Course* and a time-limited version of *LexBrief* legal briefing software and the *Lexiverse Legal Dictionary*.

The book can be packaged with *state-specific materials* at a reduced price:

California Courts
Texas Courts
Florida Courts
New York Courts
New York Civil Practice
Civil Litigation

- ***Instructor's Manual*** is free to instructors and available on CD-ROM complete with lecture notes and test questions available in files ready for word processing and printing. The CD also includes PowerPoint files for overheads and handouts.

- ***Prentice Hall Test Manager*** is available with more than 350 test questions to be selected at random or individually. Quizzes, tests, and exams can be created and printed when needed. All output can be scrambled into several different versions of the same test to discourage students from imitating one another's answers.

- *WebCT Course* for the book is fully classroom-tested and is available for Distance Learning students or as an online study enhancement to the classroom. It is a complete package with reference links, sample documents, and handouts as well as all the course management features offered as a part of any WebCT course.

- *Premium Companion Website* is available for use as a classroom study enhancement or in cartridges that easily translate into Blackboard or Course-Compass learning environments. The Prentice Hall Companion Website technology course support program includes course management, bulletin boards, and class organization features such as online syllabi.

- *FREE Companion Website* is a limited version of the Premium Companion Website. It gives students an online study guide and review with immediate hints and feedback for completing review questions.

- **LexBrief**™ software is a tool designed to help students develop the analytical, organizational, and summation skills needed to have a successful career in the legal industry. Once these skills are mastered, LexBrief™ continues its utility as an unparalleled management tool.

LexBrief™ allows users to easily and efficiently create and manage their case briefs. LexBrief™ comes with a customizable dictionary and the ability to cross-reference between briefs, as well as to organize briefs according to class.

- **The Lexiverse Dictionary** is a stand-alone, customizable legal dictionary for today's legal and paralegal students. This program allows students to augment the program's existing terminology and definitions database through the easy-to-use customization feature.

Students can now tailor their studies through the continual use of this program by building up a customized database of terms and definitions unique to the individual user. The program is ideal for use in class via a laptop, at home, or even in the office.

NOTE: Every effort has been made to provide accurate and current Internet information in this book. However, the Internet and information posted on it are constantly changing, so it is inevitable that some of the Internet addresses listed in this textbook will change.

ACKNOWLEDGMENTS

A special acknowledgement goes to Jodi McMaster at San Antonio College for hours of dedicated work and attention.

A round of applause to those whose insights contributed to the learning aspects of the book. Special thanks to:

Michael Fitch, for his guidance and encouragement early in the development of the project.

Kathryn Myers, for her generosity and kindness in allowing the use of her material on portfolios and for the guidance she unknowingly gave by her example of enthusiasm, dedication, and hard work in support of paralegal education.

The inspiring panelists and speakers at the AAfPE annual and regional meetings over the past five years, who provided insights, guidance, suggestions, and encouragement.

To the officers and members of the local and national professional associations, including NALA, NFPA, NALS, and ALA, for allowing the use of materials but mostly for their suggestions regarding topics and real life issues to be covered.

Paralegals Edie Hannah and Elma Quinn of Tom Goldman's law office, for tireless reviews, detail checking, encouragement and support, countless hours on the phone getting materials and networking with other professionals to obtain comments and input to make this textbook relevant to working paralegals as well as to students preparing for the profession.

The students in Tom Goldman's classes, for testing the text and WebCT materials in a class setting and graciously providing suggestions and feedback.

Finally, much gratitude to the reviewers, whose thorough responses helped to complete this project:

Chelsea Campbell, Lehman College CUNY
Anderson Castro, Florida International University
Stephanie Delaney, Highline Community College
Linda Hornsby, Florida International University
Nance Kriscenski, Manchester Community College
Linda Cabral Marrero, Mercy College
Leslie Miron, Mercy College
R. Eileen Mitchell, University of New Orleans
Anthony Piazza, Dan N. Myers University
Alex A. Yarborough, Virginia College at Birmingham

Henry R. Cheeseman is an award-winning author of several business law textbooks published by Prentice Hall publishing, including the definitive, highly-regarded *Business Law*. He has earned six degrees, including a Juris Doctor degree from the UCLA School of Law, an LLM degree from Boston University, and an MBA degree from the University of Chicago. Professor Cheeseman is a clinical professor of law and the Director of Legal Studies at the Marshall School of Business, University of Southern California. Students there voted him best teacher of the year, earning him the "Golden Apple" Teacher Award. Professor Cheeseman recognizes the importance of the paralegal to the practice of law, and has joined with Thomas Goldman to write this new and exciting introduction to paralegal studies.

Thomas F. Goldman is a Professor of Law and Management, Director of the Center for Legal Studies, and Director of the Paralegal Studies Program at Bucks County Community College in Pennsylvania. An accounting and economics graduate of Boston University and of Temple University School of Law, Professor Goldman now has an active international law, technology law, and litigation practice. He has worked extensively with paralegals and received the award of the Legal Support Staff Guild. He was elected the Legal Secretaries Association Boss of the Year for his contribution to cooperative education by encouraging the use of paralegals and legal assistants in law offices. He also received the Bucks County Community College Alumni Association Professional Achievement Award. He has been an educational consultant on technology to major corporations and a frequent speaker and lecturer on educational, legal, and technology issues.

The
Paralegal
Profession

CHAPTER 1
The Professional Paralegal

CHAPTER 2
Ethics, Regulation, and
Professional Responsibility

CHAPTER 3
Careers in the Paralegal Profession

CHAPTER 4
Paralegal Workplace Skills

The paralegal, or legal assistant, profession has seen explosive growth since the late 1960s. As we will discuss in Part I, opportunities and career choices for the paralegal have never been better. Possible employers are just as diverse as the duties paralegals are asked to perform. Federal, state, and local governments, including regulatory bodies, employ many paralegals.

Today's paralegals need specialized skills, and formal programs of study and continuing education programs have developed to help individuals obtain needed skills. As with other professions, ethical rules and regulations have evolved to help paralegals avoid conflicts and possible malpractice. These topics will be discussed in Part I.

CHAPTER 1

CHAPTER OBJECTIVES

After studying this chapter, you should be able to

1. Define the terms *parale-gal* and *legal assistant*.

2. Explain what paralegals do and their role in the legal profession.

3. Explore job opportunities for the paralegal.

4. Explain the need for education and training, to be recognized as a member of the paralegal profession.

5. Describe the different educational paths avail-able to become a paralegal.

6. Outline the history of the paralegal profession.

7. Understand the American Bar Association stan-dards for approval of legal assistant education programs.

8. Understand the American Association for Paralegal Education core compe-tencies for paralegals/ legal assistants.

9. Articulate your current level of skills and knowl-edge.

10. Define your personal goals.

The Professional Paralegal

The great can protect themselves, but the poor and humble require the arm and shield of the law.

ANDREW JACKSON

Introduction

The paralegal or legal assistant profession has seen an explosive growth since the late-1960s. Like other professions, this one has evolved over time to meet a need. Prior to the late 1960s, many of the functions of paralegals today were performed by those with titles such as legal secretary, lay assistant, and legal clerk or law clerk (the latter of which was usually reserved for the recent graduate of law school who had not yet passed the bar exam).

WHAT IS A PARALEGAL?

A great deal of confusion has arisen as to what the professional in this field should be called or what the professionals should call themselves. The most popular terms, *paralegal* and *legal assistant*, are used interchangeably in most of the United States. In particular, these are the terms used interchangeably by the American Bar Association (ABA), the National Federation of Paralegal Associations (NFPA), and the National Association of Legal Assistants (NALA). The confusion stems in part from the shift from the title of *secretary* to the title *administrative assistant* and, in some offices and educational institutions, *law office assistant*.

The exact definition of legal assistant has been the subject of discussions by national organizations including the ABA, NFPA, and NALA, as well as many state legislatures, supreme courts, and bar associations.

ABA definition of *paralegal* online: www.abanet.org/legal services/legalassistants/def 98.html

NFPA definition of *paralegal* online: www.paralegals.org/ development/NFPA_def.htm

The American Bar Association's 1997 version of the definition, which also has been adopted by the National Association of Legal Assistants, is:

A legal assistant or paralegal is a person, qualified by education, training, or work experience who is employed or retained by a lawyer, law office, corporation, governmental agency or other entity and who performs specifically delegated substantive legal work for which a lawyer is responsible.

The National Federation of Paralegal Associations defines a paralegal as follows:

A paralegal/legal assistant is a person qualified through education, training or work experience to perform substantive legal work that requires knowledge of legal concepts as customarily, but not exclusively performed by a lawyer. This person may be retained or employed by a lawyer, law office, governmental agency or other entity or may be authorized by administrative, statutory or court authority to perform this work.

WHAT DO PARALEGALS DO?

The primary function of paralegals is to assist attorneys in preparing for hearings, trials, meetings, and closings. In many cases paralegals do the preparatory work, helping to draft documents, assisting in the preparation of other documents and forms, coordinating the activities and functions required in some cases, and in many offices maintaining the financial records of the firm.

People tend to think of paralegals as working in a private law office directly under the supervision of attorneys. Actually, employers of the paralegal are just as diverse as the duties they are asked to perform. Many paralegals are employed by the federal government, as well as state and local governments including regulatory bodies. The paralegal's activities might include analyzing legal material for internal use and collecting and analyzing data, as well as preparing information and explanatory material, for use by the general public.

More and more paralegals are coming to the profession from other professions, such as nursing, bringing with them a specialized body of knowledge that they combine with the legal skills they learned in a paralegal program. With this expertise they frequently are hired to analyze case materials for trial attorneys, both plaintiff and defense, and also are employed as case analysts and as claims representatives for health insurance companies. Their knowledge of medicine, combined with their legal knowledge, gives them a unique ability to analyze specialized material.

Other specialties are expected to take the same career path. Those with engineering and other bachelor of science degrees also bring a special point of view to the law. A paralegal with a forensic science background, for example, may well be the ideal paralegal to work with criminal defense attorneys and prosecutors.

Prior to the recognition of a separate paralegal profession, individuals had typically acquired specialized knowledge of a narrow legal field through on-the-job training. Someone working with a lawyer, usually a secretary, would learn the daily routine tasks and become knowledgeable about that specific area of law. Many of these individuals became the resource person for information, such as the documentation requirements for real estate settlements, the preparation and filing of estate and trust accountings, and the procedures for preparing and filing cases and appeals. These were the first paralegals. Today, many of the skills and procedures formerly acquired over an extended time on the job are taught at institutions specializing in the education of paralegals or legal assistants, offering a certificate program, a two-year associate degree program, or a four-year bachelor's degree program.

In 1968 the American Bar Association formed a committee to investigate the use of lay assistants in the legal office. The result was the American Bar Association's forming the Standing Committee on Legal Assistants. The ABA gave this committee jurisdiction over training and standards for the education of legal assistants. Within this jurisdiction the Standing Committee on Legal Assistants monitors trends in the field and recommends to the House of Delegates—the policymaking body of the American Bar Association—training programs that meet its standards for quality education.

ABA Standing Committee on Legal Assistants: www.abanet.org/legalservices/legalassistants/home.html

NALA Model Standards & Guidelines: www.nala.org/stand.htm

Excerpt from the National Association of Legal Assistants Model Standards and Guidelines

Proper utilization of the services of legal assistants affects the efficient delivery of legal services. Legal assistants and the legal profession should be assured that some measures exist for identifying legal assistants and their role in assisting attorneys in the delivery of legal services. Therefore, the National Association of Legal Assistants, Inc., hereby adopts these Model Standards and Guidelines as an educational document for the benefit of legal assistants and the legal profession.

Standards. A legal assistant should meet certain minimum qualifications. The following standards may be used to determine an individual's qualifications as a legal assistant:

1. Successful completion of the Certified Legal Assistant (CLA) certifying examination of the National Association of Legal Assistants;

2. Graduation from an ABA approved program of study for legal assistants;

3. Graduation from a course of study for legal assistants which is institutionally accredited but not ABA approved, and which requires not less than the equivalent of 60 semester hours of classroom study;

4. Graduation from a course of study for legal assistants, other than those set forth in (2) and (3) above, plus not less than six months of in-house training as a legal assistant;

5. A baccalaureate degree in any field, plus not less than six months in-house training as a legal assistant;

6. A minimum of three years of law-related experience under the supervision of an attorney, including at least six months of in-house training as a legal assistant; or

7. Two years of in-house training as a legal assistant.

For purposes of these Standards, "in-house training as a legal assistant" means attorney education of the employee concerning legal assistant duties and these Guidelines. In addition to review and analysis of assignments, the legal assistant should receive a reasonable amount of instruction directly related to the duties and obligations of the legal assistant.

"Give Us Respect" Say Paralegals

Fulton County Daily Report   April 16, 2001

WANTED: Bright, articulate individual with college degree and computer skills willing to work hard in a dead-end job. About half your peers feel underpaid, but in general they find the work interesting and appreciate the flexibility this career offers.

Interested?

Then, become a paralegal, legal secretary, or legal assistant. Because that's essentially how they describe their jobs in the *Daily Report*'s survey of the salary and working conditions of legal support staff. The *Daily Report* collected data from 255 respondents at law firms, businesses, and corporations of all types and sizes around the state, including Dye, Tucker, Everitt, Long & Brewton in Augusta; Goodman McGuffey Aust & Lindsey; King & Spalding; Mead Corporation; Scientific–Atlanta; Sutherland Asbill & Brennan; Tisinger Tisinger Vance & Greer in Carrollton; Troutman Sanders; and United Parcel Service.

Those surveyed are almost evenly divided about whether they are fairly compensated: 50 percent say yes, 47 percent say no; 3 percent didn't answer. Among the paralegals surveyed, the highest percentage in one salary category earns $45,001 to $55,000; for legal assistants and legal secretaries, it's $35,001 to $45,000.

In addition to answering objective, multiple-choice questions about compensation, the respondents were invited to write detailed comments about their careers, and many did. Though some wrote glowingly about their jobs and excellent relationships with co-workers and lawyers, others worried about dwindling benefits, poor chances for advancement, as well as salaries that seem less and less adequate in light of increased workloads and escalating associate pay.

One paralegal who requested anonymity sums it up this way: "I didn't realize I would hit the proverbial ceiling so quickly," she says. "I'm in my early 30s, have been with my current employer for several years, and have already exhausted, via promotions, all advancement opportunities for paralegals with my employer."

The other thing she's exhausted is her employer's pay scale. Paralegals are a part of cash flow, she says. At firms, many do lawyer-level work, freeing up attorneys for more complex and better-paying tasks. In-house, paralegal work can reduce bills the company pays to outside counsel.

"You can't have paralegals doing attorney-level work but treat them like staff when it comes to compensation," she says. "If your clients are being billed for your services, but you're not seeing any of that at bonus time and the attorneys are, it's an annual slap in the face."

Disparities in Pay

A major factor fueling dissatisfaction with pay, according to survey responses, comes when legal support staff compares raises—usually 4 percent to 6 percent—with the double-digit increases given to greenhorn associates already earning $100,000 or more.

Of course, management and support staff see pay issues differently. That's illustrated by comments from Troutman Sanders' managing partner and some of the firm's staffers. Of the 20 Troutman Sanders support staff members who responded to the survey, 16 complained about compensation.

One Troutman legal secretary writes about lawyer–staff pay disparity through the lens of Troutman's merger with Mays & Valentine. When the merger was announced, management told staffers that it meant "partners will now experience double-digit increases in their compensation," the secretary wrote. "This was particularly galling since the staff raises have been held at 4 percent for four years, and 4 percent of $35,000 to $45,000 doesn't come close to 10 percent of $300,000."

Robert W. Webb Jr., the firm's managing partner, says he finds those survey responses upsetting. "That's just not true," he says, explaining that average merit increases have run [approximately 4] percent, and that raises have never been held at 4 percent.

In addition to merit increases, the firm spent about $350,000 on market-based pay raises for staff just this year, he says. Over the past three years, the total is $750,000. Partner pay increases were in the double digits before the Mays & Valentine merger, he says. According to the *Daily Report Dozen*, a ranking of the city's wealthiest firms, pay increases have been at 10 percent or above since 1997.

Janet L. Conley, jconley@amlaw.com

Advancement Opportunities

High associate salaries ironically may be helping paralegals get the advancement opportunities they want, says Chris Cole, director of professional staffing at Bellon & Associates, a legal recruiting firm. "As a result of the salary increases for associates, a lot of the firms have stopped hiring first-year associates," he says. "Paralegals have taken over some of those tasks."

Firms also offer supervisory positions, but there's a rub. According to Cole, supervisory paralegals usually have the same billable requirements as those without the extra responsibilities. In addition, paralegals and legal assistants are doing more of their own secretarial work—a situation shared by lawyers.

Shortage of Secretaries

Part of the shift in who handles secretarial work can be attributed to a shortage of legal secretaries. Anne Rubin, owner of the placement firm Atlanta Secretaries, says that although there's a big demand for intelligent, competent legal secretaries, there are fewer and fewer of them. Women—who hold most legal secretary jobs—now go to law school or pursue other goals, she says.

According to Rubin, the dwindling supply has pushed up pay, and top legal secretaries can make as much as $53,000. To attract good legal secretaries, she says, firms must offer more flexible working hours, especially to women with long suburban commutes and children in daycare centers that charge by the minute after 6 p.m.

Daycare Bonus at A&B

Cathy A. Benton, Alston & Bird's director of human resources, says "Alston and Bird is doing something incredible." The firm plans to open a daycare center this fall. It will be housed a few blocks from A&B's offices, and its services will be affordable and available to lawyers and support staff on an equal basis, she says.

Alston & Bird was motivated in part by Georgia's new, higher tax credits for employer-sponsored childcare, but, says Benton, "We think it is important in balancing work and family and think it is the right thing to do in today's market, to be able to recruit people and keep people."

The Benefits Factor

Benefits of all types were an important factor in job satisfaction—or dissatisfaction—according to the *Daily Report*'s survey results. Among those surveyed, 93 percent receive some form of employer-subsidized health coverage; 87 percent get life insurance; and 78 percent are covered by disability insurance. Retirement benefits also were offered widely: 89 percent had a 401(k) or other retirement plan, and 31 percent were offered a pension plan. One Georgia-Pacific Co. legal assistant praised the company's benefits: reimbursement for MARTA [rapid transportation] and membership in professional organizations, flex time, on-site daycare and access to a chiropractor.

Other support staff at other employers weren't as happy. "We have been losing benefits in the last few years," wrote one legal secretary at a firm in the 201- to 400-lawyer range. When her firm changed insurance companies recently, she says, coverage costs went up and prescription co-pays rose from $5 to $15. The firm also abolished a pension plan to which it had contributed at 4 percent of employees' salaries.

Four out of five Sutherland Asbill respondents complained about insurance benefits. One wrote next to the survey question about life insurance, "Just enough for a cheap funeral! Maybe a pine box!"

Melissa R. Todd, Sutherland Asbill's director of human resources, says secretaries get a $25,000 life insurance policy from the firm, plus a $25,000 policy for accidental death and dismemberment. Paralegals get $50,000 for each. Support staff also can purchase supplemental insurance. "Certainly that would be enough for a funeral," she says. But she adds that the firm may consider offering equal benefits to all staffers. In addition, the firm pays 90 percent of employee health insurance costs and buys monthly MARTA cards, she says.

Taking on More Work

As firms cut costs—to pay higher associate salaries, some respondents speculated—support staff are required to take on more work. Wrote one Troutman Sanders legal secretary, "The day is coming in the near future when I am going to have to take on three attorneys (some already have four people!). At that time, I will no longer have the time to do anything other than churn out a work product that I normally would never consider approving."

Webb, the firm's managing partner, says that any situations where work quality is affected by overload will be corrected. He also points out that it's not unusual among Atlanta firms for secretaries to serve three timekeepers. Troutman's firmwide ratio of secretaries to timekeepers is 2.2 to 1; the secretaries-to-lawyers ratio is 1.9 to 1, and fewer than 10 secretaries serve four lawyers, he says.

Two paralegals, each from a firm of 15 or fewer lawyers, also lament increasing workloads. "My firm doesn't replace employees when they leave—I am doing the job of three people at $14 an hour," wrote one, who also said she worked more than 40 hours a week at a firm that refused to pay overtime or bonuses.

The other paralegal wrote of being extremely disillusioned by the lack of support her firm gives its staff. "We have lost fantastic paralegals over the years due to pay and professionalism issues," she wrote. "At times, they have been replaced by individuals with no four-year degree and no formal paralegal education, causing a decline in morale of the remaining professional paralegals, who feel diminished as a class." (The jobs were necessarily "dumbed down" to accommodate the low skill level of new recruits.) "Rather than retain their experienced, professional paralegals, the firm simply finds new candidates they can pay cheaply regardless of the difference in skill-value to the practice."

Keys to Contentment

Sheri H. Kornblum, director of paralegal recruitment at The Partners Group, says firms must change to keep paralegals happy. They'll have to treat paralegals more like professionals and not micromanage them or tie them to time-clocks. But she says salaries already are pretty good, especially with overtime that's often in the $10,000 to $15,000 range. The highest base salary at which she's placed a paralegal is $62,000, she says, adding, "There are attorneys in this city who are making only $45,000." The most highly compensated paralegal in the *Daily Report*'s survey reported earning $75,000 to $85,000 and had 11 years to 15 years of experience.

Salary caps, however, may compress pay as legal support staff gain experience, Kornblum says. According to the *Daily Report* survey, about 20 percent of respondents said their employers had salary caps. But there's more to it than money, according to Kornblum. She says paralegals leave big firms for small ones because they're bored. Though smaller firms might pay less, she says, paralegals like the work because they may get to attend depositions, or sit second-chair to manage papers during a trial.

Kornblum's observation runs parallel to the survey finding that one of support staffers' biggest complaints is about poor chances for advancement. Some of the survey respondents who exhibited the most job satisfaction attributed their happiness to high levels of autonomy and responsibility.

"In my department, my job as a bankruptcy paralegal offers an opportunity for court appearances handled exclusively by paralegals," wrote one paralegal at an Atlanta firm. "Most other specialties are not as accommodating. . . . Although we deal with high-volume cases, we are treated very professionally and are given lots of freedom, and with that comes greater responsibility."

OPPORTUNITIES

Paralegals held about 188,000 jobs in 2000, according to the U. S. Department of Labor, Bureau of Labor Statistics, *Occupational Outlook Handbook.* In 2000 full-time paralegals had median annual earnings of $35,360. Salaries in the industries employing the largest numbers of paralegals in 2000 were:

- Federal government, $48,560
- Local government, $34,120
- Legal services, $34,230
- State government, $32,680

Department of Labor,
Occupational Outlook Handbook:
www.bls.gov/oco/ocos114.htm

In a 1998 survey by the American Bar Association,

Almost two-thirds of the lawyers who responded, 65.5 percent, employ legal assistants at their firms; 60.2 percent of respondents actively work with paralegals.

> The general responsibilities most often assigned to paralegals are maintaining client files, drafting correspondence, and performing factual research.
>
> Legal assistants are more likely to be employed by large firms than small firms.
>
> Lawyers in smaller firms delegate a wider array of responsibilities to legal assistants than lawyers in bigger firms do.
>
> Lawyers with business/corporate, probate/estate planning, and litigation practices make more extensive use of paralegals than do lawyers in other practice areas.

The ABA survey demonstrates that clients who choose to work with larger firms are much more likely to have a portion of their work completed by paralegals than those who choose a lawyer from a small firm. Almost all (99 percent) of the lawyers practicing in firms with more than 100 lawyers reported that their firms use legal assistants. By contrast, only 34.8 percent of those working at firms of three or fewer lawyers employ paralegals. Of the lawyers who indicated that their firms do not employ paralegals, 56.8 percent reported that their firm's size would not support legal assistants and 44.1 percent said that their secretaries assume tasks that would be assigned to legal assistants.

Exhibit 1.1 compares 2001 and 2002 salaries for paralegals, from a survey by The Affiliates, broken down by experience and size of law firm.

THE FUTURE

Clients who are unwilling or unable to pay what they see as inflated fees for lawyers may determine the future of the paralegal profession. The future also could be dictated by the courts, which, looking at the fairness of charging higher rates for attorneys' tasks that could properly be delegated to a paralegal, would result in a lower charge to the client. Two of the future concerns involving paralegals and billings are:

1. The cases in which secretarial or clerical tasks are charged to the client as paralegal fees. These tasks are considered overhead (part of the cost of running the office) and should be performed at no additional cost to the client. This is one of the areas in which the definition of paralegal has come into play in the courts. Courts are allowing charges for paralegal fees but not for secretarial fees.
2. The fairness of charging higher rates for attorneys' performing tasks that could properly be delegated to a paralegal, thereby resulting in a lower charge to the client.

ABA 1998 Survey: www.abanet. org/media/sept98/leg-asst.html

Meet THE COURTHOUSE TEAM

Introduction to the Team

As a paralegal, you will work with a number of different individuals outside of the law office. Many of these people are part of the local, state, and federal court system. Others, though located within the courthouse, are not directly part of the court system but, because of the nature of governmental administration and record keeping, might be related to your job as a paralegal. This text will introduce some of these people to you.

Most courthouses contain offices and personnel involved in administration of the legal process. Generally, the three main areas of law with separate administrative offices are: civil matters; criminal cases; and wills, probate and orphans court.

In addition, many courthouses house government offices such as the local tax authorities, recorder of deeds, central records office, district attorney/prosecutor, and public defender.

exhibit 1.1   *Survey of paralegal salaries.*

	2001	2002	% Change
SENIOR/SUPERVISING PARALEGAL (7+ years' exp.)			
Large law firm	$49,000 – $66,250	$49,000 – $65,250	–0.9%
Midsized law firm	$46,250 – $59,000	$45,750 – $57,250	–2.1%
Small/midsized law firm	$42,500 – $53,500	$40,750 – $52,500	–2.9%
Small law firm	$37,250 – $46,250	$36,500 – $46,750	–0.3%
MIDLEVEL PARALEGAL (4–6 years' exp.)			
Large law firm	$42,250 – $54,250	$42,000 – $54,250	–0.3%
Midsized law firm	$39,000 – $51,750	$39,000 – $49,750	–2.2%
Small/midsized law firm	$37,750 – $47,750	$37,000 – $46,750	–2.0%
Small law firm	$32,500 – $40,250	$33,250 – $41,750	3.1%
JUNIOR PARALEGAL (2–3 years' exp.)			
Large law firm	$33,000 – $41,000	$33,250 – $41,000	0.3%
Midsized law firm	$32,500 – $39,750	$31,750 – $39,000	–2.1%
Small/midsized law firm	$31,250 – $38,500	$30,500 – $37,750	–2.2%
Small law firm	$28,000 – $35,250	$27,250 – $35,000	–1.6%
CASE CLERK (0–2 years' exp.)			
Large law firm	$24,250 – $29,750	$25,750 – $30,500	4.2%
Midsized law firm	$24,250 – $29,250	$25,000 – $29,500	1.9%
Small/midsized law firm	$24,000 – $28,000	$24,250 – $28,250	1.0%
Small law firm	$22,000 – $26,250	$22,500 – $26,250	1.0%
LAW FIRM DEFINITIONS			
Large law firm	75+ attorneys		
Midsized law firm	35–75 attorneys		
Small/midsized law firm	10–35 attorneys		
Small law firm	up to 10 attorneys		

For instance, summarizing depositions traditionally has been a task delegated to paralegals. Assume that the paralegal takes two hours to complete the task and the paralegal's time is billed to the client at $75 per hour (don't get excited—that doesn't necessarily have any bearing on what you may be paid); the client would be charged $150. For a lawyer to do the same work, if billed out at $175 per hour, the client would be charged $350. Unless there is good reason for the lawyer to do the work, the decision not to delegate the work to a paralegal seems unfair to the client. A number of court decisions are beginning to draw upon these fundamental questions of the fairness and propriety of attorney billings for their services. As other federal and state courts weigh in on this line of decisions, law firms may have to hire more paralegals.

The U. S. Department of Labor has included the paralegal profession among the fastest growing occupations in the economy through the year 2010. This encompasses additional growth of the occupation as well as the need for individuals to replace existing employees. The Labor Department estimates might be increased further by the de facto requirement found in the court opinions that more paralegals be used to perform services instead of attorneys' performing the services. Exhibits 1.2 and 1.3 give projected job openings and replacement needs for various occupational groups.

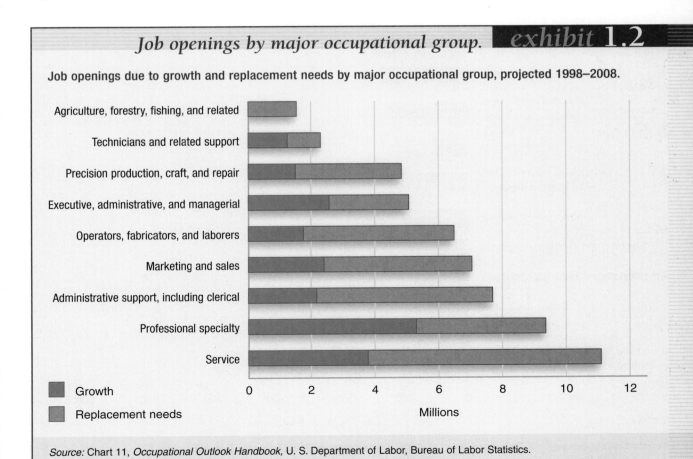

Job openings by major occupational group.   *exhibit* **1.2**

Job openings due to growth and replacement needs by major occupational group, projected 1998–2008.

Source: Chart 11, *Occupational Outlook Handbook,* U. S. Department of Labor, Bureau of Labor Statistics.

exhibit **1.3**   *Occupations with the largest numerical growth.*

Occupations with fast growth and high pay that have the largest numerical growth, projected 1998–2008.

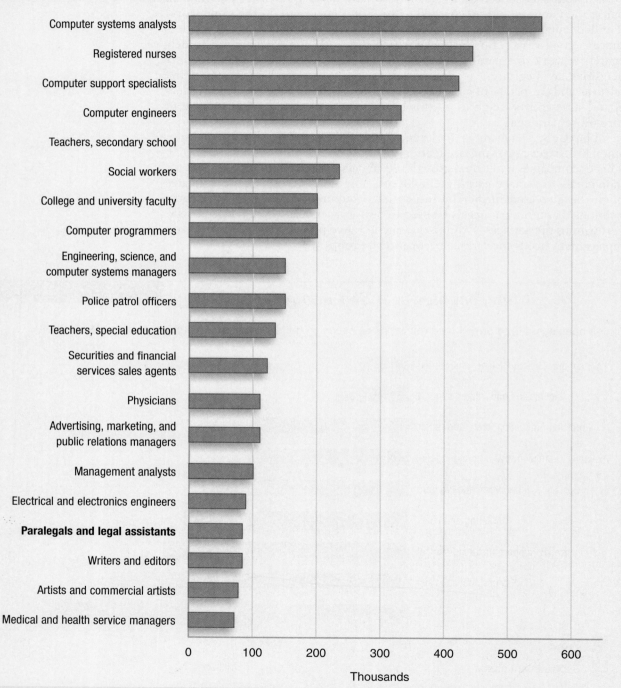

Source: Chart 8, *Occupational Outlook Handbook,* U. S. Department of Labor, Bureau of Labor Statistics.

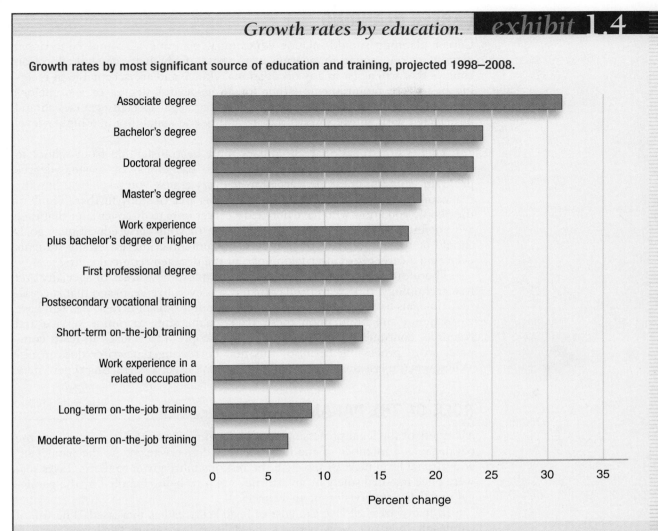

Growth rates by education.   *exhibit* 1.4

Growth rates by most significant source of education and training, projected 1998–2008.

According to the Department of Labor, "The changing pattern of occupational employment also means changes in educational requirements. Occupations requiring an associate degree or higher education, which account for 25 percent of all jobs in 1998, will account for 40 percent of job growth from 1998 to 2008." Exhibit 1.4 shows projected growth rates by amount of education and training.

The best trained, most skilled individual clearly will be the one to get the job. The challenge in obtaining your first job is demonstrating that you are the best person for the job. Consider the prospective employer comparing the resumes of a number of paralegal job applicants. One paralegal has a high school diploma and a paralegal certificate. Another applicant has an associate degree or even a bachelor's degree in paralegal studies. Which would you hire?

Monthly Labor Review,
Nov. 1999, Charles Bowman:
www.bls.gov/opub/mlr/1999/
11/art1exc.htm

CAREER PLANNING

Career planning should include educational planning. A sound educational plan builds on a sound foundation, at the base of which are general education courses that will assist in any occupational choice and are acceptable in meeting basic core requirements either for an associate's degree or a bachelor's degree. Occupation-related courses such as paralegal specialty courses should be selected with an eye toward transferability and suitability in a higher-level educational pursuit.

This is not to say that all courses must be transferable from school to school or from associate-degree program to bachelor's- or master's-degree program. Something can be learned from every course you take, including the realization that you do not wish to pursue this area of study further. Think of the people you know who have pursued a career only to discover later that they are not interested in this line of work. One of your early educational goals should be to explore areas of your actual or potential interest. Many students even find a career goal after taking one of the dreaded required courses.

Therefore, you should be prepared to explore new areas of specialty and new technology. It is clearer today than it was even five years ago that successful paralegals have a good foundation in computer skills. Further, you will have to maintain and build upon these skills as the shift to online service and resources continues to grow. Think of the people who refused to learn computer word processing because "this new correcting typewriter does it all." When was the last time you even saw, let alone used, a correcting typewriter?

ROLE OF THE PARALEGAL

Members of the legal profession and the legal community increasingly see the paralegal as a member of the legal services delivery team. As the paralegals' educational level increases, so will the responsibility given to them. Tasks that were once handled solely by an attorney are now being handled by the paralegal under the supervision of an attorney.

In many areas of law, the cost of legal services has increased. The use of paralegals in many cases permits the delivery of quality legal services at a reduced cost to the client. As concern for access to legal services increases, and discussions about mandatory pro bono service by lawyers expand, so does the possibility of involving paralegals in serving low- and moderate-income populations of the United States.

NATIONAL ASSOCIATIONS OF PARALEGALS

In addition to numerous local and state paralegal and legal assistant organizations, a number of national paralegal/legal assistant organizations support the profession. Four of these are described briefly below.

National Association of Legal Assistants

National Association of Legal Assistants: www.nala.org

National Association of Legal Assistants (NALA) is a leading professional association for legal assistants, providing continuing education and professional certification programs for paralegals. Incorporated in 1975, NALA has a membership of more than 18,000 paralegals, through individual members and through its 90 state- and local-affiliated associations.

National Federation of Paralegal Associations

National Federation of Paralegal Associations (NFPA) is a professional organization of state and local paralegal associations founded in 1974 by eight paralegal associations in response to the growing interest in development of the paralegal profession. NFPA has member associations representing more than 17,000 North American paralegals.

National Federation of Paralegal Associations: www.paralegals.org

Association of Legal Administrators

The Association of Legal Administrators (ALA) was founded in 1971 to provide support to professionals involved in the management of law firms, corporate legal departments, and government legal agencies.

Association of Legal Administrators: www.alanet.org

Legal Assistant Management Association

Legal Assistant Management Association (LAMA) is a North American management association founded in 1984. It has more than 400 members in 16 metropolitan chapters in the United States and Canada. Its members are managers of legal assistants in law firms, corporate law departments, and governmental, judicial, and legal agencies. LAMA members manage more than 5,000 legal assistants.

Legal Assistant Management Association: www.lamanet.org

QUALIFICATIONS OF A PARALEGAL

What are the qualifications that permit one to call oneself a paralegal or a legal assistant, and to be billed as a paralegal? The answer is not easy to come by. Just as the practice of law falls to the individual states for regulation, so does regulation of the paralegal profession. At present there is a lack of uniformity in regulation either by statute or by court rules. Without a state law or a court rule, perhaps the most consistent and universal recognition of minimum qualifications are those established by the educational guidelines of the American Bar Association's Standing Committee on Legal Assistants and the American Association for Paralegal Education (AAfPE), a national educational association of legal educators. The minimum educational requirements for certification of the educational institutions' program of study have become the de facto standard of the minimum qualifications to call oneself a paralegal or legal assistant.

While other state legislatures and courts wrestle with the minimum standards, California has addressed the requirements in a 2000 amendment to the Business and Professional Code that requires a paralegal to possess at least one of the following:

Emotional Labor

In an article in the *Annals of the American Academy of Political and Social Science*, Jennifer Pierce argues that paralegals function to support and maintain the emotional stability of the lawyers for whom they work, through deferential treatment and care-taking. She contends that the relationship between paralegal and attorney in large firms is a highly personal one, and this contention is supported by interviews with attorneys, who value personality traits over work performance in the hiring of legal assistants.

Source: "Emotional Labor Among Paralegals," *Annals of the Amer. Academy of Political and Social Science,* January 1999.

SIDEBAR

ABA Educational Guidelines:
www.abanet.org/legalservices/
legalassistants/resource.html

1. A certificate of completion of a paralegal program approved by the American Bar Association.

2. A certificate of completion of a paralegal program at an institution that requires a minimum of 24 semester, or equivalent, units in law-related courses, accredited by a national or regional accreditation organization or approved by the Bureau for Private Postsecondary and Vocational Education.

3. A baccalaureate or advanced degree and minimum of one year of law-related experience under an attorney who is an active member of the State Bar of California.

4. A high school diploma or general equivalency diploma and a minimum of three years' law-related experience under the supervision of a California attorney, with this training being completed before December 31, 2003.

Other states might look to the California statute in deciding the question of who is qualified by education, training, or work experience.

AAfPE: www.aafpe.org

PARALEGAL EDUCATION IN THE UNITED STATES

An estimated 800+ paralegal education programs are available in the United States. Some of these programs have obtained ABA approval of their paralegal education program. More than half of the institutions offering paralegal education programs are members of the American Association for Paralegal Education, which, as a condition of institutional membership, requires substantial compliance with the ABA guidelines for approval of a paralegal program.

The American Bar Association and the American Association for Paralegal Education are voluntary programs. Lack of approval of a program does not necessarily mean that the school or the program does not provide a good quality education but, rather, that it has chosen not to undergo the cost or process for approval by the ABA or for membership in the AAfPE.

The Navajo County Courthouse in Holbrook, Arizona.

American Bar Association Paralegal Education Standards

The American Bar Association is the largest professional legal organization in the United States. The ABA has indicated that one of its highest priorities is to increase access to legal services.

The American Bar Association Standing Committee on Legal Assistants was formed more than 25 years ago to "work within the ABA and with other groups to help make quality legal services more accessible and affordable, primarily by fostering the increasingly effective integration of legal assistants—or paralegals—into the legal services delivery team." The Committee has jurisdiction within the ABA over matters relating to the education, train-

Formal Mission Statement of the American Bar Association

Goal I To promote improvements in the American system of justice.

Goal II To promote meaningful access to legal representation and the American system of justice for all persons regardless of their economic or social condition.

Goal III To provide ongoing leadership in improving the law to serve the changing needs of society.

Goal IV To increase public understanding of and respect for the law, the legal process, and the role of the legal profession.

Goal V To achieve the highest standards of professionalism, competence, and ethical conduct.

Goal VI To serve as the national representative of the legal profession.

Goal VII To provide benefits, programs, and services that promote professional growth and enhance the quality of life of the members.

Goal VIII To advance the rule of law in the world.

Goal IX To promote full and equal participation in the legal profession by minorities, women, and persons with disabilities.

Goal X To preserve and enhance the ideals of the legal profession as a common calling and its dedication to public service.

Goal XI To preserve the independence of the legal profession and the judiciary as fundamental to a free society.

ing, and use of legal assistants or legal paraprofessionals. Through its Approval Commission, the committee sets the standards for ABA-approved educational programs for legal assistant education and training.

In 1974 the committee adopted the first guidelines for the approval of legal assistant education programs by the House of Delegates of the ABA. These guidelines require that

> the institution shall maintain a program for the education of legal assistants that is designed to qualify its graduates to be employed in law-related occupations, including public and private law practice and/or corporate or government law-related activities. (Guidelines G-301)

The process for ABA approval starts with the submission of a self-study report intended "to provide a comprehensive description of all program components with emphasis on the following areas: organization and administration; financial and other resources; advisory committee; educational program, faculty, and program leadership; admissions and student services; placement; library; and physical plant."

After submission and review of the self-study report, an onsite visit is conducted by a three-member team composed of a representative of the ABA Standing Committee on Legal Assistants, an experienced legal assistant, and an educator from another paralegal program, to verify information provided in the self-study and to acquire supplementary information essential to making an evaluation and recommendation to the House of Delegates at its semi-annual meetings in February and August. On each site visit the faculty, staff, administration, and students of the institution meet to review various documents such as course outlines, faculty evaluations, placement records, and student files.

As stated by the ABA, "Seeking approval from the American Bar Association is a voluntary process initiated by the institution offering the program. Therefore, the lack of approval does not necessarily mean a paralegal program is not of good quality and reputable."

The ABA Standing Committee Guidelines require that instruction be at the post-secondary level and contain at least 60 semester hours including general educational and legal specialty courses. Of these 60 hours, at least 18 must be general education courses and at least 18 must be legal specialty courses.

For purposes of the Guidelines, a "legal specialty course" is interpreted in Guideline G-303(c)d as a course (1) in a specific area of law, procedure, or legal process, (2) which has been developed for legal assistants and emphasizes legal assistant skills, forms, documents, procedures, and legal principles and theories, and (3) which is pertinent to the legal assistants' performance of a job.

To meet the American Bar Association requirements for approval, the program must (1) have been in operation for at least two academic years, (2) have graduated students, and (3) have satisfied the requirements of the ABA Guidelines for Paralegal Education Programs.

AAfPE Role in Paralegal Education

The American Association for Paralegal Education is a national organization of paralegal educators and institutions offering paralegal education programs. It has more than 380 members, of which more than 324 are educational institutions. Of these, 33 educational institutions are associate members (programs less than 2 years old or not meeting the criteria for institutional membership). According to the AAfPE Directory for 2001, the member schools have more than 41,000 students and more than 191,000 graduates.

Since its founding, the AAfPE has become the leading professional organization for paralegal education. Paralegal faculty and program directors

Goals of the American Association for Paralegal Education

- Promote high standards for paralegal education.

- Provide a forum for professional improvement for paralegal educators.

- Plan, promote, and hold annual conferences and seminars.

- Provide technical assistance and consultation services to institutions, educators, and employers.

- Promote research and disseminate information on the paralegal profession.

- Cooperate with the ABA and other institutions and professional associations in developing an approval process for paralegal education programs.

- Promote the goals of the AAfPE through cooperation with other national, regional, and local groups and organizations interested in paralegal education.

represent the institutional members in all aspects of the organization's decision-making. As an organization of paralegal educators, it has strived to set minimum educational standards to ensure that graduates of member institutions are well qualified to enter the workforce.

As the profession has advanced, employers and educators have recognized that successful paralegals need to possess certain basic skills. AAfPE looked at the issue and published a report that was approved and adopted by its Board of Directors, the Preamble to which states "A person must not only possess a common core of legal knowledge, but also must have acquired vital critical thinking, organizational, communication, and interpersonal skills."

Those entering the profession or seeking to develop the necessary skills and knowledge for professional growth and advancement must have an understanding of the basic skills and knowledge. They might possess some of the skills at one level of competency or another. They might have acquired some of the knowledge. They might need to further develop some skills to higher levels of competency and to gain or update additional knowledge as part of their professional education. In any case, they should look at these core competencies as skills and knowledge that should be continually upgraded and updated. Many of the core competencies can be acquired by completing a paralegal education program, whether a certificate program, associate's degree, bachelor's degree, or other continuing professional education programs and courses.

Individuals must take responsibility for their own professional education and growth. A good starting point is an honest and careful review of one's individual skill levels and knowledge in certain categories. The accompanying box, listing skills and knowledge competencies, is a useful guide.

Relevant Skills and Topics

SKILL DEVELOPMENT
- Critical thinking skills
- Organizational skills
- General communication skills
- Interpersonal skills
- Legal research skills
- Legal writing skills
- Computer skills
- Interviewing and investigation skills

ACQUISITION OF KNOWLEDGE
- Organization and operation of the legal system
- Organization and operation of law offices
- The paralegal profession and ethical obligations
- Contracts
- Torts
- Business organizations
- Litigation procedures

AAfPE Statement of Academic Quality

Selecting an appropriate educational institution for a basic education or an advanced education can be a difficult task. The AAfPE Statement of Academic Quality is a good starting point for measuring the appropriateness of an institution for an individual's education even if the institution is not a member of the association.

The AAfPE Statement of Academic Quality provides, in part:

Paralegal education is a unique academic curriculum, composed of both substantive legal knowledge and professional skills, that incorporates legal theory with an understanding of practical applications. This intellectually demanding course of study is derived from the responsibilities of paralegals as legal professionals. It is the philosophy of this organization that a person is qualified as a paralegal with (1) an associate or baccalaureate degree or equivalent course work; and (2) a credential in paralegal education completed in any of the following types of educational programs: associate degree, baccalaureate degree (major, minor or concentration), certificate, or master's degree. AAfPE recognizes these essential components of quality paralegal education programs:

Curriculum Development

Quality paralegal education programs monitor the responsibilities and competencies expected by employers on an ongoing basis. . . .

Facilities

Quality paralegal education programs have a physical learning environment that provides: (1) access to legal research library facilities that include computer-based resources; (2) classrooms that provide opportunities for interaction among students and between students and the instructor and include the necessary equipment and technology to facilitate learning; (3) a convenient physical location for administration/support staff and the provision of student services; and (4) accessibility pursuant to the Americans with Disabilities Act (ADA) requirements.

Faculty

The faculty of quality paralegal education programs consists of legal professionals and, where appropriate, other similarly qualified persons in good standing in their profession who (1) possess expertise and experience in their subject area; (2) have background working as or with paralegals; (3) can demonstrate teaching ability; (4) hold a graduate degree or possess exceptional expertise in the legal subject to be taught; and (5) are committed to the role of paralegals in the delivery of legal services. . . .

Paralegal Instruction

Quality paralegal education programs maintain standards of excellence and include, either as separate classes or with the overall course of study, the following topics: ethics, substantive and procedural law, the American legal system, delivery of legal services, law offices and related environments, the paralegal profession, legal research and writing, law-related computer skills, legal interviewing and investigation, and areas of legal practice such as those described in AAfPE's Core Competencies for Paralegal Programs; and offer an experiential learning component, such as internship, practicum, or clinical experience.

Related Competencies

Quality paralegal education programs assist their students in acquiring these essential related competencies, primarily in general education: (1) critical thinking skills (analysis, judgment, research, and problem-solving); (2) communication skills (oral, written, nonverbal, and interpersonal); (3) computer skills; (4) computational skills; (5) understanding of ethics; and (6) organizational skills. Graduates also possess a basic understanding of American history, business, and political systems.

Reprinted with the permission of the AAfPE.

Types of Programs

The goal of the educational experience is to get a job and be able to perform at a professional level. The demands on paralegals today require them to have greater skills and ability than in the past. Whereas basic typing, office, and business communications skills might have been acceptable for a starting position in a law firm twenty years ago, these are not the skills demanded for those looking for a paralegal position today. The core competencies as set by the AAfPE are essential for getting a job and succeeding in the profession today. More and more employers today also are asking for transcripts showing the courses taken and the minimum number of hours of study as spelled out in the ABA guidelines, even for graduates of educational institutions that have not obtained ABA certification of their programs. The reality is that many attorneys do not know the educational requirements to obtain a paralegal degree or certificate. And in many cases they do not know the elements of the ABA, NFPA, or NALA definitions of paralegal or legal assistant.

Paralegal/legal assistant educational programs generally fall into two categories—those offering a certificate and those offering a degree, either an associate's degree or a bachelor's degree. These programs of study may be offered by a two-year community or junior college or a four-year college or university. A number of business and private (proprietary) schools also offer paralegal/legal assistant programs of study.

Students' educational and professional backgrounds will determine, in many cases, which of the programs to select. Those with bachelor's and higher academic degrees may need only the legal specialty courses. Those who come from a specialty background, such as nursing or one heavy in science courses, may want to broaden their education by taking courses of a general nature in addition to the legal specialty courses.

Certificate Programs

Most educational institutions with paralegal/legal assistant programs, both public and private, offer a certificate. The certificate recognizes completion of a program of study that requires less than is required to receive a degree. Some certificates award college credits; some do not. For students already possessing a baccalaureate degree, obtaining additional college credits probably isn't an issue. For students without an undergraduate degree, programs that do not offer college credit can still be valuable but should be carefully considered. At the very least, the actual time spent in the classroom should be equivalent to the minimums of college credit courses.

Students' concerns should be for what is acceptable in the community in which they intend to work. Those planning to transfer should consider the acceptability of the course for transfer credit to another credit-granting institution. Even if they have no immediate intention of continuing in school, it is wise to plan ahead and not lose the hours and credits they have earned, in the event they later decide to transfer or go on to obtain a degree. Many professional paralegal organizations are reporting that a bachelor's degree is becoming more necessary to enter the paralegal field and some programs. The U. S. Attorney's Office, for example, is requiring at least a four-year degree to consider individuals for a paralegal position.

Statue of Justice, Wiblingen, Germany.

Associate Degree Programs

Many community colleges and junior colleges offer an associate degree in science (AS degree) or in arts (AA degree) or applied arts (AAS degree) in paralegal or legal assistant studies. For many students the two-year community college or junior college programs offer a community-based transition into higher education. For others it is a way of getting back into higher education while working at a full-time job or after being in another occupation. Support services for returning students or students needing additional help are often available. Many of these schools offer English courses for those for whom English is a second language and those returning to school who need a refresher course or help with study skills after years away from school. This also tends to be a cost-effective educational environment for trying different areas of study before finding an area of concentration.

Baccalaureate Programs

Some of the earliest paralegal programs were built on a model in which a bachelor's degree was the prerequisite to entering the paralegal program of study. A number of programs now offer a bachelor's degree in paralegal studies. One national organization has recommended the bachelor's degree as the minimum qualification to enter the profession. The increase in professional recognition of paralegals has resulted in their gaining more responsibility, as well as a growing demand for the skills required to perform the assigned tasks. As the standing of the paralegal on the legal team rises, so will the demand for people with a broad-based educational background to serve in those positions. Four-year programs of study are attempting to meet that demand by merging traditional four-year study core requirements and legal specialty courses.

Consider the family law attorney or paralegal. In the frequently highly charged emotional environment of custody and divorce, knowledge of family and child psychology is essential. For those in an intellectual property practice, an understanding of science and engineering is a basic requirement. The four-year timeframe allows more flexibility to explore and build skills and knowledge, as well as to meet the increasing demand for more education for paralegals.

Graduate Programs

A few colleges and universities now offer graduate degrees in legal studies. Others offer advanced degrees in related areas such as legal administration.

Specialty Certificates

Specialty certificates, such as the paralegal certificate or the legal nurse consultant certificate, offer an excellent entry point into a paralegal career. Such certificates combined with degrees in other fields of study, such as nursing, journalism, and computer science, are like a capstone program preparing one for entry into a new career. One of the greatest demands has been for those with a background in nursing combined with a paralegal education. A growing number of colleges are offering a certificate in Legal Nurse Consulting.

Paralegal Certification

The National Federation of Paralegal Associations (NFPA) administers a certification program. Its exam, known as PACE (Paralegal Advanced Competency Exam), requires that the paralegal have two years' experience and a bachelor's degree and have completed a paralegal course at an accred-

American Association of
Legal Nurse Consultants:
www.aalnc.org

NFPA PACE:
www.paralegals.org/PACE/
home.html

ited school. The two-day exam covers federal procedure and law and tests paralegal skills such as communication and interviewing, as well as areas such as family and contract law. Those who successfully pass the exam may use the designation "RP" after their names. Continued use of the designation requires 12 additional hours of continuing legal or specialty education every two years.

Since 1976, the National Association of Legal Assistants has conferred the CLA (Certified Legal Assistant) designation on those who pass its national certification program's two-day comprehensive examination. The first day contains a 1.5-hour exam on communications and a 2.5-hour exam on judgment and analytical ability. The second day consists of a 1-hour test on ethics, a 1.5-hour test on legal research, and a 2-hour test on substantive law, which includes tests on general law and four practice areas selected by the examinees. All of the sections of this exam are on the federal level, with no testing on state laws or procedures.

To maintain use of the CLA designation, the legal assistant must submit evidence of completion of 5 units of continuing legal assistant education every five years. Ten hours of education equals one unit of CLE (continuing legal education), including a college course in the field. For those who have achieved the initial designation, NALA also offers specialist credentials for those practicing in specific areas of law, including bankruptcy, intellectual property, civil litigation, probate and estate planning, corporate and business, criminal, or real estate. Successful completion of these 4-hour examinations permits the additional designation CLAS, Certified Legal Assistant–Specialty.

PERSONAL GOALS

If you are reading this book, you probably have made at least a tentative career goal to enter the paralegal profession, with the ultimate goal of obtaining a job. It should not be "just a job" but, rather, a job that will give you satisfaction and one that you will get up and go to with anticipation, not dread. The paralegal field offers many paths and many and varied specialties. One of your goals should be to take courses that will introduce you to the specialty you would enjoy most. Maybe you already are well versed in something that will lead to a specialty, such as nursing, one of the sciences, or law enforcement.

One of the first steps is to assess your own skills. What are your other educational skills? What are your personality traits? Do you like working under deadlines or working with certain groups of people, such as elderly people or those with disabilities?

As you will see, the paralegal profession offers opportunities in many areas of legal specialty and in many types of working environments. Understanding your interests, skills, and desired working conditions and job locations will help you select the best educational path toward achieving your professional goals.

NALA CLA: www.nala.org/ cert.htm

LAMA Position Paper: www.lamanet.org/resources/ pp-edu.cfm

Minimum Education

The position of the Legal Assistant Management Association (LAMA) is that a baccalaureate degree should be the minimum requirement for employment as a legal assistant. Legal assistants have assumed many responsibilities formerly handled by lawyers. Working with complex legal issues requires that a legal assistant possess clear writing, researching, and critical thinking abilities. Because a strong academic background is essential, LAMA believes that a baccalaureate degree should be the minimum requirement for employment as a legal assistant. LAMA believes this accepted professional standard of academic achievement lends greater credibility and respect to the legal profession.

Source: LAMA's *Position Paper on Legal Assistant Education.*

SIDEBAR

Collecting Lunch Stories: The Hidden Perk

Facts & Findings   August 1998

Collecting good stories is one of the top benefits of working in the legal profession. In a field that operates at an intense level most of the time and demands diligence, commitment, and excellence, it's no wonder that on occasion we crack. When this happens, we can either get upset or take a good story to Happy Hour now and then. I prefer the latter alternative. This way, when I crack, I don't think of it so much as having a breakdown as that I am contributing to the story exchange.

While working on my master's thesis, I learned four tips from legal assistants through their stories. Here are their tips and a few of their stories. Enjoy.

Tip #1: Take charge.

Refusing to take control of a situation left a legal assistant sitting in the dark—literally. Mary needed to leave on time one evening, so she asked a colleague to stay late and help an attorney who had a deadline the next day. Mary warned the paralegal before she left, "You must go in and see [the attorney] every half hour or he'll forget you're here. He'll eventually tell you to go home, but you have to go in every half hour." Mary explained that when this attorney focused on a project, he forgot everything else, including other lawyers and paralegals working with him.

The paralegal filling in for Mary didn't want to disturb the attorney, so she stayed in her office, letting the attorney come to her with work to do throughout the evening. At some point, the lawyer stopped coming, and at 4:00 a.m., after he had taken his midnight nap and gained a second wind, the attorney found the paralegal sitting in her office. He had forgotten she was there. The paralegal's fear of disturbing the attorney had kept her up all night. Worse, he was ready to work, and the paralegal was tired.

Tip #2: Learn to roll your eyes.

Sometimes it just doesn't pay to get angry. On some days it's better to do what Sabrina does: rolls her eyes and keeps on going. Sabrina, a paralegal helping a team of attorneys keep up with a hectic deposition schedule, stayed at work late one night preparing a set of documents for an attorney to use at a deposition the next day. The attorney had gone back to his hotel to work and asked Sabrina to drop off the documents on her way home.

The paralegal arrived at the hotel around 10:00 p.m. and asked the desk clerk to call up to the attorney's room to let him know she had arrived.

"He's in the bar," announced the clerk, who had gotten to know the attorney during his stay at the hotel.

Sabrina, thinking the clerk had to be mistaken, asked again. This attorney had a deposition the next day.

"In the bar," the man said, smiling, pointing toward the door.

Sabrina stepped into the bar area, and found the attorney laughing with a member of the co-counsel's trial team.

When the attorney saw Sabrina, he waved her over to the table.

"Here are your documents for tomorrow," she said.

"Oh, the deposition has been canceled. Didn't anyone call you?" the attorney grinned.

"He was the only person I was working late for that night. Who else was going to call me?" the paralegal said to me, rolling her eyes. In Sabrina's case, she respected this attorney, and the deposition cancellation was a nice break in the tough schedule.

Tip #3: Learn to laugh at yourself.

When I first moved to Massachusetts, I was working with a team of legal assistants who made fun of the way I talked and looked at me like I was a nut case when I asked the location of the closest Whataburger (only those who know Whataburger can appreciate my need . . .). It turned out no one in Massachusetts or in the several surrounding states had ever heard of Whataburger. So . . . I stood looking down at a woman on the floor surrounded by notebooks, asking her, "How much more do you lack?" (I didn't understand why she looked up at me as if I had asked why grocery stores up here keep chili on the ethnic food aisles.) "How much more do you lack?" I asked again, speaking English, I'm sure. We were tired; maybe I slurred all the words.

"How much more do I like what?" she cried. I could see frustration in her eyes. She had been working so hard. "How much more do I like sitting on the floor than I like sitting at my desk? What are you talking about?"

"I mean," I said, finally realizing I was displaying some slang (and very poor slang at that) that I had picked up in the South, "how much more do you have to do?"

She laughed. She told everyone else in the office. They laughed. We met our deadlines. We had lunch. We laughed some more.

No matter how overwhelming the situation seems, laugh. Even in the worst situations, think of yourself as if you are standing in the middle of a cartoon strip. Are the circumstances as ridiculous as the Dilbert cartoon's spoofs on corporate life?

Tip #4: Recognize the story, remember the story, repeat the story.

"Don't be too sensitive," is the advice from Karen, a legal assistant coordinator in Texas. "The way [attorneys] talk to you may be intimidating," so you can't get caught up in that.

A Boston legal assistant used all of [the above] advice (taking charge, eye rolling, . . . and laughing) to keep in perspective a heated exchange that occurred during an intense session of deposition preparation.

The paralegal went to New York to help an attorney with a deposition. She traveled with the warning that this particular attorney, though well-respected and one of the firm's top rainmakers, could be "extremely intense." During their preparation for the deposition, the attorney asked her to call another paralegal to have him send some documents for the next day. While she was in the middle of speaking into the paralegal's voice mail, the attorney barked, "Look, you have to get off the phone. We have work to do."

"Intense," was not the word that came to mind.

"Look," she said to the attorney, "you told me to call him. So just give me a break." Both stressed that the exchange allowed both paralegal and attorney to release some tension.

After the frustration wore off, she was able to recognize the situation for what it was: a great story about the well-respected attorney known for his "intensity," one that would earn respect among her colleagues.

Even if we're confident, comfortable, and able to laugh, we still experience occasional frustration; it's part of the profession. But if our polished skills don't make the situation any better, at least we'll be able to recognize a good lunch story when it happens.

Reprinted with permission of the National Association of Legal Assistants, Inc., and Charlsye Smith. This article originally appeared in the August 1998 issue of FACTS AND FINDINGS, the Journal for Legal Assistants. Inquiries should be directed to NALA, 1516 S. Boston, #200, Tulsa, OK 74119, www.nala.org.

Checklist

- My personal goals are:

- My professional goals are:

- I have these skills:
  - Languages
  - Computer
  - Academic background
  - Occupational background
  - Communication
    - Written
    - Oral
    - Public speaking
  - Organizational
  - Resourcefulness
  - Cultural awareness
  - Analytical

- Skills I need to develop:

- Skills I need to improve:

CASES FOR BRIEFING

Throughout this text, actual court cases will be presented to familiarize you with the language of law and the courts and to expose you to topics of interest, including issues of practice and ethics. Questions at the beginning of each case will guide your reading. Your instructor also might ask you to brief the case—that is, to prepare a brief abstract of the case. If briefing is assigned, read Appendix A: How to Brief a Case.

LEGAL TERMINOLOGY

American Association for Paralegal Education (AAfPE)
American Bar Association (ABA)
Associate's degree
Bachelor's degree
Certified Legal Assistant (CLA)
Legal assistant
National Association of Legal Assistants (NALA)
National Federation of Paralegal Associations (NFPA)
Paralegal (legal assistant)
Paralegal Advanced Competency Exam (PACE)
Proprietary school

Summary

What Is a Paralegal?

Definition	A paralegal, or legal assistant, is "a person qualified by education, training, or work experience who is employed or retained by a lawyer, law office, corporation, governmental agency, or other entity who performs specifically delegated substantive legal work for which a lawyer is responsible."

What Do Paralegals Do?

Functions of Paralegals	The primary function of paralegals is to assist attorneys in preparing for hearings, trials, meetings, and closings.

Opportunities

Numbers and Salaries	In 2000, paralegals held about 188,000 jobs in the United States, with median annual earnings of $35,360. The U. S. Department of Labor projects that this profession will continue to be among the fastest growing through the year 2010.

Career Planning

Education	1. General education courses. 2. Associate's degree or bachelor's degree.

Role of the Paralegal

Level of Responsibility	The paralegal is a member of the legal services delivery team with responsibilities commensurate with his or her education and experience.

National Associations of Paralegals

Major Associations	1. National Association of Legal Assistants 2. National Federation of Paralegal Associations 3. Association of Legal Administrators 4. Legal Assistant Management Association

Qualifications of a Paralegal

Minimum Qualifications	Established by the educational guidelines of the American Bar Association's Standing Committee on Legal Assistants and American Association for Paralegal Education.

(continued)

Paralegal Education in the United States	
Standards	1. American Bar Association Paralegal Education Standards 2. AAfPE in Paralegal Education 3. AAfPE Statement on Academic Quality
Types of Programs	1. Certificate programs 2. Associate degree programs 3. Baccalaureate programs 4. Graduate programs 5. Specialty certificates

Working the Web

1. Check the NFPA site at www.paralegals.org for:
   a. Various information pertaining to the paralegal profession.
   b. Current definition from your jurisdiction, in the Professional Development section.
   c. Information on career outlook, salary, and other pertinent facts, in the Career Center.

2. Visit the NALA site at www.nala.org for information on
   a. Certified Legal Assistant (CLA) program
   b. Links to recent surveys on paralegal utilization and compensation

3. Check the American Bar Association subcommittee on the utilization of legal assistants website at www.abanet.org.

4. Take a look at the American Association for Paralegal Education website at www.aafpe.org for:
   a. Core competencies
   b. A guide to quality paralegal education
   c. Links to other sites

5. Check the latest information on the paralegal occupation in the U. S. Department of Labor, Bureau of Labor Statistics' *Occupational Outlook Handbook* at www.bls.gov/oco/ocos114.htm.

Questions
CRITICAL LEGAL THINKING AND WRITING

1. Why should those planning to become paralegals or legal assistants get a well-founded education and develop the necessary skills?

2. What skills are required to be a paralegal and why are they important?

3. What is the difference between the job of a legal secretary, legal administrator, or legal assistant manager, and that of a paralegal?

4. How can a paralegal demonstrate the qualifications for employment as a paralegal?

5. How can one satisfy the court that he or she is qualified as a paralegal and not as a legal secretary?

6. Based on the AAfPE core competencies, what sorts of assignments and tasks should you expect in your paralegal education?

7. What educational plan makes the most sense for you? Why?

8. Complete the checklist "Skills & Goals." Based on your answers, how well prepared are you for a career as a paralegal? What skills need development?

9. Prepare a plan of action, based on the AAfPE core competencies, for improving your skills and knowledge.

10. Why would an employer, such as the U. S. Attorney's office, require a four-year degree for those seeking a paralegal position?

Questions
ETHICS: ANALYSIS AND DISCUSSION

1. Search your state statutes, code, or court rules for the definition of "Paralegal" or "Legal Assistant."

2. Does your state have a statute or court rule on the regulation of the paralegal or legal assistant practice?

3. Does your state have minimum educational requirements for paralegals?

Use of the Title "Paralegal"

There are few certainties in the area of ethics, for paralegals or in any profession. What qualifies as ethical conduct is in most cases based on state law and court interpretation applied to a set of facts. For the following:

- *Prepare a written statement based on your state law.*
- *Use your state bar association website as a starting point.*

You hold a bachelor's degree in paralegal studies from a prestigious college. You want to work as an independent paralegal. May you advertise in the local newspaper and put a sign on the door of your office that uses the term "paralegal," according to your state law?

Missouri v. Jenkins

Read the following case excerpts. Information on preparing a briefing is provided in Appendix A: How to Brief a Case. In your brief, prepare a written answer to each of the following questions.

1. What is the difference between "market rates" for paralegals and cost to the attorney for paralegal service?

2. Does billing for paralegal services at market rates unfairly benefit the law firm?

3. According to this court, how is a reasonable attorney's fee calculated?

4. How does the public benefit from allowing paralegals to be billed at market rates?

5. Does this court believe that a reasonable attorney's fee should include paralegal fees?

Brennan, J., delivered the opinion of the Court.

This is the attorney's fee aftermath of major school desegregation litigation in Kansas City, Missouri. We [are hearing this case to decide] should the fee award compensate the work of paralegals and law clerks by applying the market rate for their work?

I

This litigation began in 1977 as a suit by the Kansas City Missouri School District (KCMSD), the school board, and the children of two school board members, against the State of Missouri and other defendants. The plaintiffs alleged that the State, surrounding school districts, and various federal agencies had caused and perpetuated a system of racial segregation in the schools of the Kansas City metropolitan area. . . . After lengthy proceedings, including a trial that lasted 7 1/2 months during 1983 and 1984, the District Court found the State of Missouri and KCMSD liable. . . . It ordered various intradistrict remedies, to be paid for by the State and KCMSD, including $260 million in capital improvements and a magnet-school plan costing over $200 million.

The plaintiff class has been represented, since 1979, by Kansas City lawyer Arthur Benson and, since 1982, by the NAACP Legal Defense and Educational Fund, Inc. (LDF). Benson and the LDF requested attorney's fees under the Civil Rights Attorney's Fees Awards Act of 1976, 42 U.S.C. § 1988. Benson and his associates had devoted 10,875 attorney hours to the litigation, as well as 8,108 hours of paralegal and law clerk time. For the LDF, the corresponding figures were 10,854 hours for attorneys and 15,517 hours for paralegals and law clerks. Their fee applications deleted from these totals

3,628 attorney hours and 7,046 paralegal hours allocable to unsuccessful claims against the suburban school districts. With additions for postjudgment monitoring and for preparation of the fee application, the District Court awarded Benson a total of approximately $1.7 million and the LDF $2.3 million. . . .

Both Benson and the LDF employed numerous paralegals, law clerks (generally law students working part-time), and recent law graduates in this litigation. The court awarded fees for their work based on Kansas City market rates for those categories. As in the case of the attorneys, it used current rather than historic market rates in order to compensate for the delay in payment. It therefore awarded fees based on hourly rates of $35 for law clerks, $40 for paralegals, and $50 for recent law graduates. [. . .]

III

Missouri's second contention is that the District Court erred in compensating the work of law clerks and paralegals (hereinafter collectively "paralegals") at the market rates for their services, rather than at their cost to the attorney. While Missouri agrees that compensation for the cost of these personnel should be included in the fee award, it suggests that an hourly rate of $15—which it argued below corresponded to their salaries, benefits, and overhead—would be appropriate, rather than the market rates of $35 to $50. According to Missouri, § 1988 does not authorize billing paralegals' hours at market rates, and doing so produces a "windfall" for the attorney.

We begin with the statutory language, which provides simply for "a reasonable attorney's fee as part of the costs." Clearly, a "reasonable attorney's fee" cannot have been meant to compensate only work performed personally by members of the bar. Rather, the term must refer to a reasonable fee for the work product of an attorney.

Thus, the fee must take into account the work not only of attorneys but also of secretaries, messengers, librarians, janitors, and others whose labor contributes to the work product for which an attorney bills her client; and it also must take account of other expenses and profit. The parties have suggested no reason why the work of paralegals should not be similarly compensated, nor can we think of any. We thus take as our starting point the self-evident proposition that the "reasonable attorney's fee" provided for by statute should compensate the work of paralegals, as well as that of attorneys.

The more difficult question is how the work of paralegals is to be valuated in calculating the overall attorney's fee.

The statute specifies a "reasonable" fee for the attorney's work product. In determining how other elements of the attorney's fee are to be calculated, we have consistently looked to the marketplace as our guide to what is "reasonable." In *Blum v. Stenson*, 465 U.S. 886 (1984), for example, we rejected an argument that attorney's fees for nonprofit legal service organizations should be based on cost. We said: "The statute and legislative history establish that 'reasonable fees' under § 1988 are to be calculated according to the prevailing market rates in the relevant community. . . ." A reasonable attorney's fee under § 1988 is one calculated on the basis of rates and practices prevailing in the relevant market, i.e., "in line with those [rates] prevailing in the community for similar services by lawyers of reasonably comparable skill, experience, and reputation," and one that grants the successful civil rights plaintiff a "fully compensatory fee," comparable to what "is traditional with attorneys compensated by a fee-paying client."

If an attorney's fee awarded under § 1988 is to yield the same level of compensation that would be available from the market, the "increasingly widespread custom of separately billing for the services of paralegals and law students who serve as clerks," all else being equal, the hourly fee charged by an attorney whose rates include paralegal work in her hourly fee, or who bills separately for the work of paralegals at cost, will be higher than the hourly fee charged by an attorney competing in the same market who bills separately for the work of paralegals at "market rates." In other words, the prevailing "market rate" for attorney time is not independent of the manner in which paralegal time is accounted for. Thus, if the prevailing practice in a given community were to bill paralegal time separately at market rates, fees awarded the attorney at market rates for attorney time would not be fully compensatory if the court refused to compensate hours billed by paralegals or did

so only at "cost." Similarly, the fee awarded would be too high if the court accepted separate billing for paralegal hours in a market where that was not the custom.

We reject the argument that compensation for paralegals at rates above "cost" would yield a "windfall" for the prevailing attorney. Neither petitioners nor anyone else, to our knowledge, has ever suggested that the hourly rate applied to the work of an associate attorney in a law firm creates a windfall for the firm's partners or is otherwise improper under § 1988, merely because it exceeds the cost of the attorney's services. If the fees are consistent with market rates and practices, the "windfall" argument has no more force with regard to paralegals than it does for associates. And it would hardly accord with Congress' intent to provide a "fully compensatory fee" if the prevailing plaintiff's attorney in a civil rights lawsuit were not permitted to bill separately for paralegals, while the defense attorney in the same litigation was able to take advantage of the prevailing practice and obtain market rates for such work. Yet that is precisely the result sought in this case by the State of Missouri, which appears to have paid its own outside counsel for the work of paralegals at the hourly rate of $35.

Nothing in § 1988 requires that the work of paralegals invariably be billed separately. If it is the practice in the relevant market not to do so, or to bill the work of paralegals only at cost, that is all that § 1988 requires. Where, however, the prevailing practice is to bill paralegal work at market rates, treating civil rights lawyers' fee requests in the same way is not only permitted by § 1988, but also makes economic sense. By encouraging the use of lower cost paralegals rather than attorneys wherever possible, permitting market-rate billing of paralegal hours "encourages cost-effective delivery of legal services and, by reducing the spiraling cost of civil rights litigation, furthers the policies underlying civil rights statutes."

Such separate billing appears to be the practice in most communities today. In the present case, Missouri concedes that "the local market typically bills separately for paralegal services," and the District Court found that the requested hourly rates of $35 for law clerks, $40 for paralegals, and $50 for recent law graduates were the prevailing rates for such services in the Kansas City area. Under these circumstances, the court's decision to award separate compensation at these rates was fully in accord with § 1988.

IV

The courts below correctly granted a fee enhancement to compensate for delay in payment and approved compensation of paralegals and law clerks at market rates. The judgment of the Court of Appeals is therefore Affirmed.

CHAPTER 2

CHAPTER OBJECTIVES

After studying this chapter, you should be able to:

1. Explain the reasons for the Unauthorized Practice of Law (UPL) regulation.

2. Understand the basic areas of concern for the paralegal in the area of UPL.

3. Discuss issues involving the conflicting views on regulation of the paralegal profession.

4. Understand the difference between the attorneys' and the paralegals' rules of ethics and the obligations of each profession.

5. Explain the ethical responsibilities established by statutes, court decisions, and court rules.

6. Understand the concept of conflict of interest for the legal profession.

7. Explain how the ethical wall protects client confidentiality.

8. Understand how a paralegal can have a conflict of interest in working a second job.

9. Explain the concept of the work product doctrine.

10. Understand the lawyer supervision requirements and obligations in utilizing legal assistants.

Ethics, Regulation, and Professional Responsibility

Morality cannot be legislated, but behavior can be regulated. Judicial decrees may not change hearts, but they can restrain the heartless.

MARTIN LUTHER KING, JR.

Introduction

Every profession develops a set of guidelines for those in the profession to follow. These may be the rules of practice, such as court rules of procedure; ethical guidelines, such as the ABA Model Rules of Professional Conduct; or statutorily mandated rules, such as professional licensing statutes. By their own efforts, lawyers have developed a combination of organizational guidelines such as the rules of ethics, and have lobbied for licensing regulation of the profession through the courts and the legislature.

The paralegal profession is going through a growth phase in developing these guides. Even though these rules and regulations are in the development stage, the legal assistant must have some sense of the rules to be followed. The legal assistant in many workplaces today is a substitute for the recent law school graduate, frequently referred to as a junior associate, who may not have taken the bar examination and been admitted to practice. In any case, ethics rules must be followed to avoid conflict, potential violation of client rights and statutory regulation, and possible malpractice.

ABA Model Rules of Professional Conduct, 2002 Edition: www.abanet.org/cpr/mrpc/mrpc_toc.html

UNAUTHORIZED PRACTICE OF LAW (UPL)

Regulations are put into place in an attempt to prevent abuses in the practice of law. Two relevant issues involve giving advice and filling out forms.

Regulation of the Practice of Law

All of the states regulate the practice of law, in an attempt to protect the public from incompetent and unscrupulous practitioners, just as they regulate the practice of medicine and many other professions. States such as Pennsylvania have specifically addressed the issue of unauthorized practice of law by paralegals and legal assistants. The Pennsylvania statute on the unauthorized practice of law makes it a misdemeanor for "any person, including, but not limited to, *a paralegal or legal assistant* . . . within this commonwealth [to] practice law."

The Pennsylvania statute seems to address concerns that the general public will misinterpret the title of paralegal or legal assistant as denoting a person admitted to practice law in the commonwealth. An unresolved issue in Pennsylvania, and in other states, is to define what specific conduct the courts will hold to be the practice of law. Because the interpretation will vary from state to state, the paralegal must be aware of the local requirements and limitations that define the unauthorized practice of law within that jurisdiction. What constitutes the practice of law under these statutes usually is decided on a case-by-case basis.

Certain conduct required or requested by an attorney or client should at the very least cause the paralegal to pause. A client who asks you to prepare a power of attorney without "bothering the lawyer," or to "go with me to the support conference" should raise a caution flag in the paralegal's mind. The difficulty is in knowing what the individual courts allow or will permit in individual circumstances. Some jurisdictions and administrative agencies do permit those who are not admitted to practice to appear in court or before administrative law judges or referees on behalf of clients. Typically, these are law students acting under the guidance and supervision of an attorney under limited circumstances, but they may include paralegals. Depending upon the jurisdiction, nature of the action, and level of the court, the paralegal might be permitted to appear with or on behalf of a client—for example, before a Social Security Administration Administrative Law Judge.

County courthouse in Bridgeport, California.

Giving Advice

Is the giving of advice an unauthorized practice of law? Yes, if legal rights may be affected. The question of what advice is legal advice is not easy to answer. Consider the seemingly innocent question, "How should I sign my name?" In most circumstances the answer might be, "Just sign it the way you normally write your name." But when a person is signing a document in a representative capacity, for example as the officer of a corporation or on behalf of another person under a power of attorney, telling the client to just "sign your name" might be giving legal advice because the client's legal rights could be affected if he or she does not indicate representative capacity.

Filling Out Forms

Filling out forms for clients also can be a source of trouble. In some jurisdictions paralegals are permitted to assist clients in the preparation of certain documents. Other courts, however, view this assistance as rendering legal advice. One of the more interesting decisions in this context was by a federal judge who ruled the Quicken Family Lawyer computer program, which provides legal forms, as the unauthorized practice of law [*Unauthorized Practice of Law v. Parsons Tech.*, 179 F.3d 956 (5th Cir. 1999)].

REGULATION OF THE PARALEGAL PROFESSION

Regulation and licensing of the paralegal profession has been one of the hottest topics in the legal and paralegal communities. Each state, through its respective legislature and court, regulates and licenses the practice of law. The original UPL issues were simply those of the licensing of attorneys and laws preventing the unauthorized practice of law. With the development of the paralegal profession has come a new set of concerns and controversy surrounding what is the unauthorized practice of law, who should be permitted to render legal services, and under what conditions.

The conflict is between the paralegal profession and the bar organizations, such as the American Bar Association, which does not see the need for the additional time, effort, and cost for certification of paralegals and legal assistants. The ABA position is broadly based on the argument that the public is protected by the attorney's obligation to supervise the paralegal and responsibility to the public.

For the most part, the paralegal profession has sought some level of regulation, certification, or licensure. Somewhere in the middle are increasing numbers of employers of paralegals who want some level of assurance that those they hire who claim to be paralegals are qualified for those positions. As the responsibilities undertaken by paralegals have increased, so have the educational requirements. Within the profession has come a concern that those who hold themselves out as paralegals are truly qualified to perform the work they have undertaken. This is no different from the organized bar monitoring the activities of those holding themselves out as being lawyers.

State Licensing Attempts

Individual states have attempted to set up licensing systems. A case in point is the proposal rejected in 1999 by the New Jersey Supreme Court to license traditional paralegals, which had been developed after five years of study by that court's committee on paralegal education and regulation. If it had been approved, this proposal would have made New Jersey the first state to license traditional paralegals.

Ethical PERSPECTIVE

Unauthorized Practice of Law

Check those items you believe to be the unauthorized practice of law.

☐ I have been asked to appear in court for a client.

☐ The client has asked for my advice on a legal matter.

☐ The client has asked me to fill out forms that affect legal rights.

It is not always clear what conduct will be considered UPL. If you are not sure, ASK.

Ethical PERSPECTIVE

Filling Out Forms

It is the unauthorized practice of law "to fill out bankruptcy forms even when simply plugging in information and letting the computer program pick the exemptions."

In re Kaitangian, *218 B.R.102 (Bankr. S.D. Cal. 1998).*

California leads the nation in setting stringent educational requirements that may become a model for other states (refer to the California statute mentioned in Chapter 1, p. 15).

The Washington State Bar adopted a rule to establish a "Practice of Law Board" that authorizes nonlawyers to practice law in limited areas as needed to assure access to affordable legal services.

After a number of efforts, a Hawaii State Bar Association task force on paralegal certification developed a compromise "voluntary" certification proposal for consideration by the Hawaii Supreme Court, which recognized the opposition from some segments of the bar.

It is obvious to some observers that the organized bar is fearful in many cases of the incursion of the paralegal profession into the practice of law. For some, the issue is loss of income. Others are concerned for the delivery of quality legal services by all those who hold themselves out as being members of the legal profession. For the paralegal, it is a question of status as well as job opportunities. With the establishment of minimum standards for holding oneself out as a paralegal comes a status that members of a profession are entitled to enjoy. For those who have worked hard to develop the necessary paralegal skills by way of education and experience it eliminates the unqualified from taking those jobs that should be performed by qualified individuals. The stated goals of the different groups are not that far apart: delivery of quality legal services at affordable prices with a reasonable standard of living for the legal profession and the paralegal profession.

The traditional role of the attorney in advising and representing clients is limited to those who are admitted to practice as lawyers under the applicable state law. Some exemptions do exist that allow nonlawyers to perform certain services under state law, such as document preparation under California law. Under federal law, the Social Security system provides an example.

Backup Attorney

To avoid possible claims for the unauthorized practice of law, have your supervising attorney select a backup attorney with whom you are authorized to consult when your primary supervising attorney is not available. Ensure you have contact information, including home phone number, cell phone number, and pager number.

Social Security Administration

Under federal law, certain specific exemptions permit nonlawyers to act on behalf of clients and to appear before administrative agencies. Most notable is that of the Social Security Administration. Under federal regulation, a paralegal can, without supervision, represent individuals before the Social Security Administration, including appearing before Administrative Law Judges on behalf of clients. Paralegals may appear as representatives of claimants for disability claims; Medicare parts A, B, and C; and cases of overpayment and underpayment.

As representative of a claimant, the paralegal in practice before the Social Security Administration may obtain information, submit evidence, and make statements and arguments. The difference between the paralegal and the attorney is only in the matter of direct versus indirect payment for services. The Social Security Administration pays the attorney directly, whereas the paralegal must bill the client for services rendered. Within the Social Security Administration, paralegals are employed as decision writers and case technicians.

Social Security

An estimated 500,000 cases are presented annually before Administrative Law Judges of the Social Security Administration. As the population ages, that number is expected to increase.

Paralegal Regulations Encouraged

The Indiana Lawyer, February 28, 2001   Rachel E. Faulkner, Director of Public Relations, Indianapolis Bar Association

A community of legal professionals exist who are distinguished by the work they perform, yet no specific standards of regulations currently exist to mandate specific educational requirements or duties. These professionals are paralegals/legal assistants, and they provide a very necessary service to the legal community.

The American Bar Association defines a paralegal/legal assistant as an individual qualified by education, training, or work experience, who is employed or retained by a lawyer, law office, corporation, governmental agency or other entity, and who performs specifically delegated substantive legal work for which a lawyer is responsible. Similar variations of this popular definition exist from organizations such as the National Federation of Paralegal Associations, Indiana State and Indianapolis Bar Associations, the Indiana Paralegal Association, etc.

According to Edna Wallace, RP, a practicing paralegal with the law firm of Kroger, Gardis & Regas, LLP and immediate past chair of the Indianapolis Bar Association Paralegal Committee, this issue goes beyond titles and descriptions, as its significance impacts the standards of performance for the profession. Without regulation, any person employed by a lawyer, law office, corporation, government agency, or other entity can use the title of "legal assistant" without qualification by education, work experience, or training and without the knowledge to perform substantive legal work that would require knowledge of legal concepts and normally would be performed by a lawyer, and can sign [his or her] name with a designation of legal assistant, Wallace said.

Some law firms utilize the title "legal assistant" to describe their support staff who more accurately should be referred to as administrative assistants. This practice, along with the lack of regulation, perpetuates the devalued image of the profession. Many paralegals advocate formalizing standards for the profession to combat the problem and to ensure that paralegals/legal assistants truly obtain and maintain the knowledge and expertise in substantive and procedure law that their profession requires.

While mandated licensing and other regulations, such as required continuing legal education (CLE), will add value to the paralegal/legal assistant profession, like everything else it comes at a price. Will law firms agree to pay for obtaining and maintaining the license and the necessary CLE hours, as well as association dues?

Many paralegals, like Wallace, believe they should. She said that ultimately lawyers are responsible for the professional services of the paralegal/legal assistant pursuant to the Indiana Rules of Professional Responsibility (Rule 9.1). This requirement alone should inspire attorneys to take reasonable measures to ensure that their paralegal/legal assistant is experienced, qualified, and educated to maintain the integrity of the profession.

According to Wallace, encouraging regulations will work to move the profession forward. In a challenge to other paralegals/legal assistants, she asked: Are you willing to sit back and watch everything you worked hard for, went to school for, and believe in slip back to the same status as several years ago? It's an uphill battle. Are you ready for the challenge?

ETHICAL RULES AND OBLIGATIONS

Lawyers generally need to follow only one set of ethics guidelines. Although it may be a set enacted by the state legislature, it usually is one adopted by the supreme court of the state in which they practice.

The most widely adopted is the *Model Rules of Professional Conduct* (see Appendix B for excerpts of the Model Rules, 2002 edition) prepared by the American Bar Association, originally released in 1983. The prior release, the Model Code of Professional Conduct (Model Code) is still in use in some jurisdictions. Procedurally, each state reviews the Model Rules or Model Code and

Taking the Stand: Ethics

Ellen Lockwood, C.L.A.   State Bar of Texas, Chair, Ethics Committee, Legal Assisting Division

Q: How did you become the chair of the Ethics Committee?

A: The position became vacant at the time my first stint on the board of directors ended. Ethics interested me, so I asked to be appointed. The president was just thrilled to have someone volunteer!

Q: What is the most common ethics question you are asked?

A: Questions regarding giving legal advice. Usually the questions are in the gray area between giving basic information and giving legal advice.

Q: What has been the oddest ethics question you've encountered?

A: I don't recall any ethics questions that I would consider odd. I do receive many questions that surprise me because the answers appear so obvious to me.

This makes me believe that we cannot stress ethics enough in paralegal programs as well as in CLE. We particularly need examples of ethical dilemmas in everyday situations so that ethics is not just an abstract list of rules.

Q: What was the most costly ethics mistake by a paralegal that you've become aware of?

A: Other than embezzling (I'm aware of two cases in Texas), I think the most costly ethics mistake any paralegal can make is become too comfortable with your knowledge. Not only is it important to keep up your CLE; it is important to remember that you are not the attorney and cannot give legal advice. Even when you are sure of the answer, ask your attorney so you can honestly tell the client, "Attorney X asked me to tell you _____."

adopts the entire recommended set of Model Rules or the Model Code, or portions as it thinks appropriate for its jurisdiction.

Unlike the ABA for lawyers, no single source of ethical rules is set out for the legal assistant. Absent a single unified body of ethical rules, legal assistants must follow state statutes and conduct themselves in conformity with the rules of professional conduct applicable to attorneys and with the ethics opinions of their professional associations. The two major legal assistant organizations providing an ethical code for its members are the National Federation of Paralegal Associations (NFPA) and the National Association of Legal Assistants (NALA).

Although legal assistants are not governed directly by the American Bar Association ethical rules, there is an intertwined relationship between the lawyer, the client, and the paralegal. What the paralegal does or does not do can have a real impact on the lawyer's duty and obligation to the client. The lawyer is ultimately responsible for the actions of the legal assistant under the Model Rules.

www

NFPA Ethics Code: www. paralegals.org/Development/ model code.html

NALA Ethics: www.nala.org/ stand.htm

ABA Model Guidelines for the Utilization of Legal Assistant Services

In 1991 the American Bar Association's policy-making body, the House of Delegates, adopted a set of guidelines intended to govern the conduct of lawyers when utilizing paralegals or legal assistants. These guidelines are given as Exhibit 2.1.

Attorneys are bound by the ethical code adopted by the state in which they practice. The ethical guidelines for the paralegal are a combination of the ethical rules imposed on the supervising attorney and the paralegal professional association rules imposed on paralegals. As a general rule, whatever the ethical rules forbid the attorney from doing, they also forbid the paralegal from doing. Paralegals therefore can look to their state's adopted set of rules, or code, of

---

Guidelines for the utilization of legal assistant services.   exhibit 2.1

GUIDELINE 1: A lawyer is responsible for all of the professional actions of a legal assistant performing legal assistant services at the lawyer's direction and should take reasonable measures to ensure that the legal assistant's conduct is consistent with the lawyer's obligations under the ABA Model Rules of Professional Conduct.

GUIDELINE 2: Provided the lawyer maintains responsibility for the work product, a lawyer may delegate to a legal assistant any task normally performed by the lawyer except those tasks proscribed to one not licensed as a lawyer by statute, court rule, administrative rule or regulation, controlling authority, the ABA Model Rules of Professional Conduct, or these Guidelines.

GUIDELINE 3: A lawyer may not delegate to a legal assistant:

(a) Responsibility for establishing an attorney–client relationship.

(b) Responsibility for establishing the amount of a fee to be charged for a legal service.

(c) Responsibility for a legal opinion rendered to a client.

GUIDELINE 4: It is the lawyer's responsibility to take reasonable measures to ensure that clients, courts, and other lawyers are aware that a legal assistant, whose services are utilized by the lawyer in performing legal services, is not licensed to practice law.

GUIDELINE 5: A lawyer may identify legal assistants by name and title on the lawyer's letterhead and on business cards identifying the lawyer's firm.

GUIDELINE 6: It is the responsibility of a lawyer to take reasonable measures to ensure that all client confidences are preserved by a legal assistant.

GUIDELINE 7: A lawyer should take reasonable measures to prevent conflicts of interest resulting from a legal assistant's other employment or interests insofar as such other employment or interests would present a conflict of interest if it were that of the lawyer.

GUIDELINE 8: A lawyer may include a charge for the work performed by a legal assistant in setting a charge for legal services.

GUIDELINE 9: A lawyer may not split legal fees with a legal assistant or pay a legal assistant for the referral of legal business. A lawyer may compensate a legal assistant based on the quantity and quality of the legal assistant's work and the value of that work to a law practice, but the legal assistant's compensation may not be contingent, by advance agreement, upon the profitability of the lawyer's practice.

GUIDELINE 10: A lawyer who employs a legal assistant should facilitate the legal assistant's participation in appropriate continuing education and pro bono publico activities.

Source: ABA Model Guidelines for Utilization of Legal Assistant Services. Copyright © 2001 by the American Bar Association. Reprinted with permission. All rights reserved.

ABA Model Guidelines for Utilization of Legal Assistant Services: www.abanet.org/ legalassts/modguide.html

professional responsibility for guidance in deciding what is appropriate or inappropriate from an ethical perspective.

By definition, the paralegal works under the supervision of an attorney. As such, the paralegal is the agent of the attorney and therefore owes a duty to the supervising attorney similar to that of the traditional agent–servant relationship found in agency law—that of a fiduciary obligation. Among the fiduciary obligations of an agent are the duty to exercise reasonable care, skill, and diligence. The agent also owes a duty of loyalty to the principal. This includes the obligation to act for the employer's benefit rather than for his or her own benefit or the benefit of another whose interest may be adverse to that of the employer.

By extension of the rule of agency, the paralegal, as a subagent of the supervising attorney, becomes an agent of the client. The attorney is an agent of the client, and the paralegal is a subagent. As an agent of the client, the same duties that are owed to the law firm as the employer are also owed to the client.

One of the questions that arise in firms engaged in corporate practice and in securities practice is whether the paralegal can purchase stock (securities) in a client corporation. Some firms have written policies prohibiting members of the firm, including paralegals, from purchasing the securities (stock) of client corporations. At the forefront is the propriety of using the information leading to the purchase or the transaction in client securities. Among the issues is whether the purchase was made based upon material inside information, information not generally available to the public, the knowledge of which would cause a person to buy or sell a corporate security. Use of material inside information of publicly traded stocks is generally a violation of federal securities laws prohibiting insider transactions.

For the attorney, guidance is available from Model Rule 1.7 and the comments to the Model Rule and under the previous Model Code DR 5–101A, which provides that an attorney must refuse employment when personal interests, including financial interests, might sway professional judgment. To the extent that this rule applies to the attorney, good judgment would dictate that it applies to the paralegal as well.

Paralegal Associations Ethics Codes

The two leading national paralegal membership organizations are the National Federation of Paralegal Associations and the National Association of Legal Assistants. Each of these groups has formulated a set of ethical guidelines for its respective membership, as well as for others looking for ethical guidance in the regulation of the paralegal profession.

National Federation of Paralegal Associations

NFPA Guidelines for Enforcement of the Model Code: www.paralegals.org/develop ment/modelcode.html

The National Federation of Paralegal Associations, Inc. is a professional organization composed of paralegal associations and individual paralegals throughout the United States and Canada. Members of NFPA have varying backgrounds, experiences, education, and job responsibilities that reflect the diversity of the paralegal profession. NFPA promotes the growth, development, and recognition of the paralegal profession as an integral partner in the delivery of legal services. Exhibit 2.2 presents a brief version of the NFPA Model Code. The full version is reproduced in Appendix B.

More than 20 percent of the world's population is Hindu. Most Hindus live in India, where they make up about 80 percent of the population. Others live in Burma, Kenya, Malaysia, Pakistan, Singapore, Tanzania, and Uganda. Hindu law is a religious law. As such, individual Hindus apply this law to themselves regardless of their nationality or place of domicile.

Classical Hindu law rests neither on civil codes nor on court decisions but, rather, on the works of private scholars that were passed along for centuries by oral tradition and eventually were recorded in the smitris (law books). Hindu law—called dharmasastra in Sanskrit, that is, the doctrine of proper behavior—is linked to the divine revelation of Veda (the holy collection of Indian religious songs, prayers, hymns, and sayings written between 2000 and 1000 B.C.). Most Hindu law is concerned with family matters and the law of succession.

After India became a British colony, British judges applied a combination of Hindu law and common law in solving cases. Once India gained its independence, this Anglo–Hindu law, as it was called, was ousted. In the mid-1950s, India codified Hindu law by enacting the Hindu Marriage Act, the Hindu Minority and Guardianship Act, the Hindu Succession Act, and the Hindu Adoptions and Maintenance Act. Outside of India, Anglo–Hindu law applies in most other countries populated by Hindus.

In April 1997, NFPA adopted the Model Disciplinary Rules (Model Rules) to make possible the enforcement of the Canons and Ethical Considerations contained in the NFPA Model Code. At present, unlike a violation by an attorney of the state-adopted rules that can result in loss of the right to practice (disbarment), no such sanction exists for the paralegal breach of association rules except loss of membership.

NFPA Code of Ethics and Professional Responsibility.	*exhibit 2.2*

§1. NFPA model disciplinary rules and ethical considerations

1.1 A paralegal shall achieve and maintain a high level of competence.

1.2 A paralegal shall maintain a high level of personal and professional integrity.

1.3 A paralegal shall maintain a high standard of professional conduct.

1.4 A paralegal shall serve the public interest by contributing to the improvement of the legal system and delivery of quality legal services, including pro bono publico services.

1.5 A paralegal shall preserve all confidential information provided by the client or acquired from other sources before, during, and after the course of the professional relationship.

1.6 A paralegal shall avoid conflicts of interest and shall disclose any possible conflict to the employer or client, as well as to the prospective employers or clients.

1.7 A paralegal's title shall be fully disclosed.

1.8 A paralegal shall not engage in the unauthorized practice of law.

Source: Copyright © 2002 by National Federation of Paralegal Associations. Excerpts reprinted with permission.

National Association of Legal Assistants

The National Association of Legal Assistants, formed in 1975, is a leading professional association for legal assistants. NALA provides continuing professional education, development, and certification. It may best be known in the profession for its Certified Legal Assistant (CLA) examination. The ABA Standing Committee on Legal Assistants has recognized the CLA designation as a designation marking a high level of professional achievement. Exhibit 2.3 gives the NALA Code.

exhibit 2.3 | *NALA Code of Ethics and Professional Responsibility.*

A legal assistant must adhere strictly to the accepted standards of legal ethics and to the general principles of proper conduct. The performance of the duties of the legal assistant shall be governed by specific canons as defined herein so that justice will be served and goals of the profession attained.

CANON 1. A legal assistant must not perform any of the duties that attorneys only may perform nor take any actions that attorneys may not take.

CANON 2. A legal assistant may perform any task which is properly delegated and supervised by an attorney, as long as the attorney is ultimately responsible to the client, maintains a direct relationship with the client, and assumes professional responsibility for the work product.

CANON 3. A legal assistant must not: (a) engage in, encourage, or contribute to any act which could constitute the unauthorized practice of law; and (b) establish attorney–client relationships, set fees, give legal opinions or advice, or represent a client before a court or agency unless so authorized by that court or agency; and (c) engage in conduct or take any action which would assist or involve the attorney in a violation of professional ethics or give the appearance of professional impropriety.

CANON 4. A legal assistant must use discretion and professional judgment commensurate with knowledge and experience but must not render independent legal judgment in place of an attorney. The services of an attorney are essential in the public interest whenever such legal judgment is required.

CANON 5. A legal assistant must disclose his or her status as a legal assistant at the outset of any professional relationship with a client, attorney, a court or administrative agency or personnel thereof, or a member of the general public. A legal assistant must act prudently in determining the extent to which a client may be assisted without the presence of an attorney.

CANON 6. A legal assistant must strive to maintain integrity and a high degree of competency through education and training with respect to professional responsibility, local rules and practice, and through continuing education in substantive areas of law to better assist the legal profession in fulfilling its duty to provide legal service.

CANON 7. A legal assistant must protect the confidences of a client and must not violate any rule or statute now in effect or hereafter enacted controlling the doctrine of privileged communications between a client and an attorney.

CANON 8. A legal assistant must do all other things incidental, necessary, or expedient for the attainment of the ethics and responsibilities as defined by statute or rule of court.

CANON 9. A legal assistant's conduct is guided by bar associations' codes of professional responsibility and rules of professional conduct.

Copyright © 1975; revised 1979, 1988, 1995. Reprinted with permission of the National Association of Legal Assistants, www.nala.org, 1516 S. Boston, #200, Tulsa, OK 74119.

Conflict of Interest

A conflict of interest exists if the representation of one client will be directly adverse to the interest of another client. Conflict of interest may best be explained by the biblical adage that "no one can serve two masters." If the master is entitled to complete loyalty, any conflict in loyalties presents a conflict of interest in which neither master can be certain of the loyalty of his or her servant. It's easy to see the conflict that would arise in a lawyer's going to court representing both the plaintiff and the defendant. Less obvious are situations in which the attorney represents two parties with a common interest, such as a husband and wife purchasing a new home. In most cases, the interests would be the same and no conflict would exist. When these clients are seeking counseling for marital problems, however, the conflict becomes more obvious as one of them seeks a greater share of the common property or other rights and the lawyer is called upon to give legal advice as to the right to the parties. Finally, lawyers clearly cannot represent both husband and wife in court in the marital dissolution trial.

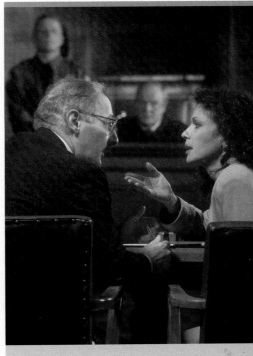

A lawyer and her client consult in court.

The American Bar Association Model Rules of Professional Conduct provide a guideline in Rule 1.7, Conflict of Interest: General Rule, which provides in part that a lawyer shall not represent a client if the representation of that client will be directly adverse to another client, unless the lawyer reasonably believes the representation "will not adversely affect the relationship with the other client; and each client consents after consultation."

The essence of the rule is that of loyalty to the client. The 1981 version of the American Bar Association Model Code of Professional Responsibility provides in Canon 5:

> A lawyer should exercise independent professional judgment on behalf of a client.

The ethical considerations comment to Canon 5 states:

> EC5–1 The professional judgment of a lawyer should be exercised, within the bounds of the law, solely for the benefit of his client and free of compromising influences and loyalties. Neither his personal interests, the interests of other clients, nor the desires of third persons should be permitted to dilute his loyalty to his client.

Clearly, a lawyer should not accept the employment if the lawyer's personal interests or desires will, or if there is a reasonable probability that they will, adversely affect the advice to be given or services to be rendered to the prospective client. The information that may be considered to create a conflict of interest is not limited solely to that of the attorney representing a client. It also includes the information held by another member of the legal team, including the legal assistant.

The National Federation of Paralegal Associations Model Code of Ethics provides in Canon 8:

> A paralegal shall avoid conflicts of interest and shall disclose any possible conflict to the employer or client, as well as to their prospective employers or clients.

The ultimate obligation to determine the conflict of interest of the paralegal or legal assistant rests with the supervising attorney. Standard procedure in law firms is to check for conflicts of interest within the law firm before accepting a new client or undertaking a new matter for an existing client. Just as other attorneys are asked to review lists of new clients and new matters, so must paralegals check to be certain they do not have a conflict of interest.

Conflicts of interest may arise for paralegals when they change from one employer to another. If the previous employer represented a client or handled certain matters for a client during the period in which the paralegal was employed, a conflict of interest may exist. A more difficult concern for the paralegal is the conflict of interest that can arise from a law firm's representation of family members and personal friends. Paralegals frequently refer family and friends to the attorney or the law firm where they work. The mere relationship or friendship itself might not create conflict but in some cases could give rise to a claim of undue influence wherein the paralegal may stand to benefit from the action of the law firm. Examples are the drafting of wills and trusts in which the paralegal may be named as a beneficiary or instances in which the paralegal may be named as the executor of the estate or as a trustee receiving compensation.

Ethical Wall

Law firms use the term *ethical wall*—also called a Chinese wall—to describe an environment in which an attorney or a paralegal is isolated from a particular case or client to avoid a conflict of interest or to protect a client's confidences and secrets. By creating this boundary or wall, any potential communications, whether written or oral, are prevented between the members of the legal team handling a particular matter or client and the person with whom there may be a conflict of interest.

In an age of consolidation of law firms in many areas, the number of individual employers has diminished while the number of clients has increased. As a result, professionals today may find themselves in firms that were on the opposite side of cases in the past. Creating an ethical wall permits the professional to accept employment with the other firm. It also permits greater mobility by professionals, as they can go to a new firm in which there may have been a conflict.

Ethical PERSPECTIVE

Uniformity of Paralegal Ethics

The paralegal profession has no unified code of ethics. State regulations and ethics opinions are not uniform. National organizations such as the National Association of Legal Assistants and the National Federation of Paralegal Associations each provide a uniform code of ethical conduct for members.

Moonlighting

Freelance or independent paralegals who work for more than one firm or attorney face the potential problem of conflict of interest. Special caution has to be taken to avoid accepting employment in cases where conflicts may exist. Freelance and independent paralegals are keenly aware of this and generally take precautions to prevent conflicts. The law firms and attorneys for whom they work usually are aware of the potential and also take special precautions to isolate potential conflict situations. Full-time paralegals who seek outside income should pay special attention to potential conflicts that may arise.

Not all of these conflicts are obvious. Consider the case of a paralegal working for a plaintiffs negligence firm handling cases against a major retail store. That paralegal's acceptance of employment at the retail store the firm is suing presents a conflict of interest. Knowledge of the strategy of the case would be of interest to the retail store employer. But divulging the information would breach the confidence of the law firm and the confidence of the law firm's client. Failure to disclose information to the retail store that directly affects its business breaches the duty of loyalty to that employer.

Attorney–Client Privilege

Attorney–client privilege is founded on the belief that clients should be able to tell their attorneys everything about their case so the attorney can give proper legal advice to the client. For the attorney, the ABA Model Rules provide in Rule 1.6, Confidentiality of Information, that "a lawyer shall not reveal information relating to representation of a client unless the client consents after consultation, except for disclosures that are impliedly authorized."

Work Product Doctrine

Work product is broadly defined to include the certain written statements and memoranda prepared by counsel in representation of a client, generally in preparation for trial. In *Hickman v. Taylor* [329 U.S. 495 (1947)] the court recognized a qualified immunity from discovery for the "work product of the lawyer"; such material could be discovered only upon a substantial showing of "necessity or justification." An exemption from discovery was necessary because, as the Hickman court stated:

> Were such materials open to opposing counsel on mere demand, much of what is now put down in writing would remain unwritten. An attorney's thoughts, heretofore inviolate, would not be his own. Inefficiency, unfairness and sharp practices would inevitably develop in the giving of legal advice and in the preparation of cases for trial. The effect on the legal profession would be demoralizing. And the interests of the clients and the cause of justice would be poorly served.

The work product doctrine is an extension of the attorney–client privilege wherein the nonlawyer is assisting the lawyer in trial preparation. Litigation practice today requires that attorneys use nonlawyers including paralegals, secretaries, law clerks, and others. The client will communicate through these members of the legal team, and the same privileges must exist [*U. S. v. Koval*, 196 F.2d 918, quoting 8 Wigmore, Evidence 2290, 2201]. The attorney's work prod-

Ethical PERSPECTIVE

The Paralegal and the Claim of Attorney–Client Privilege

As stated by the federal court in the case of Claus Von Bulow:

"The law is clear in this circuit the person claiming the attorney–client privilege has the burden of establishing all the essential elements thereof. The question is a simple one. Was Reynolds [a friend of Claus Von Bulow claiming that information given to her by the defendant was privileged] an agent of an attorney and has she presented sufficient evidence of this relationship? In other words, were communications made to her, in confidence, in her capacity as an agent of an attorney for the purpose of obtaining legal advice from that attorney? We think not.

"The attorney–client privilege is founded on the assumption that encouraging clients to make the fullest disclosure to their attorneys enables the latter to act more effectively. We have recognized that an attorney's effectiveness depends upon his ability to rely on the assistance of various aides, be they secretaries, file clerks, telephone operators, messengers, clerks not yet admitted to the bar, and aids of other sorts. The privilege must include all the persons who act as the attorney's agents."

Source: Von Bulow v. Von Bulow, 811 F. 2d 136 (2d Cir. 1987).

Federal Rules of Civil Procedure Rule 26

General Provisions Governing Discovery;
Duty of Disclosure

(b)(3) Trial Preparation: Materials. . . .
A party may obtain discovery of documents
and tangible things otherwise discoverable
. . . and prepared in anticipation of litigation or for trial by or for another party or
by or for that other party's representative
(including the other party's attorney, consultant, surety, indemnitor, insurer, or agent)
only upon a showing that the party seeking discovery has substantial need of the
materials in the preparation of the party's
case and that the party is unable without
undue hardship to obtain the substantial
equivalent of the materials by other
means. . . . The court shall protect against
disclosure of the mental impressions,
conclusions, opinions, or legal theories of
an attorney or other representative of a
party concerning a litigation.

uct has been the subject of extensive litigation. The distinction between what is discoverable and what is trial preparation
is not always clear. The courts must balance the needs of the
opposing sides.

THE FUTURE

What can you expect in the future? Certainly the demands of
employers and courts will dictate that educational requirements be increased as the paralegal becomes a more and more
important member of the legal services team. As an organization, the American Association of Legal Administrators,
representing the law office administrators who do much of the
hiring of paralegals, advocates a four-year degree as a minimum standard.

As courts mandate that certain activities be performed by
paralegals and not by lawyers, the demand for better qualified
paralegals will follow. The courts will look to credentials and
training in making determinations of who may act and bill for
services as a paralegal. If lawyers are responsible for the activities delegated to their paralegals, they will insist that paralegals
be better trained and qualified. Hiring decisions in the future
may be based on educational minimums. Years of experience
as a legal secretary may not count as much as being a graduate of an educational institution with a minimum set of
standards such as those of the American Association for Paralegal Education.

American Association of Legal
Administrators: www.alanet.
org/home.html

AAfPE Regulations Statement:
www.aafpe.org/acadqual.html

LEGAL TERMINOLOGY

Attorney–client privilege
Conflict of interest
Ethical wall
Model Guidelines for the Utilization of Legal Assistant Services
Model Rules of Professional Conduct
Unauthorized practice of law (UPL)
Work product doctrine

AAfPE Position on Educational Standards for Paralegal Regulation

The American Association for Paralegal Education (AAfPE), in existence since 1981, is the only national organization serving paralegal educators and institutions that offer paralegal programs. AAfPE presently has more than 450 members. AAfPE-member schools currently enroll more than 41,000 students and have graduated nearly 191,000 students.

As the national resource for paralegal education, AAfPE has set minimum recommended educational standards for paralegal education programs to become institutional members. AAfPE believes that the paralegal profession requires training of sufficient length, sophistication, intensity, and quality to produce a functional entry-level paralegal.

Certain educational components should be required in any paralegal regulatory plan. AAfPE recommends that state legislatures, courts, and/or bar associations considering paralegal regulation should adopt or include the AAfPE educational minimum standards described below.

FORMAL PARALEGAL EDUCATION

It is the position of AAfPE that some form of formal paralegal education should be present as a meaningful requirement in any paralegal regulation plan. This formal paralegal education should be offered through a program specifically designed to provide paralegal education.

MINIMUM LENGTH OF STUDY

A person is qualified as a paralegal with (1) an associate or baccalaureate degree or equivalent coursework, and (2) a credential in paralegal education from a paralegal program associated with an educational institution accredited by a nationally recognized agency completed in any of the following types of educational programs: associate degree, baccalaureate degree (major or minor), certificate, or master's degree.

A paralegal's education shall include, either as separate courses or within the overall course of study, coursework in substantive and procedural law, the American legal system, law offices and related environments, the paralegal profession, legal research and writing, ethics, and areas of legal practice such as those described in AAfPE's Core Competencies for Paralegal Programs.

The paralegal's credential shall include no fewer than 18 semester-credit hours of substantive paralegal classes and shall be from a paralegal education program that, at the time the paralegal credential is granted, is:

1. An institutional member of the American Association for Paralegal Education or

2. A paralegal educational program approved by the American Bar Association or

3. A paralegal education program at the post-secondary (college) level that requires the student to have completed a minimum of sixty (60) semester hours (or the equivalent) of total study prior to graduation. A semester hour is equivalent to 15 classroom hours of at least 50 minutes in duration. The course offerings may be for credit or not for credit, but they should meet these minimum time periods.

OTHER EDUCATIONAL INSTITUTION REQUIREMENTS

The educational institution should be accredited by a nationally recognized accrediting agency. Additionally, the institution should meet the educational standards described in the AAfPE Statement of Academic Quality.

Minimum educational requirements are essential in any paralegal regulation plan. Paralegal education is a unique academic curriculum, composed of both substantive legal knowledge and professional skills, which incorporates legal theory with practical application. Any proposal for regulation of paralegals should contain provisions incorporating the level of paralegal education necessary to enable graduates to meet the responsibilities of paralegals as legal professionals.

In recent years there has been a proliferation of short-term entry-level paralegal training programs of very limited duration, some with as few as 125 clock hours (which is less than 9 semester credit hours). These programs do a fundamental disservice to the legal profession by creating unrealistic expectations in both employers and students that a quality paralegal education has been delivered when such is not the case. State regulatory bodies are urged to adopt the educational minimums defined in this document as a requisite element of any paralegal regulation plan.

The AAfPE Board of Directors adopted this Position Statement on February 24, 2001, at San Antonio, Texas. Reprinted with permission of AAfPE.

Summary

CHAPTER 2 ETHICS, REGULATION, AND PROFESSIONAL RESPONSIBILITY

Unauthorized Practice of Law (UPL)

Relevant Issues	1. Regulation of the practice
	2. Giving advice
	3. Filling out forms

Regulation of the Paralegal Profession

State Function	Done by legislatures and courts of each state

Ethical Rules and Obligations

ABA Rules	1. ABA Model Rules of Professional Conduct
	2. ABA Guidelines for the Utilization of Legal Assistant Services
Paralegal Associations Ethics Codes	1. National Federation of Paralegal Associations Model Code
	2. National Association of Legal Assistants (CLA exam) Code of Ethics and Professional Responsibilities
Conflict of Interest	Association Guidelines
	1. ABA Model Rules of Professional Conduct
	2. ABA Model Code of Professional Responsibility
	3. NFPA Model Code of Ethics
Ethical Wall	Definition: An environment in which an attorney or a paralegal is isolated from a case or client to avoid a conflict of interest or to protect a client's confidences and secrets
Moonlighting	Definition: Working for more than one firm or attorney
Attorney–Client Privilege	1. Definition: A rule that says a client can tell his or her lawyer anything about the case without fear that the attorney will be called as a witness against the client
	2. Governed by ABA Model Rules, Confidentiality of Information
Work Product Doctrine	1. Work products are certain written statements and memoranda prepared by counsel in representation of a client
	2. Doctrine extends attorney–client privilege to paralegals

The Future

Education	1. NALA (recommends four-year degree)
	2. AAfPE standards

Working the Web

1. Check the NALA website at www.NALA.org for the latest ethics rules and opinions.
2. Check the NFPA at www.paralegal.org for ethics updates.
3. Check the ABA website at www.abanet.org for ethics updates.
4. Find your state bar association website, providing guidance or opinions on legal ethics, by using an Internet search engine such as www.Yahoo.com or www.google.com.
5. Check the NFPA website for agencies that allow nonlawyer practice at www.paralegals.org/Development/Roles/allow.html.

Questions

CRITICAL LEGAL THINKING AND WRITING

1. What is the general theory for regulating the practice of law? How is this applied?
2. Why is "just giving advice" potentially the unauthorized practice of law?
3. How would regulation of the paralegal profession assure the public of quality legal services?
4. What is the advantage to the paralegal in obtaining the PACE or CLA designation?
5. Why should the paralegal be familiar with the ABA Model Rules of Professional Conduct?
6. How do the ABA Model Guidelines for the Utilization of Legal Assistant Services define the role of the paralegal in the law office?
7. Do violations by a paralegal of the ethics rules of the national paralegal associations have the same impact as violation of the ethical rules of attorneys on the right to practice?
8. Would a paralegal dating a client have a conflict of interest caused by compromising influences and loyalties?
9. Under what circumstances might a paralegal have a conflict of interest in taking a new job in a law firm?
10. How does an ethical wall protect the client?
11. Does a client have an attorney–client privilege regarding information given to a paralegal during the preparation of a case?
12. Should a paralegal be considered an "other representative" under the Federal Rules of Civil Procedure, Rule 26? Why or why not?

Questions

ETHICS: ANALYSIS AND DISCUSSION

1. Are paralegals held to the same standard as attorneys when there is no supervising attorney?
2. What is the paralegal's duty to the client when the paralegal's employer breaches its duty to the client?
3. Who is responsible for the quality of the legal work performed for a client, the attorney or the paralegal?

Unauthorized Practice of Law—Form Completion

There are few certainties in the area of ethics, for paralegals or in any profession. What qualifies as ethical conduct is in most cases based on state law and court interpretation applied to a set of facts. The citation listed below represents one legal opinion and is provided as a research starting point. Do not assume that the same rule applies in your jurisdiction. For the following:

- *Prepare a written statement based on your state law.*
- *Use your state bar association website as a starting point.*

You have graduated from a paralegal program at a local college. While you are looking for a job where your talents can be properly utilized, a friend asks you to help him fill out a set of bankruptcy forms using a computer program he has purchased at the local office supply mega warehouse. The program is designed to pick out the exemptions after the requested information is plugged in. [*In Re Kaitangian*, Calif. 218 BR 102 (1998).] Is this the unauthorized practice of law?

Case

FOR DISCUSSION

In Re *Estate of Devine*   263 Ill. App.3d 799 (1994)

A paralegal working in a small office became friendly with a client of the attorney and assisted the client in personal matters outside of the office, including helping him to shop and handle personal finances. In that role the paralegal was given power to sign checks for the client. After the client died, the paralegal withdrew $165,958 from the joint account with the deceased client.

Is a lawyer responsible for the actions of a paralegal?

The court held both the paralegal and the attorney liable for breach of fiduciary duty, holding that if the attorney, who performed work including writing a will leaving a bequest to the attorney and the paralegal, was a fiduciary, so then was the paralegal as a matter of law. Further, the court noted that the law in a number of states holds the attorney liable for a paralegal's acts including the responsibility for unethical conduct by nonlawyer employees of the lawyer. The Illinois court quoted New York and New Jersey cases holding the employing attorney in violation of the Code of Professional Conduct for failing to properly supervise employed paralegals.

Questions

1. Does this case effectively extend the lawyer's ethical rules to the conduct of paralegals?
2. May a paralegal maintain a personal relationship with a client of the firm?
3. Should a paralegal be as familiar as the supervising (employing) attorney with the ABA Model Rules of Professional Conduct?

Tegman v. Accident and Medical Investigations

30 P.3d 8 (Wash. Ct. App. 2001)   Court of Appeals of Washington, Division One

Read the following case excerpted from the Court of Appeals opinion. Review and brief the case. In your brief, answer the following questions.

1. How does this court define "the practice of law"?

2. What is the standard or duty of care that this court imposes on a paralegal who does not have a supervising attorney?

3. What action does this court suggest that a paralegal take when it becomes clear that there is no supervising attorney?

4. Why should a paralegal contact the supervising attorney immediately upon being given a case to handle?

5. Based on this case, should a paralegal advise the client that he or she is a paralegal? If so, when? Why?

Becker, Mary K., A.C.J.

Between 1989 and 1991, plaintiffs Maria Tegman, Linda Leszynski, and Daina Calixto were each injured in separate and unrelated automobile accidents. After their accidents, each plaintiff retained G. Richard McClellan and Accident & Medical Investigations, Inc. (AMI) for legal counsel and assistance in handling their personal injury claims. . . . Each plaintiff signed a contingency fee agreement with AMI, believing that McClellan was an attorney and AMI a law firm. McClellan has never been an attorney in any jurisdiction. McClellan and AMI employed Camille Jescavage, . . . [a] licensed attorney. . . .

Jescavage . . . learned that McClellan entered into contingency fee agreements with AMI's clients and that McClellan was not an attorney. [Attorneys for AMI] settled a number of cases for AMI, and learned that McClellan processed settlements of AMI cases through his own bank account. . . .

In July 1991, McClellan hired Deloris Mullen as a paralegal. Mullen considered Jescavage to be her supervising attorney, though Jescavage provided little supervision. Jescavage resigned from AMI in the first week of September 1991. McClellan told Mullen that her new supervising attorney would be James Bailey. Mullen did not immediately contact Bailey to confirm that he was her supervising attorney. [He] later told Mullen he was not.

While at AMI, Mullen worked on approximately 50–60 cases, including those of [the] plaintiffs. . . .

Mullen was aware of some of McClellan's questionable practices and knew that there were substantial improprieties involved with his operation. Mullen stopped working at AMI on December 6, 1991, when the situation became personally intolerable to her and she obtained direct knowledge that she was without a supervising attorney. When she left, she did not advise any of the plaintiffs about the problems at AMI. After Mullen left, McClellan settled each plaintiff's case for various amounts without their knowledge or consent, and deposited the funds in his general account by forging their names on the settlement checks.

The "practice of law" clearly does not just mean appearing in court. In a larger sense, it includes "legal advice and counsel, and the preparation of legal instruments and contracts by which legal rights are secured." Mullen contends that her status as a paralegal precludes a finding that she was engaged in the practice of law. She argues that a paralegal is, by definition, someone who works under the supervision of an attorney, and that it is necessarily the attorney, not the paralegal, who is practicing law and owes a duty to the clients. Her argument assumes that she had a supervising attorney. The trial court's determination that Mullen was negligent was dependent on the court's finding that Mullen knew, or should have known, that she did not have a supervising attorney over a period of several months while she was at AMI. . . .

The label "paralegal" is not in itself a shield from liability. A factual evaluation is necessary to distinguish a paralegal who is working under an attorney's supervision from one who is actually practicing law. A finding that a paralegal is practicing law will not be supported merely by evidence of infrequent contact with the supervising attorney. As long as the paralegal does in fact have a supervising attorney who is responsible for the case, any deficiency in the quality of the supervision or in the quality of the paralegal's work goes to the attorney's negligence, not the paralegal's.

In this case, Mullen testified that she believed James Bailey was her supervising attorney after Jescavage left. The court found Mullen was not justified in that belief. . . . Mullen testified that she had started to distrust McClellan before he informed her that Bailey would be her supervising attorney. Mullen also testified that she did not contact Bailey to confirm that he was supervising her. Bailey testified at a deposition that he did not share Mullen's clients and she did not consult him regarding any of her ongoing cases. He also said that one of the only conversations he remembers having with Mullen with respect to AMI is one where he told her that he was not her supervising attorney after she raised the issue with him. This testimony amply supports the trial court's finding that Mullen was unjustified in her belief that Bailey was her supervising attorney.

[Mullen] continued to send out demand and representation letters after Jescavage left AMI. Letters written by Mullen before Jescavage's departure identify Mullen as a paralegal after her signature, whereas letters she wrote after Jescavage's departure lacked such identification. Even after Mullen discovered, in late November 1991, that Bailey was not her supervising attorney, she wrote letters identifying "this office" as representing the plaintiffs, neglecting to mention that she was a paralegal and that no attorney was responsible for the case. This evidence substantially supports the finding that Mullen engaged in the practice of law.

Accordingly, we conclude the trial court did not err in following *Bowers* and holding Mullen to the duty of an attorney. The duty of care owed by an attorney is that degree of care, skill, diligence, and knowledge commonly possessed and exercised by a reasonable, careful, and prudent lawyer in the practice of law in Washington. . . .

The court found that the standard of care owed by an attorney, and therefore also by Mullen, required her to notify the plaintiffs of: (1) the serious problems concerning the accessibility of their files to persons who had no right to see them, (2) the fact that client settlements were not processed through an attorney's trust account but, rather, McClellan's own account, (3) the fact that McClellan and AMI, as nonlawyers, had no right to enter into contingent fee agreements with clients and receive contingent fees, (4) the fact that McClellan was, in fact, engaged in the unlawful practice of law, and that, generally, (5) the clients of McClellan and AMI were at substantial risk of financial harm as a result of their association with AMI. Mullen breached her duty to her clients in all of these particulars.

We conclude the finding is supported by substantial evidence. Accordingly, the trial court did not err in concluding that Mullen was negligent. . . .

Although Mullen was a paralegal, she is held to an attorney's standard of care because she worked on the plaintiffs' cases during a period of several months when she had no supervising attorney. The fact that she did not render legal advice directly does not excuse her; in fact, her failure to advise the plaintiffs of the improper arrangements at AMI is the very omission that breached her duty. Under these circumstances it is not unjust to hold her accountable as a legal cause of the plaintiffs' injuries. As all the elements of negligence have been established, we affirm the judgment against Mullen. Affirmed.

WE CONCUR: AGID, J., COLEMAN, J.

This case will also be published in the Washington Appellate Reports, and if cited in the courts of Washington, will require that citation as well. This case has a Lexis number of 2001 Wash. App. LEXIS 1890.

CHAPTER 3

Careers in the Paralegal Profession

The law relating to public policy cannot remain immutable; it must change with the passage of time. The wind of change blows on it.

L. J. DANCKWERTS, *NAGLE V. FEILDEN* (1966)

Introduction

Opportunities and career choices for the paralegal have never been better. Twenty years ago the role of the paralegal was a limited, behind-the-scenes role with little client contact except, possibly, as a receptionist or a legal secretary. Today, paralegals are employed in every area of the law. They interview clients, conduct factual investigations, do legal research, prepare legal documents, assist at the counsel table in trials, and even represent clients in some administrative hearings. They are employed in law firms of all sizes, federal, state, and local government, insurance companies, and corporations.

COMPENSATION ISSUES FOR THE PARALEGAL

Paralegal compensation is as varied as the variety of working environments and regional locations. As with most jobs and professions, salaries tend to be higher in large metropolitan areas and lower in small and rural areas. Large firms tend to pay more and small firms tend to pay less. At times these variations in compensation can be justified by the costs of working in certain locations, such as higher taxation and the cost of commuting. Exhibit 3.1 gives a breakdown of hourly rates for paralegals by level and geographic region.

exhibit 3.1 *Hourly compensation for legal assistants/paralegals.*

SURVEY COVERS THREE LEVELS OF LEGAL ASSISTANT PAY

To assist in setting competitive pay levels, the *ECS Geographic Report on Professional and Technical Personnel Compensation* from Watson Wyatt Data Services breaks down the hourly wages for three levels of legal assistants/paralegals by geographic region. Highlights of the report are as follows:

FOR-PROFIT COMPANIES

Overall median rate for a legal assistant/paralegal:	$18.83/hour
Level 1, entry level, three or fewer years of experience, standardized tasks:	$15.20/hour
Highest rate: Middle Southeast states:	$17.43/hour
Level 2, intermediate, three to five years of experience, advanced skills:	$18.47/hour
Highest rate: Pacific Southwest states:	$21.16/hour
Next highest rate: Lower Mountain states:	$21.06/hour
Level 3, senior, five or more years of experience; tasks with substantial variety and complexity:	$20.90/hour
Highest rate: Pacific Southwest states:	$24.00/hour
Next highest rate: Central Plains states:	$23.04/hour

NOT-FOR-PROFIT COMPANIES

Entry-level paralegal:	$13.80/hour
Intermediate paralegal:	$15.84/hour
Senior paralegal:	$18.86/hour

SELECTING A SPECIALTY

It is never too early to set career goals. The decision to pursue a paralegal profession offers many and varied opportunities and specialties. The final career path you take will no doubt have many bends and turns as you start your first job and learn about the different areas of practice that are available to you. Your ultimate specialty or employer might result from your educational background, such as journalism or medicine, or an area of special interest such as environmental issues, or possibly just a preference to work with certain types of clients such as the elderly or infirm.

And it is never too late to make a career adjustment. Many successful individuals begin a career later in life. Colonel Sanders started Kentucky Fried Chicken late in life. Schools are full of nontraditional students seeking a career change. In the paralegal field we are seeing more and more nurses who, having worked in the medical field for years, are making a career change to the legal field.

What is important is to find a career that will give you satisfaction and in which you look forward to going to work. The decision should start with a self-evaluation of your likes and dislikes, interests, passions, and any physical or geographic limitations. If you hate to fly, you probably do not want a job that requires travel. If you are not comfortable with strangers, you probably do not want a job as a paralegal investigator for a litigation firm. If you like books and research, you might want to work as the firm librarian or researcher. Consider the characteristics in the career-planning checklist on page 61.

Paralegals as Exempt Employees Under Federal Law

Employees classified as exempt employees under the Fair Labor Standards Act are exempt from the rules requiring payment of overtime for working more than 40 hours per week. Under the Fair Labor Standards Act (FLSA), certain classes of employees—loosely defined as executive, administrative, or professional—are exempt from the Act's provisions of minimum wage and overtime pay. In many professional occupations compensation is based not on hourly labor rates but, rather, on an annual salary. As consideration for the salary, employees are not bound to the traditional 40-hour work week but may work hours in excess without being paid extra.

In certain types of practices, working in excess of the 40 hours, sometimes substantially, is common. This is particularly true in litigation practices during the course of a trial in which much preparation work is done at night and on weekends when the litigation team is not in actual court. Similarly, those in taxation practices work many extra hours during "tax season," generally mid-January to April 15. In recognition of the additional demands for time during these periods, many firms pay a flat salary and attempt to avoid hourly timekeeping altogether.

The Department of Labor, in the case of *DOL v. Page & Anderson P.C.,* attempted to have paralegals treated as nonexempt, which would have required the firm to pay overtime under the FLSA. Even though the DOL lost and abandoned its appeal with prejudice, preventing relitigating that case, the case is fact-specific to the paralegals in that firm and cannot be relied upon by other law firms.

The problem with classifying the paralegal as an exempt employee comes from the definition of "exempt employee" under the FLSA. To come under the *executive* exemption, the employee must customarily and regularly exercise discretionary powers; to come under the *administrative* exemption, one must customarily and regularly exercise discretion and independent judgment; and to come under the *professional* exemption, the work requires the consistent exercise of discretion and judgment. In describing the duties of a paralegal, most lawyers and paralegals use these phrases to describe the duties and obligations of the profession. But one of the definitions of a paralegal includes the phrase "under the direction and control of the supervising attorney." If the actions are "under the direction and control" of someone else, the person is not exercising "independent judgment and discretion," and therefore does not qualify under most interpretations of the FLSA.

Because of the rigid position of the United States Department of Labor in interpreting the FLSA, many employers classify the paralegal as an hourly employee, not out of disrespect but, rather, out of fear of a DOL audit. Failure to comply can result in claims by the DOL for willful violation of the act, which can result in penalties, including liquidated damages, and civil penalties of up to $10,000 and potential imprisonment for up to six months.

The Paralegal's Portfolio

Kathryn Myers, Coordinator, Paralegal Studies   **Saint Mary-of-the-Woods College,** Paralegal Studies Program

INTERVIEW

Q: How did the practice of assembling a portfolio come about?

A: This portfolio is actually based on the old concept of the "artist's portfolio." Anyone who is involved in a "hands-on" profession has utilized this concept for years.

Q: Instead of pictures, what do you mean when you speak of a portfolio for paralegal students?

A: A portfolio for paralegal students consists of two parts. One part is for my use in the program. The students have growth papers for each class, plus a series of other papers. I look at the collection of work to determine whether the paralegal program is doing what it says it will and whether it needs to be changed. I have modified a number of classes based on the material in this portfolio.

   The other part is a professional portfolio. The students pull material from the above portfolio and create their own professional portfolio to take on interviews. This contains a copy or copies of their resume, transcripts, selected writing samples, projects, or any other document they believe would be useful at the interview. Employers have been very impressed with this presentation.

Q: Do potential employers ever balk at seeing something that bulky? If so, how would you suggest handling it?

A: This has not been a problem for my students. As indicated earlier, we "create" two portfolios—one program-related and the other for professional purposes. I think this eliminates any problems at the interview.

Q: What is the most important thing about a portfolio?

A: The most important thing in the professional portfolio appears to be that the employer has another tool to assess the quality of the potential employee. Grades do not mean that much anymore. An "A" at [our college] may well come from a more demanding curriculum than an "A" at another institution. There is no basis for comparison unless the employer knows the grading scales/demands of the different programs. However, having a portfolio of material allows the employer to see what an interviewee can do.

Q: With that in mind, what should a paralegal student keep in mind when putting together the portfolio?

A: How a student puts a portfolio together says a lot about the student. I encourage students to incorporate both good and "not so good" work. That shows the employer that the interviewee can learn and can improve. Students collect material as they go through the program rather than waiting until the end.

   Students should highlight their growth, their abilities, and their determination. They need to provide documentation that can show abilities that counter any poor grades that might appear on the transcript. This shows potential employers that test-taking is not necessarily the be-all, end-all to grades.

   Most of all, the students need to let themselves shine through within the portfolio materials. Each students is unique and each has different talents to highlight. That is the value of the portfolio.

THE STUDENT PORTFOLIO

The following is an excerpt from Kathryn Myers' article on portfolios on the American Association for Paralegal Education website at www.aafpe.org/smwc.html.

A portfolio is a purposeful collection of student work that is accumulated over time. The material reveals the extent of student learning, achievement, and development. The "portfolio system" is intended to specify knowledge and competence in areas considered necessary to successfully work as a paralegal/ legal assistant while leaving the selection of means of documentation of competency to the individual student. Documentation of knowledge and skill acquisition can take a variety of forms including, but not limited to, letters of support

diaries

videotapes and audiotapes of work

pleadings

memoranda

course projects

registration receipts from continuing education and other conferences attended

proof of membership in professional organizations

subscriptions to legal publications

Typically, much of the material can be compiled from projects and activities required within courses.

Procedure

The portfolio shall contain documentation of knowledge and skill acquisition based on the Core Competencies established by the American Association for Paralegal Education. Those core competencies are divided into two areas—skill development and acquisition of knowledge. Within those areas are competencies based on:

Skill Development

critical thinking skills

organizational skills

general communication skills

interpersonal skills

legal research skills

legal writing skills

computer skills

interviewing and investigation skills

Acquisition of Knowledge

organization and operation of the legal system

organization and operation of law offices

the paralegal profession and ethical obligations

contracts

torts

business organizations

litigation procedures

It is understood that the areas may overlap somewhat and that these areas do not cover all competencies associated with the program, student growth, or professional success. However, students who perfect these competencies and who perform from this educational base have a foundation for success.

It is suggested that the student purchase a secure container to collect and organize the material [such as] a hanging file folder or file box. This portfolio may be maintained on computer disk; however, you will not have any graded materials if this is the only method of collection you use.

Students should keep a log of all materials completed. When completing each assignment, [they should] enter the document in the log, with a column to check for inclusion in the campus portfolio and another to check for inclusion in the professional portfolio. Some documents may, of course, overlap in their application.

Students are responsible for the contents of their portfolios. The student should periodically review the contents of the portfolio and add or remove materials based on decisions as to the extent to which the contents adequately represent knowledge and skill acquisition in each of the areas outlined below. This portfolio is not intended to be a compilation of senior level work; rather, it is useful to provide work of varying levels of efficiency to show, among other things, growth and improvement.

Content

To be a successful paralegal/legal assistant, the student must possess a common core of legal knowledge as well as acquire vital critical thinking, organizational, communication, and interpersonal skills. Courses in a student's program should provide the student with the means to develop the competencies, which have been divided into the following sections:

Area 1   Understanding the Profession and Its Ethical Obligations

Area 2   Research

Area 3   Legal Writing

Guidelines for Selecting Entries

When selecting entries, students should bear in mind that each piece is part of a much larger whole and that, together, the artifacts and rationale make a powerful statement about individual professional development. Asking the following questions may help with decision making.

1. What do I want my portfolio to show about me as a paralegal? What are my attributes as a paralegal?

2. What do I want my portfolio to demonstrate about me as a learner? How and what have I learned?

3. What directions for my future growth and development does my self-evaluation suggest? How can I show them in my portfolio?

4. What points have been made by others about me as a paralegal and learner? How can I show them in my portfolio?

5. What effect does my professionalism have upon my peers? How can I show this in my portfolio?

6. What overall impression do I want my portfolio to give a reviewer about me as a learner and as a paralegal?

When decision making about what to include becomes a challenge, it may be helpful to look at each artifact and ask yourself, "What would including this item add that has not already been said or shown?" Remember that portfolios create representative records of your professional development; they are not intended to be comprehensive.

Values and Attitudes

Values and attitudes determine the choices we make in our lives. They cross the boundaries of subject-matter areas. Thus, in this final section of your portfolio, you are asked to look at your own values and attitudes and then write a one- to three-page paper in which you reflect upon your own values. Identify one or more values that are important to you. Explain how they influence your choices as a person, parent, future paralegal, voter, and/or citizen of the global community. Include specific examples.

The following questions may help you choose a topic for your essay: What does it mean to be honest? fair? tolerant? open to new ideas and experiences? respect evidence? Which is more important—decreasing the production of greenhouse gases or preserving jobs? The right to choose how many children we want or controlling world population growth? Freedom to produce pornographic art or the right of children to be sheltered from such experiences? Spending more time with your children or getting a second job so you can buy things you want?

There are no easy answers to these questions. Have fun thinking about your own values. Remember to include specific examples from your own life!

Transcripts

Include copies of unofficial transcripts from all colleges and universities that you have attended.

Degree evaluation	Include a copy of your degree evaluation, if you received one.
Graduation evaluation	Include a copy of your graduation evaluation.
Awards or recognitions	Include copies of awards or recognitions you have received.

PROFESSIONAL PORTFOLIO

Modify this inclusive portfolio into a professional portfolio. This professional portfolio will be representative, not comprehensive. Each artifact chosen for inclusion should represent at least one significant aspect of you and/or your accomplishments that can be translated into employability. Use these guidelines to prepare your professional portfolio:

1. Prepare your portfolio as a showcase of your best work—your highest achievements. This will involve selecting from artifacts in your portfolio and adding new ones.

2. Do not send your portfolio when you apply for a job. Rather, include in your cover letter a statement concerning your portfolio. For example: "Throughout my paralegal studies program at _____ College, I developed a professional

portfolio that clearly and concisely exhibits my attributes as a paralegal. I would be pleased to share this portfolio with you during an interview."

3. If granted an interview, take your portfolio with you. Be prepared to present the highlights. Practice presenting it effectively. In some instances, you might be asked to present it at the beginning of the interview, and in other instances you might use it as a source of evidence or enhancement of a point you make in the interview. Interviewing practices vary widely from employer to employer. Portfolios are most likely to be reviewed in situations where the employer is familiar with the abilities of a paralegal.

4. If the interviewer(s) is particularly interested and would like to examine your portfolio more closely, offer to leave it if at all possible. You should make explicit arrangements for collecting it and, of course, follow through as planned. It could be that your portfolio will create the impression that tips the scales in your favor.

5. Remember—it is likely that some people in a position to hire are not familiar with professional portfolios as you know them. Take time to con-cisely explain that developing your portfolio has been a process of reflection and evaluation that has helped you to know yourself as a paralegal and to establish a foundation for career-long profes-sional development. To some extent, presenting your portfolio will inform the interviewer about both you and the portfolio concept and process.

6. Keep your portfolio up to date. As you continue to gain experience and to grow professionally, alter it to reflect your development. It is not only your first job application that may be enhanced by a well prepared and presented portfolio but developing your portfolio is an excellent founda-tion for meeting any expectation of continuing legal education.

Conclusion

It is my hope and intention that by your creating this portfolio, you have an opportunity to reflect upon your education and to emphasize to yourself and others that you are capable and qualified to per-form as a paralegal. It is time to believe in you. Good luck!

Reproduced with permission of the author.

Checklist

CAREER PLANNING

○ My current paralegal job-related skills are:

○ My special interests are:

○ My passions are:

○ My personality traits are:

○ My geographical work and living desires are:

○ My willingness to accept responsibility is:

○ My level of self-motivation is:

ASSESSING YOUR BACKGROUND

As the law has become more specialized, so has the demand for paralegals with more than just paralegal skills. Law firms specializing in an area such as medical malpractice frequently look for paralegals who also have a medical background such as nursing. Firms with large, complex litigation cases often look for someone with computer database skills who can manage the files. Paralegals with journalism experience and training frequently are sought out for their interviewing and writing skills.

Your personal background can be an asset when added to your paralegal certificate or degree. As you begin your professional training, take stock of your entire educational background, special skills, and talents, as well as personal areas of interest.

ASSESSING YOUR SKILLS

You may well have a number of personal skills that will benefit you in the future as a paralegal. You might have great interpersonal skills, communicate well orally and in writing, and be a highly motivated person—all qualities of a good paralegal. Individuals with language skills are particularly in demand in international law, as well as in working with clients who lack English-language skills. The paralegal who understands a second language and the cultural nuances of the client's background can be invaluable.

ASSESSING YOUR INTERESTS

What are your personal interests? Are you an active outdoors person in your free time, for whom working on environmental issues would be of great interest and satisfaction? Do you find yourself drawn to volunteering or working in your free time with shut-ins and elderly people?

Doing a self-assessment early in your studies offers you an opportunity to recognize your strengths and develop them and to acknowledge weaknesses that you need to work on to permit your personal and professional growth. Becoming aware of your interests and background knowledge enables you to select the elective course that can qualify you for work in a specialty field of law.

SELECTING YOUR ELECTIVES

If you have a career goal for a specific legal specialty, taking electives is a good way to gain additional knowledge in the specialty area of interest. Taking electives also is a good way to explore an area in which you think you might be interested, without committing to more than one semester or a few credits of study. Many students find new interests and a potential career direction after taking courses in areas they had not considered previously. For example, you may have been reading in newspapers and magazines, and following on television, stories about the high technology industries and wondered how your career goal as a paralegal would fit into this growth area. One of the fastest growing fields is that of intellectual property law.

In an age of dot coms, computers, and a growing global marketplace, protection of intellectual property has become a critical concern for individuals and companies alike. Taking a three-credit course in intellectual property may well introduce the paralegal student to a new area of interest in a potential growth area of the paralegal profession. This is also true for other emerging areas in the paralegal profession, such as environmental law and legal nurse consulting.

PREPARING YOUR RESUME

A resume is a short description of a person's education, a summary of work experience, and other related and supporting information that potential employers use in evaluating a person's qualifications for a position in a firm or an organization. Exhibit 3.2 provides an example. You should prepare a resume as you see yourself today. Look at your resume from the perspective of a future employer. What areas do you need to strengthen to demonstrate your ability to perform the type of job you would like to have? You should look at your resume as being a continuing work in progress. Constantly update your resume to include any new job responsibilities, part-time employment skills and qualifications, and special achievements. Add meaningful items to your resume in the form of courses, skills, and outside interests that will land you that first paralegal job after you complete your training.

After you have gathered all of the necessary information, put it into a proper resume form, then review it. Does the resume reflect the information you want to communicate to a prospective employer? Try to look at it with an open, objective mind. Employers are looking for individuals who demonstrate a good work ethic, willingness to accept responsibility and take direction, and the skills necessary for the job for which they are applying.

Set your roadmap for the job you wish to obtain. What additional educational skills are required? This will determine your future course of study. Work-study programs in your field or cooperative education are good ways of demonstrating on-the-job training. Depending upon your goals, resources, and timeframe, a specialized certificate such as a paralegal certificate, an associate's degree in paralegal studies, or a bachelor's degree in paralegal studies will certainly demonstrate your level of interest and ability to achieve the minimum level of education for the job.

Creating an Electronic Resume

A growing number of employers are using computers to search the Internet for job applicants and to sort electronically through the resumes they receive. Human resources managers search through resumes received online or through Internet sites by entering a few words or phrases that describe the required skills and qualifications for the position they are trying to fill. Only the resumes in the computer system that match these electronic sorting terms and phrases are considered for the job offered. To have your resume considered, you need to have an electronic resume in addition to the traditional printed resume.

exhibit 3.2   *Sample resume.*

JANE DOE

1234 N. Maple Street, Anytown, USA 90000   •   Home: (213) 555-1111   •   Work: (213) 555-3333   •   jane.doe@att.net

LITIGATION PARALEGAL

EDUCATION

University of Paralegal Studies, Fremont, CA
> Paralegal Specialist Certificate, 2002, Honors graduate
> Approved by ABA
> Course of study: Legal Research and Writing, Contracts, Torts, Ethics, Litigation
> > Specialization

University of California at Berkeley
> Bachelor of Arts Degree in History, 2001
> Graduated Cum Laude

SKILLS AND ABILITIES

- Ability to analyze documents, digest depositions, draft discovery, and prepare cases for trial
- Knowledge of torts and contract law, legal research techniques, and basic civil procedure
- Fluent in French, both written and spoken
- Proficient in Word for Windows, WordPerfect and Excel

LEGAL INTERNSHIP

Jones, Smith, Smythe and Smooth, Los Angeles, 2001–2002
- Digested depositions for complex litigation case
- Organized multiple documents using several software programs

WORK EXPERIENCE

Los Angeles Unified School District, 1998–1999
> Secondary School Teacher
- Arranged classroom materials
- Supervised student teachers
- Chaired English Department
- Created curricula for advanced students

PROFESSIONAL ASSOCIATIONS

Los Angeles Paralegal Association
University of Paralegal Studies Alumni Association

References and writing samples available upon request.

Checklist

RESUME

Personal information
- ○ Name
- ○ Address

Education
- ○ High school
  - ○ Year of graduation
- ○ College
  - ○ Year of graduation
  - ○ Degree
  - ○ Grade point average or class rank

Work experience
- ○ Current or last employer
  - ○ Position(s) held
- ○ Prior employer
  - ○ Position held and dates

Specific skills
- ○ Office skills   ○ Computer skills   ○ Language skills   ○ Other job-related skills

Other
- ○ Organizational memberships   ○ Licenses/certifications

Converting a Traditional Resume into an Electronic Resume

If you already have created a resume using a word-processing program, open the file containing your resume and save it as a plain ASCII text file. You will want to change the name of the new text file to distinguish it from the file name used for the traditional printed version.

Text-only files cannot accommodate type formatting and special characters, so be sure that your electronic resume appears in one simple font and one font size. You also must remove justification, tables, rules (lines), and columns. If you have tabs in your document, remove them and use the space bar to align your text (better yet, align all text at the left so that indentation problems do not occur). Change every bullet to an asterisk or a lowercase letter o, as shown in the sample electronic resume in Exhibit 3.3.

exhibit **3.3**   *Sample electronic resume.*

JANE DOE
1234 N. Maple Street
Anytown, USA 90000
Home: (213) 555-1111 * Work: (213) 555-3333
jane.doe@att.net

LITIGATION PARALEGAL

Education
University of Paralegal Studies, Fremont, CA
Paralegal Specialist Certificate, 2002, Honors graduate
Approved by ABA
Course of study: Legal Research and Writing, Contracts, Torts, Ethics, Litigation Specialization

University of California at Berkeley
Bachelor of Arts Degree in History, 2001
Graduated Cum Laude

Skills and Abilities
* Ability to analyze documents, digest depositions, draft discovery, and prepare cases for trial
* Knowledge of torts and contract law, legal research techniques, and basic civil procedure
* Fluent in French, both written and spoken
* Proficient in Word for Windows, WordPerfect 6.0, and Excel

Legal Internship
Jones, Smith, Smythe and Smooth, Los Angeles, 2001–2002
* Digested depositions for complex litigation case
* Organized multiple documents using several software programs

Work Experience
Los Angeles Unified School District, 1998–1999
Secondary School Teacher
* Arranged classroom materials
* Supervised student teachers
* Chaired English Department
* Created curricula for advanced students

Professional Associations
Los Angeles Paralegal Association
University of Paralegal Studies Alumni Association

References and writing samples available upon request.

The first line of your resume should contain only your full name. Type your street address, phone and fax numbers, and email address on separate lines below your name. Next count the number of characters in each line and create a new line whenever the number of characters (including spaces) exceeds 65. This will ensure that the text will fit on a line with appropriate margins.

Because many human resource managers search by key words, you'll want to include a key word section near the top of your resume. List nouns that describe your job-related skills and abilities. If you have work experience with specific job titles such as "paralegal," list these key words as well. Also include language proficiency or other specialty qualifications such as "nurse–paralegal" or "fluent in Spanish."

After you have created your resume, save it again as an ASCII plain text file. Email the resume to yourself or to a friend to see how it looks when sent over the Internet.

Checklist

MY CAREER ROADMAP

- ○ Skills I need to acquire:
- ○ Skills I need to strengthen:
- ○ Courses I should take:
- ○ Extracurricular activities for the resume:
- ○ Interim work experience I should seek:
- ○ Volunteer activities:
- ○ Short-term career goals:
- ○ Long-term career goals:

INTERVIEWING FOR A JOB

Most students today work at part-time or full-time jobs while pursuing their education. These might be summer jobs, holiday fill-in positions, or full-time jobs. Look at the interview for the part-time, summer, or holiday positions, or the interview for a new full-time position as an opportunity to perfect your interviewing skills. Interviewing for a job can be highly stressful. Careful interview preparation can help to eliminate some of the stress and help you put your best foot forward so you can get that dream job you want.

Checklist

Getting Ready

- ○ Write resume.
- ○ Make contacts.
- ○ Network.
- ○ Make appointments from mass mailings, telephone solicitations, and network contacts.

Before the Interview

- ○ Know your resume.
- ○ Be familiar with a typical application form.
- ○ Know something about the company or firm. Check the Martindale Hubbell or Standard and Poor's directories.
- ○ Have a list of good questions to ask the interviewer, and know when to ask them.
- ○ Rehearse your answers to possible interview questions, then rehearse again.
- ○ Plan a "thumbnail" sketch of yourself.
- ○ Know the location of the interview site and where to park, or become familiar with the public transportation schedule.
- ○ Be at least 10 minutes early.
- ○ Go alone.
- ○ Bring copies of your resume, list of references, and writing samples in a briefcase or portfolio.
- ○ Check local salary ranges for the position.
- ○ Be prepared to answer questions regarding your salary expectations.
- ○ Try to anticipate problem areas, such as inexperience or gaps in your work history.
- ○ Be prepared to handle difficult questions, and know how to overcome objections.

The Introduction

- ○ Dress the part.
- ○ Do not smoke, eat, chew gum, or drink coffee prior to or during the interview.
- ○ Maintain good eye contact and good posture.
- ○ Shake hands firmly.
- ○ Establish rapport and be cordial without being overly familiar.
- ○ Be positive—convert negatives to positives.
- ○ Keep in mind that the first impressions are lasting impressions.

(continued)

INTERVIEW STRATEGIES, continued

The Interview

- ○ Provide all important information about yourself.
- ○ Sell yourself—no one else will.
- ○ Use correct grammar.
- ○ Do not be afraid to say, "I don't know."
- ○ Ask questions of the interviewer.
- ○ Do not answer questions about age, religion, marital status, or children unless you wish to. Try to address the perceived concern.
- ○ Find out about the next interview or contact.
- ○ Find out when a decision will be made.
- ○ Shake hands at the end of the interview.

After the Interview

- ○ Immediately document the interview in your placement file.
- ○ Send personalized thank-you letters to each person who interviewed you.
- ○ Call to follow up.

Source: Adapted from *How to Land Your First Paralegal Job,* 3/e, by Andrea Wagner (Upper Saddle River, NJ: Prentice Hall, 2001), pp. 163–164.

Checklist

QUESTIONS TO ASK AT THE INTERVIEW

- ○ How does the firm evaluate paralegals?
- ○ What is the growth potential for a paralegal in the firm?
- ○ Why did the prior paralegal leave?
- ○ How is work assigned?
- ○ What support services are available to paralegals?
- ○ What consideration is given for membership in paralegal associations?
- ○ Does the firm provide any assistance for continuing education for paralegals?

After the interview, you should review what happened and the results of the interview as a way of learning how to improve your interviewing skills. Even if you obtain the job, you'll want to learn what you did correctly that helped you to get the job as well as what you could have done better for the next time.

Checklist

ANALYZING HOW I HANDLED THE INTERVIEW

○ I arrived early for the interview.

○ I greeted the interviewer warmly, with a smile and a firm handshake.

○ I maintained good posture.

○ I did not smoke or chew gum during the interview.

○ I spoke clearly, using good grammar.

○ I demonstrated enthusiasm and interest.

○ I was able to answer questions asked of me.

○ I sent a thank-you note within 24 hours after the interview.

ARRANGEMENTS AND ORGANIZATION OF LAW OFFICES AND LAW FIRMS

The classic image of the law firm was of the solo practitioner working alone in a small office in a small town. The more modern view portrayed in movies and on TV is that of a large national or global law firm. In between are small partnerships and other environments—corporations, insurance companies, government agencies, and consulting firms composed of accountants, lawyers, and management consultants. Exhibit 3.4 shows organization charts for four typical types of arrangements in which the paralegal may find work.

Solo Practice

Solo practice refers to one lawyer practicing alone without the assistance of other attorneys. The solo practitioner still exists, not only in small towns but in large metropolitan areas as well. The solo practitioner may well be the employer who is most dependent upon the skills of the paralegal in running the office, working with clients, and assisting at trial. A solo practice offers perhaps the greatest challenge for the paralegal who wishes to be involved in every aspect of a law practice. Tasks that otherwise might be assigned to an associate will fall to the legal assistant to perform.

In a litigation practice or a practice in which the attorney is frequently out of the office attending meetings, the paralegal becomes the main point of contact and coordination between clients and the supervising attorney. Jobs that might be done in larger firms by an accounting staff, such as preparation of payroll and maintenance of client escrow accounts, frequently are done by the paralegal in solo practices. Many solo practitioners consider their paralegal to be a key resource in the practice of law.

Small Offices

Small-office arrangements range from individual practitioners sharing space to partnerships. For the small practitioner, the cost of maintaining an adequate law library, conference room, office space, and office support services such as photocopy and fax machines is daunting. Therefore, practices frequently share these common services while separating client practices. The lawyers might have a similar type of practice, such as criminal law or family law, or dissimilar practices, such as family law and insurance defense work. Depending upon the arrangement, the practitioners might refer clients back and forth. The responsibility for the client and the client relationship is a personal one for the attorney.

Depending upon the arrangement, personnel, such as the receptionist, secretary, or paralegal, might be shared. In these situations the paralegal must be certain which of the attorneys is the supervising attorney with regard to each client. The paralegal who is working for more than one attorney in a sharing arrangement might be privy to confidential information that may not be shared with the other attorneys in the office. In some respects this can be thought of as an ethical wall environment. At the very least, the paralegal and the attorneys must clearly understand the ethical issues involved.

Partnerships

A partnership arrangement is two or more natural or artificial (corporation) persons who have joined together to share ownership and profit or loss. Partnerships in small-office arrangements may take the form of true partnerships, sharing all aspects of the practice, or may be partnerships in name only. In this latter case, the same ethical issues that the paralegal faces in the pure office-sharing arrangement must be considered.

If all of the attorneys are partners with complete responsibility for each other and the practice, paralegals may find themselves working for more than one of the partners. In effect, the partners share the paralegal's services. This can give rise to

Meet THE COURTHOUSE TEAM

The Courtroom

The first time you enter a courtroom, you may be surprised to find a number of people working as part of the courtroom team. Obviously there is a judge presiding. Less obvious are the support personnel—the people who keep the courtroom organized and handle trial details such as scheduling and processing documents. Also, they sometimes act as the interface between jury and judge. Depending on the state and the court, they are called minutes clerk, bailiff, or court deputy. In addition, there usually is a court reporter whose job is to make a contemporaneous record of the proceeding. Frequently the judge's law clerk will sit in on hearings as well.

Ethical PERSPECTIVE

Lawyers Who Share Offices

It is "impermissible for unaffiliated attorneys to have unrestricted access to each other's electronic files (including email and word-processing documents) and other client records. If separate computer systems are not utilized, each attorney's confidential client information should be protected in a way that guards against unauthorized access and preserves client confidences and secrets."

District of Columbia Ethics Opinion 303

certain issues for the paralegal when more than one of the partners demand something at the same time with the same sense of urgency. The fact that each of the partners will consider himself or herself to be "boss" can create a delicate situation for the paralegal.

A common solution in many offices is for one of the partners to be the primary supervising attorney for the paralegal, through whom the other partner (or partners) funnels work and requests. From an ethical point of view this solves the problem of who the supervising attorney is for the clients and files on which the paralegal is working and at the same time clarifies the lawyers' responsibilities under the lawyers' Rules of Professional Conduct.

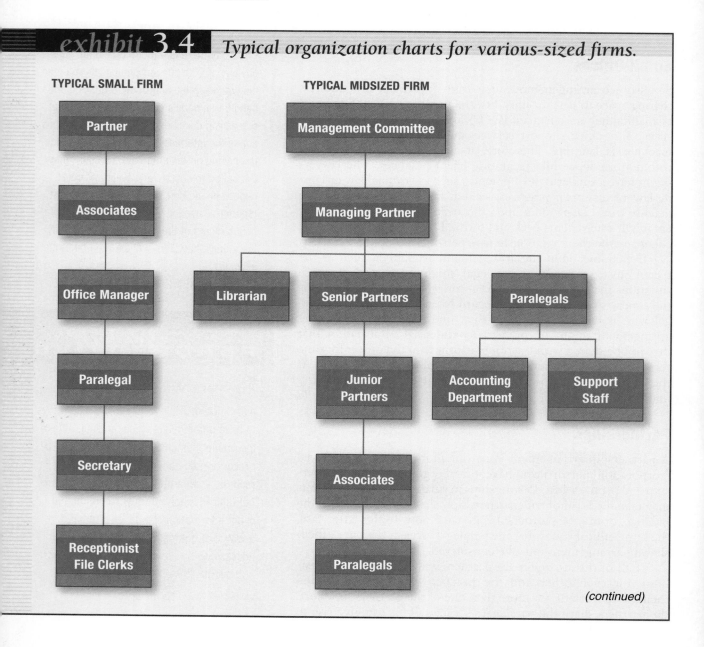

exhibit 3.4   *Typical organization charts for various-sized firms.*

TYPICAL SMALL FIRM

- Partner
- Associates
- Office Manager
- Paralegal
- Secretary
- Receptionist File Clerks

TYPICAL MIDSIZED FIRM

- Management Committee
- Managing Partner
  - Librarian
  - Senior Partners
    - Junior Partners
      - Associates
        - Paralegals
  - Paralegals
    - Accounting Department
    - Support Staff

(continued)

Continued.   *exhibit* 3.4

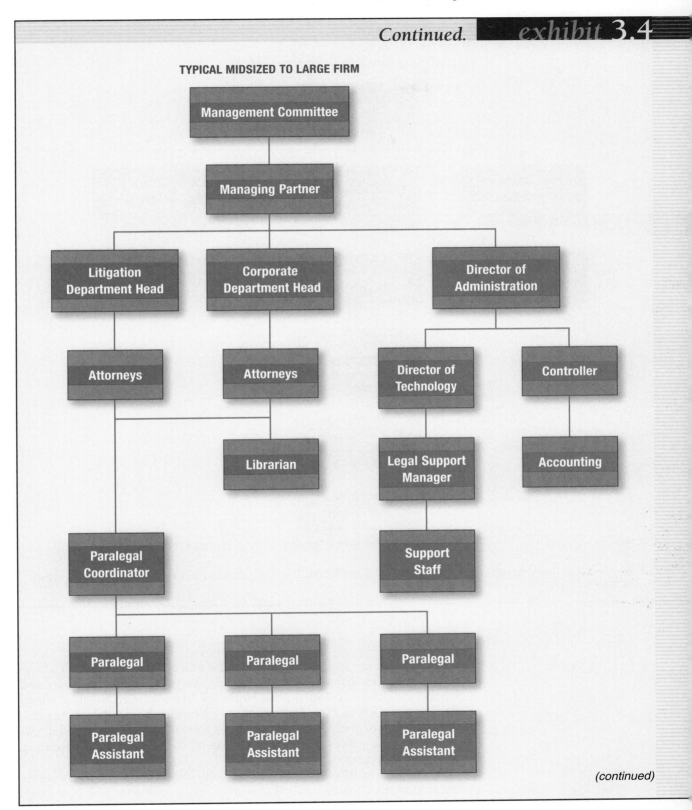

TYPICAL MIDSIZED TO LARGE FIRM

(continued)

exhibit **3.4**   *Continued.*

TYPICAL LEGAL DEPARTMENT OF CORPORATION

```
                        ┌─────────────────┐
                        │  CEO/President  │
                        └─────────────────┘
        ┌───────────────────────┼───────────────────────┐
┌─────────────────┐    ┌─────────────────┐    ┌─────────────────────┐
│  Corporation's  │    │ Legal Department│    │  General Counsel/   │
│ Other Departments│   │                 │    │ Secretary of Corporation│
└─────────────────┘    └─────────────────┘    └─────────────────────┘
        │                      │
┌─────────────────┐    ┌─────────────────┐
│ Vice Presidents │    │ General Counsel │
└─────────────────┘    └─────────────────┘
                              │
                       ┌─────────────────┐
                       │    Associate    │
                       │ General Counsel │
                       └─────────────────┘
                              │
                       ┌─────────────────┐
                       │    Paralegal    │
                       └─────────────────┘
                              │
                       ┌─────────────────┐
                       │    Secretary    │
                       └─────────────────┘
```

Source: How To Land Your First Paralegal Job, 3/e, by Andrea Wagner, © 2001. Reprinted by permission of Pearson Education, Inc., Upper Saddle River, NJ.

Large Offices

Historically, what are now viewed as large law offices are an outgrowth of traditional law offices that have expanded over the years, adding partners and associates along the way. Initially the larger law firms were regional, confined to major cities such as New York, Chicago, Philadelphia, and Los Angeles. With the growth of government at the national level, many firms found themselves establishing offices in the nation's capital to service clients appearing before federal agencies.

Continued growth of the national economy and business and corporate clients around the country resulted in many firms' establishing offices in other large cities, giving them a presence on each of the coasts as well as central locations such as Chicago, with offices in Washington, D.C., and elsewhere. Growth of the global economy has taken us one step farther, with law firms establishing offices in foreign countries. As a result, the large law firm has taken on the characteristics of many corporations, with firms merging to bring specialty areas of law within one firm while expanding the global availability of legal services.

For the paralegal the large office can be an exciting and dynamic area of practice. Paralegals may be called upon to travel with other members of the legal team or on their own as part of the practice. Even when no travel is required, the paralegal might be called upon to work with clients with diverse backgrounds, both domestically and internationally. One of the values of the large law firm for clients is the availability of a number of legal specialties within one legal services provider. For the paralegal this offers the opportunity to work in different areas of legal specialty.

Working in a large law firm also has some disadvantages. The larger the firm, the greater is the potential for less personal relationships and contacts with clients and other members of the legal team. In some firms, just as in any large organization, "playing politics" becomes very real. A paralegal's status, as well as some of the perks and benefits of the job, may depend on the status of the individual's supervising attorney. At the same time, the opportunities for advancement in a large firm might outweigh the disadvantages.

Large Firms

Unlike the small office, in which the paralegal also might be the bookkeeper, office manager, receptionist, and second chair in litigation, a department within a large firm generally hires support staff for each of these functions. The first contact for a paralegal with a large firm may be with the human resources department as part of the job application process. Bookkeeping or accounting departments usually handle payroll, check requests, and other financial issues. In the larger firms even the function of making copies takes place in a duplicating department, and the firm might have a mailroom for handling incoming and outgoing mail.

The large law firm has specialized components. In some ways this is similar to the structure of the English legal system, in which the solicitor deals directly with clients and the barrister litigates the cases. U. S. law firms frequently have litigation spe-

Courthouse built circa 1823 in Ohio.

cialists who spend their time in the actual litigation of cases while other attorneys within the same firm rarely, if ever, go to court. The role of the latter is to work with clients and, when the need arises, prepare the materials for the litigation department.

Just as the law has become more complex, lawyers also have come to specialize in narrow areas of practice such as environmental law, intellectual property law, health-care law, insurance law, tort law, and family law. This means that paralegals in large law firms also become specialists within their supervising attorney's primary field of law. Large-practice firms encourage clients to use the firm for all of their legal needs, so a lawyer within the firm frequently refers clients to other specialists in the firm while maintaining primary contact with the clients. Some firms have lawyers whose expertise is in getting new clients. These lawyers, often former politicians and government officials, are frequently referred to as the "rainmakers." They use their contacts to obtain clients and then refer the clients to the specialists within the firm.

Compensation for attorneys within large firms is generally based on how much new business the attorney has brought in, as well as how many billable hours the supervising attorneys have been able to bill for themselves and their paralegals. In this kind of environment, the paralegal who is able to maintain relationships with clients is an invaluable asset to the firm.

General Practice

A general law practice is one that handles all types of cases. This is what people usually think of as the small-town lawyer, the generalist to whom everyone in town comes for advice. The reality is that the same generalists practice in cities as well as small towns throughout the country. Their practices are as diverse as the law itself, handling everything from adoptions to zoning appeals. As general practitioners, they serve the same function in law as the general family practice doctor does in medicine.

Lawyers in this type of practice often work in several areas of law within the same day—attending a hearing in small claims court in the morning, preparing a will before lunch, having a luncheon meeting with an opposing attorney to discuss settlement of an accident case, then helping someone who is forming a corporation, and finally appearing at a municipal government meeting in the evening to seek a zoning approval. For many, the general practice is the most exciting type of practice, with a continually changing clientele offering all sorts of legal challenges. The paralegal in this environment has the opportunity to work with different types of clients on different types of legal matters on a constant basis. The challenge in this type of practice is to stay current in each of the areas of law of the practice.

Specialty Practice

A specialty practice is involved in practice in one area of law. Lawyers with specialty backgrounds, such as engineering, might choose to work in patent law or intellectual-property law. Those coming into the legal profession with accounting backgrounds might specialize in tax matters. Others have special interests and passions such as working with senior citizens in an elder law practice, or protecting the interests of children as child advocates, or practicing criminal law.

With the increasing complexity of the law, legal specialists are frequently receiving referrals from attorneys in other specialties or in general practice. The paralegal working for a specialist often acquires such a high level of knowledge in a specific area of law that it rivals that of many general practitioners. One of the dangers for the paralegal with this extent of specialty knowledge is that other attorneys could ask the paralegal questions to which the answers border on, or actually result in, the unauthorized practice of law. Because the paralegal in a specialty law practice is dependent—as are the supervising attorney and the practice—on referrals from other attorneys, the natural tendency is to accommodate referral attorneys by trying to answer questions of a legal nature. The paralegal must diplomatically avoid giving legal advice even to an attorney from another firm, to avoid a potential claim of UPL.

Maintaining relationships with other law firms and their paralegals and secretaries becomes a primary job function for the paralegal in a specialty practice. The paralegal commonly obtains referrals for the supervising attorney and the firm as a result of relationships developed in professional associations with other paralegals who recommend their friend who works for a lawyer specializing in the area sought.

In many areas of specialty, the paralegal has become a vital team member. Legal assistants with specialty skills in specific substantive areas perform services that allow the attorney to concentrate on other substantive issues of law. In addition, the legal assistant handles office management tasks and functions. These encompass intraoffice support including coordination between members of the professional team and the client. Some areas of specialty are discussed next.

Legal Nurse Consultant and Nurse Paralegal

Nurse paralegals or legal nurse consultants are nurses who have gained medical work experience and combine it with paralegal skills. Becoming a legal nurse consultant or a nurse paralegal is an ideal career opportunity for nurses with clinical nursing experience who want to work in the legal environment. Entry to most education programs requires a current license as a Registered Nurse and a minimum of 2,000 to 6,000 hours of clinical nursing experience, usually one to three years. Some programs are open to those with an associate degree in nursing, but usually a bachelor's degree in nursing is requested or desired.

Nurse paralegals draw upon their knowledge of medical terminology, medical procedures, and nursing practice to decipher medical records for the legal community. The most obvious advantage is their ability to analyze medical records from both medical and legal standpoints. Their experience also enables them to conduct more effective interviews with clients, fact witnesses, and expert witnesses in cases of medical malpractice and cases involving injury and damage investigation. Graduates of these programs often work as independent nurse consultants for law firms and insurance companies. Others find positions with insurance companies and law firms specializing in medical malpractice and personal injury.

Although the ABA considers the nurse paralegal and legal nurse consultant to be part of the paralegal profession, the American Association of Legal Nurse Consultants (AALNC) views this role as a subspecialty of nursing. In March 1998, the Standing Committee on Legal Assistants of the American Bar Association decided that "legal nurses and legal nurse consultants fall squarely within the ABA definition of 'paralegal/legal assistant.'" In contrast, AALNC has defined the legal nurse consultant as a specialty practitioner of nursing

Networking

SIDEBAR

Networking is the establishment of contact with others with whom questions and information are shared. For the paralegal, networking may be the key to obtaining a job, finding a new job, and performing at the highest level in a job. As is frequently said, it is not *what* you know but *whom* you know. Knowing the right person or a person who can refer you to the right person is a valuable asset. Many paralegals develop a referral list of other paralegals they can call to get a quick answer in their own jurisdiction and others. Most paralegals facing a deadline are not too proud to call their contacts, whether across the street, across the state, or across the nation, to meet a deadline or get the necessary form. During interviews, hiring attorneys have been known to ask about the paralegal's networking activities.

American Association of
Legal Nurse Consultants:
www.aalnc.org

whose education should be developed and presented as specialty nursing curricula by nurse educators in partnership with legal educators.

Real Estate

Paralegals or legal assistants with real estate experience in sales or from title insurance agencies can perform many of the tasks associated with a real estate practice, such as communicating between buyers and sellers, coordinating the documentation for settlement, and preparing documents for recording purposes. In most jurisdictions becoming a licensed salesperson or a real estate broker requires the completion of a course of study that provides a foundation in the practices and procedures of real estate practice and equips the paralegal with a terminology base that facilitates effective communication with the supervising attorney.

Complex Litigation

Complex litigation takes many forms, from class-action lawsuits to complex product liability cases. Paralegals working in complex litigation generally oversee the requests for document production and maintain indexes, usually on computer databases, of the paperwork generated from litigation. In large cases the paralegal might supervise a staff of other paralegals or law students in summarizing discovery documents. At trial, these paralegals frequently coordinate the production of exhibits.

In large cases, paralegals might be responsible for summarizing discovery documents.

Environmental Law

Environmental law covers everything from toxic waste dumps to protection of wildlife and the environment. A challenge for the environmental paralegal is in locating and obtaining public records and other documents necessary to establish the areas of concern and claims, some of which predate computer records, such as toxic waste dumps created during World War II and the early 1950s.

Intellectual Property

In a survey by The Affiliates, a company providing temporary and full-time legal personnel, 48 percent of the surveyed attorneys indicated intellectual property as the fastest growing field in law. The intellectual-property paralegal is concerned with the formalities of protecting intellectual-property interests including patent rights, trade secrets, and copyrights and trademarks. The two main areas are *prosecution*, which involves establishing the priority of the claims that will result in granting of the patent or copyright, and *litigation*, which protects those rights against claims by others, such as in patent infringement cases.

The Affiliates: www.futurelaw
office.com/practice.html

Elder Law

With the aging of the population has come an increased need to protect the rights of the elderly and obtain all the benefits to which they are entitled. This includes such simple tasks as assisting individuals to apply for Social Security benefits, Medicare benefits, or Medicaid benefits. It also entails working with the elderly to create estate plan documents, powers of attorney, and health-care directives. More and more, the paralegal or legal assistant is becoming an advocate for the elderly, in many cases working in a pro bono capacity or through social service agencies. Elder law has come to include the additional issues of helping the elderly work through the maze of health care and government benefits.

Legal Assistant Manager

As legal assistant staffs have grown, even at some of the smaller firms, the position of legal assistant manager has emerged. With higher turnover rates and increased specialization comes the associate's need for someone to hire, supervise, train, and evaluate legal assistants. In many firms this person is the interface between the legal assistants and the attorneys.

As paralegals gain specialized knowledge in specific fields, they find themselves working for different attorneys as their expertise demands. Attorneys, for the most part, do not have the time to handle the nonlegal aspects of managers, such as acting as leader, mentor, employee advocate, supervisor, trainer, evaluator, problem solver, and resource manager. The largest firms appoint a managing partner to handle the management tasks and human resources issues. In many smaller firms, these duties fall to the individual with the title of legal assistant manager. The new specialty is well recognized and supported by its own organization, the Legal Assistant Management Association.

Legal Assistant Management Association: www.LAMANET.org

Pro Bono Paralegals

Pro bono means working without compensation on behalf of individuals and organizations that otherwise could not afford legal assistance. Increasingly, the legal profession has taken on the role of working without compensation in legal aid offices and community legal service programs. Paralegals, as members of professional associations, participate in pro bono activities at varying levels and time commitments.

Government Employment

Federal, state, and local governments are large employers of paralegals, and paralegals are expected to be utilized even further at every level in the future. Many of the federally employed paralegals are found in administrative agencies. A good example is the work of paralegals in the Social Security Administration as decision writers, case schedulers, and case specialists. Just as the private law firm has discovered the value of the paralegal on the legal team, so have government law offices such as the U. S. Attorney's Office and the Office of the Solicitor General. These offices are involved with both criminal prosecutions and civil litigation where the government is a party. Many other agencies that conduct administrative hearings utilize paralegals at all levels.

Pro Bono Paralegals

DOMESTIC VIOLENCE PROGRAMS

The Massachusetts Paralegal Association supports a number of pro bono projects. In one of these, the Family Law Project, paralegals partner with attorneys to help handle domestic violence cases without compensation. Pro bono work is seen as part of an ethical obligation of the legal profession.

SIDEBAR

SIDEBAR

Document Specialist or Paralegal?

Under the definition enacted by the Maine legislature, anyone calling himself or herself a paralegal or legal assistant must work under the supervision of an attorney. Independent paralegals no longer can use the title *paralegal* or *legal assistant*. This has resulted in some changing the name of their freelance business to *document specialist* (*Bangor Daily News,* August 16, 1999).

The California legislature passed a law prohibiting self-help legal document service providers from receiving compensation unless the legal document assistant is registered in the county where the service is provided and provides a bond of $25,000.

The DuPont Experience

In an effort to reduce costs, DuPont, one of the largest companies in America, changed the way it uses legal assistants—elevating the work, positions, and numbers of legal assistants. Legal assistants have been given more responsibility in handling documents, technology, and investigations. In doing so, DuPont reportedly reduced by almost 90 percent the number of outside law firms and services it formerly used. As of 2000, the DuPont legal department had 51 paralegals working with 140 lawyers. In the DuPont model the legal department acts as counsel to the other DuPont-owned companies and deals with them as clients much in the way that the outside law firms had in the past.

Source: Paralegals Are Part of DuPont's Legal Team, by D. L. Hawley, *Legal Assistant Today,* March 4, 2000.

Legal Departments of Corporations

Many people think of a corporate legal department as a laid-back, conservative environment with little activity other than drafting minutes of meetings and filing corporate records with the federal and state governments. The reality today is that, in the new global economy, more and more corporations with in-house staffs are engaged in international trade. A whole body of law relates to compliance for imports and exports. For example, the transfer and sale of certain high-tech equipment and technology must have prior government approval. Sales involving shipments to other countries require letters of credit and currency conversion. International trade creates a whole host of unique issues related to the laws of the countries with which the domestic corporation may be doing business.

The paralegal is in the middle of these transactions, juggling the requirements from both the legal perspective and the sales and marketing perspective. Paralegals with foreign language skills find themselves in even greater demand in handling communication issues. Those with cultural ties to or background in the countries with which the corporation is doing business will find their knowledge frequently tapped to avoid cultural mistakes resulting from miscommunication.

Self-Employment

The paralegal has some opportunities to be self-employed, although state regulation may limit the opportunities or restrict paralegal self-employment. Where authorized by federal law, the paralegal may actively represent clients without the supervision of an attorney, such as before the Social Security Administration. Many paralegals work as freelancers for different attorneys, usually on a case-by-case basis. In addition to the normal ethical obligations regarding confidentiality and conflict of interest, the freelance paralegal must observe the ethical guidelines on advertising in the local jurisdiction and avoid creating the appearance of being available to render legal advice except where authorized.

ADMINISTRATIVE PROCEDURES IN THE LAW OFFICE

Certain administrative procedures are common to most, if not all, law offices. Two of the main administrative functions are timekeeping and conflict checking.

Timekeeping

As Abraham Lincoln has been quoted as saying, "A lawyer's time and advice are his stock-in-trade." Keeping track of billable time becomes a critical function to ensure that the law firm

Timeslips input screen.   exhibit 3.5

will be compensated properly for its advice and efforts on behalf of clients. Timekeeping extends beyond attorneys to paralegals and, in some cases, secretaries and file clerks. The task has been automated by the use of software, such as Timeslips, that accurately captures, stores, and processes this information. Exhibit 3.5 illustrates a Timeslips input screen.

Conflict Checking

Conflict checking is necessary to verify that current and prior representations of parties and matters handled will not present a conflict of interest for the firm in accepting a new client or legal matter. Checking for conflicts of interest is an essential function designed to avoid the ethical violations of representing competing interests. Many offices use computer database software for conflict checking.

Ethical PERSPECTIVE

Proof of Supervision

Accurate contemporaneously recorded time records for the paralegal and for the attorney may be used to show the level of supervision of the paralegal by the supervising attorney.

Ethical PERSPECTIVE

Adequate Screening

"The court does not subscribe to the argument that, as a matter of law, screening would be ineffective when a nonlawyer switches employment to 'the other side.' The ABA opinions indicate that a law firm can set up appropriate screening and administrative procedures to prevent nonlawyers from working on the other side of those common cases and disclosing confidential information."

Connecticut Trial Court, unpublished decision, Devine v. Beinfield, *1997 Ct. Sup. 7674, 1997 Conn Super Lexis 1966, No. CV93 0121721 S* (Jul.1,1997).

SIDEBAR

Billing for Paralegal Time

The 11th Circuit Court of Appeals has said, "We have held that paralegal time is recoverable as part of a prevailing party's award for attorney's fees and expenses, [but] only to the extent that the paralegal performs work traditionally done by an attorney." Quoting from *Allen v. United States Steel Corp.,* 665 F.2d 689, 697 (5th Cir. 1982): "To hold otherwise would be counterproductive because excluding reimbursement for such work might encourage attorneys to handle entire cases themselves, thereby achieving the same results at a higher overall cost."

Jean v. Nelson, 863 F. 2d 759 (11th Cir. 1988).

Names of clients, opposing parties, counsel, and law firms can be quickly searched electronically. Some firms still rely on a manual check of paper lists and file-card indexes containing the names of clients, opposing parties, and opposing attorneys in cases. To determine conflicts where there has been only indirect representation is difficult.

Attorneys and paralegals who change firms may have to do a preliminary conflict check before they accept or start employment. The conflict comes when the former firm and the new firm are, or were, on opposite sides of a case. It may be a conflict for someone who has had access to information about a case to switch to the firm representing the opposing party. Confidential disclosure for the limited purpose of checking for a conflict before starting employment could prevent a serious or perceived ethical breach in the form of a breach of confidentiality or conflict of interest. In some cases the conflict of interest may result from a financial interest such as stock ownership or investments. Making full disclosure of these potential conflict situations to the supervising attorney or to the appropriate conflict checker with the firm is important.

In many cases the conflict can be resolved by isolating the individual from information about the case—sometimes called building an ethical wall. An ethical wall, also known as a Chinese wall, is an attempt to shield a paralegal or lawyer from access to information about a case when there is the possibility of a conflict of interest. Most courts permit the establishment of an ethical wall to protect the parties from the conflict of interest or breach of confidentiality. But a Nevada court, based on a 1994 ethics opinion, prohibits paralegals from working for a firm that represents any client that has an adversarial relationship to any client of the former employer law firm [*Ciaffone v. District Court*, 113 Nev. 1165 (1997), 945 P.2d 950].

LEGAL TERMINOLOGY

Barrister
Conflict checking
Elective course
Ethical wall
General practice
Networking
Nurse paralegal (legal nurse consultants)
Partnership
Pro bono
Resume
Solicitor
Solo practice
Specialty practice
Timekeeping

Summary

CHAPTER 3 CAREERS IN THE PARALEGAL PROFESSION

Compensation Issues for the Paralegal

1. Salaries tend to be higher in large metropolitan areas and lower in small towns and rural areas.
2. Large firms tend to pay more and small firms, less.
3. There are regional variations.

Selecting a Specialty

1. Career satisfaction is vital.
2. Start with a self-evaluation.

Assessing Your Background

1. Personal background.
2. Paralegal certificate or degree.

Assessing Your Skills

1. Interpersonal.
2. Communication.
3. Motivation.

(continued)

Assessing Your Interests

1. Recognize your strengths.
2. Work on weaknesses.

Selecting Your Electives

1. Gain additional knowledge.
2. Explore areas of possible interest.

Preparing Your Resume

1. Traditional paper resume
2. Electronic resume
3. Constant updating

Interviewing for a Job

1. Prepare carefully to reduce stress.   2. Put your best foot forward.

Arrangements and Organization of Law Offices and Law Firms

1. Solo Practice
2. Small Offices
3. Partnerships
4. Large Offices
5. Large Firms
6. General Practice
7. Specialty Practice
    a. Legal Nurse Consultant and Nurse Paralegal
    b. Real Estate
    c. Complex Litigation
    d. Environmental Law
    e. Intellectual Property
    f. Elder Law
    g. Legal Assistant Manager
    h. Pro Bono Paralegals
8. Government Employment
9. Legal Departments of Corporations
10. Self-Employment

Administrative Procedures

1. Timekeeping
2. Conflict Checking

Working the Web

1. Check the websites of the various paralegal professional associations for information on paralegal occupational opportunities:
   a. National Association of Legal Assistants at www.nala.org
   b. National Federation of Paralegal Associations at www.paralegals .org
   c. Legal Assistant Management Association at www.lamanet.org
   d. American Association of Legal Nurse Consultants at www.aalnc.org
   e. The American Association of Nurse Attorneys at www.taana.org

2. Check online employment information source at www.monster.com

3. Check online sources for help creating resumes:
   a. Purdue University at www.owl.English.purdue.edu/files/35.html
   b. College of William and Mary at www.wm.edu/csrv/career/stualum/resmdir/contentrs.html

4. Check online career sources at:
   a. Career Resource Library at www.labor.state.ny.us/html/library.htm
   b. America's Job Bank at www.ajb.dni.us/index.html
   c. Wall Street Journal at www.careers.wsj.com
   d. CareerWEB at www.cweb.com

5. Check the Martindell-Hubbell Legal Directory for law firms in your area that have a website.

Questions

CRITICAL LEGAL THINKING AND WRITING

1. What additional costs might a paralegal incur in working in a large-city practice in contrast to a small-town office?
2. What advantages might a person have in entering the paralegal profession later in life?
3. How does assessing your interests and skills help in choosing a career path?
4. How does assessing your interests and skills help in preparing your personal resume?
5. Prepare the resume you would like to have five years from now. How would this resume help you in selecting courses, extracurricular activities, and interim employment?

6. Complete the "My Career Roadmap" checklist in this chapter.
7. Start to network by setting up a meeting with a working paralegal and preparing a list of questions to ask at that meeting.
8. Why would a paralegal who specializes in one legal field be at greater risk for unauthorized practice of law?
9. Other than revealing potential employment opportunities, what advantages does networking have for a paralegal?
10. Why is accurate timekeeping important to the paralegal and the law firm?

ETHICS: ANALYSIS AND DISCUSSION

1. In changing jobs from one firm to another, how does the paralegal avoid a conflict of interest?
2. What ethical and UPL problems do freelance paralegals face that those working in a single firm do not?
3. What ethical issues might arise in determining the paralegal's supervising attorney when the paralegal is working in a small firm of three attorneys?

Confidentiality—Conflict of Interest

There are few certainties in the area of ethics, for paralegals or in any profession. What qualifies as ethical conduct is in most cases based on state law and court interpretation applied to a set of facts. The citation listed below represents one legal opinion and is provided as a research starting point. Do not assume that the same rule applies in your jurisdiction. For the following:

- *Prepare a written statement based on your state law.*
- *Use your state bar association website as a starting point.*

You are working as a paralegal in a small law office. The office is shared by three attorneys, each of whom is a solo practitioner. To save money they share a law library and a fax machine, and they use a common computer network with separate workstations but with a common file server to save files because it has an automatic backup system. You work for each of the lawyers as the need arises, answering phones, and generally performing paralegal services. [*District of Columbia Ethics Opinion 303.*] What issues of confidentiality should be considered? As the office paralegal, are there any conflicts of interest problems for you?

Case

FOR DISCUSSION

Jean v. Nelson   863 F.2d 759 (11th Cir. 1988)

Reimbursement for Paralegal Time under Federal Statute

The district court awarded, and the 11th Circuit Court of Appeals upheld, reimbursement for time spent by paralegals and law clerks where the work was normally done by an attorney. The hourly rate awarded was $40. This is the rate at which the law firm whose paralegals and clerks were involved bills its clients.

The government challenges the rate awarded, and contends that paralegal time is compensational only at the actual cost to the plaintiffs' counsel. In the context of a Title VII case, [the court] held that paralegal time is recoverable as "part of a prevailing party's award for attorney's fees and expenses, [but] only to the extent that the paralegal performs work traditionally done by an attorney. To hold otherwise would be counterproductive because excluding reimbursement for such work might encourage attorneys to handle entire cases themselves, thereby achieving the same results at a higher overall cost."

Questions

1. Does this rationale encourage lawyers to use paralegals?
2. Does this decision facilitate the availability of lower-cost quality legal services?
3. Should an attorney be allowed to charge more than out-of-pocket costs for paralegal services?

Doe v. Condon

532 S.E.2d 879 (S.C. 2000)   Supreme Court of South Carolina

Read the following case, then review and brief the case. In your brief, answer the following questions.

1. According to this court, why is the practice of law limited to licensed attorneys?

2. What tasks does this court indicate that a paralegal may perform?

3. What tasks does this court indicate that a paralegal may not perform?

4. Why is answering legal questions about the need for a will or a trust the unauthorized practice of law (UPL)?

5. In this court's interpretation, what is the reason for prohibiting a fee-splitting arrangement between a lawyer and a paralegal?

Per curiam

This is a declaratory judgment action. Petitioner, a paralegal, has submitted a generalized list of tasks he wishes to perform and has inquired whether performing them constitutes the unauthorized practice of law. Petition also seeks a determination of the propriety of the proposed fee-splitting arrangement with his attorney–employer.

To protect the public from unsound legal advice and incompetent representation, South Carolina, like other jurisdictions, limits the practice of law to licensed attorneys.

Our Supreme Court has set forth a succinct standard for the proper role of paralegals:

> The activities of a paralegal do not constitute the practice of law as long as they are limited to work of a preparatory nature, such as legal research, investigation, or the composition of legal documents, which enables licensed attorney–employer to carry a given matter to a conclusion through his own examination, approval, or additional effort.

While the important support function of paralegals has increased through the years, the guidelines stand the test of time. The paralegal plays a supporting role to the supervising attorney. Here the roles are reversed. The attorney would support the paralegal. Petitioner would play the lead role, with no meaningful attorney supervision and the attorney's presence and involvement only surfaces on the back end. Meaningful attorney supervision must be present throughout the process. The line between what is and what is not permissible conduct by a non-attorney is sometimes unclear as a potential trap for the unsuspecting client.

The conduct of the paralegal contemplated here clearly crosses the line into the unauthorized practice of law. It is well settled the paralegal may not give legal advice, consult, offer legal explanations, or make legal recommendations.

Petitioner intends to conduct unsupervised "wills and trusts" seminars for the public, "emphasizing" living trusts during the course of his presentation. Petitioner also plans to answer estate-planning questions from the audience.

I find, as other courts have, that the very structure of such "educational" legal seminars suggests that the presenter will actually be giving legal advice on legal matters. At the very least, petitioner will implicitly advise participants that they require estate planning services. Whether a will or trust is appropriate in any given situation is a function of legal judgment. To be sure, advising a potential client when his or her need for a living trust (or other particular estate-planning instrument or device) fits squarely within the practice of law. These matters cry out for the exercise of professional judgment by a licensed attorney. Thus, in conducting these informational seminars, petitioner would engage in the unauthorized practice of law as a non-attorney offering legal advice.

I fully recognize the prevailing popularity of "financial planners" and others jump[ing] on the estate planning bandwagon. This trend in no way affects the decision before the court. This paralegal would not be presenting the estate-planning seminar as a financial planner. The seminar would be conspicuously sponsored by the paralegal's attorney–employer.

Petitioner intends to get client information and answer general estate planning questions during his proposed "initial client interviews." While petitioner may properly compile client information, petitioner may not answer estate-planning questions. Petitioner's answering legal questions would constitute the unauthorized practice of law for the reasons stated above. Wall law firm in which the petitioner is employed plans to direct clients to an attorney for follow up consultations. A paralegal may not give legal advice in any event. Moreover, permissible preparatory tasks must be performed while under the attorney supervision. The proposed after-the-fact review comes too late.

Petitioner's law firm intends to compensate him based upon the volume and type of cases he "handles." A paralegal, of course, may not handle any case. This fee arrangement directly violates Rule 5.4 of the Rules of Professional Conduct. This limitation serves to "discourage the unauthorized practice of law by lay persons and to prevent a non-lawyer from acquiring a vested pecuniary interest in an attorney's disposition of a case that could possibly take preeminence over a client's best interest. This compensation proposal arrangement, coupled with petitioner's desire to market the law firm's services via the educational seminars and meet individually with clients, creates a situation ripe for abuse. Indeed, the proposal by petitioner presents the very evil Rule 5.4 was designed to avoid. Accordingly, I find petitioner's proposed compensation plan violates both the letter and spirit of Rule 5.4 prohibiting fee-splitting with non-attorneys.

Note: If in South Carolina, include the parallel citation: 341 S.C. 22. The Lexis citation for this case is 2000 S.C. LEXIS 125.

CHAPTER 4

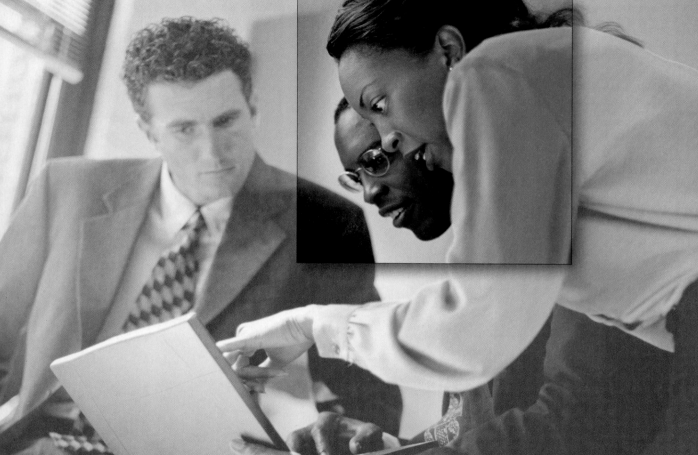

CHAPTER OBJECTIVES

After studying this chapter, you should be able to:

1. Explain what a paralegal does.
2. Describe the skills necessary to work as a paralegal.
3. Articulate personal goals and skills.
4. Understand the concept of commitment.
5. Understand the concept of resourcefulness.
6. Understand the concept of interpersonal skills.
7. Understand the concept of professional communications.
8. Understand the concept of analysis.
9. Understand the need for cultural sensitivity.

Paralegal Workplace Skills

It is when merchants dispute about their own rules that they invoke the law.

J. BRETT, *ROBINSON V. MOLLETT*, 1875

Introduction

As the paralegal profession has evolved, so, too, have the duties and roles of the paralegal within the legal system and elsewhere. The earliest legal assistant was probably a legal secretary who developed specialized skills while working for an attorney in one of the legal specialties. As the need for specialized skills became more obvious, legal assistant programs and paralegal programs were created to teach the requisite skills. In the classic sense, a paralegal performs those tasks and activities that assist the supervising attorney in representing clients. The broader view is that the paralegal performs many of the same functions that attorneys perform, under the supervision of an attorney but limited by laws and regulations on the unauthorized practice of law (UPL).

PARALEGAL TASKS AND FUNCTIONS

The actual tasks and functions the paralegal performs vary according to the type of practice, size of the firm or organization, and skill of the individual paralegal. Some of the more generic tasks include:

- Conducting interviews
- Maintaining written and verbal contacts with clients and counsel
- Setting up, organizing, and maintaining client files
- Preparing pleadings and documents
- Reviewing, analyzing, summarizing, and indexing documents and transcripts
- Assisting in preparing witnesses and clients for trial
- Maintaining calendar and tickler systems
- Performing research, both factual and legal
- Performing office administrative functions including maintaining time and billing records

Client Interviews

Many paralegals act as the first line of contact with clients. Paralegals may not ethically or legally give legal advice or set legal fees, but they frequently conduct the initial interview with the client. This might involve taking the initial client information and preparing the client data sheet (see Exhibit 4.1) or conducting a more in-depth interview to determine the facts of the matter for the attorney's review. Frequently, the paralegal continues to function as the contact point with the client and the supervising attorney or the law firm. Paralegals frequently establish rapport with clients and earn their confidence.

The paralegal always must be keenly aware of the ethical limitations in dealing with clients. This is especially true when the client develops a high level of confidence in dealing with the paralegal. Clients come to the attorney for advice. When they have confidence in a paralegal, they might tend to ask the paralegal for advice and recommendations instead of "bothering" the attorney. Providing such advice or recommendations may constitute the rendering of legal advice in violation of UPL restrictions. For example, to the client, the question "Should I make my son my power of attorney?" seems simple. But the answer is not so simple and involves many legal consequences so it must be referred to the supervising attorney. Another UPL might be to help the client complete blank legal forms, such as bankruptcy forms or will forms purchased at the stationery store.

Investigations

The paralegal may be asked to act as the direct representative of the supervising attorney in conducting an investigation into a pending case. A paralegal trained in the specific area of law understands the factual needs of a case and the sources of information available. A paralegal who has had the opportunity to observe or work with an attorney and has watched the presentation of evidence in a trial obtains a good sense of what will make good demonstrative evidence, such as models and photographs. In the case of photos, an understanding of the kind of questions that might be asked in direct examination and

---

Meet

Clerk or Minutes Clerk

The clerk is the judge's administrative assistant in the courtroom. It has been said that the clerk controls access to the judge in the courtroom. Clerks control the flow of documents to and from the bench and generally act as the judge's right hand. Frequently they arrange the schedules and coordinate requests to the judge and facilitate communication between counsel and judge. And as the judge's left and right ears, clerks convey to the judge your courtesy or lack of it. Because clerks usually are in the courtroom before anyone else, it is good practice to introduce yourself and offer a smile. When the court asks who you are, the clerk will let the court know, which is less embarrassing than having the judge ask, "Who is that?"

Client data sheet.   **exhibit 4.1**

CLIENT DATA SHEET

ACTION TAKEN/REQUIRED

1. Client Name:

2. Client/Matter Number:

3. Client Address:

4. Phone: Work:

    Home:

    Fax:

5. Email address:

6. Social Security No.:

7. Date of Birth:

8. Marital Status:

9. Client Contact:

10. Matter:

    (a) Adverse Party:

    (b) Date of Incident:

    (c) Statute of Limitations Period:

    (d) Statute of Limitations Date:

11. Opposing Counsel:

12. Opposing Counsel Address:

13. Opposing Counsel Phone:

Approximately 20 percent of the world's population is Muslim. Islam is the principal religion of Afghanistan, Algeria, Bangladesh, Egypt, Indonesia, Iran, Iraq, Jordan, Kuwait, Libya, Malaysia, Mali, Mauritania, Morocco, Niger, North Yemen, Oman, Pakistan, Qatar, Saudi Arabia, Somalia, South Yemen, Sudan, Syria, Tunisia, Turkey, and the United Arab Emirates. Islamic law (or Sharía) is the only law in Saudi Arabia. In other Islamic countries, the Sharía forms the basis of family law but coexists with other laws.

The Islamic law system is derived from the *Koran,* the Sunnah (decisions and sayings of the Prophet Muhammad), and reasoning by Islamic scholars. By 10 A.D., Islamic scholars decided that divine law could not be further improved, so they closed the door of ijtihad (independent reasoning) and froze the evolution of Islamic law at that point.

Islamic law prohibits riba, or the making of unearned or unjustified profit. Making a profit from the sale of goods or the provision of services is permitted. The most notable consequence of riba is that it forbids the payment of interest on loans. To circumvent this result, the party with the money is permitted to purchase an item and resell it to the other party at a profit or to advance the money and become a trading partner who shares in the profits of the enterprise.

Today, Islamic law is used primarily in the areas of marriage, divorce, and inheritance and, to a limited extent, in criminal law. To resolve the tension between Sharía and the practice of modern commercial law, the Sharía is often ignored in commercial transactions.

cross-examination about the photographs offered as evidence enables the paralegal to be certain that the photographs are taken from the correct angles with the correct landmarks or measurements included. Interviews conducted by the paralegal in preparation for trial could qualify as privileged for the attorney–client privilege just as they do when conducted by attorneys. The paralegal must be aware of how interview material may be used and potentially obtained by opposing parties and act to protect clients' privileged communication with the paralegal as a representative of the supervising attorney.

Legal Writing

Paralegals frequently are called upon to maintain the written communications with clients, opposing attorneys, and the court. These may be in the form of correspondence, memos of law, or briefs for the court. Many paralegals become extremely adept at drafting complaints and supporting memoranda of law and briefs. Although the content is the ultimate responsibility of the supervising attorney, the paralegal with good writing skills is an invaluable asset. Well-written and well-reasoned documentation is easy to review for signature and transmittal and is a major timesaver for the attorney.

Legal Research

In the modern law office legal research is conducted with hard copy books and also with electronic media, including extensive use of the Internet. The ability to conduct research into case law, statutory enactments, and regulatory rules and procedures gives the paralegal a major advantage in getting the job in the first place and advancing in most firms. Legal research today requires the ability to use online legal services such as Lexis, Westlaw, VersusLaw, and Loislaw, as well as the ability to find information on government websites and private websites.

www

Lexis: www.lexisnexis.com/

Westlaw: www.westlaw.com/about/

VersusLaw: www.versuslaw.com

Loislaw: www.loislaw.com

WHAT PARALEGALS IN LEGAL SPECIALTIES DO

In addition to the various generic tasks that most paralegals or legal assistants perform, paralegals working in specialty areas find themselves performing additional and more specialized tasks that frequently require special knowledge, education, or skill beyond the basic skills and knowledge required of all paralegals. Some of the tasks performed by paralegals in specialty practice are as follows.

GENERAL BUSINESS PRACTICE:

- Draft lease agreements
- Draft partnership agreements
- Draft noncompetition agreements
- Prepare agreements of sale and attend real estate settlements
- Draft contracts for business arrangements and new ventures
- Draft employee agreements

DEBTOR RIGHTS AND CREDITOR REMEDIES:

- Draft correspondence complying with state and federal regulations concerning debt collection
- Prepare documentation to support garnishment proceedings
- Arrange for execution and support judgments, including publication of notice of sales and levies on personal property
- Transfer judgments to other jurisdictions
- Prepare, file, and terminate Uniform Commercial Code financing statements (see Exhibit 4.2)
- Assist clients in filing bankruptcy petitions, including the preparation of schedules and proofs of claim
- Prepare Chapter 11 debtor's financial statements
- Attend Chapter 13 confirmation hearings

CORPORATE PRACTICE:

- Determine availability and reserve fictitious or corporate name
- Prepare and file fictitious name registrations
- Prepare articles of incorporation, minutes, and bylaws for corporation
- Prepare, issue, and transfer stock certificates
- Prepare shareholder agreements
- Prepare applications and file for employer identification numbers and tax registration numbers

exhibit 4.2   *Uniform Commercial Code Form UCC-1.*

PARTIES	FINANCING STATEMENT Uniform Commercial Code Form UCC-1 IMPORTANT — Please read instructions on reverse side of page 4 before completing

Debtor name (last name first if individual) and mailing address:

1

Debtor name (last name first if individual) and mailing address:

1a

Debtor name (last name first if individual) and mailing address:

1b

Secured Party(ies) name(s) (last name first if individual) and address for security interest information:

2

Assignee(s) of Secured Party name(s) (last name first if individual) and address for security interest information:

2a

Special Types of Parties (check if applicable):

☐ The terms "Debtor" and "Secured Party" mean "Lessee" and "Lessor," respectively.

☐ The terms "Debtor" and "Secured Party" mean "Consignee" and "Consignor," respectively.

☐ Debtor is a Transmitting Utility.

3

SECURED PARTY SIGNATURE(S)

This statement is filed with only the **Secured Party's signature** to perfect a security interest in collateral (check applicable box(es)) —

a. ☐ acquired after a **change of name, identity or corporate structure** of the Debtor.

b. ☐ as to which the **filing has lapsed.**

c. already subject to a security interest in **another county** in Pennsylvania —
   ☐ when the **collateral was moved** to this county.
   ☐ when the **Debtor's residence or place of business was moved** to this county.

d. already subject to a security interest in **another jurisdiction** —
   ☐ when the **collateral was moved** to Pennsylvania.
   ☐ when the **Debtor's location was moved** to Pennsylvania.

e. ☐ which is **proceeds** of the collateral described in block 9, in which a security interest was previously perfected (also describe proceeds in block 9, if purchased with cash proceeds and not adequately described on the original financing statement).

Secured Party Signature(s)
(required only if box(es) is checked above):

_____

_____

_____

4

Filing No. (stamped by filing officer):   **Date, Time, Filing Office** (stamped by filing officer):

5

This **Financing Statement** is presented for filing pursuant to the Uniform Commercial Code, and is to be filed with the (check applicable box):

☐ Secretary of the Commonwealth.
☐ Prothonotary of _____ County.
☐ real estate records of _____ County.

6

Number of Additional Sheets (if any):   7

Optional Special Identification (Max. 10 characters):   8

COLLATERAL

Identify collateral by item and/or type:

☐ (check only if desired) Products of the collateral are also covered.   9

Identify related real estate, if applicable: The collateral is, or includes (check appropriate box(es)) —

a. ☐ **crops** growing or to be grown on —
b. ☐ goods which are or are to become **fixtures** on —
c. ☐ **minerals** or the like (including oil and gas) as extracted on —
d. ☐ **accounts resulting from the sale of minerals** or the like (including oil and gas) at the wellhead or minehead on —

the following real estate:

Street Address:

Described at: Book _____ of (check one) ☐ Deeds ☐ Mortgages , at Page(s) _____ .
for _____ County.   Uniform Parcel Identifier _____ .
☐ Described on Additional Sheet.

Name of record owner (required only if no Debtor has an interest of record):

10

DEBTOR SIGNATURE(S)

Debtor Signature(s):

1 _____

1a _____

1b _____   11

RETURN RECEIPT TO:

STANDARD FORM — FORM UCC-1
Approved by Secretary of Commonwealth of Pennsylvania

- Prepare and file annual reports
- Prepare and file articles of dissolution
- Prepare and file securities registrations and required filings with state regulatory agencies and with the United States Securities & Exchange Commission

ENVIRONMENTAL LAW:

- Track information with regard to Superfund sites
- Determine applicability of brown fields to client property
- Research history of properties to determine environmental activity
- Obtain the appropriate information about sites from state and federal environmental agencies
- Obtain documentation and assist in the preparation of environmental audits
- Organize and index documentation

FAMILY LAW:

- Collect information from clients with regard to marital status and prior marital status
- Interview client and collect information with regard to child support (see Exhibit 4.3)
- Draft prenuptial agreements
- Draft divorce complaints and responsive pleadings
- Prepare motions for support
- Prepare motions for custody and visitation
- Prepare property settlement agreements
- Prepare protection from abuse petitions
- Prepare petitions for termination of parental rights
- Prepare adoption petitions

IMMIGRATION LAW:

- Prepare applications and petitions for filing with the Immigration and Naturalization Service (INS) (see Exhibit 4.4 for a sample)
- Coordinate translation of foreign documents
- Prepare immigration and nonimmigration visa applications
- Coordinate activities with clients in foreign jurisdictions seeking visa and entry into the United States
- Assist clients in obtaining work visa to work in foreign countries
- Assist clients in the preparation of documentation to prove claim of marital status for submission to INS

INTELLECTUAL PROPERTY:

- Prepare patent search
- Prepare trademark search
- Prepare applications for patent, trademark, or copyright (Exhibit 4.5 is a sample)

exhibit 4.3   *Child support data form.*

_____ v. _____ No. _____

THIS FORM MUST BE FILLED OUT

(If you are self-employed or if you are salaried by a business of which you are owner in whole or in part, you must also fill out the Supplemental Income Statement which appears on the last page of this Income and Expense Statement.)

INCOME AND EXPENSE STATEMENT OF

_____

I verify that the statements made in this Income and Expense Statement are true and correct. I understand that false statements herein are made subject to the penalties of 18 Pa.C.S. §4904 relating to unsworn falsification to authorities.

Date: _____   Plaintiff or Defendant _____

INCOME

Employer: _____

Address: _____

Type of Work: _____

Payroll Number: _____

Pay Period (weekly, biweekly, etc.): _____

Gross Pay per Pay Period: $ _____

Itemized Payroll Deductions: Federal Withholding $ _____
                                Social Security   _____
                                Local Wage Tax   _____
                                State Income Tax   _____
                                Retirement   _____
                                Savings Bonds   _____
                                Credit Union   _____
                                Life Insurance   _____
                                Health Insurance   _____
                                Other (specify)   _____
                                _____   _____
                                Net Pay per Pay Period $ _____

OTHER INCOME: (Fill in Appropriate Column)

	Weekly	*Monthly*	*Yearly*
Interest	$ _____	$ _____	$ _____
Dividends	_____	_____	_____
Pension	_____	_____	_____
Annuity	_____	_____	_____
Social Security	_____	_____	_____
Rents	_____	_____	_____
Royalties	_____	_____	_____
Expense Account	_____	_____	_____
Gifts	_____	_____	_____
Unemployment Comp.	_____	_____	_____
Workmen's Comp.	_____	_____	_____
Total	_____	_____	_____

TOTAL INCOME $ _____

Sample Immigration and Naturalization Service form.   *exhibit* 4.4

U.S. Department of Justice
Immigration and Naturalization Service

**Notice of Entry of Appearance
as Attorney or Representative**

Appearances - An appearance shall be filed on this form by the attorney or representative appearing in each case. Thereafter, substitution may be permitted upon the written withdrawal of the attorney or representative of record or upon notification of the new attorney or representative. When an appearance is made by a person acting in a representative capacity, his personal appearance or signature shall constitute a representation that under the provisions of this chapter he is authorized and qualified to represent. Further proof of authority to act in a representative capacity may be required. **Availability of Records** - During the time a case is pending, and except as otherwise provided in 8 CFR 103.2(b), a party to a proceeding or his attorney or representative shall be permitted to examine the record of proceeding in a Service office. He may, in conformity with 8 CFR 103.10, obtain copies of Service records or information therefrom and copies of documents or transcripts of evidence furnished by him. Upon request, he/she may, in addition, be loaned a copy of the testimony and exhibits contained in the record of proceeding upon giving his/her receipt for such copies and pledging that it will be surrendered upon final disposition of the case or upon demand. If extra copies of exhibits do not exist, they shall not be furnished free on loan; however, they shall be made available for copying or purchase of copies as provided in 8 CFR 103.10.

In re: Lim Chi	Date: 09-15-2002
	File No. A1357

I hereby enter my appearance as attorney for (or representative of), and at the request of the following named person(s):

| Name: Lim chi | ☑ Petitioner   ☐ Applicant |
| | ☐ Beneficiary |

Address: (Apt. No.) (Number & Street)	(City)	(State)	(Zip Code)
275 Swamp Road	Newtown	Pa 18940	

| Name: | ☐ Petitioner   ☐ Applicant |
| | ☐ Beneficiary |

| Address: (Apt. No.)   (Number & Street) | (City) | (State) | (Zip Code) |

Check Applicable Item(s) below:

☑ 1. I am an attorney and a member in good standing of the bar of the Supreme Court of the United States or of the highest court of the following State, territory, insular possession, or District of Columbia
  Pennsylvania _____ Supreme Court _____ and am not under a court or administrative agency
                                          Name of Court
  order suspending, enjoining, restraining, disbarring, or otherwise restricting me in practicing law.

☐ 2. I am an accredited representative of the following named religious, charitable, social service, or similar organization established in the United States and which is so recognized by the Board:

☐ 3. I am associated with _____
  the attorney of record previously filed a notice of appearance in this case and my appearance is at his request. (*If you check this item, also check item 1 or 2 whichever is appropriate.*)

☐ 4. Others (Explain Fully.)

SIGNATURE	COMPLETE ADDRESS 138 North State Street Newtown, pa 18940
NAME (Type or Print) Thomas F. Goldman	TELEPHONE NUMBER 215 555 4321

PURSUANT TO THE PRIVACY ACT OF 1974, I HEREBY CONSENT TO THE DISCLOSURE TO THE FOLLOWING NAMED ATTORNEY OR REPRESENTATIVE OF ANY RECORD PERTAINING TO ME WHICH APPEARS IN ANY IMMIGRATION AND NATURALIZATION SERVICE SYSTEM OF RECORDS:
  Thomas F. Goldman _____
                          (Name of Attorney or Representative)
THE ABOVE CONSENT TO DISCLOSURE IS IN CONNECTION WITH THE FOLLOWING MATTER:

Name of Person Consenting	Signature of Person Consenting	Date
Len Ch	*Lin Ch*	

(NOTE: Execution of this box is required under the Privacy Act of 1974 where the person being represented is a citizen of the United States or an alien lawfully admitted for permanent residence.)

This form may not be used to request records under the Freedom of Information Act or the Privacy Act. The manner of requesting such records is contained in 8CFR 103.10 and 103.20 Et.SEQ.

Form G-28 (09/26/00)Y

exhibit 4.5 Copyright form.

FORM TX

For a Nondramatic Literary Work
UNITED STATES COPYRIGHT OFFICE

REGISTRATION NUMBER

TX   TXU

EFFECTIVE DATE OF REGISTRATION

Month   Day   Year

FEE CHANGES
Fees are effective through June 30, 2002. After that date, check the Copyright Office Website at www.loc.gov/copyright or call (202) 707-3000 for current fee information.

DO NOT WRITE ABOVE THIS LINE. IF YOU NEED MORE SPACE, USE A SEPARATE CONTINUATION SHEET.

1 TITLE OF THIS WORK ▼

PREVIOUS OR ALTERNATIVE TITLES ▼

PUBLICATION AS A CONTRIBUTION If this work was published as a contribution to a periodical, serial, or collection, give information about the collective work in which the contribution appeared. Title of Collective Work ▼

If published in a periodical or serial give: Volume ▼   Number ▼   Issue Date ▼   On Pages ▼

2 a NAME OF AUTHOR ▼
DATES OF BIRTH AND DEATH
Year Born ▼   Year Died ▼

Was this contribution to the work a "work made for hire"?
☐ Yes   ☐ No

AUTHOR'S NATIONALITY OR DOMICILE
Name of Country
OR { Citizen of ▶ USA
Domiciled in ▶

WAS THIS AUTHOR'S CONTRIBUTION TO THE WORK
Anonymous?   ☐ Yes ☐ No
Pseudonymous?   ☐ Yes ☐ No
If the answer to either of these questions is "Yes," see detailed instructions.

NATURE OF AUTHORSHIP Briefly describe nature of material created by this author in which copyright is claimed. ▼
Sole Author

NOTE
Under the law, the "author" of a "work made for hire" is generally the employer, not the employee (see instructions). For any part of this work that was "made for hire" check "Yes" in the space provided, give the employer (or other person for whom the work was prepared) as "Author" of that part, and leave the space for dates of birth and death blank.

b NAME OF AUTHOR ▼
DATES OF BIRTH AND DEATH
Year Born ▼   Year Died ▼

Was this contribution to the work a "work made for hire"?
☐ Yes   ☐ No

AUTHOR'S NATIONALITY OR DOMICILE
Name of Country
OR { Citizen of ▶
Domiciled in ▶

WAS THIS AUTHOR'S CONTRIBUTION TO THE WORK
Anonymous?   ☐ Yes ☐ No
Pseudonymous?   ☐ Yes ☐ No
If the answer to either of these questions is "Yes," see detailed instructions.

NATURE OF AUTHORSHIP Briefly describe nature of material created by this author in which copyright is claimed. ▼

c NAME OF AUTHOR ▼
DATES OF BIRTH AND DEATH
Year Born ▼   Year Died ▼

Was this contribution to the work a "work made for hire"?
☐ Yes   ☐ No

AUTHOR'S NATIONALITY OR DOMICILE
Name of Country
OR { Citizen of ▶
Domiciled in ▶

WAS THIS AUTHOR'S CONTRIBUTION TO THE WORK
Anonymous?   ☐ Yes ☐ No
Pseudonymous?   ☐ Yes ☐ No
If the answer to either of these questions is "Yes," see detailed instructions.

NATURE OF AUTHORSHIP Briefly describe nature of material created by this author in which copyright is claimed. ▼

3 a YEAR IN WHICH CREATION OF THIS WORK WAS COMPLETED This information must be given in all cases.
b DATE AND NATION OF FIRST PUBLICATION OF THIS PARTICULAR WORK
Complete this information ONLY if this work has been published.
Month ▶   Day ▶   Year ▶   Nation
USA

4 COPYRIGHT CLAIMANT(S) Name and address must be given even if the claimant is the same as the author given in space 2. ▼

APPLICATION RECEIVED

ONE DEPOSIT RECEIVED

TWO DEPOSITS RECEIVED

FUNDS RECEIVED

DO NOT WRITE HERE
OFFICE USE ONLY

TRANSFER If the claimant(s) named here in space 4 is (are) different from the author(s) named in space 2, give a brief statement of how the claimant(s) obtained ownership of the copyright. ▼
By written agreement.

MORE ON BACK ▶ • Complete all applicable spaces (numbers 5-9) on the reverse side of this page.
• See detailed instructions.   • Sign the form at line 8.

DO NOT WRITE HERE
Page 1 of ____ pages

FORM TX

EXAMINED BY

CHECKED BY

CORRESPONDENCE
☐ Yes

FOR COPYRIGHT OFFICE USE ONLY

5 **DO NOT WRITE ABOVE THIS LINE. IF YOU NEED MORE SPACE, USE A SEPARATE CONTINUATION SHEET.**

PREVIOUS REGISTRATION Has registration for this work, or for an earlier version of this work, already been made in the Copyright Office?
☐ Yes ☐ No If your answer is "Yes," why is another registration being sought? (Check appropriate box.) ▼
a. ☐ This is the first published edition of a work previously registered in unpublished form.
b. ☐ This is the first application submitted by this author as copyright claimant.
c. ☐ This is a changed version of the work, as shown by space 6 on this application.
If your answer is "Yes," give: Previous Registration Number ▶   Year of Registration ▶

6 a DERIVATIVE WORK OR COMPILATION
Preexisting Material Identify any preexisting work or works that this work is based on or incorporates. ▼

b Material Added to This Work Give a brief, general statement of the material that has been added to this work and in which copyright is claimed. ▼

7 a DEPOSIT ACCOUNT If the registration fee is to be charged to a Deposit Account established in the Copyright Office, give name and number of Account.
Name ▼   Account Number ▼

b CORRESPONDENCE Give name and address to which correspondence about this application should be sent.   Name/Address/Apt/City/State/ZIP ▼

Area code and daytime telephone number ▶ 480-991-7881
Fax number ▶
Email ▶

8 CERTIFICATION* I, the undersigned, hereby certify that I am the
Check only one ▶ ☐ author
☐ other copyright claimant
☐ owner of exclusive right(s)
☐ authorized agent of _____
Name of author or other copyright claimant, or owner of exclusive right(s) ▲

of the work identified in this application and that the statements made by me in this application are correct to the best of my knowledge.

Typed or printed name and date ▼ If this application gives a date of publication in space 3, do not sign and submit it before that date.
Date ▶

Handwritten signature (X) ▼
X

9 Certificate will be mailed in window envelope to this address:

Name ▼
Number/Street/Apt ▼
City/State/ZIP ▼

YOU MUST:
• Complete all necessary spaces
• Sign your application in space 8
SEND ALL 3 ELEMENTS IN THE SAME PACKAGE:
1. Application form
2. Nonrefundable filing fee in check or money order payable to Register of Copyrights
3. Deposit material
MAIL TO:
Library of Congress
Copyright Office
101 Independence Avenue, S.E.
Washington, D.C. 20559-6000

As of July 1, 1999, the filing fee for Form TX is $30.

*17 U.S.C. § 506(e): Any person who knowingly makes a false representation of a material fact in the application for copyright registration provided for by section 409, or in any written statement filed in connection with the application, shall be fined not more than $2,500.

June 1999—200,000
WEB REV: June 1999

☆U.S. GOVERNMENT PRINTING OFFICE: 1999-454-879/49

- Assist in preparation of documentation in opposition, interference, infringement, and similar proceedings
- Coordinate activities and filings with foreign patent, trademark, and copyright attorneys and agents
- Work with engineers in preparation of applications and defense of patents and trade secrets
- Draft licensing agreements for intellectual property items

HUMAN RESOURCES LAW:

- Draft plan documents for tax-sheltered employee benefit plans
- Draft deferred compensation plans
- Prepare and file for an Internal Revenue Service determination letters of plans
- Prepare and file annual reports including 5500 series Internal Revenue Service forms
- Calculate employer and employee contribution levels and limitations
- Draft, review, and distribute summary plan descriptions

LITIGATION:

- Investigate factual allegations of case
- Help to locate witnesses and physical evidence
- Draft summons, complaint, answers, and other defenses and responsive pleadings
- Organize and maintain litigation files
- Assist in the preparation of trial notebooks
- Gather, review, summarize, and index documents for use at trial
- Locate and arrange for interviews with expert witnesses
- Prepare written interrogatories
- Assist in preparing and conducting oral depositions, including videotape depositions
- Prepare or obtain subpoenas (see sample in Exhibit 4.6) and arrange for service upon witnesses
- Coordinate, assist, and arrange for trial exhibits
- Obtain jury-pool information, and assist in the selection of appropriate jury members
- Attend trial and assist in the handling of witnesses, exhibits, and evidence
- Prepare contemporaneous summaries of witness statements during trial

PARALEGAL SKILLS

The skills needed by a paralegal are varied and depend, in some cases, on the nature of the legal specialty in which one works. Common to all paralegals are certain basic skills and attributes including communication skills, initiative, resourcefulness, commitment or "stick-to-itiveness," and self-motivation, among others.

exhibit **4.6** *Subpoena.*

Commonwealth of Pennsylvania
County of Philadelphia

In the matter of:

COURT OF COMMON PLEAS

Henry Thomas
(Plaintiff)   *(Demandante)*

October _____ Term, Yr. 2002

vs.

No. 68-96874

Thomas Cheese
(Defendant)   *(Demandado)*

Subpoena

To: Elizabeth Rhodes
        (Name of Witness)   *(Nombre del Testigo)*

1. YOU ARE ORDERED BY THE COURT TO COME TO *(El tribunal le ordena que venga a)*
Court room 654

_____, AT PHILADELPHIA, PENNSYLVANIA ON *(en Filadelfia,*

Pennsylvania el) November 4, 2002 _____, AT *(a las)* _____ 10 _____ O'CLOCK _____ A _____.M., TO

TESTIFY ON BEHALF OF *(para atestiguar a favor de)* Henry Thomas _____ IN THE ABOVE

CASE, AND TO REMAIN UNTIL EXCUSED *(en el caso arriba mencionado y permanecer hasta que le autoricen irse).*

2. AND BRING WITH YOU THE FOLLOWING *(Y traer con usted lo siguiente)*:

_____

_____

NOTICE	AVISO
If you fail to attend or to produce the documents or things required by this subpoena, you may be subject to the sanctions authorized by Rule 234.5 of the Pennsylvania Rules of Civil Procedure, including but not limited to costs, attorney fees and imprisonment.	**Si usted falla en comparecer o producir los documentos o cosas requeridas por esta cita, usted estara sujeto a las sanciones autorizadas por la regla 234.5 de las reglas de procedimiento civil de Pensilvania, incluyendo pero no limitado a los costos, remuneracion de abogados y encarcelamiento.**

INQUIRIES CONCERNING THIS SUBPOENA SHOULD BE ADDRESSED TO *(Las preguntas que tenga acerca de esta Citacion deben ser dirigidas a)*:
ISSUED BY:

Edith Hannah
                    (Attorney)   *(Abogado/Abogada)*

ADDRESS *(Direccion)* 8 North Broad Street, Philadelphia, PA

TELEPHONE NO. *(No. de Telefono)* 215 555 9999

ATTORNEY *(Abogado ID #)* A5B6

BY THE COURT *(Por El Tribunal)*
JOSEPH H. EVERS
PROTHONOTARY *(Protonotario)*

PRO _____
        (Clerk)   *(Escribano)*

10-200 (Rev. 7/99)   Completed Subpoena must be signed and sealed by the Prothonotary (Room 266 City Hall) before service.

Everyone has goals in life. You might be a great jogger who longs to win the Boston Marathon, or a skilled writer who wants to write the great American novel. Achieving most goals requires some set of skills. If your goal is to be a successful paralegal, you will need certain basic skills. You may already possess some of these, and may need to acquire others. Some of the basic skills you already have are:

- the ability to read English—unless someone is reading this book to you
- the ability to communicate at some level in writing or speaking
- initiative—because you have signed up for this course or have picked up this book to read and learn about the paralegal profession.

In addition, you may have skills such as:

- facility with computers and the Internet
- the ability to speak a second or third language
- a background in medicine, engineering, business, or other academic or occupational area.

Some other skills are less obvious—resourcefulness, commitment or stick-to-itiveness, analytical skills and interpersonal skills including cultural sensitivity—so we will explore them in more depth. We cannot all run a marathon, or type 160 words a minute, but we all can acquire most of the basic skills by making an effort to improve ourselves and attain the knowledge base to achieve most, if not all, of our goals. Many people achieve much more than they, themselves, and others believed they were capable of achieving, by just plain hard work. If you want something bad enough and are willing to work hard enough, you can achieve your personal and professional goals. A good starting point in achieving your goals is to understand your strengths and weaknesses, capitalize on the strengths, and work on improving the weaknesses.

Checklist

STRENGTHS & WEAKNESSES

○ My strengths:

○ How I can capitalize on my strengths:

○ My weaknesses:

○ How I can overcome my weaknesses:

Resourcefulness

Resourcefulness is the ability to meet and handle a situation and find solutions to problems. It is one of the most valuable skills anyone can have—and one that is not easily taught. A resourceful person in the office is sometimes referred to as the "can do" person on the team. This is the person who usually finds some creative way to accomplish what everyone else has given up on. Certainly, creativity is involved—solving the problem by thinking outside the box and not limiting the solution to tried-and-true methods.

When everyone else says, "I can't find this witness," the resourceful person tries a new approach and finds the witness. When others use only the standard telephone directories, the resourceful person uses the cross-reference directory. When local telephone directories do not yield results, resourceful people use the national telephone directories on CD and the online Internet telephone directories.

In the legal workplace the person who gets noticed is the one who finds a way to get the job done in time for the hearing, meeting, or arbitration. This is the person who is willing to use unconventional ways to get the job finished, such as when the power goes out or the computer system crashes just before a deadline. Lawyers want resourceful people on their team and reward them to keep them on the team.

> **SIDEBAR**
>
> ## Organizing
>
> The skill of organizing includes the ability to
>
> 1. Categorize
> 2. Prioritize
> 3. Organize
> 4. Utilize time efficiently

Commitment

Commitment means finishing that which one starts out to do or complete. From our childhood we remember the story of the tortoise and the hare (rabbit), in which the tortoise wins the race by being "slow and steady." The tortoise wins in part because of commitment—putting everything into the race and not stopping until the job is done.

Many people start jobs and don't finish them. Others start what seems to be an insurmountable task and—to their amazement and maybe ours—finish, and finish well. Taking on an assignment in a law office requires commitment. Team members are expected to finish the task, whether it is researching a case, writing a brief, filing a pleading, or organizing a file.

As a professional, you are expected to finish the tasks within the assigned timeframe. There is no excuse for not doing some tasks, such as filing the complaint with the court before the statute of limitations expires, or getting the brief to the court by the court-imposed deadline. Even a simple thing like getting to court on time requires commitment.

Not everyone has the necessary commitment or wants to take on the responsibility of meeting commitments. You have to decide whether you are willing to make the commitment. Others will be depending on you, and if you do not want to commit, admit it to yourself and to the others who are depending on you, and then choose some other activity or profession. Choosing a profession, whether it is the legal profession, the paralegal profession, the medical profession, or the accounting profession, requires a commitment to serve others. As a professional, you are making a commitment to your clients that you will provide the best professional advice, skill, and effort. They depend on this professionalism and the necessary commitment.

Analytical Skills

Analytical skills allow one to follow a step-by-step process to solve a problem. It could be finding a missing witness by looking in telephone books, or determining that the person is part of a group, such as a professional society or organization that publishes a membership directory. Solving these types of problems requires analytical skills to figure out, for instance, what made a bottle explode, injuring a client. Determining the actual cause requires a step-by-step analysis of the potential reasons and the narrowing down of possible causes.

One of the basic skills that law students and paralegal students are taught is *legal analysis*, the ability to identify the facts and legal issues and contrast and compare them to the law and to other cases. This is a skill that develops with time. As you learn the elements of crimes, torts, and other areas of law, you will learn the individual parts of each. In contracts law, you will learn what conduct is a valid acceptance of a contract offer, and in tort law, what constitutes reasonable conduct under the circumstances.

Thinking Outside the Box

This exercise is widely used to demonstrate thinking outside the box. Without lifting your pencil from the paper, connect all the dots with only four lines.

• • •

• • •

• • •

(Answer on p. 116)

Interpersonal Skills

Critical to paralegal success, as well as to success in other endeavors, is the ability to work with other people. To categorize people, co-workers, colleagues, and employers might be unfair, but we all do it. We think, and sometimes say, things like, "He's a pleasure to work with" or, "She has clients eating out of her hand." Conversely, we might also say things like, "She's the most negative person I know" or "He's only out for himself." These comments are a reflection of the other person's interpersonal skills, the ability to work with and effectively communicate with others.

How we relate to others can make the job easier or harder. These people include not just co-workers as members of the legal team but also clients, witnesses, and opposing parties. Obviously, everyone in the firm or on the team must have a level of trust and confidence in the others on the team. People who have a good working relationship accomplish more and enjoy doing it. In contrast, conflict and tension make the job harder and can lead to people taking shortcuts and avoiding contact, which can result in poor performance and potential malpractice.

Not everyone has the personality to deal with every type of situation and every type of personality—for example, dealing with clients. But everyone on the legal team has to develop the skills to work with people and recognize when they may have to have someone else handle certain aspects of a case or client. The skill is in recognizing when and how they can affect relationships and desired results. Some might call this "sensitivity"—to other people's needs, desires, wants, likes, and dislikes. Cultural differences are discussed later, but in the American culture, for example, people tend to be sensitive to odors—breath, body, environmental. We do not want to offend. Our use of language is another area of sensitivity. We try to avoid using words that we believe will offend the other person in a particular circumstance, such as telling off-color jokes in a religious setting in front of a person of the cloth.

The starting point in working with attorneys, paralegals, and support staff, clients and opposing counsel, court personnel and others, is to be sensitive to issues such as these. What offends you probably offends others. Being sensitive to how others react to your words, conduct, and actions can provide good clues as to what is acceptable and what is not.

In the past, how we related to others and how others perceived us was measured by direct face-to-face contact, telephone contact, and written communications. Today we have to add to those forms of communication the way we write emails and use electronic communications. These technological advances make our communications more immediate. Too many happy faces and frowning faces, such as :) or :(in an email, could be interpreted as overfamiliarity. THE USE OF ALL CAPITAL LETTERS might be interpreted as shouting at the reader. Poor spelling and bad grammar in emails are likely to be seen as less than professional or pure sloppiness or carelessness. In the past, letters were dictated, typed, proofread, and then signed. Today we dash off an email without much thought—and sometimes it reflects just that. How our clients view our capabilities and skill now might be measured by that quick email response.

The Tarrant County Courthouse in Fort Worth, Texas.

Communication Skills

Communication means expressing ideas effectively. The practice of law requires good communication, both oral and written. The lawyer and the paralegal who work together must be able to communicate assignments and information with clarity and, frequently, brevity. Over time, communication will improve, with each person coming to understand what the other is really asking or saying.

Communication is made complex by subtleties, nuances, and expressions that may require interpretation or explanation. For example, older attorneys who are used to using traditional methods of research may ask the new paralegal (who has a deep understanding of computer research methods and little traditional book experience) to "check the pocket parts." This means checking for the latest update or change to a statute or case law. Or asking a paralegal to "Shepardize" a case may have no meaning to one who has learned only the West system, in which the method for checking other cases is called KeyCiting, or the Loislaw system, which refers to this as GlobalCiting.

Although communication may not be a major issue in the typical office environment, it can be a major problem in the fast-paced office when the litigation attorney sends a message from court in the middle of a case to the support paralegal at the office, by a two-way pager, after the other side has brought up an unexpected case in argument to the court.

Creating an Impression

Unless you are intentionally trying to create a different impression, try to:

- Have a positive attitude
- Be diplomatic
- Be flexible
- Establish good rapport with others
- Be a team player
- Be resourceful
- Be adaptable
- Be thorough

Nowadays there is rarely the luxury of time to develop a common written and oral language base for communication among the paralegal, clients, opposing attorneys, and court personnel. Letters, pleadings, contracts, and other written documents must be clear and accurate. In many situations only one document must carefully communicate the idea, request, or demand. Oral communication also must be clear and precise.

The old adage still holds true: First impressions matter. If the first impression is a poorly written communication with misspelled words and unconventional grammar, or a discussion in person or by telephone that is filled with slang and poor grammar, the impression may affect the client's or court's view of the firm's professionalism, ability, and legal skills. It can influence the client's decision to stay with the firm or not, the judge's granting the request, or the court clerk's giving you the help you need.

Analyzing the Audience

There are many ways to address those with whom you communicate. Here we will point out some general differences in the way men and women communicate. The following section describes some cultural background considerations.*

IF YOUR RECEIVER IS A MAN, IT IS POSSIBLE THAT:

- He has been socialized to perform aggressively and boast of his successes.
- His childhood games taught him that competition is fun and winning is good.
- He is motivated by competition.
- He views conflict as impersonal, a necessary part of working relationships.
- He is impressed by power, ability, and achievement.
- He may hear only your literal words and miss your underlying emotion.
- He will not express his true feelings through facial expression.
- His communication style tends to be direct.

IF YOUR RECEIVER IS A WOMAN, IT IS POSSIBLE THAT:

- She has been socialized to work cooperatively and to be modest about her success.
- Her childhood games taught her to compromise and collaborate, and she continues to be motivated by affiliation.
- She competes primarily with herself—with her own expectations of what she should be able to accomplish.
- She takes conflict personally.
- She is impressed by personal disclosure and professional courage.
- She has the ability to focus on several projects at the same time.

*These discussions are adapted from *Crosstalk: Communicating in a Multicultural Workplace,* by Kenton and Valentine. Copyright © 1997 by Prentice Hall, Upper Saddle River, NJ.

Communication Skills

How well do you . . .

- Read with comprehension?
- Listen effectively and accurately and interpret nonverbal communication?
- Write in clear, concise, and grammatically correct English?
- Speak in clear, concise, and grammatically correct English?
- Use language to persuade?
- Tailor the nature of the communication to maximize understanding in the intended audience, including people with different levels of education and different cultural backgrounds?

Source: American Association for Paralegal Education.

SIDEBAR

- She is proficient at decoding your nonverbal meanings and likely to display her feelings through facial expression or body language.
- Her style will be indirect, except with other women of equal rank.

CONSIDER YOUR RECEIVER'S ATTITUDES ABOUT YOU:

- Man-to-man: He may afford you instant credibility based on similarity.
- Woman-to-woman: She may expect you to be friendly, nurturing, and concerned. She may afford you instant credibility based on similarity.
- Man-to-woman: She may expect that you will not really listen to her.
- Woman-to-man: He may expect you to be friendly and nurturing, even passive-dependent. Any aggressive behavior or deviation from his expectation can cause him discomfort and confusion, or produce negative responses. He may simply disregard you.

CULTURAL SENSITIVITY

The culturally sensitive person is aware of the reasons for differences in the way people behave, based on religious and ethnic background and belief system. As the cultural makeup of the United States has become more diverse, the need for cultural awareness and sensitivity in the legal and paralegal professions has grown. Just as men and women are said to think differently, so do Europeans, Asians, Latinos, and Africans.

To communicate effectively, you must be aware of the possible interpretations of what you are communicating and what the other person is saying. Interviewing a Latino male, for example, may require a different approach than interviewing an Asian female. Even subtleties of eye contact can affect an interview. Whereas Americans view eye contact as a sign of sincerity, some Asian cultures view it as aggressive. As you develop your communication skills, you must become sensitive to how you are perceived and learn to fashion your approach to maximize accuracy of communication.

The effectiveness of paralegals also is influenced by how well they "read" the cultural backgrounds of those with whom they interact. This involves manner of speaking, dressing, and acting, and whether one is a man or a woman in that culture. What is heard may not be what was intended. What you perceive may not be what the other person perceives, because of cultural differences that affect the interpretation of the words and body language. We will briefly highlight some general characteristics of four cultural groups.*

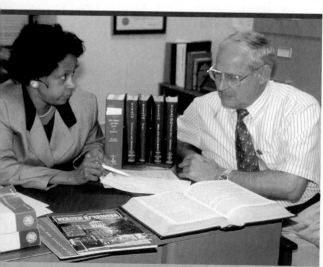

Effective communication is essential in dealings between paralegal and client.

European Background

Generally the countries of Western Europe, including Scandinavia, comprise the group of European background. This group is extraordinarily large and

*These discussions are adapted from *Crosstalk: Communicating in a Multicultural Workplace*, by Kenton and Valentine. Copyright © 1997 by Prentice Hall, Upper Saddle River, NJ.

JAG Competition Showcases Soldier Skills

Soldiers, September 2001, Volume 56, Issue 9

Deana Willis

Forget all the lawyer jokes you've heard. The 21st Theater Support Command's Office of the Staff Judge Advocate's "Iron JAG" competition demonstrated that Army attorneys and paralegals have the right stuff to bring to the battlefield—soldier-style. Iron JAG is a grueling set of events, including a 400-meter relay swim, a field march with full combat load, a modified PT test, an operational law exam, a cross-country run, and tests on common-task training and JAG mission-essential tasks.

The organizer of this year's Iron JAG, SGM Mike Broady, used his experience from a previous assignment with a ranger regiment to create a competition to reinforce the standard CTT, JAG METL, and physical training that is conducted at unit level. The 11-hour competition tested attorneys and enlisted paralegals on all facets of their missions, promoting the JAG team concept and validating and evaluating JAG training.

"The competitors happen to be lawyers, legal NCOs and legal specialists, but they're always soldiers first and they have to maintain those soldier skills," said MG John D. Altenburg, the assistant judge advocate general. "That's why we want to push this so hard."

NCOs at individual law centers throughout U. S. Army, Europe, independently trained their soldiers in annual CTT tasks and specific JAG METL tasks, then team members trained each other. Enlisted soldiers trained their officer partners in CTT, and the attorneys trained their paralegals in battlefield law to prepare for the difficult operational law test.

"The operational law test is unique," said Broady. "It's based on rules of engagement, the laws of land warfare, the Hague and Geneva conventions, collateral claims damage, and other issues that JAG teams could encounter on the battlefield."

The competition was so fierce that a winning team did not emerge until the last event. The first-place trophy was captured by the 1st Infantry Division's team number 4, CPT Joseph Ratermann and PFC Michael Rea. Second place went to CPT John Hyatt and SGT Stephen Newsome, also of the 1st Infantry Division. The 21st TSC team of CPT Robert Borcherding and SSG Geriberto Dragon placed third.

From *Soldiers*, Vol. 56, No. 9, September 2001, U. S. Government Printing Office.

complex, which limits attempts to make cultural generalities. In terms of gender differences, men and women with roots in the European culture may have different initial reactions to you and attitudes about your topic. Male and female listeners alike tend to perceive men as having more credibility than women of equal rank, experience, and training. Men tend to be more credible to other men, and women may be more credible to other women.

Now consider the cultural implications of graphic pictures of physical injuries from car crashes. These would be acceptable in the United States, but Germans tend to dislike the sight of blood, and the British are likely to be offended by violence.

According to Kenton and Valentine, if you are of European–American appearance, receivers of communication may be concerned that you will:

- Reject their opinions
- Take advantage of them or hold them back
- Consider them different in a negative way
- Deny them equal opportunities (p. 56)

Latino Background

Collectively, Latin America encompasses 51 countries. Latin American countries are generally considered to be those south of the U. S. border, including

Mexico and the countries of Central America, South America, and the Caribbean islands. With so vast an area, there are many differences from country to country and even from city to city. The languages, too, are not the same. Portuguese is spoken in Brazil, and the Spanish spoken in South America differs from the Spanish spoken in Puerto Rico. The Latino–American population has moved closer to becoming the largest minority group in the United States.

According to Kenton and Valentine, individuals with roots in the Latino culture tend to:

- Value family and loyalty to family
- Honor nationalism
- Exhibit a strong sense of honor
- Have a fatalistic view of the world
- Express passion in speech, manner, and deed (pp. 98–99)

Asian Background

More than 30 countries can be considered Asian, among them China, Malaysia, Japan, the Philippines, India, and Korea. They, too, demonstrate vast differences in the individual cultures. Some generalizations may be made, however. Being direct and to the point is generally considered rude in Asian cultures, in which relationships are considered top priority. For example, the Japanese tend to prefer an indirect style of communication. In communicating with people who have an Asian background, it might be best to begin with pleasantries about the weather, sports, or general well-being of the individual and his or her family.

Roots in the African Culture

African Americans represent the largest ethnic group in the United States. A distinction should be made between African Americans of recent immigration with stronger cultural ties to the African culture and African Americans with long family ties within the United States whose cultural roots are American. According to Kenton and Valentine, some of the African core beliefs and cultural values that may influence attitudes and behavior are:

- A holistic worldview
- Emotion and expressiveness
- A keen sense of justice or fairness
- A belief in the uniqueness of the individual as defined by the ethnic group (p. 54)

LEGAL TERMINOLOGY

Analytical skill
Commitment
Communication

Cultural sensitivity
Interpersonal skills
Resourcefulness

Summary

CHAPTER 4 PARALEGAL WORKPLACE SKILLS

Paralegal Tasks and Functions

1. Conducting interviews
2. Conducting investigations
3. Legal writing
4. Legal research
5. Review, analysis, summarizing, and indexing
6. Assisting in preparation of witnesses and clients for trial
7. Maintaining calendar and tickler systems
8. Performing research
9. Performing office administration functions

Paralegal Skills

1. Resourcefulness
2. Commitment
3. Analytical skills
4. Interpersonal skills
5. Communication skills
6. Cultural sensitivity

Analyzing the Audience

1. Men versus women
2. Cultural background

Working the Web

1. Check the online features of
   a. Westlaw at www.westlaw.com
   b. Lexis-Nexis at www.lexisnexis.com
   c. Lexisone at www.lexisone.com
2. Check the cultural awareness programs of the Office of Civil Rights of the U. S. Department of Commerce at www.doc.gov/ocr/cultural.html
3. Review Executive Order 13166: Improving Access to Services for Persons with Limited English Proficiency at www.doc.gov/ocr/eo13166.html
4. Visit the Library of Congress Country Studies website at http://lcweb2.loc.gov/frd/cs/cshome.html
5. Check the list of national holidays at the Department of State website at www.state.gov/s/cpr/rls/dpl/index.cfm?docid=3003

Questions
CRITICAL LEGAL THINKING AND WRITING

1. Why should a paralegal tell clients in the initial interview that he or she is a paralegal?
2. Why are good English writing and speaking skills important for the paralegal?
3. Complete the "Strengths & Weaknesses" checklist in this chapter.
4. How can you use the "Strengths & Weaknesses" checklist in preparing your personal career roadmap?
5. What actions have you observed in other people that demonstrated their resourcefulness? Have others ever told you that you are resourceful?
6. As a paralegal job applicant, how can you demonstrate the characteristic of commitment?
7. What cultural differences have you observed that have limited open communications?
8. Why and how might you modify your manner of dress or choice of words in interviewing a client? A witness?
9. Can you think of a situation in which an interview would be better conducted by a woman? By a man? Explain.
10. How does the "Thinking Outside the Box" activity demonstrate this type of thinking?

Questions
ETHICS: ANALYSIS AND DISCUSSION

1. Why do paralegals have to tell clients and witnesses that they are paralegals?
2. In a meeting with a client, can the paralegal use the phrase "in my opinion"?
3. Why might an ethical issue of competence be raised if the paralegal is not aware of the language and cultural differences of a client?

Unauthorized Practice of Law—Fee Splitting

There are few certainties in the area of ethics, for paralegals or in any profession. What qualifies as ethical conduct is in most cases based on state law and court interpretation applied to a set of facts. The citation listed below represents one legal opinion and is provided as a research starting point. Do not assume that the same rule applies in your jurisdiction. For the following:

- *Prepare a written statement based on your state law.*
- *Use your state bar association website as a starting point.*

You are offered the opportunity to work with a local law firm providing living trust services to the public. Your responsibility would be to make a presentation on the advantages of living trusts to community groups and in other public meetings. Any interested person would meet with you after the general session and you would fill out the forms, collect the fee, and send the completed form and half the fee collected to the law firm for review and transmittal to the client. You would retain half the amount collected as your fee. [*Cincinnati Bar Assn. v. Kathman*, 92 Ohio St.3d 92 (2001).] What ethical issues are involved? Explain.

Case FOR DISCUSSION

In Re *Busy Beaver Bldg. Centers, Inc.*   19 F.3d 833 (3rd Cir. 1994)

Paralegal Fees Based on Skill Level

In deciding the propriety of awarding paralegal fees in bankruptcy cases, the court held:

As is true with recently graduated attorneys, entry-level paralegals perform the more mundane tasks in the paralegal work spectrum, some of which may resemble those tasks generally deemed "clerical" in nature. Yet, even with these tasks, paralegals may have to bring their training or experience to bear, thereby relieving attorneys of the burden of extensive supervision and ensuring the proper completion of tasks involving the exercise, or potential exercise, of some paraprofessional judgment. Of course, the appropriate rate the attorney will command for paralegal services will ordinarily parallel the paralegal's credentials and the degree of experience, knowledge, and skill the task at hand calls for. . . . [P]urely clerical or secretarial tasks should not be billed at a paralegal rate, regardless of who performs them.

The short of it is that the market-driven approach of the [bankruptcy act] § 330 permits compensation for relatively low-level paralegal services if and only if analogous non-bankruptcy clients agree to pay for the same, and then only at that rate. [T]hose services not requiring the exercise of professional legal judgment . . . must be included in "overhead."

We cannot agree that in all cases the general ability of a legal secretary to perform some particular task determines whether a paralegal or a legal secretary is the appropriate, read most efficient, employee to perform it at any given instant. At times temporal constraints may foreclose the delegation option. At other times a paralegal—or, for that matter, an attorney—can more productively complete a clerical task, such as photocopying documents, than can a legal secretary.

Questions

1. How can the attorney prove the skill level of paralegals when seeking compensation for paralegal services?
2. Will this kind of reasoning by the court force attorneys to hire more skilled paralegals?
3. Would the existence of a certificate or degree in paralegal studies be useful in proving that the person who worked on a case was a paralegal?

Ramirez v. Plough, Inc.

12 Cal. Rptr. 2d 423 (Cal. Ct. App. 1992)*

Court of Appeal of California

* If citing in a California court, add "15 Cal. App. 4th 1110" after the case name and before the citation from the California Reporter, set off by commas. Ramirez v. Plough, Inc., 15 Cal. App. 4th 1110, 12 Cal. Rptr. 2d 423 (1992)

Read, and if assigned, brief this case. Prepare a written answer to each of the following questions.

1. How does this case illustrate the cultural differences of clients?

2. Are the views and conduct of the parent in this case the same as you have and would have taken?

3. What ethical obligation does the paralegal have to be sure the client who does not speak the same language understands the advice given? Does it matter if it is medical directions as in this case, or legal advice?

4. Does a law firm have a higher duty to a non–English-speaking client than a drug company, such as the defendant in this case, does in selling a product?

5. Does the law firm have a duty to explain cultural differences in the American legal system and its procedures to non-English speaking, non-native born clients?

Thaxter, Judge.

Jorge Ramirez, a minor, by his guardian ad litem Rosa Rivera, appeals from a summary judgment in favor of Plough, Inc. Appellant sued Plough alleging negligence, product liability, and fraud. The action sought damages for injuries sustained in March of 1986 when Jorge, who was then four months old, contracted Reye's Syndrome after ingesting St. Joseph Aspirin for Children (SJAC). Plough marketed and distributed SJAC.

Reye's Syndrome is a serious disease of unknown cause characterized by severe vomiting, lethargy, or irritability which may progress to delirium or coma.

. . . .

In December 1985, the Food and Drug Administration (FDA) requested that aspirin manufacturers voluntarily place a label on aspirin products warning consumers of the possible association between aspirin and Reye's Syndrome. Plough voluntarily complied and began including a warning and insert in SJAC packaging. On June 5, 1986, the Reye's Syndrome warning became mandatory.

In March 1986, SJAC labeling bore the following warning: "Warning: Reye's Syndrome is a rare but serious disease which can follow flu or chicken pox in children and teenagers. While the cause of Reye's Syndrome is unknown, some reports claim aspirin may increase the risk of developing this disease. Consult a doctor before use in children or teenagers with flu or chicken pox." In addition, the SJAC package insert included the following statement: "The symptoms of Reye's Syndrome can include persistent vomiting, sleepiness and lethargy, violent headaches, unusual behavior, including disorientation, combativeness, and delirium. If any of these symptoms occur, especially following chicken pox or flu, call your doctor immediately, even if your child has not taken any medication. Reye's Syndrome is serious, so early detection and treatment are vital."

Rosa Rivera purchased SJAC on March 12, 1986, and administered it to appellant, who was suffering from what appeared to be a cold or upper respiratory infection. She gave appellant the aspirin without reading the directions or warnings appearing on the SJAC packaging. The packaging was in English and Ms. Rivera can speak and understand only Spanish. She did not seek to have the directions or warnings translated from English to Spanish, even though members of her household spoke English.

The trial court granted Plough's motion for summary judgment on the grounds that "there is no duty to warn in a foreign language and there is no causal relationship between plaintiff's injury and defendant's activities."

It is undisputed SJAC was marketed and intended for the treatment of minor aches and pains associated with colds, flu, and minor viral illnesses. The SJAC box promised "fast, effective relief of fever and minor aches and pains of colds." ... In March 1986, federal regulations requiring a Reye's Syndrome warning had been promulgated and were final, although not yet effective. ... The scientific community had already confirmed and documented the relationship between Reye's Syndrome and the use of aspirin after a viral illness. There is no doubt Plough had a duty to warn of the Reye's Syndrome risk.

The question thus is whether the warning given only in English was adequate under the circumstances. Respondent argues that, as a matter of law, it has no duty to place foreign-language warnings on products manufactured to be sold in the United States and that holding manufacturers liable for failing to do so would violate public policy.

While the constitutional, statutory, regulatory, and judicial authorities relied on by respondent may reflect a public policy recognizing the status of English as an official language, nothing compels the conclusion that a manufacturer of a dangerous or defective product is immunized from liability when an English-only warning does not adequately inform non-English literate persons likely to use the product.

Plough's evidence showed that over 148 foreign languages are spoken in the United States and over 23 million Americans speak a language other than English in their homes. That evidence plainly does not prove that Plough used reasonable care in giving an English-only warning. Plough, then, resorts to arguing that the burden on manufacturers and society of requiring additional warnings is so "staggering" that the courts should preclude liability as a matter of law. We are not persuaded.

Certainly the burden and costs of giving foreign-language warnings is one factor for consideration in determining whether a manufacturer acted reasonably in using only English. The importance of that factor may vary from case to case depending upon other circumstances, such as the nature of the product, marketing efforts directed to segments of the population unlikely to be English-literate, and the actual and relative size of the consumer market which could reasonably be expected to speak or read only a certain foreign language. Plough presented no evidence from which we can gauge the extent of the burden under the facts of this case.

Ramirez submitted evidence that Plough knew Hispanics were an important part of the market for SJAC and that Hispanics often maintain their first language rather than learn English. SJAC was advertised in the Spanish media, both radio and television. That evidence raises material questions of fact concerning the foreseeability of purchase by a Hispanic not literate in English and the reasonableness of not giving a Spanish-language warning. If Plough has evidence conclusively showing that it would have been unreasonable to give its label warning in Spanish because of the burden, it did not present that evidence below.

... [I]f we accepted Plough's arguments in this case, in effect we would be holding that failure to warn in a foreign language is not negligence, regardless of the circumstances. Such a sweeping grant of immunity should come from the legislative branch of government, not the judicial. In deciding that Plough did not establish its right to judgment as a matter of law, we do not hold that manufacturers are required to warn in languages other than English simply because it may be foreseeable that non-English literate persons are likely to use their products. Our decision merely recognizes that under some circumstances the standard of due care may require such warning.

Because the evidence shows triable issues of material fact and because Plough did not establish its immunity from liability as a matter of law, its motion for summary judgment should have been denied.

Answer: Thinking Outside the Box

The instructions did not say you needed to stay within the dots!

The American Legal System

PART II

THE AMERICAN LEGAL SYSTEM

This unit introduces you to the American legal system and process. As a paralegal student, you must understand the main provisions of the U.S. Constitution and the sources of the law in the United States. These issues are addressed in Chapter 5. Chapter 6 discusses the state and federal court systems and the litigation process in the courts, as well as non-judicial alternative dispute resolution procedures such as arbitration. The next three chapters of this unit describe in sufficient detail for paralegal studies the following necessary information: administrative agencies and procedure (Chapter 7), the pretrial and trial civil litigation process (Chapter 8), and criminal law and procedure (Chapter 9). The unit ends with Chapter 10, which describes the appellate process for both civil and criminal cases. In summary, this six-chapter unit will provide you with the comprehensive knowledge of the American legal system and process that is needed for paralegal studies.

CHAPTER 5

CHAPTER OBJECTIVES

After studying this chapter, you should be able to:

1. Define *law* and describe the functions of law.

2. Describe the fairness and flexibility of the law.

3. List and describe the schools of jurisprudential thought.

4. Explain how English common law was adopted in the United States.

5. List and describe the sources of law in the United States and the doctrine of *stare decisis.*

6. Describe the concept of federalism and the doctrine of separation of powers.

7. Define and apply the Supremacy Clause of the U. S. Constitution.

8. Explain the federal government's authority to regulate commerce.

9. Explain the Bill of Rights and its freedoms.

10. Describe due process and its forms.

The Constitution and Sources of American Law

The nation's armour of defence against the passions of men is the Constitution. Take that away, and the nation goes down into the field of its conflicts like a warrior without armour.

HENRY WARD BEECHER
PROVERBS FROM PLYMOUTH PULPIT, 1887

Introduction

Every society makes and enforces laws that govern the conduct of the individuals, businesses, and other organizations that function within it. In the words of Judge Learned Hand, "Without law we cannot live; only with it can we insure the future which by right is ours. The best of men's hopes are enmeshed in its success" (*The Spirit of Liberty,* 1960).

Although U.S. law is based primarily on English common law, other legal systems, such as Spanish and French civil law, also influenced it. The sources of law in this country are the U.S. Constitution, state constitutions, federal and state statutes, ordinances, administrative agency rules and regulations, executive orders, and judicial decisions by federal and state courts.

Businesses that are organized in the United States are subject to its laws. They also are subject to the laws of other countries in which they operate. Businesses organized in other countries must obey the laws of the United States when doing business here. In addition, businesspeople owe a duty to act ethically in the conduct of their affairs, and businesses owe a responsibility not to harm society.

Paralegals need to know the history of the law in the United States and how the law developed to be what it is today. Every person in the United States, and in particular paralegals, should have knowledge of this country's constitutional framework and many of the most important provisions of the U.S. Constitution. This chapter addresses the nature and definition of law, the history and sources of law, and the U.S. Constitution.

THE COURTHOUSE TEAM

Judge's Law Clerk

Each judge has one or more law clerks to assist in researching and writing opinions. Technically not part of the courtroom team, they typically sit in the courtroom near the judge or at a table in front of the judge. Motions, briefs, and proposed orders are frequently routed through law clerks, who usually are lawyers. Some administrative law judges, however, have a paralegal serve as a "clerk." For example, Social Security Administration administrative law judges use paralegals as decision writers. They play a major role in researching and writing orders, opinions, and briefs.

Law clerks are the ones who usually communicate with the lawyers when questions arise about pleadings and other documents filed with the court. They also may set up settlement conferences and pretrial meetings. They also are a good source of information on how the judge does things. It is a good idea to take their calls almost as quickly as the judge's calls!

WHAT IS LAW?

The law consists of rules that regulate the conduct of individuals, businesses, and other organizations within society. Laws are intended to protect persons and their property from unwanted interference from others and forbid persons from engaging in certain undesirable activities.

The concept of **law** is broad. Although it is difficult to state a precise definition, *Black's Law Dictionary*, 5th edition, gives one that is sufficient for this text:

Law, in its generic sense, is a body of rules of action or conduct prescribed by controlling authority, and having binding legal force. That which must be obeyed and followed by citizens subject to sanctions or legal consequences is a law.

Functions of the Law

The law is often described by the functions it serves within a society. The primary *functions* served by U.S. law are:

1. Keeping the peace, which includes making certain activities crimes.
2. Shaping moral standards (e.g., enacting laws that discourage drug and alcohol abuse).
3. Promoting social justice (e.g., enacting statutes that prohibit discrimination in employment).
4. Maintaining the status quo (e.g., passing laws that prevent the forceful overthrow of the government).
5. Facilitating orderly change (e.g., passing statutes only after considerable study, debate, and public input).

INFORMATION TECHNOLOGY

PLUGGING INTO THE INTERNET AND THE LAW

Every year millions of students arrive on college campuses and unpack an array of items—clothes, books, furniture, decorations, and their computers. College students used to be judged by the size of their stereo speakers. Today they are judged by their computer and Internet savvy. More than 90 percent of college students now own personal computers.

The Internet has revolutionized campus life. Computer kiosks abound around college campuses, occupying space in libraries, dorm rooms, and hallways of athletic departments. Traditional libraries have become obsolete for many students as they conduct their research online. More than 60 percent of college students check out the Web daily, communicate through email, pick up course assignments, download course notes, and socialize online. Wired to modern technology, current university and college students will lead their parents and employers (and sometimes even their professors!) into the new world of high technology. Today's college students are the leaders of the e-generation.

Universities and colleges now are rated not only on how well they are connected with alumni but also on how well they are connected to computer technology. Some universities have installed software that allows their students to sit anywhere on campus with their laptops and plug into the school's computers. The computer is no longer just a study tool. It has become totally integrated into the lives of college students. The new generation of students studies online, shops online, and even dates online.

With this new technology comes one other thing that a student should know about: e-commerce and Internet law. The use of new computer technology has developed so rapidly that aspects of the law have not kept up. For example, purchase of goods and items over the Internet is exploding, but state and federal governments are struggling to develop laws to handle these transactions. How is the contract formed? What about signatures? Is a purchaser's credit card information protected? What laws protect privacy over the Internet? Can an Internet user crack a wrapper and use certain software? What criminal laws apply to fraud over the Internet? The number of legal questions pertaining to this new technology is endless.

6. Facilitating planning (e.g., designing commercial laws to allow businesses to plan their activities, allocate their productive resources, and assess the risks they take).

7. Providing a basis for compromise (approximately 90 percent of all lawsuits are settled prior to trial).

8. Maximizing individual freedom (e.g., the rights of freedom of speech, religion, and association granted by the First Amendment to the U.S. Constitution).

Fairness of the Law

On the whole, the American legal system is one of the most comprehensive, fair, and democratic systems of law ever developed and enforced. Nevertheless, some misuses and oversights of our legal system—including abuses of discretion and mistakes by judges and juries, unequal applications of the law, and procedural mishaps—allow some guilty parties to go unpunished.

In *Standefer v. United States* [447 U.S. 10, 100 S.Ct. 1999 (1980)] the Supreme Court *affirmed* (let stand) the criminal conviction of a Gulf Oil Corporation executive for aiding and abetting the bribery of an Internal Revenue Service agent. The agent had been acquitted in a separate trial. In writing the opinion of the Court, Chief Justice Warren Burger stated, "This case does no more than manifest the simple, if discomforting, reality that different juries may reach different results under any criminal statute. That is one of the consequences we accept under our jury system."

The Nature of Law

"Hardly anyone living in a civilized society has not at some time been told to do something or to refrain from doing something, because there is a law requiring it, or because it is against the law. What do we mean when we say such things? Most generally, how are we to understand statements of the form 'X is law'?"

"Introduction," *The Nature of Law: Readings in Legal Philosophy,* edited by M. P. Golding (New York: Random House, 1966).

Flexibility of the Law

One of the main attributes of American law is its *flexibility.* The law is generally responsive to cultural, technological, economic, and social changes. For example, laws that are no longer viable—such as those that restricted the property rights of women—are often repealed.

Sometimes it takes years before the law reflects the norms of society. Other times, society is led by the law. The Supreme Court's landmark 1954 decision in *Brown v. Board of Education* [347 U.S. 483, 74 S.Ct. 686 (1954)] is an example of the law leading the people. The Court's decision overturned the old "separate but equal" doctrine that condoned separate schools for Black children and White children. U.S. law evolves and changes along with the norms of society, technology, and the growth and expansion of commerce in the United States and the world.

Laws cannot be written in advance to anticipate every dispute that could arise in the future. Therefore, *general principles* are developed to be applied by courts and juries to individual disputes. This flexibility in the law leads to some uncertainty in predicting results of lawsuits. The following quote by Judge Jerome Frank addresses the value of the adaptability of law (*Law and the Modern Mind,* 1930):

> The law always has been, is now, and will ever continue to be, largely vague 7and variable. And how could this be otherwise? The law deals with human relations in their most complicated aspects. The whole confused, shifting helter-skelter of life parades before it—more confused than ever, in our kaleidoscopic age.
>
> Men have never been able to construct a comprehensive, eternalized set of rules anticipating all possible legal disputes and formulating in advance the rules which would apply to them. Situations are bound to occur which were never contemplated when the original rules were made. How much less is such a frozen legal system possible in modern times?
>
> The constant development of unprecedented problems requires a legal system capable of fluidity and pliancy. Our society would be straightjacketed were not the courts, with the able assistance of the lawyers, constantly overhauling the law and adapting it to the realities of ever-changing social, industrial, and political conditions; although changes cannot be made lightly, yet rules of law must be more or less impermant, experimental and therefore not nicely calculable.
>
> Much of the uncertainty of law is not an unfortunate accident; it is of immense social value.

Feminist Legal Theory

In the past, the law treated men and women unequally. For example, women were denied the right to vote, could not own property if they were married, were unable to have legal abortions, and could not hold the same jobs as men. The enactment of statutes, the interpretation of constitutional provisions, and the courts have changed all of these things. The Nineteenth Amendment gave women the right to vote. States have repealed constraints on the ability of women to own property. The famous U.S. Supreme Court decision in *Roe v. Wade* gave women the constitutional right to have an abortion [410 U.S. 959 (1973)].

Title VII of the Civil Rights Act of 1964 prohibits employment discrimination based on sex. In addition, the equal protection clause of the U.S. and state constitutions provides that the government cannot treat women differently from men (and vice versa) unless some imperative reason warrants different treatment.

But is it enough for women to be treated like men? Should the female perspective be taken into account when legislators and judges develop, interpret, and apply the law? A growing body of scholarship known as *feminist legal theory,* or *feminist jurisprudence,* is being created around just such a theory.

The so-called battered woman's syndrome illustrates how this type of theory works. It has been introduced into evidence to prove self-defense in homicide cases where a woman is accused of killing her husband or another male. This defense asserts that sustained domestic violence against a woman may justify such a murder. Although rejected by many courts, some courts have recognized battered woman's syndrome as a justifiable defense.

Other areas of the law in which a woman's perspective might differ from a man's include male-only combat rules in the military, rights to privacy, family law, child custody, surrogate motherhood, job security for pregnant women, rape, sexual assault, abortion, and sexual harassment.

Even the traditional "reasonable man standard," so prevalent in American law, is being attacked as gender-biased. Those who seek change argue that merely renaming it the "reasonable person theory" is not enough. They assert that women will be judged by the reasonable actions expected of men until this standard is redefined to take into account females' unique values.

This view seems to be gaining ground. For instance, in one sexual harassment case, the court recognized that a "reasonable woman standard" should be used to determine whether a male's conduct toward a female co-employee violated Title VII. The court stated, "We prefer to analyze harassment from the victim's perspective. A complete understanding of the victim's view requires, among other things, an analysis of the different perspectives of men and women. Conduct that many men consider unobjectionable may offend many women" [*Ellison v. Brady,* 924 F.2d 872 (9th Cir. 1991)].

Critics of feminist legal theory argue that existing laws adequately protect the equal rights of females in society. Feminist legal theorists counter that justice for women will remain elusive until the law recognizes the female perspective.

Schools of Jurisprudential Thought

The philosophy or science of the law is referred to as **jurisprudence.** Several different philosophies have been advanced about how the law developed. These range from the classical natural theory to modern theories of law and economics and critical legal studies. Legal philosophers can be grouped into the following major categories, which are summarized in Table 5.1.

- The *natural law school* of jurisprudence postulates that the law is based on what is "correct." Natural law philosophers emphasize a *moral theory of law*—that is, law should be based on morality and ethics. People "discover" natural law through reasoning and choosing between good and evil.

Documents such as the U.S. Constitution, the Magna Carta, and the United Nations Charter reflect this theory.

- The *historical school* of jurisprudence believes that the law is an aggregate of social traditions and customs that have developed over the centuries. Changes in the norms of society will be reflected gradually in the law. The law is an evolutionary process. Thus, historical legal scholars look to past legal decisions (precedent) to solve contemporary problems.

- The *analytical school* of jurisprudence maintains that the law is shaped by logic. Analytical philosophers believe that results are reached by applying principles of logic to the specific facts of the case. The emphasis is on the logic of the result rather than how the result is reached.

- The *sociological school* of jurisprudence asserts that the law is a means of achieving and advancing certain sociological goals. Followers of this philosophy, known as *realists*, believe that the purpose of law is to shape social behavior. Sociological philosophers are unlikely to adhere to past law as precedent.

- The philosophers of the *command school* of jurisprudence believe that the law is a set of rules developed, communicated, and enforced by the ruling party rather than reflecting the society's morality, history, logic, or sociology. This school maintains that the law changes when the ruling class changes.

- The *critical legal studies school* proposes that legal rules are unnecessary and are used as an obstacle by the powerful to maintain the status quo. Critical legal theorists (the *"crits"*) argue that legal disputes should be solved by applying arbitrary rules based on broad notions of what is "fair" in each circumstance. Under this theory, subjective decision-making by judges would be permitted.

The Law and Economics School of Jurisprudential Thought

Should free-market principles, like the supply-and-demand and cost-benefit theories, determine the outcome of lawsuits and legislation? U.S. Court of Appeals Judge Richard Posner thinks so, and so do a growing number of other judges and legal theorists. These people are members of the *law and economics school* (or the "Chicago school") of jurisprudence, which had its roots at the University of Chicago.

According to the law and economics school, which is unofficially headed by Judge Posner, promoting market efficiency should be the central goal of legal decision making. In the area of antitrust law, for example, law and economics theorists would not find corporate mergers and takeovers to be illegal simply because they resulted in market domination. Instead, they would find this practice to be illegal only if it rendered the overall market less efficient.

Focusing on cold economic categories such as market efficiency may seem appropriate when making decisions in cases that involve businesses. But proponents of law and economics theory use this type of analysis in cases involving everything from freedom of religion to civil rights. For example, in a 1983 dissenting opinion, Judge Posner suggested that the practice of appointing counsel, free of charge, to prisoners who bring civil rights cases should be abolished. If a prisoner cannot find a lawyer who will take the case on a contingency-fee basis, it probably means that the case is not worth bringing.

Despite the naysayers who warn that the morality of certain rights and liberties must be safeguarded even if it is unpopular or costly from an economic point of view, proponents of law and economics are gaining increased acceptance in law schools and increased appointments to the judiciary.

| *Comparison of schools of jurisprudential thought.* | *table 5.1* |

SCHOOL	PHILOSOPHY
Natural law	Postulates that law is based on what is "correct." Emphasizes a moral theory of law—that is, law should be based on morality and ethics.
Historical	Believes that law is an aggregate of social traditions and customs.
Analytical	Maintains that law is shaped by logic.
Sociological	Asserts that the law is a means of achieving and advancing certain sociological goals.
Command	Believes that the law is a set of rules developed, communicated, and enforced by the ruling party.
Critical legal studies	Maintains that legal rules are unnecessary and that legal disputes should be solved by applying arbitrary rules based on fairness.
Law and economics	Holds that the central concern of legal decision making should be to promote market efficiency.

HISTORY OF AMERICAN LAW

When the American colonies were first settled, the English system of law was generally adopted as the system of jurisprudence. This was the foundation from which American judges developed a common law in the United States.

English *common law* was law developed by judges who issued their opinions when deciding a case. The principles announced in these cases became **precedent** for later judges deciding similar cases. The English common law can be divided into cases decided by the law courts, chancery or equity courts, and merchant courts.

Law Courts

Prior to the Norman Conquest of England in 1066, each locality in England was subject to local laws as established by the lord or chieftain in control of the local area. There was no countrywide system of law. After 1066, William the Conqueror and his successors to the throne of England began to replace the various local laws with one uniform system of law.

To accomplish this, the king or queen appointed loyal followers as judges in all local areas. These judges were charged with administering the law in a uniform manner in what were called **law courts.** Law at this time tended to emphasize form (legal procedure) over the substance (merit) of the case. The only relief available in law courts was a monetary award for damages.

Chancery (Equity) Courts

Because of the at times unfair results and the limited remedy available in the law courts, a second set of courts—the *Court of Chancery* (or *equity court*)—was established, under the authority of the Lord Chancellor. Those who believed that the decision of the law court was unfair or that the law court could not grant an appropriate remedy could seek relief in the Court of Chancery.

The legal systems of all the states except Louisiana are based primarily on the English common law. Because of its French heritage, Louisiana bases its law on the *civil law*. Elements of California and Texas law, as well as law in other southwestern states, are rooted in civil law. In the United States, the law, equity, and merchant courts have been merged. Thus, most U.S. courts permit the aggrieved party to seek both law and equitable orders and remedies.

The importance of common law to the American legal system is described in the following excerpt from Justice William Douglas's opinion in the 1841 case of *Penny v. Little* [4 Ill. 301 (Ill. 1841)]:

The common law is a beautiful system, containing the wisdom and experiences of ages. Like the people it ruled and protected, it was simple and crude in its infancy, and became enlarged, improved, and polished as the nation advanced in civilization, virtue, and intelligence. Adapting itself to the conditions and circumstances of the people and relying upon them for its administration, it necessarily improved as the condition of the people was elevated. The inhabitants of this country always claimed the common law as their birthright, and at an early period established it as the basis of their jurisprudence.

The Chancery Court inquired into the merits of the case rather than emphasize legal procedure. The Chancellor's remedies were called *equitable remedies* because they were shaped to fit each situation. Equitable orders and remedies of the Court of Chancery took precedence over the legal decisions and remedies of the law courts.

Merchant Courts

As trade developed in the Middle Ages, the merchants who traveled about England and Europe developed certain rules to solve their commercial disputes. These rules, known as the "law of merchants" or the *law merchant*, were based upon common trade practices and usage. Eventually, a separate set of courts, called the **Merchant Court,** was established to administer these rules. In the early 1900s, the Merchant Court was absorbed into the regular law court system of England.

SOURCES OF LAW IN THE UNITED STATES

In more than 200 years since the founding of this country and the adoption of the English common law, U.S. lawmakers have developed a substantial body of law. The sources of modern law in the United States are the U.S. and state constitutions, treaties, statutes and ordinances (codified law), administrative agency rules and regulations, executive orders, and judicial decision.

Constitutions

The **Constitution of the United States of America** is the *supreme law of the land*. This means that any law—federal, state, or local—that conflicts with the U.S. Constitution is unconstitutional and, therefore, unenforceable.

The principles enumerated in the Constitution are extremely broad, as the founding fathers intended them to be applied to evolving social, technological, and economic conditions. The U.S. Constitution often is referred to as a "living document" because it is so adaptable.

The U.S. Constitution established the structure of the federal government by creating three branches of government and giving them the following powers:

1. **Legislative branch** (Congress: Senate and House of Representatives): power to make (enact) the law
2. **Executive branch** (President): power to enforce the law
3. **Judicial branch** (courts): power to interpret and determine the validity of the law

Powers not given to the federal government by the U.S. Constitution are reserved to the states. States also have their own constitutions, often patterned after the U.S. Constitution, though many are more detailed. State constitutions establish the legislative, executive, and judicial branches of state government and establish the powers of each branch. Provisions of state constitutions are valid unless they conflict with the U.S. Constitution or any valid federal law.

Treaties

The U.S. Constitution provides that the President, with the advice and consent of the U.S. Senate, may enter into **treaties** with foreign governments. Treaties become part of the supreme law of the land. With increasing international economic relations among nations, treaties will become an even more important source of law affecting business in the future.

Codified Law

Statutes are written laws that establish certain courses of conduct to which the covered parties must adhere. The U.S. Congress is empowered by the Commerce Clause and other provisions of the U.S. Constitution to enact *federal statutes* to regulate foreign and interstate commerce. Federal statutes include antitrust laws, securities laws, bankruptcy laws, labor laws, equal employment opportunity laws, environmental protection laws, consumer protection laws, and such. State legislatures enact *state statutes*, which include corporation laws, partnership laws, workers' compensation laws, the Uniform Commercial Code, and the like. The statutes enacted by the legislative branches of the federal and state governments are organized by topic into code books, often called **codified law.**

State legislatures often delegate lawmaking authority to local government bodies, including cities and municipalities, counties, school districts, water districts, and so on. These governmental units are empowered to adopt **ordinances.** Examples of ordinances are traffic laws, local building codes, and zoning laws. Ordinances are also codified.

Administrative Agencies

The legislative and executive branches of federal and state governments are empowered to establish **administrative agencies** to enforce and interpret statutes enacted by Congress and state legislatures. Many of these agencies regulate business. For example, Congress has created the Securities and Exchange Commission (SEC) and the Federal Trade Commission (FTC), among others.

The U.S. Congress or the state legislatures usually empower these agencies to adopt administrative rules and regulations to interpret the statutes that the agency is authorized to enforce. These rules and regulations have the force of law. Administrative agencies usually have the power to hear and decide disputes. Their decisions are called *orders*. Because of their power, administrative agencies are often informally referred to as the "fourth branch" of government.

Executive Orders

The executive branch of government, which consists of the President of the United States and state governors, is empowered to issue **executive orders.** This power is derived from express delegation from the legislative branch and is implied from the U.S. Constitution and state constitutions. For example, on October 8, 2001, President George W. Bush by Executive Order established within the Executive Office of the President an Office of Homeland Security to be headed by the Assistant to the President for Homeland Security.

Judicial Decisions

When deciding individual lawsuits, federal and state courts issue **judicial decisions.** In these written opinions the judge or justice usually explains the legal reasoning used to decide the case. These opinions often include interpretations of statutes, ordinances, administrative regulations, and the announcement of legal principles used to decide the case. Many court decisions are printed (reported) in books available in law libraries.

Table 5.2 summarizes the sources of law in the United States.

PRIORITY OF LAW IN THE UNITED STATES

Again, the U.S. Constitution and treaties take precedence over all other laws. Federal statutes take precedence over federal regulations, and valid federal law takes precedence over any conflicting state or local law. State constitutions rank as the highest state law, and state statutes take precedence over state regulations. Valid state law takes precedence over local laws.

The Doctrine of *Stare Decisis*

Based on the common law tradition, past court decisions become precedent for deciding future cases. Lower courts must follow the precedent established by higher courts. That is why all federal and state courts in the United States must follow the precedents established by U.S. Supreme Court decisions.

The courts of one jurisdiction are not bound by the precedent established by the courts of another jurisdiction, although they may look to each other for guidance. Thus state courts of one state are not required to follow the legal precedent established by the courts of another state.

SOURCE OF LAW	DESCRIPTION
Constitutions	The U.S. Constitution establishes the federal government and enumerates its powers. Powers not given to the federal government are reserved to the states. State constitutions establish state governments and enumerate their powers.
Treaties	The U.S. President, with the advice and consent of the U.S. Senate, may enter into treaties with foreign countries.
Codified law (statutes and ordinances)	Statutes are enacted by the U.S. Congress and state legislatures. Ordinances, enacted by municipalities and local government agencies, establish courses of conduct that the covered parties must follow.
Administrative agency rules and regulations	Administrative agencies are created by the legislative and executive branches of government. They may adopt rules and regulations that regulate the conduct of covered parties.
Executive orders	Executive orders, issued by the U.S. President and governors of states, regulate the conduct of covered parties.
Judicial decisions	Courts decide controversies. A court issues decisions that state the holding of the case and the rationale the court used in reaching that decision.

Summary of sources of law in the United States.   table 5.2

Adherence to precedent is called ***stare decisis*** ("to stand by the decision"). The doctrine of *stare decisis* promotes uniformity of law within a jurisdiction, makes the court system more efficient, and makes the law more predictable for individuals and businesses. A court may change or reverse its legal reasoning later if a new case is presented to it and change is warranted.

THE CONSTITUTION OF THE UNITED STATES OF AMERICA

Prior to the American Revolution, each of the thirteen original colonies operated as a separate sovereignty under the rule of England. In September 1774, representatives of the colonies met as a Continental Congress. In 1776, the colonies declared independence from England, and the American Revolution ensued.

The Constitutional Convention was convened in Philadelphia in May 1787, with the primary purpose of strengthening the federal government. After substantial debate, the delegates agreed to a new U.S. Constitution, reported to Congress in September 1787. State ratification of the Constitution was completed in 1788. Since that time, many amendments, including the **Bill of Rights,** have been added to the Constitution.

Stare Decisis

The doctrine of *stare decisis* is discussed in the following excerpt from Justice Musmanno's decision in *Flagiello v. Pennsylvania* [208 A.2d 193 (PA 1965)].

Without *stare decisis*, there would be no stability in our system of jurisprudence. *Stare decisis* channels the law. It erects lighthouses and flies the signals of safety. The ships of jurisprudence must follow that well-defined channel which, over the years, has been proved to be secure and worthy.

SIDEBAR

Ethical

On October 16, 1998, 14-year-old Jessica LeAnn Taylor, a junior high school cheerleader, was a passenger in a Ford Explorer SUV being driven to a homecoming football game. She never made it to the game. On the way, the left-rear Firestone ATX tire shredded, causing the SUV to roll over, killing Jessica. Randy Roberts, a small-town lawyer from East Texas, was hired by Jessica's parents to take on corporate giants Firestone Tire Company, which made the tire, and Ford Motor Company, which manufactured the Explorer SUV. At the time, Ford Explorer had become the number-one SUV in sales worldwide, and Firestone, the exclusive manufacturer of ATX and Wilderness tires for the Explorer, could hardly keep up with demand.

When attorney Roberts sought to discover any consumer complaints or other lawsuits that had been brought against Firestone concerning shredding tires, Firestone refused to disclose any documents but told Roberts that it knew of only one other similar accident. Undeterred, Roberts brought the issue to court, and the judge ordered Firestone to hand over the documents. The information, released in February 2000, showed 1,100 complaints had been reported to Firestone about its ATX and Wilderness tires shredding, and 57 lawsuits had been filed already.

Attorney Roberts notified the National Highway Traffic Safety Administration (NHTSA), the federal government administrative agency responsible for automobile safety, about the findings. The NHTSA instituted an investigation, which further found that more than 80 people had died and more than 250 people had been injured in accidents involving shredding Firestone ATX and Wilderness tires, the majority on Ford Explorer SUVs.

Further investigation showed that there had been deaths and injuries in other countries, including Saudi Arabia, Venezuela, Colombia, and Ecuador. The Firestone tires tended to shred under hot temperatures, so countries and areas of the United States with hotter temperatures witnessed more tire-shredding accidents. Evidence also showed that Ford had replaced the

Firestone tires in Saudi Arabia in the summer of 1998 but did not notify the NHTSA (no law required Ford to do so).

With mounting pressure, in August 2000 Firestone recalled more than 6 million ATX and Wilderness tires, the largest tire recall in U.S. history (the second largest involved the Firestone 500 tire scandal of the 1970s). Consumers all over America flocked to have their Firestone ATX and Wilderness tires replaced, but because of the demand Firestone began allocating recalls first to the states having the hottest climates, with others to follow. The public was incensed, so tires other than those made by Firestone were used for replacements as well, at Firestone's expense.

Ford blamed Firestone for all the problems, stating "This is a tire issue, not a vehicle issue." Firestone countered, alleging that Ford instructed its dealers to sell Ford Explorers with tires underinflated to 26 pounds per square inch (psi), instead of Firestone's suggested 30 psi. Firestone said Ford did this to lower the chance of the somewhat unstable Explorer rolling over. Ford denies responsibility.

Hundreds of civil lawsuits now have been filed against Firestone and Ford, alleging design defect, defect in manufacturing, and failure to warn. The lawsuits seek not only compensatory damages for the loss of loved ones and to pay for injuries, but also large punitive damage awards to punish Firestone and Ford for acting recklessly. It will take years for all the trials and appeals to be sorted out to determine who is financially culpable. In the meantime, substantial ethical issues have been raised questioning the conduct of Firestone and Ford.

1. Do you think Firestone acted quickly enough in instituting the recall of its ATX and Wilderness tires?

2. Did Ford act ethically in this case? Should it have done anything earlier? Explain.

3. If you were a juror in Jessica's parents' lawsuit against Firestone and Ford, would you award punitive damages? Why or why not?

The U.S. Constitution serves two major functions:

1. It creates the three branches of the federal government (the executive, legislative, and judicial branches) and allocates powers to these branches.
2. It protects individual rights by limiting the government's ability to restrict those rights.

The Constitution itself provides that it may be amended to address social and economic changes.

Federalism and Delegated Powers

The U.S. form of government is referred to as **federalism,** which means that the federal government and the 50 state governments share powers. When the states ratified the Constitution, they *delegated* certain powers to the federal government. These **enumerated powers** authorize the federal government to deal with national and international affairs. State governments have powers that are not specifically delegated to the federal government by the Constitution and are empowered to deal with local affairs.

Doctrine of Separation of Powers

The first three Articles of the Constitution divide the federal government into three branches:

1. Article I of the Constitution establishes the *legislative branch* of government, which is bicameral—consisting of the Senate and the House of Representatives—collectively referred to as *Congress.* Each state is allocated two senators. The number of representatives to the House of Representatives is determined by the population of each state. The current number of representatives is determined from the 2000 census.
2. Article II of the Constitution establishes the *executive branch* of government by providing for the election of the President and Vice President. The President is not elected by popular vote but, instead, by the *Electoral College,* whose representatives are appointed by state delegations.
3. Article III establishes the *judicial branch* of the government in the Supreme Court and provides for the creation of other federal courts by Congress.

The Polk County Courthouse in Bartow, Florida.

Checks and Balances

Certain checks and balances are built into the Constitution to ensure that no one branch of the federal government becomes too powerful. Some of the checks and balances in our system of government are as follows:

1. The judicial branch has authority to examine the acts of the other two branches of government and determine whether these acts are constitutional.
2. The executive branch can enter into treaties with foreign governments only with the advice and consent of the Senate.

Geier v. American Honda Motor Co., Inc.

120 S.Ct. 1913 (2000)   **Supreme Court of the United States**

FACTS

The United States Department of Transportation is the federal administrative agency responsible for administering and enforcing federal traffic safety laws, including the National Traffic and Motor Vehicle Safety Act of 1966. Pursuant to this Act, in 1987 the Department of Transportation adopted a Federal Motor Vehicle Safety Standard requiring automobile manufacturers to equip 10 percent of their 1987 vehicles with passive restraints, including automatic seat belts or airbags.

In 1992, Alexis Geier, driving a 1987 Honda Accord automobile in the District of Columbia, collided with a tree and was seriously injured. The car was equipped with manual shoulder and lap belts, which Geier had buckled up at the time of the accident; the car was not equipped with airbags, however.

Geier sued the car's manufacturer, the American Honda Motor Company, Inc., alleging that American Honda had negligently and defectively designed the car because it lacked a driver's side airbag, thus violating the District of Columbia's tort law.

The trial court dismissed Geier's lawsuit, finding that the District of Columbia's tort law conflicted with the federal passive restraint safety standard and was therefore preempted under the Supremacy Clause of the U.S. Constitution. The court of appeals affirmed. Geier appealed to the U.S. Supreme Court, which granted review.

ISSUE

Does the federal passive restraint safety standard preempt the District of Columbia's common law tort action in which the plaintiff claims that the defendant American Honda, which was in compliance with the federal standard, should nonetheless have equipped the 1987 automobile with airbags?

IN THE LANGUAGE OF THE COURT

Breyer, Justice.

In effect, petitioner Geier's tort action depends upon his claim that the manufacturer had a duty to install an airbag when it manufactured the 1987 Honda Accord. Such a state law—i.e., a rule of state tort law imposing such a duty—by its terms would have required manufacturers of all similar cars to install airbags rather than other passive restraint systems, such as automatic belts or passive interiors. It would have required all manufacturers to have installed airbags in respect to the entire District of Columbia-related portion of their 1987 new car fleet, even though the federal safety standard at that time required only that 10% of a manufacturer's nationwide fleet be equipped with any passive restraint device at all.

Regardless, the language of the federal passive restraint standard is clear enough: The federal standard sought a gradually developing mix of alternative passive restraint devices for safety-related reasons. The rule of state tort law for which petitioner Geier argues would stand as an "obstacle" to the accomplishment of that objective. And the federal statute foresees the application of ordinary principles of preemption in cases of actual conflict. Hence the tort action is preempted.

DECISION AND REMEDY

The U.S. Supreme Court held that the federal passive restraint safety standard preempted petitioner Geier's tort lawsuit under the District of Columbia's law against American Honda.

Questions

1. What is the purpose of the Supremacy Clause of the U.S. Constitution? What would be the consequences if there were no Supremacy Clause? Explain.

2. Do you think American Honda owed a duty to equip all of its 1987 vehicles with airbags even though federal law did not require this?

3. Do laws ever protect—rather than harm—businesses? Do you think defendant American Honda would say "There are too many laws" in this case?

3. The legislative branch is authorized to create federal courts and determine their jurisdiction and to enact statutes that change judicially made law.

Supremacy Clause

The **Supremacy Clause** establishes that the federal Constitution, treaties, federal laws, and federal regulations are the supreme law of the land [Article VI, Section 2]. State and local laws that conflict with valid federal law are unconstitutional. The concept of federal law taking precedence over state or local law is called the **preemption doctrine.**

Congress may expressly provide that a particular federal statute *exclusively* regulates a specific area or activity. No state or local law regulating the area or activity is valid if there is such a statute. More often, though, federal statutes do not expressly provide for exclusive jurisdiction. In these instances, state and local governments have *concurrent jurisdiction* to regulate the area or activity. But any state or local law that "directly and substantially" conflicts with valid federal law is preempted under the Supremacy Clause.

Commerce Clause

The **Commerce Clause** of the U.S. Constitution grants Congress the power "to regulate commerce with foreign nations, and among the several states, and with Indian tribes" [Article I, Section 8, clause 3]. Because this clause authorizes the federal government to regulate commerce, it has a greater impact on business than any other provision in the Constitution. Among other things, this clause is intended to foster the development of a national market and free trade among the states.

The Commerce Clause also gives the federal government the authority to regulate **interstate commerce.** Originally, the courts interpreted this clause to mean that the federal government could regulate only commerce that moved *in* interstate commerce. The modern rule, however, allows the federal government to regulate activities that *affect* interstate commerce.

Under the *effects on interstate commerce test*, the regulated activity does not itself have to be in interstate commerce. Thus, any local (**intrastate**) activity that has an effect on interstate commerce is subject to federal regulation. Theoretically, this test subjects a substantial amount of business activity in the United States to federal regulation.

For example, in the famous case of *Wickard, Secretary of Agriculture v. Filburn* [317 U.S. Ill, 63 S.Ct. 82 (1942)], a federal statute limited the amount of wheat a farmer could plant and harvest for home consumption. Filburn, a farmer, violated the law. The U.S. Supreme Court upheld the statute on the grounds that it prevented nationwide surpluses and shortages of wheat. The Court reasoned that wheat grown for home consumption would affect the supply of wheat available in interstate commerce.

SIDEBAR

Commerce Regulation

The federal government may regulate:

1. *Interstate* commerce that crosses state borders.

2. *Intrastate* commerce that affects interstate commerce.

State Police Power

The states did not delegate all power to regulate business to the federal government. They retained the power to regulate *intrastate* and much interstate business activity that occurs within their borders. This is commonly referred to as states' **police power.**

The Commerce Clause of the U.S. Constitution gives the federal government the exclusive power to regulate commerce with foreign nations. Direct and indirect regulation of foreign commerce by state or local governments that discriminates against foreign commerce violates the Foreign Commerce Clause and is therefore unconstitutional.

Consider the following examples. The state of Michigan is the home of General Motors Corporation, Ford Motor Company, and Chrysler Corporation, the three largest automobile manufacturers in the United States. Suppose the Michigan state legislature enacts a law imposing a 100 percent tax on any automobile imported from a foreign country that is sold in Michigan but does not impose the same tax on domestic automobiles sold in Michigan. The Michigan tax violates the Foreign Commerce Clause and therefore is unconstitutional and void.

If, on the other hand, Michigan enacts a law that imposes a 100 percent tax on all automobiles sold in Michigan, domestic and foreign, the law does not discriminate against foreign commerce and therefore does not violate the Foreign Commerce Clause. But the federal government could enact a 100 percent tax on all foreign automobiles but not domestic automobiles sold in the United States, and that law would be valid.

SIDEBAR

Police Power

States may enact laws that protect or promote the public health, safety, morals, and general welfare as long as the law does not unduly burden interstate commerce.

Police power permits states (and, by delegation, local governments) to enact laws to protect or promote the *public health, safety, morals, and general welfare.* This includes the authority to enact laws that regulate the conduct of business. Zoning ordinances, state environmental laws, corporation and partnership laws, and property laws are enacted under this power.

Bill of Rights

In 1791, the states approved the 10 amendments commonly referred to as the Bill of Rights, and they became part of the U.S. Constitution. The Bill of Rights guarantees certain fundamental rights to natural persons and protects these rights from intrusive government action. Most of these rights, or "freedoms," also have been found applicable to so-called artificial persons (i.e., corporations).

The First Amendment to the Constitution guarantees the rights of free speech, assembly, religion, and the press. Because these rights are continually litigated and are frequent subjects of U.S. Supreme Court opinions, they are singled out for special attention, along with the due process clause.

Freedom of Speech

One of the most honored freedoms guaranteed by the Bill of Rights is the *freedom of speech* of the First Amendment. Many other constitutional freedoms would be meaningless without it. The First Amendment's Freedom of Speech Clause protects speech only, not conduct. The U.S. Supreme Court places speech into three categories: (1) fully protected, (2) limited protected, and (3) unprotected speech.

1. **Fully protected speech.** *Fully protected speech* is speech that the government cannot prohibit or regulate. Political speech is an example of such speech. For example, the government could not enact a law that forbids citizens from criticizing the current administration. The First Amendment protects oral, written, and symbolic speech.

2. **Limited protected speech.** The Supreme Court has held that certain types of speech have only *limited protection* under the First Amendment. The government cannot forbid this type of speech, but it can subject this speech to time, place, and manner restrictions. The following types of speech are accorded limited protection:

- *Offensive speech* is speech that offends many members of society. (It is not the same as obscene speech, however.) The Supreme Court has held that offensive speech may be restricted by the government under time, place, and manner restrictions. For example, the Federal Communications Commission (FCC) can regulate the use of offensive language on television by limiting such language to time periods when children would be unlikely to be watching (e.g., late at night).

- *Commercial speech*, such as advertising, was once considered unprotected by the First Amendment. The Supreme Court's landmark decision in *Virginia State Board of Pharmacy v. Virginia Citizens Consumer Council, Inc.* [425 U.S. 748, 96 S.Ct. 1817 (1976)] changed this rule. In that case, the Supreme Court held that a state statute prohibiting a pharmacist from advertising the price of prescription drugs was unconstitutional because it violated the Freedom of Speech Clause. However, the Supreme Court held that commercial speech is subject to proper time, place, and manner restrictions. For example, a city could prohibit billboards along its highways for safety and aesthetic reasons as long as other forms of advertising (e.g., print media) were available.

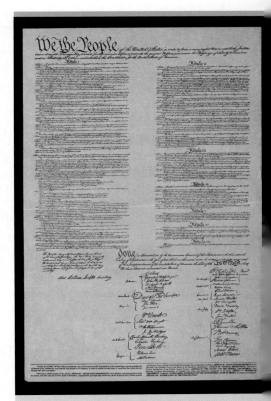

The Constitution of the United States.

3. **Unprotected speech.** The Supreme Court has held that the following types of speech are not protected by the First Amendment and may be totally forbidden by the government:

- Dangerous speech (including such things as yelling "fire" in a crowded theater when there is no fire)
- Fighting words that are likely to provoke a hostile or violent response from an average person
- Speech that incites the violent or revolutionary overthrow of the government; the mere abstract teaching of the morality and consequences of such action is protected
- Defamatory language
- Child pornography
- Obscene speech

The definition of *obscene speech* is quite subjective. One Supreme Court justice stated, "I know it when I see it" [Justice Stewart in *Jacobellis v. Ohio*, 378

Once or twice a century a new medium seems to come along that presents new problems in applying freedom-of-speech rights. This time it is the Internet. Congress enacted the *Telecommunications Act of 1996* to regulate telecommunications, including the Internet. Two provisions of this federal statute restricted the ability of cyberspace operators to transmit certain images.

1. *Computer Decency Act*. This part of the statute made it a felony to knowingly make "indecent" or "patently offensive" materials available on computer systems, including the Internet, to persons under 18 years of age.

2. *Signal Bleed Provision*. This provision of the statute required cable operators either to limit sexually explicit programming on cable channels to the hours between 10:00 P.M. and 6:00 A.M. or to scramble sexually explicit channels in full.

The Act provided for fines, prison terms, and loss of licenses for anyone convicted of violating the terms of these provisions. Immediately, cyberspace providers and users filed lawsuits challenging these provisions of the Act as violating their free speech rights granted under the First Amendment to the Constitution. Proponents of the Act countered that these provisions were necessary to protect children from indecent materials. The plaintiffs won both cases at trial, and the U.S. Supreme Court granted review to decide the free speech issues.

The Supreme Court also came down on the plaintiff's side in each case. The Court overturned the Computer Decency Act, finding that the terms "indecent" and "patently offensive" were too vague to define and criminally enforce. The Court decided that the signal-bleed provision imposed an overly broad illegal content-based restriction on speech. In both cases, the Supreme Court reasoned that limiting the content on the Internet to what is suitable for a child resulted in unconstitutional limiting of adult speech. The Court noted that children are far less likely to trip over indecent material on the Internet than on TV or radio because the information must be actively sought out on the Internet. The Court also stated that parents can regulate their children's access to the Internet and can install blocking and filtering software programs to protect their children from seeing adult materials.

The Supreme Court declared emphatically that the Internet must be given the highest possible level of First Amendment free-speech protection, greater than that afforded to TV and radio. The Court concluded that the Internet allows an individual to reach an audience of millions at almost no cost, setting it apart from TV, radio, and print media, which are prohibitively expensive to use. The Supreme Court stated, "As the most participatory form of mass speech yet developed, the Internet deserves the highest protection from government intrusion." The Court also reasoned that, because the Internet is a global medium, even if the challenged provisions of the Act were upheld, there would be no way to prevent indecent material from flowing over the Internet from abroad.

Reno v. American Civil Liberties Union, 117 S.Ct. 2329 (1997); *United States v. Playboy Entertainment Group, Inc.,* 120 S.Ct. 1878 (2000)

U.S. 184, 84 S.Ct. 1676 (1963)]. In *Miller v. California*, the Supreme Court determined that speech is obscene when

1. The average person, applying contemporary community standards, would find that the work, taken as a whole, appeals to the prurient interest.
2. The work depicts or describes, in a patently offensive way, sexual conduct specifically defined by the applicable state law.
3. The work, taken as a whole, lacks serious literary, artistic, political, or scientific value. [413 U.S. 15, 93 S.Ct. 2607 (1973)]

States are free to define what constitutes obscene speech. Movie theaters, magazine publishers, and so on are often subject to challenges that the materials they display or sell are obscene and therefore not protected by the First Amendment.

Freedom of Religion

The U.S. Constitution requires federal, state, and local governments to be neutral toward religion. The First Amendment actually contains two separate religion clauses:

1. The *Establishment Clause* prohibits the government from either establishing a state religion or promoting one religion over another. Thus, it guarantees that there will be no state-sponsored religion. The Supreme Court used this clause as its reason for ruling that an Alabama statute that authorized a one-minute period of silence in schools for "meditation or voluntary prayer" was invalid [*Wallace v. Jaffree*, 472 U.S. 38, 105 S.Ct. 2479 (1985)]. The Court held that the statute endorsed religion.

2. The *Free Exercise Clause* prohibits the government from interfering with the free exercise of religion in the United States. Generally, this clause prevents the government from enacting laws that either prohibit or inhibit individuals from participating in or practicing their chosen religion. For example, in *Church of Lukumi Babalu Aye, Inc. v. City of Hialeah, Florida* [113 S.Ct. 2217 (1993)], the U.S. Supreme Court held that a city ordinance that prohibited ritual sacrifices of animals (chickens) during church services violated the Free Exercise Clause. Of course, this right to be free from government intervention in the practice of religion is not absolute. For example, human sacrifices are unlawful and are not protected by the First Amendment.

Due Process Clause

The **Due Process Clause** provides that no person shall be deprived of "life, liberty, or property" without due process of the law. It is contained in both the Fifth and Fourteenth Amendments. The Due Process Clause of the Fifth Amendment applies to federal government action; that of the Fourteenth Amendment applies to state and local government action. The government is not prohibited from taking a person's life, liberty, or property, but the government must follow due process to do so. There are two categories of due process: *substantive* and *procedural*.

Substantive due process. **Substantive due process** requires that government statutes, ordinances, regulations, or other laws be clear on their face and not overly broad in scope. The test of whether substantive due process is met is whether a "reasonable person" could understand the law to be able to comply with it. Laws that do not meet this test are declared *void for vagueness*.

Suppose, for example, that a city ordinance made it illegal for persons to wear "clothes of the opposite sex." Such an ordinance would be held unconstitutional as void for vagueness because a reasonable person could not clearly determine whether his or her conduct violates the law.

THE CIVIL LAW SYSTEM

One of the major legal systems that has developed in the world, in addition to the Anglo–American common law system, is the **Romano–Germanic civil law system.** This legal system, commonly called the **civil law,** dates to 450 B.C., when Rome adopted the Twelve Tables, a code of laws applicable to the Romans. A compilation of Roman law, called the *Corpus Juris Civilis* (the Body of Civil Law), was completed in A.D. 534. Later, two national codes—the French Civil Code of 1804 (the Napoleonic Code) and the German Civil Code of 1896—became models for countries that adopted civil codes.

In contrast to the Anglo–American common law, in which laws are created by the judicial system as well as by congressional legislation, the Civil Code and parliamentary statutes that expand and interpret it are the sole sources of the law in most civil law countries. Thus, the adjudication of a case is simply the application of the Code or the statutes to a specific set of facts. In some civil law countries, court decisions do not have the force of law.

Today, Austria, Belgium, Greece, Indochina, Indonesia, Japan, Latin America, the Netherlands, Poland, Portugal, South Korea, Spain, Sub-Saharan Africa, Switzerland, and Turkey follow the civil law.

Procedural due process. **Procedural due process** requires that the government give a person proper *notice* and *hearing* of the legal action before that person is deprived of his or her life, liberty, or property. The government action must be fair.

For example, if the government wants to take a person's home by eminent domain to build a highway, the government must (1) give the homeowner sufficient notice of its intention, and (2) provide a hearing. Under the **Just Compensation Clause** of the Fifth Amendment, the government must pay the owner just compensation for taking the property.

LEGAL TERMINOLOGY

Administrative agencies

Bill of Rights

Civil law system

Codified law

Commerce clause

Commercial speech

Due Process Clause

Enumerated powers

Executive branch of government

Executive order

Federalism

Interstate commerce

Intrastate commerce

Judicial branch of government

Judicial decision

Jurisprudence

Just Compensation Clause

Law

Law court

Legislative branch of government

Merchant court

Ordinances

Police powers
Precedent
Preemption doctrine
Procedural due process
Stare decisis

Substantive due process
Supremacy Clause
Treaty
U.S. Constitution

Summary

CHAPTER 5 THE CONSTITUTION AND SOURCES OF AMERICAN LAW

What Is Law?

Definition	A body of rules of action or conduct prescribed by controlling authority and having binding legal force.
Functions	1. Keep the peace 2. Shape moral standards 3. Promote social justice 4. Maintain the status quo 5. Facilitate orderly change 6. Facilitate planning 7. Provide a basis for compromise 8. Maximize individual freedom
Fairness	Although the American legal system is one of the fairest and most democratic systems of law, abuses and mistakes in the application of the law still occur.
Flexibility	The law must be flexible to meet social, technological, and economic changes.

Schools of Jurisprudential Thought

Natural Law	Postulates that law is based on what is "correct"; it emphasizes a moral theory of law—that is, law should be based on morality and ethics.
Historical	Believes that law is an aggregate of social traditions and customs.
Analytical	Maintains that law is shaped by logic.
Sociological	Asserts that the law is a means of achieving and advancing certain sociological goals.
Command	Believes that the law is a set of rules developed, communicated, and enforced by the ruling party.

(continued)

Critical Legal Studies	Maintains that legal rules are unnecessary and that legal disputes should be solved by applying arbitrary rules based on fairness.
Law and Economics	Believes that promoting market efficiency should be the central concern of legal decision making.

History of American Law

Foundation of American Law	English common law (judge-made law) forms the basis of the legal systems of most states in this country. Louisiana bases its law on the French civil code.

Sources of Law in the United States

Constitutions	U.S. Constitution establishes the federal government and enumerates its powers. Powers not given to the federal government are reserved to the states. State constitutions establish state governments and enumerate their powers.
Treaties	The President, with the advice and consent of the Senate, may enter into treaties with foreign countries.
Codified Law	1. *Statutes* are enacted by Congress and state legislatures. 2. *Ordinances* and statutes are passed by municipalities and local government bodies to establish courses of conduct that must be followed by covered parties.
Administrative Agency Rules and Regulations	Administrative agencies are created by the legislative and executive branches of government; they may adopt rules and regulations that govern the conduct of covered parties.
Executive Orders	Issued by the President and governors of states, executive orders regulate the conduct of covered parties.
Judicial Decisions	Courts decide controversies by issuing decisions that state the holding of each case and the rationale the court used to reach that decision.

Doctrine of *Stare Decisis*

Definition	Means "to stand by the decision"; doctrine that provides for adherence to precedent.

Constitution of the United States of America

Scope	Consists of seven articles and 26 amendments; establishes the three branches of the federal government, enumerates their powers, and provides important guarantees of individual freedom. The Constitution was ratified by the states in 1788.

(continued)

Basic Constitutional Concepts	1. *Federalism:* The Constitution created the federal government, which shares power with the state governments.
	2. *Delegated powers:* When the states ratified the Constitution, they delegated certain powers, called *enumerated powers*, to the federal government.
	3. *Reserved powers:* Those powers not granted to the federal government by the Constitution are reserved to the states.
	4. *Separation of powers:* Each branch of the federal government has separate powers.
	   a. Legislative branch—power to make the law.
	   b. Executive branch—power to enforce the law.
	   c. Judicial branch—power to interpret the law.
	5. *Checks and balances:* Certain checks and balances are built into the Constitution to ensure that no one branch of the federal government becomes too powerful.

Supremacy Clause

Purpose	Stipulates that the U.S. Constitution, treaties, and federal law (statutes and regulations) are the *supreme law of the land*. State or local laws that conflict with valid federal law are unconstitutional. This is called the *preemption doctrine*.

Commerce Clause

Purpose	1. *Commerce Clause:* Authorizes the federal government to regulate commerce with foreign nations, among the states, and with Indian tribes. 2. *Interstate commerce:* Under the broad *effects test*, the federal government may regulate any activity (even intrastate commerce) that *affects* interstate commerce.

Bill of Rights

Scope	Consists of the first 10 amendments to the Constitution. They establish basic individual rights. The Bill of Rights was ratified in 1791.

Due Process Clause

Purpose	Provides that no person shall be deprived of "life, liberty, or property" without due process. Two categories of due process: 1. *Substantive due process:* Requires that laws be clear on their face and not overly broad in scope. Laws that do not meet this test are *void for vagueness*. 2. *Procedural due process:* Requires that the government give a person proper *notice* and *hearing* before that person is deprived of his or her life, liberty, or property. An owner must be paid *just compensation* if the government takes his or her property.

Working the Web

1. The U.S. government is the largest source of information anywhere in the world, and for the most part this information is free and available online. Two good starting points are www.uncle-sam.com, a private website, and www.firstgov.gov, an official government website.

2. The White House has made a serious commitment to provide access to government information via the Internet. Information ranging from facts about the President and Vice President and their families and events at the White House, to current executive orders and press releases is available on the White House website. One may even listen to speeches and view photos at www.whitehouse.gov.

3. Imagine you are interested in a bill that was introduced into the U.S. House of Representatives last month. You want to read the full text of the bill and find out what happened to it (its legislative history). Using the U.S. House of Representatives website at www.house.gov, retrieve a current House bill and its legislative history.

4. Get information on recent legislative actions, scheduled activities, committee information, senators and Senate leadership, Senate history, procedures, terminology, and links to other information at www.senate.gov.

5. Imagine you want to find out who your representative is in the House of Representatives. Using the U.S. House of Representatives website, determine who your representative is. Print out the biographical material about him or her. Find out what his or her email address is.

6. Suppose you want to find out what is online from the Internal Revenue Service. Using the www.firstgov.gov website, navigate your way to the Internal Revenue Service's home page.

Questions

CRITICAL LEGAL THINKING AND WRITING

1. If you briefed the case of *Lee v. Weisman* (at the end of the chapter), did your personal feelings affect the way you presented the information in your brief? Review your brief of the case; after reflection, did you write the brief from the majority or minority viewpoint?

2. What is the role of the paralegal in briefing cases for the supervising attorney?

3. Does the Establishment Clause protect the rights of the individual, or does it take them away?

4. How do the priorities of the U.S. Constitution protect the average citizen of a state?

5. How does the doctrine of *stare decisis* promote uniformity of laws?

6. How has the inherent flexibility of the American legal system enabled the United States to grow and survive challenges such as wars, domestic unrest, and terrorist threats?

7. Are money damages always a satisfactory solution to a legal dispute?

8. Should federal courts be permitted to make decisions that affect only local matters, such as the limitation on prayer in school or viewing of material on cable television?

9. What is the value in allowing the President to issue executive orders instead of Congress enacting a law?

10. Do the biblical Ten Commandments offer a sufficient set of rules of conduct for a modern society? Why or why not?

ETHICS: ANALYSIS AND DISCUSSION

1. What ethical obligations does the paralegal have in briefing cases for the supervising attorney?

2. Are there any ethical issues in allowing one's personal feelings to be expressed in working on a case? What if you have strong feelings against the position of the client, such as in the prayer in school case, or the pornography on cable case?

3. Does the American system of law depend on the legal team to put aside its personal beliefs and work diligently on unpopular cases or issues? How does this ensure equal justice and allow for change in the system?

Competent Representation

There are few certainties in the area of ethics, for paralegals or in any profession. What qualifies as ethical conduct is in most cases based on state law and court interpretation applied to a set of facts. The citation listed below represents one legal opinion and is provided as a research starting point. Do not assume that the same rule applies in your jurisdiction. For the following:

- *Prepare a written statement based on your state law.*

- *Use your state bar association website as a starting point.*

You are working in a law firm for an attorney who has had a series of strokes that have caused a permanent reading disability and memory impairment [Philadelphia Ethics Opinion 2002-12 (2000); also, see Texas Ethics Opinion 522 (1997)]. Do you have any ethical obligtation to the attorney's clients? Do you have any ethical obligation to the firm and to the attorney?

Youngstown Co. v. Sawyer, Secretary of Commerce

343 U.S. 579, 72 S.Ct. 863, 96 L.Ed.2d 1153 (1952)

5.1 FACTS

In 1951, a dispute arose between steel companies and their employees about the terms and conditions that should be included in a new labor contract. At the time, the United States was engaged in a military conflict in Korea that required substantial steel resources from which to make weapons and other military goods.

On April 4, 1952, the steelworkers' union gave notice of a nationwide strike called to begin at 12:01 A.M. on April 9. The indispensability of steel as a component in weapons and other war materials led President Dwight D. Eisenhower to believe that the proposed strike would jeopardize the national defense and that governmental seizure of the steel mills was necessary to ensure the continued availability of steel. Therefore, a few hours before the strike was to begin, the President issued Executive Order 10340, which directed the Secretary of Commerce to take possession of most of the steel mills and keep them running. The steel companies obeyed the order under protest, and brought proceedings against the President.

ISSUE

Was the seizure of the steel mills constitutional?

Bonito Boats, Inc. v. Thunder Craft Boats, Inc.

489 U.S. 141, 109 S.Ct. 971, 103 L.Ed.2d 118 (1989)

5.2 FACTS

Article 1, Section 8, clause 8 of the U.S. Constitution grants Congress the power to enact laws to give inventors the exclusive right to their discoveries. Pursuant to this power, Congress enacted federal patent laws that establish the requirements to obtain a patent. Once a patent is granted, the patent holder has exclusive rights to use the patent.

Bonito Boats, Inc. developed a hull design for a fiberglass recreational boat that it marketed under the trade name Bonito Boats Model 5VBR. The manufacturing process involved creating a hardwood model that was sprayed with fiberglass to create a mold. The mold then served to produce the finished fiberglass boats for sale. Bonito did not file a patent application to protect the utilitarian or design aspects of the hull or the manufacturing process.

After the Bonito 5VBR was on the market for six years, the Florida legislature enacted a statute prohibiting the use of a direct molding process to duplicate unpatented boat hulls and forbade the knowing sale of hulls so duplicated. The protection afforded under the state statute was broader than that provided for under the federal patent statute.

Subsequently, Thunder Craft Boats, Inc. produced and sold boats made by the direct molding process. Bonito sued Thunder Craft under Florida law.

ISSUE

Is the Florida statute valid?

Heart of Atlanta Motel v. United States

379 U.S. 241, 85 S.Ct. 348, 13 L.Ed.2d 258 (1964)

5.3 FACTS

The Heart of Atlanta Motel, in the state of Georgia, has 216 rooms available to guests. The motel is readily accessible to interstate highways 75 and 85 and to state highways 23 and 41. The motel solicits patronage from outside the state of Georgia through various national advertising media, including magazines of national circulation, and it maintains more than 50 billboards and highway signs within the state. Approximately 75 percent of the motel's registered guests are from out of state.

Congress enacted the Civil Rights Act of 1964, which made it illegal for public accommodations to discriminate against guests based on their race. Prior to that, the Heart of Atlanta Motel had refused to rent rooms to Blacks. After the act was passed, it alleged that it intended to continue not to rent rooms to Blacks. The owner of the motel brought an action to have the Civil Rights Act of 1964 declared unconstitutional, alleging that Congress, in passing the Act, had exceeded its powers to regulate commerce under the Commerce Clause of the U.S. Constitution.

ISSUE

Who wins?

Rostker, Director of the Selective Service v. Goldberg

453 U.S. 57, 101 S.Ct. 2646, 69 L.Ed.2d 478 (1981)

5.4 FACTS

In 1975, after the war in Vietnam, the U.S. government discontinued draft registration for men in this country. In 1980, after the Soviet Union invaded Afghanistan, President Jimmy Carter asked Congress for funds to reactivate draft registration. President Carter suggested that both males and females be required to register. Congress allocated funds only for the registration of males. Several men who were subject to draft registration brought a lawsuit that challenged the law as being unconstitutional in violation of the Equal Protection Clause of the U.S. Constitution. The U.S. Supreme Court upheld the constitutionality of the draft registration law, reasoning as follows.

The question of registering women for the draft not only received considerable national attention and was the subject of wide-ranging public debate, but also was extensively considered by Congress in hearings, floor debate, and in committee. The foregoing clearly establishes that the decision to exempt women from registration was not the "accidental by-product of a traditional way of thinking about women."

This is not a case of Congress arbitrarily choosing to burden one of two similarly situated groups, such as would be the case with an all-black or all-white, or an all-Catholic or all-Lutheran, or an all-Republican or all-Democratic registration. Men and women are simply not similarly situated for purposes of a draft or registration for a draft.

Justice Marshall dissented, stating that "The Court today places its imprimatur on one of the most potent remaining public expressions of 'ancient canards about the proper role of women.' It upholds a statute that requires males but not females to register for the draft, and which thereby categorically excludes women from a fundamental civic obligation. I dissent."

ISSUE

Was the decision fair? Has the law been a "progressive science" in this case? Is it ethical for males, but not females, to have to register for the draft?

Lee V. Weisman

120 L.Ed.2d 467, 112 S.Ct. 2649 (1992)   Supreme Court of the United States

Read the following case, excerpted from the U.S. Supreme Court's opinion. Review and brief the case. In your brief, answer the following questions.

1. Who are the plaintiff and defendant?
2. What does the Establishment Clause provide?
3. Was the fact that the prayer was nonsectarian important to the Supreme Court's decision?
4. What argument did the dissenting opinion make in support of allowing prayer at high school graduation ceremonies?
5. How close was the vote by the justices in this case?
6. What test did the court use to determine if the practice violates the Establishment Clause?
7. Can a school persuade a student to participate in religious exercises?
8. Is nonsectarian prayer permitted under the Establishment Clause?

Kennedy, Justice (joined by Blackmun, Stevens, O'Conner, and Souter).

Deborah Weisman graduated from Nathan Bishop Middle School, a public school in Providence, Rhode Island, at a formal ceremony in June 1989. She was about 14 years old. For many years it has been the policy of the Providence school committee and the Superintendent of Schools to permit principals to invite members of the clergy to give invocations and benedictions at middle school and high school graduations. Many, but not all, of the principals elected to include prayers as part of the graduation ceremonies. Acting for himself and his daughter, Deborah's father, Daniel Weisman, objected to any prayers at Deborah's middle school graduation, but to no avail. The school principal, petitioner Robert E. Lee, invited a rabbi to deliver prayers at the graduation exercises for Deborah's class. Rabbi Leslie Gutterman, of the Temple Beth El in Providence, accepted.

It also has been the custom of Providence school officials to provide invited clergy with a pamphlet entitled "Guidelines for Civic Occasions," prepared by the National Conference of Christians and Jews. The Guidelines recommended that public prayers at nonsectarian civic ceremonies be composed with "inclusiveness and sensitivity," though they acknowledge that "prayer of any kind may be inappropriate on some civic occasions." The principal gave Rabbi Gutterman the pamphlet before the graduation and advised him that the invocation and benediction should be nonsectarian.

Deborah's graduation was held on the premises of Nathan Bishop Middle School on June 29, 1989. Four days before the ceremony, Daniel Weisman, in his individual capacity as a Providence taxpayer and as next friend of Deborah, sought a temporary restraining order in the United States District Court for the District of Rhode Island to prohibit school officials from including an invocation or a benediction in the graduation ceremony. The court denied the motion for lack of adequate time to consider it. Deborah and her family attended the graduation, where the prayers were recited.

In July 1989, Daniel Weisman filed an amended complaint seeking a permanent injunction barring petitioners, various officials of the Providence public schools, from inviting the clergy to deliver invocations and benedictions at future graduations.

The case was submitted on stipulated facts. The District Court held that petitioners' practice of including invocations and benedictions in public school graduations violated the Establishment Clause of the First Amendment, and it enjoined petitioners from continuing the practice. The court applied the three-part Establishment Clause test. Under that test, to satisfy the Establishment Clause a governmental practice must (1) reflect a clearly secular purpose, (2) have a primary effect that neither advances nor inhibits religion, and (3) avoid excessive government entanglement with religion. On appeal, the United States Court of Appeals for the First Circuit affirmed.

These dominant facts mark and control the confines of our decision: State officials direct the performance of a formal religious exercise at promotional and graduation ceremonies for secondary schools. Even for those students who object to the religious exercise, their attendance and participation in the state-sponsored religious activity are in a fair and real sense obligatory, though the school district does not require attendance as a condition for receipt of the diploma.

The controlling precedents as they relate to prayer and religious exercise in primary and secondary public schools compel the holding here that the policy of the city of Providence is an unconstitutional one. It is beyond dispute that, at a minimum, the Constitution guarantees that government may not coerce anyone to support or participate in religion or its exercise, or otherwise act in a way which "establishes a state religion or religious faith, or tends to do so."

We are asked to recognize the existence of a practice of nonsectarian prayer within the embrace of what is known as the Judeo-Christian tradition, prayer which is more acceptable than one which, for example, makes explicit references to the God of Israel, or to Jesus Christ, or to a patron saint. If common ground can be defined which permits once conflicting faiths to express the shared conviction that there is an ethic and a morality which transcend human invention, the sense of community and purpose sought by all decent societies might be advanced. But though the First Amendment does not allow the government to stifle prayers which aspi... ends, neither does it permit the government t... take that task for itself.

The sole question presented is whether a religio... exercise may be conducted at a graduation ceremony in circumstances where, as we have found, young graduates who object are induced to conform. No holding by this Court suggests that a school can persuade or compel a student to participate in a religious exercise. That is being done here, and it is forbidden by the Establishment Clause of the First Amendment.

For the reasons we have stated, the judgment of the Court of Appeals is affirmed.

Scalia, Justice (joined by Rehnquist, White, and Thomas) dissenting, expressed the view that (1) the establishment of religion clause should not have been interpreted so as to invalidate a long-standing American tradition of nonsectarian prayer at public school graduations, (2) graduation invocations and benedictions involve no psychological coercion of students to participate in religious exercises, (3) the only coercion that is forbidden by the establishment of religion clause is that which is backed by a threat of penalty, and (4) the middle school principal did not direct or control the content of the prayers in question, and thus there was no pervasive government involvement with religious activity.

CHAPTER 6

CHAPTER OBJECTIVES

After studying this chapter, you should be able to:

1. Describe the state court systems.

2. Describe the federal court system.

3. Apply a cost-benefit analysis for bringing and defending a lawsuit.

4. Explain how a justice is chosen for the U.S. Supreme Court.

5. Explain subject-matter jurisdiction and venue of federal and state courts.

6. Describe in personam jurisdiction of courts.

7. Explain how personal jurisdiction applies to website operators.

8. Compare the Japanese and American legal systems.

9. Explain the use of arbitration.

10. Explain the use of other nonjudicial methods of alternative dispute resolution.

Judicial and Alternative Dispute Resolution

I was never ruined but twice; once when I lost a lawsuit, and once when I won one.

VOLTAIRE

Introduction

The two major court systems in the United States are: (1) the federal court system, and (2) the court systems of the 50 states and the District of Columbia. Each of these systems has jurisdiction to hear different types of lawsuits. The process of bringing, maintaining, and defending a lawsuit is called **litigation.** Litigation is a difficult, time-consuming, and costly process that must comply with complex procedural rules. Although it is not required, most parties employ a lawyer to represent them when they are involved in a lawsuit.

Several forms of *nonjudicial* dispute resolution have developed in response to the expense and difficulty of bringing a lawsuit. These methods, collectively called **alternative dispute resolution (ADR),** are being used more and more often to resolve commercial disputes.

Paralegals are especially valuable in providing support to lawyers who are engaged in litigation—that is, representing clients in lawsuits. In this area, paralegals interview clients, prepare documents submitted to courts, conduct legal research, and assist lawyers during trial.

This chapter discusses the various court systems, the jurisdiction of courts to hear and decide cases, the litigation process, and alternative dispute resolution.

U.S. Courts: www.uscourts.gov

149

STATE COURT SYSTEMS

Each state and the District of Columbia have separate court systems. Most state court systems include the following:

- Limited-jurisdiction trial courts
- General-jurisdiction trial courts
- Intermediate appellate courts
- A supreme court (or highest state court)

Limited-Jurisdiction Trial Court

State **limited-jurisdiction trial courts,** which sometimes are referred to as *inferior trial courts,* hear matters of a specialized or limited nature. Examples of these courts in many states are traffic courts, juvenile courts, justice-of-the-peace courts, probate courts, family law courts, and courts that hear misdemeanor criminal law cases and civil cases involving lawsuits less than a certain dollar amount. Because these courts are trial courts, evidence can be introduced and testimony given. Most limited-jurisdiction courts keep a record of their proceedings. Their decisions usually can be appealed to a general-jurisdiction court or an appellate court.

Many states also have created **small-claims courts** to hear civil cases involving small dollar amounts (e.g., $5,000 or less). Generally, the parties must appear individually and cannot have a lawyer represent them. The decisions of small claims courts are often appealable to general-jurisdiction trial courts or appellate courts.

General-Jurisdiction Trial Court

Every state has a **general-jurisdiction trial court.** These courts often are called **courts of record** because the testimony and evidence at trial are recorded and stored for future reference. These courts hear cases that are not within the jurisdiction of limited-jurisdiction trial courts, such as felonies, civil cases above a certain dollar amount, and so on. Some states divide their general-jurisdiction courts into two divisions, one for criminal cases and another for civil cases. General-jurisdiction trial courts hear evidence and testimony. The decisions handed down by these courts are appealable to an intermediate appellate court or the state supreme court, depending on the circumstances.

Intermediate Appellate Court

In many states, **intermediate appellate courts** (also called appellate courts or *courts of appeal*) hear appeals from trial courts. These courts review the trial court record to determine any errors at trial that would require reversal or modification of the trial court's decision. Thus, the appellate court reviews either pertinent parts or the whole trial court record from the lower court. No new evidence or testimony is permitted. The parties usually file legal briefs with the appellate court stating the law and facts that support their positions. Appellate courts usually grant a short oral hearing to the parties. Appellate court decisions are appealable to the state's highest court. In less populated states that do not have an intermediate appellate court, trial court decisions can be appealed directly to the state's highest court.

Highest State Court

Each state has a highest court in its court system. Most states call this highest court the *supreme court.* The function of a state supreme court is to hear appeals from intermediate state courts and certain trial courts. The highest court hears no new evidence or testimony. The parties usually submit pertinent parts of or the entire lower court record for review. The parties also submit legal briefs to the court and usually are granted a brief oral hearing. Decisions of state supreme courts are final, unless a question of law is involved that is appealable to the U.S. Supreme Court. Exhibit 6.1 depicts a typical state court system.

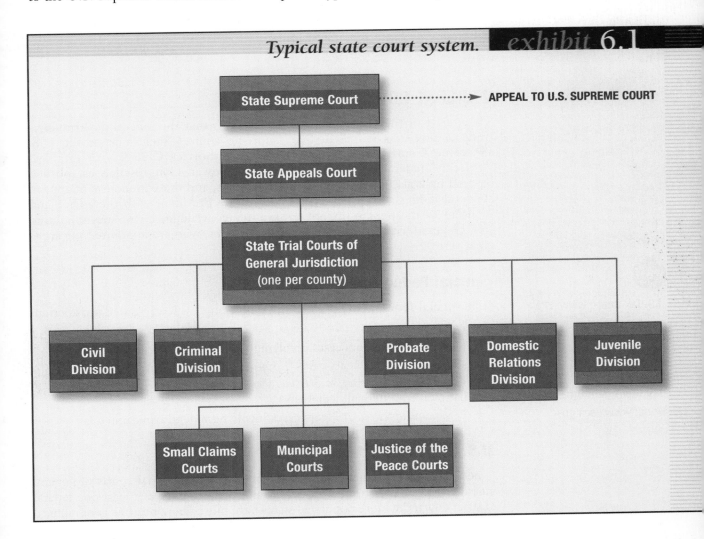

Typical state court system.   exhibit 6.1

Specialized Courts Hear Commercial Disputes

In most states, the same judges who hear and decide criminal, landlord–tenant, matrimonial, medical malpractice, and other nonbusiness-related cases also hear most business and commercial disputes. The one major exception to this standard has been the state of Delaware, where a special Chancery Court hears and decides business litigation. This special court, which deals mainly with cases involving corporate government disputes, has earned a reputation for its expertise in handling and deciding corporate matters. Perhaps the existence of this special court and a corporation code that tends to favor corporate management are the primary reasons that more than 60 percent of the corporations listed on the New York Stock Exchange are incorporated in Delaware.

New York is one state that is following Delaware's lead in this area. New York has designated four courts within its general court system to hear commercial disputes. These courts, which began operating in 1993, hear contract, sales, insurance, unfair competition, libel and slander, shareholder, business-related tort, and other commercial cases. Other states are expected to establish courts that specialize in commercial matters in the near future.

Businesses tend to favor special commercial courts because the judges presiding over them are expected to have the expertise to handle complex commercial lawsuits. Also, the courts are expected to be more efficient in deciding business-related cases, thereby saving time and money for the parties.

FEDERAL COURT SYSTEM

Article III of the U.S. Constitution provides that the federal government's judicial power is vested in one "supreme court." This court is the U.S. Supreme Court. The Constitution also authorizes Congress to establish "inferior" federal courts. Pursuant to this power, Congress has established special federal courts, the U.S. district courts, and the U.S. courts of appeal. Federal judges are appointed for life by the President with the advice and consent of the Senate (except bankruptcy court judges, who are appointed for 14-year terms, and U.S. Magistrate Judges, who are appointed for an 8-year term).

Special Federal Courts

U.S. Tax Court: www.ustax
court.gov/ustcweb.htm

U.S. Court of Federal Claims:
www.uscfc.uscourts.gov/

U.S. Court of International
Trade: www.uscit.gov/

The **special federal courts** established by Congress have limited jurisdiction. They include:

- *U.S. tax court:* Hears cases involving federal tax laws
- *U.S. claims court:* Hears cases brought against the United States
- *U.S. Court of International Trade:* Hears cases involving tariffs and international commercial disputes
- *U.S. bankruptcy court:* Hears cases involving federal bankruptcy laws

U.S. District Courts

The **U.S. district courts** are the federal court system's trial courts of general jurisdiction. The District of Columbia and each state have at least one federal district court; the more populated states have more than one. The geographical area that each court serves is referred to as a *district*. There are presently 96 federal district courts. The federal district courts are empowered to impanel juries, receive evidence, hear testimony, and decide cases. Most federal cases originate in federal district courts.

U.S. Courts Of Appeals

The **U.S. courts of appeals** are the federal court system's intermediate appellate courts. The federal court system has 13 circuits. **Circuit** refers to the geographical area served by a court. Eleven are designated by a number, such as the "First Circuit," "Second Circuit," and so on. The Twelfth Circuit court is located in Washington, D.C., and is called the District of Columbia Circuit.

As appellate courts, these circuit courts hear appeals from the district courts located in their circuit, as well as from certain special courts and federal administrative agencies. The courts review the record of the lower court or administrative agency proceedings to determine if any error would warrant reversal or modification of the lower court decision. No new evidence or testimony is heard. The parties file legal briefs with the court and are given a short oral hearing. Appeals usually are heard by a three-judge panel. After the panel renders a decision, a petitioner can request a review *en banc* by the full court.

The Thirteenth Circuit court of appeals was created by Congress in 1982. Called the **Court of Appeals for the Federal Circuit** and located in Washington, D.C., this court has special appellate jurisdiction to review the decisions of the Court of Federal Claims, the Patent and Trademark Office, and the Court of International Trade. This court of appeals was created to provide uniformity in the application of federal law in certain areas, particularly patent law.

The map in Exhibit 6.2 shows the 13 federal circuit courts of appeals.

U.S. Supreme Court

The highest court in the land is the Supreme Court of the United States, located in Washington, D.C. This court is composed of nine justices who are nominated by the President and confirmed by the Senate. The President appoints one justice as **chief justice,** responsible for the administration of the Supreme Court. The other eight justices are *associate justices.*

The Supreme Court, which is an appellate court, hears appeals from federal circuit courts of appeals and, under certain circumstances, from federal district courts, special federal courts, and the highest state courts. The Supreme Court hears no evidence or testimony. As with other appellate courts, the lower court record is reviewed to determine whether an error has been committed that warrants a reversal or modification of the decision. Legal briefs are

---

Meet THE COURTHOUSE TEAM

U.S. Magistrate Judge

Magistrate judges are appointed by the district court to serve for an 8-year term. Their duties fall into four general categories: (1) conducting most of the initial proceedings in criminal cases; (2) trying certain criminal misdemeanor cases; (3) trying civil cases with the consent of a party; and (4) conducting a wide variety of other proceedings referred to them by district judges.

www

U.S. Court for the Federal Circuit: www.fedcir.gov/

Meet THE COURTHOUSE TEAM

Courtroom Deputy Clerk

In some courts, such as the U.S. District Court for the Eastern District of Pennsylvania, each judge is assigned a courtroom deputy clerk to act as liaison between judge and counsel. The courtroom deputy clerk schedules dates and times for hearings on motions, pretrial hearings, and trials, and confers with attorneys on any special trial procedures.

exhibit 6.2   *Federal circuit courts of appeals.*

filed, and the parties are granted a brief oral hearing. The Supreme Court's decision is final.

Exhibit 6.3 illustrates the federal court system.

The U.S. Constitution gives Congress the authority to establish rules for the appellate review of cases by the Supreme Court, except in the rare case where mandatory review is required. Congress has given the Supreme Court discretion to decide what cases it will hear.

A petitioner must file a **petition for certiorari** asking the Supreme Court to hear the case. If the Court decides to review a case, it will issue a **writ of certiorari.** Because the Court issues only about 150 to 200 opinions each year, writs usually are granted only in cases involving constitutional and other important issues.

Each justice of the Supreme Court, including the chief justice, has an equal vote. The Supreme Court can issue the following types of decisions:

- *Unanimous decision.* If all of the justices voting agree as to the outcome and reasoning used to decide the case, it is a unanimous opinion. Unanimous decisions are precedent for later cases.

- *Majority decision.* If a majority of the justices agree to the outcome and reasoning used to decide the case, it is a majority opinion. Majority decisions are precedent for later cases.

- *Plurality decision*. If a majority of the justices agree to the outcome of the case, but not to the reasoning for reaching the outcome, it is a plurality opinion. A plurality decision settles the case but is not precedent for later cases.

- *Tie decision*. Sometimes the Supreme Court sits without all nine justices being present, because of illness or conflict of interest, or because a justice has not been confirmed to fill a vacant seat on the court. In the case of a tie vote, the lower court decision is affirmed. These votes are not precedent for later cases.

A justice who agrees with the outcome of a case but not the reason proffered by other justices can issue a **concurring opinion** setting forth his or her reasons for deciding the case. A justice who does not agree with a decision can file a **dissenting opinion** that sets forth the reasons for his or her dissent.

U.S. Supreme Court building, Washington D.C.

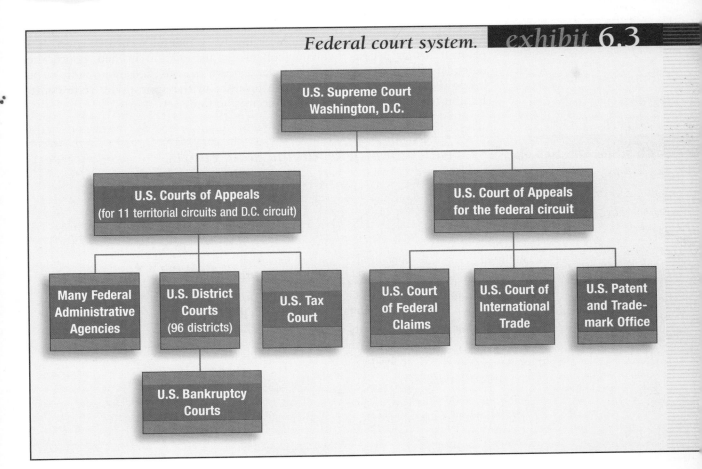

Federal court system.   exhibit 6.3

JURISDICTION OF FEDERAL AND STATE COURTS

Article III, Section 2, of the U.S. Constitution sets forth the jurisdiction of federal courts. Federal courts have *limited jurisdiction* to hear cases involving:

- **Federal questions:** Cases arising under the U.S. Constitution, treaties, and federal statutes and regulations. There is no dollar-amount limit on federal question cases that can be brought in federal court.

- **Diversity of citizenship:** Cases between (a) citizens of different states, (b) a citizen of a state and a citizen or subject of a foreign country, and (c) a citizen of a state and a foreign country where the foreign country is the plaintiff. A corporation is considered to be a citizen of the state in which it is incorporated and in which it has its principal place of business. The reason for providing diversity of citizenship jurisdiction was to prevent state court bias against nonresidents. The federal court must apply the appropriate state's law in deciding the case. The dollar amount of the controversy must exceed $75,000. If this requirement is not met, the action must be brought in the appropriate state court.

Federal courts have *exclusive jurisdiction* to hear cases involving federal crimes, antitrust, bankruptcy, patent and copyright cases, suits against the United States, and most admiralty cases. State courts cannot hear these cases.

State and federal courts have *concurrent jurisdiction* to hear cases involving diversity of citizenship and federal questions over which federal courts do not have exclusive jurisdiction (e.g., cases involving federal securities laws). If a plaintiff brings a case involving concurrent jurisdiction in state court, the defendant can remove the case to federal court. If a case does not qualify to be brought in federal court, it must be brought in the appropriate state court. Exhibit 6.4 illustrates the overlapping jurisdiction.

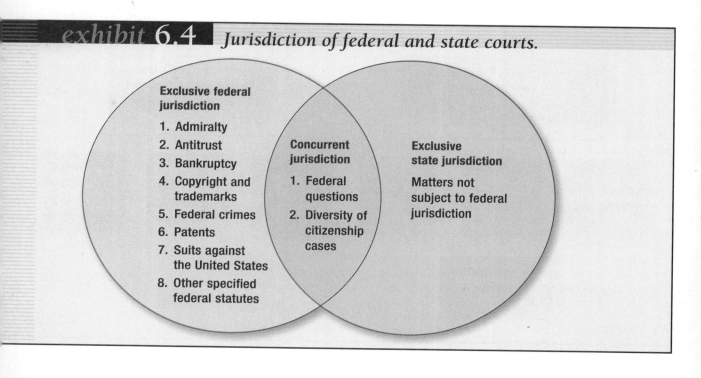

exhibit 6.4   *Jurisdiction of federal and state courts.*

Exclusive federal jurisdiction

1. Admiralty
2. Antitrust
3. Bankruptcy
4. Copyright and trademarks
5. Federal crimes
6. Patents
7. Suits against the United States
8. Other specified federal statutes

Concurrent jurisdiction

1. Federal questions
2. Diversity of citizenship cases

Exclusive state jurisdiction

Matters not subject to federal jurisdiction

Not every court has the authority to hear all types of cases. First, to bring a lawsuit in a court the plaintiff must have *standing to sue*. In addition, the court must have *jurisdiction* to hear the case, and the case must be brought in the proper *venue*.

Standing to Sue

To bring a lawsuit, a plaintiff must have **standing to sue.** The plaintiff must have some stake in the outcome of the lawsuit.

Consider this example: Linda's friend Jon is injured in an accident caused by Emily. Jon refuses to sue. Linda cannot sue Emily on Jon's behalf because she does not have an interest in the result of the case.

Courts hear and decide actual disputes involving specific controversies. Hypothetical questions will not be heard and trivial lawsuits will be dismissed.

The Franklin County Courthouse in Framington, Maine.

Types of Jurisdiction

A court must have **jurisdiction** to hear and decide a case. There are two types of jurisdiction: (1) subject-matter jurisdiction and (2) in personam, in rem, or quasi in rem jurisdiction.

1. *Subject-matter jurisdiction.* Some courts have only limited jurisdiction. To hear and decide a case, a court must have **subject-matter jurisdiction** over the type of case. For example, federal courts have jurisdiction to hear only certain types of cases (discussed later in this chapter) and certain state courts, such as probate courts and small-claims courts, can hear only designated types of cases. If a court does not have subject-matter jurisdiction, it cannot hear the case.

2. *In personam, in rem, and quasi in rem jurisdictions.* Jurisdiction over the person is called **in personam jurisdiction,** or **personal jurisdiction.** By filing a lawsuit with a court, a plaintiff gives the court in personam jurisdiction over himself or herself. The court must also have in personam jurisdiction over the **defendant,** which usually is obtained by having that person served a summons within the territorial boundaries of the state (i.e., **service of process**).

   Service of process usually is accomplished by personally serving the summons and complaint on the defendant. If this is not possible, alternative forms of notice, such as mailing the summons or publishing a notice in a newspaper, may be permitted. A corporation is subject to personal jurisdiction in the state in which it is incorporated, has its principal office, and is doing business. A party who disputes the jurisdiction of a court can make a *special appearance* in that court to argue against the imposition of jurisdiction. Service of process is not permitted during such an appearance.

A court may have jurisdiction to hear and decide a case because it has jurisdiction over the property of the lawsuit. This is called **in rem jurisdiction** ("jurisdiction over the thing"). For example, a state court would have jurisdiction to hear a dispute over the ownership of a piece of real estate located within the state. This is so even if one or more of the disputing parties lives in another state or states.

Sometimes a plaintiff who obtains a judgment against a defendant in one state will try to collect the judgment by attaching property of the defendant that is located in another state. This is permitted under **quasi in rem jurisdiction,** or **attachment jurisdiction.**

Long-Arm Statutes

In most states, a state court can obtain jurisdiction over persons and businesses located in another state or country through the state's **long-arm statute.** These statutes extend a state's jurisdiction to nonresidents who were not served a summons within the state. The nonresident must have had some *minimum contact* with the state [*International Shoe Co. v. Washington*, 326 U.S. 310, 66 S.Ct. 154, 90 L.Ed. 95 (1945)]. In addition, maintenance of the suit must uphold the traditional notions of fair play and substantial justice.

The exercise of long-arm jurisdiction is generally permitted over nonresidents who have (1) committed torts within the state (e.g., caused an automobile accident in the state), (2) entered into a contract either in the state or that affects the state (and allegedly breached the contract), or (3) transacted other business in the state that allegedly caused injury to another person.

Parties to a contract may include a **forum-selection clause** that designates a certain court to hear any dispute concerning nonperformance of the contract. In the case discussed next, under "Venue," the U.S. Supreme Court upheld a forum-selection clause in a contract.

Venue

Venue requires lawsuits to be heard by the court with jurisdiction nearest the location in which the incident occurred or where the parties reside. For example, Harry, a Georgia resident, commits a felony crime in Los Angeles County, California. The California Superior Court, located in Los Angeles, is the proper venue because the crime was committed there, the witnesses are probably from the area, and so on.

Occasionally, pretrial publicity may prejudice jurors located in the proper venue. In these cases, a *change of venue* may be requested so that a more impartial jury can be found. The courts generally frown upon *forum shopping* (i.e., looking for a favorable court without a valid reason).

ADR

Litigation is expensive and time-consuming. Businesses should consider alternative dispute resolution (ADR) to solve their disputes.

ALTERNATIVE DISPUTE RESOLUTION

Use of the court system to resolve business and other disputes can take years and cost thousands, if not millions, of dollars in legal fees and expenses. In commercial litigation, the normal business operations of the parties are often disrupted. To avoid or lessen these problems, businesses are increasingly turning to methods of alternative dispute resolution (ADR) and other aids to resolving disputes. The most common form of ADR is *arbitration.* Other forms of ADR are *mediation, conciliation, minitrial, fact-finding,* and a *judicial referee.*

Carnival Cruise Lines, Inc. v. Shute

499 U.S. 585, 111 S.Ct. 1522, 113 L.Ed.2d 622 (1991)   United States Supreme Court

FACTS

Mr. and Mrs. Shute, residents of the state of Washington, purchased passage for a seven-day cruise on the *Tropicale*, a cruise ship operated by the Carnival Cruise Lines, Inc. (Carnival). They paid the fare to the travel agent, who forwarded the payment to Carnival's headquarters in Miami, Florida. Carnival prepared the tickets and sent them to the Shutes. Each ticket consisted of five pages, including contract terms. The ticket contained a forum-selection clause that designated the state of Florida as the forum for any lawsuits arising under or in connection with the ticket and cruise. The Shutes boarded the *Tropicale* in Los Angeles, which set sail for Puerto Vallarta, Mexico. While the ship was on its return voyage and in international waters off the Mexican coast, Mrs. Shute was injured when she slipped on a deck mat during a guided tour of the ship's galley. Upon return to Washington, she filed a negligence lawsuit against Carnival in U.S. district court in Washington seeking damages. Carnival filed a motion for summary judgment contending that the suit could be brought only in a court located in the state of Florida. The district court granted Carnival's motion. The court of appeals reversed, holding that Mrs. Shute could sue Carnival in Washington. Carnival appealed to the U.S. Supreme Court.

ISSUE

Is the forum-selection clause in Carnival Cruise Line's ticket enforceable?

IN THE LANGUAGE OF THE COURT

Blackmun, Justice.

As an initial matter, we do not adopt the court of appeals' determination that a nonnegotiated forum-selection clause in a form ticket contract is never enforceable simply because it is not the subject of bargaining. Including a reasonable forum clause in form contract of this kind may well be permissible for several reasons: First, a cruise line has a special interest in limiting the fora in which it potentially could be subject to suit. Because a cruise ship typically carries passengers from many locales, it is not unlikely that a mishap on a cruise could subject the cruise line to litigation in several different fora.

Additionally, a clause establishing the forum for dispute resolution has the salutary effect of dispelling any confusion where suits arising from the contract must be brought and defended, sparing litigants the time and expense of pretrial motions to determine the correct forum, and conserving judicial resources that otherwise would be devoted to deciding these motions. Finally, it stands to reason that passengers who purchase tickets containing a forum clause like that at issue in this case benefit in the form of reduced fares reflecting the savings that the cruise line enjoys by limiting the fora in which it may be sued.

DECISION AND REMEDY

The forum-selection clause in Carnival's ticket is fair and reasonable and therefore enforceable against Mrs. Shute. If she wishes to sue Carnival, she must do so in a court in the state of Florida, not in a court in the state of Washington. The U.S. Supreme Court reversed the decision of the court of appeals.

Questions

1. Should forum-selection clauses be enforced? Why or why not?

2. Did Carnival Cruise Lines act ethically by placing the forum-selection clause in their tickets?

3. Do forum-selection clauses serve any legitimate business purpose? Explain.

Obtaining personal jurisdiction over a defendant located in another state has always been a difficult issue for the courts. States have enacted long-arm statutes that permit the courts located in one state to reach out and make people in another state come to court and defend themselves. To make sure this is not overly burdensome, the U.S. Supreme Court has held that out-of-state defendants must have had certain "minimum contacts" with the state before they are made to answer to a lawsuit there [*International Shoe Co. v. Washington,* 326 U.S. 310, 66 S.Ct. 154 (1945)].

Today, with the advent of the Internet and the ability of persons and businesses to reach millions of people in other states electronically, the application of the *International Shoe* minimum-contacts standard is even more difficult.

Several courts have decided cases involving the reach of a state's long-arm statute to obtain jurisdiction over someone in another state because of his or her Internet activities. In one case, Zippo Manufacturing Company (Zippo) sued Zippo Dot Com, Inc. (Dot Com) in federal district court in Pennsylvania. Zippo manufactures its well-known line of Zippo tobacco lighters in Bradford, Pennsylvania, and sells them worldwide. Dot Com, a California corporation with its principal place of business and its servers located in Sunnyvale, California, operates an Internet website that transmits information and sexually explicit material to its subscribers. Of Dot Com's 140,000 paying subscribers worldwide, 3,000 are located in Pennsylvania.

Zippo sued Dot Com in federal district court in Pennsylvania for trademark infringement. Dot Com alleged that it was not subject to personal jurisdiction in Pennsylvania. The district court applied the *International Shoe* "minimum-contacts" standard and held that Dot Com was subject to personal jurisdiction under the Pennsylvania long-arm statute and ordered Dot Com to defend itself there [*Zippo Manufacturing Company v. Zippo Dot Com, Inc.,* 952 F.Supp. 1119 (W.D.Pa. 1997)].

In another case, the court held that maintaining a passive website that merely provides advertising and other information is not sufficient to draw the website operator into another state's courts. The case involved Circus Circus Hotel (Circus Circus), a hotel and casino located in Las Vegas, Nevada, which maintains an Internet website advertising its services.

Janice and Robert Decker, two New Jersey residents, brought a lawsuit against Circus Circus in federal district court in New Jersey for alleged personal injuries suffered at the Las Vegas hotel. On Circus Circus's motion, the district court dismissed the action, finding that Circus Circus's passive website did not subject it to personal jurisdiction in New Jersey even though its advertisements were seen by the Deckers in New Jersey. The court held that mere Internet advertising, without selling products or services over the Internet, does not meet *International Shoe's* minimum-contacts standard necessary to haul a defendant into court [*Decker v. Circus Circus Hotel,* 49 F.Supp.2d 743 (D.N.J. 1999)].

Arbitration

In **arbitration,** the parties choose an impartial third party to hear and decide the dispute. This neutral party is called the *arbitrator.* Arbitrators usually are selected from members of the American Arbitration Association (AAA) or another arbitration association. Labor union agreements, franchise agreements, leases, and other commercial contracts often contain arbitration clauses that require disputes arising out of the contract to be submitted to arbitration. If there is no arbitration clause, the parties can enter into a *submission agreement,* whereby they agree to submit a dispute to arbitration after the dispute arises.

Federal Arbitration Act

The Federal Arbitration Act (FAA) was originally enacted in 1925 to reverse the longstanding judicial hostility to arbitration agreements that had existed as English common law and had been adopted by American courts. The Act provides that arbitration agreements involving commerce are valid, irrevocable, and enforceable contracts, unless some grounds exist at law or equity (e.g., fraud, duress) to revoke them. The FAA permits one party to obtain a court order to compel arbitration if the other party has failed, neglected, or refused to comply with an arbitration agreement.

In *Gilmer v. Interstate/Johnson Lane Corporation,* [S.Ct. 1647 (1991)], the Supreme Court upheld an arbitration clause in an employment contract. In that case, a 62-year-old employee who was dismissed from his job sued his employer for alleged age discrimination in violation of the federal Age Discrimination in Employment Act (ADEA).

The employer countered with a motion to compel arbitration. The Supreme Court upheld the motion and stated, "By agreeing to arbitrate a statutory claim, a party does not forgo the substantive rights afforded by the statute, it only submits to their resolution in an arbitral, rather than judicial, forum."

Critics contend that this gives the advantage to employers. Employers argue that arbitration is the only way to combat skyrocketing jury verdicts.

Evidence and testimony are presented to the arbitrator at a hearing held for this purpose. Less formal evidentiary rules usually are applied in arbitration hearings than at court. After the hearing, the arbitrator reaches a decision and enters an *award.* The parties often agree in advance to be bound by the arbitrator's decision and award. If the parties have not so agreed, the arbitrator's award can be appealed to court. The court gives great deference to the arbitrator's decision.

Congress enacted the Federal Arbitration Act to promote the arbitration of disputes [9 U.S.C. §§ 1 et. seq.]. About half of the states have adopted the Uniform Arbitration Act, which promotes the arbitration of disputes at the state level. Many federal and state courts have instituted programs to refer legal disputes to arbitration or another form of alternative dispute resolution.

Mediation and Conciliation

In **mediation,** the parties choose a neutral third party to act as the *mediator* of the dispute. Unlike an arbitrator, a mediator does not make a decision or award. Instead, the mediator acts as a conveyor of information between the parties and assists them in trying to reach a settlement of the dispute. A mediator often meets separately with each of the parties. If the mediator is successful, a settlement agreement is reached. If not, the case proceeds to trial. In a **conciliation,** the parties choose an interested third party, the *conciliator,* to act as the mediator.

Arbitrators and Mediators

SIDEBAR

Arbitrators usually are selected by the court, from a pool of attorneys admitted to the appointing court who have been in practice a minimum period of time and/or have taken a qualifying course for arbitrators. They usually receive a minimum payment per case, such as $100 in some jurisdictions, or a daily rate of, say, $150–$300 per day regardless of the number of cases heard. Mediators are chosen in the same manner as arbitrators but usually serve without pay as a pro bono service and must be certified as a mediator.

Businesses often complain that there are too many lawyers and too much litigation in the United States. Currently there are more than 800,000 lawyers and more than 20 million lawsuits per year in this country. In contrast, Japan, a country with about half the population of the United States, has only 15,000 lawyers and little litigation. Why the difference?

Much of the difference is cultural: Japan nurtures the attitude of avoiding confrontation. Litigious persons in Japan are looked down upon. Thus, companies rarely do battle in court. Instead, they opt for private arbitration of most of their disputes.

Other differences are built into the legal system itself. For example, there is only one place to go to become a *bengoshi,* or lawyer, in Japan—the government-operated National Institute for Legal Training. Only 2 percent of 35,000 applicants are accepted annually, and only 400 new *bengoshi* are admitted to Japan's exclusive legal club per year.

The Japanese legal system has other obstacles, too. For example, no class actions or contingency-fee arrangements are allowed. Plaintiffs must pay their lawyers a front fee of up to 8 percent of the damages sought, plus a nonrefundable filing fee to the court of one-half of 1 percent of the damages. To make matters even more difficult, no discovery is permitted. Thus, plaintiffs are denied access to an opponent's potential evidence before trial. And, even if the plaintiff wins the lawsuit, damage awards are low.

Some experts argue that Japan has more legal practitioners than the statistics reveal. For example, approximately 5,000 non-*bengoshi* patent specialists perform services similar to U.S. patent attorneys. Another 50,000 licensed tax practitioners offer services similar to U.S. tax attorneys. Many non-*bengoshi* legal experts handle tasks such as contract negotiation and drafting. In addition, sales personnel and front-line managers often act as problem-solvers.

The Japanese bias against courtroom solutions remains strong. The current system is designed to save time and money and to preserve long-term relationships. The belief that disputes can be solved amicably without litigation is a concept that U.S. businesses are starting to embrace.

Minitrial

A *minitrial* is a session, usually lasting a day or less, in which the lawyers for each side present their cases to representatives of each party who have authority to settle the dispute. In many cases, the parties hire a neutral person (e.g., a retired judge) to preside over the minitrial. Following the presentations, the parties meet to try to negotiate a settlement.

Fact-Finding

Fact-finding is a process whereby the parties hire a neutral person to investigate the dispute. The *fact-finder* reports his or her findings to the adversaries and may recommend a basis for settlement.

Judicial Referee

If the parties agree, the court may appoint a *judicial referee* to conduct a private trial and render a judgment. Referees, who often are retired judges, have most of the powers of a trial judge, and their decisions stand as a judgment of the court. The parties usually reserve their right to appeal.

LEGAL TERMINOLOGY

Alternative dispute resolution (ADR)

Arbitration

Briefs

Chief justice

Circuits

Conciliation

Concurring opinion

Court of Appeals for the Federal Circuit

Court of record

Defendant

Dissenting opinion

Diversity of citizenship

Federal question

Forum-selection clause

General-jurisdiction trial court

In personam jurisdiction (personal jurisdiction)

In rem jurisdiction

Intermediate appellate courts (courts of appeal)

Jurisdiction

Limited-jurisdiction trial courts

Litigation

Long-arm statute

Mediation

Petition for certiorari

Quasi in rem jurisdiction (attachment jurisdiction)

Service of process

Small-claims courts

Special federal courts

Standing to sue

Subject-matter jurisdiction

U.S. courts of appeal

U.S. district courts

Venue

Writ of certiorari

Summary

State Court Systems

Limited-Jurisdiction Trial Court	State court that hears matters of a specialized or limited nature (e.g., misdemeanor criminal matters, traffic tickets, civil matters under a certain dollar amount). Many states have created small claims courts that hear small-dollar-amount civil cases (e.g., under $3,000) where the parties cannot be represented by lawyers.
General-Jurisdiction Trial Court	State court that hears cases of a general nature that are not within the jurisdiction of limited-jurisdiction trial courts.
Intermediate Appellate Court	State court that hears appeals from state trial courts. The appellate court reviews the trial court record in making its decision; no new evidence is introduced at this level.
Highest State Court	Each state has a highest court in its court system. This court hears appeals from appellate courts, and where appropriate, trial courts. This court reviews the record in making its decision; no new evidence is introduced at this level. Most states call this court the supreme court.

Federal Court System

Federal Court System	1. *Special federal courts:* Federal courts that have specialized or limited jurisdiction. They include:
	
	  a. *U.S. tax court:* Hears cases involving federal tax laws.
	
	  b. *U.S. claims court:* Hears cases brought against the United States.
	
	  c. *U.S. Court of International Trade:* Hears cases involving tariffs and international commercial disputes.
	
	  d. *U.S. bankruptcy courts:* Hear cases involving federal bankruptcy law.
	
	2. *U.S. district courts:* Federal trial courts of general jurisdiction that hear cases not within the jurisdiction of specialized courts. There is at least one U.S. district court per state; more populated states have several district courts. The area served by one of these courts is called a *district.*
	
	3. *U.S. courts of appeals:* Intermediate federal appellate courts that hear appeals from district courts located in their circuit, and in certain instances from special federal courts and federal administrative agencies. There are 12 geographical *circuits* in this country. Eleven serve areas that are comprised of several states, while another is located in Washington, D.C. A thirteenth circuit court—the *Court of Appeals for the Federal Circuit*, is located in Washington, D.C., and reviews patent, trademark, and international trade cases.

(continued)

Federal Court System, *continued*	4. *U.S. Supreme Court:* Highest court of the federal court system. It hears appeals from the circuit courts and, in some instances, from special courts and U.S. district courts. The Court, located in Washington, D.C., comprises nine justices, one of whom is named chief justice.
Decisions by U.S. Supreme Court	*Petition of certiorari and writ of certiorari:* To have a case heard by the U.S. Supreme Court, a petitioner must file a *petition for certiorari* with the Court. If the Court decides to hear the case, it will issue a *writ of certiorari.*
Voting by the U.S. Supreme Court	1. *Unanimous decision:* All of the justices agree as to the outcome and reasoning used to decide the case; the decision becomes precedent. 2. *Majority decision:* A majority of justices agrees as to the outcome and reasoning used to decide the case; the decision becomes precedent. 3. *Plurality decision:* A majority of the justices agrees to the outcome but not to the reasoning; the decision is not precedent. 4. *Tie decision:* If there is a tie vote, the lower court's decision stands; the decision is not precedent. 5. *Concurring opinion:* A justice who agrees as to the outcome of the case but not the reasoning used by other justices may write a concurring opinion setting forth his or her reasoning. 6. *Dissenting opinion:* A justice who disagrees with the outcome of a case may write a dissenting opinion setting forth his or her reasoning.
Jurisdiction of Federal and State Courts	Federal courts may hear the following cases: 1. *Federal question:* Cases arising under the U.S. Constitution, treaties, and federal statutes and regulations; there is no dollar-amount limit. 2. *Diversity of citizenship:* Cases between (a) citizens of different states and (b) citizens of a state and a citizen or subject of a foreign country; federal courts must apply the appropriate state law in such cases. The controversy must exceed $75,000 for the federal court to hear the case.
Jurisdiction of State Courts	State courts hear some cases that may be heard by federal courts. 1. *Exclusive jurisdiction:* Federal courts have exclusive jurisdiction to hear cases involving federal crimes, antitrust, and bankruptcy; patent and copyright cases; suits against the United States; and most admiralty cases. State courts may not hear these matters. 2. *Concurrent jurisdiction:* State courts have concurrent jurisdiction to hear cases involving diversity of citizenship cases and federal question cases over which the federal courts do not have exclusive jurisdiction. The defendant may have the case removed to federal court. *(continued)*

Standing to Sue	To bring a lawsuit, the plaintiff must have some stake in the outcome of the lawsuit.
Subject-Matter Jurisdiction	The court must have jurisdiction over the subject matter of the lawsuit; each court has limited jurisdiction to hear only certain types of cases.
In Personam Jurisdiction (or Personal Jurisdiction)	The court must have jurisdiction over the parties to a lawsuit. The plaintiff submits to the jurisdiction of the court by filing the lawsuit there. Personal jurisdiction is obtained over the defendant by serving that person *service of process.*
In Rem Jurisdiction	A court may have jurisdiction to hear and decide a case because it has jurisdiction over the property at issue in the lawsuit (e.g., real property located in the state).
Quasi In Rem Jurisdiction (or Attachment Jurisdiction)	A plaintiff who obtains a judgment against a defendant in one state may utilize the court system of another state to attach property of the defendant's located in the second state.
Long-Arm Statutes	Permit a state to obtain personal jurisdiction over an out-of-state defendant as long as the defendant had the requisite minimum contact with the state. The out-of-state defendant may be served process outside the state in which the lawsuit has been brought.
Venue	A case must be heard by the court that has jurisdiction nearest to where the incident at issue occurred or where the parties reside. A *change of venue* will be granted if prejudice would occur because of pretrial publicity or another reason.
Forum-Selection Clause	A clause in a contract that designates the court that will hear any dispute that arises out of the contract.

Alternative Dispute Resolution (ADR)

Description	*Nonjudicial* means of solving legal disputes. ADR usually saves time and money required by litigation.

Types of ADR	1. *Arbitration:* An impartial third party, called the arbitrator, hears and decides the dispute. The arbitrator makes an award. The award is appealable to a court if the parties have not given up this right. Arbitration is designated by the parties pursuant to:
	  a. *Arbitration clause:* Agreement contained in a contract stipulating that any dispute arising out of the contract will be arbitrated.
	  b. *Submission agreement:* Agreement to submit a dispute to arbitration after the dispute arises.
	(continued)

Types of ADR, *continued*	2. *Mediation:* A neutral third party, called a *mediator*, assists the parties in trying to reach a settlement of their dispute. The mediator does not make an award.
	3. *Conciliation:* An interested third party, called a *conciliator*, assists the parties in trying to reach a settlement of their dispute. The conciliator does not make an award.
	4. *Minitrial:* A short session in which the lawyers for each side present their case to representatives of each party who have the authority to settle the dispute.
	5. *Fact-finding:* The parties hire a neutral third person, called a *fact-finder*, to investigate the dispute and report his or her findings to the adversaries.
	6. *Judicial referee:* With the consent of the parties, the court appoints a judicial referee (usually a retired judge or lawyer) to conduct a private trial and render a judgment. The judgment stands as the judgment of the court and may be appealed to the appropriate appellate court.

Working the Web

1. The official website for the U.S. Supreme Court is www.supreme courtus.gov/; however, information on the U.S. Supreme Court can also be found at the Cornell University site at www.supct.law.cornell.edu/ supct.

2. Obtain information on the U.S. Courts of Appeals at the Emory University website at www.law.emory.edu.

3. Find information on the U.S. District Courts at www.vls.law.vill.edu/ locator/fedcourt.html.

4. A number of sites offer links to state court information, and many state courts have their own Web pages. Information and links can be found at the Villanova University website at www.vls.law.vill.edu/locator/state court.htm.

5. The American Arbitration Association website, www.adr.org, offers information on alternative dispute resolution, labor relations, employment, commerce, and international disputes. It includes rules, forms, and articles about alternative dispute resolution.

6. Using the Cornell website (see above), click on the gallery of current justices. Read the biography of justice Ginsburg.

7. Using the Emory gateway (see above), find the U.S. Court of Appeals for the circuit in which your state is located. Find a recent decision.

8. Using the Emory gateway, find out if any U.S. District Courts for your state publish opinions on the Internet. List the courts and dates of coverage for each court.

9. Find the home page for courts in your state. Which courts in your state are reporting cases on the Internet? What are the dates of coverage for each court in your state?

10. Using the American Arbitration Association website (see above), click on Customer Service. Find a form for submission of a dispute resolution.

Questions
CRITICAL LEGAL THINKING AND WRITING

1. Is the action of a court in not hearing a case because of a lack of case or controversy really a decision by the court or a way of it saving time?

2. How does the Case for Briefing, *Adler v. Duval*, demonstrate the court's recognition of the case or controversy issue?

3. How does the *Adler v. Duval* case contrast with the Chapter 5 case of *Lee v. Weisman?*

4. What if an executive's calendar contains both business and personal information? Is it protected by the Fifth Amendment's privilege against self-incrimination?

5. May email be introduced as evidence to prove a case of sexual harassment?

6. How can a forum-selection clause be used to limit a client's exposure to suit?

7. What factors should be considered in advising a client in which court to bring action when there is concurrent jurisdiction?

8. What are the practical considerations in selecting a forum for trial of a case?

9. What are the advantages and the disadvantages in using the different methods of alternative dispute resolution?

10. Why might someone agree not to appeal a case decided by an arbitrator?

Questions
ETHICS: ANALYSIS AND DISCUSSION

1. May a paralegal represent a client before an arbitration panel?

2. Are a paralegal's time records or calendar subject to the attorney–client privilege?

3. May a paralegal sign a pleading?

Unauthorized Practice of Law—Court Appearance

There are few certainties in the area of ethics, for paralegals or in any profession. What qualifies as ethical conduct is in most cases based on state law and court interpretation applied to a set of facts. The citation listed below represents one legal opinion and is provided as a research starting point. Do not assume that the same rule applies in your jurisdiction. For the following:

- *Prepare a written statement based on your state law.*
- *Use your state bar association website as a starting point.*

You have been appointed as a trustee of a client's children's educational trust. You need to petition the court for a release of the funds for non-educational purposes—paying the taxes on the trust income. [*Ziegler v. Harrison Nickel*, 64 Cal. App. 4th 545; 1998 Lexis 500.] May you appear alone as the trustee and represent the trust in the court proceedings? Would a nonlawyer, nonparalegal be permitted to appear?

CASES *for Discussion*

Allison v. ITE Imperial Corp.

729 F.Supp. 45 (S.D. Miss. 1990)

6.1 FACTS

James Clayton Allison, a resident of Mississippi, was employed by the Tru-Amp Corporation as a circuit breaker tester. As part of his employment, Allison was sent to inspect, clean, and test a switch gear located at the South Central Bell Telephone Facility in Brentwood, Tennessee. On August 26, 1988, he attempted to remove a circuit breaker manufactured by ITE Corporation (ITE) from a bank of breakers, when a portion of the breaker fell off. The broken piece fell behind a switching bank and, according to Allison, caused an electrical fire and explosion. Allison was severely burned in the accident. Allison brought suite against ITE in Mississippi state court, claiming more than $50,000 in damages.

ISSUE

Can this suit be removed to federal court?

AMF Inc. v. Brunswick Corp.

621 F.Supp. 456 (E.D.N.Y. 1985)

6.2 FACTS

AMF Incorporated and Brunswick Corporation both manufacture electric and automatic bowling center equipment. In 1983 the two companies became involved in a dispute over whether Brunswick had advertised certain automatic scoring devices in a false and deceptive manner. The two parties settled the dispute by signing an agreement that any future problems between them involving advertising claims would be submitted to the National Advertising Council for arbitration. In March 1985, Brunswick advertised a new product, Armor Plate 3000, a synthetic laminated material used to make bowling lanes. Armor Plate 3000 competed with wooden lanes produced by AMF. Brunswick's advertisements claimed that bowling centers could save up to $500 per lane per year in maintenance and repair costs if they switched to Armor Plate 3000 from wooden lanes. AMF disputed this claim and requested arbitration.

ISSUE

Is the arbitration agreement enforceable?

Calder v. Jones

465 U.S. 783, 104 S.Ct. 1482, 79 L.Ed.2d 804 (1984)

6.3 FACTS

The National Enquirer, Inc., is a Florida corporation with its principal place of business in Florida. It publishes the *National Enquirer*, a national weekly newspaper with a circulation of more than 5 million copies. About 600,000 copies, almost twice the level of the next highest state, are sold in California. On October 9, 1979, the *Enquirer* published an article about Shirley Jones, an entertainer. Jones, a California resident, filed a lawsuit in California state court against the *Enquirer* and its president, a resident of Florida. The suit sought damages for alleged defamation, invasion of privacy, and intentional infliction of emotional distress.

ISSUE

Are the defendants subject to suit in California?

Burnham v. Superior Court of California

495 U.S. 604, 110 S.Ct. 2105, 109 L.Ed.2d 631 (1990)

6.4 FACTS

Dennis and Francis Burnham were married in 1976 in West Virginia. In 1977, the couple moved to New Jersey, where their two children were born. In July

1987, the Burnhams decided to separate. Mrs. Burnham, who intended to move to California, was to have custody of the children. Mr. Burnham agreed to file for divorce on grounds of "irreconcilable differences." In October 1987, Mr. Burnham threatened to file for divorce in New Jersey on grounds of "desertion." After unsuccessfully demanding that Mr. Burnham adhere to the prior agreement, Mrs. Burnham brought suit for divorce in California state court in early January 1988. In late January, Mr. Burnham visited California on a business trip. He then visited his children in the San Francisco Bay area, where his wife resided. He took the older child to San Francisco for the weekend. Upon returning the child to Mrs. Burnham's home, he was served with a California court summons and a copy of Mrs. Burnham's divorce petition. He then returned to New Jersey. Mr. Burnham made a special appearance in the California court and moved to quash the service of process.

ISSUE

Did Mr. Burnham act ethically in trying to quash the service of process? Did Mrs. Burnham act ethically in having Mr. Burnham served on his visit to California? Is the service of process good?

Adler v. Duval County School Board

112 F.3d 1475 (11th Cir. 1997)   United States Court of Appeals, Eleventh Circuit

Read the following case, excerpted from the court of appeals opinion. Review and brief the case. In your brief, answer the following questions.

1. What is the doctrine of mootness?
2. What was the action the plaintiffs complained of?
3. When would the plaintiffs have had to file and have their case heard for the court to rule on their claim?

4. How would bringing the cases as a class action have allowed the court to hear the case under the Case or Controversy requirement?
5. How does this case differ from the case of *Lee v. Weisman* in Chapter 5?

Tjoflat, Circuit Judge.

Appellants are four former high school students in the Duval County, Florida, school system who brought this action under 42 U.S.C. § 1983 (1994), alleging that a Duval County school policy permitting student-initiated prayer at high school graduation ceremonies (the "policy") violated their rights under the First and Fourteenth Amendments.

On June 7, 1993, three of the appellants graduated from Mandarin, one of the schools in the Duval County system. A fourth appellant graduated in June 1994. Because all four appellants have graduated, we find that to the extent they seek declaratory and injunctive relief, their case is moot. The only justiciable controversy in this case is the appellants' claim for money damages. We affirm the district court's grant of summary judgment for the appellees on this claim, but we do so without reviewing the merits of the district court's constitutional analysis. We begin by noting that appellants' claims for declaratory and injunctive relief are moot. All appellants have graduated, and none is threatened with harm from possible prayers in future Duval County graduation ceremonies. . . .

Article III of the Constitution limits the jurisdiction of the federal courts to the consideration of certain "Cases" and "Controversies." . . . The doctrine of mootness is derived from this limitation because an action that is moot cannot be characterized as an active case or controversy. "[A] case is moot when the issues presented are no longer 'live' or the parties lack a legally cognizable interest in the outcome." Any decision on the merits of a moot case would be an impermissible advisory opinion.

To apply the doctrine of mootness to this case, we must distinguish the appellants' claims for equitable relief from their claim for money damages. . . .

Equitable relief is a prospective remedy, intended to prevent future injuries. In contrast, a claim for money damages looks back in time and is intended to redress a past injury. The plaintiff requests money damages to redress injuries caused by the defendant's past conduct and seeks equitable relief to prevent the defendant's future conduct from causing future injury. When the threat of future harm dissipates, the plaintiff's claims for equitable relief become moot because the plaintiff no longer needs protection from future injury. This is precisely what happened in this case.

Appellants argue that, despite their graduation from high school, their claims for declaratory and injunctive relief are not moot because the original injury is "capable of repetition, yet evading review." This exception to the mootness doctrine is narrow. In the absence of a class action, the "capable of repetition, yet evading review" doctrine is limited to the situation where two elements combine: (1) the challenged action [is] in its duration too short to be fully litigated prior to its cessation or expiration, and (2) there is a reasonable expectation that the same complaining party will be subjected to the same action again. This case does not satisfy the second element. Because the complaining students have graduated from high school, there is no reasonable expectation that they will be subjected to the same injury again.

Having disposed of the appellants' claims for equitable relief, we are left with their claim for money damages, which we now address. Because the appellants' claim for money damages does not depend on any threat of future harm, this claim remains a live controversy. We accordingly turn our focus to the basis for the appellants' claim for damages. The complaint alleges that a "senior class chaplain" delivered a prayer at the June 7,

1993, Mandarin graduation ceremony at which appellants Adler, Jaffa, and Zion graduated. The only past injury for which the appellants could seek redress is being subjected to this prayer at their graduation ceremony. To prove that the appellees caused this injury, the appellants alleged in their complaint that the prayer was "a direct consequence" of the school's policy. In their answer, the appellees admitted that a student said the prayer, but denied that the prayer was a consequence of the policy.

The only issue the appellants raise on appeal is whether the district court erred in holding the policy constitutional. While the constitutionality of the policy may have been central to the now moot issue of whether equitable relief is warranted to prevent the policy from being implemented at future graduations, it does not dispose of the issue of whether the appellants should be awarded money damages for being subjected to the prayer at their graduation. In other words, any claim for damages does not depend on the constitutionality of the policy in the abstract or as applied in other Duval County schools. Even if the policy is unconstitutional, the defendants might not be liable if, for example, they did not implement the policy at the ceremony in question or if the prayer would have been delivered without the policy. On the other hand, if the district court was correct in finding the policy constitutional, defendant Epting, Mandarin's principal, might nonetheless be liable if he implemented the policy in an unconstitutional manner.

The constitutionality of the policy, therefore, has little independent relevance to the appellants' damages claim. Whether they are entitled to damages depends entirely on the circumstances under which the prayer was delivered at their graduation ceremony. In order to prevail, the appellants must have some theory connecting the individual defendants to the prayer. For these reasons, even if we were to find fault with the district court's constitutional analysis of the policy, this conclusion by itself would not answer the question of whether the court erred in granting the appellees summary judgment on the damages claim. The appellants offer no other grounds in their briefs for finding trial court error.

After considering the appellants' briefs and oral argument, we are convinced that they either fail to understand the basis for their damages claim or do not seriously seek damages. They have offered us no connection between the prayer and their damages claim; their briefs offer no indication as to any of the circumstances surrounding the Mandarin graduation prayer. They failed to argue that the prayer was a "direct consequence" of the policy, or any other theory connecting the defendants' actions to the Mandarin prayer. Their briefs do not even include the allegation made in their complaint that a prayer was delivered at Mandarin.

For all these reasons, we hold that they have waived their damages claim on appeal. We therefore affirm the district court's order to the extent it denied the appellants' motion for summary judgment and granted the appellees' motions for summary judgment on the appellants' damages claim. For the foregoing reasons, we *vacate* the district court's order granting the appellees summary judgment on the appellants' claims for declaratory and injunctive relief and *remand* the case with instructions that the district court dismiss those claims. We *affirm* the district court's denial of the appellants' motion for summary judgment and its grant of summary judgment for the appellees on the appellants' damages claim. It is *so ordered*.

UPDATE TO CASE:

After a rehearing en banc the court, upon a majority vote of the judges of the court, issued a subsequent opinion on June 3, 1999, and on March 15, 2000 on further proceeding the Court ruled that the policy on prayer did not violate the Establishment Clause. On June 19, 2000, the Supreme Court rendered a decision in *Santa Fe Independent School District v. Doe*, 530 U.S. 290, which invalidated a Texas school board's policy permitting students to vote on a prayer subject to officials' approval at home football games. The Duval Court proceeded to rehear the case based on the *Santa Fe* decision and ruled again in favor of the Duval School Board because the prayer there was not subject to official approval or input [*Adler v. Duval County Sch. Bd.*, 250 F.3d 1330 (11th Cir. 2001)].

CHAPTER 7

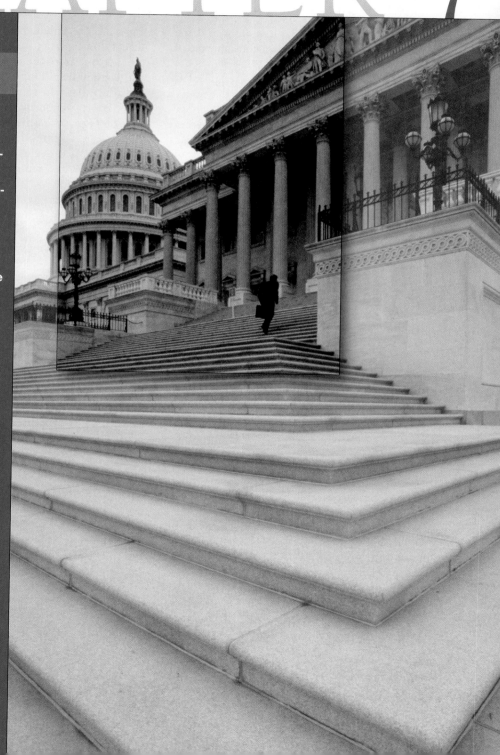

CHAPTER OBJECTIVES

After studying this chapter, you should be able to:

1. Describe general government regulation.

2. Describe specific government regulation.

3. Define an *administrative agency.*

4. Explain the scope of the Administrative Procedure Act.

5. Describe the legislative powers of administrative agencies.

6. Describe the judicial powers of administrative agencies.

7. Describe the executive powers of administrative agencies.

8. Explain how administrative agency actions are subject to judicial review.

9. Describe the protections afforded by the Freedom of Information Act.

10. List the responsibilities of the federal Food and Drug Administration.

Administrative Law and Government Regulation

I should regret to find that the law was powerless to enforce the most elementary principles of commercial morality.

LORD HERSCHELL, *REDDAWAY V. BANHAM* (1896)

Introduction

The federal government's ability to create administrative agencies is implied in the U.S. Constitution. Congress and the executive branch of government have created more than 100 federal **administrative agencies.** These agencies are intended to provide resources and expertise in dealing with complex commercial organizations and businesses. In addition, state governments have created many state administrative agencies. Since the 1960s, the numbers of administrative agencies and the regulations they produce have increased substantially. Because of their importance, administrative agencies are informally referred to as the *fourth branch of government.* (In reality, they only have the powers delegated from the actual branches of government.) Federal and state administrative agencies have adopted and enforced thousands of *rules and regulations* regarding business operations.

Many of the lawyers for whom paralegals will be working may engage in a practice of law that involves dealing with governmental administrative agencies and government regulation. These matters could include filing applications for licenses from federal and state administrative agencies, appearing at hearings before these agencies, or appealing from decisions rendered by administrative agencies. Paralegals who assist lawyers in this area of the law should have a knowledge of how administrative agencies work. This chapter discusses administrative agencies and government regulation.

GOVERNMENT REGULATION

The government's record-keeping and reporting requirements form a large part of administrative law. Other government regulations concern proper business purpose and conduct, entry restrictions into an industry, government rate setting, and the like.

Regulatory Costs

Businesses spend billions of dollars each year complying with government regulation.

General Government Regulation

Most government regulation applies to many businesses and industries collectively. For example, the National Labor Relations Board (NLRB) is empowered to regulate the formation and operation of labor unions in most industries, the Occupational Safety and Health Administration (OSHA) is authorized to formulate and enact safety and health standards for the workplace, the Consumer Product Safety Commission (CPSC) is empowered to establish mandatory safety standards for products sold in the United States, and the Securities and Exchange Commission (SEC) is authorized to enforce federal securities laws that apply to issuers of and persons who trade in securities.

Specific Government Regulation

The U.S. Congress and the executive branch have created some administrative agencies to monitor certain regulated industries. For example, the Federal Communications Commission (FCC) regulates the operation of television and radio stations, the Interstate Commerce Commission (ICC) regulates railroads, the Federal Aviation Administration (FAA) regulates commercial airlines, and the Office of the Comptroller of the Currency (OCC) regulates national banks. Although a detailed discussion of these agencies and the laws they administer is beyond the scope of this book, the reader should know that they exist.

ADMINISTRATIVE AGENCIES

Administrative agencies are established with the overall goal of creating a body of professionals who are experts in a specific field. These experts have delegated authority to regulate an individual industry or a specific area of commerce. Federal, state, and local governments create administrative agencies ranging from large, complex federal agencies, such as the Department of Health and Human Services, to local zoning boards. Many administrative

WHAT DOES "MADE IN AMERICA" MEAN?

Many goods contain the label "Made in America." What does this label really mean? In 1998, the Federal Trade Commission (FTC), the administrative agency charged with protecting consumers from deception, issued new standards that define "Made in America." These standards try to balance domestic-origin claims and the global marketplace.

The 1998 FTC guidelines require goods that are "substantially made" in the United States to bear the "Made in America" label. This new test rejects the "wholly domestic" 100 percent standard. Instead, the FTC states that a marketer may claim the "Made in America" label if either of the following "safe harbor" rules are met:

1. At least 75 percent of the total cost of manufacturing the product is U.S. manufacturing cost.

2. The final product was last "substantially transformed" in the United States. This rule requires that the manufacturing process results in a new and different article of commerce having a name, character, and use different from what existed prior to processing. For example, using foreign steel to make a new automobile qualifies, but adding a tail light to an already-made automobile would not.

The FTC guidelines also permit marketers to make qualified claims of U.S. origin even when their products would not meet the rules for the unqualified "Made in America" label. For example, a product assembled in the United States but made primarily with foreign parts could be labeled "Made in USA of foreign parts."

The labeling law is designed to protect consumers from false "Made in USA" claims. The FTC is empowered to seek sanctions against violators and to turn over fraudulent cases to the U.S. Department of Justice for criminal prosecution.

agencies are given the authority to adopt **rules and regulations** that enforce and interpret statutory law.

Federal Administrative Agencies

The most pervasive government regulations have developed from the statutes enforced by and the rules and regulations adopted by **federal administrative agencies.** Most federal administrative agencies—including the Justice Department, the Department of Housing and Urban Development, the Labor Department, the Transportation Department, and the Commerce Department—are part of the executive branch of government.

Congress has established many federal administrative agencies. These agencies are independent of the executive branch and have broad regulatory powers over key areas of the national economy. Exhibit 7.1 is an application form for an administrative hearing regarding a Social Security matter.

State Administrative Agencies

All states have created administrative agencies to enforce and interpret state law. For example, most states have a corporations department to enforce state corporations law, a banking department to regulate the operation of banks, fish

exhibit 7.1   *Application for Social Security administrative hearing.*

SOCIAL SECURITY ADMINISTRATION
OFFICE OF HEARINGS AND APPEALS

Form Approved
OMB No. 0960-0269

REQUEST FOR HEARING BY ADMINISTRATIVE LAW JUDGE
[Take or mail original and all copies to your local Social Security Office]

PRIVACY ACT NOTICE
ON REVERSE SIDE OF FORM.

1. CLAIMANT	2. WAGE EARNER, IF DIFFERENT	3. SOC. SEC. CLAIM NUMBER	4. SPOUSE's CLAIM NUMBER

5. I REQUEST A HEARING BEFORE AN ADMINISTRATIVE LAW JUDGE. I disagree with the determination made on my claim because:

An Administrative Law Judge of the Office of Hearings and Appeals will be appointed to conduct the hearing or other proceedings in your case. You will receive notice of the time and place of a hearing at least 20 days before the date set for a hearing.

6. If you have additional evidence to submit check the following block and complete the statement: ☐

I have additional evidence to submit from
(name and address of source): _____

(Please submit it to the Social Security Office within 10 days. Attach an additional sheet if you need more space.)

7. Check one of the blocks:

☐ I wish to appear at a hearing.

☐ I do not wish to appear and I request that a decision be made based on the evidence in my case.
(Complete Waiver Form HA-4608)

You have a right to be represented at the hearing. If you are not represented but would like to be, your Social Security Office will give you a list of legal referral and service organizations. (If you are represented and have not done so previously, complete and submit form SSA-1696 (Appointment of Representative).)

[You should complete No. 8 and your representative (if any) should complete No. 9. If you are represented and your representative is not available to complete this form, you should also print his or her name, address, etc. in No. 9.]

8. (CLAIMANT'S SIGNATURE)	9. (REPRESENTATIVE'S SIGNATURE/NAME)
ADDRESS	(ADDRESS) ☐ ATTORNEY; ☐ NON ATTORNEY;
CITY STATE ZIP CODE	CITY STATE ZIP CODE
DATE AREA CODE AND TELEPHONE NUMBER	DATE AREA CODE AND TELEPHONE NUMBER

TO BE COMPLETED BY SOCIAL SECURITY ADMINISTRATION-ACKNOWLEDGMENT OF REQUEST FOR HEARING

10.
Request for Hearing RECEIVED for the Social Security Administration on _____ by: _____

(TITLE)   ADDRESS

11. Was the request for hearing received within 65 days of the reconsidered determination?
☐ YES   ☐ NO

If no is checked, attach claimant's explanation for delay; and attach copy of appointment notice, letter, or other pertinent material or information in the Social Security Office.

12. Claimant not represented -
☐ list of legal referral and service organizations provided

13. Interpreter needed -
☐ enter language (including sign language): _____

14.
Check one: ☐ Initial Entitlement Case
☐ Disability Cessation Case
☐ Other Postentitlement Case

15.
Check claim type(s):

☐ RSI only ---(RSI)
☐ Title II Disability-worker or child-----------------------------(DIWC)
☐ Title II Disability-widow(er) only-----------------------------(DIWW)
☐ SSI Aged only--(SSIA)
☐ SSI Blind only--(SSIB)
☐ SSI Disability only ---(SSID)
☐ SSI Aged/Title II --(SSAC)
☐ SSI Blind/Title II ---(SSBC)
☐ SSI Disability/Title II ---(SSDC)
☐ HI Entitlement --(HIE)
☐ Other-Specify: (   )

16.
HO COPY SENT TO:_____ HO on _____
☐ CF Attached: ☐ Title II;   ☐ Title XVI; or
☐ Title II CF held in FO to establish CAPS ORBIT; or
☐ CF requested ☐ Title II;   ☐ Title XVI
(Copy of teletype or phone report attached)

17.
CF COPY SENT TO:_____ HO on _____
☐ CF Attached: ☐ Title II;   ☐ Title XVI
☐ Other Attached:

FORM HA-501-U5 (5-1996) EF (7-2000)
Issue old stock

CLAIMS FOLDER

and game departments, and workers' compensation boards. **State administrative agencies** also have a profound effect on business. Local governments and municipalities create administrative agencies, such as zoning commissions, to administer local law.

ADMINISTRATIVE LAW

Administrative law combines substantive and procedural law. Each federal administrative agency is empowered to administer a specific statute or statutes. For example, the Securities and Exchange Commission (SEC) is authorized to enforce the Securities Act of 1933, the Securities Exchange Act of 1934, and other federal statutes dealing with securities markets. These statutes are the *substantive law* that is enforced by the agency.

Administrative Procedure Act

In 1946, Congress enacted the **Administrative Procedure Act (APA)** [5 U.S.C. §§ 551 et seq.], which established certain administrative procedures that federal administrative agencies must follow in conducting their affairs. For example, the APA establishes notice and hearing requirements, rules for conducting agency adjudicative actions, and procedures for rule making. In addition, most states have enacted administrative procedural acts that govern state administrative agencies.

Delegation of Powers

Because the U.S. Constitution does not stipulate that administrative agencies are a separate branch of the government, the legislative or executive branch must create them. When an administrative agency is created, it is delegated certain powers. Under the **delegation doctrine** the agency has only the legislative, judicial, and executive powers that are delegated to it.

Thus, an agency can adopt a rule or regulation (a legislative function), prosecute a violation of the statute or rule (an executive function), and adjudicate the dispute (a judicial function). The courts generally have upheld this combined power of administrative agencies as being constitutional. If an administrative agency acts outside the scope of its delegated powers, it is an unconstitutional act.

LEGISLATIVE POWERS OF ADMINISTRATIVE AGENCIES

Administrative agencies usually are delegated certain legislative powers. These include rule-making and licensing powers.

Substantive Rule Making

Many federal statutes expressly authorize an administrative agency to issue **substantive rules.** A substantive regulation is much like a statute: It has the force of law, and the persons and businesses it covers must adhere to it.

Violators may be held civilly or criminally liable, depending on the rule. All substantive rules are subject to judicial review.

A federal administrative agency that proposes to adopt a substantive rule must follow procedures set forth in the APA. This means the agency must do the following:

1. Publish a general notice of the proposed rule making in the *Federal Register*. The notice must include
   a. The time, place, and nature of the rule-making proceeding.
   b. The legal authority pursuant to which the rule is proposed.
   c. The terms or substance of the proposed rule or a description of the subject and issues involved.
2. Give interested persons an opportunity to participate in the rule-making process. This may involve oral hearings.
3. Review all written and oral comments. Then the agency announces its *final rule making* in the matter. This procedure often is referred to as *notice-and-comment rule making*, or *informal rule making*.
4. Require, in some instances, *formal rule making*. Here, the agency must conduct a trial-like hearing at which the parties may present evidence, engage in cross-examination, present rebuttal evidence, and such.

Interpretive Rule Making

Administrative agencies can issue **interpretive rules** which explain existing statutory language. These rules do not establish new laws, and neither public notice nor public participation is required.

Statements of Policy

Administrative agencies also can issue **statements of policy**. These statements announce a proposed course of action that an agency intends to follow in the future. These statements do not have the force of law. Again, public notice and participation are not required.

EXECUTIVE POWERS OF ADMINISTRATIVE AGENCIES

Administrative agencies usually are granted **executive powers,** the authority to investigate and prosecute possible violations of statutes, administrative rules, and administrative orders. To perform these functions successfully, the agency often must obtain information from the persons and businesses under investigation as well as from other sources. If the required information is not supplied voluntarily, the agency may issue an administrative subpoena to search the business premises. As discussed shortly, however, these powers are subject to certain constitutional constraints.

**SIDEBAR**

Licensing Powers

Statutes often require the issuance of a government **license** before a person can enter certain types of industries (e.g., the operation of banks, television and radio stations, commercial airlines) or professions (e.g., doctors, lawyers, dentists, certified public accountants, contractors). Most administrative agencies have the power to determine whether to grant licenses to applicants.

Applicants must usually submit detailed applications to the appropriate administrative agency. In addition, the agency usually accepts written comments from interested parties and holds hearings on the matter. The administrative agency's decision is subject to judicial review. The courts, however, generally defer to the expertise of administrative agencies in licensing matters.

Administrative Subpoena

An **administrative subpoena** is an order that directs the subject of the subpoena to disclose the requested information. Judicial enforcement may be sought if the party does not comply with the subpoena and the agency can prove that it has reasonable grounds to believe that the information sought will prove to be a violation of the law. "Fishing expeditions" are prohibited. If a party ignores a judicial order to enforce an administrative subpoena, the party may be held in contempt of court.

Administrative Searches

Sometimes a physical inspection of a business premise is crucial to the investigation. Most inspections by administrative agencies are considered "searches" subject to the Fourth Amendment of the U.S. Constitution. The Fourth Amendment protects persons (including businesses) from unreasonable search and seizures.

Searches by administrative agencies are generally considered to be reasonable within the meaning of the Fourth Amendment if

- the party voluntarily agrees to the search.
- the search is conducted pursuant to a validly issued **search warrant.**
- a warrantless search is conducted in an emergency situation.
- the business is part of a special industry in which warrantless searches are automatically considered valid (such as liquor or firearm sales).
- the business is part of a hazardous industry and a statute expressly provides for nonarbitrary warrantless searches (such as coal mines).

Evidence from an unreasonable search and seizure ("tainted evidence") may be inadmissible in court, depending on the circumstances of the case.

JUDICIAL POWERS OF ADMINISTRATIVE AGENCIES

Many administrative agencies have the judicial authority to adjudicate cases through an administrative proceeding. Such a proceeding is initiated when an agency serves a complaint on a party the agency believes has violated a statute or administrative rule or order. The person on whom the complaint is served is called the *respondent.*

In adjudicating cases, an administrative agency must comply with the **Due Process Clause** of the U.S. Constitution (and the state constitution where applicable). **Procedural due process** requires that the respondent be given (1) proper and timely notice of the allegations or charges against him or her, and (2) an opportunity to present evidence on the matter. **Substantive due process** requires that the statute or rule that the respondent is charged with violating be clearly stated.

U. S. Department of Agriculture building, Washington D.C.

FACTS

Since the 1890s, Dow Chemical Company (Dow) has manufactured chemicals at a facility in Midland, Michigan. Its complex covers 2,000 acres and contains a number of chemical-processing plants. Many of these are "open-air" plants, with reactor equipment, loading and storage facilities, motors, transfer lines, and piping conduits located in the open areas between the buildings. Dow has undertaken elaborate precautions to secure the facility from unwelcome intrusion: An eight-foot-high chain-link fence completely surrounds the facility, security personnel guard the plant and monitor it by closed-circuit television, unauthorized entry into the facility triggers alarm systems, motion detectors indicate movement of persons within restricted areas, and the use of camera equipment by anyone other than authorized Dow personnel is prohibited. Dow considers its entire facility a trade secret.

The Environmental Protection Agency (EPA) is a federal administrative agency empowered to administer and enforce the federal Clean Air Act. In 1978, Dow denied an EPA request to conduct an on-site inspection of the Midland facility. EPA did not seek an administrative search warrant. EPA employed a commercial aerial photographer to take photographs of the facility from altitudes of 12,000, 3,000, and 1,200 feet. Using a standard floor-mounted, precision aerial-mapping camera, this firm took approximately 75 color photographs of various parts of the plant. When the photographs taken from 1,200 feet were enlarged, it was possible to discern equipment, pipes, and power lines as small as one-half inch in diameter. Several weeks later, after Dow learned about the EPA-authorized flight from independent sources, it filed suit against EPA. The district court held in favor of Dow and issued an injunction against the EPA's use of the photographs. The court of appeals reversed. Dow appealed.

ISSUE

Did EPA's aerial photography of Dow's plant constitute an unreasonable search in violation of the Fourth Amendment to the U.S. Constitution?

IN THE LANGUAGE OF THE COURT

Burger, Chief Justice.

We turn to Dow's contention that taking aerial photographs constituted a search without warrant, thereby violating Dow's rights under the Fourth Amendment. Plainly a business establishment or an industrial or commercial facility enjoys certain protections under the Fourth Amendment. Dow plainly has a reasonable, legitimate, and objective expectation of privacy within the interior of its covered buildings, and it is equally clear that expectation is one society is prepared to observe. Dow's inner manufacturing areas are elaborately secured to ensure they are not open or exposed to the public from the ground. Any actual physical entry by EPA into any enclosed area would raise significantly different questions, because the businessman, like the occupant of a residence, has a constitutional right to go about his business free from unreasonable official entries upon his private commercial property.

The issue raised by Dow's claim of search and seizure, however, concerns aerial observation of a 2,000-acre outdoor manufacturing facility without physical entry. The intimate activities associated with family privacy and the home and its curtilage simply do not reach the outdoor areas or spaces between structures and buildings of a manufacturing plant. The government has greater latitude to conduct warrantless inspections of commercial property because the expectation of privacy that the owner enjoys in such property differs significantly from the sanctity accorded an individual's home. We emphasized that unlike a homeowner's interest in his dwelling, the interest of the owner of commercial property is not one in being free from any inspections. And with regard to regulatory inspections, we have held that what is observable by the public is observable without warrant, by the government inspector as well.

Here, EPA was not employing some unique sensory device that, for example, could penetrate the walls of buildings and record conversations in Dow's plants, offices, or laboratories, but rather a conventional, albeit precise, commercial camera commonly used in map making. It may well be, as the government concedes, that the surveillance of private property by using highly sophisticated surveillance equipment not generally available to the public, such as satellite technology, might be constitutionally proscribed absent warrant. But the photographs here are not so revealing of intimate details as to raise constitutional concerns. Although they undoubtedly give EPA more detailed information than naked-eye views, they remain limited to an outline of the facility's buildings and equipment. The mere fact that human vision is enhanced somewhat, at least to the degree here, does not give rise to constitutional problems.

DECISION AND REMEDY

The Supreme Court held that the taking of photographs of an industrial plant complex from navigable airspace is not a search prohibited by the Fourth Amendment. Affirmed.

Questions

1. Should the government be given greater latitude to conduct warrantless searches of business property than personal homes? Why or why not?

2. Did EPA act ethically in this case?

3. Could Dow have in any way protected itself from the search conducted in this case?

Paralegal Representation at Ohio Unemployment Compensation Hearing

Ohio Adm. Code 4146–19–01 Representation before [Unemployment Compensation Board of Review] referee or board:

"At any proceeding before a Referee or the board, any interested party may appear in person, by counsel, or an authorized representative."

This rule reflects the board's long-standing policy of permitting nonlawyers to assist parties in presenting their claims. The proceedings are designed and function as alternatives to judicial dispute resolution so that the services of a lawyer are not a requisite to receiving a fair hearing and just decision.

In this regard, claimants traditionally are accompanied by friends, co-workers, family, and union representatives, or are assisted by legal-aid societies that provide paralegals without charge to assist the worker in presenting the claim. [*Enize v. Giles,* 22 Ohio St.3d 213 (1986), 490 N.E.2d 585]

Illinois View of Representation Before Administrative Agency

"The legislature has authorized the representation of participants in proceedings before the Department. . . . Any individual or entity in any proceeding before the Director or his representative, or the Referee or the Board of Review, may be represented by a union or any duly authorized agent" [820 ILCS 405/806].

In Illinois, only licensed attorneys are permitted to practice law [705 ILCS 205/1]. The legislature has no authority to grant a nonattorney the right to practice law even if limited to practice before an administrative agency [*People ex rel. Chicago Bar Association v. Goodman* (1937), 366 Ill. 346, 352].

"Based on the foregoing, we hold that Gates' correspondence with the Department in behalf of Emro did not constitute the practice of law. Our holding is a narrow one confined to the facts of this case. We specifically do not reach the question of whether Gates' actions would have constituted the practice of law if, as in Goodman, Gates had participated in the hearing.

"Nor do we speculate . . . at what point, if any, in the Department's administrative proceedings the participation of nonattorneys constitutes the unauthorized practice of law. . . . Consequently, we need not determine whether there is a point in the administrative proceedings where participation by a nonattorney constitutes the unauthorized practice of law" [*Perto v. Board of Review,* 274 Ill. App.3d 485 (1995), 654 N.E.2d 232].

Procedures for Administrative Adjudication

Administrative law judges (ALJs) preside over administrative proceedings and decide questions of law and fact concerning the case. There is no jury. The ALJ is an employee of the administrative agency.

Both the administrative agency and the respondent may be represented by counsel. Witnesses may be examined and cross-examined, evidence may be introduced, objections may be made, and so forth. Agency rules allow more liberal introduction of evidence than do court rules.

The ALJ's decision is issued in the form of an *order*, which must state the reasons for the ALJ's decision. The order becomes final if it is not appealed. An appeal consists of a review by the agency, and the agency review can result in new findings of fact and law. Further appeal can be made to the appropriate federal court (in federal agency actions) or state court (in state agency actions).

Table 7.1 summarizes the powers of administrative agencies.

Judicial Review of Administrative Agency Actions

Many federal statutes expressly provide for judicial review of administrative agency actions. Where an enabling statute does not provide for review, the Administrative Procedure Act authorizes judicial review of federal administra-

table 7.1   *Powers of administrative agencies.*

POWER	DESCRIPTION
Legislative Powers	
1. Substantive rule making	To adopt rules that advance the purpose of the statutes the agency is empowered to enforce. These rules have the force of law, and public notice and participation are required.
2. Interpretive rule making	To adopt rules that interpret statutory language. These rules do not establish new laws, and neither public notice nor participation is required.
3. Statements of policy	To announce a proposed course of action the agency plans to take in the future. These statements do not have the force of law, and public participation and notice are not required.
4. Licensing	To grant licenses to applicants (e.g., television station licenses, bank charters) and to suspend or revoke licenses.
Executive Powers	
	To prosecute violations of statutes and administrative rules and orders, including the power to investigate suspected violations, issue administrative subpoenas, and conduct administrative searches.
Judicial Powers	
	To adjudicate cases through an administrative proceeding, including the power to issue a complaint, hold a hearing by an administrative law judge (ALJ), and issue an order deciding the case and assessing remedies.

Appeal of a federal administrative agency rule, order, or decision.   exhibit 7.2

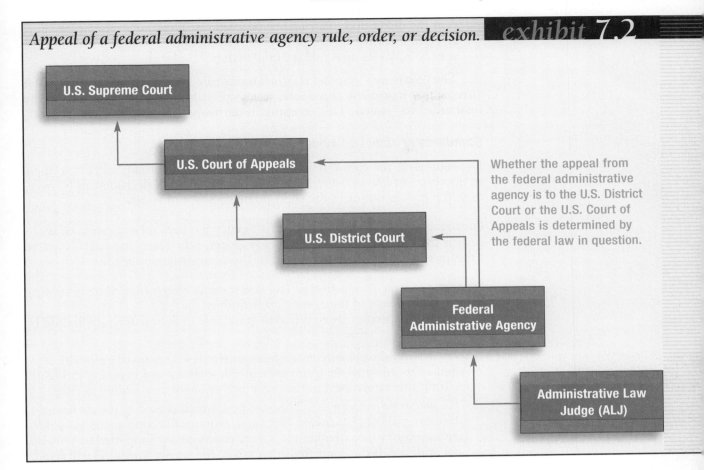

Whether the appeal from the federal administrative agency is to the U.S. District Court or the U.S. Court of Appeals is determined by the federal law in question.

tive agency actions. The party appealing the decision of an administrative agency is called the **petitioner.**

Decisions of federal administrative agencies are appealed to the appropriate federal court, and decisions of state administrative agencies may be appealed to the proper state court. A court may order the agency to prepare a detailed writing of the reasons for its decision. The federal appeal process is illustrated in Exhibit 7.2.

Conditions for Judicial Review

Before a petitioner can appeal an action of an administrative agency to a reviewing court, the following conditions must be satisfied.

1. The case must be *ripe for review*. For example, a petitioner cannot seek review of an administrative agency's rule, order, policy, or other action unless it specifically applies to the petitioner.

2. The petitioner must have *exhausted all administrative remedies.* For example, a petitioner cannot seek judicial review of a decision of an ALJ if an appeal to the full commission is available.

3. The decision of the administrative agency must be final before judicial review can be sought. Called the **final order rule,** it is intended to pre-

vent the disruption of an agency proceeding. Thus, an accused party in an administrative agency proceeding cannot appeal to the courts until the agency issues its final ruling in the matter.

The courts may suspend the final order rule if the petitioner would suffer "irreparable injury" or "economic hardship" if he or she had to wait until a final order was issued. This exception is narrowly construed by the courts.

Standards of Judicial Review

Depending on the circumstances, different standards of judicial review apply to questions of law and questions of fact. The agency's decision can be overturned if it does not meet the appropriate standard of review.

Questions of law. If the administrative agency has decided a question of law—such as the interpretation of statutory language—the reviewing court is free to substitute its own judgment for that of the administrative agency.

Questions of fact. A question of fact is not easily overturned. The reviewing court usually defers to the agency's fact-finding.

The APA specifies three different standards of review for fact-finding by administrative agencies:

1. *The arbitrary, capricious abuse-of-process test.* This standard generally is applied to informal decisions such as rule-making and licensing [5 U.S.C. § 706]. It is rarely used to reverse a discretionary fact-finding decision.

2. *The substantial-evidence test.* This standard, which is used to review formal decision-making [5 U.S.C. § 706(2)(e)], requires the court to examine the entire record to see whether the agency's decision was supported by substantial evidence. If the court finds that it was, the agency's decision will stand.

3. *The unwarranted-by-the-facts test* (or the *de novo* standard of review). This test, which is rarely used, requires the reviewing court to try the case as if it had not been heard previously [5 U.S.C. § 706(2)(f)]. This type of review is available if the agency's fact-finding procedure was inadequate or if new issues arise on appeal.

Immunity of Agency Employees

Federal administrative agency employees are immune from lawsuits for personal liability regarding the actions and decisions they make while performing their agency duties. This places administrative agency employees on a par with judges, legislators, and others involved in the judicial process who are accorded similar immunity.

Consider this example: Suppose a group of persons wishes to form a new national bank. Under the law, a national bank cannot be formed without the approval of the comptroller of the currency (Comptroller), a federal government official. Assume that the Comptroller does not approve the formation of the bank. The applicants may appeal the Comptroller's decision to the proper court, but they may not sue the Comptroller personally for denying their application.

The immunity of agency employees is not absolute. For example, an agency employee who intentionally injures someone while performing agency business is subject to personal liability.

PUBLIC DISCLOSURE OF AGENCY ACTIONS

Public concern over possible secrecy of administrative agency actions led Congress to enact several statutes that (1) promote public disclosure of federal administrative agency actions, and (2) protect parties from overly obtrusive agency actions. These statutes are the Freedom of Information Act, the Government in the Sunshine Act, the Equal Access to Justice Act, and the Privacy Act.

Freedom of Information Act

The **Freedom of Information Act** (FOIA) [5 U.S.C. § 552] was enacted to give the public access to most documents in the possession of federal administrative agencies. For purposes of privacy, the following documents are exempt from disclosure:

1. Documents classified by the President to be in the interests of national security.
2. Documents that are statutorily prohibited from disclosure.
3. Records whose disclosure would interfere with law enforcement proceedings.
4. Documents describing agency personnel practices.
5. Intraagency and interagency memoranda.
6. Medical, personnel, and similar files.
7. Documents containing trade secrets or other confidential or privileged information.
8. Documents pertaining to the operation of financial institutions.
9. Geological and geophysical data and maps.

The courthouse in Clarksville, Tennessee.

The Freedom of Information Act requires federal administrative agencies to publish agency procedures, rules, regulations, interpretations, and other such information in the *Federal Register*. The Act also requires agencies to publish quarterly indexes of certain documents. In addition, the Act specifies time limits for agencies to respond to requests for information, sets limits on copying charges, and provides for disciplinary action against agency employees who refuse to honor proper requests for information.

Decisions by federal administrative agencies not to publicly disclose documents requested under the Act are subject to judicial review in the proper U.S. district court. The court may award attorneys' fees to a successful petitioner. (The Department of Justice's Freedom of Information Act form appears later in the text, as Figure 18.7.)

Government in the Sunshine Act

The **Government in the Sunshine Act** [5 U.S.C. § 552(b)] was enacted to open certain federal administrative agency meetings to the public. Only federal administrative agencies that are headed by two or more persons appointed by the President are subject to this Act. Exceptions to this rule include meetings (1) about things that are exempt from disclosure under the Freedom of Information Act, (2) where a person is accused of a crime, (3) concerning an agency's issuance of a subpoena, (4) where attendance of the public would significantly frustrate implementation of a proposed agency action, and (5) concerning day-to-day operations. Decisions by federal administrative agencies to close a meeting to the public are subject to judicial review in the proper U.S. district court.

Equal Access to Justice Act

Congress enacted the **Equal Access to Justice Act** [5 U.S.C. § 504] to protect persons from harassment by federal administrative agencies. Under this Act, a private party who is the subject of an unjustified federal administrative agency action can sue to recover attorneys' fees and other costs. The courts generally have held that the agency's conduct must be extremely outrageous before they will make an award under the Act. A number of states have similar statutes.

Privacy Act

The federal **Privacy Act** [5 U.S.C. § 552(a)] stipulates that federal administrative agencies can maintain only information about an individual that is relevant and necessary to accomplish a legitimate agency purpose. The Act affords individuals the right to have access to agency records concerning themselves and to correct these records. Many states have enacted similar privacy acts.

FOOD AND DRUG ADMINISTRATION (FDA)

The Food and Drug Administration is involved in the regulation of food, drugs, cosmetics, and medicinal devices. The first federal statute regulating the wholesomeness of food and drug products was enacted in 1906. A much more comprehensive act—the federal Food, Drug, and Cosmetic Act (FDCA) [21 U.S.C. § 301]—was enacted in 1938. This Act, as amended, provides the basis for the regulation of much of the testing, manufacture, distribution, and sale of foods, drugs, cosmetics, and medicinal products and devices in the United States. The FDA can seek search warrants and conduct inspections; obtain orders for the seizure, recall, and condemnation of products; seek injunctions; and seek criminal penalties against willful violations. The U.S. Department of Justice has the authority to bring lawsuits to enforce the FDCA.

Required FDA Approval

Before certain food additives, drugs, and medicinal devices can be sold to the public, they must receive FDA approval. An applicant must submit an application to the FDA that contains relevant information about the safety and uses of the product. After considering the evidence, the FDA will either approve or deny the application. The FDA can sue and obtain a seizure order and injunction against further sales of unapproved items.

Regulation of Food

The federal government has enacted a comprehensive set of statutes that regulates the manufacture, processing, distribution, and sale of food. These laws are intended to (1) ensure the wholesomeness of food, (2) encourage accuracy in labeling and packaging, and (3) prevent injury to health.

A Hidden Source of Protein in Peanut Butter

You take a big bite of a peanut butter sandwich and savor the taste. It has been processed by a food manufacturer and inspected by the federal government, so you think it is pure peanut butter. Not necessarily. Under federal FDA guidelines, peanut butter may contain up to 30 insect fragments per 3 1/2 ounces and still be considered "safe" for human consumption.

The FDA has set ceilings or "action levels" for certain contaminants, or "defects," as the FDA calls them, for various foods. Several of these action levels are

Golden raisins—35 fly eggs per 8 ounces

Popcorn—two rodent hairs per pound

Shelled peanuts—20 insects per 100 pounds

Canned mushrooms—20 maggots per 3½ ounces

Tomato juice—10 fly eggs per 3½ ounces

The FDA can mount inspections and raids to enforce its action levels. If it finds that the federal tolerance system has been violated, it can seize the offending food and destroy it at the owner's expense. For example, in the Great Peanut Raid of 1991, the FDA seized 8.5 million pounds of peanuts shipped to the United States from foreign countries. The FDA found that these peanuts contained illegal levels of contamination and sent them back to their home countries.

The courts have upheld the presence of some contamination in food as lawful under the federal Food, Drug, and Cosmetic Act. For example, in one case the court found that 28 insect parts in nine pounds of butter did not violate the Act. The court stated, "Few foods contain no natural or unavoidable defects. Even with modern technology, all defects in foods cannot be eliminated" [*United States v. Capital City Foods, Inc.*, 345 F.Supp. 277 (N.D. 1972)].

Adulterated food. The FDCA prohibits the shipment, distribution, or sale of adulterated food. Food is deemed adulterated if it consists in whole or in part any "filthy, putrid, or decomposed substance" or if it is otherwise "unfit for food." Note that food does not have to be entirely pure to be distributed or sold; it only has to be unadulterated.

Misbranded food. The FDCA also prohibits false and misleading labeling of food products. In addition, it mandates affirmative disclosure of information on food labels, including the name of the food, the name and place of the manufacturer, and a statement of ingredients. A manufacturer may be held liable for deceptive labeling or packaging.

Regulation of Drugs

The FDCA gives the FDA the authority to regulate the testing, manufacture, distribution, and sale of drugs. The *Drug Amendment to the FDCA*, enacted in 1962, gives the FDA broad powers to license new drugs in the United States. After a new drug application is filed, the FDA holds a hearing and investigates the merits of the application. This process can take many years. The FDA also may withdraw approval of any previously licensed drug.

This law requires all users of prescription and nonprescription drugs to receive proper directions for use (including the method and duration of use)

Seafood Processing

SIDEBAR

In 1995, the federal Food and Drug Administration (FDA) issued new regulations that establish safety standards for seafood and shellfish. The FDA is authorized to conduct inspections of seafood processors to ensure compliance with these regulations.

The FDA & Drugs

The FDA may speed up the approval process for experimental drugs that hold promise in treating incurable diseases (e.g., AIDS).

and adequate warnings about any related side effects. The manufacture, distribution, or sale of adulterated or misbranded drugs is prohibited.

Regulation of Cosmetics

The FDA's definition of cosmetics includes substances and preparations for cleansing, altering the appearance of, and promoting the attractiveness of a person. For example, eye shadow and other facial makeup are cosmetics subject to FDA regulation. Ordinary household soap is expressly exempted from this definition.

The FDA has issued regulations that require cosmetics to be labeled, to disclose ingredients, and to contain warnings if they are carcinogenic (cancer-causing) or otherwise dangerous to a person's health. The manufacture, distribution, or sale of adulterated or misbranded cosmetics is prohibited. The FDA may remove from commerce cosmetics that contain unsubstantiated claims of preserving youth, increasing virility, growing hair, and the like.

Ethical PERSPECTIVE — *Less Baloney on the Shelves*

For much of its existence, the federal FDA was a paper tiger led by wine-and-dine-with-the-industry regulators. In April 1991, the FDA shocked the food industry by having U.S. marshals seize 24,000 half-gallon cartons of Citrus Hill Fresh Choice orange juice, which is made by mammoth food processor Procter & Gamble (P&G). After trying for a year to get P&G to remove the word *fresh* from the carton—the product is made from concentrate and is pasteurized—the FDA finally got tough. P&G gave in after two days and agreed to remove the word *fresh* from its Citrus Hill products.

Next on the FDA's hit list were Best Foods, which markets Mazola Corn Oil; Great Foods of America, makers of HeartBeat Canola Oil; and again P&G, manufacturer of Crisco Corn Oil. These companies had prominently advertised their cooking oils as having "no cholesterol," and some even added cute little hearts to the labels. Although the claim was literally true (these oils do not contain cholesterol), they are in fact 100% fat—which is not good for the heart. The FDA believed that these companies were hoodwinking the public and ordered the companies to take the "no cholesterol" labels off their vegetable oils.

In late 1990, Congress passed a sweeping truth-in-labeling law called the Nutrition Labeling and Education Act. The statute requires food manufacturers and processors to provide more nutritional information on virtually all foods and bars them from making scientifically unsubstantiated health claims.

This law requires the more than 20,000 food labels found on grocery store shelves to disclose the number of calories derived from fat and the amount of dietary fiber, saturated fat, cholesterol, and a variety of other substances. The law applies to packaged foods as well as fruit, vegetables, and raw seafood. Meat, poultry, and egg products, which are regulated by the Department of Agriculture, are exempt from the Act, as are restaurant food and prepared dishes sold in supermarkets and delicatessens.

In December 1992, the FDA announced final regulations to implement the Act. The regulations require food processors to provide uniform information about serving sizes and nutrients on labels of the food products they sell and establish standard definitions for *light, low-fat, natural,* and other terms routinely bandied about by food processors.

Many food processors in the United States and across the world genetically modify some foods by adding genes from other organisms to help crops grow faster or to ward off pests. In the past, food processors did not notify consumers that they were purchasing genetically modified agricultural products. Although the companies insist that genetically altered foods are safe, consumers and many countries began to demand that these foods be clearly labeled so buyers could decide for themselves. When most large food processors balked at this idea, the consumers went to their lawmakers.

The most concerned countries in the world regarding this issue were in Europe. Led by Germany, many European countries wanted to require genetically engineered food products to be labeled as such and to be transported separately from nonaltered agricultural products. Some European countries wanted genetically altered foods to be banned completely. The United States—a major exporter of agricultural products and the leader in the development of biotech foods—argued that these countries were using this issue to erect trade barriers to keep U.S.-produced food products out of their countries in violation of international trade treaties and conventions administered by the World Trade Organization (WTO), which had reduced or eliminated many international trade restrictions.

In January 2000, a compromise was reached when 138 countries, including the United States, agreed to the United Nations-sponsored Biosafety Protocol. After much negotiation, the countries agreed that all genetically engineered foods would be clearly labeled with the phrase "May contain living modified organisms." This allows consumers to decide on their own whether to purchase altered food products. In addition, the boxes and containers in which the goods are shipped must be clearly marked as containing genetically altered food products. This compromise assures that biosafety labeling rules will coexist with the free-trade agreements of the WTO.

Regulation of Medical Devices

In 1976, Congress enacted the Medicinal Device Amendment to the FDCA. This amendment gave the FDA authority to regulate medicinal devices, such as heart pacemakers, kidney dialysis machines, defibrillators, surgical equipment, and other diagnostic, therapeutic, and health devices. The mislabeling of such devices is prohibited and the FDA is empowered to remove "quack" devices from the market.

LEGAL TERMINOLOGY

Administrative agency	Interpretive rules
Administrative law judge (ALJ)	License
Administrative Procedure Act (APA)	Petitioner
Administrative subpoena	Privacy Act
Delegation doctrine	Procedural due process
Due Process Clause	Rules and regulations
Equal Access to Justice Act	Search warrant
Executive powers	State administrative agencies
Federal administrative agencies	Statements of policy
Final order rule	Substantive due process
Freedom of Information Act	Substantive rules
Government in the Sunshine Act	

Summary

CHAPTER 7　ADMINISTRATIVE LAW AND GOVERNMENT REGULATION

Government Regulation

General Government Regulation	Government-enacted laws that regulate businesses and industries collectively.
Specific Government Regulation	Government-enacted laws that regulate certain industries only.

Administrative Agencies

Description	Created by federal and state legislative and executive branches; consist of professionals having expertise in a certain area of commerce, who interpret and apply designated statutes.
Rules and Regulations	Administrative agencies are empowered to adopt rules and regulations that interpret and advance the laws they enforce.
Administrative Procedure Act (APA)	Federal act that establishes procedures (e.g., notice, hearing) to be followed by federal agencies in conducting their affairs. States have enacted their own procedural acts to govern state agencies.

(continued)

Delegation Doctrine	When an administrative agency is created, it is delegated certain legislative, judicial, and executive powers. If an administrative agency acts outside the scope of its delegated powers, it is an unconstitutional act.

Legislative Powers of Administrative Agencies

Substantive Rule Making	Administrative agencies have the power to adopt *substantive rules* that have the force of law and must be adhered to by covered persons and businesses.
Interpretive Rule Making	Rules that interpret existing statutory language.
Statement of Policy	Announces a proposed course of action that an agency intends to follow in the future.
Licensing Powers	Administrative agencies are authorized to issue *licenses* before a person or business can enter certain types of industries.

Executive Powers of Administrative Agencies

Administrative Subpoena	An order that directs the subject of the subpoena to disclose the requested information.
Administrative Search	Inspection of business premises; subject to the Fourth Amendment's protection against *unreasonable search and seizure*.

Judicial Powers of Administrative Agencies

Complaint	Administrative agency serves a complaint on the party it believes has violated the law. This party is called the *respondent*.
Administrative Law Judge (ALJ)	Employee of the administrative agency who presides over the administrative proceeding; decides questions of law and fact, issues a decision in the form of an *order*.

Judicial Review of Administrative Agency Actions

Petitioner	Party appealing the decision of an administrative agency.
Conditions for Judicial Review	1. The case must be *ripe for review*. 2. The petitioner must have *exhausted all administrative remedies*. 3. The *final-order rule* requires that the decision of the administrative agency must be final before judicial review can be sought.
Immunity	Administrative agency employees are immune from lawsuits for personal liability regarding actions and decisions they make while performing their agency duties. *(continued)*

Public Disclosure of Agency Actions

Freedom of Information Act	Federal law that gives the public access to most documents in the possession of federal administrative agencies. Also requires federal administrative agencies to publish agency procedures, rules, regulations, interpretations, and other information in the *Federal Register*.
Government in the Sunshine Act	Federal law that opens certain federal administrative agency meetings to the public.
Equal Access to Justice Act	Federal law that protects persons from harassment by federal administrative agencies and provides certain penalties for its violation.
Privacy Act	Federal law that (a) restricts information a federal administrative agency can maintain about an individual, and (b) gives individuals the right to access agency records concerning themselves.

Federal Food and Drug Administration (FDA)

Description	Federal administrative agency empowered to interpret and enforce the Federal Food, Drug, and Cosmetic Act and other federal consumer protection laws.
Federal Food, Drug, and Cosmetic Act (FDCA)	Federal statute that regulates the testing, manufacture, distribution, and sale of foods, food additives, drugs, cosmetics, and medicinal products.
Powers of the FDA	The FDA has the power to approve or deny applications by private companies to distribute drugs, food additives, and medicinal devices to the public.
Regulation of Food, Drugs, and Cosmetics	The FDA prohibits the shipment, distribution, or sale of *adulterated* or *misbranded* food, drugs, cosmetics, or medicinal devices.

Working the Web

1. Find out what a regulation is, why it matters, where to find a particular rule, or horror stories and outrages involving federal regulations at www.regulation.org.

2. Stay abreast of recent developments in state and federal administrative law at ABA's www.abanet.org/adminlaw/home.html.

3. To download the handbook of *Freedom of Information Act* (FOIA), see the American Civil Liberties Union (ACLU) website at www.ACLU.org/library/foia.html.

4. Learn more about the products regulated by the Food and Drug Administration and the latest safety alerts and FDA news at www.fda.gov.

Questions
CRITICAL LEGAL THINKING AND WRITING

1. Can the legislature of your state authorize paralegals to represent parties before administrative agencies? If so, have they?

2. Which, if any, administrative agencies in your state permit paralegals to represent parties before them?

3. The Colorado Supreme Court has set a standard for unlicensed practice of law where "there are few or no disputed legal principles involved and the monetary amount in issue is too small to justify hiring an attorney" [*Denver Bar Association v. Public Utilities Commission*, 154 Colo. 273 (1964)]. Do you agree or disagree with the standard? Is it valid today in cases of paralegals who have graduated with degrees and certificates in paralegal studies?

4. Should the government by federal regulation require building owners to make buildings accessible for persons with disabilities?

5. Does the ability to appeal an action by an administrative agency protect the individual from arbitrary enforcement of federal regulation?

6. What standards would you like to see adopted that would permit paralegals to represent parties before more state and federal agencies? Why is this a reasonable standard?

7. Should the courts regulate the appearance before administrative agencies by nonlawyers? Why?

8. What protections exist to prevent administrative agencies from enacting arbitrary rules and regulations?

9. How does the Freedom of Information Act help an individual in dealing with the federal administrative agency bureaucracy?

10. Do the Food and Drug Administration and the Department of Agriculture have completely independent areas of responsibility? Explain.

Questions
ETHICS: ANALYSIS AND DISCUSSION

1. What ethical quidelines apply to the representation of parties before administrative agencies by a paralegal?

2. May paralegals advertise their availability to appear before administrative agencies?

3. Does the paralegal appearing before an administrative agency have a duty of candor to the agency?

Unauthorized Practice of Law—Completing Forms

There are few certainties in the area of ethics, for paralegals or in any profession. What qualifies as ethical conduct is in most cases based on state law and court interpretation applied to a set of facts. The citation listed below represents one legal opinion and is provided as a research starting point. Do not assume that the same rule applies in your jurisdiction. For the following:

- *Prepare a written statement based on your state law.*
- *Use your state bar association website as a starting point.*

As a recent graduate of a four-year degree program, you wish to get started in your career. You purchase a copy of Quicken Family Lawyer at your local computer store. You invite a group of friends and relatives to your place and offer to use the program to prepare powers of attorney and living wills (advance medical directives) for them. [*Unauthorized Practice of Law v. Parsons Tech.*, 179 F.3d 956 (5th Cir. 1999).] Are there any UPL issues? Explain.

CASES *for Discussion*

Federal Communications Commission v. Midwest Video Corporation

440 U.S. 689, 99 S.Ct. 1435 (1979)

7.1 FACTS

The Federal Communications Commission (FCC) is a federal administrative agency that is empowered to enforce the Communications Act of 1934. This Act, as amended, gives FCC power to regulate broadcasting of radio and television. The Act provides that "broadcasting shall not be deemed a common carrier." In *United States v. Midwest Video Corporation* [406 U.S. 649, 92 S.Ct. 1860 (1972)], the U.S. Supreme Court held that FCC also has the power to regulate cable television.

In May 1976, FCC promulgated rules requiring cable television operators that have 3,500 or more subscribers to (1) develop a 20-channel capacity, (2) make four channels available for use by public, educational,

local, governmental, and leased-access users (with one channel assigned to each), (3) make equipment available for those utilizing these public-access channels, and (4) limit the fees that cable operators could charge for their services.

ISSUE

Do these rules exceed the statutory authority of FCC?

Bowman Transportation, Inc. v. Arkansas–Best Freight System, Inc.

419 U.S. 281, 95 S.Ct. 438 (1974)

7.2 FACTS

The Interstate Commerce Commission (ICC) is a federal administrative agency empowered to regulate motor carriers involved in interstate commerce. Trucking companies must apply to ICC and obtain a license before they can offer trucking services on a route. The Interstate Commerce Act empowers ICC to grant an application for a license if it finds that (1) the applicant is fit, willing, and able to properly perform the service proposed, and (2) the service proposed is or will be required by the present or future "public convenience or necessity."

Thirteen motor carriers applied to offer trucking services between points in the Southwest and Southeast. After reviewing the applications and extensive written evidence (including the testimony of more than 900 witnesses), ICC granted licenses to three of the applicants. Arkansas–Best Freight Systems, Inc., a rejected applicant, brought an action seeking to annul ICC's order.

ISSUE

Should ICC's grant of the licenses be overturned on appeal?

United States v. Gel Spice Co., Inc.

601 F.Supp. 1205 (E.D.N.Y. 1984)

7.3 FACTS

Barry Engel owned and operated Gel Spice Co., Inc., which specialized in the importation and packaging of various food spices for resale. All of the spices that Gel Spice imported were unloaded at a pier in New York City and taken to a warehouse on McDonald Avenue. Storage and repackaging of the spices took place in the warehouse.

Between July 1976 and January 1979, the McDonald Avenue warehouse was inspected four times by investigators from the FDA. The investigators found live rats in bags of basil leaves, rodent droppings in boxes of chili peppers, and mammalian urine in bags of sesame seeds. The investigators produced additional evidence that showed that spices packaged and sold from the warehouse contained insects, rodent excreta pellets, rodent hair, and rodent urine. The FDA brought criminal charges against Engel and Gel Spice.

ISSUE

Are they guilty?

Donovan, Secretary of Labor v. Dewey

452 U.S. 594, 101 S.Ct. 2534 (1981)

7.4 FACTS

The Federal Mine Safety and Health Act of 1977 requires the secretary of labor to develop detailed mandatory health and safety standards to govern the operation of the nation's mines. The act provides that federal mine inspectors are to inspect underground mines at least four times a year and surface mines at least twice a year to ensure compliance with these standards and to make the following inspections to determine whether previously discovered violations have been corrected. The act also grants mine inspectors "a right of entry to, upon or through any coal or other mine" and states that "no advance notice of an inspection shall be provided to any person."

In July 1978, a federal mine inspector attempted to inspect quarries owned by Waukesha Lime and Stone Company (Waukesha) to determine whether all 25 safety and health violations uncovered during a prior inspection had been corrected. Douglas Dewey, Waukesha's president, refused to allow the inspector to inspect the premises without first obtaining a search warrant.

ISSUE

Are the warrantless searches of stone quarries authorized by the Mine Safety and Health Act constitutional? Did Dewey act ethically in refusing to allow the inspections?

FMC Corp. v. U.S. Department of Commerce

76 F.Supp. 471 (1992)

U.S. District Court, Eastern District of Penn.

Read the following case, excerpted from the district court's opinion. Review and brief the case. In your brief, answer the following questions.

1. Is the United States government subject to administrative regulations?

2. Where are federal regulations found?

3. What is the source of the federal regulations in this case?

4. What is CERCLA and who enacted it?

Newcomer, District Judge.

This action is brought pursuant to the Comprehensive Environmental Response, Compensation and Liability Act of 1980, as amended ("CERCLA"), and the Declaratory Judgment Act. Plaintiff FMC Corporation ("FMC") owned and operated, from 1963 to 1976, the Avtex site in Front Royal, Virginia ("the Facility"), a site which has been listed on the National Priorities List since 1986. FMC seeks indemnification from the defendants for some portion of its present and future response costs of response in performing removal actions and other response actions at the Facility. FMC bases its claim on the United States Government ("Government") activities during the period of January 1942 through 1945 relating to the operation of a rayon manufacturing facility at the Avtex site, and contends that these activities render the Government liable as an "owner," "operator," and/or "arranger" under section 107 of CERCLA.

During World War II, after the bombing of Pearl Harbor and the Japanese conquest of Asia, the United States suffered a loss of 90% of its crude rubber supply. An urgent need arose for natural rubber substitute to be used in manufacturing airplane tires, jeep tires, and other war-related items. The best rubber substitute available was high-tenacity rayon tire cord. The Facility was one of the major producers of high-tenacity rayon yarn, which was twisted and woven into high-tenacity rayon tire cord. FMC presented evidence at trial showing that during the World War II period, the Government participated in managing and controlling the Facility, which was then owned by American Viscose Corporation ("American Viscose"), requiring the Facility to manufacture increasing quantities of high-tenacity rayon yarn, which involved the treatment of hazardous materials and necessitated the disposal of

hazardous materials. FMC also presented evidence showing that the Government-owned "facilities" and equipment at the plant used in the treatment and disposal of hazardous materials.

The evidence included the following:

1. During World War II, the Government took over numerous plants which, for a multitude of reasons, failed to meet production requirements, including a plant producing high-tenacity rayon yarn. Beginning no later than 1943, the rayon tire cord program received constant attention from the highest officials of the War Production Board (WPB), as well as top officials of the War Department and other Government departments and agencies.

2. Once the WPB determined that there was a need for substantial expansion of the production capabilities at the Facility, Government personnel were assigned to facilitate and expedite construction. The rayon tire cord program, in general, and the implementation of the program at the Facility, in particular, required and received far more involvement, participation, and control by the Government than the vast majority of the production programs implemented during World War II.

3. The disposal or treatment of hazardous substance is inherent in the production of high-tenacity rayon yarn. The Government was familiar with the Facility's process for producing high-tenacity rayon yarn. The Government knew or should have known that the disposal or treatment of hazardous substances was inherent in the manufacture of high-tenacity rayon yarn and that its production requirements caused a significant increase in the

amount of hazardous substances generated and disposed of at the Facility.

The District Court concluded that the United States, through the actions and authority of the WPB and other departments, agencies, and instrumentalities of the United States Government, "operated" the Facility, from approximately January 1942 to at least November 1945, as defined by Section 101(20) of CERCLA. During the period the Government operated the Facility, wastes containing "hazardous substances," as defined by Section 101(14) of CERCLA, and as identified in 40 C.F.R. Part 302, Table 302.4 (1990), were "disposed of" at the Facility.

There has been a "release or threatened release" of hazardous substances from facilities which were owned by the United States. Such release or threatened release of hazardous substances has caused and will continue to cause FMC to incur "necessary costs of response" within the meaning of Section 107 of CERCLA, including without limitation the costs which FMC has incurred and will incur in monitoring, assessing, and evaluating the release or threatened release of hazardous substances and performing removal and/or remedial activities and taking other actions required or requested by the EPA, as well as attorneys' fees and expenses associated with this lawsuit.

Liability of an owner or operator of a facility as defined by § 107(a) for the cost of removal "is strict and joint and several." The United States Government as owner is responsible for costs resulting from responses to the release of hazardous substances.

And it is so ordered.

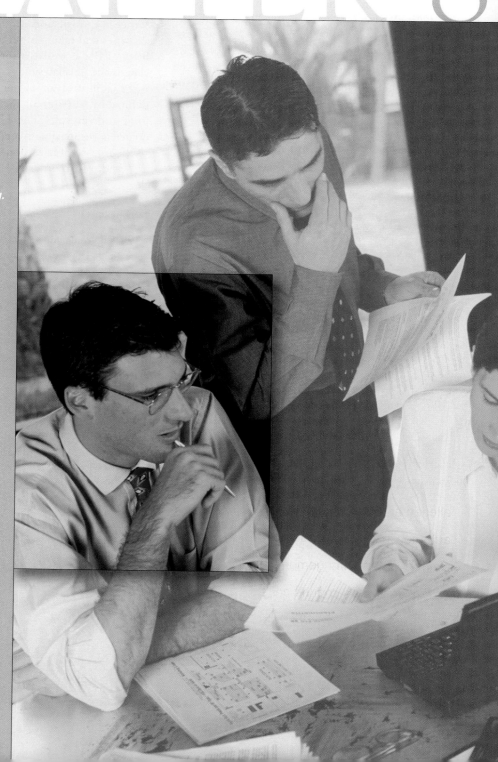

Civil Litigation

The law wherein, as in a magic mirror, we see reflected, not only our own lives, but the lives of all men that have been! When I think on this majestic theme, my eyes dazzle.

OLIVER WENDELL HOLMES, THE LAW, SPEECHES 17 (1913)

Introduction

The bringing, maintaining, and defense of a lawsuit comprise the **litigation process,** or **litigation. Civil litigation** involves legal action to resolve disputes between parties as contrasted with criminal litigation, which is brought by the government against a party accused of violating the law. The parties to the civil litigation may be individuals, businesses, or in some cases, government agencies. The fundamental process is the same, but the court and the procedure may vary.

Many lawyers specialize in civil litigation, in which a plaintiff sues a defendant to recover money damages or other remedy for the alleged harm caused by the defendant to the plaintiff. This may be an automobile accident case, a suit alleging a breach of a contract, a claim of patent infringement, or any of a myriad of other civil wrongs. A paralegal often spends considerable time researching, preparing documents, interviewing clients, and consulting with the attorney on civil litigation matters. This chapter discusses the process of civil litigation in detail.

THE LITIGATION PROCESS

The American litigation process is sometimes called an *adversarial system*. From the point of view of the layperson and some foreigners, it is a derogatory term. But "adversarial system" merely means that both of the litigants present their side of the case before a fact finder in the form of a jury or a judge. Each side tests the other side through questions before a neutral finder of fact who must determine the truth of the allegations made by each side. Also, with limited exception, by statute or court rule, each side typically pays its own cost of litigation, including attorney's fees and court costs irrespective of who wins or loses. In contrast, some foreign jurisdictions provide for the winner to be reimbursed for some of the cost of litigating the claim. Exhibit 8.1 is an example of a litigation timeline.

exhibit **8.1**   *Key events before trial.*

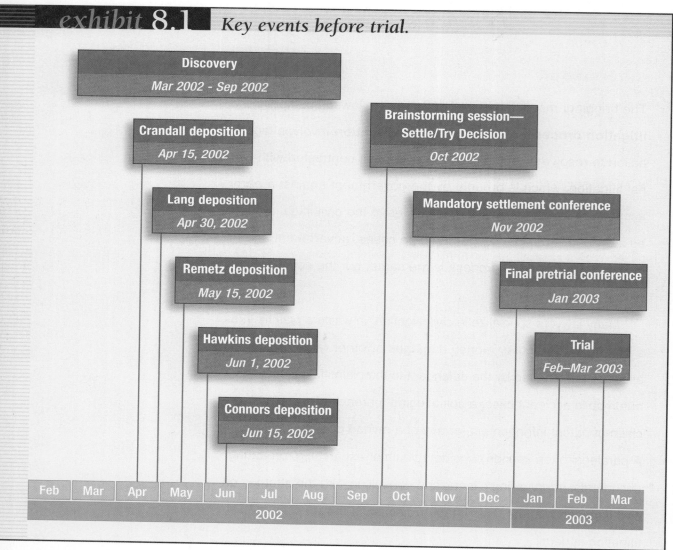

Prepared with TimeMap, courtesy of CaseSoft, a division of DecisionQuest.

Cases or Controversies

The first issue is: Is there an actual legal dispute? This is also referred to as *cases or controversies*. Courts will not attempt to answer hypothetical questions. If there is an actual controversy, the party seeking a remedy must be the one who has been wronged or aggrieved by the defendant.

Before a court may hear a case, it must have the authority or the "power" to hear the case. The judicial power of the federal courts comes from the U.S. Constitution. Cases not within the power of the federal courts are within the authority of the state courts, which derive their authority from the individual state constitutions.

Differences Between Civil and Criminal Actions

The most significant difference between a civil action and a criminal action is the burden of proof required. In a criminal case, every accused is presumed innocent and the prosecution must prove the defendant guilty "beyond a reasonable doubt." In civil actions, cases are decided in favor of the party that has the *preponderance of the evidence*, when one party has presented slightly more evidence than the other party. In a civil action, both sides place in turn their evidence on the scales of justice, and one side wins.

The result of a conviction in a criminal action is usually a loss of freedom, which could be incarceration—in jail or under house arrest—or probation, and the possible loss of property in the form of fines, forfeiture, and costs. Civil suits, in contrast, generally result in the payment of damages in the form of money, or a court prohibition, under the penalty of being held in **contempt of court,** against certain forms of action, called an **injunction,** or an order to do something. In a civil action, the parties each pay for their own lawyers. In criminal cases, the government pays the lawyers who prosecute the cases. Persons accused of crimes pay for their own private counsel or, if the accused can't afford to pay for an attorney, the government provides and pays for a lawyer.

PRELITIGATION

Many cases that are brought to a lawyer are resolved before institution of suit. This may involve as little effort as a letter from the lawyer advising the other party of a claim that results in settlement. For example, a collection letter from a lawyer may result in the debt being paid. It may involve correspondence between attorneys for the parties and telephone discussions that result in an agreement to settle negotiated between attorneys. A majority of cases in which litigation is commenced by the filing of pleadings are settled before actual trial of the case.

Key events before trial are shown in the timeline of Exhibit 8.1. The pretrial litigation process can be divided into the following major phases:

Cost–Benefit Analysis of a Lawsuit

The choice of whether to bring or defend a lawsuit should be analyzed like any other business decision. This includes performing a *cost–benefit analysis* of the lawsuit. For the plaintiff, it may be wise not to sue. For the defendant, it may be wise to settle.

FACTORS IN DECIDING WHETHER TO BRING OR SETTLE A LAWSUIT

☐ The probability of winning or losing.

☐ The amount of money to be won or lost.

☐ Lawyers' fees and other costs of litigation.

☐ Loss of time by managers and other personnel.

☐ The long-term effects on the relationship and reputations of the parties.

☐ The amount of prejudgment interest provided by law.

☐ The aggravation and psychological costs associated with a lawsuit.

☐ The unpredictability of the legal system and the possibility of error.

☐ Other factors peculiar to the parties and lawsuit.

1. Pleadings
2. Discovery
3. Pretrial motions
4. Settlement conference.

Pleadings

The paperwork that is filed with the court to initiate and respond to a lawsuit is referred to as the **pleadings.** The major pleadings are the complaint, the answer, the cross-complaint, and the reply.

Complaint and Summons

The party who is suing (the **plaintiff**) must file a **complaint,** also called a plaintiff's original petition or summons in some jurisdictions, with the proper court. The content and form of the complaint will vary depending on local court procedural rules. Many courts follow the federal practice of "notice pleading." Other state courts follow the traditional form requiring detailed allegations of the basis for the action. The complaint must name the parties to the lawsuit, allege the ultimate facts and law violated, and state the remedy desired, and the "prayer for relief" to be awarded by the court. The complaint can be as long as necessary, depending on the case's complexity. Exhibit 8.2 is a sample state trial court complaint filed in Pennsylvania. Exhibit 8.3 is a federal pleading. Exhibit 8.4 is a bilingual notice to plead a complaint.

Once a complaint has been filed with the court, the court issues a **summons,** a court order directing the **defendant** to appear in court and answer the complaint. A fundamental requirement is that notice be given to the defendant. A sheriff, another government official, or a private process server may serve the complaint and, where required, the summons on the defendant. In some cases, the defendant may be served by other means, such as by publication when the defendant cannot otherwise be found to be served personally.

Answer

The defendant must file an **answer** to the plaintiff's complaint. The defendant's answer is filed with the court and served on the plaintiff. In the answer, the defendant admits or denies the allegations contained in the plaintiff's complaint. A judgment will be entered against a defendant who admits to all of the allegations in the complaint. The case will proceed if the defendant denies all or some of the allegations.

If the defendant does not answer the complaint, a **default judgment** is entered against him or her. A default judgment establishes the defendant's liability. The plaintiff then has only to prove damages.

In addition to answering the complaint, a defendant's answer can assert *affirmative defenses.* For example, if a complaint alleges that the plaintiff was personally injured by the defendant, the defendant's answer could state that he or she acted in self-defense. Another affirmative defense would be an assertion

IN THE COURT OF COMMON PLEAS OF BUCKS COUNTY, PA.
CIVIL ACTION-LAW

COUNTY LINE FENCE CO., INC.   :   NO.
2051 W. County Line Road
Warrington, PA 18976   :

    V.   ATTORNEY I.D. #12204

WAYNE YARNELL   :
5707 Dunbar Court
Bensalem, PA 19020   :

<u>COMPLAINT</u>

1. Plaintiff is County Line Fence Company, Inc., a Pennsylvania corporation duly authorized to do business in Pennsylvania, with a place of business at 2051 W. County Line Road, Warrington, Bucks County, Pennsylvania.

2. Defendant, WAYNE YARNELL, is an adult individual residing at 5707 Dunbar Court, Bensalem, Pennsylvania.

3. On or about April 30, 2002, Defendant entered into a contract with the Plaintiff for a 140 ft. Bufftech fence to be installed on Defendant's property at 5707 Dunbar Court, Bensalem, PA 19020. (See Exhibit "A")

4. Plaintiff properly and adequately installed the fencing per the contract.

5. Defendant agreed to pay a total of $5,300.00 for the fence.

6. Demand was made upon the Defendant by Plaintiff for payment of the amount due for fencing and installation.

7. In spite of the demand for payment, Defendant has failed and refused, and continues to fail and refuse to pay Plaintiff the balance due.

WHEREFORE, Plaintiff demands judgment in the amount of $5,300.00, together with attorneys fees, costs of suit and any additional amounts as the court deems proper.
THOMAS F. GOLDMAN & ASSOCIATES

Thomas F. Goldman

Thomas F. Goldman, Esquire
Attorney for Plaintiff

exhibit 8.3   *Complaint filed in federal court.*

UNITED STATES DISTRICT COURT
FOR THE DISTRICT OF COLUMBIA

UNITED STATES OF AMERICA	) CASE NUMBER 1:01CV01660
	) JUDGE: Ricardo M. Urbina
	) DECK TYPE: General Civil
Plaintiff,	) DATE STAMP: 08/01/2002
	)
v.	)
	) Civ. No.
	) COMPLAINT FOR CIVIL
ENHANCED SERVICES BILLING, INC.	) PENALTIES, PERMANENT
BILLING CONCEPTS, INC.,	) INJUNCTION, CONSUMER
Delaware Corporations,	) REDRESS AND OTHER
both with their principal place of business at	) EQUITABLE RELIEF
411 John Smith Drive, Suite 200	)
San Antonio, Texas 78229,	)
	)
NEW CENTURY EQUITY HOLDINGS CORP.	)
A Delaware Corporation,	)
10101 Reunion Place, Suite 450	)
San Antonio, Texas 78216	)
	)
	)
	)
Defendants.	)

Plaintiff, the United States of America, acting upon notification and authorization to the Attorney General by the Federal Trade Commission ("FTC" or "Commission"), for its complaint alleges that:

1. Plaintiff brings this action under Sections 5(a)(1), 5(m)(1)(A), 9, 13(b), 16(a) and 19 of the Federal Trade Commission Act, 15 U.S.C. §§45(a)(1),

45(m)(1)(A), 49, 53(b), 56(a) and 57b, and the Telephone Disclosure and Dispute Resolution Act of 1992 ("TDDRA"), 15 U.S.C. §§ 5701 *et. seq.*, to obtain injunctive relief and consumer redress for violations of Section 5(a)(1) of the Federal Trade Commission Act, 15 U.S.C. § 45(a)(1), and to obtain monetary civil penalties, consumer redress and injunctive and other relief for Defendants' violations of the Commission's Trade Regulation Rule Pursuant to the Telephone Disclosure and Dispute Resolution Act of 1992 ("900-Number Rule"), 16 C.F.R. Part 308.

JURISDICTION AND VENUE

2. This court has jurisdiction over this matter under 28 U.S.C. §§ 1331, 1337(a), 1345 and 1355 and under 15 U.S.C. §§ 45(m)(1)(A), 49, 53(b), 56(a), 57b, 5721 and 5723. This action arises under 15 U.S.C. § 45(a)(1).

3. Venue in the District of Columbia is proper under 15 U.S.C. § 53(b) and 28 U.S.C. §§ 1391(b) and (c) and 1395(a).

DEFENDANTS

4. Defendant Enhanced Services Billing, Inc. is a Delaware corporation with its principal place of business at 7411 John Smith Drive, Suite 200, San Antonio, Texas 78229. Enhanced Services Billing, Inc. provides or provided billing and collection services for vendors who market Internet Web sites, psychic memberships, voice mail and hospital telephone and television rental, and other enhanced services. Enhanced Services Billing, Inc. was incorporated on March 17, 1994. Enhanced Services Billing, Inc. transacts or has transacted business in this district.

5. Defendant Billing Concepts, Inc. is a Delaware corporation with its principal place of business at 7411 John Smith Drive, Suite 200, San Antonio, Texas 78229. Billing Concepts, Inc. provides or provided billing and collection services for vendors who market . . .

exhibit **8.4**   *Bilingual notice to plead a complaint.*

IN THE COURT OF COMMON PLEAS
OF PHILADELPHIA COUNTY, PENNSYLVANIA
CIVIL ACTION LAW

KATHRYN KELSEY

vs.

KATHRYN CARROLL

: NO.

: ATTORNEY I.D. NO.

: COMPLAINT IN EQUITY

COMPLAINT – CIVIL ACTION

NOTICE

You have been sued in court. If you wish to defend against the claims set forth in the following pages, you must take action within twenty (20) days after this complaint and notice are served, by entering a written appearance personally or by attorney and filing in writing with the court your defenses or objections to the claims set forth against you. You are warned that if you fail to do so the case may proceed without you and a judgment may be entered against you by the court without further notice for any money claimed in the complaint or for any other claims or relief requested by the plaintiff. You may lose money or property or other rights important to you.

You should take this paper to your lawyer at once. If you do not have a lawyer or cannot afford one, go to or telephone the office set forth below to find out where you can get legal help.

Philadelphia Bar Association
Lawyer Referral and
Information Service
One Reading Center
Philadelphia, Pennsylvania 19107
215-238-1701

AVISO

Le han demandado a usted en la corte. Si usted quiere defenderse de estas demandas expuestas en las paginas siguientes, usted tiene veinte (20) dias de plazo al partir de la fecha de la demanda y la notificacion. Hace falta asentar una compancia escrita o en persona o con un abogado y entregar a la corte en forma escrita sus defensas o sus objeciones a las demandas en contra de su persona. Sea avisado que si usted no se defiende, la corta tomara medidas y puede continuar la demanda en contra suya sin previo aviso o notificacion. Ademas, la corte puede decidir a favor del demandante y requiere que usted cumpla con todas las provisiones de esta demanda. Usted puede perer dinero o sus propiedades u oetros derechos importantes para usted.

Lieva esta demanda a un abogado immediatamente. Si no tiene abogado o si no tiene el dinero suficiente de pagartal servicio, vaya en persona o llame por telefono a la oficina cuya direccion se encuentra escrita abajo para averiguar donde se puede conseguir asistencia legal.

Asociacion de Licenciados de Filadelfia
Servicio de Referencia e
Informacion Legal
One Reading Center
Filadelfia, Pennsylvania 19107
215-238-1701

that the plaintiff's lawsuit is barred because the **statute of limitations** (time within which to bring the lawsuit) has expired. Exhibit 8.5 is a sample answer in state court, and Exhibit 8.6 recaps the pleadings process.

Cross-Complaint and Reply

A defendant who believes that he or she has been injured by the plaintiff can file a **cross-complaint,** or counterpetition as it is called in some jurisdictions, against the plaintiff in addition to an answer. In the cross-complaint, the defendant (now the *cross-complainant*) sues the plaintiff (now the *cross-defendant*) for damages or some other remedy. The original plaintiff must file a **reply** (answer) to the cross-complaint. The reply—which can include affirmative defenses—must be filed with the court and served on the original defendant.

Intervention and Consolidation

If other persons have an interest in a lawsuit, they may step in and become parties to the lawsuit. This is called an **intervention.** For instance, a bank that has made a secured loan on a piece of real estate can intervene in a lawsuit between parties who are litigating ownership of the property.

If several plaintiffs have filed separate lawsuits stemming from the same fact situation against the same defendant, the court can initiate a **consolidation** of the cases into one case if it would not cause undue prejudice to the parties. Suppose, for example, that a commercial airplane crashes, killing and injuring many people. The court could consolidate all of the lawsuits against the defendant airplane company.

Statute of Limitations

For some crimes, such as murder, there is no limitation on the time in which a defendant can be charged. In civil actions, however, the plaintiff must bring suit within a certain period of time after the action that gives rise to the complaint or lose the right to use the courts to enforce the civil right and remedy.

A statute of limitations establishes the period during which a plaintiff must bring a lawsuit against a defendant. If a lawsuit is not filed within this period, the plaintiff loses his or her right to sue. A statute of limitations usually begins to "run" at the time the plaintiff first has the right to sue the defendant (e.g., when the accident happens, or when the breach of contract occurs). Depending on state law, it also may begin to run when the plaintiff knows or should have known of the defendant's wrongful action that gives rise to a cause of action. In the case of minors, the statute may not begin to run—regardless of the time of discovery of the accrual of the cause of action—until the minor reaches the age of majority.

Federal and state governments have established statutes of limitations for each type of lawsuit. Most are from one to four years, depending on the type of lawsuit. For example, a one-year statute of limitations is common for ordinary negligence actions. Thus, if on July 1, 2000, Otis negligently causes an automobile accident in which Cha-Yen is injured, Cha-Yen has until July 1, 2001, to bring a negligence lawsuit against Otis. If she waits longer than that, she loses her right to sue him.

THE COURTHOUSE TEAM

Sheriff

In most jurisdictions, the sheriff's office performs several tasks related to the administration of court proceedings. In civil cases, the sheriff may be the designated official for serving all complaints and carrying out additional components of the litigation process. In criminal court cases, sheriffs may act as guards and escorts for prisoners and maintain the courthouse holding facility. Increasingly, sheriffs also provide courthouse security for the building and the individual courtrooms.

exhibit **8.5**   *Sample state answer.*

DATZ and GOLDBERG

BY: MARC C. BENDO, ESQUIRE

IDENTIFICATION NO.   80075   ATTORNEY FOR   DEFENDANT

1311 SPRUCE STREET

PHILADELPHIA, PENNSYLVANIA 19107

(215) 545-7960

COUNTY LINE FENCE CO., INC.   *COURT OF COMMON PLEAS*
2051 W. County Line Road
Warrington, PA 18976
                                                 BUCKS COUNTY DIVISION

vs.   *TERM*

WAYNE YARNALL
5707 Dunbar Court
Bensalem, PA 19020   *NO.* 99004879-23-1

ANSWER OF DEFENDANT, WAYNE YARNALL, TO PLAINTIFF'S CIVIL ACTION
WITH NEW MATTER

1. Denied. Plaintiff is without knowledge or information sufficient to form a belief as to the truth or falsity of this
   averment. Accordingly, same is denied with strict proof
   demanded at time of Trial.

2. Admitted. By way of further answer, however, Plaintiff's
   Civil Action has misspelled Defendant's proper name, which is
   Wayne Yarnall.

3. Denied. These allegations constitute conclusions of law to
   which no response is required pursuant to the applicable
   Pennsylvania Rules of Civil Procedure . . .

INFORMATION TECHNOLOGY

E-FILINGS IN COURT

When litigation ensues, the clients, lawyers, and judges involved in the case usually are buried in paper—pleadings, interrogatories, documents, motions to the court, briefs, and memoranda; the list goes on and on. By the time a case is over, reams of paper are stored in dozens, if not hundreds, of boxes. Further, court appearances, no matter how small the matter, must be made in person. For example, lawyers often wait hours for a 10-minute scheduling or other conference with the judge. Additional time is required to drive to and from court, which in an urban area may amount to hours.

Some forward-thinking judges and lawyers envision a day when the paperwork and hassle are reduced or eliminated in a "virtual courthouse." The technology currently is available for implementing electronic filing—*e-filing*—of pleadings, briefs, and other documents related to a lawsuit. E-filing would include using CD-ROMs for briefs, scanning evidence and documents into a computer for storage and retrieval, and e-mailing correspondence and documents to the court and the opposing counsel. Scheduling and other conferences with the judge or opposing counsel could be held via telephone conferences and email.

Some courts have instituted e-filing already. For example, in the Manhattan bankruptcy court, e-filing is now mandatory. Other courts around the world are doing the same. Companies such as Microsoft and Lexis-Nexis have developed systems to manage e-filings of court documents.

Court personnel in some venues are resisting the "electronic courthouse" because they perceive it as a means of reducing personnel needs and court funding. Some lawyers are resisting e-filing because they have to learn how to deal with new technology and because it might reduce their billable hours when they no longer get paid for shuffling paper or sitting and waiting to appear before a judge. Eventually, though, courts and lawyers will be brought into this new technological age.

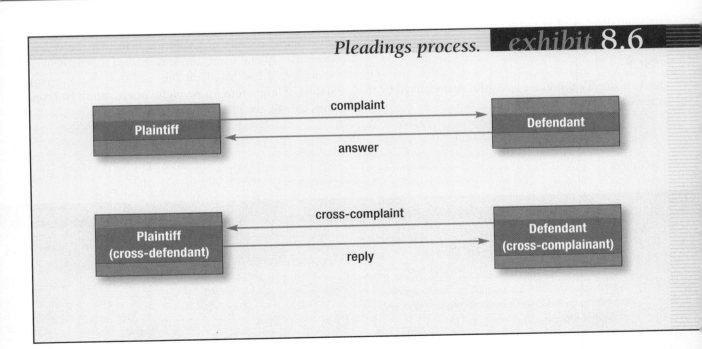

Pleadings process. **exhibit 8.6**

Norgart v. the Upjohn Company

21 Cal.4th 383, 87 Cal.Rptr.2nd 453 (1999)   Supreme Court of California

FACTS

Kristi Norgart McBride lived with her husband in Santa Rosa, California. Kristi suffered from manic-depressive mental illness (now called bipolar disorder). In this disease, the person cycles between manic (ultrahappy, expansive, extrovert) episodes to depressive episodes. The disease is often treated with prescription drugs. In April 1984, Kristi attempted suicide. A psychiatrist prescribed an antianxiety drug. In May 1985, Kristi attempted suicide again by overdosing on drugs. The doctor prescribed Halcion, a hypnotic drug, and added Darvocet-N, a mild narcotic analgesic. On October 16, 1985, after descending into a severe depression, Kristi committed suicide by overdosing on Halcion and Darvocet-N.

On October 16, 1991, exactly six years after Kristi's death, Leo and Phyllis Norgart, Kristi's parents, filed a lawsuit against the Upjohn Company, the maker of Halcion, for wrongful death based on Upjohn's alleged failure to warn of the unreasonable dangers of taking Halcion. The trial court granted Upjohn's motion for summary judgment based on the fact that the one-year statute of limitations for wrongful death actions had run. The court of appeals reversed, and Upjohn appealed to the Supreme Court of California.

ISSUE

Is the plaintiff's action for wrongful death barred by the one-year statute of limitations?

IN THE LANGUAGE OF THE COURT

Mosk, Justice.

Statute of limitations is the collective term commonly applied to a great number of acts that prescribe the periods beyond which a plaintiff may not bring a cause of action. It has a purpose to protect defendants from the stale claims of dilatory plaintiffs. It has a related purpose to stimulate plaintiffs to assert fresh claims against defendants in a diligent fashion. Inasmuch as it necessarily fixes a definite period of time, it operates conclusively across the board and not flexibly on a case-by-case basis.

Under the statute of limitations, a plaintiff must bring a cause of action from wrongful death within one year of accrual. The limitations period is thus defined by the Legislature. That means that the date of accrual of a cause of action for wrongful death is the date of death. Under the statute of limitations, the Norgarts had to bring the cause of action for wrongful death within one year of accrual. They did not do so. Pursuant to this rule, the Norgarts were too late, exactly five years too late.

DECISION AND REMEDY

The supreme court of California held that the defendant, the Upjohn Company, was entitled to judgment as a matter of law based on the fact that the one-year statute of limitations for wrongful death actions had run, thus barring the plaintiff's lawsuit. Reversed.

Questions

1. What is the public policy behind having statutes of limitations? What is the public policy against having such statutes? Which policy should dominate and why?

2. Was it ethical for the Upjohn Company to avoid facing the merits of the lawsuit by asserting the one-year statute of limitations?

3. What are the business implications for having statutes of limitations?

Discovery

The legal process provides for a detailed pretrial procedure called **discovery.** During discovery, both parties engage in various activities to learn facts of the case from the other party and witnesses prior to trial. Discovery serves several functions, including preventing surprise, allowing parties to prepare thoroughly for trial, preserving evidence, saving court time, and promoting the settlement of cases. The major forms of discovery are depositions, interrogatories, production of documents, and physical and mental examination.

Depositions

A **deposition** is the oral testimony given, under oath, by a party or witness prior to trial. The person giving the deposition is called the **deponent.** The *parties* to the lawsuit must give their depositions, if the other party calls them to do so. The deposition of a **witness** can be given voluntarily or pursuant to a **subpoena** (court order). The deponent can be required to bring documents to the deposition.

Depositions are used to preserve evidence (e.g., if the deponent is deceased, ill, or otherwise not available at trial) and to impeach testimony given by witnesses at trial. Most depositions are taken at the office of one of the attorneys. The deponent is placed under oath and then asked oral questions by one or both of the attorneys. The questions and answers are recorded in written form by a court reporter. Depositions also can be videotaped. The deponent is given an opportunity to correct his or her answers prior to signing the deposition, depending on local practice or rules.

Interrogatories

Interrogatories are written questions submitted by one party to a lawsuit to another party. The questions can be very detailed, as illustrated by the sample interrogatory in Exhibit 8.7. In addition, in some jurisdictions it might be necessary to attach certain documents to the answers. A party is required to answer the interrogatories in writing within a specified time period (e.g., 60 to 90 days). An attorney usually helps with the preparation of the answers. The answers are signed under oath.

Production of Documents

Often, particularly in complex business cases, a substantial portion of the lawsuit may be based on information contained in documents (e.g., memoranda, correspondence, company records). One party to a lawsuit may request that the other party produce all documents that are relevant to the case

Can a Paralegal Be Deposed?

A Pennsylvania case has held that a certified paralegal who was also a registered nurse could be deposed as to what she observed during an independent medical examination (IME) of the client because she might be called to impeach the doctor performing the IME. The court did state, however, that the attorney's work-product shield would apply and the deposition would be limited to the paralegal's factual observation of the IME. [*Dienes v. Markey,* PICS case no. 99-0247 (C.P. York Feb. 8, 1999)]

The Appomatox Courthouse in Appomatox, Virginia, site of General Robert E. Lee's surrender on April 9, 1865.

Video Deposition Know-How

Ann T. Greeley, Ph.D., DecisionQuest

While transcribed and video depositions have many similarities, there are a number of important skills involved in effective video deposition testimony that are not involved in a transcribed deposition. The most important thing to remember is that the "camera doesn't forget"! This fact has three important implications:

You're on Stage

Witnesses must look credible at all times—not only during responses, but also between questions, between answers, and during any delays. When giving a video deposition, a witness must develop a level of self-awareness beyond that which is required for a transcribed deposition.

Nonverbal Behaviors Are Key

Nonverbal behaviors are extremely important in communicating credibility, and due to the nature of the camera, these behaviors are magnified. Therefore, distracting behaviors must be eliminated or minimized. Straightening a tie, twirling a piece of hair, adjusting glasses, or shifting around in a chair are signs of nervousness. Nervousness can be interpreted as defensiveness or as having something to hide. A calm and credible presence is crucial in a video deposition.

Possible Trial Testimony

In some states, video depositions can be used in lieu of live testimony even if the witness is present in the courtroom. As such, you need to prepare the witness as you would for testimony in front of a jury. Substantive preparation is extremely important for video depositions because unprepared deponents not only make errors, but they also appear nervous. As noted earlier, the camera exaggerates this appearance.

Given these aspects of video depositions, keep in mind the following points for effective testimony.

1. Be aware of nonverbal communication.
2. Conservative clothing is a must for a video deposition.
3. Keep the background simple.
4. Be aware that time has greater significance in a video deposition.
5. Beware of technical problems and plan ahead.

Overall, the video deposition presents distinct challenges for attorneys and witnesses. We find the best way to assure that a video deposition is successful is to conduct the witness preparation on videotape, before the actual deposition takes place. The attorney and a communications specialist can provide feedback to the witness long before the session is scheduled. In this way, you can be assured that the witness's performance will be one you and the camera won't want to forget.

prior to trial. This is called **production of documents.** If the documents sought are too voluminous to be moved or are in permanent storage, or if moving the documents would disrupt the ongoing business of the party who is to produce them, the requesting party may be required to examine the documents at the other party's premises. Exhibit 8.8 is an example of a request for production of documents.

Physical and Mental Examination

In cases that concern the physical or mental condition of a party, a court can order the party to submit to certain physical or mental examinations to determine the extent of the alleged injuries. This would occur, for example, where the plaintiff has been injured in an accident and is seeking damages for physical injury and mental distress.

Sample interrogatory.   *exhibit* 8.7

THOMAS F. GOLDMAN & ASSOCIATES
138 N. State Street
Newtown, PA 18940
(123) 555-1234

KATHRYN KELSEY	: COURT OF COMMON PLEAS
	: PHILADELPHIA COUNTY
	:
vs.	: APRIL TERM, 2002
	:
KATHRYN CARROLL	: NO. 1234

INTERROGATORIES ADDRESSED TO KATHRYN KELSEY

You are to answer the following interrogatories under oath or verification pursuant to the Pa. R.C.P. 4005 and 4006 within thirty days from the service hereof. The answering party is under a duty to supplement responses to any questions with information discovered after these answers were given.

Also, a party or expert witness must amend prior responses if he/she obtains information upon the basis of which:

(a) he/she knows the response was incorrect when made; or

(b) he/she knows that the response, though correct when made, is no longer true.

The words "your vehicle" as used in the following interrogatories are defined as the motor vehicle you were operating at the time of the accident.

When a Standard Interrogatory uses the word: "identify", the party served with the Interrogatory must identify all documents, things and persons known to that party or to that party's attorney, and the address of all persons identified MUST be set forth.

Where a Standard Interrogatory is marked with an asterisk (*), a Request for Production may accompany the Interrogatory.

STANDARD INTERROGATORIES PURSUANT TO PHILADELPHIA RULE OF CIVIL PROCEDURE *4005

INJURIES AND DISEASES ALLEGED

1. State in detail the injuries or diseases that you allege that you suffered as a result of the accident referred to in the Complaint.

MEDICAL TREATMENT & REPORTS*

2. If you received medical treatment or examinations (including x-rays) because of injuries or diseases you suffered as a result of the accident, identify:

   (a) Each hospital at which you were treated or examined;

   (b) The dates on which each such treatment or examination at a hospital was rendered and the charges by the hospital for each;

   (c) Each doctor or practitioner by whom you were treated or examined;

exhibit 8.7   *Sample interrogatory, continued.*

(d) The dates on which each such treatment or examination by a doctor or practitioner was rendered and the charges for each;

(e) All reports regarding any medical treatment or examinations, setting forth the author and date of such reports.

OTHER EXPENSES*

3. If you have incurred any bills or expenses in connection with the injuries or diseases which you suffered because of the accident referred to in the Complaint, identify each such bill or expense, the service for which the bill or expense was incurred, and the identity of the person who rendered the bill or who was involved in the expense.

PRIOR OR SUBSEQUENT INJURIES OR DISEASES

4. Either prior to or subsequent to the accident referred to in the Complaint, have you ever suffered any injuries or diseases in those portions of the body claimed by you to have been affected by the accident referred to in the Complaint?
    If so, identify:

(a) The injuries or diseases you suffered;

(b) The date and place of any accident, if such an injury or disease was caused by an accident;

(c) All hospitals, doctors or practitioners who rendered treatment or examinations because of any such injuries or diseases;

(d) Anyone against whom a claim was made, and the Court, term or number of any claim or lawsuit that was filed, in connection with any such injuries or diseases.

EARNINGS BEFORE THE ACCIDENT*

5. For the period of three years immediately preceding the date of the accident referred to in the complaint, state:

(a) The name and address of each of your employers or, if you were self-employed during that period, each of your business addresses and the name of the business while self-employed;

(b) The dates of commencement and termination of each of your periods of employment or self-employment;

(c) A detailed description of the nature of your occupation in each employment or self-employment;

(d) The amount of income from employment and self-employment for each year. (Attach your federal income tax return for each year.)

EARNINGS AFTER THE ACCIDENT*

6. If you have engaged in one or more gainful occupations subsequent to the date of the accident referred to in the Complaint, state:

(a) The name and address of each of your employers or if you were self-employed, each of your business addresses and the name of the business while self-employed;

(b) The dates of commencement and termination of each of your periods of employment or self-employment;

(c) A detailed description of the nature of your occupation in each employment or self-employment;

(d) The wage, salary or rate of earnings received by you in each employment or self-employment. (Attach your federal income tax return for each year subsequent to the accident);

(e) The dates of all absences from your occupation resulting from the injuries and diseases suffered in this accident. Set forth the amount of any earnings or other benefits lost by you because of such absences.

LIMITATIONS OF DUTIES AND ACTIVITIES AFTER THE ACCIDENT

7. State whether, as a result of this accident, you have been unable to perform any of your customary occupational duties or social or other activities in the same manner as prior to the accident, stating with particularity (a) the duties and/or activities you have been unable to perform, (b) the periods of time you have been unable to perform, and (c) the names and last known addresses of all persons who have knowledge thereof.

WITNESSES AND THOSE WITH KNOWLEDGE OF ACCIDENT

8. (a) Identify each person who (1) was a witness to the accident through sight or hearing and/or (2) has knowledge of facts concerning the happening of the accident or conditions or circumstances at the scene of the accident prior to, after, or at the time of the accident.

    (b) With respect to each person identified in the answer to the interrogatory above, state that person's exact location and activity at the time of the accident.

STATEMENTS

9. Have you or has anyone acting on your behalf obtained from any person any statement (as defined by the Rules of Civil Procedure) concerning this action or its subject matter?
    If so, identify:

    (a) Each such person;

    (b) When, where, by whom and to whom each statement was made, and whether it was reduced to writing or otherwise recorded;

    (c) Any person who has custody of any such statements that were reduced to writing or otherwise recorded.

STATEMENTS MADE BY PARTY TO WHOM INTERROGATORY IS ADDRESSED*

10. Have you given any statement (as defined by the Rules of Civil Procedure) concerning this action or its subject matter?
    If so, identify:

    (a) Each person to whom a statement was given;

    (b) When and where each statement was given;

    (c) Any person who has custody of any such statements that were reduced to writing or otherwise recorded.

DEMONSTRATIVE EVIDENCE*

11. Do you or does anyone acting on your behalf know of the existence of any photographs, motion pictures, video recordings, maps, diagrams or models of the site of the accident, the parties or any other subject matter involved in this action?
    If the answer is in the affirmative, identify:

    (a) The date(s) when they were made and what they are;

    (b) The name and address of the person making them;

    (c) The subject that each represents or portrays.

TRIAL PREPARATION MATERIAL

12. Have you or has anyone on your behalf conducted any investigations of the accident which is the subject matter of the complaint?
    If the answer is in the affirmative, identify:

exhibit **8.7**   *Sample interrogatory, continued.*

(a) Each person, and the employer of each person, who conducted any investigation;

(b) The dates of the investigations;

(c) All notes, reports or other documents prepared during or as a result of the investigations and the identity of the persons who have possession thereof.

EXPERTS*

13. (a) State the name and address of each person whom you expect to call as an expert witness at trial and state the subject matter on which the expert is expected to testify.

(b) For each such expert, have the expert state the substance of the facts and opinions to which the expert is expected to testify and summarize the grounds for each such opinion.

(c) Set forth the qualifications of each expert, listing the schools attended, years of attendance, degrees received, and experience in any particular field of specialization or expertise.

INSURANCE

14. (a) State whether you are covered by any type of insurance including any excess or umbrella insurance, in connection with this accident.

If the answer is in the affirmative, state the following with respect to each policy:

(b) The name of the insurance carrier which issued each policy of insurance;

(c) The name insured under each policy and the policy number;

(d) The type of each policy and the effective dates;

(e) The amount of coverage provided for injury to each person, for each occurrence, and in the aggregate for each policy;

(f) Each exclusion, if any, in the policy which is applicable to any claim thereunder and the reasons why you or the company claims the exclusion is applicable.

(g) Whether you have made a claim under the policy and if so set forth the nature of the claim, the amount recovered and the date of recovery.

NONSTANDARD INTERROGATORIES

15. State your full name, address, date of birth and social security number.

16. Have you ever used any names other than the one listed above? If yes, state all names used and when each additional name was used.

17. To the extent known to you, your attorney or other representative, set forth the name and home and business address of the following:

(a) Those who actually saw the accident;

(b) Those who were present at or near the scene at the time of the accident;

(c) Those who have any knowledge of, or information concerning the circumstances and manner in which the accident occurred or the nature of the injuries sustained in the accident.

18. At the time of the accident or immediately thereafter, did you have any conversation with or make any statements to any of the parties or witnesses, or did any of them make any statements to you or in your presence? If so state the substance of any such conversation or statement and in whose presence it took place.

19. If you, your representative, attorney, consultant, surety, indemnitor, insurer or agent obtained a statement or statements as defined in Pennsylvania Rules of Civil Procedure 4003.4(1) and (2), concerning this action and/or its subject matter from any party to this action, any witness, or any person not a party to this action then state:

    (a) The name and address of the person who gave such statement, including the name and address of each person's employer;

    (b) The date each statement was given;

    (c) The name and address of the person who obtained each statement;

    (d) The date when each statement was obtained;

    (e) The place where each statement was obtained;

    (f) Whether each statement is written, signed by the person making it or if there is a stenographic, mechanical, electrical or other recording, or a transcription thereof;

    (g) The names and addresses of all persons and/or entities who presently have custody of each original statement identified in your answer above;

    (h) Please attach to your Answer to Interrogatories a copy or like reproduction of each statement identified in your answer above.

20. State the exact date, time and place the accident occurred and describe in detail how you claim the accident occurred.

21. State:

    (a) The exact portion of the highway where the accident occurred;

    (b) The positions of the respective vehicles prior to impact;

    (c) Distance from you when you first observed the other vehicle;

    (d) Positions of vehicles after impact;

    (e) What part of your vehicle came in contact with what part of the other vehicle;

    (f) The weather and road conditions at the time of the accident;

    (g) If weather was inclement, state whether windshield wipers were in use at the time of the collision;

    (h) What type of traffic signals controlled the place where the accident occurred;

    (i) Speed of all vehicles immediately prior to impact;

    (j) Lighting conditions at time of accident, including whether any artificial light illuminated place of accident. If there were artificial lights, state type and distance from accident.

22. State the name and address of the owner of the vehicle in which you were traveling.

23. State the registration number, year, make and model of above vehicle.

24. With regard to the vehicle listed above, state the name, address, age and driver's license number of operator of vehicle.

25. State whether the vehicle or any part thereof in which you were traveling at the time of the accident was defective, or not in safe working order. Identify defects, if any:

26. State whether repairs were made to the vehicle after accident. If yes, identify name and address of person/business making repairs, date and type of work performed. Attach copy of repair bill.

27. State where you were coming from and where you were going at time of the accident.

28. State how long you had been traveling and approximately how many miles traveled prior to the accident.

29. State whether you had been at the location of the accident previously; if yes, approximately how many times.

30. State whether you had consumed any alcohol, medication or drugs within 24 hours of the accident. If so, identify substance and when, where, and amount consumed.

31. State whether you have a prescription for any corrective lenses. If so, identify type of prescription and whether you were wearing same at time of accident.

32. Please identify your driver's license number and the State which issued the license. Identify any restriction on your license.

exhibit **8.7**   *Sample interrogatory, continued.*

33. If your driver's license has ever been revoked, suspended or withdrawn, state where, when and for what offense.

34. State when you first experienced pain following accident.

35. State nature of pain experienced.

36. State name and address of family physician.

37. State name and address of all physicians, clinics, hospitals, therapists, etc. where you sought consultation or treatment within five (5) years prior or subsequent to this accident and reason for consultation and/or treatment.

38. Did you know any of the witnesses or the individuals in any of the other vehicles involved in this accident or any of the witnesses to the occurrences?

    (a) If answer is yes, state name(s) of individual(s) you knew, how long you knew the individual(s) and the nature of your relationship with the individual(s) named.

    (b) As to the individual(s) named in 38(a) who were in another vehicle involved in this accident, did you know the individual(s) would be traveling near you on the highway?

39. As to each party traveling in the vehicle you were in, state your relationship (i.e., friend, relative, stranger, etc.).

40. As to each party named in #39, state how long you have known this person.

41. As to each witness, state your relationship (i.e., friend, relative, stranger, etc.) and where each witness was at the time of the accident.

42. State whether or not you knew or had ever before seen any of the occupants of the other vehicle(s) involved in this accident. If yes, state:

    (a) Who it is you knew or had seen prior to this accident;

    (b) How you know the person(s) identified;

    (c) For what length of time prior to the accident you knew this person(s);

    (d) Whether you knew the individual(s) named above would be traveling near you;

    (e) Whether you were traveling to the same location for the same purpose.

43. State whether or not you reside in a household where a relative owns a motor vehicle. Identify this individual and his/her relationship to you.

    (a) Identify the vehicle owned by year, make, model, license and vehicle identification number.

    (b) State whether this vehicle is insured. If yes, attach a copy of the declaration page indicating whether or not the limited tort option was selected.

44. State whether or not the police were called to the locale of the accident. If yes, state:

    (a) Who called police;

    (b) Whether or not the police responded to the call;

    (c) How long it took the police to respond;

    (d) The name(s) and badge(s) of the officer(s);

    (e) Whether you left the location prior to the police arrival;

    (f) Whether you provided your name to the police;

    (g) What, if anything, you told police;

    (h) Whether or not a police report was prepared. If answer is yes, please attach a copy of the police report and/or identify police department involved and police reference number for accident report.

45. If you were taken to the hospital for treatment, state how and by whom you were transported.

THOMAS F. GOLDMAN & ASSOCIATES
BY: _____

THOMAS F. GOLDMAN & ASSOCIATES
138 N. State Street
Newtown, PA 18940
(123) 555-1234

KATHRYN KELSEY	:	COURT OF COMMON PLEAS
	:	PHILADELPHIA COUNTY
vs.	:	APRIL TERM, 2002
KATHRYN CARROLL	:	NO. 1259

REQUEST TO PRODUCE UNDER PA R.C.P. 4033 and 4009
<u>DIRECTED TO PLAINTIFFS</u>

Within thirty (30) days of service, please produce for inspection and copying at the office of THOMAS F. GOLDMAN & ASSOCIATES, 138 North State Street, Newtown, Pennsylvania 18940, the following:

1. All photographs and/or diagrams of the area involved in this accident or occurrence, the locale or surrounding area of the site of this accident or occurrence, or any other matter or things involved in this accident or occurrence.

2. All property damage estimates rendered for any object belonging to the Plaintiffs which was involved in this accident or occurrence.

3. All property damage estimates rendered for any object belonging to the Defendant which was involved in this accident or occurrence.

4. All statements concerning this action or its subject matter previously made by any party or witness. The statements referred to here are defined by Pa. R.C.P. 4003.4.

5. All transcriptions and summaries of all interviews conducted by anyone acting on behalf of the Plaintiff or Plaintiff's insurance carrier of any potential witness and/or person(s) who has any knowledge of the accident or its surrounding circumstances.

6. All inter-office memorandum between representative of Plaintiffs' insurance carrier or memorandum to Plaintiffs' insurance carrier's file concerning the manner in which the accident occurred.

7. All inter-office memorandum between representative of Plaintiffs' insurance carrier or memorandum to Plaintiffs' insurance carrier's file concerning the injuries sustained by the Plaintiffs.

8. A copy of any written accident report concerning this accident or occurrence signed by or prepared by Plaintiff for Plaintiffs' insurance carrier or Plaintiff's employers.

9. A copy of the face sheet of any policy of insurance providing coverage to Plaintiffs for the claim being asserted by Plaintiff in this action.

10. All bills, reports, and records from any and all physicians, hospitals, or other health care providers concerning the injuries sustained by the Defendants from this accident or occurrence.

11. All photographs and/or motion pictures of any and all surveillance of Defendant performed by anyone acting on behalf of Plaintiff, Plaintiffs' insurer and/or Plaintiffs' attorney.

12. All photographs taken of Plaintiffs' motor vehicle which depict any damage to said vehicle which was sustained as a result of this accident.

13. All photographs taken of defendant's motor vehicle which depict any damage to said vehicle which was sustained as a result of this accident.

14. Any and all reports, writings, memorandum, Xeroxed cards and/or other writings, lists or compilations of the Defendant and others with similar names as indexed by the Metropolitan Index Bureau, Central Index Bureau or other Index Bureau in possession of the Plaintiffs or the Plaintiffs' insurance carrier.

Pretrial Motions

Parties to a lawsuit can make several pretrial motions to try to dispose of all or part of a lawsuit prior to trial. The two major pretrial motions are the motion for judgment on the pleadings, and the motion for summary judgment.

Motion for Judgment on the Pleadings

Either party can make a **motion for judgment on the pleadings** once the pleadings are complete. This motion alleges that if all of the facts presented in the pleadings are true, the party making the motion would win the lawsuit when the proper law is applied to these facts. In deciding this motion, the judge cannot consider any facts outside the pleadings.

Motion for Summary Judgment

The trier of the fact (i.e., the jury, or, if no jury, the judge) determines *factual issues*. A **motion for summary judgment** asserts that there are no factual disputes to be decided by the jury and that the judge should apply the relevant

Ethical PERSPECTIVE *Calendars Ordered Into the Daylight*

Most executives keep some form of calendar that contains lists of things to do, appointments, and "what I've done" notes. If a calendar contains business-related information exclusively, it is discoverable by the prosecution in a criminal case. If the calendar is personal in nature, its owner can shield it from discovery under the Fifth Amendment's self-incrimination privilege. What if an executive's calendar contains both business and personal information? Is it discoverable or not? The court had to decide this issue in the following case.

John Doe I and John Doe II are two executives of a company that is the subject of an ongoing grand jury investigation into possible illegal price-fixing in a certain industry. Both executives kept calendars that contained both business and personal notes. The grand jury sought production of the calendars, but the executives refused to produce them, alleging Fifth Amendment protection. After examining the evidence, the district court determined that the calendars were corporate in nature and ordered them disclosed. The court also issued an order holding the executives in contempt for their failure to turn over their calendars. The executives appealed.

The court of appeals decided that where a calendar contains a mixture of business and personal notes, a mul-

tifactor approach should be applied to determine if they are discoverable. The court will look at ownership, preparation, access, content, purpose, and ratio of business to personal entries in determining whether a document is corporate or personal in nature. This balancing test asks, "What is the essential nature of the document?" No single factor is dispositive, and the final determination whether the calendar is business or personal in nature is a question of fact.

Applying this multifactor approach to the instant case, the court found that the executives' calendars contained a majority of business-related entries. There were notes concerning business travel, job-related "to do" lists, and entries about compensation at work. The court found that the executives' self-serving affidavits to the contrary were not credible. The court of appeals stated, "In the totality of these circumstances, the district court's conclusion that the daytimers were prepared, maintained, and used for business, not personal purposes, is not clearly erroneous."

The court held that the executives' calendars were discoverable and were not protected by the Fifth Amendment's privilege against self-incrimination. [In Re *Grand Jury Proceedings,* 55 F.3d 1012 (1995)]

Email has made it faster and easier to communicate with others, whether for business or personal reasons. Email messages also have become a source of evidence to be used at both criminal and civil trials. Consider the following case.

Karen Strauss worked for Microsoft Corporation as an assistant editor for the *Microsoft Systems Journal*. When she was passed over for a promotion and subsequently dismissed from her job, she brought a sex-discrimination case against Microsoft. She alleged that her supervisor, Jon Lazarus, sexually harassed her by making certain remarks and sending messages to her by email. She alleged that Lazarus referred to another woman in the office as "Spandex Queen," told another woman that he would pay her $500 if he could call her "Sweet Georgia Brown," and referred to himself as the "president of the Amateur Gynecology Club." Strauss also wanted to introduce email evidence that Lazarus followed these remarks with email messages to Strauss containing a satirical essay entitled "Alice in UNIX Land," an advertisement for the replacement of "Mouse Balls," and a parody on a play entitled *A Girl's Guide to Condoms*.

The email messages had been erased, but the plaintiff retrieved them from backup tapes automatically made by the company's computer network.

Microsoft made a motion to the court to preclude this evidence, including the email messages, from being introduced at trial. The district court denied Microsoft's motion. The court stated that the email messages, when viewed in light of Strauss's other evidence, could lead a reasonable jury to conclude that Microsoft engaged in the challenged conduct. The court noted that although the email messages may be embarrassing to Microsoft, such evidence is admissible. The court stated, "The Federal Rules of Evidence favor placing even the nastier side of human nature before the jury if to do so would aid its search for the truth." The court permitted Strauss to sue Microsoft for sexual harassment using the email messages as evidence.

As email continues to increase in use, it will become a greater—and very tangible—source of evidence at criminal and civil trials. [*Strauss v. Microsoft Corporation,* 68 Fair Empl. Prac. Cases (BNA) 1576 (S.D.N.Y. 1995)]

law to the undisputed facts to decide the case. Motions for summary judgment, which can be made by either party, are supported by evidence outside the pleadings. Affidavits from the parties and witnesses, documents (e.g., a written contract between the parties), depositions, and such are common forms of evidence. If, after examining the evidence, the court finds no factual dispute, it can decide the issue or issues raised in the summary judgment motion. This may dispense with the entire case or with part of the case. If the judge finds that a factual dispute exists, the motion will be denied and the case will go to trial.

Pretrial Settlement Conference

Federal court rules and most state court rules permit the court to direct the attorneys or parties to appear before the court for a **pretrial hearing,** or **settlement conference.** One of the major purposes of these hearings is to facilitate settlement of the case. Pretrial conferences often are held informally in the judge's chambers. If no settlement is reached, the pretrial hearing is used to identify the major trial issues and other relevant factors.

U.S. Magistrate Judge

In the federal court system, a magistrate judge typically handles pretrial criminal matters. Under some local rules, by virtue of the authority in 28 U.S.C. 636(c), this judge may conduct, upon consent of all parties in a civil case, any or all proceedings, including a jury or non-jury trial, and order the entry of a final judgment. Appeals of a judgment may be made directly to the Court of Appeals, unless in the parties' consent they elected to have the case reviewed by the appropriate district judge (in which event any further appeal to the court of appeals would only be by petition for leave to appeal).

PERSPECTIVE

Oregon Rule on Visiting Adversaries' Websites

Visiting the website of a client's adversary in litigation does not violate the rule against lawyers' communicating with persons known to be represented by other counsel.

[Oregon State Bar Legal Ethics Commission Opinion 2001–164]

Utah Rule on Unencrypted Email

In ordinary circumstances a lawyer may use unencrypted Internet email to transmit client confidential information. *[Utah 00–01]*

More than 90 percent of all cases are settled before they go to trial. In cases that do proceed to trial, the trial judge may advise the attorneys of the rules or timetable of the individual judge. The judges also will advise the attorneys of any deadlines for discovery and the deadline for submitting any final motions with regard to what may be offered at the trial, called *motions in limine.*

In a number of jurisdictions, cases are referred to arbitration or other forms of alternative dispute resolution. Depending on the amount of money in controversy, some cases are required to be submitted before court-approved panels of attorneys sitting as arbitrators of the dispute. In other courts, the litigants may elect to have the case heard before an arbitration panel. Appeal rights from arbitration panel decisions vary, but cases typically may be appealed *de novo* to the trial court as if no arbitration had occurred, except possibly the payment of an appeal fee to cover part of the cost of the arbitration.

THE TRIAL

Pursuant to the Seventh Amendment to the U.S. Constitution, a party to an action at law is guaranteed the right to a *jury trial* in cases in federal court. Most state constitutions contain a similar guarantee for state court actions. If either party requests a jury, the trial will be by jury. If both parties waive their right to a jury, the trial will be without a jury. In non-jury trials, the judge sits as the **trier of fact.** These trials also are called *waiver trials* or **bench trials.** At the time of trial, the parties usually submit trial briefs to the judge that contain legal support for their side of the case.

Trials are usually divided into the following phases:

- Jury selection
- Opening statements
- Plaintiff's case
- Defendant's case
- Rebuttal and rejoinder
- Closing arguments
- Jury instructions
- Jury deliberation
- Entry of judgment

Jury Selection

The pool of the potential jurors usually is selected from voter or automobile registration lists. Potential jurors are asked to fill out a questionnaire such as that shown in Exhibit 8.9. Individuals are selected to hear specific cases through the process called **voir dire** ("to speak the truth"). Lawyers for each party and the judge can ask prospective jurors questions to determine if they would be biased in their decision. Jurors can be "stricken for cause" if the court believes that the potential juror is too biased to render a fair verdict. Lawyers may also use preemptory challenges to exclude a juror from sitting on a particular case without giving any reason for the dismissal. Once the appropriate number of jurors is selected (usually 6 to 12 jurors), they are impaneled to hear the case and are sworn in. The trial is ready to begin. In cases in which the Court is concerned for the safety of the jury, such as a high-profile murder case, it can **sequester,** or separate it from the outside world. Jurors are paid minimum fees for their service. Courts can hold people in contempt and fine or jail them for willful refusal to serve as a juror.

Opening Statements

Each party's attorney is allowed to make an **opening statement** to the jury. In opening statements, attorneys usually summarize the main factual and legal issues of the case and describe why they believe their client's position is valid. The information given in this statement is not considered as evidence. It is the attorney's opportunity to tell the trier of fact what he or she intends to tell them through witnesses and evidence.

Plaintiff's Case

Plaintiffs bear the **burden of proof** to persuade the trier of fact of the merits of their case. This is called the **plaintiff's case.** The plaintiff's attorney calls witnesses to give testimony. After a witness has been sworn in, the plaintiff's attorney examines (questions) the witness. This is called **direct examination.** Documents and other evidence can be introduced through each witness. After the plaintiff's attorney has completed his or her questions, the defendant's attorney can question the witness in **cross-examination.** The defendant's attorney can ask questions only about the subjects that were brought up during the direct examination. After the defendant's attorney completes his or her questions, the plaintiff's attorney can ask questions of the witness in **redirect examination.** The defendant's attorney can then again ask questions of the witness. This is called **recross examination.** Exhibit 8.10 illustrates this process.

Defendant's Case

After the plaintiff has concluded his or her case, the **defendant's case** proceeds. The defendant's case must

1. rebut the plaintiff's evidence.
2. prove any affirmative defenses asserted by the defendant.
3. prove any allegations contained in the defendant's cross-complaint.

The defendant's witnesses are examined in much the same way as the plaintiff's attorney cross-examines each witness. This is followed by redirect and recross examination.

Attorneys' Fees

In most civil lawsuits, each party is responsible for paying its own attorney's fees, whether the party wins or loses. This is called "the American rule." The court can award attorney's fees to the winning party if a statute so provides, if the parties have so agreed (e.g., in a contract), or if the losing party has acted maliciously or pursued a frivolous case. Accused parties in criminal cases are responsible for paying their own attorney's fees if they can afford to do so. If the accused is indigent, the government will provide an attorney (e.g., a public defender) free of charge.

An attorney in a civil lawsuit can represent the plaintiff on an hourly, project, or contingency fee basis. Hourly fees usually range from $75 to $500 per hour, depending on the type of case, the expertise of the lawyer, and the locality of the lawsuit. Under a *contingency fee arrangement,* the lawyer receives a percentage of the amount recovered for the plaintiff upon winning or settling the case. Contingency fees normally range from 20 to 50 percent of the award or settlement, with an average of about 35 percent. Lawyers for defendants in lawsuits normally are paid on an hourly basis.

exhibit **8.9**   *Sample jury questionnaire.*

JURY QUESTIONNAIRE

(Please Print)

NAME _____   JUROR NO. _____

     (Last)   *(First)*   *(Middle initial)*

SECTION OF CITY _____

    (Currently)   *(Other sections of city lived in within past ten years)*

Marital Status ☐ Married ☐ Single ☐ Divorced ☐ Separated ☐ Widowed

Occupation _____

    (Currently)   *(Other occupations within past ten years)*

Occupation of ☐ Spouse *(or deceased spouse)* ☐ Other

_____

    (Currently)   *(Other occupations within past ten years)*

No. of Male Children _____ Ages _____

No. of Female Children _____ Ages _____

Your Level of Schooling Completed _____

Race ☐ White ☐ Hispanic ☐ Black ☐ Other

STOP HERE
Writing below this line is prohibited until the juror video is shown

---

QUESTIONS TO BE ANSWERED IN THE JURY ASSEMBLY ROOM

1. Do you have any physical or psychological disability or are you presently taking any medication? ☐ YES ☐ NO

2. (a) Have you ever been a juror before? ☐ YES ☐ NO
   (b) If so, were you ever on a hung jury? ☐ YES ☐ NO

Questions 3 through 15 apply to criminal cases only

3. Do you have any religious, moral or ethical beliefs that would prevent you from sitting in judgment in a criminal case and rendering a fair verdict? ☐ YES ☐ NO

4. Have you or anyone close to you ever been a victim of a crime? ☐ YES ☐ NO

5. Have you or anyone close to you ever been charged with or arrested for a crime, other than a traffic violation? ☐ YES ☐ NO

6. Have you or anyone close to you ever been an eyewitness to a crime, whether or not it ever came to Court? ☐ YES ☐ NO

7. Have you, or has anyone close to you, ever worked as a police officer or in other law enforcement jobs? This includes prosecutors, public defenders, private criminal defense lawyers, detectives, and security or prison guards. ☐ YES ☐ NO

Sample jury questionnaire, continued.   *exhibit* **8.9**

8. Would you be more likely to believe the testimony of a police officer or any other law enforcement officer just because of his job?   ☐ YES ☐ NO

9. Would you be less likely to believe the testimony of a police officer or any other law enforcement officer just because of his job?   ☐ YES ☐ NO

10. Would you have any problem following the Court's instruction that the defendant in a criminal case is presumed to be innocent until proven guilty beyond a reasonable doubt?   ☐ YES ☐ NO

11. Would you have any problem following the Court's instruction that the defendant in a criminal case does not have to take the stand or present evidence, and it cannot be held against the defendant if he or she elects to remain silent?   ☐ YES ☐ NO

12. Would you have any problem following the Court's instruction in a criminal case that just because someone is arrested, it does not mean that the person is guilty of anything?   ☐ YES ☐ NO

13. In general, would you have any problem following and applying the judge's instructions on the law?   ☐ YES ☐ NO

14. Would you have any problem during jury deliberations in a criminal case discussing the case fully but still making up your own mind?   ☐ YES ☐ NO

15. Is there any other reason you could not be a fair juror in a criminal case?   ☐ YES ☐ NO

Questions 16 through 24 apply to civil cases only

16. Have you or anyone close to you ever sued someone, been sued, or been a witness?   ☐ YES ☐ NO

17. Have you or anyone close to you been employed as a lawyer or in a law-related job?   ☐ YES ☐ NO

18. Have you or anyone close to you been employed as a doctor or nurse or in a medical-related job?   ☐ YES ☐ NO

19. In a civil case, would you have any problem following the Court's instruction that the plaintiff has the burden or proof, but unlike in a criminal case, the test is not beyond a reasonable doubt but "more likely than not"?   ☐ YES ☐ NO

20. In a civil case, would you have any problem putting aside sympathy for the plaintiff and deciding the case solely on the evidence?   ☐ YES ☐ NO

21. In a civil case, would you have any problem following the Court's instruction to award money for damages for things like pain and suffering, loss of life's pleasures, etc., although it is difficult to put a dollar figure on them?   ☐ YES ☐ NO

22. Would you have any problem during jury deliberations in a civil case discussing the case fully but still making up your own mind?   ☐ YES ☐ NO

23. Is there any reason in a civil case that you cannot follow the Court's instructions on the law?   ☐ YES ☐ NO

24. Is there any reason in a civil case that you cannot otherwise be a fair juror?   ☐ YES ☐ NO

exhibit 8.10   *Sequence for examining witnesses.*

Rebuttal and Rejoinder

After the defendant's attorney has completed calling witnesses, the plaintiff's attorney can call witnesses and put forth evidence to rebut the defendant's case. This is called a **rebuttal.** The defendant's attorney can call additional witnesses and introduce other evidence to counter the rebuttal. This is called the *rejoinder.*

Closing Arguments

At the conclusion of the evidence, each party's attorney is allowed to make a **closing argument** to the jury. Each attorney tries to convince the jury to render a verdict for his or her clients by pointing out the strengths in the clients' case and the weaknesses in the other side's case. Information given by the attorneys in their closing statements is not evidence. It is a chance for the attorneys to tell the jury what they said they would tell the jury through witness and evidence in the opening statements and how they had done that during the trial.

Jury Instructions

Once the closing arguments are completed, the judge reads **jury instructions** (or **charges**) to the jury. These instructions inform the jury about what law to apply in deciding the case (see Exhibit 8.11). For example, in a criminal trial the judge will read the jury the statutory definition of the crime charged. In an accident case, the judge will read the jury the legal definition of *negligence.*

Jury Deliberation

The jury then goes into the jury room to deliberate its findings. **Jury deliberation** can take from a few minutes to many weeks. After deliberation, the jury announces its **verdict.** In a civil case, the jury also assesses damages. The judge assesses penalties in criminal cases.

6.01J (Civ) PROPERTY DAMAGE

The plaintiff is entitled to be compensated for the harm done to his (her) property. If you find that the property was a total loss, damages are to be measured by either its market value or its special value to plaintiff, whichever is greater. If the property was not a total loss, damages are measured by (the difference in value before and after the harm) (the reasonable cost of repairs) and you may consider such evidence produced by defendant by way of defense to plaintiff's claim. In addition, plaintiff is entitled to be reimbursed for incidental costs or losses reasonably incurred because of the damage to the property, such as (rental of a replacement vehicle during repairs), (towing charges), (loss of use of the property), (etc.).

SUBCOMMITTEE NOTE

Damage to property is covered generally by Restatement of Torts, §§ 927 and 928. Section 927 provides for damages to be measured by the "market value" or "damages based upon its special value to [plaintiff] if that is greater than its market value." Restatement of Torts, § 927, Comment c (1934). Section 928 provides, in the case of damages not amounting to total destruction, damages measured by "the difference between the value of the chattel before the harm and the value after the harm or, at plaintiff's election, the reasonable cost of repair or restoration." This accounts for the parenthesized phrases (the difference in value before and after the harm) and (the reasonable cost of repairs).

Incidental costs will depend on the nature of the property damage. Rental of a substitute vehicle has long been recognized as one such compensable item. *Bauer v. Armour & Co.*, 84 Pa.Super. 174 (1924). Compensation for loss of use is specifically authorized by Restatement of Torts, § 928(b), in the case of less than total loss. The Subcommittee can see no logical reason why such damages should not be awarded under Section 927 in the case of total loss. *Nelson v. Johnson*, 55 D. & C. 2d 21 (Somerset C.P. 1970). Any further expense, proximately resulting from the loss or damage is recoverable under general provisions of tort law. *Nelson v. Johnson, supra*, at 33-34.

In the case of damage to automobiles, however, the appellate courts have adhered to the ancient rule requiring testimony of the one who supervised or made the repairs, prior to admission of damage estimates. *Mackiw v. Pennsylvania Threshermen & Farmers Mut. Cas. Ins. Co.*, 201 Pa.Super. 626, 193 A.2d 745 (1963). This rule has been criticized as time-consuming and "technical" by the very courts adhering to it. *Mackiw, supra*, 193 A.2d at 745. It further creates an intolerable burden on the courts, in a period when backlog has led to "compulsory" arbitration in many counties of cases valued below $10,000. E.g., *Loughery v. Barnes*, 181 Pa.Super. 352, 124 A.2d 120 (1956) (appeal after verdict of $341.30 for property damage); *Wilk v. Borough of Mt. Oliver*, 152 Pa.Super. 539, 33 A.2d 73 (1943) (new trial ordered after verdict of $175). The Subcommittee therefore adopts a rule requiring only the submission of a repair bill or estimate in proof of damages to automobiles (such bill being submitted prior to trial to defense counsel); should defendant wish to challenge such an estimate, he may do so through cross-examination and through the introduction of evidence in his own case. See *Watsontown Brick Co. v. Hercules Powder Co.*, 265 F.Supp. 268, 275 (M.D.Pa.), *aff'd*, 387 F.2d 99 (3rd Cir. 1967) (after introduction of damage evidence, burden shifts to defendant to show reduction).

Absent stipulation, the issue of reasonable compensation remains a jury issue.

6.01F (Civ) FUTURE PAIN AND SUFFERING

The plaintiff is entitled to be fairly and adequately compensated for such physical pain, mental anguish, discomfort, inconvenience and distress as you believe he (she) will endure in the future as a result of his (her) injuries. [. . .]

Entrepreneurs have been leaders in developing start-up companies that currently dominate the area of e-commerce and the Internet. Entrepreneur Bill Gates created Microsoft Corporation and is now the richest person in the world. The entrepreneurs who started Netscape, Yahoo, AOL, Amazon.com, and eBay are also multimillionaires. Many new entrepreneurs are hatching the successful Internet and e-commerce businesses of the future in their dorm rooms, juice bars, and chat rooms on the Net. These Internet and e-commerce entrepreneurs are members of a new breed who think big, move fast, and are willing to take risks.

These new cyberspace entrepreneurs need a new type of lawyer who understands their mindset. These lawyers practice "entrepreneur law" in that they must be able to give competent legal and business advice on a moment's notice. Although having to be careful to protect the interests of their clients, and to give correct legal advice, entrepreneurial lawyers must recognize that e-commerce and Internet businesses sometimes must act faster than traditional businesses. In such cases, the client may be willing to skip some of the minute details that lawyers would insist on for traditional clients. These "techie-owners" often find "Wall Street" lawyers too slow, too expensive, and too risk-adverse. The new entrepreneur lawyer is more to their liking.

There is a growing need for lawyers who know e-commerce and Internet law, have specialized skills in handling transactional law, and know small-client management. At the start, entrepreneur lawyers need strong skills in finance law, e-commerce contract law, selecting and drafting business entity formation documents, preparing transactional documents of shipping, drawing licensing agreements, drafting shareholder agreements, drafting employment agreements, and protecting trademarks, service marks, and trade secrets. Eventually, the lawyer would be looking at handling the Internet company's initial public offering (IPO) and debt financing. It is hoped that after the Internet company is successful, it will not trade in its entrepreneur lawyer for the "traditional" lawyer.

Civil cases include personal injury cases, such as those against airlines, in which a judgment may be awarded to the plaintiff if successful.

Entry of Judgment

After the jury has returned its verdict, in most cases the judge enters **judgment** to the successful party based on the verdict. This is the official decision of the court. But the court may overturn the verdict if it finds bias or jury misconduct. This is called a **judgment notwithstanding the verdict** or **judgment n.o.v.** or **j.n.o.v.,** for the Latin *judgment non obstante verdicto.* In a civil case, the judge may reduce the amount of monetary damages awarded by the jury if he or she finds the jury to have been biased, emotional, or inflamed. This is called *remittitur.* The trial court usually issues a *written memorandum* setting forth the reasons for the judgment. This memorandum, together with the trial transcript and evidence introduced at trial, constitutes the permanent *record* of the trial court proceeding.

LEGAL TERMINOLOGY

Answer

Bench trial

Burden of proof

Civil litigation

Closing arguments

Complaint

Consolidation

Contempt of court

Cross-complaint

Cross-examination

Default judgment

Defendant

Defendant's case

Deponent

Deposition

Direct examination

Discovery

Injunction

Interrogatories

Intervention

Judgment

Judgment notwithstanding the verdict (j.n.o.v.)

Jury deliberation

Jury instructions/charges

Litigation/litigation process

Motion for judgment on the pleadings

Motion for summary judgment

Opening statement

Plaintiff

Plaintiff's case

Pleadings

Pretrial hearing (or settlement conference)

Production of documents

Rebuttal

Recross examination

Redirect examination

Reply

Sequester

Settlement conference

Statute of limitations

Subpoena

Summons

Trier of fact

Verdict

Voir dire

Witness

Summary

The Pleadings

Description	Paperwork that initiates and responds to a lawsuit.
Complaint	Filed by the plaintiff with the court and served with a summons on the defendant. It sets forth the basis of the lawsuit.
Answer	Filed by the defendant with the court and served on the plaintiff. It usually denies most allegations of the complaint.
Cross-Complaint	Filed and served by the defendant if he or she countersues the plaintiff. The defendant is the cross-complainant and the plaintiff is the cross-defendant. The cross-defendant must file and serve a reply (answer).
Intervention	A person who has an interest in a lawsuit may intervene and become a party to the lawsuit.
Consolidation	Separate cases against the same defendant arising from the same incident may be consolidated by the court into one case if it would not cause prejudice to the parties.

Discovery

Description	The pretrial litigation process for discovering facts of the case from the other party and witnesses.
Depositions	Oral testimony given by a *deponent*, either a party or witness. Depositions are transcribed.
Interrogatories	Written questions submitted by one party to the other party. They must be answered within a specified period of time.
Production of Documents	A party to a lawsuit may obtain copies of all relevant documents from the other party.
Physical and Mental Examination	These examinations of a party are permitted upon order of the court where injuries are alleged that could be verified or disputed by such examination.

Dismissals and Pretrial Judgments

Motion for Judgment on the Pleadings	Alleges that if all facts as pleaded are true, the moving party would win the lawsuit. No facts outside the pleadings may be considered.

(continued)

Motion for Summary Judgment	Alleges that there are no factual disputes, so the judge may apply the law and decide the case without a jury. Evidence outside the pleadings may be considered (e.g., affidavits, documents, depositions).

Pretrial Settlement Conference

Description	Conference prior to trial between the parties in front of the judge to facilitate the settlement of the case. Also called *pretrial hearing*. If a settlement is not reached, the case proceeds to trial.

The Trial

Jury Selection	Jury selection. Done through a process called *voir dire*. Biased jurors are dismissed and replaced.
Opening Statements	Made by the parties' lawyers. Are not evidence.
The Plaintiff's Case	The plaintiff bears the burden of proof. The plaintiff calls witnesses and introduces evidence to try to prove his or her case.
The Defendant's Case	The defendant calls witnesses and introduces evidence to rebut the plaintiff's case and to prove affirmative defenses and cross-complaints.
Rebuttal and Rejoinder	The plaintiff and defendant may call additional witnesses and introduce additional evidence.
Closing Arguments	Made by the parties' lawyers. Are not evidence.
Jury Instructions	Judge reads instructions to the jury as to what law they are to apply to the case.
Jury Deliberation	Jury retires to the jury room and deliberates until it reaches a *verdict*.
Entry of Judgment	The judge may: a. Enter the verdict reached by the jury as the court's *judgment*. b. Grant a motion for *judgment* n.o.v. if the judge finds the jury was biased. This means that the jury's verdict does not stand. c. Order *remittitur* (reduction) of any damages awarded if the judge finds the jury to have been biased or emotional.

Working the Web

1. Use the court links in the federal courts website to locate the U.S. District Court for your jurisdiction and download, if available, the local rules at www.uscourts.gov/links.html.
2. Visit the national archives and review the grant of judicial power in Article III of the U.S. Constitution at www.nara.gov/exhall/charters/constitution/constitution.html.
3. Read the rights granted by the Fifth Amendment to the Constitution at www.nara.gov/exhall/charters/billrights/billrights.html.
4. Use the Lexisone website state resource locator to find the online resources of your state at www.lexisone.com/legalresearch/legalguide/states/states_resources_index.htm.
5. Use the Martindale–Hubbell website to locate available expert witnesses and process servers in your jurisdiction at www.martindale.com/xp/martindale/experts_and_services/search_experts_and_services/leg_search.xml.

Questions

CRITICAL LEGAL THINKING AND WRITING

1. What is the reason for having a statute of limitations in civil actions?
2. Why would a court in the administration of justice ever make a finding of judgment notwithstanding the verdict?
3. What is the possible reason for granting a summary judgment? When will it be granted?
4. Why is the burden of proof in civil cases different from that in criminal cases?
5. Do you believe that the general availability of liability insurance influences jury awards? Would knowing that a defendant was insured affect your judgment as a member of a jury?
6. Why would a named defendant not file an answer to a complaint?
7. If both sides of a case have taken complete and thorough discovery in a case, are they more or less likely to settle before trial? Why?
8. What are the advantages, disadvantages, and benefits of using video depositions?
9. What characteristics would you want in a juror in a case involving a charge of possession of drugs for personal use by a college student, an automobile accident involving a senior citizen, and an injury to a child caused by a defective toy resulting in visible scarring to the lower leg? Why?

10. How does the legal team determine that there are sufficient facts to go to a jury?

Questions
ETHICS: ANALYSIS AND DISCUSSION

1. Is there an ethical obligation not to file certain lawsuits?
2. What are the implications for a paralegal in failing to file a pleading before expiration of the statute of limitations? For the supervising attorney? For the client?
3. Should the email of lawyers and paralegals be treated as confidential and not subject to use as evidence in a case? Why or why not?

Unauthorized Communication

There are few certainties in the area of ethics, for paralegals or in any profession. What qualifies as ethical conduct is in most cases based on state law and court interpretation applied to a set of facts. The citation listed below represents one legal opinion and is provided as a research starting point. Do not assume that the same rule applies in your jurisdiction. For the following:

- *Prepare a written statement based on your state law.*
- *Use your state bar association website as a starting point.*

You have been advised in your orientation of the ethical rule prohibiting communication with an opponent who is represented by counsel. While surfing the web, you decide to see if the opposing party has a website, you locate it and check it carefully for any information that might help the investigation of the case assigned to you. You send a request to the site and get back information related to the lawsuit. [Oregon State Bar Op2001–164.] Have you violated the ethical prohibition barring communications with a represented party?

CASES *for Discussion*

Conrad v. Delta Airlines, Inc.

494 F.2d 914 (7th Cir. 1974)

8.1 FACTS

Captain Conrad was a pilot for Delta Airlines. In 1970, Conrad was forced to resign by the airline. He sued, alleging that he was discharged because of his pro-union activities and not because of poor job performance, as claimed by Delta.

During discovery, a report written by a Delta flight operations manager was produced that stated: "More than a few crew members claimed that Conrad professed to being a leftist-activist. His overactivity with the local pilots' union, coupled with inquiries regarding company files to our secretary, led to the conclusion that potential trouble will be avoided by acceptance of his resignation."

Conrad claims that the report is evidence of the anti-union motivation for his discharge. Delta made a summary judgment motion to the trial court.

ISSUE

Should its summary judgment motion be granted?

Haviland & Co. v. Montgomery Ward & Co.

31 F.R.D. 578 (S.D.N.Y. 1962)

8.2 FACTS

Haviland & Company filed suit against Montgomery Ward & Company in U.S. district court, claiming that Ward used the trademark "Haviland" on millions of dollars worth of merchandise. As the owner of the mark, Haviland & Company sought compensation from Ward. Ward served notice to take the deposition of Haviland & Company's president, William D. Haviland. The attorneys for Haviland told the court that Haviland was 80 years old, lived in Limoges, France, and was too ill to travel to the United States for the deposition. Haviland's physician submitted an affidavit confirming these facts.

ISSUE

Must Haviland give his deposition?

Simblest v. Maynard

427 F.2d 1 (2d Cir. 1970)

8.3 FACTS

On November 9, 1965, Mr. Simblest was driving a car that collided with a fire engine at an intersection in Burlington, Vermont. The accident occurred on the night on which a power blackout left most of the state without lights. Mr. Simblest, who was injured in the accident, sued the driver of the fire truck for damages. During the trial, Simblest testified that when he entered the intersection, the traffic light was green in his favor. All of the other witnesses testified that the traffic light had gone dark at least 10 minutes before the accident. Simblest testified that the accident was caused by the fire truck's failure to use any warning lights or sirens. Simblest's testimony was contradicted by four witnesses who testified that the fire truck had used both its lights and sirens. The jury found that the driver of the fire truck had been negligent and rendered a verdict for Simblest. The defense made a motion for judgment n.o.v.

ISSUE

Who wins?

Harris v. Time, Inc.

191 C.A.3d 449, 237 Cal. Rptr. 584 (Cal.App. 1987)

8.4 FACTS

One day Joshua Gnaizda, a three-year-old, received in the mail what he (or his mother) thought was a tantalizing offer from Time, Inc. The front of the envelope contained a see-through window that revealed the following statement: "Joshua Gnaizda, I'll give you this versatile new calculator watch free just for opening this envelope before Feb. 15, 1985." Beneath the offer was a picture of the calculator watch itself. When Joshua's mother opened the envelope, she realized that the see-through window had not revealed the full text of Time's offer. Not viewable through the see-through window were the following words: "and mailing this certificate today." The certificate required Joshua to purchase a subscription to *Fortune* magazine in order to receive the free calculator watch.

Joshua (through his father, a lawyer) sued Time in a class action, seeking compensatory damages in an amount equal to the value of the calculator watch and $15 million in punitive damages. The trial court dismissed the lawsuit as being too trivial for the court to hear. Joshua appealed.

ISSUE

Should Joshua be permitted to maintain his lawsuit against Time, Inc.? Did Time act ethically? Should Joshua's father have sued for $15 million?

Gnazzo v. G.D. Searle & Co.

973 F.2d 136 (1992)   United States Court of Appeals, Second Circuit

Read the following case, excerpted from the court of appeals opinion. Review and brief the case. In your brief, answer the following questions.

1. What is a statute of limitations? What purposes does such a statute serve?

2. What was the Connecticut statute of limitations for the injury alleged by the plaintiff?

3. What is summary judgment? When will it be granted?

4. What was the decision of the trial court? Of the court of appeals?

Pierce, Circuit Judge.

On November 11, 1974, Gnazzo had a CU-7 intrauterine device (IUD) inserted in her uterus for contraceptive purposes. The IUD was developed, marketed, and sold by G.D. Searle & Co. (Searle). When Gnazzo's deposition was taken, she stated that her doctor had informed her that "the insertion would hurt, but not for long," and that she "would have uncomfortable and probably painful periods for the first three to four months." On October 11, 1975, Gnazzo found it necessary to return to her physician due to excessive pain and cramping. During this visit she was informed by her doctor that he thought she had pelvic inflammatory disease (PID). She recalled that he stated that the infection was possibly caused by venereal disease or the use of the IUD. The PID was treated with antibiotics and cleared up shortly thereafter. Less than one year later, Gnazzo was again treated for an IUD-associated infection. This infection was also treated with antibiotics. Gnazzo continued using the IUD until it was finally removed in December of 1977.

Following a laparoscopy in March of 1989, Gnazzo was informed by a fertility specialist that she was infertile because of PID-induced adhesions resulting from her prior IUD use. Subsequent to this determination, and at the request of her then-attorneys, Gnazzo completed a questionnaire dated May 11, 1989. In response to the following question, "When and why did you first suspect that your IUD had caused you any harm?," Gnazzo responded "sometime in 1981" and explained: "I was married in April 1981, so I stopped using birth control so I could get pregnant—nothing ever happened (of course), then I started hearing and reading about how damaging IUDs could be. I figured that was the

problem; however, my marriage started to crumble, so I never pursued the issue."

On May 4, 1990, Gnazzo initiated the underlying action against Searle. In an amended complaint, she alleged that she had suffered injuries as a result of her use of the IUD developed by Searle. Searle moved for summary judgment on the ground that Gnazzo's claim was time-barred by Connecticut's three-year statute of limitations for product liability actions. Searle argued, inter alia, that Gnazzo knew in 1981 that she had suffered harm caused by her IUD. Gnazzo contended that her cause of action against Searle accrued only when she learned from the fertility specialist that the IUD had caused her PID and subsequent infertility.

In a ruling dated September 18, 1991, the district court granted Searle's motion for summary judgment on the ground that Gnazzo's claim was time-barred by the applicable statute of limitations. In reaching this result, the court determined that Connecticut law provided no support for Gnazzo's contention that she should not have been expected to file her action until she was told of her infertility and the IUD's causal connection. This appeal followed.

On appeal, Gnazzo contends that the district court improperly granted Searle's motion for summary judgment because a genuine issue of material fact exists as to when she discovered, or reasonably should have discovered, her injuries and their causal connection to the defendant's alleged wrongful conduct. Summary judgment is appropriate when there is no genuine issue as to any material fact and the moving party is entitled to judgment as a matter of law. We consider the record in the light most favorable to the non-movant. However, the non-movant "may not rest upon the mere allegations of denials of her pleading, but must set forth specific facts showing that there is a genuine issue for trial."

Under Connecticut law, a product liability claim must be brought within "three years from the date when the injury is first sustained or discovered or in the exercise of reasonable care should have been discovered." In Connecticut, a cause of action accrues when a plaintiff suffers actionable harm. Actionable harm occurs when the plaintiff discovers or should discover, through the exercise of reasonable care, that he or she has been injured and that the defendant's conduct caused such injury.

Gnazzo contends that "the mere occurrence of a pelvic infection or difficulty in becoming pregnant does not necessarily result in notice to the plaintiff of a cause of action." Thus, she maintains that her cause of action did not accrue until 1989 when the fertility specialist informed her both that she was infertile and that this condition resulted from her previous use of the IUD.

Under Connecticut law, however, "the statute of limitations begins to run when the plaintiff discovers some form of actionable harm, not the fullest manifestation thereof. Therefore, as Gnazzo's responses to the questionnaire indicate she suspected "sometime in 1981" that the IUD had caused her harm because she had been experiencing trouble becoming pregnant and had "started hearing and reading about how damaging IUDs could be and had figured that was the problem."

Thus, by her own admission, Gnazzo had recognized, or should have recognized, the critical link between her injury and the defendant's causal connection to it. In other words, she had "discovered, or should have discovered through the exercise of reasonable care, that she had been injured and that Searle's conduct caused such injury." However, as Gnazzo acknowledged in the questionnaire, she did not pursue the "issue" at the time because of her marital problems. Thus, even when viewed in the light most favorable to Gnazzo, the non-moving party, we are constrained to find that she knew by 1981 that she had "some form of actionable harm." Consequently, by the time she commenced her action in 1990, Gnazzo was time-barred by the Connecticut statute of limitations.

Since we have determined that Gnazzo's cause of action commenced in 1981, we need not address Searle's additional contention that Gnazzo's awareness in 1975 of her PID and her purported knowledge of its causal connection to the IUD commenced the running of the Connecticut statute of limitations at that time.

We are sympathetic to Gnazzo's situation and mindful that the unavoidable result we reach in this case is harsh. Nevertheless, we are equally aware that "it is within the Connecticut General Assembly's constitutional authority to decide when claims for injury are to be brought. Where a plaintiff has failed to comply with this requirement, a court may not entertain the suit." The judgment of the district court is affirmed.

CHAPTER 9

CHAPTER OBJECTIVES

After studying this chapter, you should be able to:

1. Distinguish between felonies, misdemeanors, and violations.

2. Define and list the essential elements of a crime.

3. Describe criminal procedure, including arrest, indictment, arraignment, and the criminal trial.

4. List and describe crimes against persons and property.

5. Define major white-collar crimes, such as embezzlement, mail fraud, and bribery.

6. Explain the elements necessary to find criminal fraud.

7. Explain the constitutional safeguards against unreasonable searches and seizures.

8. Describe the Fifth Amendment's privilege against self-incrimination.

9. Explain the scope of the Foreign Corrupt Practices Act.

10. List and describe laws involving computer and Internet crimes.

Criminal Law and Process

It is better that ten guilty persons escape, than that one innocent suffer.

SIR WILLIAM BLACKSTONE,
COMMENTARIES ON THE LAWS OF ENGLAND (1809)

Introduction

For members of society to coexist peacefully and commerce to flourish, people and their property must be protected from injury by other members of society. Federal, state, and local governments' **criminal laws** are intended to accomplish this by providing an incentive for persons to act reasonably in society and imposing penalties on persons who violate them.

The United States has one of the most advanced and humane criminal law systems in the world. It differs from many other criminal law systems in several respects. First, a person charged with a crime in the United States is *presumed innocent until proven guilty.* The **burden of proof** is on the government to prove that the accused is guilty of the crime charged. Further, the accused must be found guilty "beyond a reasonable doubt." Conviction requires unanimous jury vote. Under many other legal systems, a person accused of a crime is presumed guilty unless the person can prove that he or she is not. A person charged with a crime in the United States also is provided with substantial constitutional safeguards during the criminal justice process—the protections against unreasonable search and seizure, against self-incrimination, against double jeopardy, and against cruel and unusual punishment, and the right to a public jury trial.

Some private lawyers specialize in criminal law by representing clients accused of criminal wrongdoing. Other lawyers work for the government, either for the prosecution team that represents the government in the criminal lawsuit against the defendant, or for a government-appointed defense counsel representing defendants who cannot afford a private attorney to represent them. Paralegals work for all of these criminal lawyers, and therefore require knowledge of the criminal legal process.

DEFINITION OF A CRIME

A **crime** is defined as any act done by an individual in violation of those duties that he or she owes to society and for the breach of which the law provides that the wrongdoer shall make amends to the public. Many activities have been considered crimes throughout the ages, whereas other crimes are of recent origin.

Penal Codes and Regulatory Statutes

Statutes are the primary source of criminal law. Most states have adopted comprehensive **penal codes** that define in detail the activities considered to be crimes within their jurisdiction and the penalties that will be imposed for committing these crimes. A comprehensive federal criminal code defines federal crimes (Title 18 of the U.S. Code). In addition, state and federal regulatory statutes often provide for criminal violations and penalties. The state and federal legislatures are continually adding to the list of crimes.

The penalty for committing a crime may be the imposition of a fine, imprisonment, both, or some other form of punishment (e.g., probation). Generally, imprisonment is imposed to

1. Incapacitate the criminal so he or she will not harm others in society.
2. Provide a means to rehabilitate the criminal.
3. Deter others from similar conduct.
4. Inhibit personal retribution by the victim.

Parties to a Criminal Action

In a criminal lawsuit, the government (not a private party) is the **plaintiff.** A lawyer called the **prosecutor, district attorney,** or in the federal system United States Attorney, represents the gov-

THE COURTHOUSE TEAM

Criminal Clerk of Court

In most jurisdictions the civil court records and the criminal court records are maintained in separate offices. The office of the criminal clerk of court maintains the official court files of criminal cases, including indictments, court proceedings, sentences and costs of prosecution records. Criminal defense requests and motions are also filed with the clerk of courts in most jurisdictions.

ernment. The accused is the **defendant.** The **defense attorney** represents the accused. If the accused cannot afford a defense lawyer, the government will provide one free of charge, called a **public defender.**

CLASSIFICATION OF CRIMES

All crimes can be classified into one of these categories: felonies, misdemeanors, or violations.

Felonies

Felonies are the most serious kinds of crimes. They include crimes that are *mala in se*—inherently evil. Most crimes against the person (murder, rape, and the like) and certain business-related crimes (such as embezzlement and bribery) are felonies in most jurisdictions. Felonies usually are punishable by imprisonment. In some jurisdictions, certain felonies (e.g., first-degree murder) are punishable by death. Federal law and some state laws require mandatory sentencing for specified crimes. Many statutes define different degrees of crimes (e.g., first-, second-, and third-degree murder) with each degree earning different penalties.

"This, ladies and gentleman, is Exhibit A, the sneakers that urged my client to Just Do It."

© The New Yorker Collection 1992 Arnie Levin from cartoonbank.com. All Rights Reserved.

Misdemeanors

Misdemeanors are less serious than felonies. They are crimes *mala prohibita*—not inherently evil but prohibited by society. This category includes many crimes against property, such as robbery, burglary, and violations of regulatory statutes. Misdemeanors carry lesser penalties than felonies; they usually are punishable by fine and/or imprisonment for one year or less.

Violations

Crimes such as traffic violations and jaywalking are neither felonies nor misdemeanors. Called **violations,** these crimes usually are punishable by a fine. Occasionally, a few days of imprisonment are imposed.

ESSENTIAL ELEMENTS OF A CRIME

For a person to be found guilty of most crimes, a criminal act and criminal intent must be proven.

Criminal Act

The defendant must have actually performed the prohibited act. Under the common law, actual performance of the criminal act is called the *actus reus* (guilty act). Under the Model Penal Code, the prohibited act may be analyzed in terms of conduct, circumstances, and results. Killing someone without legal justification is an example of *actus reus*. Sometimes the omission of an act constitutes the requisite *actus reus*. For example, a crime has been committed if a taxpayer who is under a legal duty to file a tax return fails to do so. Merely thinking about committing a crime is not a crime because no action has been taken.

Criminal Intent

To be found guilty of a crime, the accused must be found to have possessed the requisite subjective state of mind (i.e., specific or general intent) when the act was performed. This is called the **mens rea** (evil intent) under the traditional common law analysis and *culpable mental state* under the Model Penal Code. The Model Penal Code has four levels of culpable mental state:

1. Purposeful (or intentional)
2. Knowingly
3. Recklessly
4. With criminal negligence.

Specific intent is found where the accused purposefully, intentionally, or with knowledge commits a prohibited act. *General intent* is found where there is a showing of recklessness or a lesser degree of mental culpability. The individual criminal statutes state whether the crime requires a showing of specific or general intent. Juries may infer an accused's intent from the facts and circumstances of the case. There is no crime if the requisite *mens rea* cannot be proven. Thus, no crime is committed if one person accidentally injures another person.

Some statutes impose criminal liability based on *strict* or *absolute liability*. A finding of *mens rea* is not required. Criminal liability is imposed if the prohibited act is committed. Absolute liability is often imposed by regulatory statutes, such as environmental laws.

CRIMINAL ACTS AS BASIS FOR TORT ACTIONS

An injured party may bring a *civil tort action* against a wrongdoer who has caused the party injury during the commission of a criminal act. Civil lawsuits are separate from the government's criminal action against the wrongdoer. In many cases, a person injured by a criminal act will not sue the criminal to recover civil damages. This is because the criminal is often *judgment proof*—that is, the criminal does not have the money to pay a civil judgment. Table 9.1 compares civil and criminal law.

Criminal Procedure

Federal rules of criminal procedure govern all criminal proceedings in the courts of the United States (federal courts). [F.R.C.P. Rule 1]

CRIMINAL PROCEDURE

The court procedure for initiating and maintaining a criminal action is quite detailed. It encompasses both pretrial procedures and the actual trial. Pretrial criminal procedure consists of several distinct stages, including *arrest*, *indictment* or *information*, *arraignment*, and possible *plea bargaining*.

INFORMATION TECHNOLOGY
FEDERAL LAW HELPS VICTIMS OF IDENTITY FRAUD

For centuries, some individuals—for various purposes, mostly financial in nature—have attempted to take the identity of other persons. Today, taking on the identity of another can be extremely lucrative, earning the spoils of another's credit cards, bank accounts, Social Security benefits, and such. The use of new technology—computers and the Internet—has made such identity fraud even easier. The victim of such fraud may be left with funds stolen, a dismantled credit history, and thousands of dollars in costs trying to straighten out the mess.

Identity fraud is the fastest growing financial fraud in the United States. Credit reporting firms say identity fraud cases have increased from 10,000 in 1990 to more than 500,000 cases per year today.

To combat such fraud, Congress passed the Identity Theft and Assumption Deterrence Act of 1998.

This law criminalizes identity fraud, making it a federal felony punishable with prison sentences ranging from 3 to 25 years. The Act also appoints a federal administrative agency, the Federal Trade Commission (FTC), to help victims restore their credit and erase the impact of the imposter. Law-enforcement officials suggest that you:

1. Never put your Social Security number on any document unless it is legally required.

2. Obtain and review copies of your credit report at least twice each year.

3. Use passwords other than maiden names and birthdays on bank accounts and other accounts that require personal identification numbers (PINs).

Arrest

Before the police can arrest a person for committing a crime, they usually must obtain an **arrest warrant** based upon a showing of **probable cause**—the substantial likelihood that the person either committed or is about to commit a crime. If the police do not have time to obtain a warrant (e.g., if the police arrive during the commission of a crime, when a person is fleeing from the scene of the crime, or when it is likely that evidence will be destroyed), the

	Civil and criminal law compared.	table 9.1
ISSUE	**CIVIL LAW**	**CRIMINAL LAW**
Party who brings the action	Plaintiff	Government
Trial by jury	Yes, except actions for equity	Yes
Burden of proof	Preponderance of evidence	Beyond a reasonable doubt
Jury vote	Judgment for plaintiff requires specific jury vote (e.g., 9 of 12 jurors)	Conviction requires unanimous jury vote
Sanctions and penalties	Monetary damages and equitable remedies (e.g., injunction, specific performance)	Imprisonment, capital punishment, fine, probation

police still may arrest the suspect. *Warrantless arrests*, too, are judged by the probable-cause standard. After a person is arrested, he or she is taken to the police station for *booking*—the administrative proceeding for recording the arrest, fingerprinting, and so on.

Indictment or Information

Accused persons must be formally charged with a crime before they can be brought to trial. This usually is done by the issuance of a *grand jury indictment* or a *magistrate's* (judge's) *information statement*. Evidence of serious crimes, such as murder, is usually presented to a *grand jury*. Most grand juries consist of between 6 and 24 citizens who are charged with evaluating the evidence presented by the government. Grand jurors sit for a fixed time, such as one year. If the grand jury determines that there is sufficient evidence to hold the accused for trial, it issues an **indictment**. Note that the grand jury does not determine guilt. If an indictment is issued, the accused will be held for later trial.

After arrest, the detainee is taken to the police station for booking.

For lesser crimes (burglary, shoplifting, and such), the accused will be brought before a *magistrate* (judge). A magistrate who finds that there is enough evidence to hold the accused for trial will issue *information*. The case against the accused is dismissed if neither an indictment nor an information is issued.

Arraignment

If an indictment or information is issued, the accused is brought before a court for an **arraignment** proceeding during which the accused is (1) informed of the charges against him or her, and (2) asked to enter a *plea*. The accused may plead *guilty, not guilty*, or *nolo contendere*. A plea of *nolo contendere* means that the accused agrees to the imposition of a penalty but does not admit guilt. A *nolo contendere* plea cannot be used as evidence of liability against the accused at a subsequent civil trial. Corporate defendants often enter this plea. The government has the option of accepting a *nolo contendere* plea or requiring the defendant to plead guilty or not guilty. Depending on the nature of the crime, the accused may be released upon posting bail.

Plea Bargaining

Sometimes the accused and the government enter into a **plea bargain** agreement. The government engages in plea bargaining to save costs, avoid the risks of a trial, and prevent further overcrowding of the prisons. This type of arrangement allows the accused to admit to a lesser crime than charged. In return, the government agrees to impose a lesser penalty or sentence than might have been obtained had the case gone to trial. In the federal system, more than 90 percent plead guilty rather than go to trial.

THE CRIMINAL TRIAL

The criminal trial and the civil action trial have many similarities. The functions of the judge and jury are the same. The jury acts as the **trier of fact.** In cases in which the defendant exercises the right to proceed without a jury, also known as a **bench trial** (or *waiver trial*), the judge acts as the trier of fact. The judge also acts as the arbiter of procedural rules covering the conduct of the trial, and the judge is ultimately the one who applies the law to findings of fact, and guilt or innocence of the charges and who determines the sentence, fine, or other permitted forfeiture in cases of guilt. In some cases, such as murder trials, the jury also decides the sentence.

The order and presentation of evidence also are similar. The prosecution goes first and puts on its case, followed by the defense's presentation of its evidence. Motions for dismissal at the close of the prosecution's case are also similar to those in the civil action.

A significant difference is the concern in many cases to protect the record (the trial transcript). The defense counsel tends to be especially concerned with making appropriate objections on the record that can be used as the basis of an appeal. Prosecutors also are concerned that they not say anything on the record that the defendant can use as a basis for appeal in the event of a conviction.

Pretrial Discovery

A limited amount of pretrial discovery is permitted, with substantial restrictions to protect the identity of government informants and to prevent intimidation of witnesses. Defense attorneys often file motions to suppress evidence, which ask the court to exclude evidence from trial that the defendant believes the government obtained in violation of the defendant's constitutional rights, statute, or procedural rule. The government is under an obligation to provide **exculpatory** evidence to the defense attorney.

Under the Federal Rules of Criminal Procedure Rule 16, upon the defendant's request, the government must disclose and make available for inspection, copying, or photographing any relevant written or recorded statements made by defendant within the possession, custody, or control of the government, the existence of which is known, or where the exercise of due diligence may become known to the attorney for the government.

Determination of Guilt

At a criminal trial, unlike a civil-action trial, all jurors must *unanimously* agree before the accused is found *guilty* of the crime charged. If even one juror disagrees (i.e., has reasonable doubt) about the guilt of the

Meet THE COURTHOUSE TEAM

District Attorney–Prosecutor

In most jurisdictions, the individual who prosecutes criminal cases on behalf of the state is called the district attorney (DA) or prosecutor. In the federal system, the United States Attorney is the one who prosecutes federal criminal cases. The U.S. Attorney is appointed, whereas a district attorney is usually an elected official.

Subpoenas in Federal Criminal Cases

F.R.C.P. Rule 17 provides that the clerk of court or the magistrate judge hearing the matter shall issue subpoenas. These must be served by a person, not a party, who is no younger than 18 years of age. There is no provision for service by mail. All subpoenas must be accompanied by a check for the witness fee (typically $40 per day) and mileage (roundtrip to the courthouse), unless the subpoena is issued on behalf of the United States or the court has determined upon *ex parte* motion that the defendant is financially unable to pay.

SIDEBAR

accused, the accused is *not guilty* of the crime charged. If all of the jurors agree that the accused did not commit the crime, the accused is *innocent* of the crime charged.

After trial, the following rules apply:

- If the defendant is found guilty, he or she may appeal.
- If the defendant is found innocent, the government cannot appeal.
- If the jury cannot come to a unanimous decision about the defendant's guilt, the jury is considered a **hung jury.** The government may choose to retry the case before a new judge and jury.

CRIMES AFFECTING BUSINESS

Many crimes are committed against business property, often involving the theft, misappropriation, or fraudulent taking of property. The most important types of crimes against business property are discussed in the following paragraphs.

THE COURTHOUSE TEAM

Public Defender

Persons who are unable to afford private counsel to defend them in a criminal prosecution are appointed counsel by the court, either from a list of private counsels compensated by the court or through the public defender's office from its staff or by its request for court appointment of outside counsel.

Robbery

At common law, **robbery** is defined as the taking of personal property from another person by the use of fear or force. For example, if a robber threatens to physically harm a storekeeper unless the victim surrenders the contents of the cash register, this is robbery. If a criminal pickpockets somebody's wallet, it is not robbery because there has been no use of force or fear. Robbery with a deadly weapon is generally considered *aggravated robbery* (or armed robbery) and carries a harsher penalty.

Burglary

At common law, **burglary** was defined as "breaking and entering a dwelling at night" with the intent to commit a felony. Modern penal codes have broadened this definition to include daytime thefts and thefts from offices and commercial and other buildings. In addition, most modern definitions of burglary have abandoned the "breaking-in" element. Thus, unauthorized entering of a building through an unlocked door is sufficient. Aggravated burglary (or armed burglary) carries stiffer penalties.

Larceny

At common law, **larceny** is defined as the wrongful and fraudulent taking of another person's personal property. Most personal property—including tangible property, trade secrets, computer programs, and other business property—is subject to larceny. The stealing of automobiles and car stereos, pickpocketing, and such are larceny. Neither the use of force nor the entry of a building is required. Some states distinguish between *grand larceny* and *petit larceny,* depending on the value of the property taken.

Theft

Some states have dropped the distinction among the crimes of robbery, burglary, and larceny. Instead, these states group these crimes under the general crime of *theft*. Most of these states distinguish between *grand theft* and *petit theft*, depending upon the value of the property taken.

Receiving Stolen Property

It is a crime for a person to (1) knowingly receive stolen property, and (2) intend to deprive the rightful owner of that property. Knowledge and intent can be inferred from the circumstances. The stolen property can be any tangible property (e.g., personal property, money, negotiable instruments, stock certificates, and so on).

Arson

At common law, **arson** was defined as the malicious or willful burning of the dwelling of another person. Modern penal codes expanded this definition to include the burning of all types of private, commercial, and public buildings. Thus, in most states, an owner who burns his or her own building to collect insurance proceeds can be found liable for arson. If arson is found, the insurance company does not have to pay the proceeds of any insurance policy on the burned property.

Forgery

The crime of **forgery** occurs if a written document is fraudulently made or altered and that change affects the legal liability of another person. Examples of forgery are counterfeiting, falsifying public records, and the material altering of legal documents. One of the most common forms of forgery is the signing of another person's signature to a check or changing the amount of a check. Note that signing another person's signature without intent to defraud is not forgery. For instance, forgery has not been committed if one spouse signs the other spouse's payroll check for deposit in a joint checking or savings account at the bank.

Extortion

The crime of **extortion** means the obtaining of property from another, with his or her consent, induced by wrongful use of actual or threatened force, violence, or fear. For example, extortion occurs when a person threatens to expose something about another person unless that other person gives money or property. The truth or falsity of the information is immaterial. Extortion of private persons is commonly called *blackmail*. Extortion of public officials is called *extortion "under color of official right."*

Sentencing Guidelines

The United States Sentencing Commission established the Sentencing Guidelines for the federal criminal justice system [18 U.S.C. § 3551 et. seq.]. If a defendant is found guilty, the court probation office prepares a report for the court and applies the Sentencing Guidelines to the individual defendant and the crimes for which he or she has been found guilty.

During sentencing, the court may consider the evidence produced at trial and also all relevant information that may be provided by the pretrial services officer, the U.S. attorney, and the defense attorney. In unusual circumstances, the court may depart from the sentence calculated according to the Sentencing Guidelines.

A sentence may include time in prison, a fine to be paid to the government, and monetary restitution to pay to crime victims. The court's probation officers assist the court in enforcing any conditions that are imposed as part of the criminal sentence.

SIDEBAR

Money Laundering

The term *money laundering* refers to the process by which criminals convert tainted proceeds into apparently legitimate funds or property. It applies equally to an international wire transfer of hundreds of millions of dollars in drug proceeds and the purchase of an automobile with funds robbed from a bank.

Money laundering is a federal crime. The following activities are among those that were criminalized by the Money Laundering Control Act:

- Knowingly engaging in a *financial transaction* involving the proceeds of some form of specified unlawful activity. Transactions covered include the sale of real property, personal property, intangible assets, and anything of value. [18 U.S.C. § 1956]

- Knowingly engaging in a *monetary transaction* by, through, or to a financial institution involving property of a value greater than $10,000, which is derived from specified unlawful activity. Monetary transaction is defined as a deposit, withdrawal, transfer between accounts, and use of a monetary instrument. [18 U.S.C. § 1957]

"Specified unlawful activity" includes narcotics activities and virtually any white-collar crime.

Money laundering statutes have been used to go after entities and persons involved in illegal check-cashing schemes, bribery, insurance fraud, Medicaid fraud, bankruptcy fraud, bank fraud, fraudulent transfer of property, criminal conspiracy, environmental crime, and other types of illegal activities.

Conviction for money laundering carries stiff penalties. Persons can be fined up to $500,000 or twice the value of the property involved, whichever is greater, and sentenced to up to 20 years in federal prison. In addition, violation subjects the defendant to provisions that mandate forfeiture to the government of any property involved in or traceable to the offense [18 U.S.C. §§ 981–982]. Any financial institution convicted of money laundering can have its charter revoked or its insurance of deposit accounts terminated.

To avoid running afoul of these increasingly complex statutes, banks and businesses must develop and implement policies and procedures to detect criminal activity and report money laundering by customers to the federal government.

Credit-Card Crimes

Substantial purchases in the United States are made with credit cards. This poses a problem if someone steals and uses another person's credit cards. Many states have enacted statutes that make the misappropriation and use of credit cards a separate crime. In other states, credit-card crimes are prosecuted under the forgery statute.

Bad Checks

Many states have enacted *bad check legislation*, which makes it a crime for a person to make, draw, or deliver a check at a time when that person knows that funds in the account are insufficient to cover the amount of the check. Some states require proof that the accused intended to defraud the payee of the check.

White-Collar Crimes

Certain types of crime that are prone to be committed by businesspersons are often referred to as **white-collar crimes.** These crimes usually involve cunning and deceit rather than physical force. Many of the white-collar crimes are discussed in the paragraphs that follow.

At Taubman Trial, Lovely Paralegal Holds the Balance

New York Observer, December 10, 2001   Ralph Gardner, Jr.

The surprise star of *U.S.A. v. Alfred Taubman* may turn out to be not Diana (Dede) Brooks, Sotheby's former chief executive, whom the defense spent the better part of the trial's final week attempting to portray as a sort of dominatrix in pearls and pumps, but Jade Burns. You need not feel inadequate if you've never heard of Ms. Burns. She's not a former member of Sotheby's titled board, or the ultimate expert on Rembrandt, or the recipient of a sweetheart loan from the auction house in exchange for the opportunity to sell her grandmother's Monet water lilies. Ms. Burns is a paralegal employed by the Department of Justice. And throughout the trial, she's sat at the prosecution table and ably and discreetly operated one of the computers that projects Sotheby's and Christie's notes, memos, board minutes, consignment contracts and other documents, incriminating or not, depending on your point of view, onto a giant screen and a collection of TV monitors strategically placed around the courtroom.

Mr. Taubman, Sotheby's former chairman and still its largest shareholder, is charged with conspiring with Sir Anthony Tennant, his opposite number at Christie's, to fix the auction business so that clients couldn't play the two houses against each other in search of more favorable terms. Sir Anthony is in Great Britain, where he can't be extradited; he's denied any wrongdoing. Ms. Brooks has pled guilty to collusion and awaits sentencing. She hopes that in exchange for her testimony against Mr. Taubman, she'll receive little (or, better yet, no) jail time. The jury spent the better part of Dec. 4 in deliberations, requesting documents and, before they quit for the night, a reading of the antitrust laws.

In light of all this, Ms. Burns, the government's last witness, showing up in the trial's final hours and on the spur of the moment, it seemed, appears an awfully small fish. However, since price-fixing never does much to stir the imagination, the case may turn on which side seems more sympathetic to the working-class jury. And in that regard, the paralegal, who is only 24, had very little competition: There seemed to be no heroes in this trial. The witness list included its share of overcompensated and overweight middle-aged men.

Ms. Burns' star turn came in response to a defense witness named Christine Nelson, an economic consul-

tant who was being paid $425 an hour to testify that Mr. Taubman had done nothing wrong, based on her examination of data supplied to her by Sotheby's and Christie's. The prosecution has made much of a 1993 memo in Sir Anthony's handwriting that allegedly lays out the terms of his collusion deal with Mr. Taubman. However, in several areas where they'd agreed to stop competing, for example, in ceasing to give advances on single lots, or loans below Libor, the British equivalent of the prime rate, Ms. Nelson's analysis proved that the deal was disregarded. Of course, her study only examined the years 1993 to 1995. "Her chart simply started too early and ended too early," prosecutor John C. Greene charged in his summation rebuttal, rather than continuing on to 1999, when the alleged conspiracy started to unravel. She also ignored a possible logical explanation for her counter-intuitive findings, one offered by Christopher Davidge, Christie's former chief executive, when he testified earlier in the trial on loans below Libor: namely, that "the business was improving" and that, while the sheer number of such loans might be increasing, as a percentage of all transactions it might actually be diminishing. Finally, as the prosecution brought out on cross-examination, Ms. Nelson had no way of knowing whether the consignment contracts she studied may have been subject to preexisting, pre-1993 agreements between the auction houses and particular clients.

When Ms. Burns took the witness stand, one couldn't help but compare her to Ms. Nelson, whose Goody Two-Shoes manner didn't appear to endear her to the jury. (It's impossible to handicap a jury, but this one has offered few signs of affection for Mr. Taubman or his team. And shortly after Ms. Nelson stepped down after parts of two days spent on the witness stand, one of the jurors instructed Scott Muller, a Taubman lawyer, to turn off a light on a projection machine that was shining in the jury's eyes. When the lawyer promptly obeyed, the juror turned to a couple of buddies on the jury and gave them a wink and a "See, that'll show 'em" nod.)

Leave a person on a witness stand long enough, and they start to remind you of someone you hated in high school. And Ms. Nelson, particularly as she gamely sparred with Patricia Jannaco, the government lawyer cross-examining her, recalled the teacher's pet who scores 100 on the math final and throws off the entire grading curve. Ms. Burns also happens to be extremely pretty, perhaps even beautiful, though it's hard to tell since she keeps her hair pulled back and wears those nerdy, dark-framed glasses of the sort Tina Fey sports while giving the "Weekend Update" on Saturday Night Live. While the Berkeley philosophy major spent only a few fleeting moments on the witness stand, the government was able to get into evidence the fact that her charts covered the years up to and including 1998, unlike Ms. Nelson's (making one wonder what she might have been hiding), and also that Ms. Burns' data included information on sellers' commissions, the essence of the alleged collusion between Mr. Taubman and Mr. Tennant, showing the rates had gone up.

Besides Ms. Nelson, the defense called 13 other witnesses (the government offered five), whose contributions were of a more impressionistic nature. They testified to Mr. Taubman's excellence as a human being, even if he was a little vague on occasion, and to Ms. Brooks' unsympathetic tendencies.

Perhaps the most damaging testimony to Ms. Brooks came at the start of the defense's presentation, when Donaldson Pillsbury, Sotheby's in-house lawyer, testified that he never heard Mr. Taubman tell her, as she'd claimed, "You'll look good in stripes" during a meeting when he supposedly feared she'd squeal to the feds. Rather, Mr. Pillsbury said, Mr. Taubman actually asked rather amiably, "How do you think I'd look in stripes?" The ultimate question, of course, is whether the jury is wondering the same thing.

Mr. Taubman is little short of Sphinx-like as he sits at the defense table, the very model of aristocratic comportment, with the jury left to connect the dots as best it can to form a picture of his personality, one that's based mostly on the testimony of minions, some of whom had only fleeting contact with him. They painted a picture of an individual neither liked nor disliked, let alone loved or loathed, whose habits were more reminiscent of a brown bear than of a swashbuckling billionaire. (Mr. Taubman's net worth was estimated by his lawyers during their opening statements at between $700 million and $1 billion.)

Bernard Winograd, a former executive with Mr. Taubman's investment company in Michigan, whose holdings include Sotheby's, testified that "he does have a sleeping disorder and can occasionally fall asleep involuntarily." William Sheridan, Sotheby's current chief financial officer, volunteered that at board meetings his boss "was more concerned with what time lunch was going to be served and what was for lunch."

Ms. Brooks, on the other hand, was portrayed as the C.E.O. from heck, if not quite from hell, a Valkyrie in a business suit. George Bailey, Sotheby's managing director for Europe, recalled that she balked at agendas different from her own, including Mr. Taubman's. "She's a very emotional person," Mr. Bailey, whose British accent was as thick as Lyle's Golden Syrup, testified. "She used to get very upset." Michael Curle, a former Sotheby's finance director for Europe, once heard her snap at Mr. Bailey, "Alfred Taubman doesn't run this company, I do." And the billionaire apparently took it. "Mr. Taubman was pretty meek for a guy who owned all that stock," Mr. Sheridan said. "He'd just crawl back into his shell."

The central mystery of the case, of course, is who is Alfred Taubman, and why would he risk his reputation and immense wealth in something as potentially obvious as a price-fixing scheme? In answer to the latter question, lead prosecutor Greene quoted Adam Smith from 1776 (right around the time both auction houses were founded) in his closing argument, even though the defense fought mightily to prevent him from doing so. "People in the same trade seldom meet together for merriment and diversion," the economist observed, "but a conversation ends in a conspiracy against the public or in some contrivance to raise prices."

And then, of course, there's the possibility that Mr. Taubman is innocent. Sotheby's insiders have said that his defense team's portrayal of him as disinterested in the business isn't a cynical tactic to save him from the slammer, but the truth. He bought Sotheby's to mingle with lords and ladies, Kennedys and Duponts, they say, and left the nuts and bolts of crunching numbers to others. He really was out to lunch.

Mr. Taubman's true crime, the working-class jury may decide in these patriotic times, is that he seems to have aspired to being British. It was Mr. Bailey who stated that even though he wasn't aware that his chairman had met with Sir Anthony Tennant, it didn't surprise him. "No disrespect to Mr. Taubman," he stated delicately, "but he particularly enjoyed meeting people of title and position in the U.K." With that comment, it became clear whom Mr. Taubman models himself after as he sits there at the defense table, exquisitely well fed and beautifully tailored in his three-piece suits, not an American captain of business, but a British lord.

In his closing argument, Mr. Greene attacked what he described as the defense's "dumb and hungry" defense, pointing out that individuals who amass huge fortunes from scratch tend to have a certain faculty for numbers. Furthermore, Mr. Taubman sat on the boards of both Chase Manhattan Bank and Macy's. "Do you think they'd keep him on the boards if he is a know-nothing who only asked what is for lunch?" Mr. Greene inquired.

In Mr. Taubman's defense, at the time the conspiracy is alleged to have taken place, Sotheby's did have an excellent in-house chef. So if the chairman did often ask what was on the menu, the question may have been more a testimony to the sophistication of his palate than to a preoccupation with his animal needs. However, Mr. Taubman's attorney, Robert B. Fiske, Jr., chose not to highlight his client's good taste when his turn came to offer a summation. Rather, he called Mr. Greene's remark about the "dumb and hungry" defense "kind of an insult. It's an insult to Mr. Taubman and to the fine witnesses who came in here and testified."

What they testified to, according to Mr. Fiske, was that his client was a good and honorable man, and that Ms. Brooks was fully capable of hatching a conspiracy on her own and had the capacity and motive to do so. Mr. Fiske recalled his opening statement at the start of the 14-day trial, when he argued that Ms. Brooks found herself in dire straits back in 1994, shortly after becoming the C.E.O. of Sotheby's Holdings, when a contemporary sale cratered and the price of the company's stock plummeted, imperiling her nascent personal fortune in Sotheby's stock options.

The case was rather quite simple, Mr. Fiske told the haphazardly attentive jury (one of whom dozed on occasion; another, fortunately an alternate, appeared to be in R.E.M. sleep). It all boiled down to whom you believed. Ms. Brooks or Mr. Taubman. "You simply cannot believe Ms. Brooks, and you cannot believe her beyond a reasonable doubt," the lawyer, a former Whitewater prosecutor, charged. "She has no remorse about this at all."

Mr. Fiske dismissed Christopher Davidge, Christie's former chief executive and the government's other main witness, who, along with Christie's, received amnesty from prosecution for squealing first to the government about the alleged conspiracy, as someone who was being paid for his testimony and thus was not even worth considering. Mr. Fiske was referring to an $8 million severance package that Mr. Davidge received from Christie's in exchange for cooperating with the government's investigation into Sotheby's. "This is a one-witness case," Mr. Fiske told the jury. "She is an admitted liar with a powerful motive," that motive being to stay out of jail.

While Mr. Greene's summation was as focused as a satellite-guided missile hitting an Al Qaeda cave complex, "The agreement itself is the crime," he instructed the jury; "whether it is ever carried out, or succeeds or failed, doesn't matter," Mr. Fiske's closing argument was more complicated. For example, he reminded the jury that the only charge in the indictment concerned whether a conspiracy existed to fix sellers' prices, not such issues as guarantees, single-lot advances, or loans below Libor, describing those areas as a "side show." But he then went on to praise Ms. Nelson, whose charts dealt specifically with single-lot advances, loans below Libor, etc., but not at all with seller's commissions, describing her data as "unassailable." Ms. Burns' brief but charming testimony, alas, wasn't evoked by either the prosecution or the defense.

Perhaps the only masterpiece displayed at trial was a poster the prosecution created and had placed on an easel in front of the jury that showed the 12 meetings between Mr. Taubman and Sir Anthony. Though not quite rising to the level of Cubist collage, the government had cut-and-pasted the entries from Mr. Taubman's, his secretaries', and his handlers' daily planners into a sort of color-field painting, punctuated with Twomblyesque scribbled references to meetings with "a gentleman," "Tony," and, in one case, an individual denoted simply with four asterisks. Mr. Fiske characterized the meetings as wholly above board, however. "They were social friends," he noted, and besides, as chairman of their respective auction houses, the two had many legitimate subjects to discuss.

No matter how the case turns out, the jury seems to be getting along famously, at least those who manage to remain sentient, and they invariably enter the courtroom chuckling over some aside one of them has made to the others. And the members of the standing-room-only audience on the trial's last day, reporters, lawyers and a smattering of art-world types, seem to have no particular fear that the wounds this trial opened won't heal completely, even if Mr. Taubman's and Ms. Brooks' reputations lay in ruin. "I was thinking," said one Upper East Sider, "we should have an end-of-the-trial cocktail party with striped food."

Embezzlement

Unknown at common law, the crime of **embezzlement** is now a statutory crime. Embezzlement is the fraudulent conversion of property by a person to whom that property was entrusted. Typically, embezzlement is committed by an employer's employees, agents, or representatives (e.g., accountants, lawyers, trust officers, treasurers). Embezzlers often try to cover their tracks by preparing false books, records, or entries.

The key element here is that the stolen property was *entrusted* to the embezzler. This differs from robbery, burglary, and larceny, in which property is taken by someone not entrusted with the property. Consider this example: Embezzlement has been committed if a bank teller absconds with money that was deposited by depositors. The employer (the bank) entrusted the teller to take deposits from its customers.

"I plead guilty, Your Honor, but only in a nice, white-collar sort of way."

Criminal Fraud

Obtaining title to property through deception or trickery constitutes the crime of **criminal fraud,** also known as *false pretenses* or *deceit*. Consider this example: Robert Anderson, a stockbroker, promises Mary Greenberg, a prospective investor, that he will use any money she invests to purchase interests in oil wells. Based on this promise, Ms. Greenberg decides to make the investment. Mr. Anderson never intended to invest the money. Instead, he used the money for his personal needs. This is criminal fraud.

Mail and Wire Fraud

Federal law prohibits the use of mails or wires (e.g., telegraph or telephone) to defraud another person. These crimes are called **mail fraud** and **wire fraud,** respectively. The government often prosecutes a suspect under these statutes if there is insufficient evidence to prove the real crime that the criminal was attempting to commit or did commit. Wire fraud statutes are also sometimes used to prosecute Internet fraud.

Bribery

Bribery is one of the most prevalent forms of white-collar crime. A bribe can be in the form of money, property, favors, or anything else of value. The crime of commercial bribery prohibits the payment of bribes to private persons and businesses. This type of bribe is often called a *kickback* or a *payoff*. Intent is a necessary element of this crime. The offeror of a bribe commits the crime of bribery when the bribe is tendered. The offeree is guilty of the crime of bribery when he or she accepts the bribe. The offeror can be found liable for the crime of bribery even if the person to whom the bribe is offered rejects the bribe.

Consider this example: Harriet Landers is the purchasing agent for the ABCD Corporation and is in charge of purchasing equipment to be used by the corporation. Neal Brown, the sales representative of a company that makes equipment that can be used by the ABCD Corporation, offers to pay her a 10

Lawyer Charged with Bribing Skadden Paralegal in Insider Trading Scheme

New York Law Journal, November 21, 2000   Mark Hamblett

White Plains, N.Y., attorney Robert C. Schuster tried to bribe a paralegal at one of New York's largest law firms to obtain inside information on approaching mergers and acquisitions, federal prosecutors charged Monday. But authorities say the paralegal, who worked at Skadden, Arps, Slate, Meagher & Flom, turned the tables on Schuster by reporting the bribe attempt and then working as a confidential informant to help snare the attorney. Schuster, 32, allegedly offered the paralegal as much as $15,000 for advance notice of mergers and acquisitions being handled by Skadden.

In a complaint unsealed Monday following Schuster's arrest, prosecutors said the sole practitioner and former assistant district attorney was captured on tape talking to the paralegal and referring to the master stock market manipulator played by actor Michael Douglas in the movie "Wall Street."

"I'm not Gordon Gekko," Schuster reportedly said, "but . . . no risk, no reward."

Schuster, a prosecutor with the Cayuga County District Attorney's Office in Auburn from 1996 to 1997, pleaded not guilty to charges of securities fraud, wire fraud, and commercial bribery before Southern District Magistrate Judge Michael H. Dolinger. He was released on personal recognizance after he and his wife pledged their home to meet the bond of $200,000. The Millwood, N.Y., resident, a 1995 graduate of the Georgetown University Law Center, was also accused of violating securities laws in a civil complaint filed Monday by the Securities and Exchange Commission.

Assistant U.S. Attorney Timothy J. Coleman said in the complaint and an accompanying news release that Schuster was representing the paralegal on another matter when on Sept. 9 he offered $10,000—or $15,000, if necessary—for inside information on corporate mergers and acquisitions.

The paralegal, who remains unnamed, refused the offer and immediately reported the incident to Skadden management, which then alerted the authorities. However, the paralegal was persuaded to help with the investigation and draw Schuster into making incriminating statements on the phone and in person. The paralegal also agreed to wear a recording device when meeting Schuster in person to discuss the arrangement.

During meetings in October, Schuster was allegedly taped while promising the paralegal a "cut" of his profits should the scheme succeed, adding on one occasion that "the whole strategy has to be to know something before anyone else does." The Federal Bureau of Investigation had the paralegal give Schuster a fictitious tip about an upcoming takeover of a real company and, according to the complaint, Schuster ran with it, using his account at Fidelity Brokerage Services to buy 3,000 shares of the company for $153,750. He later gave the paralegal a $500 down payment for participating in the scheme.

On Oct. 4, the complaint continues, Schuster said he assumed that his "co-conspirator" was not wearing a recording device, stating "I am extremely security conscious . . . so I will be very, very cautious." Later, during the same conversation, Schuster muttered the old stockpicker's adage, "Pigs get fat; hogs get slaughtered."

Thomas Lee represented Schuster at arraignment.

percent kickback if she buys equipment from him. She accepts the bribe and orders the equipment. Both parties are guilty of bribery.

At common law, the crime of bribery was defined as the giving or receiving of anything of value in corrupt payment for an "official act" by a public official. Public officials include legislators, judges, jurors, witnesses at trial, administrative agency personnel, and other government officials. Modern penal codes also make it a crime to bribe public officials. For example, a developer who is constructing an apartment building cannot pay the building inspector to overlook a building code violation.

Ethical PERSPECTIVE · *Hughes Aircraft Downed as a Criminal Conspirator*

Hughes Aircraft Co., Inc. (Hughes), an aircraft manufacturer, contracted with the U.S. government to manufacture micro-electronic circuits, known as "hybrids," which are used as components in weapons defense systems. The contract required Hughes to perform tests on each hybrid. A Hughes employee, Donald LaRue, was the supervisor responsible for ensuring the accuracy of the hybrid testing process. LaRue falsely reported that all tests had been performed and that each hybrid had passed the test. When LaRue's subordinates called his actions to the attention of LaRue's supervisors, they did nothing about it. Instead, they responded that LaRue's decisions were his own and were not to be questioned. The United States sued Hughes and LaRue, charging criminal conspiracy to defraud the government. At trial, LaRue was acquitted, but Hughes was convicted of criminal conspiracy and fined $3.5 million. Hughes appealed its conviction, asserting that it should not be convicted of criminal conspiracy if its alleged co-conspirator, LaRue, was acquitted.

Should Hughes be acquitted as a matter of law because the same jury that convicted Hughes acquitted its alleged co-conspirator of the charge of criminal conspiracy? No. The court of appeals held that Hughes may be found guilty of criminal conspiracy even though its co-conspirator had been acquitted of the same crime, and affirmed.

The court of appeals, as a matter of law, held that the inconsistency of the jury verdicts of two defendants charged with criminal conspiracy does not mean that the convicted defendant should also be acquitted. The court noted that the jury may have been more lenient with defendant LaRue, an individual, than they were with Hughes, the corporate defendant. Moreover, the court stated that the jury could have found Hughes guilty of the required act of conspiracy based on evidence provided at trial by the other Hughes's employees that were called as witnesses. [*United States v. Hughes Aircraft Company, Inc.*, 20 F.3d 974 (9th Cir. 1994)]

Racketeer Influenced and Corrupt Organizations Act (RICO)

Organized crime has a pervasive influence on many parts of the U.S. economy. In 1980, Congress enacted the Organized Crime Control Act. The **Racketeer Influenced and Corrupt Organizations Act (RICO)** is part of this Act [18 U.S.C. §§ 1961–1968]. Originally, RICO was intended to apply only to organized crime, but the broad language of the RICO statute has been used against nonorganized crime defendants as well. RICO, which provides for both criminal and civil penalties, is one of the most important laws affecting business today.

RICO makes it a federal crime to acquire or maintain an interest in, use income from, or conduct or participate in the affairs of an "enterprise" through a "pattern" of "racketeering activity." An "enterprise" is defined as a corporation, a partnership, a sole proprietorship, another business or organization, and the government. *Racketeering activity* consists of a number of specifically enumerated federal and state crimes, including activities such as gambling, arson, robbery, counterfeiting, dealing in narcotics, and so on. Business-related crimes, such as bribery, embezzlement, mail fraud, wire fraud, and the like, also are considered racketeering.

During the 1970s, several scandals were uncovered in which American companies were found to have bribed foreign government officials to obtain lucrative contracts. Congressional investigations discovered that making such payments—or bribes—was pervasive in conducting international business. To prevent American companies from engaging in this type of conduct, the U.S. Congress enacted the Foreign Corrupt Practices Act of 1977 (FCPA) [15 U.S.C. § 78m]. Congress amended the FCPA as part of the Omnibus Trade and Competitiveness Act of 1988.

The FCPA attacks the problem in two ways. First, it requires firms to keep accurate books and records of all foreign transactions and install internal accounting controls to ensure that transactions and payments are authorized. Inadvertent or technical errors in maintaining books and records do not violate the FCPA.

Second, the FCPA makes it illegal for American companies, or their officers, directors, agents, or employees, to bribe a foreign official, a foreign political party official, or a candidate for foreign political office. A bribe is illegal only if it is meant to influence the awarding of new business or the retaining of a continuing business activity. Payments to secure ministerial, clerical, or routine government action (such as scheduling inspections, signing customs documents, unloading and loading of cargo, and the like) do not violate the FCPA.

The FCPA imposes criminal liability only in circumstances in which persons knowingly fail to maintain the proper system of accounting, pay the illegal bribe themselves, or supply a payment to a third party or agent knowing that it will be used as a bribe. A firm can be fined up to $2 million and an individual can be fined up to $100,000 and imprisoned for up to five years for violations of the FCPA.

The 1988 amendments created two defenses. One excuses a firm or a person charged with bribery under the FCPA if the firm or person can show that the payment was lawful under the written laws of that country. The other allows a defendant to show that a payment was a reasonable and bona fide expenditure related to the furtherance or execution of a contract.

Some people argue that the FCPA is too soft and permits U.S. firms to engage in the payment of bribes internationally that would otherwise be illegal in the United States. Others argue that the FCPA is difficult to interpret and apply, and that U.S. companies are placed at a disadvantage in international markets where commercial bribery is commonplace and firms from other countries are not hindered by laws similar to the FCPA.

To prove a *pattern of racketeering*, at least two predicate acts must be committed by the defendant within a 10-year period. For example, committing two different frauds would be considered a pattern. Individual defendants found criminally liable for RICO violations can be fined up to $25,000 per violation, imprisoned for up to 20 years, or both. In addition, RICO provides for the *forfeiture* of any property or business interests (even interests in a legitimate business) that were gained because of RICO violations. This provision allows the government to recover investments made with monies derived from racketeering activities. The government also may seek civil penalties for RICO violations. These include injunctions, orders of dissolution, reorganization of business, and divestiture of the defendant's interest in an enterprise.

Racketeering

In 1992, mob boss John Gotti was sentenced to life in prison after being convicted of criminal racketeering and murder charges. Gotti died in prison in 2002.

SIDEBAR

The Internet and Information Age ushered in a whole new world for education, business, and consumer transactions. But with it followed a new rash of digital crimes. Prosecutors and courts wrestled over how to apply existing laws written in a nondigital age to new Internet-related abuses. In many instances, criminal cases were dismissed because the statutory language of existing criminal laws could not be stretched to reach unauthorized computer breaches.

In 1996, Congress responded by enacting the Information Infrastructure Protection Act (IIP Act). In this new federal law, Congress addressed computer-related crimes as distinct offenses. Previously, the Computer Abuse Act outlawed knowingly damaging federal computers, but this Act did not cover nonfederal interest computers owned by businesses and individuals. Also, existing criminal acts required that unauthorized access to computer data had to be for the defendant's commercial benefit before it was illegal. The IIP Act cleared up both of these deficiencies in criminal law in the following ways:

- The IIP Act applies to all "protected computers," not only to federal computers. By statutory definition, a protected computer includes any computer that is used in interstate or foreign commerce.

Thus, the IIP Act provides protection for any computer attached to the Internet.

- The IIP Act does not require that the defendant accessed a protected computer for commercial benefit. The Act makes it clear that simply accessing and obtaining information from a protected computer in excess of one's authorization is unlawful.

The IIP Act makes it a criminal offense for anyone to intentionally access and obtain information from a protected computer without authorization. Thus, persons who transmit a computer virus over the Internet or hackers who trespass into Internet-connected computers may be criminally prosecuted under the IIP Act. Even merely observing data on a protected computer without authorization is sufficient to meet the requirement that the defendant has accessed a protected computer. Criminal penalties for violating the IIP Act include imprisonment for up to 10 years and fines.

The IIP Act gives the federal government a much-needed weapon for directly prosecuting cyber-crooks, hackers, and others who enter, steal, destroy, or look at others' computer data without authorization.

INCHOATE CRIMES

In addition to the substantive crimes discussed, a person can be held criminally liable for committing an **inchoate crime,** which includes incomplete crimes and crimes committed by nonparticipants. The most important inchoate crimes are discussed in the following paragraphs.

Criminal Conspiracy

When two or more persons enter into an *agreement* to commit a crime it is termed **criminal conspiracy.** To be liable for a criminal conspiracy, the conspirators must take an *overt act* to further the crime. The crime itself does not have to be committed, however.

Consider this example: Two securities brokers agreed over the telephone to commit a securities fraud. They also obtained a list of potential victims and prepared false financial statements necessary for the fraud. Because they entered into an agreement to commit a crime and took overt action, the brokers are guilty of the crime of criminal conspiracy even if they didn't carry out the securities fraud. The government usually brings criminal conspiracy charges if (1) the defendants have been thwarted in their efforts to commit the substantive crime, or (2) insufficient evidence is available to prove the substantive crime.

Attempt to Commit a Crime

The **attempt to commit a crime** is itself a crime. For example, suppose a person wants to kill his neighbor. He shoots at her but misses. The perpetrator is not liable for the crime of murder, but he is liable for the crime of attempted murder.

Aiding and Abetting the Commission of a Crime

Sometimes persons assist others in the commission of a crime. The act of **aiding and abetting** the commission of a crime is itself a crime. This concept, which is very broad, encompasses rendering support, assistance, or encouragement to the commission of a crime. Harboring a criminal after he or she has committed a crime is also considered aiding and abetting.

CONSTITUTIONAL SAFEGUARDS

When our forefathers drafted the U.S. Constitution, they included provisions that protect persons from unreasonable government intrusion and provide safeguards for those accused of crimes. Although these safeguards originally applied only to federal cases, the Fourteenth Amendment's Due Process Clause made them applicable to state criminal law cases as well. The most important constitutional safeguards and privileges are discussed in the following paragraphs.

SIDEBAR

Computer Crime

The use of computers to commit business crimes is increasing. Businesses must implement safeguards to prevent computer crimes.

Corporate Criminal Liability

A corporation is a fictitious legal person that is granted legal existence by the state only after meeting certain requirements. A corporation cannot act on its own behalf. Instead, it must act through *agents* such as managers, representatives, and employees.

The question of whether a corporation can be held criminally liable has intrigued legal scholars for some time. Originally, under the common law, it was generally held that corporations lacked the criminal mind (*mens rea*) to be held criminally liable. Modern courts, however, are more pragmatic. These courts have held that corporations are criminally liable for the acts of their managers, agents, and employees. In any event, because corporations cannot be put in prison, they usually are sanctioned with fines, loss of a license or franchise, and the like.

Corporate directors, officers, and employees are individually liable for crimes they personally commit, whether for personal benefit or on behalf of the corporation. In addition, under certain circumstances a corporate manager can be held criminally liable for the criminal activities of his or her subordinates. To be held criminally liable, the manager must have failed to supervise the subordinate appropriately. This is an evolving area of the law.

Fourth Amendment Protection Against Unreasonable Searches and Seizures

The *Fourth Amendment* to the U.S. Constitution protects persons and corporations from overzealous investigative activities by the government. It protects the rights of the people from **unreasonable search and seizure** by the government and permits people to be secure in their persons, houses, papers, and effects.

"Reasonable" search and seizure by the government is lawful. **Search warrants** based on probable cause are necessary in most cases. These warrants specifically state the place and scope of the authorized search. General searches beyond the specified area are forbidden. *Warrantless searches* generally are permitted only (1) incident to arrest, (2) where evidence is in "plain view," or (3) where evidence likely will be destroyed. Warrantless searches also are judged by the probable-cause standard.

Sevier County Courthouse completed 1896 in Sevierville, Tennessee.

Evidence obtained from an unreasonable search and seizure is considered tainted evidence ("fruit of a poisonous tree"). Under the **exclusionary rule,** such evidence can be prohibited from introduction at a trial or administrative proceeding against the person searched. This evidence, however, is freely admissible against other persons. The U.S. Supreme Court created a *good-faith exception* to the exclusionary rule. This exception allows evidence otherwise obtained illegally to be introduced as evidence against the accused if the police officers who conducted the unreasonable search reasonably believed they were acting pursuant to a lawful search warrant.

Generally, the government does not have the right to search business premises without a search warrant. But businesses in certain hazardous and regulated industries—such as sellers of firearms and liquor, coal mines, vehicle dismantling and automobile junkyards, and the like—are subject to warrantless searches if proper statutory procedures are met. A business also may give consent to search the premises, including employee desks and computers, because of the lack of privacy in those items.

Fifth Amendment Privilege Against Self-Incrimination

The *Fifth Amendment* to the U.S. Constitution provides that no person "shall be compelled in any criminal case to be a witness against himself." Thus, a person cannot be compelled to give testimony against himself or herself, although nontestimonial evidence (fingerprints, body fluids, and the like) may be required. A person who asserts this right is described as having "taken the Fifth." This protection applies to federal cases and is extended to state and local criminal cases through the Due Process Clause of the Fourteenth Amendment.

The protection against **self-incrimination** applies only to natural persons who are accused of crimes. Therefore, artificial persons (such as corporations and partnerships) cannot raise this protection against incriminating testimony. Thus, business records of corporations and partnerships are not protected

Kyllo v. United States

121 S.Ct. 2038 (2001)   Supreme Court of the United States

FACTS

In 1992, government agents suspected that marijuana was being grown in the home of Danny Kyllo, part of a triplex building in Florence, Oregon. Indoor marijuana growth typically requires high-intensity lamps. To determine whether an amount of heat was emanating from Kyllo's home consistent with the use of such lamps, federal agents used a thermal imager to scan the triplex. Thermal imagers detect infrared radiation and produce images of the radiation. The scan of Kyllo's home, which was performed from an automobile on the street, showed that the roof over the garage and a side wall of Kyllo's home were "hot." The federal agents concluded that Kyllo was using halide lights to grow marijuana in his house. The agents used this scanning evidence to obtain a search warrant authorizing a search of Kyllo's home. During the search, the agents found an indoor growing operation involving more than 100 marijuana plants.

Kyllo was indicted for manufacturing marijuana, a violation of federal criminal law. Kyllo moved to suppress the imaging evidence and the evidence it led to, arguing that it was an unreasonable search that violated the Fourth Amendment to the U.S. Constitution. The trial court disagreed with Kyllo and let the evidence be introduced and considered at trial. Kyllo then entered a conditional guilty plea and appealed the trial court's failure to suppress the challenged evidence. The court of appeals affirmed. The U.S. Supreme Court granted *certiorari* to hear the appeal.

ISSUE

Is the use of a thermal-imaging device aimed at a private home from a public street to detect relative amounts of heat within the home a "search" within the meaning of the Fourth Amendment?

IN THE LANGUAGE OF THE COURT

Scalia, Justice.

At the very core of the Fourth Amendment stands the right of a man to retreat into his own home and there be free from unreasonable governmental intrusion. With few exceptions, the question whether a warrantless search of a home is reasonable and hence constitutional must be answered no. On the other hand, the lawfulness of warrantless visual surveillance of a home has still been preserved. If fact we have held that visual observation is no "search" at all. We have applied the test on different occasions in holding that aerial surveillance of private homes and surrounding areas does not constitute a search. [*California v. Ciraolo*, 476 U.S. 207, 213, 106 S.Ct. 1809 (1986), and *Florida v. Riley*, 488 U.S. 445, 109 S.Ct. 693 (1989)]

The present case involves officers on a public street engaged in more than naked-eye surveillance of a home. The question we confront today is what limits there are upon this power of technology to shrink the realm of guaranteed privacy. We think that obtaining by sense-enhancing technology any information regarding the interior of the home that could not otherwise have been obtained without physical intrusion into a constitutionally protected area constitutes a search. This assures preservation of that degree of privacy against government that existed when the Fourth Amendment was adopted. On the basis of this criterion, the information obtained by the thermal imager in this case was the product of a search.

DECISION AND REMEDY

The U.S. Supreme Court held that the use of a thermal-imaging device aimed at a private home from a public street to detect relative amounts of heat within the home is a "search" within the meaning of the Fourth Amendment. The Supreme Court reversed and remanded the case for further proceedings.

Questions

1. Is the Fourth Amendment's prohibition against unreasonable search and seizure an easy standard to apply? Explain.

2. Did the police act ethically in obtaining the evidence in this case? Did Kyllo act ethically in trying to suppress the evidence?

3. How can the government catch entrepreneurs such as Kyllo? Explain.

Fifth Amendment

It is improper for a jury to infer guilt from the defendant's exercise of his or her constitutional right to remain silent.

Immunity

Some persons who are granted immunity are placed in witness protection programs. They are usually given a new identity, relocated, and found a job.

from disclosure, even if they incriminate individuals who work for the business. But certain "private papers" of businesspersons (such as personal diaries) are protected from disclosure.

Immunity from Prosecution

On occasion, the government wants to obtain information from a suspect who has asserted his or her Fifth Amendment privilege against self-incrimination. The government can try to achieve this by offering the suspect **immunity from prosecution,** in which the government agrees not to use any evidence given by a person who has been granted immunity against that person. Once immunity is granted, the suspect loses the right to assert his or her Fifth Amendment privilege. Grants of immunity often are given when the government wants the suspect to give information that will lead to the prosecution of other, more important criminal suspects. Partial grants of immunity also are available. For example, a suspect may be granted immunity from prosecution for a serious crime but not a lesser crime, in exchange for information.

Attorney–Client Privilege and Other Privileges

To obtain a proper defense, the accused person must be able to tell his or her attorney facts about the case without fear that the attorney will be called as a witness against the accused. The **attorney–client privilege** is protected by the Fifth Amendment. Either the client or the attorney can raise this privilege. For the privilege to apply, the information must be told to the attorney in his or her capacity as an attorney, and not as a friend or neighbor or other such relationship.

The following privileges also have been recognized under the Fifth Amendment:

1. Psychiatrist/psychologist–patient privilege,
2. Priest/minister/rabbi–penitent privilege,
3. Spouse–spouse privilege, and
4. Parent–child privilege.

There are some exceptions. For example, a spouse or a child who is beaten by a spouse or a parent may testify against the accused.

Fifth Amendment Protection Against Double Jeopardy

The **double jeopardy** clause of the Fifth Amendment protects persons from being tried twice for the same crime. For example, if the state tries a suspect for the crime of murder and the suspect is found innocent, the state cannot bring another trial against the accused for the same crime. But if the same criminal act involves several different crimes, the accused may be tried for each of the crimes without violating the double jeopardy clause. Suppose the accused kills two people during a robbery. The accused may be tried for two murders and the robbery.

If the same act violates the laws of two or more jurisdictions, each jurisdiction may try the accused. For instance, if an accused person kidnaps a person in one state and brings the victim across a state border into another state, the act violates the laws of two states and the federal government. Thus, three jurisdictions can prosecute the accused without violating the double jeopardy clause.

Sixth Amendment Right to a Public Jury Trial

The *Sixth Amendment* guarantees that criminal defendants have these rights:

1. The right to be tried by an impartial jury of the state or district in which the alleged crime was committed.
2. The right to confront (cross-examine) the witnesses against the accused.
3. The right to have the assistance of a lawyer.
4. The right to have a speedy trial.

The Speedy Trial Act requires that a criminal defendant be brought to trial within 70 days after indictment [18 U.S.C. § 3161(c)(1)]. The court may grant continuances to serve the "ends of justice."

Miranda 2000

Most people have not read and memorized the provisions of the U.S. Constitution. The U.S. Supreme Court recognized this fact when it decided the landmark case *Miranda v. Arizona* in 1966 [384 U.S. 436, 86 S.Ct. 1602]. In that case, the Supreme Court held that the Fifth Amendment privilege against self-incrimination is not useful unless a criminal suspect has knowledge of this right. Therefore, the Supreme Court required that the following warning—colloquially called the **Miranda rights**—be read to a criminal suspect before he or she is interrogated by the police or other government officials:

- You have the right to remain silent.
- Anything you say can and will be used against you.
- Your have the right to consult a lawyer, and to have a lawyer present with you during interrogation.
- If you cannot afford a lawyer, a lawyer will be appointed free of charge to represent you.

Any statements or confessions obtained from a suspect prior to being read his or her *Miranda* rights can be excluded from evidence at trial. *Miranda* has been criticized for letting guilty defendants go free. To combat this problem, the U.S. Congress enacted a statute, 18 U.S.C. Section 3501, which provided that a statement or confession by a suspect is admissible into evidence if it is "voluntarily" given even if the suspect has not been read his or her *Miranda* rights. Under this federal statute, many courts admitted into evidence confessions and other statements by defendants.

In 2000, the U.S. Supreme Court decided to revisit *Miranda* in *Dickerson v. United States* [120 S.Ct. 2326] to

test the lawfulness of Section 3501 (voluntary admission of guilt). In that case, the criminal defendant Dickerson was indicted for bank robbery. Before trial, Dickerson moved to suppress an incriminating statement he had made to the Federal Bureau of Investigation (FBI) prior to being read his *Miranda* rights. The court of appeals applied Section 3501 and admitted the statement at trial. Dickerson appealed to the U.S. Supreme Court to keep the statement out of trial.

In a closely watched case, the Supreme Court upheld the *Miranda* ruling, finding that the *Miranda* decision was constitutionally based, and that Congress's attempt to lessen it by enacting Section 3501 was unconstitutional. In reaching its decision, the Supreme Court stated:

We do not think there is justification for overruling *Miranda. Miranda* has become embedded in routine police practice to the point where the warnings have become part of our national culture. Whether or not we would agree with *Miranda's* reasoning and its resulting rule, were we addressing the issue in the first instance, the principles of stare decisis weigh heavily against overruling it now. We conclude that *Miranda* announced a constitutional rule that Congress may not supercede legislatively. Following the rule of stare decisis, we decline to overrule *Miranda* ourselves.

Thus, rather than being overturned or chipped away at, *Miranda* has been resurrected in its strict liability format: Police and government officials must read criminal suspects their *Miranda* rights. Otherwise the suspect's statements and confessions are inadmissible at trial.

Little did Christopher Columbus know in 1503 when he sailed past the Cayman Islands in the Caribbean that these tiny islands would become a bastion of international finance in the late twentieth and early twenty-first centuries. These tiny islands of 35,000 people host about 600 banks with more than $500 million in deposits. Why is so much money being hoarded there? The answer is: bank secrecy laws.

Every nation has banking laws, but all banking laws are not equal. What the Cayman Islands banking law provides is confidentiality. In most instances, no party other than the depositor has the right to know the identity of the depositor, account number, or amount in the account. In fact, most accounts are held in the name of trusts instead of the depositor's actual name. This bank secrecy law has attracted many persons to park their ill-gotten gains in a Cayman Islands bank. Often the bank is no more than a lawyer's office.

Switzerland was once the primary location for depositing money that did not want to be found. After some pressure from the United States and other countries, however, Switzerland entered into memoranda of understanding agreeing to cooperate with criminal investigations by these countries and to help uncover money deposited in Switzerland made through securities frauds and other crimes. Therefore, Switzerland has lost some of its luster as an international money hideout.

So Switzerland has been replaced by other places offering even more secret bank secrecy laws. The Cayman Islands is now the "Switzerland of the Caribbean," and there are several other bank secrecy hideouts around the world, including the Bahamas in the Caribbean, the country of Liechtenstein in Europe, the Isle of Jersey off Great Britain, and the micro-island of Niue in the South Pacific. These tiny countries and islands follow the adage: "Write a good law and they will come."

Eighth Amendment Protection Against Cruel and Unusual Punishment

The *Eighth Amendment* protects criminal defendants from **cruel and unusual punishment.** For example, it prohibits the torture of criminals. This clause, however, does not prohibit capital punishment.

Accountant–Client Privilege?

The common law has long recognized an attorney–client privilege that protects communications between a client and his or her lawyer from discovery in a lawsuit. This means that lawyers cannot testify against their own clients. The rationale for this rule is that if an attorney could be called to testify against a client, the client might choose to withhold information from the attorney. This might prevent the attorney from preparing the best defense.

Although a similar situation occurs when accountants are supplied with information and documents by their clients,

the U.S. Supreme Court has found that there is no corresponding accountant–client privilege under federal law [*Couch v. U.S.*, 409 U.S. 322, 93 S.Ct. 611 (1973)]. Thus, an accountant could be called as a witness in cases involving federal securities laws, federal mail or wire fraud, or federal RICO.

Nevertheless, approximately 20 states have enacted special statutes that create an accountant–client privilege. An accountant cannot be called as a witness against a client in a court action in a state where these statutes are in effect. Federal courts do not recognize these laws, though.

Federal Antiterrorism Act of 2001

The devastating suicide attack on the World Trade Center in New York and the Pentagon in Washington, D.C., on September 11, 2001, shocked the nation. The attacks were organized and orchestrated by terrorists who crossed nations' borders easily, secretly planned and prepared for the attacks undetected, and financed the attacks with money located in banks in the United States, Great Britain, and other countries.

In response, Congress held hearings investigating how to counter such terrorist activities. Congress enacted a new federal Antiterrorism Act that assists the government in detecting and preventing terrorist activities, and investigating and prosecuting terrorists. The bill was signed into law by President George W. Bush on October 26, 2001. The Act contains the following main features.

- *Special intelligence court.* The Act authorizes a special intelligence court to issue expanded wiretap orders and subpoenas to obtain evidence of suspected terrorism.

- *Nationwide search warrant.* The Act created a nationwide search warrant to obtain evidence of terrorist activities. Previously, search warrants were limited to specific geographical locations.

- *Roving wiretaps.* The Act permits "roving wiretaps" on a person suspected of involvement in terrorism so that any telephone or electronic device used by the person may be monitored. Previously, officials had to obtain separate wiretap orders for each phone a suspect used, which increased the difficulty of monitoring terrorists who used multiple telephones, including cellular phones.

- *Sharing of information.* The Act permits sharing of evidence obtained during grand jury proceedings, and evidence obtained by government law enforcement and intelligence agencies such as the Federal Bureau of Investigation (FBI), Central Intelligence Agency (CIA), National Security Administration (NSA), Immigration and Naturalization Service (INS), U.S. Treasury Department, and other government agencies. Previously, sharing of such information was restricted.

- *Detention of noncitizens.* The Act gives the federal government authority to detain a nonresident in the United States for up to seven days without filing charges against that person if he or she is certified by the U.S. Attorney General as being under suspicion of involvement in terrorist activities. Nonresidents who are certified by a court as a threat to national security may be held for up to six months without a trial. Aliens who raise funds for terrorist organizations may be deported.

- *Bioterrorism provision.* The Act makes it illegal for people or groups to possess substances that can be used as biological or chemical weapons for any purpose besides a "peaceful" one.

- *Anti–money laundering provisions.* The Act includes several provisions to discover, trace, and impound bank accounts used to fund terrorist activities. The Act requires U.S. banks to determine sources of large overseas private bank accounts. Banks that refuse to disclose information on such accounts to U.S investigators are subject to sanctions, including loss of license to conduct banking operations. The U.S. Treasury Department may cut off all dealings in the United States of foreign banking institutions located in nations with bank secrecy laws that refuse to disclose information on bank accounts to U.S. investigators. U.S. banks are barred from doing business with offshore shell banks that have no connection to any regulated banking industry.

Proponents of the federal Antiterrorism Act argue that the new investigative and other powers granted by the Act are necessary to give law enforcement and intelligence agencies necessary tools to detect and prevent terrorist activities and to investigate and prosecute terrorists. Critics of the Act argue that civil liberties and many constitutional freedoms are trampled by provisions of the Act.

LEGAL TERMINOLOGY

Actus reus

Aiding and abetting

Arraignment

Arrest warrant

Arson

Attempt to commit a crime

Attorney–client privilege

Bench trial/waiver trial

Bribery

Burden of proof

Burglary

Crime

Criminal conspiracy

Criminal fraud

Criminal law

Cruel and unusual punishment

Defendant

Defense attorney

District attorney

Double jeopardy

Embezzlement

Exclusionary rule

Exculpatory

Extortion

Felony

Forgery

Hung jury

Immunity from prosecution

Inchoate crime

Indictment

Larceny

Mail fraud

Mens rea

Miranda rights

Misdemeanor

Penal code

Plaintiff

Plea bargain

Probable cause

Prosecutor

Public defender

Racketeer Influenced and Corrupt
    Organizations Act (RICO)

Robbery

Search warrant

Self-incrimination

Trier of fact

Unreasonable search and seizure

Violation

White-collar crime

Wire fraud

Summary

What Is a Crime?

Specifics of a Criminal Trial	1. The accused is *presumed innocent until proven guilty.* 2. The plaintiff (the government) bears the *burden of proof.* 3. The government must prove *beyond a reasonable doubt* that the accused is guilty of the crime charged. 4. The accused does not have to testify against himself or herself.
Definition	Any act done by a person in violation of those duties that he or she owes to society and for the breach of which the law provides a penalty.
Penal Codes	State and federal statutes that define many crimes. Criminal conduct is also defined in many *regulatory statutes.*
Parties to a Criminal Lawsuit	1. *Plaintiff:* The government, which is represented by the *prosecuting attorney* (or *prosecutor*). 2. *Defendant:* The person or business accused of the crime, who is represented by a *defense attorney.*
Classification of Crimes	1. *Felonies:* The most serious kinds of crimes. *Mala in se* (inherently evil). Usually punishable by imprisonment. 2. *Misdemeanors:* Less serious crimes. *Mala prohibita* (prohibited by society). Usually punishable by fine and/or imprisonment for less than one year. 3. *Violations:* Not a felony nor a misdemeanor. Generally punishable by a fine.
Elements of a Crime	1. *Actus reus:* guilty act. 2. *Mens rea:* evil intent.

Criminal Procedure and Process

Pretrial Criminal Procedure	1. *Arrest:* Made pursuant to an *arrest warrant* based upon a showing of "probable cause," or, where permitted, by a *warrantless* arrest. 2. *Indictment or information:* Grand juries issue *indictments;* magistrates (judges) issue *informations.* These formally charge the accused with specific crimes. 3. *Arraignment:* Accused is informed of the charges against him or her and enters a *plea* in court. The plea may be *not guilty, guilty,* or *nolo contendere.* 4. *Plea bargaining:* Government and accused may negotiate a settlement agreement wherein the accused agrees to admit to a lesser crime than charged. *(continued)*

Criminal Trial

Criminal Trial	1. *Conviction:* Requires unanimous vote of jury. 2. *Innocent:* Requires unanimous vote of jury. 3. *Hung jury:* Nonunanimous vote of the jury; the government may prosecute the case again.
Appeal	1. *Defendant:* May appeal his or her conviction. 2. *Plaintiff (government):* May not appeal a verdict of innocent.

Crimes Affecting Business

Robbery	The taking of personal property from another by fear or force.
Burglary	The unauthorized entering of a building to commit a felony.
Larceny	The wrongful taking of another's property other than from his person or building.
Theft	The wrongful taking of another's property, whether by robbery, burglary, or larceny.
Receiving Stolen Property	A person knowingly receives stolen property with the intent to deprive the rightful owner of that property.
Arson	The malicious and willful burning of another's building.
Forgery	Fraudulent making or altering of a written document that affects the legal liability of another person.
Extortion	Threat to expose something about another person unless that person gives up money or property.
Credit-card Crimes	The misappropriation or use of another person's credit card.
Bad check legislation	The making, drawing, or delivery of a check by a person when that person knows that there are insufficient funds in the account to cover the check.

White-Collar Crimes

Definition	Crimes that are prone to be committed by businesspersons that involve cunning and trickery rather than physical force.
Embezzlement	The fraudulent conversion of property by a person to whom the property was entrusted.
Criminal Fraud	Obtaining title to another's property through deception or trickery. Also called *false pretenses* or *deceit.*
Mail Fraud	The use of mail to defraud another person.

(continued)

Wire Fraud	The use of wire (telephone or telegraph) to defraud another person.
Bribery	The offer of payment of money or property or something else of value in return for an unwarranted favor. The payor of a bribe is also guilty of the crime of bribery. 1. *Commercial bribery* is the offer of a payment of a bribe to a private person or a business. This is often referred to as a *kickback* or *payoff*. 2. Bribery of a public official for an "official act" is a crime.
Racketeer Influenced and Corrupt Organizations Act (RICO)	Makes it a federal crime to acquire or maintain an interest in, use income from, or conduct or participate in the affairs of an "enterprise" through a "pattern" of "racketeering activity." Criminal penalties include the *forfeiture* of any property or business interests gained by a RICO violation.

Inchoate Crimes

Definition	Crimes that are incomplete or that are committed by nonparticipants.
Criminal Conspiracy	When two or more persons enter into an *agreement* to commit a crime and take some *overt act* to further the crime.
Attempt to Commit a Crime	The attempt to commit a crime is a crime even if the commission of the intended crime is unsuccessful.
Aiding and Abetting the Commission of a Crime	Rendering support, assistance, or encouragement to the commission of a crime, or knowingly harboring a criminal after he or she has committed a crime.

Constitutional Safeguards

Fourth Amendment Protection Against Unreasonable Searches and Seizures	Protects persons and corporations from *unreasonable searches and seizures.*
	
	1. *Reasonable searches and seizures* based on *probable cause* are lawful:
	  a. *Search warrant:* Stipulates the place and scope of the search.
	  b. *Warrantless search:* Permitted only:
	    i. Incident to an arrest.
	    ii. Where evidence is in plain view.
	    iii. Where it is likely that evidence will be destroyed.
	2. *Exclusionary rule:* Evidence obtained from an unreasonable search and seizure is *tainted evidence* that may not be introduced at a government proceeding against the person searched.
	3. *Business premises:* Protected by the Fourth Amendment, except that certain *regulated industries* may be subject to warrantless searches authorized by statute.

Fifth Amendment Privilege Against Self-Incrimination	Provides that no person "shall be compelled in any criminal case to be a witness against himself." A person asserting this privilege is said to have taken the Fifth. *(continued)*

Fifth Amendment Privilege Against Self-Incrimination, *continued*	1. *Nontestimonial evidence:* This evidence (e.g., fingerprints, body fluids, etc.) is not protected.
	2. *Businesses:* The privilege applies only to natural persons; businesses cannot assert the privilege.
	3. *Miranda rights:* A criminal suspect must be informed of his or her Fifth Amendment rights before the suspect can be interrogated by the police or government officials.
	4. *Immunity from prosecution:* Granted by the government to obtain otherwise privileged evidence. The government agrees not to use the evidence given against the person who gave it.
	5. *Attorney–client privilege:* An accused's lawyer cannot be called as a witness against the accused.
	6. *Other privileges:* The following privileges have been recognized, with some limitations:
	   a. psychiatrist/psychologist–patient
	   b. priest/minister/rabbi–penitent
	   c. spouse–spouse; parent–child
	7. *Accountant–client privilege:* None recognized at the federal level. Some states recognize this privilege in state law actions.

Fifth Amendment Protection Against Double Jeopardy	Protects persons from being tried twice by the same jurisdiction for the same crime. If the act violates the laws of two or more jurisdictions, each jurisdiction may try the accused.
Sixth Amendment Right to a Public Jury Trial	Guarantees criminal defendants the following rights: 1. To be tried by an impartial jury 2. To confront the witness 3. To have the assistance of a lawyer 4. To have a speedy trial
Eighth Amendment Protection Against Cruel and Unusual Punishment	Protects criminal defendants from cruel and unusual punishment. Capital punishment is permitted.

Working the Web

1. Check the U.S. Department of Justice website for information on the Freedom of Information Act and the principal FOIA contacts at various federal agencies at www.usdoj.gov/04foia/04_3.html.

2. Obtain a copy of *Your Right to Federal Records Questions and Answers on the Freedom of Information Act and Privacy Act* at www.pueblo.gsa.gov/cic_text/fed_prog/foia/foia.htm.

3. View the Privacy Act of 1974 at www.usdoj.gov/04foia/privstat.htm.

4. View a copy of the original document and information on the Bill of Rights at www.nara.gov/exhall/treasuresofcongress/page_3.html.

5. Obtain information on the United States Sentencing Commission at www.ussc.gov.

Questions
CRITICAL LEGAL THINKING AND WRITING

1. What obligation does the prosecution have to reveal to a defense attorney information helpful to the defense?

2. Why is counsel provided to criminal defendants without charge if they cannot afford to hire a lawyer?

3. Why is the burden of proof different in a criminal case than in a civil case?

4. What is the value in a plea bargain to the government? The defendant?

5. Why is the government not permitted to appeal a finding of not guilty in a criminal case?

6. Why would a person want to waive his or her Fifth Amendment right against self-incrimination?

7. When can a person be tried twice for the same act and not violate the double-jeopardy provision of the Fifth Amendment?

8. How can a corporation be punished for criminal acts?

9. How does the exclusionary rule protect the rights of the individual?

10. Should the standards of protection provided by the Constitution apply to nonresidents of the United States for crimes committed in the United States? Why or why not?

Questions
ETHICS: ANALYSIS AND DISCUSSION

1. Does the attorney–client privilege apply to those working as experts, such as accountants, for an attorney preparing a criminal case for trial? Would this be an extension of the attorney–client privilege?

2. Is the information given to a paralegal by a criminal client covered under the Fifth Amendment when he or she interviews a criminal?

3. What obligation does a paralegal have to make available exculpatory evidence discovered during investigation of a case?

Attorney–Client Privilege—Work Product Doctrine

There are few certainties in the area of ethics, for paralegals or in any profession. What qualifies as ethical conduct is in most cases based on state law and court interpretation applied to a set of facts. The citation listed below represents one legal opinion and is provided as a research starting point. Do not assume that the same rule applies in your jurisdiction. For the following:

- *Prepare a written statement based on your state law.*
- *Use your state bar association website as a starting point.*

You are working at a firm with a large client base that does not speak English. You are fluent in three languages and you are asked to translate for a firm attorney during an interview of a client in a criminal case. You take notes as you translate to be sure you are properly translating what is said. [*Von Bulow by Auersperg v. Von Bulow*, 811 F. 2nd 136 (2nd Cir. 1987).] Are the notes covered under the work product doctrine? Does the attorney–client privilege apply to what you heard?

CASES *for Discussion*

People v. Paulson

216 Cal.App.3d 1480, 265 Cal.Rptr. 579 (Cal.App. 1990)

9.1 FACTS

Lee Stuart Paulson owns the liquor license for "My House," a bar in San Francisco. The California Department of Alcoholic Beverage Control is the administrative agency that regulates bars in that state. The California Business and Professions Code, which the department administers, prohibits "any kind of illegal activity on licensed premises." On February 11, 1988, an anonymous informer tipped the department that narcotic sales were occurring on the premises of "My House" and that the narcotics were kept in a safe behind the bar on the premises.

A special department investigator entered the bar during its hours of operation, identified himself, and informed Paulson that he was conducting an inspection. The investigator, who did not have a search warrant,

opened the safe without seeking Paulson's consent. Twenty-two bundles of cocaine, totaling 5.5 grams, were found in the safe. Paulson was arrested. At his criminal trial, Paulson challenged the lawfulness of the search.

ISSUE

Was the warrantless search of the safe a lawful search?

Center Art Galleries–Hawaii, Inc. v. United States

875 F.2d 747 (9th Cir. 1989)

9.2 FACTS

The Center Art Galleries–Hawaii sells artwork. Approximately 20 percent of its business involves art by Salvador Dali. The federal government, which suspected the center of fraudulently selling forged Dali artwork, obtained identical search warrants for six locations controlled by the center. The warrants commanded the executing officer to seize items which were "evidence of violations of federal criminal law." The warrants did not describe the specific crimes suspected and did not stipulate that only items pertaining to the sale of Dali's work could be seized. There was no evidence of any criminal activity unrelated to that artist.

ISSUE

Is the search warrant valid?

United States v. John Doe

465 U.S. 605, 104 S.Ct. 1237, 79 L.Ed.2d 552 (1984)

9.3 FACTS

John Doe is the owner of several sole-proprietorship businesses. In 1980, during the course of an investigation of corruption in awarding county and municipal contracts, a federal grand jury served several subpoenas on John Doe demanding the production of certain business records. The subpoenas demanded the production of the following records: (1) general ledgers and journals, (2) invoices, (3) bank statements and canceled checks, (4) financial statements, (5) telephone-company records, (6) safe-deposit box records, and (7) copies of tax returns. John Doe filed a motion in federal court seeking to quash the subpoenas, alleging that producing these business records would violate his Fifth Amendment privilege of not testifying against himself.

ISSUE

Do the records have to be disclosed?

People v. Shaw

10 Cal.App.4th 969, 12 Cal.Rptr.2d 665 (Cal. App. 1992)

9.4 FACTS

In 1979, Leo Shaw, an attorney, entered into a partnership agreement with three other persons to build and operate an office building. From the outset, it was agreed that Shaw's role was to manage the operation of the building. Management of the property was Shaw's contribution to the partnership; the other three partners contributed the necessary capital. In January 1989, the other partners discovered that the loan on the building was in default and that foreclosure proceedings were imminent. Upon investigation, they discovered that Shaw had taken approximately $80,000 from the partnership's checking account. After heated discussions, Shaw repaid $13,000. In May 1989, when no further payment was forthcoming, a partner filed a civil suit against Shaw and notified the police. The state filed a criminal complaint against Shaw on March 15, 1990. On April 3, 1990, Shaw repaid the remaining funds as part of a civil settlement. At his criminal trial in November 1990, Shaw argued that the repayment of the money was a defense to the crime of embezzlement.

ISSUE

Did Shaw act ethically in this case? Would your answer be different if he had really only "borrowed" the money and had intended to return it?

Department of Justice v. Landano

508 U.S. 165 (1993)

Read the following case, excerpted from the U.S. Supreme Court's opinion. Review and brief the case. In your brief, answer the following questions:

1. Under what circumstances may a defendant obtain information under the Freedom of Information Act (FOIA)?

2. When may the government in a criminal case refuse to divulge information under the FOIA?

3. Is all information provided to the Federal Bureau of Investigation confidential and therefore not available under the FOIA?

4. Who has the burden of proof in FOIA cases?

O'Connor, J., delivered the opinion for a unanimous Court.

Exemption 7(D) of the Freedom of Information Act, 5 U.S.C. § 552 (FOIA), exempts from disclosure agency records "compiled for law enforcement purposes by criminal law enforcement authority in the course of a criminal investigation" if release of those records "could reasonably be expected to disclose" the identity of or information provided by a "confidential source" [§ 552(b)(7)(D)]. This case concerns the evidentiary showing that the Government must make to establish that a source is "confidential" within the meaning of Exemption 7(D). We are asked to decide whether the Government is entitled to a presumption that all sources supplying information to the Federal Bureau of Investigation (FBI or Bureau) in the course of a criminal investigation are confidential sources.

Respondent Vincent Landano was convicted in New Jersey state court for murdering Newark, New Jersey, police officer John Snow in the course of a robbery. The crime received considerable media attention. Evidence at trial showed that the robbery had been orchestrated by Victor Forni and a motorcycle gang known as "the Breed." There was testimony that Landano, though not a Breed member, had been recruited for the job. Landano always has maintained that he did not participate in the robbery, and that Forni, not he, killed Officer Snow. He contends that the prosecution withheld material exculpatory evidence in violation of *Brady v. Maryland*, 373 U.S. 83 (1963).

Landano apparently is currently pursuing a Brady claim in the state courts. Seeking evidence to support that claim, Landano filed FOIA requests with the FBI for information that the Bureau had compiled in the course of its involvement in the investigation of Officer Snow's murder. Landano sought release of the Bureau's files on both Officer Snow and Forni. The FBI released several hundred pages of documents. The Bureau redacted some of these, however, and withheld several hundred other pages altogether.

The information withheld under Exemption 7(D) included information provided by five types of sources: regular FBI informants; individual witnesses who were not regular informants; state and local law enforcement agencies; other local agencies; and private financial and commercial institutions. In the Government's view, all such sources should be presumed confidential. The deleted portions of the files were coded to indicate which type of source each involved.

Relying on legislative history, the court stated that a source is confidential within the meaning of Exemption 7(D) if the source received an explicit assurance of confidentiality or if there are circumstances "from which such an assurance could reasonably be inferred." An "assurance of confidentiality," the court said, is not a promise of absolute anonymity or secrecy, but "an assurance that the FBI would not directly or indirectly disclose the cooperation of the interviewee with the investigation unless such a disclosure is determined by the FBI to be important to the success of its law enforcement objective."

Exemption 7(D) permits the Government to withhold "records or information compiled for law enforcement purposes, but only to the extent that the production of such law enforcement records or information . . . could reasonably be expected to disclose the identity of a confidential source, including a state, local, or foreign agency or authority or any private institution which furnished information on a confidential basis, and, in the case of a record or information compiled by criminal law enforcement authority in the course of a criminal investigation, information furnished by a confidential source" [§ 552(b)(7)(D)]. The Government bears the burden of establishing that the exemption applies.

When FOIA was enacted in 1966, Exemption 7 broadly protected "'investigatory files compiled for law enforcement purposes except to the extent available by law to a private party.'" Congress adopted the current version of Exemption 7(D) in 1986. The 1986 amendment expanded "records" to "records or information," replaced the word "would" with the phrase "could reasonably be expected to," deleted the word "only" from before "confidential source," and clarified that a confidential source could be a state, local, or foreign agency or a private institution.

Under Exemption 7(D), the question is not whether the requested document is of the type that the agency usually treats as confidential, but whether the particular source spoke with an understanding that the communication would remain confidential. According to the Conference Report on the 1974 amendment, a source is confidential within the meaning of Exemption 7(D) if the source provided information under an express assurance of confidentiality or in circumstances from which such an assurance could be reasonably inferred. In this case, the Government has not attempted to demonstrate that the FBI made explicit promises of confidentiality to particular sources. That sort of proof apparently often is not possible: The FBI does not have a policy of discussing confidentiality with every source, and when such discussions do occur, agents do not always document them.

The precise question before us, then, is how the Government can meet its burden of showing that a source provided information on an implied assurance of confidentiality. The parties dispute two issues: the meaning of the word "confidential," and whether, absent specific evidence to the contrary, an implied assurance of confidentiality always can be inferred from the fact that a source cooperated with the FBI during a criminal investigation.

FOIA does not define the word "confidential." In common usage, confidentiality is not limited to complete anonymity or secrecy. A statement can be made "in confidence" even if the speaker knows the communication will be shared with limited others, as long as the speaker expects that the information will not be published indiscriminately. A promise of complete secrecy would mean that the FBI agent receiving the source's information could not share it even with other FBI personnel. Such information, of course, would be of little use to the Bureau.

We assume that Congress was aware of the Government's disclosure obligations under Brady and applicable procedural rules when it adopted Exemption 7(D). Congress also must have realized that some FBI witnesses would testify at trial. We therefore agree with the Court of Appeals that the word "confidential," as used in Exemption 7(D), refers to a degree of confidentiality less than total secrecy. A source should be deemed confidential if the source furnished information with the understanding that the FBI would not divulge the communication except to the extent the Bureau thought necessary for law enforcement purposes.

Considerations of "fairness" also counsel against the Government's rule. The Government acknowledges that its proposed presumption, though rebuttable in theory, is in practice all but irrebuttable. Once the FBI asserts that information was provided by a confidential source during a criminal investigation, the requester—who has no knowledge about the particular source or the information being withheld—very rarely will be in a position to offer persuasive evidence that the source in fact had no interest in confidentiality.

We agree with the Government that, when certain circumstances characteristically support an inference of confidentiality, the Government similarly should be able to claim exemption under Exemption 7(D) without detailing the circumstances surrounding a particular interview. Neither the language of Exemption 7(D) nor Reporters Committee, Page 178, however, supports the proposition that the category of all FBI criminal investigative sources is exempt.

But Congress did not expressly create a blanket exemption for the FBI; the language that it adopted requires every agency to establish that a confidential source furnished the information sought to be withheld under Exemption 7(D). In short, the Government offers no persuasive evidence that Congress intended for the Bureau to be able to satisfy its burden in every instance simply by asserting that a source communicated with the Bureau during the course of a criminal investigation. Had Congress meant to create such a rule, it could have done so much more clearly.

The Government has argued forcefully that its ability to maintain the confidentiality of all of its sources is vital to effective law enforcement. A prophylactic rule protecting the identities of all FBI criminal investigative sources undoubtedly would serve the Government's objectives, and would be simple for the Bureau and the courts to administer. But we are not free to engraft that policy choice onto the statute that Congress passed. For the reasons we have discussed, and consistent with our obligation to construe FOIA exemptions narrowly in favor of disclosure, we hold that the Government is not entitled to a presumption that a source is confidential within the meaning of Exemption 7(D) whenever the source provides information to the FBI in the course of a criminal investigation.

More narrowly defined circumstances, however, can provide a basis for inferring confidentiality. For example, when circumstances such as the nature of the crime investigated and the witness' relation to it support an inference of confidentiality, the Government is entitled to a presumption. In this case, the Court of Appeals incorrectly concluded that it lacked discretion to rely on such circumstances. Accordingly, we vacate the judgment of the Court of Appeals and remand the case for further proceedings consistent with this opinion. It is so ordered.

CHAPTER 10

CHAPTER OBJECTIVES

After studying this chapter, you should be able to:

1. Name the issues that can be used as the basis for an appeal in a civil case.

2. Name the issues that can be used as the basis for an appeal in a criminal case.

3. Describe the function of the appellate courts in the legal system.

4. Explain the procedures in appealing a case.

5. Describe the nature of the procedural rules of appealing a case in the federal courts.

6. Outline the rules and procedures of the U.S. Supreme Court.

7. Describe the role of the paralegal in the appellate process.

8. Explain the right to make an oral argument in an appeal.

9. Describe the types of actions appellate courts may take.

10. Point out the ethical issues in the appeal of a case.

The Appellate Process

Discourage litigation. Persuade your neighbors to compromise whenever you can. Point out to them how the nominal winner is often a real loser—in fees, and expenses, and waste of time. As a peacemaker the lawyer has a superior opportunity of being a good man. There will still be business enough.

ABRAHAM LINCOLN, *NOTES ON THE PRACTICE OF LAW* (1850)

Introduction

In a civil case, either party can **appeal** the trial court's decision once a final judgment is entered. In a criminal case, only the defendant can appeal. The appeal is made to the appropriate appellate court. A notice of appeal must be filed within a pre-scribed time after judgment is entered (usually within 60 or 90 days). The appealing party is called the **appellant, or petitioner.** The responding party is called the **appellee, or respondent.** The appellant often is required to post an appeal bond (e.g., one-and-one-half times the judgment) on appeal.

A paralegal who works for an attorney who is involved in han-dling litigation and appeals should learn the appellate process, which is covered in this chapter.

THE COURTHOUSE TEAM

Court Reporter

The *court reporter* is a person regularly assigned to the specific judge or is a floating or temporary reporter. His or her job is to take down the proceedings and prepare a written transcript.

The court reporter has the difficult job of making a transcript of a hearing or trial. This becomes even more difficult when two or more people are speaking at the same time, or answering with visual signs such as nodding their heads. Court reporters also have to know who is who at the trial table so they can accurately reflect the proper person when that person speaks. Therefore, members of the trial team should give their business card to the court reporter before the court action starts.

Court reporters can be a major source of information on the likes and dislikes of the trial judge and the procedures that individual judges follow. This is particularly true in the court systems where a reporter is assigned to and works exclusively with one judge. Most court reporters are eager to help and give advice. They also may be willing to get you a copy of the transcript on an expedited basis. Good relations with them are beneficial.

U.S. Supreme Court Rules:
ww.supremecourtus.gov/ct rules/ctrules.html

U.S. Court of Appeals:
www.uscourts.gov/courtsof appeals.html

FUNCTION OF THE APPELLATE COURT

Unlike the trial court, whose main function is to make finding of facts, the appellate court's main function is to make *findings of law*. The trial court first must make *finding of facts*. This is the job of the jury or a trial judge sitting without a jury. After the facts are determined, the judge applies the law to the facts or instructs the jury to apply the law as it applies to the case based on the facts as they find them to be. During the trial, issues may arise requiring rulings from the court on matters of procedure, referred to as **procedural law**—in contrast to **substantive law,** the law of the case (such as the law of negligence, trespass, invasion of privacy, and the like). Procedural law is concerned with the way the trial is conducted, what questions may be asked, what evidence may be presented to the jury, and what the trial attorneys may say in presenting and arguing their case.

The appellate court on appeal may be asked to rule on the propriety of the rulings of the lower court trial judge on these matters of procedural law. In other cases they may be asked to rule on the underlying theory of law of the case, such as whether certain conduct comes within the law of negligence.

FEDERAL APPELLATE PROCEDURE

The **Federal Rules of Civil Procedure** govern civil trials in the federal system. The *Federal Rules of Criminal Procedure* govern criminal trials in the federal system. The **Federal Rules of Appellate Procedure (F.R.A.P.),** and in the case of the United States Supreme Court the rules of the Supreme Court of the United States, govern appeals in both civil and criminal cases to the federal appellate court.

Because the Rules of Civil Procedure and the Rules of Appellate Procedure are frequently amended, it is essential to have a current copy of the rules in preparing any appeal.

In addition to these general rules of procedure, individual courts may have local rules governing things such as electronic filing and submitting briefs in electronic form such as compact disc. Therefore, it also is necessary to secure the local rules of court before proceeding.

UNITED STATES COURTS OF APPEALS

Appeals from the decisions of the U.S. district courts are made to the U.S. courts of appeals, of which there are thirteen. An appeal, which is permitted as a matter of right, from a district court to a court of appeals is taken by the filing of a notice of appeal within the time period provided by the Federal Rules of Appellate Procedure (F.R.A.P. 4).

Generally, the notice of appeal in civil cases must be filed with the district clerk within 30 days after entry of the judgment or order appealed from. But

INFORMATION TECHNOLOGY

WHAT IS PACER?

Public Access to Court Electronic Records (**PACER**) is an electronic public-access service that allows users to obtain case and docket information from federal appellate, district, and bankruptcy courts, and from the U.S. Party/Case Index. Currently, most courts are accessible on the Internet, and links to these courts are provided from PACER's website, http://pacer.psc.uscourts.gov. A few systems, however, are not available on the Internet and must be dialed directly using communication software (such as ProComm Plus, pcAnywhere, or Hyperterminal) and a modem.

Electronic access is available for most courts by registering with the PACER Service Center, the judiciary's centralized registration, billing, and technical support center. Each court maintains its own databases with case information. Because PACER database systems are maintained within each court, each jurisdiction will have a different URL or modem number. Accessing and querying information from each service is comparable, but the format and content of information provided may differ slightly. Links and toll-free modem numbers are provided to most jurisdictions.

PACER is a service of United States Judiciary. The Administrative Office of the United States Courts runs the PACER Service Center.

---

when the United States or its officer or agency is a party, the notice appeal may be filed by any party within 60 days after entry of the judgment or order appealed from. In criminal cases, a defendant's notice of appeal must be filed in the district court within 10 days after entry of the judgment or order or the following of the government's notice of appeal. In criminal cases, the government is entitled to appeal within 30 days.

Exhibit 10.1 sets forth the form for appellate rules for United States courts of appeals.

PACER System:
http://pacer.psc.uscourts.gov/

UNITED STATES SUPREME COURT

The rules for appealing to the United States Supreme Court are found in the *Rules of the Supreme Court of the United States.* The time limit for seeking review by the United States Supreme Court is generally 90 days after the entry of the judgment for which judicial review is sought. As the rules clearly state, review by the Supreme Court is "not a matter of right, but of judicial discretion" and "a petition for *writ of certiorari* will be granted only for compelling reasons" (Rule 10).

As textbooks say, in the United States you can appeal your legal case all the way to the Supreme Court. In reality, however, the chance of ever having your case heard by the highest court is slim to none. Each year, more than 7,000 petitioners pay the $300 filing fee to ask the Supreme Court to hear their case. In addition, these petitioners usually pay big law firms from $30,000 to $100,000 or more to write the appeal petition.

Discovery of Electronic Documents

GP Solo, March 2001

Essentially, the rules that govern the discoverability of electronic documents are identical to those that guide the courts in their rulings regarding traditional documents. Electronic documents are subject to the same protections as traditional documents. This article surveys the legal concepts and practical considerations both counsel and their clients must grasp in this new era of discovery.

Rule 34 of the Federal Rules of Civil Procedure allows any party to serve on any other party a request to produce, and permit the party making the request to inspect and copy, any designated documents, or to inspect and copy, test, or sample any tangible things that constitute or contain matters within the scope of Rule 26(b) and that are in the custody or control of the party on whom the request is served.

The inclusive description of "documents" makes clear that Rule 34 applies to electronic data compilations from which information can be obtained only with the use of detection devices, and that when the data can be made usable by the discovering party only through respondent's devices, respondent may be required to use his or her devices to translate the data into usable form.

What Have Courts Ordered Parties to Produce?

The fact that information has been produced in traditional form does not preclude production of identical information in electronic format. In some cases, courts have required such production to prevent the requesting parties from having to bear the cost of any necessary encoding of such information for analysis. Courts have reasoned that because much of our information is transmitted by computer, it is not unreasonable to require a party to produce the information on computer disk for the plaintiff.

Courts sometimes require parties to make an extensive effort to be certain that document requests are satisfied. For example, a court may require conversion of the format of electronic documents, reasoning that the normal and reasonable translation of electronic data into a form the discovering party can use should be the ordinary and foreseeable burden of a respondent absent a showing of extraordinary hardship.

A trial court may also require a party to create or manufacture data or documents previously nonexis-tent. For example, a court has required a plaintiff to create a computer tape of information that the plaintiff had printed from its computer and produced to the defendant so that the information could be read by the defendant's computer.

Courts recognize that inaccessibility does not relieve a party from its responsibility to make the information available, explaining that Rule 34 contemplates that when data are in an inaccessible form, the party responding to the request for documents must make the data available.

Any analysis associated with the prospect of discovery into a party's computer or hard drive must consider the risk of damage to a party's system and the exposure to confidential information. However, inspection of another's hard drive in an attempt to retrieve data purportedly "purged" from a system may be allowed if the requesting party presents evidence of the likelihood of retrieving purged information, and of there being no other less intrusive manner to obtain the information. In such an event, the order must define parameters of time and scope, and must place sufficient access restrictions to prevent compromising confidentiality and to prevent harm to the defendant's computer and databases.

Duty to Preserve

The risk of spoliation of electronic documents is more pronounced than with traditional ones. However, the rules for when a duty to preserve data arises and what sanctions attach in the event of spoliation are the same for electronic and traditional documents. A party does not have a duty to preserve evidence unless it has notice of its relevance. Specifically, counsel should be aware that a complaint "may alert a party," and that a discovery request places a party on notice that particular information is relevant or sought.

How to Protect Electronic Documents from Discovery

Certain documents, regardless of their form, will be protected from discovery: those subject to the attorney–client privilege, the work product doctrine, and trade secret protections. Before litigation arises, clients should categorize those files believed to be pro-

Sheila J. Carpenter and Shaunda A. Patterson

tected by privileges to avoid inadvertent disclosures in responding to discovery requests. E-mail to and from counsel should be labeled "privileged."

Become familiar with your client's computer system. One bar committee advises counsel to ask their clients the following questions to ensure that the client will preserve and collect all potentially relevant electronic information.

- Where are all of the potential sources of electronic information?
- What is the client's retention policy, and what procedures does the client have in order to enforce the policy?
- How is information stored on the system?
- What are the backup procedures used by the client? Are copies made daily, weekly, or monthly? How is the backup material stored? Is the information compressed during the backup procedures? How frequently are the media used for backup recycled, if at all?
- When information is deleted from the system, is it merely designated to be overwritten, or does the system have a program that actually overwrites the deleted file with a garbled date and random characters? Does the system have an "undelete" program that can restore deleted files?

Advise clients to institute/follow a records retention policy. The benefits to a company in developing and following a sound records retention policy are twofold: it prevents obsolete, unnecessary, or potentially harmful documents from lying around just long enough to be subject to inevitable discovery; and it provides a defense if unwarranted allegations of spoliation arise. Additionally, when a document destruction issue arises, a party can assert that the document was destroyed in good faith.

Advise clients to invest in software that fully erases deleted data. When a user elects to delete data from his or her computer, operating systems typically do not actually remove the information from the file or hard drive. Instead, the file's address is merely changed, and the information is retrievable for some time. These deletion programs are useless if backup disks are made and kept indefinitely. Backup information should have a business purpose.

Special Concerns Associated with E-mail

Because e-mail communications are more casual than traditional avenues of correspondence, users often engage in a reckless exchange. A company can do three basic things to minimize negative ramifications from the use of e-mail: adopt a formal document retention policy specifically for its e-mail system; organize or archive its e-mail system so that important business-related and privileged documents can be retrieved without confusion or delay; and train its employees to exercise care in drafting e-mail messages. Counsel should require that the client's employees be trained in accordance with the company-wide e-mail policy on appropriate usage, which should include the following provisions:

- The e-mail system is the property of the employer.
- E-mail is to be used only for valid business purposes.
- E-mail must not be used for personal matters or to comment about others.
- E-mail correspondence is to be kept confidential by the employee/user.
- The employee agrees and is aware that e-mail may be monitored and disclosed by the employer.
- Humor and sarcasm should not be communicated in e-mail.
- Employees should not compose e-mail messages when they are angry.
- E-mail message recipient lists and text should be thoroughly reviewed by the composer for accuracy before being sent.
- Employees should archive important messages by subject and delete groups when no longer needed.
- Archived and current messages will be subject to review and production in litigation.
- E-mail messages that are not archived will be deleted 30 days after they are sent.

Moreover, the policy should include penalties or disciplinary actions that will be enforced if an employee uses the system in an inappropriate manner.

From GP Solo, Vol. 18, No. 2, March 2001. Copyright © 2001 American Bar Association. Reprinted with permission.

---

exhibit 10.1   *Form 1 of appellate rules.*

United States District Court for the ___Eastern___

District of ___Pennsylvania___

File Number ___US3CA 01234___

Ethan Marshall

           v.   )
)   Notice of Appeal
)
Sara Elliott   )

Notice is hereby given that ___Ethan Marshall___ (plaintiffs)
in the above named case,* hereby appeal to the United States Court of Appeals for the
___Third___ Circuit ___from the final judgment___ entered in this
action on the __06__ day of __February__ , __2002__ .

(s) _____
Thomas F. Goldman

_____
(Address)
Attorney for ___Plaintiff___
Address: ___138 North State Street___
___Newtown, Pa, 18940___

* See Rule 3(c) for permissible ways of identifying appellants.

Costs on Appeal

In recent years, the Supreme Court has accepted only about 100 of these cases for full review each term.

As mentioned in Chapter 6, each of the nine Supreme Court justices has three law clerks who often assist them in reading the appellate petitions. The clerks then write a short *memorandum* discussing the key issues raised by the appeal and recommend to the justices whether they should grant or deny a review. The justices meet once a week to discuss what cases merit a review. The votes of four justices are necessary to grant an appeal and schedule an oral argument before the court. Written opinions by the justices usually are issued many months later.

Checklist

BRIEFS IN FEDERAL COURTS OF APPEALS

Covers

- ○ Appellant brief—Blue
- ○ Appellee brief—Red
- ○ Amicus brief—Green
- ○ Reply brief—Gray

Content of cover

- ○ Number of the case centered at top
- ○ Name of court
- ○ Title of case
- ○ Nature of proceedings and name of court, agency, or board below
- ○ Title of the brief (party or parties for whom brief filed)
- ○ Counsel representing party for whom brief filed
- ○ Name
- ○ Address
- ○ Telephone number

Binding

- ○ Does not obscure text
- ○ Permits brief to lie reasonably flat when opened
- ○ Secure

Paper

- ○ 8 1/2 x 11 inches
- ○ Double-spaced
- ○ Margins at least 1 inch on all sides
- ○ One side only used
- ○ Opaque and unglazed
- ○ Headings and footnotes single-spaced
- ○ Page numbers in margins (but no text)
- ○ Clarity equal to or greater than laser printer

Typeface

- ○ If proportionally spaced, must include serifs and be 14 point or larger
- ○ Monospaced face may not contain more than $10^{1}/_{2}$ characters per inch
- ○ Plain, roman style
- ○ Italics and boldface may be used for emphasis
- ○ Case names must be italicized and underlined

Page limit

- ○ Principal briefs 30 pages (no more than 14,000 words or 1,300 lines of monospaced face text)
- ○ Reply briefs 15 pages (or half the 14,000 word or 1,300 lines limit for principal briefs)

The Process of Choosing a Supreme Court Justice

In an effort to strike a balance of power between the executive and legislative branches of government, Article II, Section 2 of the U.S. Constitution gives the President the power to appoint Supreme Court justices "with the advice and consent of the Senate." In recent years, however, many conservative and liberal critics have charged that this process has become nothing more than a political tennis match in which the hapless nominee is the ball.

Some of the most notorious fights over Supreme Court nominations in U.S. history took place during the Ronald Reagan administration. President George Bush was given the chance to cast a conservative shadow over the court's decisions when Justice Thurgood Marshall, one of the most liberal members of the Court, retired in 1991 after serving 24 years. Also, he had been the only Black person to serve on the Supreme Court. Bush nominated

Clarence Thomas, a Black conservative serving as a judge of the U.S. Court of Appeals in the District of Columbia, to replace Marshall.

The election of Bill Clinton as President swung the pendulum back to the Democrats. Clinton got an early opportunity to nominate a candidate when Justice Byron R. White, the only Democrat-appointed member of the court, retired. Clinton nominated Judge Ruth Bader Ginsburg, who is considered a moderate liberal, had ruled in favor of abortion rights, and was a pioneer in the area of women's rights. Ginsburg was approved by a bipartisan vote of the Senate and took office for the Supreme Court's 1993–94 term. She is the second woman to serve on the Court, joining Sandra Day O'Connor, who was nominated by Reagan. Ginsburg is also the first Jewish person to serve on the Court since Justice Abe Fortas resigned in 1969.

What does it take to win a review by the Supreme Court? Often it requires a *split opinion* in the circuit courts of appeal—that is, several circuit courts have decided the legal issue differently. For example, the Supreme Court recently decided a case where several courts of appeal had held that Title VII, which prohibits sex discrimination in employment, prohibited same-sex discrimination, but several other circuit courts had held that Title VII did not apply to same-sex discrimination. The Supreme Court decided that Title VII did prohibit same-sex discrimination. The court's ruling then resolved the split among the circuit courts and became the "law of the land."

In addition, the U.S. Supreme Court usually decides to hear cases involving major constitutional questions such as freedom of speech, freedom of religion, and due process. The court, therefore, rarely decides day-to-day legal issues such as breach of contract, tort liability, or corporate law unless a more important constitutional or federal law question is involved. So the next time you hear someone say, "I'll take you to the U.S. Supreme Court!" just say "not!"

STATE APPEALS COURTS

The overall organization of the state appeals courts is the same as the federal system—a trial court and one or more appeals courts. As with the federal system, each of the courts publishes its own rules of procedure governing trial and appeal. Just as the individual federal district courts and appellate courts may have local rules, so may the different state courts in different counties or parishes. Although some differences in local rules might not seem to be significant, failure to follow them can result in rejection of an appeal with no time to re-file before the deadline. For example, some courts require a colored backer, such as blue for the appellant and yellow for the appellee, or that the documents be printed on traditional legal-size paper as opposed to letter-size paper.

Paralegals working in the appellate process usually are under significant deadlines and need to be aware of these local rule changes and differences. We commonly see paralegals filing documents with backup copies on different-size paper and with extra copies of blue, yellow, brown, and tan backers and, of course, a trusty stapler to reassemble the documents in the event the rules have been amended or misinterpreted.

The appeal process for the paralegal may include the appeal of cases from the minor judiciary or small-claims court, as they sometimes are called. In many jurisdictions a small-claims court has a limited amount of jurisdiction and matters are heard by lay judges, who are people from the community without a law degree elected by their peers to sit as judges. In some states these are called justices of the peace. Although most cases are resolved without additional proceedings, appeals are heard from time to time.

Generally the process is to appeal **de novo,** or appeal to a higher court as if there had been no prior decision. These appeals are generally to the state trial court. The rules for appealing these matters are found in the Rules for the Minor Judiciary in some states or in the Trial Court Rules of Civil Procedure in other states. Typically, the rules set deadlines and requirements to give notice of the appeal to the opposing party and the lower-court judge. If the appealing party was the original initiating plaintiff, he or she may be required, as a part of the appellate process, to file a complaint or summons or other document under the local Rules of Civil Procedure for the trial court. When a party appealing the action was the responding party or defendant in the lower court action, proper notice is required to give the other party an opportunity to file his or her complaint or summons as required under the local Rules of Civil Procedure.

Decisions of state trial courts may be appealed to state appeals courts. Many states have two or more appeals courts, an intermediate appeals level and a state supreme court or, as it is called in some states, the superior court. In some states separate intermediate appeals courts exist to hear certain types of case appeals, such as criminal appeals or municipal government law issue appeals. The functions of the appeals courts are the same: to hear questions of law, procedural and substantive.

An attorney presents her case before the 3rd District Appellate Court, Texas.

Forwarding the Record on Appeal

The paralegal typically will be asked to take care of "forwarding the record." Under F.R.A.P. 11 the appellant must order from the court reporter the transcript of the proceedings not already on file and "do whatever else is necessary to enable the clerk to assemble and forward the record."

SIDEBAR

ROLE OF THE PARALEGAL IN THE APPELLATE PROCESS

The paralegal's role in the appellate process varies according to the nature of the case, the internal structure of the law firm, and the skill of the paralegal. The paralegal who is fortunate enough to sit through a trial may be in the best position to analyze the trial transcript for errors in application of the procedural rules during trial that may give rise to an appeal. The paralegal observing the trial usually is not subject to the pressures that trial counsels have trying to formulate questions and anticipate answers while thinking on their feet. Paralegals observing the trial proceedings are better able to keep track of procedural rulings. These notes enable them to review the transcript for potential errors in the trial court rulings on matters of procedure such as the admission or exclusion of evidence.

The paralegal may be asked to summarize the transcript of the trial, looking for the procedural errors and errors by the court in applying the rules of law. Ultimately the attorney must make the decision on what legal issues to raise on appeal. In any given case, a number of potential issues may be considered as potential grounds for appeal. The decision on which to pursue typically is based on a search of the law—constitutional, statutory, and case law. The paralegal may be given the assignment to do the research on these points of law.

Normally a time limit exists within which to file the appeal. It may be or seem to be relatively short, particularly when there is an extensive trial transcript to review and a number of legal issues to research. Like a statute of limitations, the client's rights may be cut off if the appeal is not filed on time or "perfected." In this regard, the paralegal usually feels the same pressure of the deadline. Paralegals in appellate litigation soon realize this is not an area of law for the traditional 9-to-5 employee.

Bexar County Courthouse in San Antonio, Texas.

FILING BRIEFS, ORAL ARGUMENTS

The parties may designate all or relevant portions of the trial record to be submitted to the appellate court for review. The appellant's attorney may file an opening brief with the court, setting forth legal research and other information to support his or her contentions on appeal. The appellee can file a responding brief answering the appellant's contentions.

In some appeals, the attorneys submit their case on "brief" only and ask the court to make a decision based upon the written submission. In other cases, the attorneys on their own or at the request of the court make oral arguments to support their position and clarify what they believe to be the appropriate law. Appellate courts usually permit a brief oral argument at which each party's attorney is heard.

Not every appellate court, however, permits or allows oral argument in every case. Many cases are decided on the brief submitted. In some courts, it is necessary, at the time of filing, to make any desired request for oral argument or indicate a willingness to have the matter decided on the briefs alone. In some cases, the oral argument is allowed automatically, and in others a reason for the desired oral argument must be stated.

In the federal court of appeals, oral argument is allowed unless a panel of three judges unanimously agrees, after reviewing the briefs, that the oral argument is unnecessary because the appeal is

Appeals on "Brief"

In some appeals, attorneys will submit their case on "brief" only and ask the court to make a decision based on the written submission without oral argument.

frivolous, the dispositive issues have been authoritatively decided, or the facts and argument are adequately presented in the briefs and record and the decisional process would not be aided by oral argument [F.R.A.P. 344].

Typically, oral arguments are made before the court without the presence of clients or witnesses. Because no additional fact-finding is permitted, it is merely a matter of making appropriate legal arguments to attempt to persuade the court to rule in favor of the legal position being argued. Many appellate courts establish a time limit for each side. In some courts, the time limit is enforced by the flashing of a light when the time has expired, and in other courts by a warning light when the time has almost been used, to allow for final statements.

The judges may waive the time limits particularly when they use up the attorneys' allotted time by asking questions. Local practice, however, is what determines how the court will treat the time limit. Paralegals can contact the local court and the clerk of court, or the law clerk to the individual judges, to determine the local rule in procedure so they may advise their supervising attorney and prepare accordingly.

ACTIONS BY THE APPELLATE COURTS

After review of the briefs, the record in the form of the trial court transcript, and oral arguments by the attorneys, an appellate court may affirm, reverse, or remand the case to the lower court.

If the appellate court believes there had been no errors in application of the procedural law or the substantive law, it will *affirm* the decision of lower court and the lower court decision will stand. If the appellate court rules that the lower court has made a substantial error, either in the procedural law or the substantive law of the case, it may **reverse** the decision of lower court.

Standard of Clear Error

"We will not reverse a determination for clear error unless it strikes us as wrong with the force of a 5-week-old, unrefrigerated, dead fish." [*Parts and Elec. Motors, Inc. v. Sterling Elec., Inc.,* 866 F.2d 228, 233 (7th Cir. 1988)]

SIDEBAR

Awarding Attorneys' Fees

Some clients attempt to use their financial power to gain an advantage over their opponents in litigation. One of the ways the courts can prevent this unequal footing is the award of attorney's fees. For example, the Lanham Act provides that the court "in exceptional cases may award reasonable attorney fees to the prevailing party" [15 U.S.C. § 1117(a)]. The standard is not whether the claimant filed suit in good faith but, rather, whether plaintiff's action was oppressive.

Under the Lanham Act, an award of attorney's fees is committed to the trial court's sound discretion. Some state statutes, such as the Illinois Consumer Act, also permit the recovery of lawyers' fees if "special circumstances" exist.

Discussing the Illinois case, the Seventh Circuit elaborated on what a prevailing defendant must show to obtain fees under both statutes: that the plaintiff's suit was "oppressive."

By way of example, the court explained that "a suit can be oppressive because of lack of merit and cost of defending even though the plaintiff honestly though mistakenly believes that he has a good case and is not trying merely to extract a settlement based on the suit's nuisance value." The court warned that the standard is not bad faith but, rather "malicious, fraudulent, deliberate, or willful" conduct. [*Door Sys., Inc. v. Pro-Line Door Sys.,* 126 F.3d 1028, 1030-32 (7th Cir. 1997)]

FACTS

Inda Crawford was employed as a legal assistant by the law firm of Hicks, Thomas & Lilienstern (HTL) for a number of years prior to May 1999. During her employment with the HTL law firm, HTL represented Michael Rubin and other real estate agents in a lawsuit against Westgate Petroleum and other defendants. Crawford worked on this case as a legal assistant for HTL and billed 170 hours of work on the case.

In May 1999, Crawford left her employment at HTL and went to work for the law firm Templeton, Smithee, Hayes, Fields, Young & Heinrich (Templeton). Templeton represented Westgate Petroleum and the other defendants in the previously-mentioned lawsuit. Rubin and the other real estate agents in this case filed a writ of mandamus with trial court judge the Honorable Ron Enns to have the Templeton firm disqualified as counsel for Westgate et al. because Crawford had now switched firms.

Rubin argued that because Crawford had previously worked on the case for the HTL firm, the opposing counsel she now worked for should be disqualified from representing the opposing side in the lawsuit. The trial court judge denied the petitioners' write of mandamus. The petitioners appealed.

ISSUE

Should the writ of mandamus be approved disqualifying a law firm that represents one side of a lawsuit because a legal assistant who worked for the law firm that represented the other side of the lawsuit has now switched firms and works for the law firm sought to be disqualified?

IN THE LANGUAGE OF THE COURT

Boyd, Chief Justice. In *Phoenix Founders, Inc. v. Marshall*, 887 S.W.2d 831, 835 (Tex. 1994), the court had occasion to discuss at some length circumstances such as the one before us in which a paralegal has changed employment from a law firm on one side of a case to a law firm on the other side of the case. In doing so, it recognized the countervailing interests involved and noted with approval the ABA suggestion that any restrictions on the nonlawyer's employment should be held to the minimum standard necessary to protect confidentiality of client information. In the course of its discussion, the court held that a paralegal or legal assistant who changes employment and who has worked on a case is subject to a conclusive presumption that confidences and secrets were imparted. While the presumption that a legal assistant obtained confidential information is not rebuttable, the presumption that the information was shared with a new employer is rebuttable.

Such distinction was created to ensure that a non-lawyer's mobility would not be unduly restricted. However, the court emphasized that the only way the rebuttable presumption could be overcome would be (1) to instruct the legal assistant not to work on any matter on which the paralegal worked during the prior employment, or regarding which the paralegal had information relating to the former employer's representation; and (2) "to take other reasonable steps to ensure that the paralegal does not work in connection with the matters on which the paralegal worked during the prior employment, absent client consent."

The trial court also had before it copies of a May 17, 1999, memo from Joe Hayes, managing partner of the Templeton firm, addressed to all the lawyers and staff of the Templeton firm. In the memo, Hayes designated two cases (one of which underlies this proceeding) as those about which Crawford might possess confidential information. In the memo, the recipients were instructed that Texas Disciplinary Rules 1.05(b)(1) and 5.03(a) prohibited them, as Crawford's supervising employers, "from revealing any confidential information she might have regarding the cases." The memo also advised that to satisfy the requirements of the Disciplinary Rules, as well as those set forth by the supreme court in the *In Re American Home Products Corporation* case, the firm was implementing the following six policies and procedures, effective immediately:

1. Inda shall not perform any work or take any action in connection with the *Westgate* case or the *Seger* case [the second, unrelated, case].

2. Inda shall not discuss the *Westgate* case or the *Seger* case, or disclose any information she has concerning these cases, with anyone.

3. No lawyer or staff member shall discuss the *Westgate* case or the *Seger* case with Inda, or in her presence.

4. All computer information relating to the *Westgate* case and the *Seger* case shall be removed from the firm's computer system. No future information concerning either the *Westgate* case or the *Seger* case shall be stored in any electronic medium, but rather kept solely in hard copy form with the files in the respective case.

5. The files in the *Westgate* case and the *Seger* case shall be kept in locked files under my supervision. No one shall have access to those files other than me, and those to whom I have given specific authority to access these files. Inda shall not have access to these files or the area where the files are to be maintained. At the close of each business day, all documents relating to these cases shall be placed in their respective files, which shall be returned to their storage places, which shall then be locked.

6. Inda shall not be given access to any of the files pertaining to the *Westgate* case or the *Seger* case, or their contents. None of the documents pertaining to either of these cases shall be disclosed to Inda, discussed with her, or discussed in her presence.

Our review of the record before the trial court convinces us that we cannot say he abused his discretion in arriving at his decision to deny the motion to disqualify the Templeton law firm. Accordingly, relators' petition seeking mandamus relief must be, and is, denied.

DECISION AND REMEDY

The court of appeals affirmed the trial court's denial of the writ of mandamus, thus permitting Crawford to work for the second law firm, which had imposed sufficient safeguards to assure that confidential information obtained at the first law firm was not disclosed to the second law firm.

Questions

1. Does the court's "rebuttable presumption" test work? Would any other test work better?

2. Using the court's "rebuttable presumption" test, would there be some temptation on the part of the second law firm to obtain confidential information that the paralegal learned at the first law firm?

3. Do the ethics standards of the American Bar Association and paralegal associations adequately address ethical conflicts that paralegals face? Discuss.

The court also may find that the lower court has made an error that can be corrected, by sending the case back to the lower court, and **remand** the case to the lower court, to take additional action or conduct further proceedings. For example, the lower court may be directed to hold further proceedings in which a jury hears testimony related to the issue of damages and makes an award of monetary damages.

An appellate court will reverse a lower court decision if it finds an *error of law* in the record. An error of law occurs if the jury was improperly instructed by the trial court judge, prejudicial evidence was admitted at trial when it should have been excluded, prejudicial evidence was obtained through an unconstitutional search and seizure, and the like. An appellate court will not reverse a finding of fact unless such finding is unsupported by the evidence or is contradicted by the evidence.

LEGAL TERMINOLOGY

Appeal

Appellant/petitioner

Appellee/respondent

De novo

Federal Rules of Appellate Procedure (F.R.A.P.)

Federal Rules of Civil Procedure (F.R.C.P.)

PACER

Procedural law

Remand

Reverse

Substantive law

Summary

CHAPTER 10 THE APPELLATE PROCESS

Appellate Court	
Functions	1. Unlike the trial court, whose main function is to make findings of facts, the appellate court's main function is to make findings of law. 2. In a civil case, unlike a criminal case, either party can appeal the trial court's decision once a final judgment is entered. In a criminal case, only the defendant can appeal. The appeal is made to the appropriate appellate court.
Procedure	Civil trials in the federal system are governed by the Federal Rules of Civil Procedure. Criminal trials in the federal system are governed by the Federal Rules of Criminal Procedure. Appeals in both civil and criminal cases to the Federal Appellate Courts are governed by the Federal Rules of Appellate Procedure (F.R.A.P.) and in the case of the United States Supreme Court by the rules of the Supreme Court of the United States. *(continued)*

United States Courts of Appeals

Procedure	1. Appeals from the decisions of the United States district courts are made to one of thirteen United States courts of appeals.
	2. The time limit for seeking review by the United States Supreme Court is generally 90 days after the entry of the judgment for which judicial review is sought. Review by the Supreme Court is "not a matter of right, but of judicial discretion," and "a petition for *writ of certiorari* will be granted only for compelling reasons" (Rule 10).

State Appeals Courts

Procedure	The general organization of the state courts is the same as the federal system: a trial court and one or more appeals courts. As with the federal system, each of the courts publishes its own rules of procedure governing trial and appeal. Just as the individual federal district courts and appellate courts may have local rules, so may the different state courts in different counties or parishes.

Oral Arguments

Rules	In some appeals, the attorneys submit their case on "brief" only and ask the court to make a decision based upon the written submission. In other cases, the attorneys, on their own or at the request of the court, make an oral argument to support their position and clarify what they believe to be the appropriate law. Not every appellate court permits or allows oral argument in every case.

Actions by the Appellate Courts

Affirm	The appellate court believes there have been no errors in the application of the procedural law or the substantive law and allows the prior decision to stand.
Reverse	The appellate court rules that the lower court has made a substantial error either in the procedural or substantive law of the case.
Remand	The court finds that the lower court has made an error that can be corrected by sending the case back to the lower court.

Working the Web

1. Check the Rules of the U.S. Supreme Court at its website at www.supremecourtus.gov/.
2. Read the information on the U.S. courts of appeals at the federal judiciary website at www.uscourts.gov/.
3. Check the links to information available for the federal courts at www.uscourts.gov/allinks.html.
4. Check the PACER website for reasons for using the service at http://pacer.psc.uscourts.gov/.
5. Use the PACER training site to learn how to use the system at http://pacer.train.uscourts.gov/.

Questions

CRITICAL LEGAL THINKING AND WRITING

1. Based on the court opinion in the *Palsgraf* case in Appendix A, what, if any, grounds are there for a further appeal? Explain.
2. How can the courts prevent wealthy litigants from using their financial power to defeat an opposing party with a legitimate claim?
3. Is it morally proper for a company, such as Microsoft, that is in the middle of a trial that could result in the limitation or prohibition against the release of a new product, such as a new software operating system, to take steps to delay the litigation process, including the taking of appeals to the U.S. Supreme Court, until after the release of the product?
4. How would knowledge of how individual justices of the Supreme Court voted in earlier cases help in making a decision to appeal a case?
5. Why is the average case unlikely to be appealed to the U.S. Supreme Court?
6. How may appeals be filed electronically in the federal court system?
7. Why is the U.S. Supreme Court more likely to take a case where there is a "split" in the circuit courts of appeals than other cases?
8. How important is the selection of a U.S. Supreme Court justice to the average citizen?
9. Why is there no need for clients and witnesses to be present at the oral argument of a case on appeal?
10. Why would the appellate court want a copy of the lower court trial transcript?

Questions
ETHICS: ANALYSIS AND DISCUSSION

1. Does the legal team have any obligations when they know an appeal is without legal basis and is only to delay or harass the opposing side?

2. What ethical issues are created when a paralegal is hired who works on a case for the opposing side that is now on appeal by the new employer?

3. What are the ethical obligations of the supervising attorney when hiring a new paralegal who has worked for a competing firm?

Unauthorized Practice of Law—Pro Se Assistance

There are few certainties in the area of ethics, for paralegals or in any profession. What qualifies as ethical conduct is in most cases based on state law and court interpretation applied to a set of facts. The citation listed below represents one legal opinion and is provided as a research starting point. Do not assume that the same rule applies in your jurisdiction. For the following:

- *Prepare a written statement based on your state law.*
- *Use your state bar association website as a starting point.*

A former client of the firm where you work sees you on the street at a local lunch stand and shows you a copy of a judgment rendered against him in a small-claims court. He tells you he is out of work and cannot afford to hire a lawyer. [Pennsylvania comments to Ethics Rule 5.5.] Can you help the client proceed *pro se* (on his own, acting as his own lawyer)? Can you help him prepare the paperwork to appeal the judgment? Does any of this constitute the unauthorized practice of law?

CASES *for Discussion*

Ray, Governor of Washington v. Atlantic Richfield Co.

435 U.S. 151, 98 S.Ct. 988, 55 L.Ed.2d 179 (1978)

10.1 FACTS

In 1972, Congress enacted a federal statute called the Ports and Waterways Safety Act, which established uniform standards for the operation of boats on inland waterways in the United States. The Act coordinated its provisions with those of foreign countries so that there was a uniform body of international rules that applied to vessels that traveled between countries.

Pursuant to the Act, a federal rule was adopted that regulated the design, length, and size of oil tankers, some of which traveled the waters of the Puget Sound area in the state of Washington. Oil tankers from various places entered Puget Sound to bring crude oil to refineries located in Washington.

In 1975, the state of Washington enacted a statute that established different designs, smaller lengths, and smaller sizes for oil tankers serving Puget Sound than the federal law allowed. Oil tankers used by the Atlantic Richfield Company (ARCO) to bring oil into Puget Sound met the federal standards but not the state standards.

ARCO sued to have the state statute declared unconstitutional.

ISSUE

In what court should this case have been brought? To what court would an appeal be taken? What needs to be done to file an appeal with the United States Supreme Court?

Yanase v. Automobile Club of Southern California

212 Cal.App.3d 468, 260 Cal.Rptr. 513 (Cal.App. 1989)

10.2 FACTS

In January 1984, George Yanase was a paying guest at the Royal Lodge–Downtown Motel in San Diego, California. Yanase was a member of the Automobile Club of Southern California. The Auto Club publishes a "Tourbook" in which it lists hotels and motels and rates the quality of their services, including the cleanliness of rooms, quality of the restaurant, level of personal service, and the like. Yanase had selected the Royal from the Tourbook. On the night of his stay at the Royal, Yanase was shot in the parking lot adjacent to the motel and died as a result of his injuries. Yanase's widow sued Auto Club for negligence.

ISSUE

If both parties are from California, in what court should this case have been brought? To what court would an appeal be taken?

Thomas v. Review Board of the Indiana Employment Security Division

450 U.S. 707, 101 S.Ct. 1425, 67 L.Ed.2d 624 (1981)

10.3 FACTS

Eddie C. Thomas, a Jehovah's Witness, was initially hired to work in a roll factory at Blaw-Knox Company. The function of the department was to fabricate sheet steel for a variety of industrial uses. On his application, Thomas listed that he was a Jehovah's Witness. Approximately one year later, the roll foundry closed and Blaw-Knox transferred Thomas to a department that fabricated turrets for military tanks. On the first day of this new job, Thomas realized that the work he was doing violated his religious beliefs because it was weapon-related. Because there were no other jobs available, Thomas quit and filed for unemployment compensation.

The state of Indiana denied his claim on the grounds that Thomas quit his job for personal reasons. Thomas sued, alleging that the government's denial of unemployment benefits violated his right to freedom of religion.

ISSUE

Is this the type of issue the United States Supreme Court would hear? To have an appeal to the U.S. Supreme Court accepted by the Court, what must a petitioner do?

United States v. Eichman

496 U.S. 310, 110 S.Ct. 2404, 110 L.Ed.2d 287 (1990)

10.4 FACTS

In 1989, Congress enacted the Flag Protection Act, which made it a crime to knowingly mutilate, deface, physically defile, burn, or trample the U.S. flag. The law provided for fines and up to one year in prison upon conviction [18 U.S.C. § 700]. Certain individuals set fire to several U.S. flags on the steps of the U.S. Capitol in Washington, D.C., to protest various aspects of the federal government's foreign and domestic policy.

In a separate incident, other individuals set fire to a U.S. flag to protest the Act's passage. All of these individuals were prosecuted for violating the Act. The district courts held the Act unconstitutional in violation of the defendants' First Amendment free-speech rights and dismissed the charges. The government appealed to the U.S. Supreme Court, which consolidated the two cases.

ISSUE

Is this the type of case that is heard by the U.S. Supreme Court? Why or why not? Did the flag burners exhibit any morals?

Phoenix Founders Inc. v. Marshall

887 S.W.2d 831 (Tex. 1994)

Read the following case, excerpted from the state supreme court's opinion. Review and brief the case. In your brief, answer the following questions.

1. What is the danger in hiring a paralegal who has worked at a competing law firm when handling a case on appeal?

2. What is the supervising attorney's responsibility in hiring a paralegal who has worked at another law firm?

3. What steps must be taken when hiring a paralegal who worked at another law firm that represents an opposing party?

4. What instructions should the paralegal who worked at another firm be given when hired?

5. Under what general circumstances will a law firm be disqualified after hiring a paralegal?

Spector, Justice, delivered the opinion of the Court, in which Hillips, Chief Justice, and Gonzalez, Hightower, Hecht, Doggett, Cornyn, and Gammage, Justices join.

In this original proceeding, we consider whether a law firm must be disqualified from ongoing litigation because it rehired a legal assistant who had worked for opposing counsel for three weeks. We hold that disqualification is not required if the rehiring firm is able to establish that it has effectively screened the paralegal from any contact with the underlying suit. Because this standard had not been adopted in Texas prior to the trial court's disqualification order, we deny mandamus relief without prejudice to allow the trial court to reconsider its ruling in light of today's opinion.

The present dispute arises from a suit brought by Phoenix Founders, Inc. and others ("Phoenix") to collect a federal-court judgment against Ronald and Jane Beneke and others. The law firm of Thompson & Knight represented Phoenix in the original federal-court suit, which began in 1990 and ended in 1991, and has also represented them in the collection suit since its commencement in 1992. The Benekes have been represented in the latter suit by the firm of David & Goodman.

In July of 1993, Denise Hargrove, a legal assistant at Thompson & Knight, left her position at that firm to begin working for David & Goodman as a paralegal. While at David & Goodman, Hargrove billed six-tenths of an hour on the collection suit for locating a pleading. She also discussed the case generally with Mark Goodman, the Benekes' lead counsel. After three weeks at David & Goodman, Hargrove returned to Thompson & Knight to resume work as a paralegal. At the time of the rehiring, Thompson & Knight made no effort to question Hargrove in regard to potential conflicts of interest resulting from her employment at David & Goodman.

Three weeks after Hargrove had returned, counsel for the Benekes wrote to Thompson & Knight asserting that its renewed employment of Hargrove created a conflict of interest. The letter demanded that the firm withdraw from its representation of Phoenix. Hargrove resigned from Thompson & Knight the next week, after having been given the option of either resigning with severance pay or being terminated. The firm itself, however, refused to withdraw from the case. The Benekes then filed a motion to disqualify.

This Court has not previously addressed the standards governing a disqualification motion based on the hiring of a nonlawyer employee. With respect to lawyers, however, this Court has adopted a standard requiring disqualification whenever counsel undertakes representation of an interest that is adverse to that of a former client, as long as the matters embraced in the pending suit are "substantially related" to the factual matters involved in the previous suit. This strict rule is based on a conclusive presumption that confidences and secrets were imparted to the attorney during the prior representation [Coker, 765 S.W.2d at 400].

We agree that a paralegal who has actually worked on a case must be subject to the presumption set out in Coker; that is, a conclusive presumption that confidences and secrets were imparted during the course of the paralegal's work on the case. We disagree, however, with the argument that paralegals should be conclusively presumed to share confidential information with members of their firms. The Disciplinary Rules require a lawyer having direct supervisory authority over a nonlawyer to make reasonable efforts to ensure that the nonlawyer's conduct is compatible with the professional obligations of the lawyer.

The Texas Committee on Professional Ethics has considered the application of these rules in the context of a "right hand" legal secretary or legal assistant leaving one small firm and joining another that represents an adverse party. The Committee concluded that the Rules do not require disqualification of the new law firm, provided that the supervising lawyer at that firm complies with the Rules so as to ensure that the nonlawyer's conduct is compatible with the professional obligations of a lawyer. This view is consistent with the weight of authority in other jurisdictions. The American Bar Association's Committee on Professional Ethics, after surveying case law and ethics opinions from a number of jurisdictions, concluded that the new firm need not be disqualified, as long as the firm and the paralegal strictly adhere to the screening process set forth in the opinion, and as long as the paralegal does not reveal any information relating to the former employer's clients to any person in the employing firm. A number of courts have since relied on the ABA's opinion to allow continued representation under similar conditions.

Underlying these decisions is a concern regarding the mobility of paralegals and other nonlawyers. A potential employer might well be reluctant to hire a particular nonlawyer if doing so would automatically disqualify the entire firm from ongoing litigation. This problem would be especially acute in the context of massive firms and extensive, complex litigation. Recognizing this danger, the ABA concluded "any restrictions on the nonlawyer's employment should be held to the minimum necessary to protect confidentiality of client information" [ABA Op. 1526].

We share the concerns expressed by the ABA, and agree that client confidences may be adequately safeguarded if a firm hiring a paralegal from another firm takes appropriate steps in compliance with the Disciplinary Rules. Specifically, the newly hired paralegal should be cautioned not to disclose any information relating to the representation of a client of the former employer. The paralegal should also be instructed not to work on any matter on which the paralegal worked during the prior employment, or regarding which the paralegal has information relating to the former employer's representation. Additionally, the firm should take other reasonable steps to ensure that the paralegal does not work in connection with matters on which the paralegal worked during the prior employment, absent client consent after consultation. Each of these precautions would tend to reduce the danger that the paralegal might share confidential information with members of the new firm. Thus, while a court must ordinarily presume that some sharing will take place, the challenged firm may rebut this presumption by showing that sufficient precautions have been taken to guard against any disclosure of confidences.

Absent consent of the former employer's client, disqualification will always be required under some circumstances, such as (1) when information relating to the representation of an adverse client has in fact been disclosed, or (2) when screening would be ineffective or the nonlawyer necessarily would be required to work on the other side of a matter that is the same as or substantially related to a matter on which the nonlawyer has previously worked. Ordinarily, however, disqualification is not required as long as "the practical effect of formal screening has been achieved."

In reconsidering the disqualification motion, the trial court should examine the circumstances of Hargrove's employment at Thompson & Knight to determine whether the practical effect of formal screening has been achieved. The factors bearing on such a determination will generally include the substantiality of the relationship between the former and current matters; the time elapsing between the matters; the size of the firm; the number of individuals presumed to have confidential information; the nature of their involvement in the former matter; and the timing and features of any measures taken to reduce the danger of disclosure. The fact that the present case involves representation of adverse parties in the same proceeding, rather than two separate proceedings, increases the danger that some improper disclosure may have occurred. Evidence regarding the other factors, however, may tend to rebut the presumption of shared confidences.

The ultimate question in weighing these factors is whether Thompson & Knight has taken measures sufficient to reduce the potential for misuse of confidences to an acceptable level. Because we have modified the controlling legal standard, the writ of mandamus is denied without prejudice to allow the trial court to reconsider the disqualification motion in light of today's opinion. The stay order previously issued by this Court remains in effect only so long as necessary to allow the trial court to act.

Substantive

Legal

Topics

PART III

SUBSTANTIVE
LEGAL TOPICS

Part III introduces paralegals
to many important and substantive areas of the law,
providing the thorough
understanding of basic law
required by paralegals. The
seven chapters in Part III
describe the major laws that
a paralegal will encounter in
her or his career, beginning
with tort law and strict liability,
and contract and commercial
law. The coverage then continues to personal and real
property law; agency and
employment law, including
equal opportunity laws; business organizations and forms
for conducting business; and
family law, wills, trusts, and
estates. Chapter 16 covers
the evolving area of intellectual property laws, Internet
laws, and e-commerce laws.

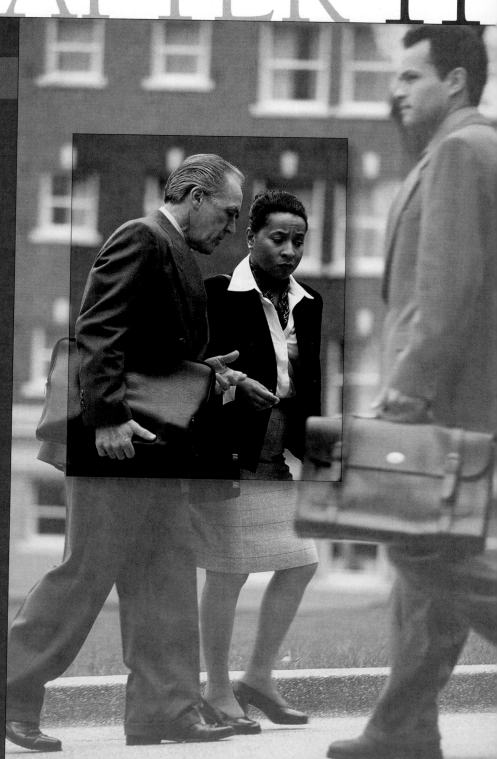

CHAPTER 11

CHAPTER OBJECTIVES

After studying this chapter, you should be able to:

1. List and describe intentional torts against persons.

2. List and describe intentional torts against property.

3. Define the tort of false imprisonment and apply merchant-protection statutes.

4. Describe the torts of invasion of privacy and misappropriation of the right to publicity.

5. Define the tort of defamation.

6. List and explain the elements necessary to prove negligence.

7. Apply special negligence doctrines such as negligence per se, negligent infliction of emotional distress, and *res ipsa loquitur.*

8. Describe the tort of professional malpractice.

9. Describe and apply the doctrine of strict liability.

10. Explain when punitive damages are awarded in strict liability actions.

Torts and Strict Liability

Negligence is not actionable unless it involves the invasion of a legally protected interest, the violation of a right. Proof of negligence in the air, so to speak, will not do.

C. J. CARDOZO, *PALSGRAF V. LONG ISLAND RAILROAD CO.* (1928)

Introduction

Tort is the French word for a "wrong." Tort law protects a variety of injuries and provides remedies for them. Under tort law an injured party can bring a civil lawsuit to seek compensation for a wrong done to the party or to the party's property. Many torts originate in common law. The courts and legislatures have extended tort law to reflect changes in modern society.

Tort damages are monetary damages sought from the offending party, intended to compensate the injured party for the injury suffered. They may consist of past and future medical expenses, loss of wages, pain and suffering, mental distress, and other damages caused by the defendant's tortious conduct. If the victim of a tort dies, his or her beneficiaries can bring a *wrongful death action* to recover damages from the defendant. **Punitive damages,** which are awarded to punish the defendant, may be recovered in intentional tort and strict liability cases. Other remedies, such as injunctions, may be available, too.

Tort lawsuits make up a substantial portion of the civil lawsuits in this country. Therefore, a paralegal should have a knowledge of the major tort principles and the elements of each tort. This chapter covers various tort laws, including intentional torts, negligence, and strict liability.

INTENTIONAL TORTS AGAINST PERSONS

The law protects a person from unauthorized touching, restraint, or other contact. In addition, the law protects a person's reputation and privacy. Violations of these rights are actionable as torts. Intentional torts against the person are discussed in the paragraphs that follow.

Assault

Assault is (1) the threat of immediate harm or offensive contact or (2) any action that arouses reasonable apprehension of imminent harm. Actual physical contact is unnecessary. For example, suppose a 6-foot-5-inch, 250-pound male makes a fist and threatens to punch a 5-foot, 100-pound woman. If the woman is afraid that the man will physically harm her, she can sue him for assault. If she is a black-belt karate champion and laughs at the threat, there is no assault because the threat does not cause any apprehension.

Battery

Battery is unauthorized and harmful or offensive physical contact with another person. Basically, the interest protected here is each person's reasonable sense of dignity and safety. For example, intentionally hitting someone is considered battery because it is harmful. Note that there does not have to be direct physical contact between the victim and the perpetrator. If an injury results, throwing a rock, shooting an arrow or a bullet, knocking off a hat, pulling a chair out from under someone, and poisoning a drink are all instances of actionable battery. The victim need not be aware of the harmful or offensive contact (e.g., it may take place while the victim is asleep). Assault and battery often occur together, although they do not have to (e.g., the perpetrator hits the victim on the back of the head without any warning).

Sometimes a person acts with the intent to injure one person but actually injures another. The *doctrine of transferred intent* applies to these situations. Under this doctrine, the law transfers the perpetrator's intent from the target to the actual victim of the act. The victim then can sue the defendant.

False Imprisonment

The intentional confinement or restraint of another person without authority or justification and without that person's consent constitutes **false imprisonment.** The victim may be restrained or confined by physical force, barriers, threats of physical harm, or the perpetrator's false assertion of legal authority (i.e., *false arrest*). A threat of future harm or moral pressure is not considered false imprisonment. The false imprisonment must be complete. For example, merely locking one door to a building when other exits are not locked is not false imprisonment. A person is not obliged to risk danger or an affront to his or her dignity by attempting to escape.

Shoplifting causes substantial losses to merchants each year. Almost all states have enacted **merchant protection statutes,** also known as the *shopkeeper's privilege.* These statutes allow merchants to stop, detain, and investigate suspected shoplifters without being held liable for false imprisonment if:

Wal-Mart Shopper Wins $3.2 Million

GOODMAN V. WAL-MART (AL 1999)

On Christmas Eve 1995, LaShawna Goodman went to the local Wal-Mart store in Opelika, Alabama, to do some last-minute holiday shopping. She brought along her two young daughters and a telephone, which she had purchased earlier at Wal-Mart, to exchange. She presented the telephone and receipt to a Wal-Mart employee, who took the telephone. Unable to find another telephone she wanted, Goodman retrieved the previously purchased telephone from the employee, bought another item, and left.

Outside, Ms. Goodman was stopped by Wal-Mart security personnel and was accused of stealing the phone. Goodman offered to show the Wal-Mart employees the original receipt, but the Wal-Mart employees detained her and called the police. Ms. Goodman was handcuffed in front of her children. Wal-Mart filed criminal charges against Ms. Goodman.

At the criminal trial Ms. Goodman was acquitted of all charges. Now it was Ms. Goodman's turn: She filed a civil lawsuit against Wal-Mart Stores, Inc., to recover damages for falsely accusing her of stealing the telephone. She presented the evidence as outline above. Wal-Mart asserted the defense that it was in its rights to have detained Ms. Goodman as it did and to prosecute Ms. Goodman based on its investigation. Wal-Mart asserted that the merchant-protection statute protected its actions in this case. Wal-Mart alleged that it had reasonable grounds to suspect Ms. Goodman of shoplifting, that it conducted the investigation in a reasonable manner, and that it had sufficient grounds to have Ms. Goodman prosecuted criminally based on its investigation.

But the jury did not accept Wal-Mart's plea that it had acted reasonably. The jury rejected Wal-Mart's defenses, including the shopkeeper's privilege and its allegations that it had not maliciously prosecuted her. The jury determined that Ms. Goodman should be awarded $200,000 in compensatory damages for her suffering. The jury then decided that Wal-Mart had acted so badly in this case that it tacked on $3 million in punitive damages in its award to Ms. Goodman, just to teach Wal-Mart a lesson.

1. There are reasonable grounds for the suspicion,
2. Suspects are detained for only a reasonable time, and
3. Investigations are conducted in a reasonable manner.

Defamation of Character

A person's reputation is a valuable asset. Therefore, every person is protected during his or her lifetime from false statements by others. This protection ends upon a person's death. The tort of **defamation of character** requires a plaintiff to prove that (1) the defendant made an *untrue statement of fact* about the plaintiff, and (2) the statement was intentionally or accidentally *published* to a third party. In this context, publication simply means that a third person heard or saw the untrue statement. It does not just mean appearance in newspapers, magazines, or books.

The term for an oral defamatory statement is **slander.** A false statement that appears in a letter, newspaper, magazine, book, photograph, movie, video, and the like is called **libel.** Most courts hold that defamatory statements in radio and television broadcasts are considered libel because of the permanency of the media.

Publishing an untrue statement of fact is not the same as publishing an opinion. The publication of opinions is usually not actionable. "My lawyer is lousy" is an opinion. Because defamation is defined as an untrue statement of fact, truth is an absolute defense to a charge of defamation.

In *New York Times Co. v. Sullivan* [376 U.S. 254, 84 S.Ct. 710 (1964)], the U.S. Supreme Court held that *public officials* cannot recover for defamation unless they can prove that the defendant acted with "actual malice." Actual malice means that the defendant made the false statement knowingly or with reckless disregard of its falsity. This requirement has since been extended to *public figure* plaintiffs such as movie stars, sports personalities, and other celebrities.

Misappropriation of the Right to Publicity

Each person has the exclusive legal right to control and profit from the commercial use of his or her name and personality during his or her lifetime. This is a valuable right, particularly to well-known persons such as sports figures and movie stars. Any attempt by another person to appropriate a living person's name or identity for commercial purposes is actionable. The wrongdoer is liable for the tort of **misappropriation of the right to publicity** (also called the *tort of appropriation*).

In such cases, the plaintiff can (1) recover the unauthorized profits made by the offending party, and (2) obtain an injunction against further unauthorized use of his or her name or identity. Many states provide that the right to publicity survives a person's death and may be enforced by the deceased's heirs.

Invasion of the Right to Privacy

The law recognizes each person's right to live his or her life without being subjected to unwarranted and undesired publicity. Violation of this right constitutes the tort of **invasion of the right to privacy.** Examples of this tort are reading someone else's mail, wiretapping, and such. In contrast to defamation, the fact does not have to be untrue. Therefore, truth is not a defense to a charge of invasion of privacy. If the fact is public information, there is no claim to privacy. But a fact that was once public (e.g., the commission of a crime) may become private after the passage of time.

Placing someone in a "false light" constitutes an invasion of privacy. For example, sending an objectionable telegram to a third party and signing another's name would place the purported sender in a false light in the eyes of the receiver. Falsely attributing beliefs or acts to another also can form the basis of a lawsuit.

Intentional Infliction of Emotional Distress

In some situations a victim might suffer mental or emotional distress without first being physically harmed. The Restatement (Second) of Torts provides that a person whose *extreme and outrageous conduct* intentionally or recklessly causes severe emotional distress to another is liable for that emotional distress. This is called the tort of **intentional infliction of emotional distress,** or the *tort of outrage.* The plaintiff must prove that the defendant's conduct was "so outrageous in character and so extreme in degree as to go beyond all possible bounds of decency, and to be regarded as atrocious and utterly intolerable in a civilized society." An indignity, an annoyance, rough language, or an occasional inconsiderate or unkind act does not constitute outrageous behavior.

However, repeated annoyances or harassment coupled with threats are considered "outrageous."

The tort does not require any publication to a third party or physical contact between the plaintiff and defendant. For example, a credit collection agency making harassing telephone calls to a debtor every morning between 1:00 and 5:00 A.M. is outrageous conduct.

The mental distress suffered by the plaintiff must be severe. Many states require that this mental distress be manifested by some form of physical injury, discomfort, or illness, such as nausea, ulcers, headaches, or miscarriage. This requirement is intended to prevent false claims. Some states have abandoned this requirement. The courts have held that shame, humiliation, embarrassment, anger, fear, and worry constitute severe mental distress.

INTENTIONAL TORTS AGAINST PROPERTY

The two general categories of property are real property and personal property. *Real property* consists of land and anything permanently attached to that land. *Personal property* consists of things that are movable, such as automobiles, books, clothes, pets, and such. The law recognizes certain torts against real and personal property. These torts are discussed in the paragraphs that follow.

Trespass to Land

Interference with an owner's right to exclusive possession of land constitutes the tort of **trespass to land.** There does not have to be any interference with the owner's use or enjoyment of the land; the ownership itself is what counts. Thus, unauthorized use of another person's land is trespass even if the owner is not using it. Actual harm to the property is not necessary.

Examples of trespass to land are entering another person's land without permission, remaining on the land of another after permission to do so has expired (e.g., a guest refuses to leave), or causing something or someone to enter another's land (e.g., one person builds a dam that causes another person's land to flood). A person who is pushed onto another's land or enters that land with good reason is not liable for trespass. For example, a person may enter another person's land to save a child or a pet from harm.

Trespass to and Conversion of Personal Property

The tort of **trespass to personal property** occurs whenever one person injures another person's personal property or interferes with that person's enjoyment of his or her personal property. The injured party can sue for damages. For example, breaking another's car window is trespass to personal property.

Police officers investigate an accident at an intersection in California.

Depriving a true owner of the use and enjoyment of his or her personal property by taking over such property and exercising ownership rights over it

Liability for Frivolous Lawsuits

Entrepreneurs and others often believe they have a reason to sue someone to recover damages or other remedies. If the plaintiff has a reason to bring the lawsuit and does so, but the plaintiff does not win the lawsuit, he or she does not have to worry about being sued by the person whom he or she sued. A losing plaintiff does have to worry about being sued by the defendant in a second lawsuit for **malicious prosecution** if certain elements are met, however.

In a lawsuit for malicious prosecution, the original defendant sues the original plaintiff. In this second lawsuit, which is a *civil* action for damages, the original defendant is the plaintiff and the original plaintiff is the defendant. The courts do not look favorably on malicious prosecution lawsuits because they think these inhibit the original plaintiff's incentive to sue. Thus, to succeed in a malicious prosecution lawsuit, the courts require the plaintiff to prove all of the following:

- The plaintiff in the original lawsuit (now the defendant) instituted or was responsible for instituting the original lawsuit.
- There was no *probable cause* for the first lawsuit; that is, it was a frivolous lawsuit.
- The plaintiff in the original action brought it with *malice*. [Caution: This is a difficult element to prove.]
- The original lawsuit was terminated in favor of the original defendant (now the plaintiff).
- The current plaintiff suffered injury as a result of the original lawsuit.

A successful case of malicious prosecution involves proof of malicious conduct, which is an intentional tort. Therefore, punitive damages can be awarded in a malicious prosecution case. The moral of the story is simple: Make sure you have probable cause for instituting an action before bringing a lawsuit.

---

constitutes the tort of **conversion of personal property.** Conversion also occurs when someone who originally is given possession of personal property fails to return it (e.g., fails to return a borrowed car). The rightful owner can sue to recover the property. If the property was lost or destroyed, the owner can sue to recover its value.

UNINTENTIONAL TORTS (NEGLIGENCE)

Under the doctrine of **unintentional tort,** commonly referred to as **negligence,** a person is liable for harm that is the *foreseeable consequence* of his or her actions. Negligence is defined as "the omission to do something which a reasonable man would do, or doing something which a prudent and reasonable man would not do" [*Blyth v. Birmingham Waterworks Co.*, 11 Exch. 781, 784 (1856)]. Consider this example: A driver who causes an automobile accident becuase he or she fell asleep at the wheel is liable for any resulting injuries caused by his or her negligence.

Elements of Negligence

To be successful in a negligence lawsuit, the plaintiff must prove that (1) the defendant owed a *duty of care* to the plaintiff, (2) the defendant *breached* this duty of care, (3) the plaintiff suffered *injury*, and (4) the defendant's negligent act *caused* the plaintiff's injury. Each of these elements is discussed in the paragraphs that follow.

Duty of Care

To determine whether a defendant is liable for negligence, it first must be ascertained whether the defendant owed a **duty of care** to the plaintiff. Duty of care refers to the obligation we all owe each other—the duty not to cause any unreasonable harm or risk of harm. For example, each person owes a duty to drive his or her car carefully, not to push or shove on escalators, not to leave skateboards on the sidewalk, and the like. Businesses owe a duty to make safe products, not to cause accidents, and so on.

The courts decide whether a duty of care is owed in specific cases by applying a *reasonable person standard.* Under this test, the courts attempt to determine how an *objective, careful, and conscientious person would have acted in the same circumstances*, and then measure the defendant's conduct against this standard. The defendant's subjective intent ("I did not mean to do it") is immaterial in asserting liability. Certain impairments do not affect the reasonable person standard. For instance, there is no reasonable alcoholics standard.

Defendants with a specific expertise or competence are measured against a *reasonable professional standard.* This standard is applied in much the same way as the reasonable person standard. For example, a brain surgeon is measured against a reasonable brain surgeon standard rather than a lower reasonable doctor standard. Children are generally required to act as a *reasonable child* of similar age and experience would act.

Ouch! The Coffee's Too Hot!

Studies have shown that people don't care about how good their coffee tastes if it is hot. So restaurants, coffee shops, and other sellers make their coffee hot. McDonald's, however, ended up in hot water for making its coffee *too* hot. Consider this case.

Stella Liebeck, an 81-year-old resident of Albuquerque, New Mexico, visited a drive-through window of a McDonald's restaurant with her grandson. Her grandson, the driver of the vehicle, placed the order. When it came, he handed a cup of hot coffee to Liebeck. As her grandson drove away from the drive-through window, Liebeck took the lid off the coffee cup she held in her lap. The coffee spilled on Liebeck, who suffered third-degree burns on her legs, groin, and buttocks. She required medical treatment, was hospitalized, and has permanent scars from the incident.

Liebeck sued McDonald's for selling coffee that was too hot and for failing to warn her of the danger of the hot coffee it served. McDonald's rejected Liebeck's pretrial offer to settle the case for $300,000.

At trial, McDonald's denied that it had been negligent and asserted that Liebeck's own negligence—opening a hot-coffee cup on her lap—caused her injuries. The jury heard evidence that McDonald's enforces a quality-control rule that requires its restaurants and franchises to serve coffee at 180 to 190 degrees Fahrenheit. Evidence showed that this was 10 to 30 degrees hotter than coffee served by competing restaurant chains, and approximately 40 to 50 degrees hotter than normal house-brewed coffee.

Based on this evidence, the jury concluded that McDonald's acted recklessly and awarded Liebeck $200,000 compensatory damages (reduced by $40,000 for her own negligence), and $2.7 million punitive damages. After the trial court judge reduced the amount of punitive damages to $480,000, the parties reached an out-of-court settlement for an undisclosed amount. Because of this case, McDonald's and other purveyors of coffee have reduced the temperature at which they sell coffee and have placed warnings on their coffee cups.

Breach of Duty

Once a court finds that the defendant actually owed the plaintiff a duty of care, it must determine whether the defendant breached this duty. A **breach of the duty of care** is the failure to exercise care. It is the failure to act as a reasonable person would act. A breach of this duty may consist of either an action (e.g., throwing a lit match on the ground in a forest and causing a fire) or a failure to act when there is a duty to act (e.g., a firefighter who refuses to put out a fire). Generally, passersby are not expected to rescue others gratuitously to save them from harm.

Injury to Plaintiff

Even though a defendant's act might have breached a duty of care owed to the plaintiff, this breach is not actionable unless the plaintiff suffers injury. For example, a business's negligence causes an explosion and fire at its factory at night. No one is injured and there is no damage to the neighbor's property. The negligence is not actionable.

The damages recoverable depend on the effect of the injury on the plaintiff's life or profession. Now suppose two men injure their hands when a train door malfunctions. The first man is a professional basketball player. The second is a college professor. The first man can recover greater damages.

Causation

A person who commits a negligent act is not liable unless this act was the *cause* of the plaintiff's injuries. Courts have divided causation into two categories—causation in fact and proximate cause—and require each to be shown before the plaintiff may recover damages.

1. *Causation in fact.* The defendant's negligent act must be the **causation in fact** (or **actual cause**) of the plaintiff's injuries. For example, suppose a corporation negligently pollutes the plaintiff's drinking water. The plaintiff dies of a heart attack unrelated to the polluted water. Although the corporation has acted negligently, it is not liable for the plaintiff's death. There was a negligent act and an injury, but there was no *cause-and-effect* relationship between them. If, instead, the plaintiff had died from the pollution, there would have been causation in fact, and the polluting corporation would have been liable. If two (or more) persons are liable for negligently causing the plaintiff's injuries, both (or all) can be held liable to the plaintiff if acts by each of them are substantial factors in causing the plaintiff's injuries.

2. *Proximate cause.* Under the law, a negligent party is not necessarily liable for all damages set in motion by his or her negligent act. Based on public policy, the law establishes a point along the damage chain after which the negligent party is no longer responsible for the consequences of his or her actions. This limitation on liability is referred to as **proximate cause** (or **legal cause**). The general test of proximate cause is *foreseeability*. A negligent party who is found to be the actual cause—but not the proximate cause—of the plaintiff's injuries is not liable to the plaintiff. Situations are examined on a case-by-case basis.

The landmark case establishing the doctrine of proximate cause is *Palsgraf v. Long Island Railroad Company* [248 N.Y. 339, 162 N.E. 99 (1928)]. Helen Palsgraf was standing on a platform waiting for a passenger train. The Long Island Railroad Company owned and operated the trains and employed the station guards. As a man carrying a package wrapped in a newspaper tried to board the moving train, railroad guards tried to help him. As they did so, the

Is a Singer Liable When Someone Acts Upon His Lyrics?

Many people, particularly youths, are influenced by singers, musicians, sports figures, movie stars, and other celebrities. Some listeners, readers, or watchers will be moved to love; others to tears; some to creativity, spirituality, or fear. But what happens when a person is so moved by a song, a movie, or a book that he or she commits a crime or engages in other dangerous conduct? Is the songwriter, singer, author, scriptwriter, or movie company liable for this conduct? This question was posed to the court in *McCollum v. CBS, Inc., and Osbourne*.

John "Ozzie" Osbourne is a well-known singer of rock-and-roll music and has become a cult figure. The words and music of his songs demonstrate a preoccupation with unusual, antisocial, and even bizarre attitudes and beliefs, often emphasizing such things as satanic worship, the mocking of religious beliefs, death, and suicide. CBS Records (CBS) produced and distributed Osbourne's albums.

On Friday night, October 26, 1984, John Daniel McCollum (John) listened again and again to certain music recorded by Osbourne. He was a 19-year-old youth who had a problem with alcohol abuse as well as serious emotional problems. John was in his bedroom using headphones to listen to the final side of Osbourne's two-record album, *Speak to the Devil*, when he placed a .22 caliber handgun next to his right temple and took his own life.

One of the songs that John had been listening to was called "Suicide Solution." Three of the verses of the song stated:

Wine is fine but whiskey's quicker
Suicide is slow with liquor
Take a bottle, drown your sorrows

Then it floods away tomorrow
Made your bed, rest your head
But you lie there and moan
Suicide is the only way out
Don't you know what it's really about?
Ah know people
You really know where it's at
You got it
Why try, why try
Get the gun and try it
Shoot, shoot, shoot

John's relative, Jack McCollum, and John's estate sued Ozzie Osbourne and CBS for negligence, alleging that the lyrics of Osbourne's music incited John to commit suicide. When the trial court dismissed the action, the plaintiffs appealed. The appellate court held that, although Osbourne's lyrics might have been an actual cause of John's suicide, they were not the proximate cause of the suicide. The court stated:

John's tragic self-destruction, while listening to Osbourne's music, was not a reasonably foreseeable risk or consequence of defendant's remote artistic activities. It is simply not acceptable to a free and democratic society to impose a duty upon performing artists to limit and restrict their creativity in order to avoid the dissemination of ideas in artistic speech that may adversely affect emotionally troubled individuals. Such a burden would quickly have the effect of reducing and limiting artistic expression to only the broadest standard of taste and acceptance and the lowest level of offense, provocation, and controversy.

[*McCollum v. CBS, Inc., and Osbourne*, 202 Cal.App.3d 989, 249 Cal.Rptr. 187 (Cal.App. 1988)]

package was dislodged from the man's arm, fell to the railroad tracks, and exploded. The package contained hidden fireworks. The explosion shook the railroad platform, causing a scale on the platform to fall on Palsgraf, injuring her. She sued the railroad for negligence. Justice Cardoza denied her recovery, finding that the railroad was not the proximate cause of her injuries.

SPECIAL NEGLIGENCE DOCTRINES

The courts have developed many *special negligence doctrines.* The most important of these are discussed in the paragraphs that follow.

Negligent Infliction of Emotional Distress

Some jurisdictions have extended the tort of emotional distress to include the **negligent infliction of emotional distress.** The most common examples of this involve bystanders who witness the injury or death of a loved one that is caused by another's negligent conduct. Under this tort, the bystander, even though not personally physically injured, can sue the negligent party for his or her own mental suffering.

Generally, to be successful in this type of case, the plaintiff must prove that (1) a relative was killed or injured by the defendant, (2) the plaintiff suffered severe emotional distress, and (3) the plaintiff's mental distress resulted from a sensory and contemporaneous observance of the accident. Some states require that the plaintiff's mental distress be manifested by some physical injury; other states have eliminated this requirement.

Negligence Per Se

Statutes often establish duties that one person owes to another. Violating a statute that proximately causes an injury is **negligence per se.** The plaintiff in such an action must prove that (1) a statute existed, (2) the statute was enacted to prevent the type of injury suffered, and (3) the plaintiff was within a class of persons the statute meant to protect.

Consider this example: Most cities have an ordinance that places the responsibility for fixing public sidewalks in residential areas on the homeowners whose homes front the sidewalk. A homeowner is liable if he or she fails to repair a damaged sidewalk in front of his or her home and a pedestrian trips and is injured because of the damage. The injured party does not have to prove that the homeowner owed the duty, because the statute establishes that.

Res Ipsa Loquitur

If a defendant is in control of a situation in which a plaintiff has been injured and has superior knowledge of the circumstances surrounding the injury, the plaintiff might have difficulty proving the defendant's negligence. In such a situation, the law applies the doctrine of ***res ipsa***

Professional Malpractice

Professionals, including doctors, lawyers, architects, accountants, and others, owe a duty of ordinary care in providing their services. This duty is known as the *reasonable professional standard.* A professional who breaches this duty of care is liable for the injury his or her negligence causes. This liability is commonly referred to as **professional malpractice.**

Consider these examples: a doctor who amputates a wrong leg is liable for *medical malpractice.* A lawyer who fails to file a document with the court on time, causing the client's case to be dismissed, is liable for *legal malpractice.* An accountant who fails to use reasonable care, knowledge, skill, and judgment when providing auditing and other accounting services to a client is liable for *accounting malpractice.*

Professionals who breach this duty are liable to their patients or clients. They also may be liable to some third parties.

loquitur (Latin for "the thing speaks for itself"). This doctrine raises a presumption of negligence and switches the burden to the defendant to prove that he or she was *not* negligent. *Res ipsa loquitur* applies in cases where the following elements are met:

1. The defendant had exclusive control of the instrumentality or situation that caused the plaintiff's injury.
2. The injury ordinarily would not have occurred "but for" someone's negligence.

Consider this example: Haeran goes in for major surgery and is given anesthesia to put her to sleep during the operation. Sometime after the operation it is discovered that a surgical instrument has been left in Haeran during the operation. She suffers severe injury because of the left-in instrument. Haeran would be hard-pressed to identify which doctor or nurse had been careless and left the instrument in her body. In this case, the court can apply the doctrine of *res ipsa loquitur* and place the presumption of negligence on the defendants. Any defendant who can prove he or she did not leave the instrument in Haeran escapes liability; any defendant who does not disprove his or her negligence is liable. Other typical *res ipsa loquitur* cases involve commercial airplane crashes, falling elevators, and the like.

Courthouse in Appomatox, Virginia.

Good Samaritan Laws

In the past, exposure to liability made many doctors, nurses, and other medical professionals reluctant to stop and render aid to victims in emergency situations, such as highway accidents. Almost all states have enacted **Good Samaritan laws** that relieve medical professionals from liability for injury caused by their ordinary negligence in such circumstances.

Good Samaritan laws protect medical professionals only from liability for their *ordinary negligence*, not for injuries caused by their gross negligence or reckless or intentional conduct. Most Good Samaritan laws protect licensed doctors and nurses and laypersons who have been certified in CPR. Good Samaritan statutes generally do not protect laypersons who are not trained in CPR—that is, they are liable for injuries caused by their ordinary negligence in rendering aid.

Consider this example: Sam is injured in an automobile accident and is unconscious in his automobile alongside the road. Doctor Pamela Heathcoat, who is driving by the scene of the accident, stops, pulls Sam from the burning wreckage, and administers first-aid. In doing so, Pamela negligently breaks Sam's shoulder. If Pamela's negligence is ordinary negligence, she is not liable to Sam because the Good Samaritan law protects her from liability. If Pamela was grossly negligent or reckless in administering aid to Sam, she is liable to him for the injuries she caused.

It is a question of fact for the jury to decide whether a doctor's conduct was ordinary negligence or gross negligence or recklessness. If Cathy, a layperson not trained in CPR, had rendered aid to Sam and caused Sam injury because of her ordinary negligence, the Good Samaritan law would not protect her and she would be liable to Sam.

Dram Shop Acts

Many states have enacted **Dram Shop Acts** that make a tavern and bartender civilly liable for injuries caused to or by patrons who are served too much alcohol. The alcohol must be either served in sufficient quantity to make the patron intoxicated or served to an already intoxicated person. Both the tavern and the bartender are liable to third persons injured by the patron and for injuries the patron suffered. They also are liable for injuries caused by or to minors served by the tavern, regardless of whether the minor is intoxicated.

Guest Statutes

Many states have enacted **guest statutes** providing that if a driver voluntarily and without compensation gives a ride in a vehicle to another person (e.g., a hitchhiker), the driver is not liable to the passenger for injuries caused by the driver's ordinary negligence. If the passenger pays compensation to the driver, however, the driver owes a duty of ordinary care to the passenger and will be held liable. The driver is always liable to the passenger for wanton and gross negligence—for example, injuries caused because of excessive speed.

Fireman's Rule

Under the **fireman's rule,** a firefighter who is injured while putting out a fire may not sue the party whose negligence caused the fire. This rule has been extended to police officers and other government workers. The bases for this rule are that (1) people might not call for help if they could be held liable; (2) firefighters, police officers, and other such workers receive special training for their jobs; and (3) these workers have special medical and retirement programs paid for by the public.

"Danger Invites Rescue" Doctrine

The law recognizes a **"danger invites rescue" doctrine.** Under this doctrine, a rescuer who is injured while going to someone's rescue can sue the person who caused the dangerous situation. For example, a passerby who is injured while trying to rescue children from a fire set by an arsonist can bring a civil suit against the arsonist.

Social Host Liability

Several states have adopted the **social host liability** rule. This rule provides that a social host is liable for injuries caused by guests who are served alcohol at a social function (e.g., a birthday party, a wedding reception) and later cause injury because they are intoxicated. The injury may be to a third person or to the guest himself or herself. The alcohol served at the social function must be the cause of the injury. A few states have adopted statutes that relieve social hosts from such liability.

Liability of Landowners

Owners and renters of real property owe certain duties to protect visitors from injury while on the property. A landowner's and tenant's liability generally depends on the visitor's status. Visitors fall into the following two categories:

1. *Invitees and licensees.* An *invitee* is a person who has been expressly or impliedly invited onto the owner's premises for the *mutual benefit* of both parties (e.g., guests invited for dinner, the mail carrier, and customers of a business). A *licensee* is a person who, *for his or her own benefit*, enters the premises with the express or implied consent of the owner (e.g., Avon representative, encyclopedia salesperson, Jehovah's Witnesses). An owner owes a **duty of ordinary care** to invitees and licensees. An owner is liable if he or she negligently causes injury to an invitee or licensee. For example, a homeowner is liable if she leaves a garden hose across the walkway on which an invitee or a licensee trips and is injured.

2. *Trespassers.* A *trespasser* is a person who has no invitation, permission, or right to be on another's property. Burglars are a common type of trespasser. Generally, an owner does not owe a duty of ordinary care to a trespasser. For example, if a trespasser trips and injures himself on a bicycle the owner negligently left out, the owner is not liable. An owner, however, does owe a **duty not to willfully or wantonly injure a trespasser.** Thus, an owner cannot set traps to injure trespassers.

A few states have eliminated the invitee–licensee–trespasser distinction. These states hold that owners and renters owe a duty of ordinary care to all persons who enter the property.

Liability of Common Carriers and Innkeepers

The common law holds common carriers and innkeepers to a higher standard of care than most other businesses. Common carriers and innkeepers owe a **duty of utmost care**—rather than a duty of ordinary care—to their passengers and guests. For example, innkeepers must provide security for their guests. The concept of utmost care is applied on a case-by-case basis. Obviously, a large hotel must provide greater security to guests than a "mom-and-pop" motel has to provide. Some states and cities have adopted specific statutes and ordinances relating to this duty.

DEFENSES AGAINST NEGLIGENCE

A defendant in a negligence lawsuit may raise several defenses to the imposition of liability. These defenses are discussed in the following paragraphs.

Superseding or Intervening Event

Under negligence, a person is liable only for foreseeable events. Therefore, an original negligent party can raise a *superseding* (or *intervening*) *event* as a defense to liability. For example, assume that an avid golfer negligently hits a spectator with a golf ball, knocking the spectator unconscious. While lying on the ground waiting for an ambulance to come, the spectator is struck by a bolt

FACTS

On April 11, 1991, Wilkie Cheong and Drew R. Antablin, longtime friends and experienced skiers, skied together at Alpine Meadows, a resort near Tahoe City, California. While skiing, Antablin accidentally collided with Cheong, causing injury to him. Cheong sued Antablin to recover damages for negligent skiing. The trial court granted Antablin's motion for summary judgment, holding that the doctrine of assumption of risk barred Cheong's claim and dismissed the lawsuit. The court of appeals affirmed. Cheong appealed to the California Supreme Court.

ISSUE

Does the doctrine of assumption of risk bar recovery?

IN THE LANGUAGE OF THE COURT

As a general rule, persons have a duty to use due care to avoid injuring others. This general rule, however, does not apply to coparticipants in a sport, where conditions or conduct that otherwise might be viewed as dangerous often are an integral part of the sport itself. Courts should not hold a sports participant liable to a coparticipant for ordinary careless conduct committed during the sport because in the heat of an active sporting event a participant's normal energetic conduct often includes accidentally careless behavior. Vigorous participation in such sporting events likely would be chilled if legal liability were to be imposed on a participant on the basis of his or her ordinary careless conduct.

For these reasons, the general test is that a participant in an active sport breaches a legal duty of care to other participants—i.e., engages in conduct that properly may subject him or her to financial liability—only if the participant intentionally injures another player or engages in conduct that is so reckless as to be totally outside the range of the ordinary activity involved in the sport.

DECISION AND REMEDY

The state supreme court held that the doctrine of assumption of risk barred recovery in this case.

Questions

1. Do you think the law should recognize the doctrine of assumption of risk? Why or why not?

2. Should Cheong have sued Antablin? Discuss.

3. Should the doctrine of assumption of risk be applied as a defense when spectators are injured at professional sports events? Explain.

of lightning and killed. The golfer is liable for the injuries caused by the golf ball. He is not liable for the death of the spectator, however, because the lightning bolt was an unforeseen intervening event.

Assumption of the Risk

If a plaintiff knows of and voluntarily enters into or participates in a risky activity that results in injury, the law recognizes that the plaintiff assumed, or took on, the risk involved. Thus, the defendant can raise the defense of **assumption of the risk** against the plaintiff. This defense assumes that the plaintiff (1) had knowledge of the specific risk, and (2) voluntarily assumed that risk. For example, under this theory, a race car driver assumes the risk of being injured or killed in a crash. Assumption of the risk was raised as a defense in the Case for Discussion above.

Contributory Negligence

Under the common law doctrine of **contributory negligence,** a plaintiff who is partially at fault for his or her own injury cannot recover against the negligent defendant. For example, suppose a driver who is driving faster than the speed limit negligently hits and injures a pedestrian who is jaywalking. Suppose the jury finds that the driver is 80 percent responsible for the accident and the jaywalker is 20 percent responsible. The pedestrian suffered $100,000 in injuries. Under the doctrine of contributory negligence, the pedestrian cannot recover any damages from the driver.

The doctrine of contributory negligence has one major exception: The defendant has a duty under the law to avoid the accident if at all possible. This rule is known as the *last clear chance rule.* For example, a driver who sees a pedestrian walking across the street against a "Don't Walk" sign must avoid hitting him or her if possible. When deciding cases involving this rule, the courts consider the attentiveness of the parties and the amount of time each had to respond to the situation.

Comparative Negligence

As seen, application of the doctrine of contributory negligence could reach an unfair result where a party only slightly at fault for his or her injuries could not recover from an otherwise negligent defendant. Many states have replaced the doctrine of contributory negligence with the doctrine of **comparative negligence.** Under this doctrine, damages are apportioned according to fault. When the comparative negligence rule is applied to the previous example, the result is much fairer. The plaintiff–pedestrian can recover 80 percent of his or her damages (or $80,000) from the defendant–driver. This is an example of *pure comparative negligence.* Several states have adopted *partial comparative negligence*, which provides that a plaintiff must be less than 50 percent responsible for causing his or her own injuries to recover under comparative negligence; otherwise, contributory negligence applies.

Doctrine of Strict Liability

In the landmark case *Greenmun v. Yuba Power Products, Inc.* [59 Cal.2d 57, 27 Cal.Rptr. 697 (1963)], the California Supreme Court adopted the **doctrine of strict liability in tort** as a basis for product liability actions. Most states now have adopted this doctrine as a basis for product liability actions. The doctrine of strict liability removes many of the difficulties for the plaintiff associated with other theories of product liability. In the remainder of this chapter, we will examine the scope of the strict liability doctrine.

Restatement of Torts

The doctrine of strict liability is not part of the Uniform Commercial Code (UCC). The most widely recognized articulation of the doctrine is found in Section 402A of the Restatement (Second) of Torts, which provides:

(1) One who sells any product in a defective condition unreasonably dangerous to the user or consumer or to his property is subject to liability for physical harm thereby caused to the ultimate user or consumer, or to his property, if

    (a) the seller is engaged in the business of selling such a product, and

    (b) it is expected to and does reach the user or consumer without substantial change in the condition in which it is sold.

(2) The rule stated in Subsection (1) applies although

    (a) the seller has exercised all possible care in the preparation and sale of his product, and

    (b) the user or consumer has not bought the product from or entered into any contractual relation with the seller.

Liability Without Fault

Unlike negligence, strict liability does not require the injured person to prove that the defendant breached a duty of care. *Strict liability is imposed irrespective of fault.* A seller can be found strictly liable even though he or she has exercised all possible care in the preparation and sale of his or her product.

The doctrine of strict liability applies to sellers and lessors of products who are engaged in the business of selling and leasing products. Casual sales and transactions by nonmerchants are not covered. Thus, a person who sells a defective product to a neighbor in a casual sale is not strictly liable if the product causes injury.

Strict liability applies only to products, not services. In hybrid transactions involving both services and products, the dominant element of the transaction dictates whether strict liability applies. For example, in a medical operation that requires a blood transfusion, the operation would be the dominant element and strict liability would not apply. Strict liability may not be disclaimed.

All in the Chain of Distribution Are Liable

All parties in the **chain of distribution** of a defective product are strictly liable for the injuries caused by that product. Thus, all manufacturers, distributors, wholesalers, retailers, lessors, and subcomponent manufacturers may be sued under this doctrine. This view is based on public policy. Lawmakers presume that sellers and lessors will insure against the risk of a strict liability lawsuit and spread the cost to their consumers by raising the price of products.

Consider this example: Suppose a subcomponent manufacturer produces a defective tire and sells it to a truck manufacturer. The truck manufacturer places the defective tire on one of its new model trucks. The truck is distributed by a distributor to a retail dealer. Ultimately, the retail dealer sells the truck to a buyer. The defective tire causes an accident in which the buyer is injured. All of the parties in the tire's chain of distribution can be sued by the injured party. In this case, the liable parties are the subcomponent manufacturer, the truck manufacturer, the distributor, and the retailer.

A defendant who has not been negligent but who is made to pay a strict liability judgment can bring a separate action against the negligent party in the chain of distribution to recover its losses. In the preceding example, the retailer could sue the manufacturer to recover the strict liability judgment assessed against it. Exhibit 11.1 compares the doctrines of negligence and strict liability.

Doctrines of negligence and strict liability compared.   *exhibit* **11.1**

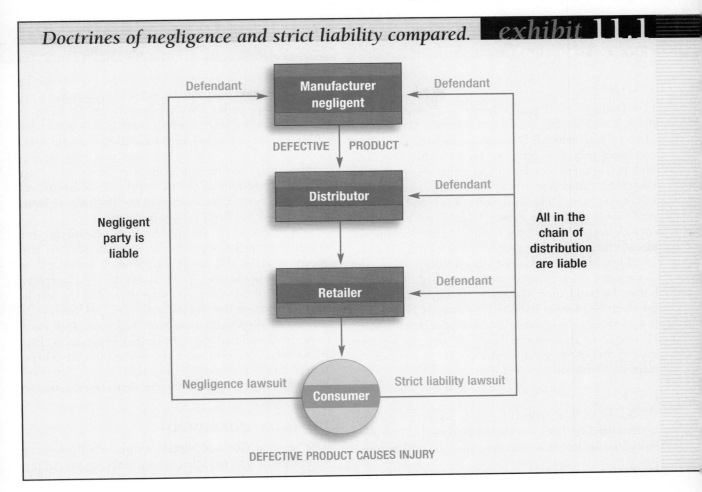

Parties Who Can Recover for Strict Liability

Because strict liability is a tort doctrine, privity of contract between the plaintiff and the defendant is not required. The doctrine applies even if the injured party had no contractual relations with the defendant. Under strict liability, sellers and lessors are liable to the ultimate user or consumer. Users include the purchaser or lessee, family members, guests, employees, customers, and persons who passively enjoy the benefits of the product (e.g., passengers in automobiles).

Most jurisdictions have judicially or statutorily extended the protection of strict liability to bystanders. The courts have stated that bystanders should be entitled to even greater protection than a consumer or user. This is because consumers and users have the chance to inspect for defects and to limit their purchases to articles manufactured by reputable manufacturers and sold by reputable retailers, whereas bystanders do not have the same opportunity.

Damages Recoverable for Strict Liability

The damages recoverable in a strict liability action vary by jurisdiction. Damages for personal injuries are recoverable in all jurisdictions that have adopted the doctrine of strict liability, although some jurisdictions limit the

Shoshone Coca-Cola Bottling Co. v. Dolinski

420 P.2d 855 (1967) **Supreme Court of Nevada**

FACTS

Leo Dolinski purchased a bottle of "Squirt," a soft drink, from a vending machine at a Sea and Ski plant, his place of employment. Dolinski opened the bottle and consumed part of its contents. He immediately became ill. Upon examination, it was found that the bottle contained the decomposed body of a mouse, mouse hair, and mouse feces. Dolinski visited a doctor and was given medicine to counteract nausea. Dolinski suffered physical and mental distress from consuming the decomposed mouse and possessed an aversion to soft drinks.

The Shoshone Coca-Cola Bottling Company (Shoshone) manufactured and distributed the Squirt bottle. Dolinski sued Shoshone, basing his lawsuit on the doctrine of strict liability. The state of Nevada had not previously recognized the doctrine of strict liability. However, the trial court adopted the doctrine of strict liability and the jury returned a verdict in favor of the plaintiff. Shoshone appealed.

ISSUE

Should the state of Nevada judicially adopt the doctrine of strict liability? If so, was there a defect in the manufacture of the Squirt bottle that caused the plaintiff's injuries?

IN THE LANGUAGE OF THE COURT

Thompson, Justice. We affirm the verdict and judgment since, in our view, public policy demands that one who places upon the market a bottled beverage in a condition dangerous for use must be held strictly liable to the ultimate user for injuries resulting from such use, although the seller has exercised all reasonable care. Though appellant Shoshone suggests that only the legislature may declare the policy of Nevada on this subject, the weight of the case authority is contra. As indicated, most states approving the doctrine of strict liability have done so by court declaration.

In the case at hand, Shoshone contends that insufficient proof was offered to establish that the mouse was in the bottle of "Squirt" when it left Shoshone's possession. The plaintiff offered the expert testimony of a toxicologist who examined the bottle and contents on the day the plaintiff drank from it. It was his opinion that the mouse "had been dead for a long time" and that the dark stains (mouse feces) that he found on the bottom of the bottle must have been there before the liquid was added. The jury apparently preferred the latter evidence that traced cause to the defendant.

DECISION AND REMEDY

The Supreme Court of Nevada adopted the doctrine of strict liability and held that the evidence supported the trial court's finding that there was a defect in manufacture. Affirmed.

Questions

1. Should the courts adopt the theory of strict liability? Why or why not?

2. Was it ethical for Shoshone to argue that it was not liable to Dolinski?

3. Should all in the chain of distribution of a defective product—even those parties who are not responsible for the defect—be held liable under the doctrine of strict liability? Or should liability be based only on fault?

dollar amount of the award. Property damage is recoverable in most jurisdictions, but economic loss (e.g., lost income) is recoverable in only a few jurisdictions. *Punitive damages* are generally allowed if the plaintiff can prove that the defendant either intentionally injured him or her or acted with reckless disregard for his or her safety.

Ethical PERSPECTIVE

GM Hit with Punitive Damages

On Christmas Eve, Patricia Anderson was driving her Chevrolet Malibu automobile, which was manufactured by the General Motors (GM) Corporation, home from church. Her four young children, ages 1 through 9, and a neighbor were also in the car. The Chevy Malibu was stopped at a stoplight at 89th Place and Figueroa Street in Los Angeles when a drunken driver plowed his car into the back of the Malibu at 50 to 70 mph. The Malibu burst into flames as its gas tank ruptured and ignited. Although no one died in the crash, the occupants of the Malibu were severely burned. Many required substantial and multiple skin grafts.

The two injured women and four injured children sued GM for product liability. They alleged that the fuel tank of the Chevy Malibu was defectively designed and placed too close to the rear bumper. GM countered that the tragic accident was the fault of the driver who struck the Malibu. The accident victims produced evidence that showed that GM knew that the car's fuel-tank design was unsafe but had not changed the design because of cost.

The Chevy Malibu was one of GM's A-Class cars, which also include the Pontiac Grand Am, the Oldsmobile Cutlass, and the Chevrolet Monte Carlo, all of which have similar fuel-tank designs. The plaintiffs produced GM memos that said it would cost GM $8.59 per vehicle to produce and install a safer fuel tank design, but that it would cost the company only an estimated $2.40 per car not to fix the cars and pay damages to injured victims.

After a 10-week trial, the jurors returned a verdict of $107 million in compensatory damages to the plaintiffs for injuries, disfigurement, and pain and suffering caused to them by the accident. The jury then tacked on $4.9 billion as punitive damages to punish GM. This was the largest amount ever awarded in a personal-injury lawsuit. GM, the world's largest automobile company, reported annual earnings of $3 billion in 1998, the year of the verdict. After the trial one juror stated: "We're just like numbers. Statistics. That's something that is wrong."

GM asked the trial judge to throw out the trial. GM claimed that it was not given a fair trial because the trial court judge refused to allow the jury to hear evidence that (1) the driver of the other car was drunk and went to jail, and (2) crash-test data showed the safety history of the vehicle. GM also claimed that the jury was prejudiced by repetitive personal attacks on GM as a "soulless company" and its lawyers as "hired guns" who consumed "cappuccinos and designer muffins." GM did not convince the judge that such animosity influenced the jury.

GM also alleged that the jury was allowed to hear evidence that it should not have heard—namely, that GM had lobbied Congress in the 1970s not to adopt tougher standards for protecting fuel tanks in crashes.

In its post-trial motions, GM argued that the award of damages, specifically the $4.8 billion of punitive damages, was the result of bias and prejudice of the jury, and asked the trial court judge to reduce the award of damages. This the trial court judge did do: He let the compensatory damages award stand but reduced the award of punitive damages to $1 billion. The revised award is equivalent to 2 percent of GM's net worth and 10 times the compensatory damages. GM faced more than 30 other lawsuits involving fuel tank explosions in its A-Class cars.

1. Should General Motors have designed the fuel tank placement differently? Explain.

2. Was an award of punitive damages warranted in this case? Why or why not?

LEGAL TERMINOLOGY

Assault

Assumption of the risk

Battery

Breach of duty of care

Causation in fact/actual cause

Chain of distribution

Comparative negligence

Contributory negligence

Conversion of personal property

"Danger invites rescue" doctrine

Defamation of character

Doctrine of strict liability in tort

Dram Shop Act

Duty not to willfully or wantonly injure a trespasser

Duty of care

Duty of ordinary care

Duty of utmost care

False imprisonment

Fireman's rule

Good Samaritan law

Guest statute

Intentional infliction of emotional distress

Invasion of right to privacy

Libel

Malicious prosecution

Merchant protection statute

Misappropriation of the right to publicity

Negligence

Negligence per se

Negligent infliction of emotional distress

Professional malpractice

Proximate cause/legal cause

Punitive damages

Res ipsa loquitur

Slander

Social host liability

Tort

Trespass to land

Trespass to personal property

Unintentional tort

Summary

Intentional Torts Against Persons

Assault	Threat of immediate harm or offensive contact, or any action that arouses reasonable apprehension of imminent harm.
Battery	The unauthorized and harmful or offensive physical contact with another person. *Transferred intent doctrine:* If a person intends to injure one person but actually harms another person, the law transfers the perpetrator's intent from the target to the actual victim.
False Imprisonment	Intentional confinement or restraint of another person without authority or justification and without that person's consent.
Merchant Protection	These statutes permit businesses to stop, detain, and investigate suspected shoplifters (and not be held liable for false imprisonment) if the following requirements are met: 1. There are reasonable grounds for the suspicion. 2. Suspects are detained for only a reasonable time. 3. Investigations are conducted in a reasonable manner.
Defamation of Character	The defendant makes an untrue statement of fact about the plaintiff that is published to a third party. Truth is an absolute defense. Types of defamation: 1. *Slander:* Oral defamation 2. *Libel:* Written defamation Public figure plaintiffs must prove the additional element of *malice*.
Misappropriation of the Right to Publicity	Appropriating another person's name or identity for commercial purposes without that person's consent. Also called *tort of appropriation*.
Invasion of Privacy	Unwarranted and undesired publicity of a private fact about a person. The fact does not have to be untrue. Truth is not a defense.
Intentional Infliction of Emotional Distress	Extreme and outrageous conduct intentionally or recklessly done that causes severe emotional distress. Some states require that the mental distress be manifested by physical injury. Also known as *tort of outrage*.
Malicious Prosecution	A successful defendant in a prior lawsuit can sue the plaintiff if the first lawsuit was frivolous. *(continued)*

Intentional Torts Against Property

Trespass to Land	Interference with a landowner's right to exclusive possession of his or her land.
Trespass to Personal Property	A person injures another person's personal property or interferes with that person's enjoyment of his or her property.
Conversion of Personal Property	Taking over another person's personal property and depriving him or her of the use and enjoyment of the property.

Unintentional Torts (Negligence)

Definition of Negligence	The omission to do something which a reasonable man would do, or doing something which a prudent and reasonable man would not do.

Elements of Negligence	To establish negligence, the plaintiff must prove:
	
	 1. The defendant owed a *duty of care* to the plaintiff.
	 2. The defendant *breached this duty*.
	 3. The plaintiff suffered *injury*.
	 4. The defendant's negligent act *caused* the plaintiff's injury. Two types of causation must be shown:
	
	    a. *Causation in fact* (or *actual cause*): The defendant's negligent act was the actual cause of the plaintiff's injury.
	
	    b. *Proximate cause* (or *legal cause*): The defendant is liable only for the *foreseeable* consequences of his or her negligent act.

Special Negligence Doctrines

Negligent Infliction of Emotional Distress	A person who witnesses a close relative's injury or death may sue the negligent party who caused the accident to recover damages for any emotional distress suffered by the bystander. To recover for *negligent infliction of emotional distress*, the plaintiff must prove: 1. A relative was killed or injured by the defendant. 2. The plaintiff suffered severe emotional distress. 3. The plaintiff's mental distress resulted from a sensory and contemporaneous observance of the accident. Some states require that the mental distress be manifested by physical injury.
Professional Malpractice	Doctors, lawyers, architects, accountants, and other professionals owe a duty of ordinary care in providing their services. They are judged by a *reasonable professional standard*. Professionals who breach this duty are liable to clients and some third parties for *professional malpractice*.

(continued)

Negligence *Per Se*	A statute or ordinance establishes the duty of care. A violation of the statute or ordinance constitutes a breach of this duty of care.
Res Ipsa Loquitur	A presumption of negligence is established if the defendant had exclusive control of the instrumentality or situation that caused the plaintiff's injury and the injury would not have ordinarily occurred but for someone's negligence. The defendants may rebut this presumption.
Good Samaritan Laws	Relieve doctors and other medical professionals from liability for ordinary negligence when rendering medical aid in emergency situations.
Dram Shop Acts	State statutes that make taverns and bartenders liable for injuries caused to or by patrons who are served too much alcohol and cause injury to themselves or others.
Guest Statutes	Provide that a driver of a vehicle is not liable for ordinary negligence to passengers he or she gratuitously transports. The driver is liable for gross negligence.
Fireman's Rule	Firefighters, police officers, and other government employees who are injured in the performance of their duties cannot sue the person who negligently caused the dangerous situation that caused the injury.
"Danger Invites Rescue" Doctrine	A person who is injured while going to someone's rescue may sue the person who caused the dangerous situation.
Social Host Liability	Some states make social hosts liable for injuries caused by guests who are served alcohol at a social function and later cause injury because they are intoxicated.
Liability of Landowners	Landowners (and tenants) owe the following duties to persons who come upon their property: 1. *Invitees:* Duty of ordinary care 2. *Licensees:* Duty of ordinary care 3. *Trespassers:* Duty not to willfully and wantonly injure trespassers
Liability of Common Carriers and Innkeepers	Owe a *duty of utmost care* rather than the duty of ordinary care, to protect their passengers and patrons from injury.

Defenses Against Negligence

Superseding Event	An intervening event caused by another person that caused the plaintiff's injuries that relieves the defendant from liability.

(continued)

Assumption of the Risk	A defendant is not liable for the plaintiff's injuries if the plaintiff had knowledge of a specific risk and voluntarily assumed that risk.
Plaintiff Partially at Fault	States have adopted one of the following two rules that affect a defendant's liability if the plaintiff had been partially at fault for causing his or her own injuries: 1. *Contributory negligence:* A plaintiff cannot recover anything from the defendant. 2. *Comparative negligence:* Damages are apportioned according to the parties' fault. Also called *comparative fault.*

Doctrine of Strict Liability

Strict Liability in Tort	A manufacturer or seller who sells a defective product is liable to the ultimate user who is injured thereby. All in the chain of distribution are liable irrespective of fault. Sometimes called *vertical liability.*

Working the Web

1. Using the Findlaw search engine, find materials on torts.
2. Check the latest summary of legal news from a variety of newspapers and periodicals and ethics and practice issues at the ABA Tort and Insurance Practice Section at www.abanet.org/tips/home.html.
3. Visit the Cornell Legal Information Institute for an overview of tort law and links to information on damages and product liability at www.law.cornell.edu/topics/torts.html.
4. See the U.S. Consumer Product Safety Commission website for information on hazardous products, recalls, injury statistics, and current press releases at www.cpsc.gov/.
5. Find information from the U.S. Consumer Product Safety Commission website in Spanish at www.cpsc.gov/cpscpub/spanish/spanish.html.

Questions
CRITICAL LEGAL THINKING AND WRITING

1. What is the legal purpose for allowing a person to sue for defamation of character?
2. Should the right to publicity be a protected right? Why or why not?
3. Should the tort of intentional infliction of emotional distress be recognized by the law? What difficulties arise in trying to apply this tort?

4. What are the elements necessary to prove negligence? Describe each element.

5. Explain the doctrine of proximate cause. Give an example of this doctrine's application.

6. Should the law recognize the doctrine of negligent infliction of emotional distress? Are the elements easy to meet?

7. Compare the doctrine of contributory negligence to the doctrine of comparative negligence.

8. What does the Good Samaritan law provide? Do you think this law serves a good purpose?

9. What does the doctrine of strict liability provide? Do you think this doctrine is fair?

10. What are punitive damages? What public policies are served by an award of punitive damages?

ETHICS: ANALYSIS AND DISCUSSION

1. What, if any, obligations does the legal team have when they know a client is using superior resources to harass someone by bringing a frivolous lawsuit?

2. What ethical obligation does the legal team have to inform clients, even when the client does not ask for advice, of actions they should take to avoid liability in light of decisions like the one in the case against McDonald's for damages from hot coffee?

3. What is the "reasonable professional standard" for a paralegal?

Conflict of Interest

There are few certainties in the area of ethics, for paralegals or in any profession. What qualifies as ethical conduct is in most cases based on state law and court interpretation applied to a set of facts. For the following:

- *Prepare a written statement based on your state law.*
- *Use your state bar association website as a starting point.*

As a recent graduate with school loans to pay, you also work at a local food market at night. You are working on a slow Tuesday evening and instead of walking the aisle of the store you take a coffee break in the back of the store. A customer slips on a small bunch of grapes, which are in the aisle, breaking a bone in the leg. The injured customer is also a long-time client of the law firm where you work. Is there any conflict of interest? Can the conflict be resolved? How?

Manning v. Grimsley

643 F.2d 20 (1st Cir. 1981)

11.1 FACTS

On September 16, 1975, the Baltimore Orioles professional baseball team was at Boston's Fenway Park to play the Boston Red Sox. Ross Grimsley was a pitcher for the visiting Baltimore club. During one period of the game, Grimsley was warming up in the bullpen, throwing pitches to a catcher. During this warmup, Boston spectators in the stands heckled Grimsley. After Grimsley had completed warming up and the catcher had left from behind the plate in the bullpen, Grimsley wound up as if he were going to throw the ball in his hand at the plate, then turned and threw the ball at one of the hecklers in the stand. The ball traveled at about 80 miles an hour, passed through a wire fence protecting the spectators, missed the heckler that Grimsley was aiming at, and hit another spectator, David Manning, Jr., causing injury. Manning sued Grimsley and the Baltimore Orioles.

ISSUE

Are the defendants liable?

Johnson v. Kmart Enterprises, Inc.

297 N.W.2d 74 (Wis.App. 1980)

11.2 FACTS

At about 7:30 P.M. on September 8, 1976, Deborah A. Johnson entered a Kmart store located in Madison, Wisconsin, to purchase some diapers and several cans of motor oil. She took her young child along to enable her to purchase the correct-size diapers, carrying the child in an infant seat that the mother had purchased at Kmart two or three weeks previously. A large Kmart price tag was still attached to the infant seat. Johnson purchased the diapers and oil and some children's clothes. She was in a hurry to leave because it was 8:00 P.M., her child's feeding time, and she hurried through the checkout lane. She paid for the diapers, the oil, and the clothing.

Just after leaving the store, she heard someone ask her to stop. She turned around and saw a Kmart security officer. He showed her a badge and asked her to come back into the store, which she did. The man stated, "I have reason to believe that you have stolen this car seat." Johnson explained that she had purchased the seat previously. She demanded to see the manager, who was called to the scene. When Johnson pointed out that the seat had cat hairs, food crumbs, and milk stains on it, the man said, "I'm really sorry. There's been a terrible mistake. You can go." Johnson looked at the clock when she left, which read 8:20 P.M. Johnson sued Kmart for false imprisonment.

ISSUE

Is Kmart liable?

Karns v. Emerson Electric Co.

817 F.2d 1452 (1987)

11.3 FACTS

The Emerson Electric Co. manufactures and sells a product called the Weed Eater Model XR-90. The Weed Eater is a multipurpose weed-trimming and brush-cutting device. It consists of a handheld gasoline-powered engine connected to a long drive shaft, at the end of which can be attached various tools for cutting weeds and brush. One such attachment is a 10-inch circular sawblade capable of cutting through growth up to 2 inches in diameter. When this sawblade is attached to the Weed Eater, approximately 270 degrees of blade edge are exposed when in use.

The owner's manual contained the following warning: "Keep children away. All people and pets should be kept at a safe distance from the work area, at least 30 feet, especially when using the blade."

Donald Pearce, a 13-year-old boy, was helping his uncle clear an overgrown yard. The uncle was operating a Weed Eater XR-90 with the circular sawblade attachment. When Pearce stooped to pick up something off the ground about 6 to 10 feet behind and slightly to the left of where his uncle was operating the Weed Eater, the sawblade on the Weed Eater struck something near the ground. The Weed Eater kicked back to the left and cut off Pearce's right arm to the elbow. Pearce, through his mother, Charlotte Karns, sued Emerson to recover damages under strict liability.

ISSUE

Is Emerson liable?

Luque v. McLean, Trustee

8 Cal.3d 136, 104 Cal.Rptr. 443 (Cal. 1972)

11.4 FACTS

Celestino Luque lived with his cousins Harry and Laura Dunn in Millbrae, California. The Dunns purchased a rotary lawn mower from Rhoads Hardware. The lawn mower was manufactured by Air Capital Manufacturing Company and was distributed by Garehime Corporation. On December 4, 1965, neighbors asked Luque to mow their lawn. While Luque was cutting the lawn, he noticed a small carton in the path of the lawn mower. Luque left the lawn mower in a stationary position with its motor running and walked around the side of the lawn mower to remove the carton. As he did so, he suddenly slipped on the wet grass and fell backward. Luque's left hand entered the unguarded hole of the lawn mower and was caught in the revolving blade, which turns at 175 miles per hour and 100 revolutions per second. Luque's hand was severely mangled and lacerated. The word *Caution* was printed above the unguarded hole on the lawn mower.

Luque sued Rhoads Hardware, Air Capital, and Garehime Corporation for strict liability. The defendants argued that strict liability does not apply to *patent* (obvious) defects.

ISSUE

Was it ethical for the defendants to argue that they were not liable for patent defects? Would patent defects ever be corrected if the defendants' contention were accepted by the court? Who wins?

Braun v. Soldier of Fortune Magazine, Inc.

968 F.2d 1110 (1992)   United States Court of Appeals, Eleventh Circuit

Read the following case, excerpted from the court of appeals opinion. Review and brief the case. In your brief, answer the following questions:

1. Who are the plaintiffs? What are they suing for?

2. When does a magazine owe a duty to refrain from publishing an advertisement?

3. Was the advertisement the proximate cause of the plaintiff's injuries?

4. Should the award of punitive damages have been reduced?

Anderson, Circuit Judge.

In January 1985, Michael Savage submitted a personal service advertisement to Soldier of Fortune (SOF). After several conversations between Savage and SOF's advertising manager, Joan Steel, the following advertisement ran in the June 1985 through March 1986 issues of SOF:

> GUN FOR HIRE: 37-year-old professional mercenary desires jobs. Vietnam Veteran. Discrete [sic] and very private. Body guard, courier, and other special skills. All jobs considered. Phone (615) 436-9785 (days) or (615) 436-4335 (nights), or write: Rt. 2, Box 682 Village Loop Road, Gatlinburg, TN 37738.

Savage testified that, when he placed the ad, he had no intention of obtaining anything but legitimate jobs. Nonetheless, Savage stated that the overwhelming majority of the 30 to 40 phone calls a week he received in response to his ad sought his participation in criminal activity such as murder, assault, and kidnapping. The ad also generated at least one legitimate job as a bodyguard, which Savage accepted.

In late 1984 or early 1985, Bruce Gastwirth began seeking to murder his business partner, Richard Braun. Gastwirth enlisted the aid of another business associate, John Horton Moore, and together they arranged for at least three attempts on Braun's life, all of which were unsuccessful. Responding to Savage's SOF ad, Gastwirth and Moore contacted him in August 1985 to discuss plans to murder Braun.

On August 26, 1985, Savage, Moore, and another individual, Sean Trevor Doutre, went to Braun's suburban Atlanta home. As Braun and his 16-year-old son Michael were driving down the driveway, Doutre stepped in front of Braun's car and fired several shots into the car with a MAC 11 automatic pistol. The shots hit Michael in the thigh and wounded Braun as well. Braun managed to roll out of the car, but Doutre walked over to Braun and killed him by firing two more shots into the back of his head as Braun lay on the ground.

On March 31, 1988, appellees Michael and Ian Braun filed this diversity action against appellants in the United States District Court for the Middle District of Alabama, seeking damages for the wrongful death of their father. Michael Braun also filed a separate action seeking recovery for the personal injuries he received at the time of his father's death. The district court consolidated these related matters.

Trial began on December 3, 1990. Appellees contended that, under Georgia law, SOF was liable for their injuries because SOF negligently published a personal service advertisement that created an unreasonable risk of the solicitation and commission of violent criminal activity, including murder. To show that SOF knew of the likelihood that criminal activity would result from placing an ad like Savage's, appellees introduced evidence of newspaper and magazine articles published prior to Braun's murder which described links between SOF and personal service ads and a number of criminal convictions including murder, kidnapping, assault, extortion, and attempts thereof. Appellees also presented evidence that, prior to SOF's acceptance of Savage's ad, law enforcement officials had contacted SOF staffers on two separate occasions in connection with investigations of crimes.

In his trial testimony, SOF president Robert K. Brown denied having any knowledge of criminal activity associated with SOF's personal service ads at any time prior to Braun's murder in August 1985. Both Jim Graves, a former managing editor of SOF, and Joan Steel, the advertising manager who accepted Savage's advertisement, similarly testified that they were not aware of other crimes connected with SOF ads prior to running Savage's ad. Steel further testified that she had understood the term "Gun for Hire" in Savage's ad to refer to a "bodyguard or protection service-type thing" rather than to any illegal activity.

The jury returned a verdict in favor of appellee and awarded compensatory damages on the wrongful death claim in the amount of $2,000,000. The jury also awarded appellee Michael Braun $375,000 in compensatory damages and $10,000,000 in punitive damages for his personal injury claim.

To prevail in an action for negligence in Georgia, a party must establish the following elements:

(1) A legal duty to conform to a standard of conduct raised by the law for the protection of others against unreasonable risks of harm,

(2) a breach of this standard,

(3) a legally attributable causal connection between the conduct and the resulting injury, and

(4) some loss or damage flowing to the plaintiff's legally protected interest as a result of the alleged breach of the legal duty.

To the extent that SOF denies that a publisher owes any duty to the public when it publishes personal service ads, its position is clearly inconsistent with Georgia law. We believe, however, that the crux of SOF's argument is not that it had no duty to the public but that, as a matter of law, there is a risk to the public when a publisher prints an "unreasonable" advertisement only if the ad openly solicits criminal activity.

SOF further argues that imposing liability on publishers for the advertisements they print indirectly threatens core, noncommercial speech to which the Constitution accords its full protection. Supreme Court cases discussing the limitations the First Amendment places on state defamation law indicate that there is no constitutional infirmity in Georgia law holding publishers liable under a negligence standard with respect to the commercial advertisements they print. Past Supreme Court decisions indicate, however, that the negligence standard the First Amendment permits is a "modified" negligence standard. The Court's decisions suggest that Georgia law may impose tort liability on publishers for injury caused by the advertisements they print only if the ad on its face, without the need to investigate, makes it apparent that there is a substantial danger of harm to the public.

We conclude that the First Amendment permits a state to impose upon a publisher liability for compensatory damages for negligently publishing a commercial advertisement where the ad on its face, and without the need for investigation, makes it apparent that there is a substantial danger of harm to the public. The absence of a duty requiring publishers to investigate the advertisements they print and the requirement that the substance of the ad itself must warn the publisher of a substantial danger of harm to the public guarantee that the burden placed on publishers will not impermissibly chill protected commercial speech.

Our review of the language of Savage's ad persuades us that SOF had a legal duty to refrain from publishing it. Savage's advertisement (1) emphasized the term "Gun for Hire," (2) described Savage as a "professional mercenary," (3) stressed Savage's willingness to keep his assignments confidential and "very private," (4) listed legitimate jobs involving the use of a gun—bodyguard and courier—followed by a reference to Savage's "other special skills," and (5) concluded by stating that Savage would consider "all jobs."

The ad's combination of sinister terms makes it apparent that there was a substantial danger of harm to the public. The ad expressly solicits all jobs requiring the use of a gun. When the list of legitimate jobs—i.e., bodyguard and courier—is followed by "other special skills" and "all jobs considered," the implication is clear that the advertiser would consider illegal jobs. We agree with the district court that "the language of this advertisement is such that, even though couched in terms not explicitly offering criminal services, the publisher could recognize the offer of criminal activity as readily as its readers obviously did." We find that the jury had ample grounds for finding that SOF's publication of Savage's ad was the proximate cause of Braun's injuries.

For the foregoing reasons, we affirm the district court's judgment.

CHAPTER 12

CHAPTER OBJECTIVES

After studying this chapter, you should be able to:

1. List the elements necessary to form a valid contract.

2. Describe and distinguish between express and implied-in-fact contracts.

3. Define an offer and an acceptance.

4. Define consideration and analyze whether contracts are lacking in consideration.

5. Identify illegal contracts that are contrary to statutes and that violate public policy.

6. List and describe the contracts that must be in writing under the Statute of Frauds.

7. Describe compensatory, consequential, and liquidated damages.

8. Define the equitable remedies of specific performance, injunction, reformation, and quasi-contract.

9. Define sales contracts governed by Article 2 of the UCC and lease contracts governed by Article 2A of the UCC.

10. Describe the writing and signature requirements for Internet contracts provided by the Federal Electronic Signature Act.

Contracts and Commercial Transactions

The movement of the progressive societies has hitherto been a movement from status to contract.

SIR HENRY MAINE, *ANCIENT LAW*

Introduction

Contracts are the basis of many of our daily activities. They provide the means for individuals and businesses to sell and otherwise transfer property, services, and other rights. The purchase of goods, such as books and automobiles, is based on sales contracts; the hiring of employees is based on service contracts; and the lease of an apartment is based on a rental contract. The list is almost endless. Without enforceable contracts, commerce would collapse.

Contracts are voluntarily entered into by parties. The terms of the contract become *private law* between the parties. The contract between parties is the law between them, and the courts are obliged to give legal effect to such contracts according to the true interests of the parties.

The law of contracts makes up a substantial portion of many lawyers' practices. Lawyers are called upon to prepare and review all sorts of contracts, including contracts for the sale of personal property and real property, commercial sales and lease contracts, licenses, and other contracts. Lawyers rely heavily on the help of paralegals in drafting and reviewing contracts. This chapter introduces you to the study of contract law and commercial transactions governed by the Uniform Commercial Code (UCC). The discussion includes the definition of a contract, requirements for forming a contract, the performance of contracts, and remedies for the breach of contracts.

DEFINITION OF AND PARTIES TO A CONTRACT

A **contract** is an agreement that is enforceable by a court of law or equity. A simple and widely recognized definition of a contract is provided by the Restatement (Second) of Contracts: "A contract is a promise or a set of promises for the breach of which the law gives a remedy or the performance of which the law in some way recognizes a duty [Restatement (Second) of Contracts, § 1].

Every contract involves at least two parties. The **offeror** is the party who makes an offer to enter into a contract. The **offeree** is the party to whom the offer is made (see Exhibit 12.1). In making an offer, the offeror promises to do—or to refrain from doing—something. The offeree then has the power to

Evolution of the Modern Law of Contracts

The use of contracts goes back to ancient times. The common law of contracts developed in England around the fifteenth century. American contract law evolved from the English common law.

At first the United States adopted a *laissez-faire* approach to the law of contracts. The central theme of this theory was *freedom of contract*. The parties (such as consumers, shopkeepers, farmers, and traders) generally dealt with one another face-to-face, had equal knowledge and bargaining power, and had the opportunity to inspect the goods prior to sale. Contract terms were openly negotiated. There was little, if any, government regulation of the right to contract. This "pure" or classical law of contracts produced objective rules, which, in turn, produced certainty and predictability in the enforcement of contracts. It made sense until the Industrial Revolution.

The Industrial Revolution changed many of the underlying assumptions of pure contract law. For example, as large corporations developed and gained control of crucial resources, the traditional balance of parties' bargaining power shifted: Large corporations now had the most power. The chain of distribution for goods also changed because (1) buyers did not have to deal face-to-face with sellers, and (2) there was not always an opportunity to inspect the goods prior to sale.

Eventually sellers began using *form contracts* that offered their goods to buyers on a take-it-or-leave-it basis. Most contracts in the United States today are form contracts. Examples of form contracts are automobile contracts, mortgage contracts, and sales contracts for consumer goods.

Federal and state governments alike enacted statutes intended to protect consumers, creditors, and others from unfair contracts. In addition, the courts began to develop certain common law legal theories that allowed some oppressive or otherwise unjust contracts to be avoided. Today, under this modern law of contracts, there is substantial government regulation of the right to contract.

Parties to a contract.   *exhibit* **12.1**

offer

Offeror   **Offeree**

acceptance

Offeror makes an   Offeree has the power to accept
offer to the offeree   the offer and create a contract.

create a contract by accepting the offeror's offer. A contract is created if the offer is accepted. No contract is created if the offer is not accepted.

REQUIREMENTS OF A CONTRACT

To be an enforceable contract, the following four basic requirements must be met:

1. *Agreement.* To have an enforceable contract, there must be an agreement between the parties.
2. *Consideration.* The promise must be supported by a bargained-for consideration that is legally sufficient.
3. *Contractual capacity.* The parties to a contract must have the capacity to contract.
4. *Lawful object.* The object of the contract must be lawful, or legal.

The following text discusses these requirements in greater detail.

Agreement

Agreement is the manifestation by two or more persons of the substance of a contract. It requires an *offer* and *acceptance*. The process of reaching an agreement usually proceeds as follows: Prior to entering into a contract, the parties may engage in preliminary negotiations about price, time of performance, and such. At some point during these negotiations, one party makes an **offer.** The person who makes the offer is called the offeror, and the person to whom the offer is made is called the offeree. The offer sets forth the terms under which the offeror is willing to enter into the contract. The offeree has the power to create an agreement by accepting the offer.

Requirements of the Offer

Section 24 of the Restatement (Second) of Contracts defines an offer as: "The manifestation of willingness to enter into a bargain, so made as to justify another person in understanding that his assent to that bargain is invited and will conclude it." To be effective:

The Uniform Commercial Code

One of the major frustrations of businesspersons conducting interstate business is that they are subject to the laws of each of the states in which they operate. To address this problem, in 1949 the National Conference of Commissioners on Uniform State Laws promulgated the **Uniform Commercial Code (UCC).** The UCC is a *model act* containing uniform rules that govern commercial transactions. To create this uniformity, individual states had to enact the UCC as their commercial law statute. In fact, they did, and every state (except Louisiana, which has adopted only parts of the UCC) enacted the UCC as a commercial statute.

The UCC is divided into articles, each of which establishes uniform rules for a facet of commerce in the United States. The articles of the UCC are

Article 1	General provisions
Article 2	Sales
Article 2A	Leases
Revised	

Article 3	Negotiable instruments
Article 4	Bank deposits and collections
Article 4A	Wire transfers
Article 5	Letters of credit
Article 6	Bulk transfers
Article 7	Documents of title
Article 8	Investment securities
Article 9	Secured transactions

The UCC is continually being revised to reflect changes in modern commercial practices and technology. Example: Article 2A was drafted to govern leases of personal property, and Article 4A was added to regulate the use of wire transfers in the banking system. Articles 3 and 4, which cover the creation and transfer of negotiable instruments and the clearing of checks through the banking system, were amended substantially in 1990. Article 2, which covers the sale of goods, is currently in the initial stages of revision.

1. The offeror must *objectively intend* to be bound by the offer.
2. The terms of the offer must be definite or reasonably *certain*.
3. The offer must be *communicated* to the offeree.

Consider the following examples: A question such as "Are you interested in selling your building for $2 million?" is not an offer. It is an invitation to make an offer or an invitation to negotiate. But the statement "I will buy your building for $2 million" is a valid offer because it indicates the offeror's present intent to contract.

Suppose the owner of Company A has lunch with the owner of Company B. In the course of their conversation, Company A's owner exclaims in frustration, "For two dollars I'd sell the whole computer division!" A valid contract cannot result from that offer made in anger.

Termination of the Offer

A valid offer gives the offeree the power to accept the offer and thereby create a contract. This power, however, does not continue indefinitely. An offer can be terminated by the *action of the parties*.

Under the common law, an *offeror* may revoke (withdraw) an offer any time prior to its acceptance by the offeree. Generally, this is so even if the offeror promised to keep the offer open for a longer period of time. An offer is terminated if the *offeree* rejects it. Any subsequent attempt by the offeree to accept the offer is ineffective and is construed as a new offer that the original offeror (now the offeree) is free to accept or reject.

A **counteroffer** by the *offeree* simultaneously terminates the offeror's offer and creates a new offer. A counteroffer might be: "I think $250,000 is too high for the computers. I will pay you $200,000." With this, the original offer is terminated and the counteroffer is a new offer that the other is free to accept or reject.

Acceptance

Acceptance is a manifestation of assent by the offeree to the terms of the offer in a manner invited or required by the offer as measured by the objective theory of contracts. Recall that generally (1) unilateral contracts can be accepted only by the offeree's performance of the required act, and (2) a bilateral contract can be accepted by an offeree who promises to perform (or, where permitted, by performance of) the requested act.

Only the offeree has the legal power to accept an offer and create a contract. Third persons usually do not have the power to accept an offer. If an offer is made individually to two or more persons, each has the power to accept the offer. Once an offeree accepts the offer, though, it terminates as to the other offerees. An offer that is made to two or more persons jointly must be accepted jointly.

Express and Implied Contracts

An actual contract (as distinguished from a quasi-contract, discussed later in this chapter) may be either *express* or *implied-in-fact*.

1. **Express contracts** are stated in oral or written words. Examples of such contracts include an oral agreement to purchase a neighbor's bicycle and a written agreement to buy an automobile from a dealership.

2. **Implied-in-fact contracts** are implied from the conduct of the parties. Implied-in-fact contracts leave more room for questions. The following elements must be established to create an implied-in-fact contract:

    a. The plaintiff provided property or services to the defendant.

    b. The plaintiff expected to be paid by the defendant for the property or services and did not provide the property or services gratuitously.

    c. The defendant was given an opportunity to reject the property or services provided by the plaintiff but failed to do so.

Consideration

Consideration is a necessary element for a contract to exist. Consideration is defined as the thing of value given in exchange for a promise. Consideration can come in many forms. The most common types consist of either a tangible

Option Contracts

SIDEBAR

An offeree can prevent the offeror from revoking his or her offer by paying the offeror compensation to keep the offer open for an agreed-upon period of time. This is called an *option contract*, in which the offeror agrees not to sell the property to anyone but the offeree during the option period. The death or incompetency of either party does not terminate an option contract unless it is for the performance of a personal service.

Example: Anne Mason offers to sell a piece of real estate to Harold Greenberg for $1 million. Mr. Greenberg wants time to make a decision, so he pays Ms. Mason $20,000 to keep her offer open to him for 6 months. At any time during the option period, Mr. Greenberg may exercise his option and pay Ms. Mason the $1 million purchase price. If he lets the option expire, however, Ms. Mason may keep the $20,000 and sell the property to someone else.

Ethical PERSPECTIVE *Owner of Scrabble Spelled "L-O-S-E-R"*

Implied-in-fact contracts are implied from the conduct of the parties. Consider the following case: Selchow & Richter (S&R) owns the trademark to the famous board game *Scrabble*. Mark Landsberg wrote a book on strategy for winning at Scrabble and contacted S&R to request permission to use the Scrabble trademark. In response, S&R requested a copy of Landsberg's manuscript, which he provided. After prolonged negotiations between the parties regarding the possibility of S&R's publication of the manuscript broke off, S&R brought out its own Scrabble strategy book. No express contract was ever entered into between Landsberg and S&R. Landsberg sued S&R and its subsidiary, Scrabble Crossword Game Players, Inc., for damages for breach of an implied contract.

Was there an implied-in-fact contract between the parties? The district court and appellate court held that an implied-in-fact contract had been formed between the parties and that the contract was breached by the defendants. The court noted that the law allows for recovery for the breach of an implied-in-fact contract when the recipient of a valuable idea accepts and uses the information without paying for it, even though he knows that compensation is expected.

Here, the court found that (1) Landsberg's disclosure of his manuscript was confidential and for the limited purpose of obtaining approval for the use of the Scrabble mark, and (2) given Landsberg's express intention to exploit his manuscript commercially, the defendant's use of any portion of it was conditioned on payment. Landsberg was awarded $440,300 damages.

1. Did Selchow & Richter act ethically in this case?

2. Is the doctrine of implied-in-fact contracts needed? Explain.

payment (e.g., money or property) or the performance of an act (e.g., providing legal services). Less-usual forms of consideration include the forbearance of a legal right (e.g., accepting an out-of-court settlement in exchange for dropping a lawsuit) and noneconomic forms of consideration (e.g., refraining from drinking, using tobacco, swearing, or playing cards or billiards for money for a specified time period).

Written contracts are presumed to be supported by consideration. This is a rebuttable presumption that may be overcome by sufficient evidence. A few states provide that contracts made under seal cannot be challenged for lack of consideration.

Gift Promises

Gift promises, also called **gratuitous promises,** are unenforceable because they lack consideration. To change a gift promise into an enforceable promise, the promisee must offer to do something in exchange—that is, consideration—for the promise. Suppose Mrs. Colby promised to give her son $10,000 and then rescinded the promise. The son would have no recourse because it was a gift promise that lacked consideration. If, however, Mrs. Colby promised her son $10,000 for getting an "A" in his business law course and the son performed as required, the contract would be enforceable. A completed gift promise cannot be rescinded for lack of consideration.

Capacity to Contract

Generally, the law presumes that the parties to a contract have the requisite **contractual capacity** to enter into the contract. Certain persons, however, do not have this capacity. They include minors, mentally incompetent persons, and intoxicated persons. The common law of contracts and many state statutes protect persons who lack contractual capacity from having contracts enforced against them. The party asserting incapacity or his or her guardian, conservator, or other legal representative bears the burden of proof.

Minors

Minors do not always have the maturity, experience, or sophistication needed to enter into contracts with adults. States have enacted statutes that specify the *age of majority*. The most prevalent age of majority is 18 years for males and females alike. Any age below the statutory age of majority is called the *period of minority*.

To protect minors, the law recognizes the **infancy doctrine,** which allows minors to **disaffirm** (or cancel) most contracts they have entered into with adults. A minor's right to disaffirm a contract is based on public policy, with the reasoning that minors should be protected from unscrupulous behavior of adults.

A Contract Is a Contract Is a Contract

Mighty Morphin Power Rangers was a phenomenal success as a television series. The Power Rangers battled to save the universe from all sorts of diabolical plots and bad guys. They also were featured in a profitable line of toys and garments bearing the Power Rangers' logo. The Power Rangers' name and logo are known to millions of children and their parents worldwide. The claim of ownership of the logo for the Power Rangers ended up in a battle itself, this time in a courtroom.

David Dees is a designer who works as d/b/a David Dees Illustration. Saban Entertainment, Inc. (Saban), which owns the copyright and trademark to Power Ranger figures and the name "Power Ranger," hired Dees as an independent contractor to design a logo for the Power Rangers. The contract signed by the parties was entitled "Work-for-Hire/Independent Contractor Agreement." The contract was drafted by Saban with the help of its attorneys; Dees signed the agreement without the representation of legal counsel.

Dees designed the logo currently used for the Power Rangers and was paid $250 to transfer his copyright ownership in the logo. Subsequently, Dees sued Saban to recover damages for copyright and trademark infringement. Saban defended, arguing that a contract is a contract is a contract, and Dees was bound by the agreement he had signed.

The trial court agreed with Saban, finding that the "Work-for-Hire/Independent Contractor Agreement" was an enforceable contract between the parties and that Dees had transferred his ownership interests in the logo to Saban. Dees appealed. The court of appeals affirmed the judgment for Saban, stating, "The disputed agreement transferred plaintiff's copyright in the Mighty Morphin Power Rangers' logo with as much specificity as the law requires." The court found that a contract is a contract is a contract, at least in this case. Dees' appeal to the U.S. Supreme Court was denied. [*Dees, d/b/a David Dees Illustration v. Saban Entertainment, Inc.,* 131 F.3d 146 (1997)]

Under the infancy doctrine, a minor has the option of choosing whether to enforce the contract (i.e., the contract is *voidable* by a minor). The adult party is bound to the minor's decision. If both parties to the contract are minors, both parties have the right to disaffirm the contract.

A minor can expressly disaffirm a contract orally, in writing, or by the minor's conduct. No special formalities are required. The minor may disaffirm the contract at any time prior to reaching the age of majority plus a "reasonable time." The designation of a reasonable time is determined on a case-by-case basis.

Minors are obligated to pay for the **necessaries of life** that they contract for. Otherwise, many adults would refuse to sell these items to them. There is no standard definition of what is a *necessary of life*, but items such as food, clothing, shelter, medical services, and the like are generally understood to fit this category. Goods and services such as automobiles, tools of trade, education, and vocational training also have been found to be necessaries of life in some situations. The minor's age, lifestyle, and status in life influence what is considered necessary.

Mentally Incompetent Persons

Mental incapacity may arise because of mental illness, brain damage, mental retardation, senility, and the like. The law protects people suffering from substantial mental incapacity from enforcement of contracts against them because these persons may not understand the consequences of their actions in entering into a contract.

Intoxicated Persons

Most states provide that contracts entered into by certain intoxicated persons are voidable by that person. The intoxication may occur because of alcohol or drug use. The contract is not voidable by the other party if that party had contractual capacity. Under the majority rule, the contract is voidable only if the person was so intoxicated when the contract was entered into that he or she was incapable of understanding or comprehending the nature of the transaction. In most states, this rule holds even if the intoxication was self-induced. A contract disaffirmed based on intoxication generally must be returned to the status quo.

Lawful Object

As an essential element for the formation of a contract, the object of the contract must be *lawful*. A contract to perform an illegal act is called an **illegal contract.** Illegal contracts are void; they cannot be enforced by either party to the contract. Because illegal contracts are void, the parties cannot sue for nonperformance. Further, if an illegal contract is executed, the court will generally leave the parties where it finds them. Most contracts are presumed to be lawful. The burden of proving that a contract is unlawful rests on the party who asserts its illegality.

Illegality—Contracts Contrary to Statutes

Federal and state legislatures alike have enacted statutes prohibiting certain types of conduct. Contracts to perform an activity that is prohibited by statute

You're out on a date and your partner whispers sweet nothings in your ear. What's a guy or girl to do? Quick, whip out a **nondisclosure agreement**—or **NDA,** as they are called—and have the other side sign it before you respond. That is what many entrepreneurs and techies are doing—having their boyfriends, girlfriends, family members, friends, and others sign NDAs before revealing anything about what they are doing.

NDAs have been around for a long time. Traditionally they have been used by lawyers, investment bankers, and others involved in secret takeovers and other large corporate deals. NDAs swear the signatory to secrecy about confidential ideas, trade secrets, and other nonpublic information revealed by the party proffering the NDA. But today, many entrepreneurs, particularly those in Internet and high-tech industries, are handing out NDAs as fast as business cards.

They serve a purpose in that they protect people who have a great idea (or so they think) and want to share it with a potential partner, investor, lawyer, or investment banker, but want an assurance that the recipient of the information will not steal or reveal the information to anyone else.

NDAs are enforceable contracts, so if someone violates it, the disclosing party can sue the breaching party for damages. Bill Gates of Microsoft has plumbers and others who work on his house sign NDAs. Sabeer Bhatia, founder of Hotmail, collected more than 400 NDAs in 2 years before selling his company to Microsoft for $400 million.

Although it may not be hard to get some people to sign NDAs, others balk. Some friends and relatives refuse to sign NDAs thrust on them because NDAs present an aura of distrust. And it is particularly insulting to sign an NDA and then to hear a hairpin idea from the disclosing party. Industry bigwigs—venture capitalists, securities analysts, and successful technology companies—routinely refuse to sign NDAs because they see too many similar ideas and do not want their tongues tied by any single one.

NDAs will continue to increase in use, though. So the next time you are at a party and you ask someone what they do for a living, don't be surprised if you are NDA'd!

are illegal contracts. These contracts include gambling contracts, contracts that provide for usurious rates of interest, and contracts that violate Sabbath laws and licensing statutes.

Illegality—Contracts Contrary to Public Policy

Certain contracts are illegal because they are **contracts contrary to public policy.** Although *public policy* eludes a precise definition, the courts have held contracts to be contrary to public policy if they have a negative impact on society or interfere with the public's safety and welfare.

STATUTE OF FRAUDS—WRITING REQUIREMENT

All states have enacted a **Statute of Frauds** that requires certain types of contracts to be in *writing*. This statute is intended to ensure that the terms of important contracts are not forgotten, misunderstood, or fabricated.

Flood v. Fidelity & Guaranty Life Insurance Co.

394 So.2d 1311 (1981)

Court of Appeals of Louisiana

FACTS

Ellen and Richard Alvin Flood, who were married in 1965, lived in a mobile home in Louisiana. Richard worked as a maintenance man and Ellen was employed at an insurance agency. Evidence at trial showed that Ellen was unhappy with her marriage. Ellen took out a life insurance policy on the life of her husband and named herself as beneficiary. The policy was issued by Fidelity & Guaranty Life Insurance Co. (Fidelity).

In June 1972, Richard became unexpectedly ill. He was taken to the hospital, where his condition improved. After a visit at the hospital from his wife, Richard died. Ellen was criminally charged with the murder of her husband by poisoning. Evidence showed that six medicine bottles at the couple's home, including Tylenol and paregoric bottles, contained arsenic. The court found that Ellen had fed Richard ice cubes laced with arsenic at the hospital.

Ellen was tried and convicted of the murder of her husband. As beneficiary of Richard's life insurance policy, Ellen requested Fidelity to pay her the benefits. Fidelity refused to pay the benefits and returned all premiums paid on the policy. This suit followed. The district court held in favor of Ellen Flood and awarded her the benefits of the life insurance policy. Fidelity appealed.

ISSUE

Was the life insurance policy an illegal contract that is void?

IN THE LANGUAGE OF THE COURT

Lear, Judge.

Louisiana follows the majority rule that holds, as a matter of public policy, that a beneficiary named in a life insurance policy is not entitled to the proceeds of the insurance if the beneficiary feloniously kills the insured.

The genesis of this litigation is the escalating criminal action of Ellen Flood, bent on taking the life of her lawful husband. Our courts have previously adjudicated (1) the issue of the cause of death of Richard Flood, (2) the culprit in that death, and (3) the motives for the death. Under the peculiar circumstances of the case, it was unreasonable of the trial court not to consider and to assign great weight to the mountain of evidence tending to prove Mrs. Flood's scheme to defraud both the insurer, Fidelity, and the insured, Mr. Flood. It is clear to us that the entirety of the transaction here reviewed is tainted with the intendment of Ellen Flood to contravene the prohibitory law.

Life insurance policies are procured because life is, indeed, precarious and uncertain. Our law does not and cannot sanction any scheme that has as its purpose the certain infliction of death for, *inter alia*, financial gain through receipt of the proceeds of life insurance. To sanction this policy in any way would surely shackle the spirit, letter, and life of our laws.

DECISION AND REMEDY

The appellate court held that the life insurance policy that Ellen Flood had taken out on the life of her husband was void based on public policy. Reversed.

Questions

1. Should Ellen Flood have been allowed to retain the insurance proceeds in this case?

2. Did Ellen Flood act unethically in this case? Did she act illegally?

3. What would be the economic consequences if persons could recover insurance proceeds for losses caused by their illegal activities (e.g., murder, arson)?

Ethical PERSPECTIVE   *Don't Be Taken by Fraud*

Contracting parties must be careful not to be taken by fraud. Basically, if a deal sounds "too good to be true," it is a signal that the situation might be fraudulent. Other frauds are difficult to detect. If there is fraud, the innocent party can get out of the contract and recover his or her losses. To prove **fraud,** the following elements must be shown:

1. The wrongdoer made a false representation of material fact.
2. The wrongdoer intended to deceive the innocent party.
3. The innocent party justifiably relied on the misrepresentation.
4. The innocent party was injured.

MATERIAL MISREPRESENTATION OF FACT

A misrepresentation may occur by words (oral or written) or by the conduct of the party. To be actionable as fraud, the misrepresentation must be of a past or existing material fact. This means that the misrepresentation must have been a significant factor in inducing the innocent party to enter into the contract. It does not have to be the sole factor. Statements of opinion or predictions about the future generally do not form the basis for fraud.

INTENT TO DECEIVE

To prove fraud, the person making the misrepresentation must have either had knowledge that the representation was false or made it without sufficient knowledge of the truth. This is called *scienter* ("guilty mind"). The misrepresentation must have been made with the intent to deceive the innocent party. Intent can be inferred from the circumstances.

RELIANCE ON THE MISREPRESENTATION

A misrepresentation is not actionable unless the innocent party to whom the misrepresentation was directed acted upon it. Further, an innocent party who acts in reliance on the misrepresentation must justify his or her reliance. Justifiable reliance generally is found unless the innocent party knew that the misrepresentation was false or was so extravagant as to be obviously false. For example, reliance on a statement such as, "This diamond ring is worth $10,000, but I'll sell it to you for $100" would not be justified.

INJURY TO THE INNOCENT PARTY

To recover damages, the innocent party must prove that the fraud caused economic injury. The measure of damages is the difference between the value of the property as represented and the actual value of the property. This measure of damages gives the innocent party the "benefit of the bargain." In the alternative, the buyer can rescind the contract and recover the purchase price.

Generally, an *executory contract* that is not in writing even though the Statute of Frauds requires it to be is unenforceable by either party. (If the contract is valid in all other respects, however, it may be voluntarily performed by the parties.) The Statute of Frauds is usually raised by one party as a defense to enforcement of the contract by the other party. But if an oral contract that should have been in writing under the Statute of Frauds is already executed (fully performed), neither party can seek to rescind the contract on the ground of noncompliance with the Statute of Frauds. Contracts that are required to be in writing under the Statute of Frauds are discussed in the following paragraphs.

Contracts Involving Interests in Land

Any contract that transfers an ownership interest in real property must be in writing to be enforceable under the Statute of Frauds. Real property includes the land itself, buildings, trees, soil, minerals, timber, plants, crops, fixtures, and things permanently affixed to the land or buildings. Certain personal property that is permanently affixed to the real property—for example, built-in cabinets in a house—are *fixtures* that become part of the real property.

Other contracts that transfer an ownership interest in land must be in writing under the Statute of Frauds. For example, borrowers often give a lender an interest in real property as security for the repayment of a loan. This must be done through a written mortgage or deed of trust. A *lease* is the transfer of the right to use real property for a specified period of time. Most Statutes of Frauds require leases for a term of more than one year to be in writing.

One-Year Rule

According to the Statute of Frauds, an executory contract that cannot be performed by its own terms within one year of its formation must be in writing. This **one-year rule** is intended to prevent disputes about contract terms that otherwise may occur toward the end of a long-term contract. If performance of the contract is possible within the one-year period, the contract may be oral.

Contracts for the Sale of Goods

Section 201 of the UCC is the basic Statute of Frauds provision for sales contracts. It requires that contracts for the sale of goods costing *$500 or more* must be in writing to be enforceable. If the contract price of an original sales contract is below $500 and does not have to be in writing under the UCC Statute of Frauds, but if a modification of the contract increases the sales price to $500 or more, the modification has to be in writing to be enforceable [UCC § 2-209(3)].

Formality of the Writing

Many written commercial contracts are long, detailed documents that have been negotiated by the parties and drafted and reviewed by their lawyers. Other written contracts are preprinted forms that are prepared in advance to be used in recurring situations.

To be legally binding, a written contract does not have to be either drafted by a lawyer or formally typed. Generally, the law only requires a writing containing the essential terms of the parties' agreement. Under this rule, any writing—letters, telegrams, invoices, sales receipts, handwritten agreements written on scraps of paper, and such—can be an enforceable contract.

Required Signature

The Statute of Frauds and the UCC require the written contract, whatever its form, to be signed *by the party against whom the enforcement is sought.* The signature of the person who is enforcing the contract is not necessary. Thus, a written contract may be enforceable against one party but not the other party.

You may "seal a deal" with a handshake, but the contract behind the deal may need to be in writing to be enforceable.

In the world of pen-and-paper, it used to be, "Sign on the dotted line," "Put your John Hancock right here," or "Sign by the X." No more. In the e-commerce world, it is now, "What is your mother's maiden name?" "Slide your smart card in the sensor," or "Look into the iris scanner." But are electronic signatures sufficient to form an enforceable contract? The courts and state legislatures of the 50 states have wrestled with this question, often reaching inconsistent decisions on whether electronic contracts meet the writing and signature requirements of the state Statutes of Frauds.

In 2000, the federal government stepped into the breach and enacted the Electronic Signature in Global and National Commerce Act. This is a federal statute enacted by Congress and signed by the President, and therefore has national reach. The act is designed to place the world of electronic commerce on par with the world of paper contracts in the United States.

ELECTRONIC SIGNATURE

One of the main features of the federal law is that it recognizes an *electronic signature,* or *e-signature.* The act gives an e-signature the same force and effect as a pen-inscribed signature on paper. The act is technology-neutral, however, in that the law does not define or decide which technologies should be used to create a legally binding signature in cyberspace.

Loosely defined, a digital signature is some electronic method that identifies an individual. The challenge is to make sure that someone who uses a digital signature is the person he or she claims to be. The act provides that a digital signature can be verified in one of three ways:

1. By something the signatory knows, such as a secret password, a pet's name, and so forth.
2. By something a person has, such as a smart card, which looks like a credit card and stores personal information.
3. By biometrics, which uses a device that digitally recognizes fingerprints or the retina or iris of the eye.

The verification of electronic signatures creates a need for the use of scanners and other methods for verifying personal information.

WRITING REQUIREMENTS

The act recognizes electronic contracts as meeting the writing requirement of the Statute of Frauds for most contracts. Statutes of Frauds are state laws that require certain types of contracts to be in writing. The new federal act provides that electronically signed contracts cannot be denied effect because they are in electronic form or delivered electronically. The act also provides that record retention requirements are satisfied if the records are stored electronically.

The federal law was passed with several provisions to protect consumers.

1. Consumers must consent to receiving electronic records and contracts.
2. To receive electronic records, consumers must be able to demonstrate that they have access to the electronic records.
3. Businesses must tell consumers that they have the right to receive hard-copy documents of the transaction.

The new federal act preempts conflicting state law except where states have enacted the e-signature provisions of the model Uniform Electronic Transactions Act (UETA); those states are exempted from this provision. This provision was a conciliation of Congress to tread lightly on states rights and give states an incentive to adopt the more comprehensive UETA for regulating electronic contracts.

One of the shortfalls of the new federal act is that it does not—and cannot—provide a global solution. Some countries have enacted electronic commerce statutes, but with different provisions and requirements from U.S. law. Many other countries do not have e-commerce laws at all. Global contracting requires an international solution, such as an e-commerce treaty signed by the members of the World Trade Organization (WTO).

Ethical PERSPECTIVE — *Unconscionable Contract*

The general rule of freedom of contract holds that if (1) the object of a contract is lawful and (2) the other elements for the formation of a contract are met, the courts will enforce a contract according to its terms. Although it is generally presumed that parties are capable of protecting their own interests when contracting, it is a fact of life that dominant parties sometimes take advantage of weaker parties. As a result, some lawful contracts are so oppressive or manifestly unfair that they are unjust.

To prevent the enforcement of such contracts, the courts developed the equitable doctrine of unconscionability, which is based on public policy. A contract found to be unconscionable under this doctrine is called an **unconscionable contract,** or a *contract of adhesion.*

The courts are given substantial discretion in determining whether a contract or contract clause is unconscionable. There is no single definition of *unconscionability.* The doctrine may not be used merely to save a contracting party from a bad bargain.

The following elements must be shown to prove that a contract or clause in a contract is unconscionable:

- The parties possessed severely unequal bargaining power.
- The dominant party unreasonably used its unequal bargaining power to obtain oppressive or manifestly unfair contract terms.
- The adhering party had no reasonable alternative.

If the court finds that a contract or contract clause is unconscionable, it may (1) refuse to enforce the contract, (2) refuse to enforce the unconscionable clause but enforce the remainder of the contract, or (3) limit the applicability of any unconscionable clause so as to avoid any unconscionable result. The appropriate remedy depends on the facts and circumstances of each case. Note that because unconscionability is a matter of law, the judge may opt to decide the case without a jury trial.

1. Explain the doctrine of unconscionability.
2. Does the doctrine of unconscionability promote ethics? Explain.

Generally, the signature may appear anywhere on the writing. In addition, it does not have to be a person's full legal name. The person's last name, first name, nickname, initials, seal, stamp, engraving, or other symbol or mark (e.g., an X) that indicates the person's intent can be binding. The signature may be affixed by an authorized agent.

PERFORMANCE

In contracts, parties make certain promises to each other. These promises may be classified as *covenants* or *conditions.* Performance may be classified as complete performance, substantial performance (minor breach), or inferior performance (material breach).

Covenants

A **covenant** is an unconditional promise to perform. Nonperformance of a covenant is a breach of contract that gives the other party the right to sue. For example, if Medcliff Corporation borrows $100,000 from a bank and signs a promissory note to repay this amount plus 10 percent interest in one year, this promise is a covenant. It is an unconditional promise to perform.

Conditions Precedent

If the contract requires the occurrence (or nonoccurrence) of an event before a party is obligated to perform a contractual duty, there is a **condition precedent.** The happening (or nonhappening) of the event triggers the contract or duty of performance. If the event does not occur, no duty to perform arises because there is a failure of condition.

Consider this example: Suppose X Company offers Joan Andrews a job as an industrial engineer upon her graduation from college. If Ms. Andrews graduates, the condition has been met. If the employer refuses to hire Ms. Andrews at that time, she can sue the employer for breach of contract. But if Ms. Andrews does not graduate, X company is not obligated to hire her because there has been a failure of condition.

Complete Performance

Most contracts are discharged by the **complete** (or *strict*) **performance** of the contracting parties. Complete performance occurs when a party to a contract renders performance exactly as required by the contract. A fully performed contract is called an *executed contract.*

Tender of performance also discharges a party's contractual obligations. Tender is an unconditional and absolute offer by a contracting party to perform his or her obligations under the contract.

Consider this example: Suppose Ashley's Dress Shops, Inc., contracts to purchase dresses from a dress manufacturer for $25,000. Ashley's has performed its obligation under the contract once it tenders the $25,000 to the manufacturer. If the manufacturer fails to deliver the dresses, Ashley's can sue it for breach of contract.

Substantial Performance (Minor Breach)

Substantial performance occurs when there has been a **minor breach** of contract. It occurs when a party to a contract renders performance that deviates only slightly from complete performance. The nonbreaching party may (1) convince the breaching party to elevate his or her performance to complete performance, or (2) deduct the cost to repair the defect from the contract price and remit the balance to the breaching party, or (3) sue the breaching party to recover the cost to repair the defect if the breaching party has already been paid.

Consider this example: Suppose Donald Trump contracts with Big Apple Construction Co. to have Big Apple construct an office building for $50 million. The architectural plans call for installation of three-ply windows in the building. Big Apple constructs the building exactly to plan except that it installs two-ply windows. There has been substantial performance. It would cost $300,000 to install the correct windows. If Big Apple agrees to replace the windows, its performance is elevated to complete performance and Trump must remit the entire contract price. But if Trump has to hire someone else to replace the windows, he may deduct this cost of repair from the contract price and remit the difference to Big Apple.

Inferior Performance (Material Breach)

A **material breach** of a contract occurs when a party fails to perform certain express or implied obligations that impair or destroy the essence of the contract. Because there is no clear line between a minor breach and a material breach, determination is made on a case-by-case basis. Where there has been a material breach of a contract, the nonbreaching party has two choices:

1. The nonbreaching party may *rescind* the contract, seek restitution of any compensation paid under the contract to the breaching party, and be discharged from any further performance under the contract.
2. The nonbreaching party may treat the contract as being in effect and sue the breaching party to recover *damages*.

Suppose a university contracts with a general contractor to build a new three-story building with classroom space for 1,000 students. But the completed building can support the weight of only 500 students because the contractor used inferior materials. The defect cannot be repaired without rebuilding the entire structure. Because this is a material breach, the university may rescind the contract and require removal of the building. The university is discharged of any obligations under the contract and is free to employ another contractor to rebuild the building. Alternatively, the university could accept the building and deduct from the contract price the damages caused by the defect.

REMEDIES

The most common remedy for a breach of contract is an award of *monetary damages*. This is often called the "law remedy." But if a monetary award does not provide adequate relief, the court may order any one of several *equitable remedies*, including specific performance, injunction, reformation, and quasi-contract. Equitable remedies are based on the concept of fairness.

Monetary Damages

Monetary damages are of three types: compensatory, consequential, and liquid.

Compensatory Damages

Compensatory damages are intended to compensate a nonbreaching party for the loss of the bargain. They place the nonbreaching party in the same position as if the contract has been fully performed by restoring the "benefit of the bargain."

Consider this example: Suppose Lederle Laboratories enters into a written contract to employ a manager for three years at a salary of $6,000 per month. Before work is to start, the manager is informed that he will not be needed. This is a material breach of contract.

Assume that the manager finds another job, but it pays only $5,000 a month. The manager may recover $1,000 per month for 36 months (total $36,000) from Lederle Laboratories as compensatory damages. These damages place the manager in the same situation as if the contract with Lederle had been performed.

Consequential Damages

In addition to compensatory damages, a nonbreaching party sometimes can recover *special* or **consequential damages** from the breaching party. Consequential damages are *foreseeable* damages that arise from circumstances outside the contract. To be liable for consequential damages, the breaching party must know or have reason to know that the breach will cause special damages to the other party.

Consider this example: Suppose Soan-Allen Co., a wholesaler, enters into a contract to purchase 1,000 men's suits for $150 each from the Fabric Manufacturing Co., a manufacturer. Prior to contracting, the wholesaler tells the manufacturer that the suits will be resold to retailers for $225. The manufacturer breaches the contract by failing to manufacture the suits. The wholesaler cannot get the suits manufactured by anyone else in time to meet his contracts. He can recover $75,000 of lost profits on the resale contracts (1,000 suits x $75 profit) as consequential damages from the manufacturer because the manufacturer knew of this special damage to Soan-Allen Co. if it were to breach the contract.

Liquidated Damages

Under certain circumstances, the parties to a contract may agree in advance to the amount of damages payable upon a breach of contract. These are called **liquidated damages.** To be lawful, the actual damages must be difficult or impracticable to determine, and the liquidated amount must be reasonable in the circumstances. An enforceable liquidated damage clause is an exclusive remedy even if actual damages are later determined to be different.

A liquidated damage clause is considered a *penalty* if actual damages are clearly determinable in advance or the liquidated damages are excessive or unconscionable. If a liquidated damage clause is found to be a penalty, it is unenforceable. The nonbreaching party may then recover actual damages.

Exterior of Tippecanoe County Courthouse, Lafayette, Indiana.

Mitigation of Damages

If a contract has been breached, the law places a duty on the innocent nonbreaching party to take reasonable efforts to *mitigate* (i.e., avoid and reduce) the resulting damages. The extent of mitigation required depends on the type of contract involved. For example, if an employer breaches an employment contract, the employee owes a duty to mitigate damages by trying to find substitute employment. The employee is required only to accept comparable employment. In determining the comparability of jobs, the courts consider factors such as compensation, rank, status, job description, and geographical location.

Equitable Remedies

Equitable remedies include specific performance, injunction, reformation, and quasi-contract.

Specific Performance

An award of **specific performance** orders the breaching party to *perform* the acts promised in the contract. The courts have the discretion to award this remedy if the subject matter of the contract is unique. This remedy is available to enforce land contracts because every piece of real property is considered unique. Works of art, antiques, items of sentimental value, rare coins, stamps, heirlooms, and such also fit the requirement for uniqueness. Most other personal property does not. Specific performance of personal-service contracts is not granted because the courts would find it difficult or impracticable to supervise or monitor performance of the contract.

Injunction

An **injunction** is a court order that "prohibits" a person from doing a certain act. To obtain an injunction, the requesting party must show that he or she will suffer irreparable injury unless the injunction is issued.

For example, suppose a professional football team enters into a five-year employment contract with a "superstar" quarterback. The quarterback breaches the contract and enters into a contract to play for a competing team. Here,

Article 2 (Sales) of Uniform Commercial Code

Article 2 (Sales) of the UCC applies to *transactions in goods,* that is, the sale of goods [UCC 2-102]. All states except Louisiana have adopted some version of Article 2 of the UCC. A "sale" consists of the passing of title from a seller to a buyer for a price [UCC 2-106(1)].

For example, the purchase of a book is a sale subject to Article 2. This is so whether the book was paid for by cash, check, credit card, or other form of consideration.

Article 2 establishes a uniform law covering the formation, performance, and default of sales contracts.

Goods are defined as tangible things that are movable at the time of their identification to the contract [UCC 2-105(1)]. Specially manufactured goods and the unborn young of animals are examples of goods.

Money and intangible items, such as stocks, bonds, and patents, are not tangible goods. Therefore, they are not subject to Article 2.

Real estate is not subject to Article 2 either, because it is not movable [UCC 2-105(1)]. Minerals, structures, growing crops, and other things that are severable from real estate may be classified as goods subject to Article 2, however. For example, the sale and removal of a chandelier in a house is a sale of goods subject to Article 2 because its removal would not materially harm the realty. However, the sale and removal of the furnace would be a sale of real property because its removal would cause material harm [UCC 2-107(2)].

Contracts for the provision of services—including legal services, medical services, dental services, and such—are not covered by Article 2. Sometimes, however, a sale involves both the provision of a service and a good in the same transaction. This is referred to as a *mixed sale.* Article 2 applies to mixed sales only if the goods are the predominant part of the transaction. The UCC provides no guidance for deciding cases based on mixed sales. Therefore, the courts decide these issues on a case-by-case basis.

Article 2A (Leases) of the Uniform Commercial Code

Personal property leases are a billion-dollar industry. Consumer rentals of automobiles or equipment and commercial leases of items such as aircraft and industrial machinery fall into this category.

Article 2A of the UCC was promulgated in 1987. This article, cited as the Uniform Commercial Code—Leases, directly addresses personal property leases [UCC 2A-101]. It establishes a comprehensive, uniform law covering the formation, performance, and default of leases in goods [UCC 2A-102, 2A-103(h)].

Article 2A is similar to Article 2. In fact, many Article 2 provisions were changed to reflect leasing terminology and practices and carried over to Article 2A. Many states have adopted Article 2A, and many more are expected to do so in the future.

A *lease* is a transfer of the right to the possession and use of the named goods for a set term in return for certain consideration [UCC 2A-103(1)(i)(x)]. The leased goods can be anything from a hand tool leased to an individual for a few hours to a complex line of industrial equipment leased to a multinational corporation for a number of years.

In an ordinary lease, the *lessor* is the person who transfers the right of possession and use of goods under the lease [UCC 2A-103(1)(p)]. The *lessee* is the person who acquires the right to possession and use of goods under a lease [UCC 2A-103(1)(n)].

A *consumer lease* is one with a value of $25,000 or less between a lessor regularly engaged in the business of leasing or selling and a lessee who leases the goods primarily for a personal, family, or household purpose [UCC 2A-103(1)(e)].

A *finance lease* is a three-party transaction consisting of the lessor, the lessee, and the *supplier* (or vendor) [UCC 2A-103(1)(g)].

Consider this example: The Dow Chemical Company decides to use robotics to manufacture most of its products. It persuades Ingersoll-Rand to design the robotic equipment that will meet its needs. To finance the purchase of the equipment, Dow Chemical goes to Citibank, which purchases the robotics equipment from Ingersoll-Rand and leases it to Dow Chemical. Citibank is the lessor, Dow Chemical is the lessee, and Ingersoll-Rand is the supplier.

the first team can seek an injunction to prevent the quarterback from playing for the other team.

Reformation

Reformation is an equitable doctrine that permits the court to *rewrite* a contract to express the parties' true intentions. For example, suppose a clerical error is made during the typing of the contract and both parties sign the contract without discovering the error. If a dispute later arises, the court can reform the contract to correct the clerical error to read what the parties originally intended.

Quasi-contract

A **quasi-contract** (also called *quantum meruit* or an *implied-in-law contract*) is an equitable doctrine that permits the recovery of compensation even though no enforceable contract exists between the parties because of lack of consideration, the Statute of Frauds has run out, or the like. Such contracts are imposed by law to prevent unjust enrichment. Under quasi-contract, a party can recover the reasonable value of the services or materials provided. For example, a physician who stops to render aid to an unconscious victim of an automobile accident may recover the reasonable value of his services from that person.

U.N. CONVENTION ON CONTRACTS FOR THE INTERNATIONAL SALE OF GOODS (CISG)

Businesspersons who engage in international commerce face the daunting task of trying to comply with the laws of many nations. To ease this burden, more than 60 countries are signatories to the **United Nations Convention on Contracts for the International Sale of Goods (CISG).** This treaty took more than 50 years to negotiate and incorporates rules from all the major legal systems of the world.

The CISG establishes uniform rules for the formation and enforcement of contracts involving the international sale of goods. Many of its provisions are remarkably similar to the provisions of the American UCC. The CISG applies if the buyer and seller have their places of business in different countries and both nations are parties to the convention.

The contracting parties may agree to exclude (i.e., opt out of) the CISG and let other laws apply. The parties to any international contract can agree that the CISG controls, even if one or both of their countries are not signatories to the convention.

LEGAL TERMINOLOGY

Acceptance

Agreement

Article 2 (Sales) of Uniform Commercial Code

Article 2A (Leases) of Uniform Commercial Code

Compensatory damages

Complete performance

Condition precedent

Consequential damages

Consideration

Contract

Contracts contrary to public policy

Contractual capacity

Counteroffer

Covenant

Deed of trust

Disaffirm

Express contract

Force majeure clause

Fraud

Gift promise (gratuitous promise)

Illegal contract

Implied-in-fact contract

Infancy doctrine

Injunction

Liquidated damages

Material breach—inferior performance

Minor breach—substantial performance

Necessaries of life

Nondisclosure agreement (NDA)

Offer

Offeree

Offeror

One-year rule

Quasi-contract (implied-in-law contract)

Reformation

Specific performance

Statute of Frauds

Tender of performance

UCC Section 201 (Statute of Frauds)

Unconscionable contract

Uniform Commercial Code (UCC)

Summary

Definition of and Parties to a Contract

Definition	A promise or set of promises for the breach of which the law gives a remedy or the performance of which the law in some way recognizes a duty.
Parties to a Contract	1. *Offeror:* Party who makes an offer to enter into a contract. 2. *Offeree:* Party to whom the offer is made.

Requirements of a Contract

Elements	1. Agreement 2. Consideration 3. Contractual capacity 4. Lawful object
Agreement	1. *Offer:* Manifestation by one party of a willingness to enter into a contract. 2. *Offeror:* Party who makes an offer. 3. *Offeree:* Party to whom an offer is made. This party has the power to create an agreement by accepting the terms of the offer.
Termination of an Offer by Action of the Parties	1. *Revocation:* The offeror may *revoke* (withdraw) an offer any time prior to its acceptance by the offeree. 2. *Rejection:* An offer is terminated if the offeree rejects the offer by his or her words or conduct. 3. *Counteroffer:* A counteroffer by the offeree terminates the offeror's offer (and creates a new offer).
Acceptance	Manifestation of assent by the offeree to the terms of the offer. Acceptance of the offer by the offeree creates a contract.
Express and Implied Contracts	1. *Express contract:* A contract expressed in oral or written words. 2. *Implied-in-fact contract:* A contract implied from the conduct of the parties.
Consideration	Thing of value given in exchange for a promise. May be tangible or intangible property, performance of a service, forbearance of a legal right, or another thing of value.
Capacity to Contract	1. *Infancy doctrine:* Minors under the age of majority may *disaffirm* (cancel) most contracts they have entered into with adults. The contract is *voidable* by the minor but not by the adult.

(continued)

Capacity to Contract, *continued*	2. *Mental incompetence:* Contracts by persons who are insane are *voidable* by the insane person but not by the competent party to the contract. 3. *Intoxicated persons:* Contracts by *intoxicated* persons are *voidable* by the intoxicated person but not by the competent party to the contract.
Lawful Object	An illegal contract is *void*. Therefore, the parties cannot sue for nonperformance. If the contract has been executed, the court will *leave the parties where it finds them.* 1. Contracts that violate statutes are illegal, void, and unenforceable. 2. Contracts that violate public policy are illegal, void, and unenforceable.

Statute of Frauds

Writing Requirement	A state statute requires the following contracts to be in writing: 1. *Contracts involving the transfer of interests in real property:* Includes contracts for the sale of land, buildings, and items attached to land, mortgages, leases for a term of more than one year, and express easements. 2. Contracts that cannot be performed within one year of their formation (*one-year rule*). 3. *Contracts for the sale of goods* costing $500 or more (UCC 201).
Sufficiency of the Writing	1. *Formality of the writing:* A written contract does not have to be formal or drafted by a lawyer to be enforceable. Informal contracts, such as handwritten notes, letters, invoices, and the like, are enforceable contracts. 2. *Required signature:* The party against whom enforcement of the contract is sought must have signed the contract. The signature may be the person's full legal name, last name, first name, nickname, initials, or other symbol.
Electronic Signatures	*Electronic Signature in Global and National Commerce Act (E-Sign Act):* A federal statute that recognizes and gives electronic signatures—e-signatures—the same force and effect as a pen-inscribed signature on paper. The act is technology-neutral in that the law does not define or decide which technologies should be used to create a legally binding signature in cyberspace.

Performance

Covenant	Unconditional promise to perform. Nonperformance of a covenant is a breach of contract that gives the other party the right to sue.
Conditions Precedent	Requires the occurrence or nonoccurrence of an event before a party is obligated to perform.
Levels of Performance	1. *Complete performance:* A party renders performance exactly as required by the contract. That party's contractual duties are discharged.

(continued)

	2. *Substantial performance:* A party renders performance that deviates only slightly from complete performance. There is a *minor breach*. The nonbreaching party may recover damages caused by the breach. 3. *Inferior performance:* A party fails to perform express or implied contractual duties that impair or destroy the essence of the contract. There is a *material breach*. The nonbreaching party may either (1) rescind the contract and recover restitution or (2) affirm the contract and recover damages.
Remedies	
Monetary Damages	1. *Compensatory damages:* Damages that compensate a nonbreaching party for loss of the contract. Restore the "benefit of the bargain" to the nonbreaching party as if the contract had been fully performed. 2. *Consequential damages:* Foreseeable damages that arise from circumstances outside the contract and of which the breaching party either knew or had reason to know. Also called *special damages*. 3. *Liquidated damages:* Damages payable upon breach of contract that are agreed on in advance by the contracting parties. Liquidated damages substitute for actual damages.
Mitigation of Damages	The duty the law places on a nonbreaching party to take reasonable efforts to avoid or reduce the resulting damages from a breach of contract. To mitigate a breach of an employment contract, the nonbreaching party must only accept "comparable" employment.
Equitable Remedies	*Equitable remedies* are available if the nonbreaching party cannot be adequately compensated by a legal remedy or to prevent unjust enrichment. 1. *Specific performance:* Court order that requires the breaching party to perform his or her contractual duties. Available only if the subject matter of the contract is *unique*. 2. *Injunction:* Court order that prohibits a person from doing a certain act. The requesting party must show that he or she will suffer irreparable injury if the injunction is not granted. 3. *Reformation:* Permits the court to rewrite a contract to express the parties' true intention. Available to correct clerical and mathematical errors. 4. *Quasi-contract:* Permits the court to order recovery of compensation even though no enforceable contract exists between the parties. Used to prevent unjust enrichment. Also called an *implied-in-law contract* or *quantum meruit*.
Unconscionable Contracts	
Definition	Contracts that are oppressively unfair or unjust. Also called *contracts of adhesion*.

(continued)

Elements	1. The parties possessed severely unequal bargaining power.
	2. The dominant party unreasonably used its power to obtain oppressive or manifestly unfair contract terms.
	3. The adhering party had no reasonable alternative.
Remedies	Where a contract or contract clause is found to be unconscionable, the court may do one of the following:
	1. Refuse to enforce the contract.
	2. Refuse to enforce the unconscionable clause but enforce the remainder of the contract.
	3. Limit the applicability of any unconscionable clause so as to avoid any unconscionable result.

Working the Web

1. Use Findlaw to find documents such as the Uniform Commercial Code and journal articles about contract law, torts, and real estate at www.find law.com.

2. Find an overview of contracts at the Cornell University Law School Legal Information Institute at www.law.cornell.edu/topics/contracts.html.

3. Use the state locator at the Legal Information Institute to find the version of the Uniform Commercial Code adopted by your state at www.law.cornell.edu/uniform/ucc.html.

4. Check the Contracting and Organizations Research Institute at the University of Missouri (CORI), whose mission is to improve understanding of how the economic system works by facilitating and enabling interdisciplinary empirical research on contracting and organizational structure. Search its digital contracts at http://cori.missouri.edu/index.htm.

5. Check Pace University's website on International Commercial Law and the CISG, the United Nations Convention on Contracts for the International Sale of Goods at http://cisgw3.law.pace.edu/.

Questions

CRITICAL LEGAL THINKING AND WRITING

1. Describe an offer and an acceptance. When is a contract made?

2. What is an implied-in-fact contract? Why does the law recognize these contracts?

3. Explain a gift promise. Why are these contracts unenforceable?

4. What does the infancy doctrine provide? What public policy does this doctrine serve?

5. What does the Statute of Frauds provide? Why is the Statute of Frauds necessary?

6. What are the main provisions of the Federal Electronic Signature Act? Why was this law enacted?

7. What is an unconscionable contract? Why does the law recognize this doctrine?

8. What is the difference between complete performance, substantial performance, and inferior performance of a contract?

9. What is an equitable remedy? Why does the law provide for equitable remedies?

10. What do Article 2 and Article 2A of the Uniform Commercial Code provide? What is the difference between the common law of contracts and Articles 2 and 2A?

ETHICS: ANALYSIS AND DISCUSSION

1. What are the ethical implications of using a standard form contract, such as an employment contract with a non-compete clause, from a set of practice books that is sold and distributed nationally?

2. Is it ethical to copy into your word processor, and use as your own, a standard form real estate contract that contains a copyright notice from the state association of Realtors?

3. You have been asked to witness the signature of a client's spouse who is not present. Are there any ethical issues?

Compensation from the Unauthorized Practice of Law

There are few certainties in the area of ethics, for paralegals or in any profession. What qualifies as ethical conduct is in most cases based on state law and court interpretation applied to a set of facts. The citation listed below represents one legal opinion and is provided as a research starting point. Do not assume that the same rule applies in your jurisdiction. For the following:

- *Prepare a written statement based on your state law.*
- *Use your state bar association website as a starting point.*

You are a paralegal not otherwise licensed to practice law. Because of your substantial expertise, you are requested to prepare a complex set of legal documents for a former client. You enter into a fee agreement and are paid upon completion of the work. The "clients" then seek return of the funds paid, claiming they did not understand the significance of the UPL law in the state. [*Vista Designs v. Silverman*, 774 So.2d 884 (Fla.App. 4 Dist. 2001).] Can you be compelled to return the fee paid? Has the client breached its contract?

Bobby Floars Toyota, Inc. v. Smith

269 S.E. 320 (N.C.App. 1980)

12.1 FACTS

Infancy Doctrine. Charles Edwards Smith, a minor, purchased an automobile from Bobby Floars Toyota on August 15, 1973. Smith executed a security agreement to finance part of the balance due on the purchase price, agreeing to pay off the balance in 30 monthly installments. On September 25, 1973, Smith turned 18, the age of majority. Smith made 10 monthly payments after turning 18. He then decided to disaffirm the contract and stopped making the payments. Smith claims that he may disaffirm the contract entered into when he was a minor. Toyota argues that Smith had ratified the contract since attaining the age of majority.

ISSUE

Who is correct?

Welch v. Metro-Goldwyn-Mayer Film Co.

207 Cal.App.3d 165, 254 Cal.Rptr. 645 (Cal.App. 1989)

12.2 FACTS

Damages. Raquel Welch, a movie actress, appeared in about 30 films between 1965 and 1980. Considered a sex symbol, her only serious dramatic role was a roller derby queen in *Kansas City Bomber*. About 1980, Michael Phillips and David Ward developed a film package based on the John Steinbeck novella *Cannery Row*. In early 1981, Metro-Goldwyn-Mayer Film Co. (MGM) accepted to produce the project and entered into a contract with Welch to play the leading female character, a prostitute named Suzy. At 40 years old, Welch relished the chance to direct her career toward more serious roles. Welch was to receive $250,000 from MGM, with pay-

ment being divided into weekly increments during filming. Filming began on December 1, 1980. On December 22, 1980, MGM fired Welch and replaced her with another actress, Debra Winger. Welch sued MGM to recover the balance of $194,444 that remained unpaid under the contract.

ISSUE

Who wins?

Liz Claiborne, Inc. v. Avon Products, Inc.

530 N.Y.S.2d 425, 141 A.D.2d 329 (N.Y. Sup.App. 1988)

12.3 FACTS

Specific Performance. Liz Claiborne, Inc., is a large maker of women's better sportswear in the United States and a well-known name in fashion, with sales of more than $1 billion a year. Claiborne distributes its products through 9,000 retail outlets in the United States. Avon Products, Inc., is a major producer of fragrances, toiletries, and cosmetics, with sales of more than $3 billion a year. Claiborne, who desired to promote its well-known name on perfumes and cosmetics, entered into a joint venture with Avon whereby Claiborne would make available its name, trademarks, and marketing experience and Avon would engage in the procurement and manufacture of the fragrances, toiletries, and cosmetics. The parties would equally share the financial requirements of the joint venture.

In 1986, its first year of operation, the joint venture had sales of more than $16 million. In the second year, sales increased to $26 million, making it one of the fastest-growing fragrance and cosmetic lines in the country. In 1987, Avon sought to "uncouple" the joint venture. Avon thereafter refused to procure and manufacture the line of fragrances and cosmetics for the joint venture. When Claiborne could not obtain the necessary fragrances and cosmetics from any other source for the fall/Christmas season, Claiborne sued Avon for breach of contract, seeking specific performance of the contract by Avon.

ISSUE

Is specific performance an appropriate remedy in this case?

Walgreen Co. v. Sara Creek Property Co.

966 F.2d 273 (7th Cir. 1992)

12.4 FACTS

Walgreen Company operated a pharmacy in the Southgate Mall in Milwaukee since 1951, when the mall opened. Its lease, signed in 1971 and carrying a 30-year term, contains an exclusivity clause in which the landlord, Sara Creek Property Company, promises not to lease space in the mall to anyone else who wants to operate a pharmacy or a store containing a pharmacy.

In 1990, after its anchor tenant went broke, Sara Creek informed Walgreen that it intended to lease the anchor tenant space to Phar-Mor Corporation. Phar-Mor, a "deep discount" chain, would occupy 100,000 square feet, of which 12,000 square feet would be occupied by a pharmacy the same size as Walgreen's. The entrances to the two stores would be within a few hundred feet of each other.

Walgreen sued Sara Creek for breach of contract and sought a permanent injunction against Sara Creek's leasing the anchor premises to Phar-Mor.

ISSUE

Do the facts of this case justify issuing a permanent injunction? Did Sara Creek act ethically in not living up to the contract?

CASE FOR BRIEFING

Carnival Leisure Industries, Ltd. v. Aubin

938 F.2d 624 (1991)   United States Court of Appeals, Fifth Circuit

Read the following case, excerpted from the court of appeals opinion. Review and brief the case. In your brief, answer the following questions.

1. What were the plaintiff's contentions on appeal?

2. What law was applied by the court in this case, Bahamian law or Texas law? Why was that law applied?

3. What is the consequence of finding an illegal contract? Apply this rule to the facts of this case.

4. Did Aubin act ethically in avoiding an obligation that he knowingly made? Do you think he would have given back the money if he had won at gambling?

Garwood, Circuit Judge.

During a January 1987 visit to the Bahamas, George J. Aubin, a Texas resident, visited Cable Beach Hotel and Casino (the Casino), which was owned and operated by Carnival Leisure Industries, Ltd. (Carnival Leisure). While gambling at the Casino, Aubin received markers or chips from the Casino and the Casino received drafts drawn on Aubin's bank accounts in Texas. Aubin spent all of the markers provided on gambling, although he also could have spent them on food, beverages, souvenirs, or lodging at the Casino. Aubin ultimately gambled and lost $25,000, leaving the Casino with the same amount in bank drafts.

Carnival Leisure was unable to cash the bank drafts because Aubin had subsequently directed his bank to stop payment. Carnival Leisure sued Aubin in the United States District Court for the Southern District of Texas to enforce the debt. The district court granted Carnival Leisure's motion for summary judgment against Aubin in the amount of $25,000 and attorney's fees and costs. Carnival Leisure claimed that the debt was enforceable under Texas law because public policy had changed and now favored enforcement of gambling debts. The district court agreed. Aubin raises on appeal only the issue of whether public policy in Texas continues to prevent the enforcement of gambling debts.

Carnival Leisure claims, however, that since 1973 the public policy of Texas toward gambling and the legality of gambling debts has changed. Although gambling is generally proscribed in Texas, there has been an exception for the "social" gambler since 1973. The Texas legislature enacted the Bingo Enabling Act in 1981, the Texas Racing Act in 1986, and the Charitable Raffle Enabling Act in 1989. Provisions were added to the Texas Penal Code excepting these three activities from its general proscription against gambling.

The enactment of statutes legalizing some forms of gambling admittedly evidences some dissipation or narrowing of public disapproval of gambling. However, such statutes hardly introduce a judicially cognizable change in public policy with respect to gambling generally. The social gambling permitted is confined to private places where no one receives any benefit other than his personal winnings and all participants are subject to the same risks, a categorically vastly different kind of activity from the sort involved here. The racing, bingo, and raffling exceptions are narrow, strictly regulated exceptions to a broad public policy in Texas against most forms of gambling. Further, the kind of gambling engaged in here is not of the sort permitted by any of these exceptions.

Even if gambling legislation in Texas were evidence sufficient to warrant judicial notice of a shift in public policy with respect to legalized gambling, such a shift would not be inconsistent with a continued public policy disfavoring gambling on credit. Although Aubin could have used the loaned markers for nongambling purposes at the Casino, it is undisputed that they were in fact used exclusively for gambling. Aubin's gambling debt therefore fits squarely within the terms of the public policy of Texas prohibiting the enforcement of gambling debts owed to gambling participants incurred for the purpose of gambling.

We hold that the public policy in Texas against gambling on credit prevents enforcement of the debt incurred for the purpose of gambling and provided by a participant in the gambling activity. The district court's grant of summary judgment in favor of Carnival Leisure is accordingly reversed and this case is remanded to the district court for further proceedings consistent with this opinion.

CHAPTER 13

CHAPTER OBJECTIVES

After studying this chapter, you should be able to:

1. Define *personal property* and describe the methods for acquiring ownership.

2. Explain bailments and the parties to a bailment.

3. List and describe the four types of real property.

4. Describe ownership interests in surface, subsurface, and air rights.

5. Identify the types of co-ownership.

6. Name and describe the types of freehold estates.

7. Explain the real estate transaction, or transfer of deed.

8. Identify and describe the various types of leaseholds and explain the landlord–tenant relationship.

9. Explain some features of land-use control, including zoning laws.

10. Describe how environmental laws protect the environment.

Property and the Environment

Property and law are born and must die together.

JEREMY BENTHAM, *PRINCIPLES OF THE CIVIL CODE*

Introduction

Private ownership of property forms the foundation of our economic system. As such, a comprehensive body of law has been developed to protect property rights. The law protects the right of property owners to use, sell, dispose of, control, and prevent others from trespassing on their rights.

Many lawyers practice in the real estate law area. A paralegal is often called upon to assist an attorney in preparing the necessary documents for the sale of real property and for the recording of transfers of real property. This chapter covers the topics of personal property, real property, landlord–tenant relationships, insurance, devising property through gift or inheritance, and protection of the environment.

PERSONAL PROPERTY

The two kinds of property are real property and personal property. **Real property** includes land and property that is permanently attached to it. For example, minerals, crops, timber, and buildings that are attached to land are generally considered real property. **Personal property** (sometimes referred to as *goods* or *chattels*) consists of everything that is not real property. Real property can become personal property if it is removed from the land. For example, a tree that is part of a forest is real property; a tree that is cut down is personal property.

361

SIDEBAR

Estray Statutes

Most states have enacted **estray statutes** that permit a finder of *mislaid* or *lost* property to clear title to the property if

1. The finder reports the found property to the appropriate government agency and then turns over possession of the property to this agency,

2. Either the finder or the government agency posts notices and publishes advertisements describing the lost property, and

3. A specified time (usually a year or a number of years) has passed without the rightful owner's reclaiming the property.

Many state estray statutes require that the government receive a portion of the value of the property. Some statutes provide that title cannot be acquired in found property that is the result of illegal activity. For example, title has been denied to finders of property and money deemed to have been used for illegal drug purchases.

Consider the following case: While hunting on unposted and unoccupied property in Oceola Township, Michigan,

Duane Willsmore noticed an area with branches arranged in a crisscross pattern. When he kicked aside the branches and sod, he found a watertight suitcase in a freshly dug hole. Willsmore informed the Michigan state police of his find. A state trooper and Willsmore together pried open the suitcase and discovered $383,840 in cash. The state police took custody of the money, which was deposited in an interest-bearing account.

Michigan's estray statute provides that the finder and the township in which the property was found must share the value of the property if the finder publishes required notices and the true owner does not claim the property within one year. Willsmore published the required notices and brought a declaratory judgment action seeking the determination of ownership of the money. After one year had gone by and the rightful owner had not claimed the briefcase, the court ordered that Willsmore and the Township of Oceola were equal one-half owners of the briefcase and its contents. [*Willsmore v. Township of Oceola, Michigan,* 308 N.W.2d 796 (Mich.App. 1981)]

Personal property that is permanently affixed to land or buildings is called a *fixture*. Such property, which includes things such as heating systems and storm windows, is categorized as real property. Unless otherwise agreed, fixtures remain with a building when it is sold. Personal property (e.g., furniture, pictures, and other easily portable household items) may be removed by the seller prior to sale.

Personal property can be either tangible or intangible. **Tangible property** includes physically defined property such as goods, animals, and minerals. **Intangible property** represents rights that cannot be reduced to physical form, such as stock certificates, certificates of deposit, bonds, and copyrights.

BAILMENTS

A **bailment** occurs when the owner of personal property delivers his or her property to another person to be held, stored, or delivered, or for some other purpose. In a bailment, the owner of the property is the **bailor** and the party to whom the property is delivered for safekeeping, storage, or delivery (e.g., warehouse or common carrier) is the **bailee** (see Exhibit 13.1).

A bailment is different from a sale or a gift because title to the goods does not transfer to the bailee. Instead, the bailee must follow the bailor's directions concerning the goods. For example, suppose Hudson Corp. is relocating its

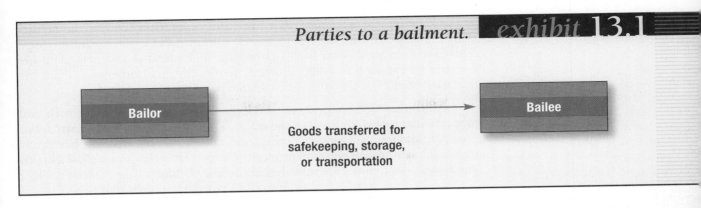

Parties to a bailment.   *exhibit* 13.1

| Bailor | → | Bailee |

Goods transferred for
safekeeping, storage,
or transportation

offices and hires American Van Lines to move its office furniture and equipment to the new location. American Van Lines (the bailee) must follow Hudson's (the bailor) instructions regarding delivery. The law of bailments establishes the rights, duties, and liabilities of parties to a bailment.

Mutual Benefit Bailments

Mutual benefit bailments are bailments that *benefit both parties*. The bailee owes a **duty of reasonable care** (or **ordinary care**) to protect the bailed goods. This means that the bailee is liable for any goods that are lost, damaged, or destroyed because of his or her negligence. Consider this example: Suppose ABC Garment Co. delivers goods to Lowell, Inc., a commercial warehouseman, for storage. A fee is charged for this service. ABC Garment Co. receives the benefit of having its goods stored, and Lowell, Inc., receives the benefit of being paid compensation for storing the goods. In this example, Lowell, Inc. (the bailee), owes a duty of ordinary care to protect the goods.

REAL PROPERTY

Property and ownership rights in real property play an important part in this country's society and economy. Individuals and families own or rent houses, farmers and ranchers own farmland and ranches, and businesses own or lease commercial and office buildings. Real property includes the following:

1. *Land and buildings.* **Land** is the most common form of real property. A landowner usually purchases the *surface rights* to the land—that is, the right to occupy the land. The owner may use, enjoy, and develop the property as he or she sees fit, subject to any applicable government regulations. *Buildings* constructed on land—such as houses, apartment buildings, manufacturing plants, and office buildings—are real property. Things such as radio towers, bridges, and the like are considered real property as well.

2. *Subsurface rights.* The owner of land possesses **subsurface rights** (or **mineral rights**) to the earth located beneath the surface of the land. These rights can be valuable. For example, gold, uranium, oil, or natural gas may lie beneath the surface of land. Theoretically, mineral rights extend to the center of the earth. In reality, mines and oil wells usually extend only several miles into the earth. Subsurface rights may be sold separately from surface rights.

3. *Plant life and vegetation.* **Plant life and vegetation** growing on the surface of land are considered real property. This includes natural plant life (e.g., trees) and cultivated plant life (e.g., crops). When land is sold, any plant life growing on the land is included unless the parties agree otherwise. Plant life that is severed from the land is considered personal property.

4. *Fixtures.* Certain personal property is associated so closely with real property that it becomes part of the realty. These items are called **fixtures.** For example, kitchen cabinets, carpeting, and doorknobs are fixtures, but throw rugs and furniture are personal property. Unless otherwise provided, if a building is sold, the fixtures are included in the sale. If the sale agreement is silent as to whether an item is a fixture, the courts make their determinations on the basis of whether the item can be removed without causing substantial damage to the realty.

FREEHOLD ESTATES

A person's ownership rights in real property are called an *estate in land* (or *estate*). An estate is defined as the bundle of *legal rights* that the owner has to possess, use, and enjoy the property. The type of estate that an owner possesses is determined from the deed, will, lease, or other document that transferred the ownership rights to him or her.

A **freehold estate** is one in which the owner has a *present possessory interest* in the real property; that is, the owner may use and enjoy the property as he or she sees fit, subject to any applicable government regulation or private restraint. The two types of freehold estates are *estates in fee* and *life estates*.

Estates in Fee

A **fee simple absolute** (or **fee simple**) is the highest form of ownership of real property because it grants the owner the fullest bundle of legal rights that a person can hold in real property. It is the type of ownership that most people connect with "owning" real property. A fee simple owner has the right to exclusively possess and use his or her property to the extent that the owner has not transferred any interest in the property (e.g., by lease).

A **fee simple defeasible** (or **qualified fee**) grants the owner all the incidents of a fee simple absolute except that it may be taken away if a specified *condition* occurs or does not occur. For example, a conveyance of property to a church "as long as the land is used as a church or for church purposes" creates a qualified fee. The church has all of the rights of a fee simple absolute owner except that its ownership rights are terminated if the property is no longer used for church purposes.

Life Estate

A **life estate** is an interest in real property that lasts for the life of a specified person, usually the grantee. For example, a conveyance of real property "to Anna for her life" creates a life estate. A life estate also may be measured by the

---

Air Rights: Value in the Heavens

Common law provided that the owners of real property owned that property from the center of the earth to the heavens. This rule has been eroded by modern legal restrictions such as land-use control laws, environmental protection laws, and air navigation requirements. Even today, however, the owners of land may sell or lease air space parcels above their land.

An **air-space parcel** is a three-dimensional cube of air above the surface of the earth. Air-space parcels are valuable property rights, particularly in densely populated metropolitan areas where building property is scarce. For example, many developments have been built in air-space parcels in New York City. The most notable are Madison Square Garden and Two Penn Plaza, which were built in air-space parcels above Penn Station.

life of a third party (e.g., "to Anna for the life of Benjamin"). This is called an **estate** *pur autre vie*. A life estate may be defeasible (e.g., "to John for his life, but only if he continues to occupy this residence"). Upon the death of named person, the life estate terminates and the property reverts to the grantor or the grantor's estate or other designated person.

A life tenant is treated as the owner of the property during the duration of the life estate. He or she has the right to possess and use the property except to the extent that it would cause permanent *waste* of the property. A life tenant may sell, transfer, or mortgage his or her estate in the land. The mortgage, however, cannot exceed the duration of the life estate. A life tenant is obligated to keep the property in repair and to pay property taxes.

FUTURE INTERESTS

A person may be given the right to possess property in the *future* rather than in the present. This right is called a **future interest**. The two forms of future interests are *reversion* and *remainder* (see Exhibit 13.2).

Reversion

A **reversion** is a right of possession that returns to the *grantor* after the expiration of a limited or contingent estate. Reversions do not have to be expressly stated because they arise automatically by law. For example, if a grantor conveys property "to M. R. Harrington for life," the grantor has retained a reversion in the property. That is, when Harrington dies, the property reverts to the grantor or, if he or she is not living, then to his or her estate.

Remainder

If the right of possession returns to a *third party* upon the expiration of a limited or contingent estate, it is called a **remainder**. The person who is entitled to the future interest is called a **remainderman**. For example, a conveyance of property "to Joe for life, remainder to Meredith" is a vested remainder—the only contingency to Meredith's possessory interest is Joe's death.

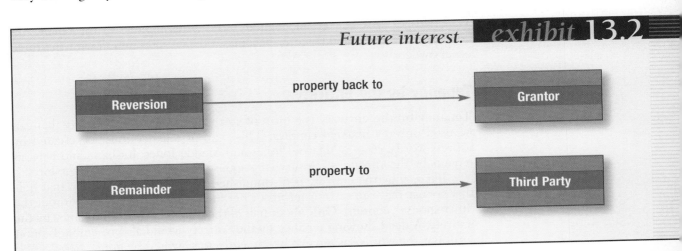

Future interest.   **exhibit 13.2**

CONCURRENT OWNERSHIP

Two or more persons may own a piece of real property. This is called **co-ownership** or **concurrent ownership.** The following forms of co-ownership are recognized: *joint tenancy, tenancy in common, tenancy by the entirety, community property, condominium,* and *cooperative.*

Joint Tenancy

To create a joint tenancy, words that clearly show a person's intent to create a joint tenancy must be used. Language such as "Marsha Leest and James Leest, as joint tenants" is usually sufficient. The most distinguishing feature of a **joint tenancy** is the co-owners' **right of survivorship.** This means that upon the death of one of the co-owners (or *joint tenants*), the deceased person's interest in the property automatically passes to the surviving joint tenants. Any contrary provision in the deceased's will is ineffective.

Consider this example: Jones, one of four people who own a piece of property in joint tenancy, executes a will leaving all of his property to a university. Jones dies. The surviving joint tenants—not the university—acquire his interest in the piece of property. Each joint tenant has a right to sell or transfer his or her interest in the property, but such conveyance terminates the joint tenancy. The parties then become tenants in common. Exhibit 13.3 is a deed showing joint tenancy.

Tenancy in Common

In a **tenancy in common,** the interests of a surviving *tenant in common* pass to the deceased tenant's estate and not to the co-tenants. A tenancy in common may be created by express words, such as "Iran Cespedes and Joy Park, as tenants in common." Unless otherwise agreed, a tenant in common can sell, give, devise, or otherwise transfer his or her interest in the property without the consent of the other co-owners. A deed showing tenancy in common would resemble Exhibit 13.3, but the words "as tenants in common" would replace "as joint tenants . . . ."

Consider this example: Lopez, one of four tenants in common who own a piece of property, has a will that leaves all of his property to his granddaughter. When Lopez dies, the granddaughter receives his interest in the tenancy in common, and the granddaughter becomes a tenant in common with the three other owners.

Tenancy by the Entirety

Tenancy by the entirety is a form of co-ownership of real property that can be used only by married couples. This type of tenancy must be created by express words, such as "Harold Jones and Maude Jones, husband and wife, as tenants by the entireties." A surviving spouse has the right of survivorship.

Tenancy by the entirety is distinguished from a joint tenancy in that neither spouse may sell or transfer his or her interest in the property without the other spouse's consent. Only about half of the states recognize a tenancy by the entirety. A deed showing tenancy by the entirety would also resemble Exhibit 13.3, but the words "as tenants by the entireties" would be used.

Deed showing joint tenancy.   *exhibit* **13.3**

For Simple/Trustees' Deed

This Indenture Made this   day of

Between

KATHRYN KELSEY and WILLIAM KELSEY

(hereinafter called the Grantor s),

SUSAN CARROLL and PATRICK CARROLL, as joint-tenants with right of survivorship

(hereinafter called the Grantee s),

Witnesseth That the said Grantor s for and in consideration of the sum of

lawful money of the United States of America, unto   them   well and truly paid by the said Grantee s, at or before the sealing and delivery hereof, the receipt whereof is hereby acknowledged, they   granted, bargained and sold, released and confirmed, and by these presents   do   grant, bargain and sell, release and confirm unto the said Grantee s,   their heirs   and assigns, as joint-tenants with right of survivorship,

Together with all and singular the   improvements, ways, streets, alleys, driveways, passages, waters, water-courses, rights, liberties, privileges, hereditaments and appurtenances, whatsoever unto the hereby granted premises belonging, or in any wise appertaining, and the reversions and remainders, rents, issues, and profits thereof; and all the estate, right, title, interest, property, claim and demand whatsoever of the said Grantor , as well at law as in equity, of, in, and to the same.

To have and to hold the said lot   or piece   of ground above described with the   hereditaments and premises hereby granted, or mentioned, and intended so to be, with the appurtenances, unto the said Grantee ,   and assigns and assigns, to and for the only proper use and behoof of the said Grantee .   and assigns forever.

And the said   and Assigns, that   do   by these presents, covenant, grant and agree, to and with the said   the said   all and singular the Hereditaments and premises herein above described and granted, or mentioned and intended so to be with the Appurtenances unto the said   the said   and against all and every Person or Persons and Assigns, against   whomsoever lawfully claiming or to claim the same or any part thereof, by from, or under   or any of them, shall and will WARRANT and forever DEFEND.

(SPECIAL WARRANTY)

OR

the said   do   covenant, promise and agree, to and with the said and assigns, by these presents, that   the said   has/have not done, committed or knowingly or willingly suffered to be done or committed, any act, matter or thing whatsoever whereby the premises hereby granted, or any part thereof, is, are, shall or may be impeached, charged or incumbered, in title, charge, estate, or otherwise howsoever.

(TRUSTEES' WARRANTY)

In Witness Whereof, the said Grantor   has/have caused these presents to be duly executed dated the day and year first above written.

Sealed and Delivered
IN THE PRESENCE OF US:

COMMONWEALTH OF   }
COUNTY OF   } SS.
On this, the   day of   , A.D.   , before me, the undersigned officer, personally appeared   whose name   is (are) subscribed to the within known to me (or satisfactorily proven) to be the person   executed the same for the purposes therein contained. instrument, and acknowledged that   he   **In Witness Whereof**, I hereunto set my hand and official seal.

_____
Notary Public
My Commission Expires:

COMMONWEALTH OF   }
COUNTY OF   } SS.
On this, the   day of   , A.D.   , before me, the undersigned officer, personally appeared   of himself (herself) to be the   he as such   a corporation and that   he as such   who acknowledged being authorized to do so, executed the foregoing instrument for the purposes therein contained by signing the name of the corporation by himself (herself) as
In Witness Whereof, I hereunto set my hand and official seal.

_____
Notary Public
My Commission Expires:

Community Property

Nine states—Arizona, California, Idaho, Louisiana, Nevada, New Mexico, Texas, Washington, and Wisconsin—recognize a form of co-ownership known as **community property.** This method of co-ownership applies only to married couples and is based on the notion that a husband and wife should share equally in the fruits of the marital partnership.

Under these laws, each spouse owns an equal one-half share of the income of both spouses and the assets acquired during the marriage regardless of who earns the income. Property that is acquired through gift or inheritance either before or during marriage remains separate property.

When a spouse dies, the surviving spouse automatically receives one-half the community property. The other half passes to the heirs of the deceased spouse as directed by will or by state intestate statute if there is no will.

For example, a husband and wife have community property assets of $1.5 million and the wife dies with a will. The husband automatically has a right to receive $750,000 of the community property. The remaining $750,000 passes as directed by the wife's will. Any separate property owned by the wife, such as jewelry she inherited, also passes in accordance with her will. Her husband has no vested interest in that property.

During the marriage, neither spouse can sell, transfer, or gift community property without the consent of the other spouse. Upon a divorce, each spouse has a right to one-half of the community property.

The location of the real property determines whether community property law applies. For example, if a married couple who lives in a non–community property state purchases real property located in a community property state, community property laws apply to that property.

table 13.1 *Summary of concurrent ownership.*

FORM OF OWNERSHIP	RIGHT OF SURVIVORSHIP	TENANT MAY UNILATERALLY TRANSFER HIS OR HER INTEREST
Joint tenancy	Yes, deceased tenant's interest automatically passes to co-tenants.	Yes, tenant may transfer his or her interest without the consent of co-tenants. Transfer severs joint tenancy.
Tenancy in common	No, deceased tenant's interest passes to his or her estate.	Yes, tenant may transfer his or her interest without the consent of co-tenants. Transfer does not sever tenancy in common.
Tenancy by the entirety	Yes, deceased tenant's interest automatically passes to his or her spouse.	No, neither spouse may transfer his or her interest without the other spouse's consent.
Community property	Yes, when a spouse dies the surviving spouse automatically receives one half of the community property. The other half passes to the heirs of the deceased spouse as directed by a valid will or by state intestate statute if there is no will.	No, neither spouse may transfer his or her interest without the other spouse's consent.

Condominiums

Condominiums are a common form of ownership in multiple-dwelling buildings. Purchasers of a condominium (1) have title to their individual units and (2) own the common areas (e.g., hallways, elevators, parking areas, and recreational facilities) as tenants in common with the other owners. Owners may sell or mortgage their units without the permission of the other owners. Owners are assessed monthly fees for the maintenance of common areas. In addition to dwelling units, the condominium form of ownership is offered for office buildings, boat docks, and such.

Cooperatives

A **cooperative** is a form of co-ownership of a multiple-dwelling building in which a corporation owns the building and the residents own shares in the corporation. Each cooperative owner then leases a unit in the building from the corporation under a renewable, long-term, proprietary lease. Individual residents may not secure loans with the units they occupy. The corporation may borrow money on a blanket mortgage, and each shareholder is jointly and severally liable on the loan. Usually, cooperative owners may not sell their shares or sublease their units without the approval of the other owners.

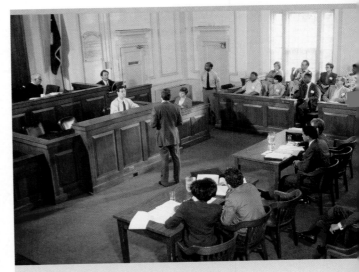

A courtroom scene with a trial in progress.

TRANSFER OF OWNERSHIP OF REAL PROPERTY

Ownership of real property may be transferred from one person to another. Title to real property may be transferred by sale, tax sale, gift, will, or inheritance. **Deeds** are used to convey real property by sale or gift. The seller or donor is called the **grantor.** The buyer or recipient is called the **grantee.** A deed may be used to transfer a fee simple absolute interest in real property or any lesser estate (e.g., life estate).

State laws recognize different types of deeds that provide differing degrees of protection to grantees. A **warranty deed** contains the greatest number of warranties and provides the most protection to grantees. A **quitclaim deed** provides the least amount of protection because the grantor conveys only whatever interest he or she has in the property.

Sale of Real Estate

A sale or conveyance is the most common method for transferring ownership rights in real property. An agreement for the sale of real property under the state Statute of Frauds must be in writing to be enforceable. Exhibit 13.4 shows the parties to a real estate sale. The seller delivers a deed to the buyer and the buyer pays the purchase price at the closing or settlement.

A copy of an agreement form for the sale of real estate is set forth in Exhibit 13.5. A settlement form is shown in Exhibit 13.6. Exhibit 13.7 shows a notice of property defects.

exhibit 13.4   *Parties to and documents in a real estate transaction.*

Recording Statutes

Every state has a recording statute that provides that copies of deeds and other documents concerning interests in real property (e.g., mortgages, liens, easements) may be filed in a government office where they become public records open to viewing by the public. Recording statutes are intended to prevent fraud and to establish certainty in the ownership and transfer of property. Instruments usually are filed in the *county recorder's office* of the county in which the property is located. A fee is charged to record an instrument.

Persons interested in purchasing the property or lending on the property check these records to determine if the grantor or borrower actually owns the property and whether any other parties (e.g., lienholders, mortgagees,

easement holders) have an interest in the property. The recordation of a deed is not required to pass title from the grantor to the grantee. Recording the deed gives *constructive notice* to the world of the owner's interest in the property.

A party who is concerned about his or her ownership rights in a parcel of real property can bring a **quiet title** action to have a court determine the extent of those rights. Public notice of the hearing must be given so that anyone claiming an interest in the property may appear and be heard. After the hearing, the judge declares who has title to the property—that is, the court "quiets title" by its decision.

Agreement for the sale of real property.   *exhibit* **13.5**

AGREEMENT FOR THE SALE OF REAL ESTATE   S & C 1969A Residential
COPYRIGHT PENNSYLVANIA ASSOCIATION OF REALTORS® 1973   (Rev. 7-90)

COPIES
1. White............Seller
2. Yellow...........Agent
3. Pink.............Buyer
4. Blue.........Mortgagee
5. Gold ....
6. Green ....Buyer's copy at time of signing

┌─ AGENT FOR THE SELLER ─┐   ┌─ SUBAGENT FOR SELLER ─┐

└─ PA. LICENSED BROKER ─┘   └─ PA. LICENSED BROKER ─┘

𝕿𝖍𝖎𝖘 𝕬𝖌𝖗𝖊𝖊𝖒𝖊𝖓𝖙, this .... day of .... A.D. ....

1. PRINCIPALS (1-78) Between ....

(residing at .... Zip Code.............) **hereinafter called Seller,**

and ....

(residing at .... Zip Code.............) **hereinafter called Buyer.**

2. PROPERTY (4-89) Seller hereby agrees to sell and convey to Buyer, who hereby agrees to purchase:
ALL THAT CERTAIN lot or piece of ground with buildings and improvements thereon erected, if any, known as:

.... in the.................. of ....

County of .... **State of** ...., **Zip Code**..........

Zoning Classification
Failure of this agreement to contain the zoning classification (except in cases where the property {and each parcel thereof, if subdividable} is zoned solely or primarily to permit single-family dwellings) shall render this agreement voidable at the option of the Buyer, and, if voided, any deposits tendered by the Buyer shall be returned to the Buyer without any requirement for court action.

3. TERMS (3-85) (A) Purchase Price .... **Dollars**

which shall be paid to the Seller by the Buyer as follows:

(B) Cash or check at signing this agreement: .... $..........

(C) Cash or check to be paid on or before: .... 19.... $..........

(D) .... $..........

(E) Cash or certified check at time of settlement: .... **TOTAL** $_____

(F) Written approval of Seller to be on or before:................................ 19....

(G) Settlement to be made on or before:... 19....

(H) Conveyance from Seller will be by fee simple deed of special warranty.

(I) Payment of transfer taxes will be divided equally between Buyer and Seller.

(J) The following shall be apportioned pro-rata as of and at time of settlement: taxes as levied and assessed, rents, interest on mortgage assumptions, condominium fees and homeowner association fees, if any, water and or sewer rents, if any, together with any other lienable municipal services.

4. MORTGAGE CONTINGENCY (4-89) This sale is NOT contingent upon any mortgage financing except as hereinafter provided.

(A) Mortgage terms required by Buyer. Amount of mortgage loan $ .... Term .... years,
Type of mortgage ....
Interest rate............. %; **however, Buyer agrees to accept the interest rate as may be committed by the mortgage lender, not to exceed a maximum interest rate of**............. %.

(B) Within ten(10) days of Seller's approval of this agreement, Buyer shall make a completed mortgage application to a responsible mortgage lending institution through the office of Subagent for the Seller, if any, otherwise through the office of Agent for the Seller, **who for the purposes of negotiating for the said mortgage loan, shall be considered the Agent for the Buyer.**

(C) (1) Buyer will, upon receipt of a mortgage commitment, promptly provide a copy to Seller, Agent and/or Subagent, if any.
(2) Mortgage commitment date .... If a written commitment is not received by the above date, **Buyer agrees to extend the commitment date until Seller terminates this agreement in writing.**
(3) Should the mortgage commitment:
(a) not be valid until the date of settlement, or
(b) be conditioned upon the **sale and settlement of any other property**, or
(c) contain any other condition not specified in this Agreement,
Seller has the option to terminate this Agreement in writing.
(4) In the event that the Seller terminates this agreement as specified in paragraphs 4(C) (2) or (3), OR
(a) the mortgage commitment is not obtained by or valid until the date of settlement, or
(b) the mortgage commitment is conditioned upon the **sale and settlement of any other property** which do not occur by the date of settlement, or
(c) the mortgage commitment contains any other condition not specified in this Agreement which the Buyer is unable to satisfy by the date of settlement,
the Buyer shall not be required to purchase the property and all deposit monies paid on account shall be returned to the Buyer, except any payments made by Buyer as described in Paragraph 7(C) (1), (2), and (3).

(D) Seller hereby agrees to permit inspections by authorized appraisers, reputable certifiers and/or Buyer as may be required by the lending institution or insuring agencies.

5. SPECIAL CLAUSES

exhibit **13.5**   *Agreement for the sale of real property, continued.*

6. **NOTICES & ASSESSMENTS (7-90)**
   (A) Seller represents as of the approval date of this agreement, that no public improvement, condominium or homeowner association assessments have been made against the premises which remain unpaid and that no notice by any government or public authority has been served upon the Seller or anyone on the Seller's behalf, including notices relating to violations of zoning, housing, building, safety or fire ordinances which remain uncorrected unless otherwise specified herein.
   (B) If required by law, Seller shall deliver to Buyer on or before settlement, a certification from the appropriate municipal department or departments disclosing notice of any uncorrected violation of zoning, housing, building, safety or fire ordinances.
   (C) Buyer is advised that access to a public road may require issuance of a highway occupancy permit from the Department of Transportation.
   (D) Seller will be responsible for any notice of improvements or assessments received on or before the date of Seller's approval of this agreement, unless improvements consist of sewer or water lines not in use.
   (E) Buyer will be responsible for any notice served upon Seller after the approval date of this agreement and for the payment thereafter of any public improvement, condominium or homeowner association assessments.

7. **TITLE AND COSTS (1-86)**
   (A) The premises are to be conveyed free and clear of all liens, encumbrances, and easements, EXCEPTING HOWEVER, the following: existing building restrictions, ordinances, easements of roads, easements visible upon the ground, privileges or rights of public service companies, if any, otherwise the title to the above described real estate shall be good and marketable and such as will be insured by a reputable Title Insurance Company at the regular rates.
   (B) In the event the Seller is unable to give a good and marketable title and such as will be insured by a reputable Title Company, subject to aforesaid, Buyer shall have the option of taking such title as the Seller can give without abatement of price or of being repaid all monies paid by Buyer to the Seller on account of the purchase price and the Seller will reimburse the Buyer for any costs incurred by the Buyer for those items specified in paragraph 7(C) items (1), (2), (3), and in paragraph 7(D); and in the latter event there shall be no further liability or obligation on either of the parties hereto and this agreement shall become NULL AND VOID and all copies will be returned to Seller's Agent for cancellation.
   (C) The Buyer will pay for the following:
      (1) The premium for mechanics lien insurance and/or title search, or fee for cancellation of same, if any.
      (2) The premiums for flood insurance and/or fire insurance with extended coverage, insurance binder charges or cancellation fee, if any.
      (3) Appraisal fees and charges paid in advance to mortgagee if any.
      (4) Buyer's normal settlement costs and accruals.
   (D) Any survey or surveys which may be required by the Title Insurance Company or the abstracting attorney, for the preparation of an adequate legal description of the premises (or the correction thereof), shall be secured and paid for by the Seller. However, any survey or surveys desired by the Buyer or required by his/her mortgage shall be secured and paid for by the Buyer.

8. **FIXTURES, TREES, SHRUBBERY, ETC. (1-81)** All existing plumbing, heating and lighting fixtures (including chandeliers) and systems appurtenant thereto and forming a part thereof, and other permanent fixtures, as well as all ranges, laundry tubs, T.V. antennas, masts and rotor systems, together with wall to wall carpeting, screens, storm sash and/or doors,shades, awnings, venetian blinds, couplings for automatic washers and dryers, etc., radiator covers, cornices, kitchen cabinets, drapery rods, drapery rod hardware, curtain rods, curtain rod hardware, all trees, shrubbery, plantings now in or on property, if any, unless specifically excepted in this agreement, are included in the sale and purchase price. None of the above mentioned items shall be removed by the Seller from the premises after the date of this agreement. Any remaining heating and/or cooking fuels stored on the premises at time of settlement are also included under this agreement. Seller hereby warrants that he will deliver good title to all of the articles described in this paragraph, and any other fixtures or items of personalty specifically scheduled and to be included in this sale.

9. **DEPOSIT AND RECOVERY FUND (4-89)** Deposits, regardless of the form of payment and the person designated as payee, shall be paid to Agent for the Seller who shall retain them in an escrow account until consummation or termination of this Agreement in conformity with all applicable laws and regulations. Agent for the Seller may, at his or her sole option, hold any uncashed check tendered as deposit, pending the acceptance of this offer. Buyer and Seller agree that, in the event the Agent and/or Subagent are/is joined in litigation for the return of deposit monies, the Agent's and/or Subagent's attorneys fees and costs will be paid by the party joining the Agent or Subagent.
   A Real Estate Recovery Fund exists to reimburse any persons who have obtained a final civil judgment against a Pennsylvania real estate licensee owing to fraud, misrepresentation, or deceit in a real estate transaction and who have been unable to collect the judgement after exhausting all legal and equitable remedies. For complete details about the Fund, call (717) 783-3658.

10. **POSSESSION AND TENDER (3-85)**
   (A) Possession is to be delivered by deed, keys and physical possession to a vacant building (if any) broom clean, free of debris at day and time of settlement, or by deed and assignment of existing lease(s) at time of settlement if premises are tenant occupied. Buyer will acknowledge existing lease(s) by initialing said lease(s) at time of signing of this agreement, unless otherwise specified herein. Buyer will acknowledge existing lease(s) by initialing said lease(s) at time of signing of this agreement of sale if tenant occupied.
   (B) Seller will not enter into any new leases, written extension of existing leases, if any, or additional leases for the premises without expressed written consent of the Buyer.
   (C) Formal tender of an executed deed and purchase money is hereby waived.
   (D) Buyer reserves the right to make a pre-settlement inspection of the subject premises.

11. **MAINTENANCE AND RISK OF LOSS (3-85)**
   (A) Seller shall maintain the property (including all items mentioned in paragraph #8 herein) and any personal property specifically scheduled herein in its present condition, normal wear and tear excepted.
   (B) Seller shall bear risk of loss from fire or other casualties until time of settlement. In the event of damage to any property included in this sale by fire or other casualties, not repaired or replaced prior to settlement, Buyer shall have the option of rescinding this agreement and receiving all monies paid on account or of accepting the property in its then condition together with the proceeds of any insurance recovery obtainable by Seller. Buyer is hereby notified that he may insure his equitable interest in this property as of the time of the acceptance of this agreement.

12. **RECORDING (3-85)** This agreement shall not be recorded in the Office for the Recording of Deeds or in any other office or place of public record and if Buyer causes or permits this agreement to be recorded, Seller may elect to treat such act as a breach of this agreement.

13. **ASSIGNMENT (3-85)** This agreement shall be binding upon the parties, their respective heirs, personal representatives, guardians and successors, and to the extent assignable, on the assigns of the parties hereto, it being expressly understood, however, that the Buyer shall not transfer or assign this agreement without the written consent of the Seller.

14. **DEFAULT-TIME OF THE ESSENCE (1-79)** The said time for settlement and all other times referred to for the performance of any of the obligations of this agreement are hereby agreed to be of the essence of this agreement. Should the Buyer:
   (A) Fail to make any additional payments as specified in paragraph #3, or
   (B) Furnish false or incomplete information to the Seller, the Seller's Agent, or the mortgage lender, concerning the Buyer's legal or financial status, or fail to cooperate in the processing of the mortgage loan application, which acts would result in the failure to obtain the approval of a mortgage loan commitment, or
   (C) Violate or fail to fulfill and perform any other terms or conditions of this agreement,
   then in such case, all deposit money and other sums paid by the Buyer on account of the purchase price, whether required by this agreement or not, may be retained by the Seller: (1) On account of the purchase, or (2) As monies to be applied to the Seller's damages, or (3) As liquidated damages for such breach, as the Seller may elect, and in the event that the Seller elects to retain the monies as liquidated damages in accordance with paragraph #14(3), the Seller shall be released from all liability or obligations and this agreement shall be NULL AND VOID and all copies will be returned to the Seller's Agent for cancellation.

15. **AGENT(S) (3-85)** It is expressly understood and agreed between the parties that the named Agent, Broker, and any Subagent, Broker and their salespeople, employees, officers and or partners, are Agent(s) for the Seller, not the Buyer, however, the Agent(s) may perform services for the Buyer in connection with financing, insurance and document preparation.

16. **REPRESENTATIONS (3-85)** It is understood that Buyer has inspected the property, or hereby waives the right to do so and has agreed to purchase it as a result of such inspection and not because of or in reliance upon any representation made by the Seller or any other officer, partner or employee of Seller, or by the Agent, Subagent, if any, of the Seller, their salespeople and employees, officers and or partners, The Buyer has agreed to purchase it in its present condition unless otherwise specified herein. It is further understood that this agreement contains the whole agreement between the Seller and the Buyer and there are no other terms, obligations, covenants, representations, statements or conditions, oral or otherwise of any kind whatsoever concerning this sale. Furthermore, this agreement shall not be altered, amended, changed or modified except in writing executed by the parties.

APPROVAL BY BUYER

WITNESS AS
TO BUYER ....   BUYER .... (SEAL)
WITNESS AS
TO BUYER ....   BUYER .... (SEAL)

APPROVAL BY SELLER   BUYER .... (SEAL)

Seller hereby approves the above contract this .... day of .... A.D. ....

and in consideration of the services rendered in procuring the Buyer, Seller agrees to pay the named Agent a fee of ....
of/from the herein specified sale price. In the event Buyer defaults hereunder, any monies paid on account shall be divided .... Seller,

WITNESS AS
TO SELLER .... Agent, but in no event will the sum paid to the Agent be in excess of the above specified Agent's fee.
WITNESS AS
TO SELLER ....   SELLER .... (SEAL)

AGENT BY: ....   SELLER .... (SEAL)

                                                      SELLER .... (SEAL)

TO: .... (Agent)   Date ....

In conjunction with the purchase of the premises described in this agreement of sale attached hereto, I/We hereby authorize your firm to perform the services as indicated below by my/our initials.
A. Order Title insurance in any reputable title insurance company .... (INITIALS)
B. Order insurance in the amount of $ .... ⎵ Homeowners ⎵ Fire & Extended Coverage ⎵ Flood .... (INITIALS)
C. .... (INITIALS)

Settlement statement.   *exhibit* **13.6**

A. Settlement Statement

U.S. Department of Housing and Urban Development

OMB Approval No. 2502-0265

B. Type of Loan

1. ☐ FHA 2. ☐ FmHA 3. ☐ Conv. Unins. 4. ☐ VA 5. ☐ Conv. Ins.

6. File Number:

7. Loan Number:

8. Mortgage Insurance Case Number:

C. Note: This form is furnished to give you a statement of actual settlement costs. Amounts paid to and by the settlement agent are shown. Items marked "(p.o.c.)" were paid outside the closing; they are shown here for informational purposes and are not included in the totals.

D. Name & Address of Borrower:	E. Name & Address of Seller:	F. Name & Address of Lender:
Ethan & Ariel Marshall 52 Moritz Way Anyplace, PA 55555	Sara and Natasha Elliot 138 Weisser Place Anyplace, PA 55555	4th National Bank OneSouth Main St. Newcity, PA 44444

G. Property Location:
1 Zollinger Way

H. Settlement Agent:
Roberts

Place of Settlement:
Newcity

I. Settlement Date:
08-19-2002

J. Summary of Borrower's Transaction		**K. Summary of Seller's Transaction**	
100. Gross Amount Due From Borrower		**400. Gross Amount Due To Seller**	
101. Contract sales price	150000	401. Contract sales price	150000
102. Personal property		402. Personal property	
103. Settlement charges to borrower (line 1400)	21000	403.	
104.		404.	
105.		405.	
Adjustments for items paid by seller in advance		**Adjustments for items paid by seller in advance**	
106. City/town taxes 08-19-2002 to 12-31-2002	650	406. City/town taxes 08-19-2002 to 12-31-2002	650
107. County taxes to		407. County taxes to	
108. Assessments to		408. Assessments to	
109.		409.	
110.		410.	
111.		411.	
112.		412.	
120. Gross Amount Due From Borrower	152750	**420. Gross Amount Due To Seller**	150650
200. Amounts Paid By Or In Behalf Of Borrower		**500. Reductions In Amount Due To Seller**	
201. Deposit or earnest money		501. Excess deposit (see instructions)	
202. Principal amount of new loan(s)		502. Settlement charges to seller (line 1400)	9000
203. Existing loan(s) taken subject to		503. Existing loan(s) taken subject to	
204.		504. Payoff of first mortgage loan	75000
205.		505. Payoff of second mortgage loan	
206.		506.	
207.		507.	
208.		508.	
209.		509.	
Adjustments for items unpaid by seller		**Adjustments for items unpaid by seller**	
210. City/town taxes to		510. City/town taxes to	
211. County taxes to		511. County taxes to	
212. Assessments to		512. Assessments to	
213.		513.	
214.		514.	
215.		515.	
216.		516.	
217.		517.	
218.		518.	
219.		519.	
220. Total Paid By/For Borrower	135000	**520. Total Reduction Amount Due Seller**	84000
300. Cash At Settlement From/To Borrower		**600. Cash At Settlement To/From Seller**	
301. Gross Amount due from borrower (line 120)	152750	601. Gross amount due to seller (line 420)	150650
302. Less amounts paid by/for borrower (line 220)	(135000)	602. Less reductions in amt. due seller (line 520)	(84000)
303. Cash ☑ From ☐ To Borrower	17750	**603. Cash** ☑ To ☐ From Seller	

Section 5 of the Real Estate Settlement Procedures Act (RESPA) requires the following: • HUD must develop a Special Information Booklet to help persons borrowing money to finance the purchase of residential real estate to better understand the nature and costs of real estate settlement services; • Each lender must provide the booklet to all applicants from whom it receives or for whom it prepares a written application to borrow money to finance the purchase of residential real estate; • Lenders must prepare and distribute with the Booklet a Good Faith Estimate of the settlement costs that the borrower is likely to incur in connection with the settlement. These disclosures are manadatory.

Section 4(a) of RESPA mandates that HUD develop and prescribe this standard form to be used at the time of loan settlement to provide full disclosure of all charges imposed upon the borrower and seller. These are third party disclosures that are designed to provide the borrower with pertinent information during the settlement process in order to be a better shopper.

The Public Reporting Burden for this collection of information is estimated to average one hour per response, including the time for reviewing instructions, searching existing data sources, gathering and maintaining the data needed, and completing and reviewing the collection of information.

This agency may not collect this information, and you are not required to complete this form, unless it displays a currently valid OMB control number.

The information requested does not lend itself to confidentiality.

Previous editions are obsolete

Page 1 of 2

form **HUD-1** (3/86) ref Handbook 4305.2

exhibit **13.7** *Notice of property defect.*

1:23:59 pm Jun 13, 2002

TEST SITE ADDRESS
112 SCHAN DRIVE
CHURCHVILLE, BUCKS COUNTY
PA 18966

MARTIN GOLDMAN [BUYER]

To Whom It May Concern:

The results of your radon evaluation for the property listed above is

*** 0.79 pCi/l *** for the location: 1ST FLOOR DINING ROOM.

The laboratory data at the bottom of this page were used to calculate the radon exposure level for this location. Interpretation of these results should be done in compliance with the U.S. EPA radon testing protocols and your state and local health and environmental offices. Currently the EPA has set a remediation action guideline equal to the yearly average exposure equivalent of 4.0 pCi/l.

If your results are above this 4.0 pCi/l guideline level, you should conduct another test to confirm that remediation is, in fact, necessary prior to seeking remediation services. This step is especially important if the results of this screening test show radon levels less than 20 pCi/l, as radon emissions can be higher than average for short periods of time due to unusual environmental conditions. We have included information from the U.S. EPA, as well as from the radon offices of the Pennsylvania DER and New Jersey DEP to assist you in making specific follow-up decisions. If you desire additional information, contact the Franklin Environmental Lab directly, or the government's radon office in your area. Franklin Environmental will be happy to supply you with referral information for these offices. In the event that you have questions, comments or complaints about radon services you may direct these to:

The PA Dept. of Environmental Resources, (717) 787-2480

The NJ Dept. of Environmental Protection & Energy, (609) 987-6393

The DE Div. of Public Health/Office of Radiation Control, (302) 739-3787, for radon testing & remediation services conducted in these states.

FRANKLIN ENVIRONMENTAL ANALYSIS
P.O. Box 554
Feasterville, PA 19053-0554
Telephone: (215) 744-9212

Exposure Start Time:	09:00
Exposure Start Date:	06-10-02
Exposure Stop Time:	14:15
Exposure Stop Date:	06-12-02
Canister Id Numb:	500057
Canister Initial Weight:	166.83
Canister Final Weight:	167.21
Canister Type:	4.00 in. DB
Measurement Time:	13:09
Measurement Date:	06-13-02
Counting Efficiency:	0.312
Background Counts:	168.600
Elapsed Time:	600
Gross Counts:	1844
Radon Concentration:	0.79

U.S. EPA ID#: 1219000
PA/DER Cert#: 0520
NJ/DEP Cert#: MEB90005
NJ/DEP LAB #: 77931
DE/ORC REG #: 118RT

1ST FLOOR DINING ROOM

Marketable Title

Marketable title means that the title is free from any encumbrances, defects in title, or other defects that are not disclosed but would affect the value of the property. A buyer of real property can purchase **title insurance** from a title insurance company. The title insurance policy lists any defects in the title of the property, if any, and ensures against unlisted defects in title.

The title insurer must reimburse the insured for any losses caused by undiscovered defects in the title. Each time a property is transferred, a new title insurance policy must be obtained. Exhibit 13.8 shows the opening two pages of a title insurance policy.

Adverse Possession

In most states, a person who wrongfully possesses someone else's real property obtains title to that property if certain statutory requirements are met. This is called **adverse possession.** Property owned by federal and state governments is not subject to adverse possession.

Under this doctrine, the transfer of the property is involuntary and does not require delivery of a deed. For a person to obtain title under adverse possession, the wrongful possession must be

- *For a statutorily prescribed period of time.* In most states, this period is between 10 and 20 years.
- *Open, visible, and notorious.* The adverse possessor must occupy the property so as to put the owner on notice of the possession.
- *Actual and exclusive.* The adverse possessor must physically occupy the premises. The planting of crops, grazing of animals, or building of a structure on the land constitutes physical occupancy.
- *Continuous and peaceful.* The occupancy must be uninterrupted for the required statutory period. Any break in normal occupancy terminates the adverse possession. This means that the adverse possessor may leave the property to go to work, to the store, on a vacation, and such. The adverse possessor cannot take the property by force from an owner.
- *Hostile and adverse.* The possessor must occupy the property without the express or implied permission of the owner. Thus, a lessee cannot claim title to property under adverse possession.

If the elements of adverse possession are met, the adverse possessor acquires clear title to the land. But title is acquired only as to the property actually possessed and occupied during the statutory period, and not the entire tract. For example, an adverse possessor who occupies one acre of a 200,000-acre ranch for the statutory period of time acquires title to only the one acre.

THE COURTHOUSE TEAM

Meet

Registrar of Deeds

Records of all transfers of real estate, claims against real estate, and the form of mortgages and means are generally maintained in a separate office under the direction of the Registrar, or Recorder, of Deeds. The Registrar of Deeds may be an elected or appointed official and is responsible for recording documents related to the transfer of real estate, and documents related to claims against property in the form of mortgages and liens. These records may be hardcopy or electronic copies, or a combination.

The Registrar of Deeds office is concerned with the authenticity of the deeds filed and proper authentication by way of notarization. In filing documents it is necessary to determine the standards of the individual office with regard to the form of the notarization and any additional paperwork required before it will accept the document for recording. This office also may collect the taxes as an agent for the taxing authority, whether local or state, and additional paperwork is required in this regard. The Registrar also generally charges a fee for filing documents, which may include additional charges when the pages exceed a certain number. It is always best to check with the office to determine the number and amounts of the checks, drafts, or other forms of payment required.

exhibit 13.8 Title insurance policy.

FIRST AMERICAN TITLE INSURANCE COMPANY

OWNERS FORM

SCHEDULE A

Policy Number
0000000000

Date of Policy
January 1, 2004

Amount of Insurance
$200,500.00

File Number **ABC 12345**

1. Name of Insured on the Owner's Policy:

   Mary Jane Smith

2. The estate or interest in the land described in this Schedule and which is encumbered by the insured mortgage is Fee Simple.

3. The estate or interest referred to herein is at Date of Policy vested in the insured:

   The Insured by virtue of a Deed from Thomas Jones dated 12/31/2001 and recorded 1/1/2002 in Maricopa County in Land Record Book 1111 page 111.

4. The land herein described is encumbered by the following mortgage or trust deed, and assignments:

   $150,500.00   Mary Jane Smith to Country Bank dated 12/31/2001 and recorded 1/1/2002 in Maricopa County in land Record Book 1111 page 222. and the mortgage or trust deeds, if any, shown in Schedule B hereof.

5. The land referred to in this policy is situated in the State of Arizona, County of Maricopa and is described as follows:

   See attached Exhibit "A"
   Commonly known as:

   County Parcel Number **12-12-12-12-12**
   123 Main Street
   Main Township
   Maricopa County, Arizona

PA–3

Form No. PA 13
(10-17-92)
ALTA Owner's Policy

POLICY OF TITLE INSURANCE

ISSUED BY

First American Title Insurance Company

SUBJECT TO THE EXCLUSIONS FROM COVERAGE, THE EXCEPTIONS FROM COVERAGE CONTAINED IN SCHEDULE B AND THE CONDITIONS AND STIPULATIONS, FIRST AMERICAN TITLE INSURANCE COMPANY, a California corporation, herein called the Company, insures, as of Date of Policy shown in Schedule A, against loss or damage, not exceeding the Amount of Insurance stated in Schedule A, sustained or incurred by the insured by reason of:

1. Title to the estate or interest described in Schedule A being vested other than as stated therein;
2. Any defect in or lien or encumbrance on the title;
3. Unmarketability of the title;
4. Lack of a right of access to and from the land.

The Company will also pay the costs, attorneys' fees and expenses incurred in defense of the title, as insured, but only to the extent provided in the Conditions and Stipulations.

First American Title Insurance Company

BY _Barbara S. Kennedy_ PRESIDENT

ATTEST _Mark R. Arneson_ SECRETARY

BY _____ COUNTERSIGNED

Many parts of the United States, particularly the West, were settled by "squatters" who came, staked a claim to open property, farmed or ranched the property, and acquired title to it from the government. The federal government encouraged such activity by holding "land rushes" that awarded title to the first person who staked a claim to the designated lands. Although the days of the Wild West are past, many states recognize modern-day squatters' rights under the doctrine of adverse possession. Consider the following case.

Edward and Mary Shaughnessey purchased a 16-acre tract in St. Louis county in 1954. Subsequently, they subdivided 12 acres into 18 lots offered for sale and retained possession of the remaining 4-acre tract. In 1967, Charles and Elaine Witt purchased lot 12, which is adjacent to the 4-acre tract. The Witts constructed and moved into a house on their lot. In 1968, they cleared an area of land that ran the length of their property and extended 40 feet onto the 4-acre tract. The Witts constructed a pool and a deck, planted a garden, made a playground for their children, set up a dog run, and built a fence along the edge of the property line, which included the now-disputed property. Neither the Witts nor the Shaughnesseys realized that the Witts had encroached on the Shaughnesseys' property.

In February 1988, the Shaughnesseys sold the 4-acre tract to Thomas and Rosanne Miller. When a survey showed the encroachment, the Millers demanded that the Witts remove the pool and cease using the property. When the Witts refused to do so, the Millers sued to quiet title. The Witts defended, arguing that they had obtained title to the disputed property by adverse possession.

The court of appeals agreed with the Witts. The court held that the Witts had proven the necessary elements for adverse possession under state law. The Witts' occupation of the land was open and notorious, actual and exclusive, hostile and adverse, continuous and peaceful, and had been so for the statutory period of 10 years. The court issued an order quieting title to the disputed property in the Witts' favor.

Questions

1. Did the Millers act ethically in trying to eject people who had occupied the land for 20 years?

2. Did the Witts act ethically in claiming title to someone else's land? Should they be allowed to benefit from their own mistake?

Easements

An **easement** is an interest in land that gives the holder the right to make limited use of another's property without taking anything from it. Typical easements include common driveways, party walls, right-of-ways, and such.

Easements may be *expressly* created by *grant* (where an owner gives another party an easement across his or her property) or *reservation* (where an owner sells land he or she owns but reserves an easement on the land). They also may be *implied* by (1) *implication*, where an owner subdivides a piece of property with a well, path, road, or other beneficial appurtenant that serves the entire parcel, or by (2) *necessity*; for example, "landlocked" property has an implied easement across surrounding property to enter and exit the landlocked property. Easements also can be created by adverse possession.

exhibit 13.9   *Dominant and servient easement.*

exhibit 13.10   *Easement by necessity—easement appurtenant.*

Exhibit 13.9 shows a dominant and servient easement with a common driveway. Exhibit 13.10 shows a landlocked real property and easement by necessity.

LANDLORD–TENANT RELATIONSHIP

Landlord–tenant relationships are common in the United States because (1) more than half of the population rent their homes, and (2) many businesses lease office space, stores, manufacturing facilities, and other commercial property. The parties to the relationship have certain legal rights and duties governed by a mixture of real estate and contract law.

A landlord–tenant relationship is created when the owner of a freehold estate (i.e., an estate in fee or a life estate) transfers a right to exclusively and temporarily possess the owner's property. The tenant receives a *nonfreehold estate* in the property—that is, the tenant has a right to possession of the property but not title to the property.

Types of Tenancy

The tenant's interest in the property is called a **leasehold estate,** or **leasehold.** The owner who transfers the leasehold estate is called the **landlord,** or **lessor.** The party to whom the leasehold estate is transferred is called the **tenant,** or **lessee.** *Tenancies* are of four types:

1. *Tenancy for years.* A **tenancy for years** is created when the landlord and the tenant agree on a specific duration for the lease. Any lease for a stated period—no matter how long or short—is called a tenancy for years. Examples of these arrangements include office space leased in a high-rise office building on a 30-year lease and a cabin leased for the summer. A tenancy for years terminates automatically, without notice, upon the expiration of the stated term.

2. *Periodic tenancy.* A **periodic tenancy** is created when a lease specifies intervals at which payments are due but does not specify the duration of the lease. A lease that states, "Rent is due on the first day of the month" establishes a periodic tenancy. Many such leases are created by implication. A periodic tenancy may be terminated by either party at the end of any payment interval, but adequate notice of the termination must be given. At common law, the notice period equaled the length of the payment period. Therefore, a month-to-month tenancy requires a one-month notice of termination.

3. *Tenancy at will.* A lease that may be terminated at any time by either party is termed a **tenancy at will.** A tenancy at will may be created expressly (e.g., "to tenant as long as landlord wishes") but more likely is to be created by implication. Most states have enacted statutes requiring minimum advance notice for the termination of a tenancy at will. The death of either party terminates a tenancy at will.

4. *Tenancy at sufferance.* A **tenancy at sufferance** is created when a tenant retains possession of the property after the expiration of another tenancy or a life estate without the owner's consent. That is, the owner suffers the *wrongful possession* of his or her property by the holdover tenant. This is not really a true tenancy but merely the possession of property without right. Technically, a tenant at sufferance is a trespasser. A tenant at sufferance is liable for the payment of rent during the period of sufferance. To evict a holdover tenant, most states require an owner to go through certain legal proceedings, called *eviction proceedings* or *unlawful detainer actions.* A few states allow owners to use self-help to evict a holdover tenant as long as force is not used.

The Lease

The rental agreement between the landlord and the tenant is called the **lease.** Leases generally can be either oral or written, except that most statutes of frauds require written leases for periods of time longer than one year. The lease must contain the essential terms of the parties' agreement. The lease is often a form contract prepared by the landlord and presented to the tenant. This is particularly true of residential leases. Other leases are negotiated between the parties. For example, a bank's lease of a branch office would be negotiated with the owner of the building. Exhibit 13.11 shows the opening two pages of a form lease agreement. Lease forms are often considerably longer than two pages.

Implied Warranty of Habitability

The courts of many jurisdictions hold that an **implied warranty of habitability** applies to residential leases for their duration. This warranty provides that the leased premises must be fit, safe, and suitable for ordinary residential use. On the one hand, unchecked rodent infestation, leaking roofs, and unworkable bathroom facilities have been held to breach the implied warranty of habitability. On the other hand, a small crack in the wall or some paint peeling from a door does not breach this warranty.

If the landlord's failure to maintain or repair the leased premises affects the tenant's use or enjoyment of the premises, state statutes and judicial decisions provide various remedies. Generally, the tenant may (1) withhold from his or her rent the amount by which the defect reduced the value of the premises to him or her, (2) repair the defect and deduct the cost of repairs from the rent due for the leased premises, (3) cancel the lease if the failure to repair constitutes constructive eviction, or (4) sue for damages for the amount the landlord's failure to repair the defect reduced the value of the leasehold.

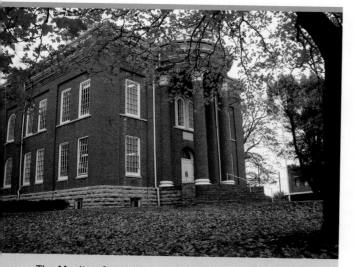

The Manitou County Court House in Missouri.

LAND-USE CONTROL

Although the United States has the most advanced private-property system in the world, ownership and possession of real estate are not free of government regulation. Pursuant to constitutional authority, federal, state, and local governments have enacted myriad laws that regulate ownership, possession, and use of real property. These laws are collectively referred to as **land-use control**.

Most counties and municipalities have enacted zoning ordinances to regulate land use. **Zoning ordinances** (1) establish use districts within the municipality (i.e., areas usually are designated residential, commercial, or industrial), (2) restrict the height, size, and location of buildings on a building site, and (3) establish aesthetic requirements or limitations for the exterior of buildings.

A zoning commission usually formulates zoning ordinances, conducts public hearings, and makes recommendations to the city council, which must vote to enact an ordinance. Once enacted, the zoning commission enforces the zoning ordinance. If landowners believe that a zoning ordinance is illegal or that it has been applied unlawfully to them or their property, they may

Form lease agreement. *exhibit* **13.11**

TEXAS ASSOCIATION OF REALTORS®

RESIDENTIAL LEASE AGREEMENT

USE OF THIS FORM BY PERSONS WHO ARE NOT MEMBERS OF THE TEXAS ASSOCIATION OF REALTORS® IS NOT AUTHORIZED.
©Texas Association of REALTORS®, Inc. 1997

NOTICE:
Landlord's broker, _____, ☐ will ☐ will not act as the property manager.
Future inquires about this Lease, rental payments, and security deposits should be directed to ☐ Landlord's broker ☐ Landlord.
Landlord's broker ☐ does ☐ does not have authority to bind Landlord to this Lease under another agreement or power of attorney.

1. **PARTIES:** The parties to this agreement (Lease) are the owner of the Property_____
_____(Landlord) and _____
_____(Tenant).

2. **PROPERTY:** Landlord leases to Tenant that certain real property known as_____
_____(address)_____(city) Texas_____ (zip code)
or as described on attached exhibit together with all its improvements including the following non-real estate items_____
_____, (the Property)
also described as (legal description recommended if lease is for one year or more):_____
_____.

3. **TERM:** This Lease commences on _____ (Commencement Date) and ends on
_____(Termination Date).

4. **AUTOMATIC RENEWAL AND NOTICE OF TERMINATION:** <u>This lease will automatically renew on a month-to-month basis
unless either party provides the other party written notice of termination at least thirty (30) days before the Termination Date or the
end of any renewal period.</u> VERBAL NOTICE IS NOT SUFFICIENT UNDER ANY CIRCUMSTANCES.   If this Lease is
automatically renewed on a month-to-month basis, either party may terminate the renewal of this Lease by providing written
notice to the other party and the renewal will terminate:

☐ A. on the last day of the month in which the notice is given if notice is given on the first day of the month. If the notice is given
on a day other than the first day of the month, the renewal will terminate on the last day of the month following the month in
which the notice is given.

☐ B. on the date designated in the notice but not sooner than thirty (30) days after the notice is given and, if necessary, rent will
be prorated on a daily basis.

If neither of the above choices is checked, box A will be deemed checked. Time is of the essence for providing notice of
termination (strict compliance with dates by which notice must be provided is required).

5. **RENT:**

A. <u>Monthly Rent</u>: Tenant will pay monthly rent in the amount of _____ for each full month during
this Lease. The first full month's rent is due and payable no later than _____ .
Thereafter, Tenant will pay the monthly rent on or before the first day of each month during this Lease. Weekends and
holidays do not delay or excuse Tenant's obligation to timely pay rent.

B. <u>Prorated Rent</u>: Tenant will pay as prorated rent from the Commencement Date to the first day of the following month the sum
of _____ on or before _____.

C. <u>Place of Payment</u>: Tenant will pay all rent to _____ (name of
payee) at _____
(address) in _____ (city) _____ (state) _____ (zip) or at
such other place as Landlord may designate from time to time in writing.

D. <u>Method of Payment</u>: Tenant must pay all rent timely and without demand, deduction, or offset, except as permitted by this
Lease. Time is of the essence for the payment of rent (strict compliance with rental due dates is required). Tenant must pay
all rent by check, money order, cashier's check, or other means acceptable to Landlord. If multiple Tenants occupy the

(TAR-2001) 10-01-97   Initialed for Identification by Tenants: _____, _____, _____, _____ and Landlord _____, _____   Page 1 of 8

GDAR 7161 10/97

exhibit **13.11**   *Form lease agreement, continued.*

Residential Lease concerning_____

Property, Landlord may require Tenants to pay monthly rents by one check or draft. By providing written notice to Tenant, Landlord may require Tenant to pay the amounts due under this Lease by certified funds.

   E.   <u>Common Areas</u>: Landlord is not obligated to pay any non-mandatory or user fees for Tenant's use of any common areas or facilities (such as pool or tennis courts).

   F.   <u>Rent Increases</u>: There will be no rent increases through the Termination Date. If this Lease is renewed automatically on a month-to-month basis, Landlord may increase the rent during the renewal period by providing written notice to Tenant that becomes effective the month following the 30th day after the notice is provided.

6.   **LATE CHARGES:**   If Tenant fails to timely pay any month's rent, Tenant will pay Landlord an initial late charge of _____ plus additional late charges of _____ per day thereafter until rent is paid in full. If Landlord <u>receives</u> the monthly rent by the _____ day of the month, Landlord will waive the late charges for that month. Any waiver of late charges under this paragraph will not affect or diminish any other right or remedy Landlord may exercise for Tenant's failure to timely pay rent (including reporting late payments to consumer reporting agencies).

7.   **RETURNED CHECKS:**   Tenant will pay _____ *(not to exceed $25)* for each check Tenant tenders to Landlord which is returned by the institution on which it is drawn for any reason, <u>plus initial and additional late charges</u> until Landlord has received payment.

8.   <u>**APPLICATION OF FUNDS:**</u>   <u>Landlord will apply all funds received from Tenant first to any non-rent obligations of Tenant including late charges, returned check charges, charge-backs for repairs, brokerage fees, and periodic utilities,   then to rent regardless of any notations on a check.</u>

9.   **PETS:**   THERE WILL BE NO PETS, unless authorized by a separate written pet agreement.   Tenant must not permit any pet, including mammals, reptiles, birds, fish, rodents, or insects on the Property, <u>even temporarily</u>, unless otherwise agreed by a separate written pet agreement. If Tenant violates the pet restrictions of this Lease, Tenant will pay Landlord a fee of _____ per day per pet for each day Tenant violates the pet restrictions as additional rent for any unauthorized pet. Landlord may remove or cause to be removed any unauthorized pet and deliver it to appropriate local authorities by providing at least 24-hour written notice to Tenant of Landlord's intention to remove the unauthorized pet. Landlord will not be liable for any harm, injury, death, or sickness to any unauthorized pet. Tenant is responsible and liable for any damage or required cleaning to the Property caused by any unauthorized pet and for all costs Landlord may incur in removing or causing any unauthorized pet to be removed.

10.   **DELAY OF OCCUPANCY:**   If Tenant is unable to occupy the Property on the Commencement Date because of construction on the Property or a prior tenant's holding over of the Property, Landlord will not be liable to Tenant for such delay and this Lease will remain enforceable. Landlord will abate rent on a daily basis during any delay. If Tenant is unable to occupy the Property after the third (3rd) day after the Commencement Date because of construction on the Property or a prior tenant's holding over of the Property, Tenant may terminate this Lease by giving written notice to Landlord before the Property becomes available to be occupied by Tenant, and Landlord will refund to Tenant the security deposit and any rent paid. These conditions do not apply to any delay in occupancy caused by cleaning or repairs.

11.   **SECURITY DEPOSIT:**

   A.   <u>Security Deposit</u>: Upon execution of this Lease, Tenant will pay a security deposit to Landlord in the amount of _____. "Security deposit" has the meaning assigned to that term in §92.102 of the Texas Property Code. No interest will be paid to Tenant on the security deposit. Landlord may place the security deposit in an interest bearing account and any interest earned will be paid to Landlord or Landlord's representative. **Notice: §92.108 of the Texas Property Code provides that Tenant may not withhold payment of any portion of the last month's rent on grounds that the security deposit is security for unpaid rent. Bad faith violations of §92.108 may subject Tenant to liability up to three times the rent wrongfully withheld and the Landlord's reasonable attorney's fees.**

   B.   <u>Refund</u>: Subchapter C of Chapter 92 of the Texas Property Code governs the obligations of the parties regarding the security deposit. <u>Tenant must give Landlord at least thirty (30) days written notice of surrender before Landlord is obligated to refund or account for the security deposit.</u> **Notice: The Texas Property Code does not obligate Landlord to return or account for the security deposit until 30 days after Tenant surrenders the Property (vacating and returning all keys and access devices) and gives Landlord a written statement of Tenant's forwarding address.**

   C.   <u>Deductions</u>:

      (1)   Landlord may deduct reasonable charges from the security deposit for:

         (a)   unpaid or accelerated rent;

(TAR-2001) 10-01-97   Initialed for Identification by Tenants: ____, ____, ____, ____ and Landlord ____, ____   Page 2 of 8 institute a court proceeding seeking judicial review of the ordinance or its application.

An owner who wishes to use his or her property for a use different from that permitted under a current zoning ordinance may seek relief from the ordinance by obtaining a **variance.** To do this, the landowner must prove that the ordinance causes an undue hardship by preventing him or her from making a reasonable return on the land as zoned. Variances tend to be difficult to obtain.

Zoning laws act prospectively; that is, uses and buildings that already exist in the zoned area are permitted to continue even though they do not fit within new zoning ordinances. Such uses are called **nonconforming uses.** For example, if a new zoning ordinance is enacted making an area a residential zone, an existing funeral parlor is a nonconforming use.

ENVIRONMENTAL PROTECTION

In the 1970s, the federal government began enacting statutes to protect our nation's air and water from pollution. Federal legislation also was enacted to regulate hazardous wastes and to protect wildlife. In many instances, states enacted their own environmental laws that now coexist with federal law as long as they do not directly conflict with the federal law or unduly burden interstate commerce. These laws provide both civil and criminal penalties. The development of such a vast body of law in such a short time is unprecedented in U.S. history. Environmental protection is one of the most important, and costly, issues facing business and society today.

In 1970, Congress created the **Environmental Protection Agency (EPA)** to coordinate the implementation and enforcement of the federal environmental protection laws. The EPA has broad rule-making powers to adopt regulations advancing the laws it is empowered to administer. The agency also has adjudicative powers to hold hearings, make decisions, and order remedies for violations of federal environmental laws. In addition, the EPA can initiate judicial proceedings in court against suspected violators of federal environmental laws.

Natural Resources Defense Council, Inc. v. EPA

824 F.2d 1146 (1987)   United States Court of Appeals, District of Columbia Circuit

FACTS

Vinyl chloride, a gaseous synthetic chemical used in the manufacture of plastics, is a strong carcinogen. The EPA issued a notice of proposed rule making to establish emission standards for vinyl chloride as a toxic pollutant under Section 112 of the Clean Air Act. Section 112 stipulates that the EPA must set minimum emission standards for toxic air pollutants at the level that in its judgment "provides an ample margin of safety to protect the public health." The EPA issued a final order requiring emissions of vinyl chloride to be set at a level that would provide an ample margin of safety for human beings. The National Resources Defense Council, Inc. (NRDC), an environmental activist organization, sued the EPA, alleging that its final order violated Section 112. The NRDC argued that the EPA must set a zero level of emissions of vinyl chloride.

ISSUE

Must the EPA set a zero level of emissions of the toxic pollutant vinyl chloride?

IN THE LANGUAGE OF THE COURT

Bork, Circuit Judge.

To accept the NRDC's contention, we would have to conclude that Congress mandated massive economic and social dislocations by shutting down entire industries. The EPA has determined that zero-emissions standard for toxic pollutants would result in the elimination of such activities as the generation of electricity from either coal burning or nuclear energy; the manufacture of steel; the mining, smelting, or refining of virtually any mineral (e.g., copper, iron, lead, zinc, and limestone); the manufacture of synthetic organic chemicals; and the refining, storage, or dispensing of any petroleum product. It is simply not possible that Congress intended such havoc in the American economy, and not a single representative or senator mentioned the fact. Thus, we find no support for the NRDC's extreme position in the language or legislative history of the act.

The EPA's decision does not require a finding that "safe" means "risk-free" or a finding that the determination is free from uncertainty. Instead, we find only that the EPA's decision must be based upon an expert judgment with regard to the level of emission that will result in an "acceptable" risk to health. In this regard, the EPA must determine what inferences should be drawn from available scientific data and decide what risks are acceptable in the world in which we live.

DECISION AND REMEDY

The court of appeals held that the EPA must reach a determination of what amount of vinyl chloride is "safe" and then set emission standards accordingly to provide for an "ample margin of safety."

Questions

1. Should emission levels of toxic pollutants be set at "risk-free" levels rather than just "safe" levels? Explain.

2. Do environmental activist groups and organizations serve an important public purpose? Explain.

3. Can you think of instances in which environmental laws should be used to shut down whole industries? Explain.

LEGAL TERMINOLOGY

Adverse possession

Air-space parcel

Bailee

Bailment

Bailor

Community property

Condominium

Cooperative

Co-ownership (concurrent
  ownership)

Deed

Duty of ordinary care

Duty of reasonable care (duty of
  ordinary care)

Easement

Environmental Protection Agency

Estate *pur autre vie*

Estray statute

Fee simple absolute (fee simple)

Fee simple defeasible (qualified fee)

Fixture

Freehold estate

Future interest

Grantee

Grantor

Implied warranty of habitability

Intangible property

Joint tenancy

Land

Landlord/lessor

Land-use control

Lease

Leasehold estate (leasehold)

Life estate

Mutual benefit bailment

Nonconforming uses

Periodic tenancy

Personal property

Plant life and vegetation

Quiet title

Quitclaim deed

Real property

Remainder

Remainderman

Reversion

Right of survivorship

Subsurface rights (mineral rights)

Tangible property

Tenancy at sufferance

Tenancy at will

Tenancy by the entirety

Tenancy for years

Tenancy in common

Tenant/lessee

Title insurance

Variance

Warranty deed

Zoning ordinance

Summary

Personal Property

Definition	Everything that is not real property; sometimes referred to as *goods* or *chattels*.
Types of Property	1. *Tangible property:* Physically defined property such as goods, animals, and minerals. 2. *Intangible property:* Rights that cannot be reduced to physical form, such as stock certificates, bonds, and copyrights.

Bailments

Description	Bailments occur when the owner of personal property delivers the property to another person to be held, stored, or delivered, or for some other purpose.
Parties	1. *Bailor:* Owner of the property. 2. *Bailee:* Party to whom the property is delivered.
Mutual Benefit Bailment	Arises when both parties benefit from the bailment. This includes commercial bailments. The bailee owes a duty of *reasonable care* (or *ordinary care*) and is liable for *ordinary negligence*.

Real Property

Nature of Real Property	*Real property* is immovable; it includes land, buildings, subsurface rights, air rights, plant life, and fixtures.

Freehold Estates

Definition	Estates where the owner has a present possessory interest in the real property.
Estates in Fee	1. *Fee simple absolute* (or *fee simple*): Highest form of ownership. 2. *Fee simple defeasible* (or *qualified fee*): Estate that ends if a specified condition occurs.
Life Estates	An interest in real property that lasts for the life of a specified person; called an *estate pour autre vie* if the time is measured by the life of a third person.
Future Interest	Right to possess real property in the future rather than currently.

(continued)

Reversion	Right to possession that returns to the grantor after the expiration of a limited or contingent estate.
Remainder	Right to possession that goes to a third person after the expiration of a limited or contingent estate; the third person is called a *remainderman*.

Concurrent Ownership

Concurrent Ownership	Where two or more persons jointly own real property.
Joint Tenancy	Owners may transfer their interests without the consent of co-owners; transfer severs the joint tenancy. Under the *right of survivorship*, the interest of a deceased owner passes to his or her co-owners.
Tenancy in Common	Owners may transfer their interests without the consent of co-owners; transfer does not sever the tenancy in common. Interest of a deceased owner passes to his or her estate.
Tenancy by the Entirety	Form of co-ownership that can be used only by a married couple; neither spouse may transfer his or her interest without the other spouse's consent. A surviving spouse has the right of survivorship.
Community Property	Form of co-ownership that applies only to a married couple; neither spouse may transfer his or her interest without the other spouse's consent. When a spouse dies, the surviving spouse automatically receives one-half of the community property.
Condominium	Owners have title to their individual units and own the common areas as tenants in common; owners may transfer their interests without the consent of other owners.
Cooperative	A corporation owns the building and the residents own shares of the corporation. Usually, owners may not transfer their shares without the approval of the other owners.

Transfer of Ownership of Real Property

Sale of Real Estate	An owner sells his or her property to another for consideration.
Marketable Title	A title free of encumbrances, defects in title, or other defects.
Deed	Instrument used to convey real property by sale or gift. 1. *Warranty deed:* Provides the most protection to the grantee because the grantor makes warranties against defect in title. 2. *Quitclaim deed:* Provides least amount of protection to the grantee because the grantor transfers only the interest he or she has in the property.

(continued)

Adverse Possession	A person who occupies another's property acquires title to the property if the occupation has been: 1. For a statutory period of time (in many states, 10 to 20 years) 2. Open, visible, and notorious 3. Actual and exclusive 4. Continuous and peaceful 5. Hostile and adverse
Easement	An interest in land that gives the holder the right to make limited use of another's property without taking anything from it (e.g., driveways, party walls).

Landlord–Tenant Relationship

Definition	Created when an owner of a freehold estate transfers a right to another to exclusively and temporarily possess the owner's property.
Types of Tenancy	1. *Tenancy for years:* Tenancy for a specified period of time. 2. *Periodic tenancy:* Tenancy for a period of time determined by the payment interval. 3. *Tenancy at will:* Tenancy that may be terminated at any time by either party. 4. *Tenancy at sufferance:* Tenancy created by the wrongful possession of property.
Lease	The rental agreement between the landlord and the tenant that contains the essential terms of the parties' agreement.

Land-Use Control

Public Regulation of Land Use	*Zoning ordinances:* Laws adopted by local governments that restrict use of property, set building standards, and establish architectural requirements. 1. *Variance:* Permits an owner to make a nonzoned use of his or her property; requires permission from a zoning board. 2. *Nonconforming use:* A nonzoned use that is permitted (grandfathered in) when an area is rezoned.

Environmental Protection

Laws	Federal and state governments have enacted environmental protection statutes to control pollution and to penalize those who violate these statutes.
Environmental Protection Agency (EPA)	Federal administrative agency created in 1970 that is empowered to implement and enforce federal environmental protection statutes. The EPA can adopt regulations to interpret and enforce the laws it is authorized to administer.

Working the Web

1. Using the Findlaw search engine, find materials on real estate contracts.

2. Search Legal Online, an Internet periodical for lawyers, for useful articles about real property. Visit at www.legalonline.com.

3. Search the ABA Guide to Home Ownership at www.abanet.org/publiced/practical/books/home_ownership/home.html.

4. Find U.S. Department of Housing and Urban Development (HUD) information for home buyers at www.hud.gov.

5. Find a copy of the Federal Fair Housing Act at Cornell Law School's Legal Information Institute at www.law.cornell.edu/uscode/42/ch45.html.

6. Obtain an overview of landlord–tenant law at Cornell Law School's Legal Information Institute, with links to both federal and state materials, at www.law.cornell.edu/topics/landlord_tenant.html.

7. Visit the ABA section of real property, probate, and trust law, including the Environmental Land Use Committee, at www.abanet.org/rppt/home.html.

Questions
CRITICAL LEGAL THINKING AND WRITING

1. Describe personal property. How does this differ from real property?

2. What does an estray statute provide? What public policy underlies an estray statute?

3. Describe how a bailment occurs. Who are the parties to a bailment? How is liability for lost or damaged goods assessed?

4. What is a fee simple absolute (or fee simple) estate? How does this differ from a life estate?

5. Describe the differences between a joint tenancy, tenancy in common, and tenancy by the entirety.

6. What is the purpose of a recording statute?

7. Describe the doctrine of adverse possession. Why does the law recognize this doctrine?

8. What is an easement? Describe the difference between an express easement and an implied easement.

9. Describe the differences between tenancy for years, periodic tenancy, tenancy at will, and tenancy by sufferance.

10. What purpose is served by environmental protection laws? Has the law gone far enough to protect the environment?

Questions

ETHICS: ANALYSIS AND DISCUSSION

1. What obligation does the legal team have in advising clients that live in one state but own property in another?

2. Does the preparation of a report for a client showing the history of the ownership of a property, as shown in public records, and claims against the property, as shown in public records, constitute the practice of law?

3. In your jurisdiction is there a priority given based upon the time of filing of deeds to real estate? Is the failure to promptly file a deed malpractice?

Contingent Fees

There are few certainties in the area of ethics, for paralegals or in any profession. What qualifies as ethical conduct is in most cases based on state law and court interpretation applied to a set of facts. The citation listed below represents one legal opinion and is provided as a research starting point. Do not assume that the same rule applies in your jurisdiction. For the following:

- *Prepare a written statement based on your state law.*
- *Use your state bar association website as a starting point.*

As an experienced paralegal, you have investigated many complex cases and developed a reputation for discovering little-known facts and obtaining information not normally obtained by investigators. A law firm proposes to have its client hire you to conduct the investigation of a complex and troublesome environmental case involving a major corporation that appears to be hiding information. [*Ethics Opinion 510, Texas Professional Ethics Committee Opinions.*] Can you accept the case with your compensation based on a contingent fee if paid directly from the client from his or her award, if any? From the firm? Can you accept a "substantial" bonus from the law firm?

CASES *for Discussion*

Naab v. Nolan

327 S.E.2d 151 (WV 1985)

13.1 FACTS

In 1973, Joseph and Helen Naab purchased a tract of land in a subdivision of Williamstown, West Virginia. At the time of purchase, the property had both a house and a small concrete garage. Evidence showed that the garage had been erected sometime prior to 1952 by one of the Naabs' predecessors in title. In 1975, Roger and Cynthia Nolan purchased a lot contiguous to that owned by the Naabs. The following year, the Nolans had their property surveyed. The survey indicated that one corner of the Naabs' garage encroached 1.22 feet onto the Nolans' property and the other corner encroached 0.91 feet over the property line. The Nolans requested that the Naabs remove the garage from their property. When the Naabs refused, the lawsuit ensued.

ISSUE

Who wins?

Hill v. Pinelawn Memorial Park, Inc.

282 S.E.2d 779 (N.C. 1981)

13.2 FACTS

On October 13, 1972, Johnnie H. Hill and his wife, Clara Mae, entered into an installment sales contract with Pinelawn Memorial Park (Pinelawn) to purchase a mausoleum crypt. They made it clear they wanted to buy crypt "D," which faced eastward toward Kinston. The Hills paid $1,035 down payment and continued to make $33.02 monthly payments.

On February 13, 1974, William C. Shackleford and his wife, Jennie L., entered into an agreement with Pinelawn to purchase crypt D. They paid $1,406 down payment and two annual installments of $912. The Hills

were first put on notice of the second contract when they visited Pinelawn in February 1977 and saw the Shackleford name on crypt D. The Hills then tendered full payment to Pinelawn for crypt D. On April 25, 1977, the Hills sued Pinelawn and the Shacklefords. They demanded specific performance on the contract and the deed to crypt D. Upon being served with summons, the Shacklefords discovered that they had no deed to the crypt and demanded one from Pinelawn. Pinelawn delivered them a deed dated August 18, 1977, which the Shackelfords recorded in the County Register on September 9, 1977.

ISSUE

Who owns crypt D?

Love v. Monarch Apartments

771 P.2d 79 (Kan.App. 1989)

13.3 FACTS

Sharon Love entered into a written lease agreement with Monarch Apartments for apartment 4 at 441 Winfield in Topeka, Kansas. Shortly after moving in, she experienced serious problems with termites. Her walls swelled, clouds of dirt came out, and when she checked on her children one night, she saw termites flying around the room. She complained to Monarch, which arranged for the apartment to be fumigated.

When the termite problem persisted, Monarch moved Love and her children to apartment 2. Upon moving in, Love noticed that roaches crawled over the walls, ceilings, and floors of the apartment. She complained, and Monarch called an exterminator, who sprayed the apartment. When the roach problem persisted, Love vacated the premises.

ISSUE

Did Love lawfully terminate the lease?

Souders v. Johnson

501 So.2d 745 (Fla.App. 1987)

13.4 FACTS

When Dr. Arthur M. Edwards died, leaving a will disposing of his property, he left the villa-type condominium in which he lived, its "contents," and $10,000 to his stepson, Ronald W. Souders. Edwards left the residual of his estate to other named legatees. In administering the estate, certain stock certificates, passbook savings accounts, and other bank statements were found in Edwards' condominium. Souders claimed that these items belonged to him because they were "contents" of the condominium. The other legatees opposed Souders' claim, alleging that the disputed property was intangible property and not part of the contents of the condominium.

The value of the property was as follows: condominium, $138,000; furniture in condominium, $4,000; stocks, $377,000; and passbook and other bank accounts, $124,000.

ISSUE

Who is entitled to the stocks and bank accounts? Do you think Souders acted ethically in this case?

Walker v. Quillen

Read the following case, excerpted from the court of appeals opinion. Review and brief the case. In your brief, answer the following questions:

1. Who were the plaintiffs (appellees)? Who was the defendant (appellant)?

2. Describe the tract of land owned by the plaintiffs and defendant.

3. What was the issue in this case? How did the court decide this issue?

Moore, Justice.

Pursuant to Supreme Court Rule 25(a), appellees, Elizabeth Star Ayres and Clara Louise Quillen, have moved to affirm a judgment of the Court of Chancery granting an implied easement in favor of appellees' servient estate, as against the dominant estate of appellant, Irvin C. Walker ("Walker"). The appellees contend that sufficient evidence supports the findings of the Court of Chancery and that there was no abuse of discretion in granting the implied easement. We agree and affirm.

The appellees own in fee simple absolute a tract of land in Sussex County known as "Bluff Point." The tract is surrounded on three sides by Rehoboth Bay and is landlocked on the fourth side by Walker's land. At one time, the two tracts in question were held by a common owner. In 1878, Bluff Point was sold in fee simple absolute apart from the other holdings, thereby landlocking the parcel. A narrow dirt road, which traverses Walker's land, connects Bluff Point to a public road and is its only means of access.

Under the doctrine of implied easement or easement by necessity, the Court of Chancery found that the appellees were entitled to cross over a portion of Walker's land for access to Bluff Point. The court also found that water access, even if a reasonable substitute for land access, was not feasible because of the shallowness of the water surrounding Bluff Point. There is ample evidence in the record to support the finding that the two tracts originated from the unified holdings of one owner, and that an implied easement was created by the severance that landlocked Bluff Point. The record also sufficiently supports the finding that navigable access to Bluff Point was not feasible. Now, therefore, it is ordered that the judgment of the Court of Chancery be, and the same hereby is, affirmed.

CHAPTER 14

Agency and Employment Law

Let every eye negotiate for itself, and trust no agent.

WILLIAM SHAKESPEARE, *MUCH ADO ABOUT NOTHING*

Introduction

If businesspeople had to conduct all of their business personally, the scope of their activities would be severely curtailed. Partnerships would not be able to operate; corporations could not act through managers and employees; and sole proprietorships would not be able to hire employees. The use of agents (or agency), which allows one person to act on behalf of another, solves this problem.

There are many examples of agency relationships, including a salesperson who sells goods for a store, an executive who works for a corporation, a partner who acts on behalf of a partnership, an attorney who is hired to represent a client, a real estate broker who is employed to sell a house, and so on. Agency is governed by a large body of common law, known as *agency law*.

Employment law is a burgeoning area of the law. The U.S. Congress has created many federal laws that protect job applicants and employees from discrimination in employment. Paralegals will be called on to conduct research, assist lawyers in the preparation and review of employment contracts, and prepare for litigation in this exciting area of the law. Agency law and employment law are discussed in this chapter.

exhibit 14.1 *The principal–agent relationship.*

THE NATURE OF AGENCY

Agency relationships are formed by the mutual consent of a principal and an agent. Section 1(1) of the Restatement (Second) of Agency defines *agency* as a *fiduciary relationship* "which results from the manifestation of consent by one person to another that the other shall act in his behalf and subject to his control, and consent by the other so to act." The Restatement (Second) of Agency is the reference source of the rules of agency. A party who employs another person to act on his or her behalf is called a **principal.** A party who agrees to act on behalf of another is called an **agent.** The principal–agent relationship is commonly referred to as an **agency.** This relationship is depicted in Exhibit 14.1

Any person who has the capacity to contract can appoint an agent to act on his or her behalf. Generally, persons who lack contractual capacity, such as insane persons and minors, cannot appoint an agent. However, the court can appoint a legal guardian or other representative to handle the affairs of insane persons, minors, and others who lack capacity to contract. With court approval, these representatives can enter into enforceable contracts on behalf of the persons they represent.

An agency can be created only to accomplish a lawful purpose. Agency contracts that are created for illegal purposes or are against public policy are void and unenforceable. For example, a principal cannot hire an agent to kill another person. Some agency relationships are prohibited by law. For example, unlicensed agents cannot be hired to perform the duties of certain licensed professionals (e.g., doctors and lawyers).

KINDS OF EMPLOYMENT RELATIONSHIPS

Businesses usually have three kinds of employment relationships: (1) employer–employee relationships; (2) principal–agent relationships; and (3) principal–independent contractor relationships. Table 14.1 summarizes these relationships.

Employer–Employee Relationship

An **employer–employee relationship** exists when an employer hires an employee to perform some form of physical service. For example, a welder on General Motors Corporation's assembly line is employed in an employer–employee relationship because he performs a task.

An employee is not an agent unless he or she is specifically empowered to enter into contracts on the principal employer's behalf. Employees may enter into only the contracts that are within the scope of their employment. The welder in the previous example is not an agent because he cannot enter into contracts on behalf of General Motors Corporation. If the company empowers him to enter into contracts, he becomes an agent.

Principal–Agent Relationship

A **principal–agent relationship** is formed when an employer hires an employee and gives that employee authority to act and enter into contracts on his or her behalf. The extent of this authority is governed by any express agreement between the parties and implied from the circumstances of the agency. For example, the president of a corporation usually has the authority to enter into major contracts on the corporation's behalf, but a supervisor on the corporation's assembly line may have the authority only to purchase the supplies necessary to keep the line running.

Principal–Independent Contractor Relationship

A **principal–independent contractor relationship** exists when principals employ outsiders—persons and businesses who are not employees—to perform certain tasks on their behalf. These persons and businesses are called **independent contractors.** Professionals and tradespeople who commonly act as independent contractors include doctors, dentists, stockbrokers, architects, certified public accountants, real estate brokers, and plumbers.

A principal can authorize an independent contractor to enter into contracts. Principals are bound by the authorized contracts of their independent contractors. For example, if a client authorizes an attorney to settle a case within a certain dollar amount and the attorney does so, the settlement agreement is binding.

Summary of employment relationships.   *table* 14.1

TYPE OF RELATIONSHIP	DESCRIPTION
Employer–employee	The employer has the right to control the physical conduct of the employee.
Principal–agent	The agent has the authority to act on behalf of the principal as authorized by the principal and implied from the agency. An employee is often the agent of his employer.
Principal–independent contractor	The principal has no control over the details of the independent contractor's conduct. An independent contractor is usually not an agent of the principal.

Employment-at-Will

Employees who are offered express employment contracts for a definite term cannot be discharged in violation of the contract. Most employees, however, do not have employment contracts; their status is termed **employment-at-will.**

Under common law, an at-will employee could be discharged by an employer at any time for any reason. This laissez-faire doctrine gave the employer great flexibility in responding to its changing needs. It also caused unfair results for some employees. Today, there are many statutory, contract, public policy, and tort exceptions to the at-will doctrine. These exceptions are:

- **Statutory exception.** Federal and state statutes that restrict the employment-at-will doctrine include federal labor laws that prohibit employers from discharging employees who are members of labor unions in violation of labor laws or collective bargaining agreements. Title VII and other federal and state antidiscrimination laws that prohibit employers from engaging in race, sex, religious, age, disability, or other forms of discrimination are additional examples of such laws.

- **Contract exception.** The courts have held that an implied-in-fact contract can be created between an employer and an employee. Implied-in-fact contracts develop from the conduct of the parties. For example, a company bulletin, handbook, or personnel policy might mention that employees who do their jobs properly will not be discharged. This can be construed as an implied promise that an employee can be discharged only for good cause. Thus, the employer's ability to discharge an employee at will is removed. An employee who is discharged in violation of an implied-in-fact contract can sue the employer for breach of contract.

- **Public policy exception.** The most used common-law exception to the employment-at-will doctrine is the *public policy exception*. This rule states that an employee cannot be discharged if such discharge violates the public policy of the jurisdiction. Examples of violations of public policy are discharging an employee for serving as a juror, refusing to do an act in violation of the law (e.g., refusing to engage in dumping of toxic wastes in violation of environmental protection laws), refusing to engage in illegal research (e.g., research that violates patent laws or animal protection laws), and refusing to distribute defective products.

An employee who has been wrongfully discharged can sue his or her employer for damages and other remedies (reinstatement, back pay, and such). Punitive damages may be recovered if the employer has engaged in fraud or other intentional conduct.

FORMATION OF THE AGENCY RELATIONSHIP

An agency and the resulting authority of an agent can arise in any of these four ways: (1) express agency, (2) implied agency, (3) apparent agency, and (4) agency by ratification. Each of these types of agencies is discussed in the paragraphs that follow.

Express Agency

The most common form of agency is **express agency.** In an express agency, the agent has the authority to contract or otherwise act on the principal's behalf as expressly stated in the agency agreement. In addition, the agent may possess certain implied or apparent authority to act on the principal's behalf (as discussed later in this chapter).

Express agency occurs when a principal and an agent expressly agree to enter into an agency agreement with each other. Express agency contracts can be either oral or written unless the Statute of Frauds stipulates that they must be written. For example, in most states a real estate broker's contract to sell real estate must be in writing.

If the principal and agent enter into an **exclusive agency contract,** the principal cannot employ any agent other than the exclusive agent. If the principal does so, the exclusive agent can recover damages from the principal. If an agency is not an exclusive agency, the principal can employ more than one agent to try to accomplish a stated purpose. When multiple agents are employed, the agencies with all of the agents terminate when any one of the agents accomplishes the stated purpose.

A **power of attorney** is one of the most formal types of express agency agreements. It is often used to give an agent the power to sign legal documents, such as deeds to real estate, on behalf of the principal. The two kinds of powers of attorney are (1) **general,** which confers broad powers on the agent to act in any matters on the principal's behalf; and (2) **special,** which limits the agent to acts specifically enumerated in an agreement. The agent is called an **attorney-in-fact** even though he or she does not have to be a lawyer. Powers of attorney must be written, and usually they must be notarized. A general power of attorney is shown in Exhibit 14.2.

Implied Agency

In many situations, a principal and an agent do not expressly create an agency. Instead, the agency is implied from the conduct of the parties. This type of agency is referred to as **implied agency.** The extent of the agent's authority is determined from the facts and circumstances of the particular situation. Implied authority can be conferred by (1) industry custom, (2) prior dealing between the parties, (3) the agent's position, and (4) the acts deemed necessary to carry out the agent's duties. The court may deem other factors relevant as well. Implied authority cannot conflict with express authority or with stated limitations on express authority.

Often, even an express agency agreement does not provide enough detail to cover all contingencies that may arise in the future regarding the performance of the agency. In this case, the agent possesses certain implied authority to act. This implied authority is sometimes referred to as *incidental authority*. Certain emergency situations may arise in the course of an agency. If the agent cannot contact the principal for instructions, the agent has implied emergency powers to take all actions reasonably necessary to protect the principal's property and rights.

Apparent Agency

Apparent agency (or **agency by estoppel**) arises when a principal creates the appearance of an agency that in actuality does not exist. Where an apparent agency is established, the principal is estopped from denying the agency relationship and is bound to contracts entered into by the apparent agent while acting within the scope of the apparent agency. Note that it is the principal's actions—not the agent's—that create an apparent agency.

exhibit **14.2** *Sample general power of attorney.*

POWER OF ATTORNEY

Know All Men by These Presents: That _____ the undersigned (jointly and severally, if more than one) hereby make, constitute and appoint _____ My true and lawful Attorney for me and in my name, place and stead and for my use and benefit:

(a) To ask, demand, sue for, recover, collect and receive each and every sum of money, debt, account, legacy, bequest, interest, dividend, annuity and demand (which now is or hereafter shall become due, owing or payable) belonging to or claimed by me, and to use and take any lawful means for the recovery thereof by legal process or otherwise, and to execute and deliver a satisfaction or release therefor, together with the right and powers to compromise or compound any claim or demand;

(b) To exercise any or all of the following powers as to real property, any interest therein and/or any building thereon: To contract for, purchase, receive and take possession thereof and of evidence of title thereto; to lease the same for any term or purpose, including leases for business, residence, and oil and/or mineral development; to sell, exchange, grant or convey the same with or without warranty; and to mortgage, transfer in trust, or otherwise encumber or hypothecate the same to secure payment of a negotiable or non-negotiable note or performance of any obligation or agreement;

(c) To exercise any or all of the following powers as to all kinds of personal property and goods, wares and merchandise, chosen in action and other property in possession or in action: To contract for, buy, sell, exchange, transfer and in any legal manner deal in and with the same and to mortgage, transfer in trust, or otherwise encumber or hypothecate the same to secure payment of a negotiable or non-negotiable note or performance of any obligation or agreement;

(d) To borrow money and to execute and deliver negotiable or non-negotiable notes therefor with or without security, and to loan money and receive negotiable or non-negotiable notes therefor with such security as said Attorney shall deem proper;

(e) To create, amend, supplement and terminate any trust and to instruct and advise the trustee of any trust wherein I am or may be trustor or beneficiary; to represent and vote stock, exercise stock rights, accept and deal with any dividend, distribution or bonus, join in any corporate financing reorganization, merger, liquidation, consolidation or other action and the extension, compromise, conversion, adjustment, enforcement or foreclosure, singly or in conjunction with others of any corporate stock, bond, note, debenture or other security; to compound, compromise, adjust, settle and satisfy any obligation secured or unsecured, owing by or to me and to give or accept any property and/or money whether or not equal to or less in value than the amount owing in payment, settlement or satisfaction thereof;

(f) To transact business of any kind or class and as my act and deed to sign, execute, acknowledge and deliver any deed, lease, assignment of lease covenant, indenture, indemnity, agreement, mortgage, deed of trust, assignment of mortgage or of the beneficial interest under deed of trust, extension or renewal of any obligation, subordination or waiver or priority, hypothecation, bottomry, charter-party, bill of lading, bill of sale, bill, bond, note, whether negotiable or non-negotiable, receipt, evidence of debt, full or partial release or satisfaction of mortgage, judgment and other debt, request for partial or full reconveyance of deed of trust and such other instruments in writing of any kind or class as may be necessary or proper in the premises.

Giving and Granting unto my said Attorney full power and authority to do and perform all and every act and thing whatsoever, requisite, necessary or appropriate to be done in and about the premises as fully to all intents, and purposes as I might or could do it personally present, hereby ratifying all that my said Attorney shall lawfully do or cause to be done by virtue of these presents. The powers and authority hereby conferred upon my said Attorney shall be applicable to all real and personal property or interests therein now owned or hereafter required by me and whenever situate.

My said Attorney is empowered hereby to determine in said Attorney's sole discretion the time when, purpose for and manner in which any power herein conferred upon said Attorney shall be exercised, and the conditions, provisions and covenants of any instrument or document which may be executed by said Attorney pursuant hereto and in the acquisition or disposition of real or personal property, my said Attorney shall have exclusive power to fix the terms thereof for cash, credit and/or property, and if on credit with or without security.

The undersigned, if a married person, hereby further authorizes and empowers my said Attorney, as my duly authorized agent, to join in my behalf, in the execution of any instrument by which any community real property or any interest therein, now owned or hereafter acquired by my spouse and myself, or either of us, is sold, leased, encumbered, or conveyed.

When the context to requires, the masculine gender includes the feminine and/or neuter, and the singular number includes the plural.

Witness my hand this _____ day of _____ 20_____

STATE OF CALIFORNIA, COUNTY OF _____ SS.

On _____ before me, the undersigned, a Notary Public in and for said State personally appeared _____

_____

personally known to me (or proved to me on the basis of satisfactory evidence) to be the person _____ whose name _____ subscribed to the within instrument and acknowledge that _____ executed the same.

WITNESS my hand and official seal.

Signature _____

Name *(Typed or Printed)* _____

(This area for official seal)

Apparent Agency

Franchising has become a major form of conducting business in the United States. In a franchise agreement, one company (called the franchisor) licenses another company (called the franchisee) to use its trade name, trademarks and service marks, and trade secrets. Many fast-food restaurants, gasoline stations, motels and hotels, and other businesses are operated in this fashion.

The franchisor and franchisee are independently owned businesses. A principal–agent relationship usually is not created by the franchise. If no express or implied agency is created, the franchisor would not normally be civilly liable for the tortious conduct (e.g., negligence) of the franchisee. Liability could be imposed on the franchisor, however, if an apparent agency is shown. Consider the following case.

The Howard Johnson Company (HJ) operates a chain of hotels, motels, and restaurants across the United States. Approximately 75 percent of the HJ motor lodges are owned and operated by franchisees licensed by HJ to do business under the "Howard Johnson" trade name and trademarks. The rest are company-owned.

Orlando Executive Park, Inc. (OEP) is a corporate franchisee that owns and operates an HJ motor lodge franchise in Orlando, Florida. The motor lodge is part of a large complex known as "Howard Johnson's Plaza," located off Interstate 4. The motor lodge contains approximately 300 guest rooms in six separate buildings.

P.D.R. (name withheld by the court), a 35-year-old married woman and mother of a young child, worked as a supervisor for a restaurant chain. Her work occasionally required her to travel and stay overnight in Orlando. On October 22, 1975, P.D.R. stopped to stay at the HJ motor lodge in Orlando. At approximately 9:30 P.M., P.D.R. registered for her previously reserved room at the lodge. The registration form did not inform her that the hotel was an HJ franchisee. P.D.R. parked her car in the motor lodge parking lot and proceeded with her suitcase to her ground-floor room in Building A, which was located directly behind the registration office. P.D.R. then went back to her car to get some papers. After obtaining the papers from her car, P.D.R. returned to Building A. As she proceeded down an interior hallway of the building toward her room, she was accosted by a man she had previously seen standing behind the registration office. The man struck her in the throat and neck and choked her until she became semiconscious. When P.D.R. fell to the floor, her assailant sat on top of her and stripped her of her jewelry. He then dragged her down the hallway and beneath a secluded stairway, where he brutally beat her. The assailant then disappeared into the night and has never been identified.

P.D.R. suffered serious physical and psychological injury, including memory loss, mental confusion, and an inability to tolerate and communicate with people. Within one year of the assault, she lost her job. P.D.R. suffers permanent injury that requires expensive, long-term medical and psychiatric treatment. P.D.R. brought a tort action against OEP and HJ and sought actual and punitive damages against both of them.

The jury had little trouble finding that OEP had breached its duty of care and was liable. Evidence showed that other criminal activity had occurred previously on the premises but that OEP failed to warn guests, including P.D.R., of the danger. In fact, OEP management actively discouraged criminal investigations by the sheriff's deputies, thereby minimizing any deterrent effect they might have had. Further evidence showed that the dark and secluded stairwell area where P.D.R. was dragged was a security hazard that should have been boarded up or better lit.

The jury also found HJ liable to P.D.R. under the doctrine of apparent agency. The appellate court stated: "While OEP might not be HJ's agent for all purposes, the signs, national advertising, uniformity of building design, and color schemes allow the public to assume that this and other similar motor lodges are under the same ownership. An HJ official testified that it was the HJ marketing strategy to appear as a 'chain that sells a product across the nation.'"

The court continued, "There was sufficient evidence for the jury to reasonably conclude that HJ represented to the traveling public that it could expect a particular level of service at a Howard Johnson Motor Lodge. The uniformity of signs, design, and color schemes easily leads the public to believe that each motor lodge is under common ownership or conforms to common standards, and the jury could find they are intended to do so." The appellate court upheld an award of $750,000 compensatory damages against OEP and HJ jointly. [*Orlando Executive Park, Inc. v. P.D.R.*, 402 So.2d 442 (Fla.App. 1981)]

Consider this example: Suppose Georgia Pacific, Inc., interviews Albert Iorio for a sales representative position. Mr. Iorio, accompanied by Jane Franklin, the national sales manager, visits retail stores located in the open sales territory. While visiting one store, Jane tells the store manager, "I wish I had more sales reps like Albert." Nevertheless, Albert is not hired. If Albert later enters into contracts with the store on behalf of Georgia Pacific and Jane has not controverted the impression of Albert she left with the store manager, the company will be bound to the contracts.

Agency by Ratification

Agency by ratification occurs when (1) a person misrepresents himself or herself as another's agent when in fact he or she is not, and (2) the purported principal ratifies (accepts) the unauthorized act. In such cases, the principal is bound to perform and the agent is relieved of any liability for misrepresentation.

Consider this example: Bill Levine sees a house for sale and thinks his friend Sherry Maxwell would want it. Bill enters into a contract to purchase the house from the seller and signs the contract "Bill Levine, agent for Sherry Maxwell." Because Bill is not Sherry Maxwell's agent, she is not bound to the contract. However, if Sherry agrees to purchase the house, there is an agency by ratification. The ratification "relates back" to the moment Bill Levine entered into the contract. Upon ratification of the contract, Sherry Maxwell is obligated to purchase the house.

County courthouse in Dallas, Texas.

CONTRACT LIABILITY TO THIRD PARTIES

A principal who authorizes an agent to enter into a contract with a third party is liable on the contract. Thus, the third party can enforce the contract and recover damages if the principal fails to perform it.

The agent also can be held liable on the contract in certain circumstances. Imposition of such liability depends upon whether the agency is classified as (1) *fully disclosed,* (2) *partially disclosed,* or (3) *undisclosed.*

Fully Disclosed Agency

A **fully disclosed agency** results if the third party entering into the contract knows (1) that the agent is acting as an agent for a principal, and (2) the actual identity of the principal. The third party has the requisite knowledge if the principal's identity is disclosed to the third party by either the agent or some other source.

In a fully disclosed agency, the contract is between the principal and the third party. Thus, the principal, who is called a fully disclosed principal, is liable on the contract. The agent, however, is not liable on the contract because the third party relied on the principal's credit and reputation when the contract was made. An agent is liable on the contract if he or she guarantees that the principal will perform the contract.

Partially Disclosed Agency

A **partially disclosed agency** occurs if the agent discloses his or her agency status but does not reveal the principal's identity and the third party does not know the principal's identity from another source. The nondisclosure may be because (1) the principal instructs the agent not to disclose his or her identity to the third party, or (2) the agent forgets to tell the third party the principal's identity. In this kind of agency, the principal is called a partially disclosed principal.

In a partially disclosed agency, both the principal and the agent are liable on third-party contracts. This is because the third party must rely on the agent's reputation, integrity, and credit because the principal is unidentified. If the agent is made to pay the contract, the agent can sue the principal for indemnification. The third party and the agent can agree to relieve the agent's liability.

Undisclosed Agency

An **undisclosed agency** occurs when the third party is unaware of either the existence of an agency or the principal's identity. The principal is called an *undisclosed principal*. Undisclosed agencies are lawful. They often are used when the principal thinks the terms of the contract would be changed if his or her identity were known. For example, a wealthy person may use an undisclosed agency to purchase property if he thinks the seller would raise the price of the property if his identity were revealed.

In an undisclosed agency, both the principal and the agent are liable on the contract with the third party. This is because the agent, by not divulging that he or she is acting as an agent, becomes a principal to the contract. The third party relies on the reputation and credit of the agent in entering into the contract. If the principal fails to perform the contract, the third party can recover against the principal or the agent. If the agent is made to pay the contract, he or she can recover indemnification from the principal.

Agent Exceeding the Scope of Authority

An agent who enters into a contract on behalf of another party impliedly warrants that he or she has the authority to do so. This is called the agent's *implied warranty of authority*. If the agent exceeds the scope of his or her authority, the principal is not liable on the contract unless the principal ratifies it. The agent, however, is liable to the third party for breaching the implied warranty of authority. To recover, the third party must show (1) reliance on the agent's representation, and (2) ignorance of the agent's lack of status.

Consider this example: Suppose Sam, Sara, Satchel, Samantha, and Simone form a rock band called SSSSex. SSSSex is just a voluntary association without any legal status. Sam enters into a contract with

Signing Properly as an Agent

The agent's signature on a contract entered into on the principal's behalf is important. It can establish the agent's status and, therefore, his liability. For instance, in a fully disclosed agency the agent's signature must clearly indicate that he is acting as an agent for a specifically identified principal. Examples of proper signatures are "Allison Adams, agent for Peter Perceival," "Peter Perceival, by Allison Adams, agent," and "Peter Perceival, by Allison Adams."

An agent who is authorized to sign a contract for a fully disclosed principal but fails to properly do so can be held personally liable on the contract. For example, in the prior example a partially disclosed agency would be created if the contract were signed "Allison Adams, agent." If Adams merely signed the contract "Allison Adams," the agency would be an undisclosed agency. In both these instances the agent is liable on the contract.

SIDEBAR

Rocky's Musical Instruments to purchase instruments and equipment for the band on credit and signs the contract, "Sam, for SSSSex." When SSSSex fails to pay the debt, Rocky's can sue Sam and recover. Sam must pay the debt because he breached his implied warranty of authority when he acted as an agent for a *nonexistent principal*; that is, the purported principal was not a legal entity upon which liability could be imposed.

TORT LIABILITY TO THIRD PARTIES

The principal and the agent are each personally liable for their own tortious conduct. The principal is liable for the tortious conduct of an agent who is acting within the scope of his or her authority. The agent, however, is liable only for the tortious conduct of the principal if he or she directly or indirectly participates in or aids and abets the principal's conduct.

The courts have applied a broad and flexible standard in interpreting scope of authority in the context of employment. Although other factors also may be considered, the courts rely on the following factors to determine whether an agent's conduct occurred within the scope of his or her employment:

- Was the act specifically requested or authorized by the principal?
- Was it the kind of act that the agent was employed to perform?
- Did the act occur substantially within the time period of employment authorized by the principal?
- Did the act occur substantially within the location of employment authorized by the employer?
- Was the agent advancing the principal's purpose when the act occurred?

Where liability is found, tort remedies are available to the injured party. These remedies include recovery for medical expenses, lost wages, pain and suffering, and emotional distress, and, in some cases, punitive damages. The three main sources of tort liability for principals and agents are misrepresentation, negligence, and intentional torts.

Misrepresentation

Intentional misrepresentations are also known as **fraud** or *deceit.* They occur when an agent makes statements that he or she knows are not true. An *innocent misrepresentation* occurs when an agent negligently makes a misrepresentation to a third party.

A principal is liable for the intentional and innocent misrepresentations made by an agent acting within the scope of employment. The third party can either (1) rescind the contract with the principal and recover any consideration paid, or (2) affirm the contract and recover damages.

Consider this example: Assume that (1) a car salesman is employed to sell the principal's car, and (2) the principal tells the agent that the car was repaired after it was involved in a major accident. If the agent intentionally tells the buyer that the car was never involved in an accident, the agent has made an intentional misrepresentation. Both the principal and the agent are liable for this misrepresentation.

Intentional Torts

Intentional torts include such acts as assault, battery, false imprisonment, and other intentional conduct that causes injury to another person. A principal is not liable for the intentional torts of agents and employees that are committed outside the principal's scope of business. For example, if an employee attends a sporting event after working hours and gets into a fight with another spectator at the event, the employer is not liable.

However, a principal is liable under the doctrine of vicarious liability for intentional torts of agents and employees committed within the agent's scope of employment. The courts generally apply one of the following tests in determining whether an agent's intentional torts were committed within the agent's scope of employment.

Motivation Test

Under the **motivation test,** if the agent's motivation in committing the intentional tort is to promote the principal's business, the principal is liable for any injury caused by the tort. But if the agent's motivation in committing the intentional tort was personal, the principal is not liable even if the tort took place during business hours or on business premises. For example, a principal is not liable if his agent was motivated by jealousy to beat up someone on the job who dated her boyfriend.

Work-Related Test

Some jurisdictions have rejected the motivation test as too narrow. These jurisdictions apply the *work-related test* instead. Under this test, if an agent commits an intentional tort within a work-related time or space—for example, during working hours or on the principal's premises—the principal is liable for any injuries caused by the agent's intentional torts. Under this test, the agent's motivation is immaterial.

Principals are liable for the negligent conduct of agents acting within the scope of their employment.

Negligence

Principals are liable for the negligent conduct of agents acting within the scope of their employment. This liability is based on the common law doctrine of *respondeat superior* ("let the master answer"), which, in turn, is based on the legal theory of *vicarious liability* (liability without fault). The principal is liable because of his or her employment contract with the negligent agent, not because the principal was personally at fault.

This doctrine rests on the principle that if someone (i.e., the principal) expects to derive certain benefits from acting through others (i.e., an agent), that person also should bear the liability for injuries caused to third persons by the negligent conduct of an agent who is acting within the scope of his or her employment.

Frolic and Detour

Agents sometimes do things during the course of their employment to further their own interests rather than the principal's. For example, an agent might take a detour to run a personal errand while on assignment for the principal.

This is commonly referred to as a **frolic and detour.** Negligence actions stemming from frolic and detour are examined on a case-by-case basis. Agents always are personally liable for their tortious conduct in such situations. Principals generally are relieved of liability if the agent's frolic and detour is substantial. If the deviation is minor, however, the principal is liable for the injuries caused by the agent's tortious conduct.

Consider these examples: A salesperson stops home for lunch while on an assignment for his principal. While leaving his home, the agent hits and injures a pedestrian with his automobile. The principal is liable if the agent's home was not too far out of the way from the agent's assignment. But the principal would not be liable if an agent who is supposed to be on assignment to Los Angeles flies to San Francisco to meet a friend and is involved in an accident. The facts and circumstances of each case determine its outcome.

The "Coming and Going" Rule

Under the common law, a principal generally is not liable for injuries caused by its agents and employees while they are on their way to or from work. This so-called **"coming and going" rule** applies even if the principal supplies the agent's automobile or other transportation or pays for gasoline, repairs, and other automobile operating expenses. This rule is quite logical. Because principals do not control where their agents and employees live, they should not be held liable for tortious conduct of agents on their way to and from work.

Dual-Purpose Mission

Sometimes principals request that agents run errands or conduct other acts on their behalf while the agent or employee is on personal business. In this case, the agent is on a **dual-purpose mission.** That is, he or she is acting partly for himself or herself and partly for the principal. Most jurisdictions hold both the principal and the agent liable if the agent injures someone while on such a mission.

Consider this example: Suppose a principal asks an employee to drop off a package at a client's office on the employee's way home. If the employee negligently injures a pedestrian while on this dual-purpose mission, the principal is liable to the pedestrian.

INDEPENDENT CONTRACTOR

Section 2 of the Restatement (Second) of Agency defines an independent contractor as "A person who contracts with another to do something for him who is not controlled by the other nor subject to the other's right to control with respect to his physical conduct in the performance of the undertaking." Independent contractors usually work for a number of clients, have their own offices, hire employees, and control the performance of their work.

Merely labeling someone an "independent contractor" is not enough. The crucial factor in determining whether someone is an employee or an independent contractor is the *degree of control* that the employer has over the agent. Critical factors in determining independent contractor status include:

- Whether the worker is engaged in a distinct occupation or an independently established business
- The length of time the agent has been employed by the principal

CASE FOR DISCUSSION
Edgewater Motels, Inc. v. Gatzke and Walgreen Co.
277 N.W.2d 11 (1979)   **Supreme Court of Minnesota**

FACTS

Arlen Gatzke (Gatzke) was a district manager for the Walgreen Company (Walgreen). In August 1979, Gatzke was sent to Duluth, Minnesota, to supervise the opening of a new Walgreen store. In Duluth, Gatzke stayed at the Edgewater Motel (Edgewater). While in Duluth, Gatzke was "on call" 24 hours a day to other Walgreen stores located in his territory.

About midnight on the evening of August 23, 1979, Gatzke, after working 17 hours that day, went with several other Walgreen employees to a restaurant and bar to drink. Within one hour's time, Gatzke had consumed three "doubles" and one single brandy Manhattan. About 1:30 A.M., he went back to the Edgewater Motel and filled out his expense report. Soon thereafter a fire broke out in Gatzke's motel room. Gatzke escaped, but the fire spread and caused extensive damage to the motel. Evidence showed that Gatzke smoked two packs of cigarettes a day. An expert fire reconstruction witness testified that the fire started from a lit cigarette in or next to the wastepaper basket in Gatzke's room.

Edgewater Motels, Inc., sued Gatzke and Walgreen. The parties stipulated that the damage to the Edgewater Motel was $330,360. The jury returned a verdict against defendants Gatzke and Walgreen. The court granted Walgreen's posttrial motion for judgment notwithstanding the verdict. Plaintiff Edgewater and defendant Gatzke appealed.

ISSUE

Was Gatzke's act of smoking within his "scope of employment," making his principal, the Walgreen Company, vicariously liable for his negligence?

IN THE LANGUAGE OF THE COURT

Scott, Justice.

The question of whether smoking can be within an employee's scope of employment is a close one, but after careful consideration of the issue, we are persuaded by the reasoning of the courts that hold that smoking can be an act within an employee's scope of employment. It seems only logical to conclude that an employee does not abandon his employment as a matter of law while temporarily acting for his personal comfort when such activities involve only slight deviations from work that are reasonable under the circumstances. We hold that an employer can be held vicariously liable for his employee's negligent smoking of a cigarette if he was otherwise acting in the scope of his employment at the time of the negligent act.

The record contains a reasonable basis from which a jury could find that Gatzke was involved in serving his employer's interests at the time he was at the bar. Gatzke testified that, while at the Bellows, he discussed the operation of the newly opened Walgreen's store with other Walgreen employees. But more important, even assuming that Gatzke was outside the scope of his employment while he was at the bar, there is evidence from which a jury could reasonably find that Gatzke resumed his employment activities after he returned to his motel room and filled out his expense account.

Additionally, the record indicates that Gatzke was an executive type of employee who had no set working hours. He considered himself a 24-hour-a-day man; his room at the Edgewater Motel was his "office away from home." It was therefore also reasonable for the jury to determine that the filling out of his expense account was done within authorized time and space limits of his employment. In light of the above, we hold it was reasonable for the jury to find that Gatzke was acting within the scope of his employment when he completed his expense account.

DECISION AND REMEDY

The state supreme court held that Gatzke's negligent act of smoking was within the scope of his employment while acting as an employee of the Walgreen Company. The supreme court reinstated the jury's verdict awarding damages to plaintiff Edgewater Motels, Inc.

Questions

1. Should smoking cigarettes be held to be within an employee's "scope of employment"? Why or why not?

2. Do employers owe a duty to police the personal habits of their employees?

3. Because of the dangers of smoking, would employers be justified in hiring only nonsmokers as employees?

- The amount of time that the agent works for the principal
- Whether the principal supplies the tools and equipment used in the work
- The method of payment, whether by time or by the job
- The degree of skill necessary to complete the task
- Whether the worker hires employees to assist him or her
- Whether the employer has the right to control the manner and means of accomplishing the desired result

If an examination of these factors shows that the principal asserts little control, the person is an independent contractor. Substantial control indicates an employer–employee relationship.

Generally, a principal is not liable for the torts of its independent contractors. Independent contractors are personally liable for their own torts. The rationale behind this rule is that principals do not control the means by which the results are accomplished. Nevertheless, this rule has several exceptions:

- *Nondelegable duties.* Certain duties may not be delegated. For example, railroads owe a duty to maintain safe railroad crossings. They cannot escape this liability by assigning the task to an independent contractor.
- *Special risks.* Principals cannot avoid strict liability for dangerous activities assigned to independent contractors. For example, the use of explosives, clearing land by fire, crop dusting, and such involve special risks that are shared by the principal.
- *Negligence in the selection of an independent contractor.* A principal who knowingly hires an unqualified or dangerous person as an independent contractor is liable if that person injures someone while on the job.

Checklist

DETERMINING INDEPENDENT CONTRACTOR STATUS

- ○ Whether the worker is engaged in a distinct occupation or an independently established business.

- ○ The length of time the agent has been employed by the principal.

- ○ The amount of time the agent works for the principal.

- ○ Whether the principal supplies the tools and equipment used in the work.

- ○ The method of payment, whether by time or by the job.

- ○ The degree of skill necessary to complete the task.

- ○ Whether the worker hires employees to assist him or her.

- ○ Whether the employer has the right to control the manner and means of accomplishing the desired result.

Ethical PERSPECTIVE — *Microsoft Violates Employment Law*

Microsoft Corporation, headquartered in the state of Washington, is the world's largest provider of computer operating systems, software programs, and Internet browsers. The company has made one of its founders, Bill Gates, the richest person in the world. But the company was caught nickel-and-diming some of its workers out of their stock option benefits. It all started with an Internal Revenue Service (IRS) investigation. Here is the story.

In addition to having regular employees, Microsoft used the services of other workers classified as *independent contractors* (called *freelancers)* and temporary agency employees (called *temps).* Most of these special employees worked full-time for Microsoft doing jobs that were identical to jobs performed by Microsoft's regular employees. Microsoft paid the special employees by check as outside workers.

In 1990, the IRS conducted an employment tax examination and determined that Microsoft had misclassified these special workers as independent contractors and that the workers in these positions should be reclassified as "employees" for federal tax purposes.

The IRS used the following factors to reach the conclusion that the special workers were Microsoft employees rather than independent contractors:

- The party that has the right to control the manner and means by which the service or product is produced
- The degree of skill required
- The source of the instrumentalities and tools

- The location of the work
- The duration of the relationship between the parties
- The extent of the hiring party's discretion over when and how long to work
- The hiring party's role in hiring and paying assistants
- Whether the work is part of the regular business of the hiring party

The IRS applied these factors to both the freelancers and the temps who worked at Microsoft and found both to be employees of Microsoft. But that was not the end of the story. Plaintiff Donna Vizcaino and other freelancers sued Microsoft in a class action lawsuit alleging that they were denied employment benefits, especially employee stock options, that were paid to regular employees. Microsoft contributed 3 percent of an employee's salary to the stock option plan.

The court of appeals agreed with the plaintiffs, citing the Internal Revenue Code that requires such stock-option plans to be available to all employees. Thus, Microsoft's attempt to define certain full-time employees as freelancers and temps was rebuffed by the courts [*Vizcaino v. United States District Court for the Western District of Washington,* 173 F.3d 713 (9th Cir. 1999)].

1. Did Microsoft act ethically in this case?
2. Why did Microsoft classify these employees as "freelancers" and "temps"?

TERMINATION OF AN AGENCY AND EMPLOYMENT CONTRACT

An agency contract is similar to other contracts in that it can be terminated either by an act of the parties or by operation of law. These different methods of termination are discussed next. Note that once an agency relationship is terminated, the agent no longer can represent the principal or bind the principal to contracts.

Termination by Acts of the Parties

The parties to an agency contract can terminate an agency contract by agreement or by their actions. The four methods of termination of an agency relationship by acts of the parties are:

Minimum Wage and Overtime Pay

The Fair Labor Standards Act (FLSA) establishes minimum wage and overtime pay requirements for workers. Managerial, administrative, and professional employees are exempt from the Act's wage and hour provisions. As outlined below, the FLSA requires employers to pay covered workers at least the minimum wage for their regular work hours. Overtime pay is also mandated.

- *Minimum wage.* The minimum wage is set by Congress and can be changed. Currently, it is set at $5.15 per hour. The Department of Labor permits employers to pay less than the minimum wage to students and apprentices. An employer may reduce minimum wages by an amount equal to the reasonable cost of food and lodging provided to employees.

- *Overtime pay.* Under the FLSA, an employer cannot require nonexempt employees to work more than 40 hours per week unless they are paid one-and-a-half times their regular pay for each hour worked in excess of 40 hours. Each week is treated separately. For example, if an employee works 50 hours one week and 30 hours the next, the employer owes the employee 10 hours of overtime pay. [29 U.S.C. §§ 201 et seq.]

1. *Mutual agreement.* As with any contract, the parties to an agency contract can mutually agree to terminate their agreement. By doing so, the parties relieve each other of any further rights, duties, obligations, or powers provided for in the agency contract. Either party can propose the termination of an agency contract.

2. *Lapse of time.* Agency contracts are often written for a specific period of time. The agency terminates when the specified time period elapses. Suppose, for example, that the principal and agent enter into an agency contract "beginning January 1, 2002, and ending December 31, 2005." The agency automatically terminates on December 31, 2005. If the agency contract does not set forth a specific termination date, the agency terminates after a reasonable time has elapsed. The courts often look to the custom of an industry in determining the reasonable time for termination of the agency.

3. *Purpose achieved.* A principal can employ an agent for the time it takes to accomplish a certain task, purpose, or result. Such agencies automatically terminate once they are completed. Suppose a principal employs a licensed real estate broker to sell his house. The agency terminates when the house is sold and the principal pays the broker the agreed-upon compensation.

4. *Occurrence of a specified event.* An agency contract can specify that the agency exists until a specified event occurs. The agency terminates when the specified event happens. For example, if a principal employs an agent to take care of her dog until she returns from a trip, the agency terminates when the principal returns from the trip.

Wrongful Termination of an Agency or Employment Contract

Generally, agency and employment contracts that do not specify a definite time for their termination can be terminated at will by either the principal or the agent without liability to the other party. When a principal terminates an agency contract, it is called a *revocation of authority.* When an agent terminates an agency, it is called a *renunciation of authority.*

Unless an agency is irrevocable, both the principal and the agent have an individual power to unilaterally terminate any agency contract. Note that having the power to terminate an agency agreement is not the same as having the right to terminate it. The unilateral termination of an agency contract may be wrongful. If the principal's or agent's termination of an agency contract breaches the contract, the other party can sue for damages for **wrongful termination of an agency.**

Consider this example: A principal employs a licensed real estate agent to sell his house. The agency contract gives the agent an exclusive listing for three months. After one month, the principal unilaterally terminates the agency. The principal has the power to do so, and the agent can no longer act on behalf of the principal. Because the principal did not have the right to terminate the contract, however, the agent can sue him and recover damages (i.e., lost commission) for wrongful termination.

WORKERS' COMPENSATION

Many types of employment are dangerous, and each year many workers are injured on the job. At common law, employees who were injured on the job could sue their employer for negligence. This time-consuming process placed the employee at odds with his or her employer. In addition, there was no guarantee that the employee would win the case. Ultimately, many injured workers—or the heirs of deceased workers—were left uncompensated.

Workers' compensation acts were enacted in response to the unfairness of that result. These acts create an administrative procedure for workers to receive compensation for injuries that occur on the job. First, the injured worker files a claim with the appropriate state government agency (often called the workers' compensation board or commission). Next, that entity determines the legitimacy of the claim. If the worker disagrees with the agency's findings, he or she may appeal the decision through the state court system. Workers' compensation benefits are paid according to preset limits established by statute or regulation. The amounts that are recoverable vary from state to state.

Employment-Related Injury

To be compensable under workers' compensation, the claimant must prove that the injury arose out of and in the course of his or her employment. An accident that occurs while an employee is actively working is clearly within the scope of this rule. Accidents that occur at a company cafeteria or while on a business lunch for an employer are covered. Accidents that happen while the employee is at an off-premises restaurant during his or her personal lunch hour are not covered. Many workers' compensation acts include stress as a compensable work-related injury.

Exclusive Remedy

Workers' compensation is an *exclusive remedy*. Thus, workers cannot sue their employers in court for damages. The one exception to this rule is: If an employer intentionally injures a worker, the worker can collect workers' compensation benefits and sue the employer. Workers' compensation acts do not bar injured workers from suing responsible third parties to recover damages.

TITLE VII OF THE CIVIL RIGHTS ACT OF 1964

After substantial debate, Congress enacted the **Civil Rights Act of 1964.** **Title VII** of that Act (entitled the Fair Employment Practices Act) was intended to eliminate job discrimination based on the following *protected classes:* (1) *race*, (2) *color*, (3) *religion*, (4) *sex*, or (5) *national origin* [42 U.S.C. §§ 2000e et seq.]. As amended by the Equal Employment Opportunity Act of 1972, Section 703(a)(2) of Title VII provides in pertinent part that

Family and Medical Leave Act

In February 1993, Congress enacted the Family and Medical Leave Act. This law guarantees workers unpaid time off from work for medical emergencies. The Act, which applies to companies with 50 or more workers as well as federal, state, and local governments, covers about half of the nation's workforce. To be covered by the Act, an employee must have worked for the employer for at least one year and have performed more than 1,250 hours of service during the previous 12-month period.

Covered employers are required to provide up to 12 weeks of unpaid leave during any 12-month period due to the

1. Birth of, and care for, a son or daughter
2. Placement of a child for adoption or in foster care
3. Serious health condition that makes the employee unable to perform his or her duties

4. Care for a spouse, child, or parent with a serious health problem

Leave because of the birth of a child or the placement of a child for adoption or foster care cannot be taken intermittently unless the employer agrees. Other leaves may be taken on an intermittent basis. The employer may require medical proof of claimed serious health conditions.

An eligible employee who takes leave must, upon returning to work, be restored to either the same or an equivalent position with equivalent employment benefits and pay. The restored employee is not entitled to the accrual of seniority during the leave period, however. A covered employer may deny restoration to a salaried employee who is among the highest-paid 10 percent of that employer's employees if the denial is necessary to prevent "substantial and grievous economic injury" to the employer's operations.

Family and Medical Leave Act:
www.dol.gov/dol/esa/fmla.htm

It shall be an unlawful employment practice for an employer

(1) to fail or refuse to hire or to discharge any individual, or otherwise to discriminate against any individual with respect to his compensation, terms, conditions, or privileges of employment, because of such individual's race, color, religion, sex, or national origin; or

(2) to limit, segregate, or classify his employees or applicants for employment in any way which would deprive or tend to deprive any individual of employment opportunities or otherwise adversely affect his status as an employee, because of such individual's race, color, religion, sex, or national origin.

Scope of Coverage of Title VII

Title VII prohibits discrimination in hiring, decisions regarding promotion or demotion, payment of compensation and fringe benefits, availability of job training and apprenticeship opportunities, referral systems for employment, decisions regarding dismissal, work rules, and any other "term, condition, or privilege" of employment. Any employee of covered employers, including undocumented aliens, may bring actions for employment discrimination under Title VII.

Race, Color, and National Origin Discrimination

Title VII of the Civil Rights Act of 1964 was enacted primarily to prohibit employment discrimination based on race, color, and national origin. *Race* refers to broad categories such as Black, Caucasian, Asian, and American Indian. *Color* refers to the color of a person's skin. *National origin* refers to the country of a person's ancestors or cultural characteristics.

Sex Discrimination

Although the prohibition against **sex discrimination** applies equally to men and women, the overwhelming majority of Title VII sex discrimination cases are brought by women. An example of such discrimination is the old airline practice of ignoring the marital status of male flight attendants but hiring only single female flight attendants.

Sexual Harassment

In the modern work environment, co-workers sometimes become sexually interested or involved with each other voluntarily. On other occasions, though, a co-worker's sexual advances are not welcome.

Refusing to hire or promote someone unless he or she has sex with the manager or supervisor is sex discrimination that violates Title VII. Other forms of conduct, such as lewd remarks, touching, intimidation, posting pinups, and other verbal or physical conduct of a sexual nature, constitute **sexual harassment** and violate Title VII. To determine what conduct creates a hostile work environment, the U.S. Supreme Court stated [*Harris v. Forklift Systems, Inc.*, 114 S.Ct. 367 (1993)]:

> We can say that whether an environment is "hostile" or "abusive" can be determined only by looking at all the circumstances. These may include the frequency of the discriminatory conduct; its severity; whether it is physically threatening or humiliating, or a mere offensive utterance; and whether it unreasonably interferes with an employee's work performance.

Exhibit 14.3 sets forth an employer's policies against sexual harassment.

Religious Discrimination

Title VII prohibits employment discrimination based on a person's religion. Religions include traditional religions, other religions that recognize a supreme being, and religions based on ethical or spiritual tenets. Many religious discrimination cases involve a conflict between an employer's work rule and an employee's religious beliefs (e.g., when an employee is required to work on his or her religious holiday).

The right of an employee to practice his or her religion is not absolute. Under Title VII, an employer is under a duty to *reasonably accommodate* the religious observances, practices, or beliefs of its employees if it does not cause an *undue hardship* on the employer. The courts must apply these general standards to specific fact situations. In making their decisions, the courts must consider factors such as the number of employees of the employer, the importance of the employee's position, and the availability of alternative workers.

Bona Fide Occupational Qualification (BFOQ)

Discrimination based on protected classes (other than race or color) is permitted if it is shown to be a **bona fide occupational qualification (BFOQ).** To be legal, a BFOQ must be both *job-related* and a *business necessity*. For example, allowing only women to be locker-room attendants in a women's gym is a valid BFOQ, but prohibiting males from being managers or instructors at the same gym would not be a BFOQ.

exhibit 14.3   *Policies against sexual harassment.*

Many businesses have taken steps to prevent sexual harassment in the workplace. For example, some businesses have explicitly adopted policies (see below) forbidding sexual harassment, implemented procedures for reporting incidents of sexual harassment, and conducted training programs to sensitize managers and employees about the issue.

Statement of Prohibited Conduct

The management of Company considers the following conduct to illustrate some of the conduct that violates Company's Sexual Harassment Policy:

A. Physical assaults of a sexual nature, such as

   1. Rape, sexual battery, molestation, or attempts to commit these assaults.

   2. Intentional physical conduct that is sexual in nature, such as touching, pinching, patting, grabbing, brushing against another employee's body, or poking another employee's body.

B. Unwanted sexual advances, propositions, or other sexual comments, such as

   1. Sexually oriented gestures, noises, remarks, jokes, or comments about a person's sexuality or sexual experience directed at or made in the presence of any employee who indicates or has indicated in any way that such conduct is unwelcome in his or her presence.

   2. Preferential treatment or promises of preferential treatment to an employee for submitting to sexual conduct, including soliciting or attempting to solicit any employee to engage in sexual activity for compensation or reward.

   3. Subjecting, or threats of subjecting, an employee to unwelcome sexual attention or conduct or intentionally making performance of the employee's job more difficult because of the employee's sex.

C. Sexual or discriminatory displays or publications anywhere in Company's workplace by Company employees, such as

   1. Displaying pictures, posters, calendars, graffiti, objects, promotional materials, reading materials, or other materials that are sexually suggestive, sexually demeaning, or pornographic, or bringing into Company's work environment or possessing any such material to read, display, or view at work.

       A picture will be presumed to be sexually suggestive if it depicts a person of either sex who is not fully clothed or in clothes that are not suited to or ordinarily accepted for the accomplishment of routine work in and around the workplace and who is posed for the obvious purpose of displaying or drawing attention to private portions of his or her body.

   2. Reading or otherwise publicizing in the work environment materials that are in any way sexually revealing, sexually suggestive, sexually demeaning, or pornographic.

   3. Displaying signs or other materials purporting to segregate an employee by sex in any area of the workplace (other than restrooms and similar semi-private lockers/changing rooms).

AGE DISCRIMINATION IN EMPLOYMENT ACT

In the past, some employers discriminated against employees and prospective employees based on their age. For example, employers often refused to hire older workers. The Age Discrimination in Employment Act (ADEA), which prohibits certain age discrimination practices, was enacted in 1967 [29 U.S.C. §§ 621–634].

The ADEA prohibits age discrimination in all employment decisions, including hiring, promotions, payment of compensation, and other terms and conditions of employment. Originally, ADEA prohibited employment discrimination against persons between 40 and 65 years of age. In 1978, its coverage was extended to persons up to 70 years of age. Further amendments completely eliminated an age ceiling, so ADEA now applies to employees who are 40 and older.

AMERICANS WITH DISABILITIES ACT

Americans with Disabilities Act: www.usdoj.gov/crt/ada/adahom1.htm

The **Americans with Disabilities Act (ADA),** signed into law on July 26, 1990 [42 U.S.C. §§ 1201 et seq.], is the most comprehensive piece of civil rights legislation since the Civil Rights Act of 1964. The ADA imposes obligations on employers and providers of public transportation, telecommunications, and public accommodations to accommodate individuals with disabilities.

Title I of the ADA prohibits employment discrimination against qualified individuals with disabilities in regard to job application procedures, hiring, compensation, training, promotion, and termination. It requires an employer to make reasonable accommodations to individuals with disabilities that do not cause undue hardship to the employer. Reasonable accommodations may include making facilities readily accessible to individuals with disabilities, providing part-time or modified work schedules, acquiring equipment or devices, modifying examination and training materials, and providing qualified readers or interpreters.

Employers are not obligated to provide accommodations that would impose an *undue burden*, or actions that would require significant difficulty or expense. The courts consider factors such as the nature and cost of accommodation, the employer's overall financial resources, and the employer's type of operation. Obviously, what may be a significant difficulty or expense for a small employer may not be an undue hardship for a large employer.

LEGAL TERMINOLOGY

Agency
Agency by ratification
Agent
Americans with Disabilities Act (ADA)
Apparent agency (agency by estoppel)
Attorney-in-fact
Bona fide occupational qualification (BFOQ)
Color discrimination
"Coming and going" rule
Dual-purpose mission
Employer–employee relationship
Employment-at-will
Employment-related injury
Exclusive agency contract
Express agency
Frolic and detour
Fully disclosed agency
General power of attorney

Implied agency
Independent contractor
Intentional misrepresentation (fraud)
Intentional tort
Motivation test
National origin discrimination
Negligence
Partially disclosed agency
Power of attorney
Principal
Principal–agent relationship
Principal–independent contractor relationship
Sex discrimination
Sexual harassment
Special power of attorney
Title VII of Civil Rights Act of 1964
Undisclosed agency
Wrongful termination of an agency

Summary

CHAPTER 14 AGENCY AND EMPLOYMENT LAW

The Nature of Agency

Definition	A fiduciary relationship that results from the manifestation of consent by one person to act on behalf of another person with that person's consent.
Parties	1. *Principal:* Party who employs another person to act on his or her behalf. 2. *Agent:* Party who agrees to act on behalf of another person.

(continued)

Kinds of Employment Relationships

Employer–Employee Relationship	An employer hires an employee to perform some form of physical service. An employee is not an agent unless the principal authorizes him or her to enter into contracts on the principal's behalf.
Principal–agent relationship	An employer hires an employee and authorizes the employee to enter into contracts on the employer's behalf.
Principal–Independent Contractor Relationship	Principal employs a person who is not an employee of the principal. The independent contractor has authority to enter into only those contracts authorized by the principal.

Formation of the Agency Relationship

Express Agency	Principal and agent expressly agree in words to enter into an agency agreement. The agency contract may be oral or written unless the Statute of Frauds requires it to be in writing.
Implied Agency	An agency is implied (inferred) from the conduct of the parties.
Apparent Agency	Arises when a principal creates an appearance of an agency that in actuality does not exist. Also called *agency by estoppel* or *ostensible agency*.
Agency by Ratification	Occurs when a person misrepresents him- or herself as another's agent when he or she is not and the purported principal ratifies (accepts) the unauthorized act.

Contract Liability to Third Parties

Fully Disclosed Agency	The third party entering into the contract knows that the agent is acting for a principal and knows the identity of the principal. The principal is liable on the contract; the agent is not liable on the contract.
Partially Disclosed Agency	The third party knows that the agent is acting for a principal but does not know the identity of the principal. Both the principal and the agent are liable on the contract.
Undisclosed Agency	The third party does not know that the agent is acting for a principal. Both the principal and the agent are liable on the contract.

Tort Liability to Third Parties

Description	Principals are liable for the *tortious conduct* of an agent who is acting within the *scope of his authority*. Liability is imposed for misrepresentation, negligence, and intentional torts.

(continued)

Misrepresentation	Principals are liable for intentional and innocent misrepresentations made by an agent acting within the scope of his or her employment.
Negligence	Principals are liable for the negligent conduct of agents acting within the scope of their employment. Special negligence doctrines include: 1. *Frolic and detour:* Principals are generally relieved of liability if the agent's negligent act occurred on a substantial frolic and detour from the scope of employment. 2. *"Coming and going" rule:* Principals are not liable if the agent's tortious conduct occurred while on the way to or from work. 3. *Dual-purpose mission:* If the agent is acting on his or her own behalf and on behalf of the principal, the principal is generally liable for the agent's tortious conduct.
Intentional Torts	States apply one of the following rules: 1. *Motivation test:* The principal is liable if the agent's intentional tort was committed to promote the principal's business. 2. *Work-related test:* The principal is liable if the agent's intentional tort was committed within a work-related time or space. Agents are personally liable for their own tortious conduct.

Independent Contractor

Liability for Independent Contractor's Torts	Generally, principals are not liable for the tortious conduct of independent contractors. Exceptions to the rule are for: 1. *Nondelegable duties* 2. *Special risks* 3. *Negligence in selecting an independent contractor* Independent contractors are personally liable for their own torts.

Termination of an Agency and Employment Contract

Termination by Acts of the Parties	The following *acts of the parties* terminate agency contracts: 1. *Mutual agreement.* 2. *Lapse of time.* 3. *Purpose achieved.* 4. *Occurrence of a specified event.*
Wrongful Termination of an Agency Contract	If an agency is for an agreed-upon term or purpose, the *unilateral termination* of the agency contract by either the principal or the agent constitutes the *wrongful termination* of the agency. The breaching party is liable to the other party for damages caused by the breach.

(continued)

Workers' Compensation

Workers' Compensation Acts	State statutes that create an administrative procedure for workers to receive payments for job-related injuries. Most states require employers to carry private or government-sponsored *workers' compensation insurance*. Some states permit employers to self-insure.
Employment-Related Injury	To be compensable under workers' compensation, the claimant must prove that the injury arose out of and in the course of his or her employment.
Exclusive Remedy	Workers' compensation is an exclusive remedy. Thus, workers cannot sue their employers to recover damages for job-related injuries.

Title VII of the Civil Rights Act of 1964

Description	Federal statute that prohibits job discrimination based on the (1) race, (2) color, (3) religion, (4) sex, or (5) national origin of the job applicant.
Scope of Coverage of Title VII	*Employment decisions subject to Title VII:* Decisions regarding hiring; promotion; demotion; payment of salaries, wages, and fringe benefits; job training and apprenticeships; work rules; or any other "term, condition, or privilege of employment."
Protected Classes	Employment discrimination based on the following protected classes is forbidden by Title VII: 1. *Race:* Broad class based on common physical characteristics 2. *Color:* Skin color 3. *National origin:* A person's national heritage 4. *Sex:* Male or female 5. *Religion:* Discrimination solely because of a person's religious beliefs or practices. An employer has a duty to *reasonably accommodate* an employee's religious beliefs if it does not cause an *undue hardship* on the employer.
Sexual Harassment	Lewd remarks, touching, intimidation, posting pinups, and other verbal or physical conduct of a sexual nature that occurs on the job. Sexual harassment that creates a *hostile work environment* violates Title VII [*Meritor Savings Bank v. Vinson*, 477 U.S. 57 (1986)].

Age Discrimination in Employment Act (ADEA)

Description	Federal statute that prohibits employment discrimination against applicants and employees who are 40 years of age and older. *(continued)*

Americans with Disabilities Act (ADA)	
Description	Federal law that imposes obligations on employers and providers of public transportation, telecommunications, and public accommodations to accommodate individuals with disabilities.
Title I of ADA	Federal law that prohibits employment discrimination against qualified individuals with disabilities. Requires employers to make *reasonable accommodations* to accommodate employees with disabilities that do not cause *undue hardship* to the employer.

Working the Web

1. Find information on labor law in the United States from the U.S. Department of Labor at www.dol.gov/dol/esa/public/whd_org.htm.
2. Locate basic information on the Family and Medical Leave Act at www.dol.gov/dol/esa/fmla.htm.
3. Find an overview of agency law at the Cornell University Law School Legal Information Institute at www.law.cornell.edu/topics/agency.html.
4. Search for the U.S. Equal Employment Opportunity Commission (EEOC), established by Title VII of the Civil Rights Act of 1964, at www.eeoc.gov/welcome.html.
5. Find information on the Americans with Disabilities Act at the U.S. Department of Justice Americans with Disabilities Act home page at www.usdoj.gov/crt/ada/adahom1.htm.

Questions
CRITICAL LEGAL THINKING AND WRITING

1. Define an agency. What purpose does an agency serve?
2. Define an independent contractor. What factors does a court look at in determining whether an independent contractor status exists?
3. Explain the doctrine of apparent agency. Why did the courts adopt this doctrine.
4. What is the contract liability of the principal and the agent in a fully disclosed agency, partially disclosed agency, and undisclosed agency?
5. What does the doctrine of respondent superior provide? What is the public policy behind this doctrine?

6. Explain the tort liability of a principal and agent. Explain the tort liability of a principal and an independent contractor.

7. What are the protected classes under Title VII of the Civil Rights Act of 1964?

8. Describe the protections afforded by the Family and Medical Leave Act. Why did Congress pass this act?

9. Define *sexual harassment*. Give some examples of sexual harassment.

10. Describe the protections afforded by the Americans with Disabilities Act (ADA).

ETHICS: ANALYSIS AND DISCUSSION

1. What ethical issues may be involved when a paralegal acts under a power of attorney for a client of the firm?

2. Is a paralegal who is investigating the facts of a case acting as an agent for the client or for the law firm? Does the answer change the ethical obligations of the paralegal?

3. Is the failure of a paralegal to properly advise a client on how to sign a document malpractice or a breach of an ethical obligation?

UPL: Representation at Depositions

There are few certainties in the area of ethics, for paralegals or in any profession. What qualifies as ethical conduct is in most cases based on state law and court interpretation applied to a set of facts. The citation listed below represents one legal opinion and is provided as a research starting point. Do not assume that the same rule applies in your jurisdiction. For the following:

- *Prepare a written statement based on your state law.*
- *Use your state bar association website as a starting point.*

A corporate client is concerned about testimony that an employee may give in a pending civil action even though the corporation has not been named as a defendant. [Colorado Bar Association Ethics Opinion 79.] May a paralegal attend depositions for the sole purpose of taking notes on testimony given or taken in the action?

Grinder v. Bryans Road Building & Supply Co., Inc.

432 A.2d 453 (Md.App. 1981)

14.1 FACTS

G. Elvin Grinder of Marbury, Maryland, was a building contractor who, prior to May 1, 1973, did business as an individual and traded as "Grinder Construction." Grinder maintained an open account, on his individual credit, with Bryans Road Building & Supply Co., Inc. Grinder would purchase materials and supplies from Bryans on credit and later pay the invoices.

On May 1, 1973, G. Elvin Grinder Construction, Inc., a Maryland corporation, was formed with Grinder personally owning 52 percent of the stock of the corporation. Grinder did not inform Bryans that he had incorporated, and continued to purchase supplies on credit from Bryans under the name "Grinder Construction."

In May 1978, after certain invoices were not paid by Grinder, Bryans sued Grinder personally to recover. Grinder asserted that the debts were owed by the corporation. Bryans amended its complaint to include the corporation as a defendant.

ISSUE

Who is liable to Bryans?

Largey v. Intrastate Radiotelephone, Inc.

136 C.A.3d 660, 186 C.R. 520 (Cal.App. 1982)

14.2 FACTS

Intrastate Radiotelephone, Inc., a public utility, supplies radiotelephone utility service to the general public for radiotelephones, pocket pagers, and beepers. Robert Kranhold, an employee of Intrastate, was authorized to use his personal vehicle on company business. On the morning of March 9, 1976, when Kranhold was driving his vehicle to Intrastate's main office, he negligently struck a motorcycle driven by Michael S. Largey, causing severe and permanent injuries to Largey. The accident occurred at the intersection where Intrastate's main office is located.

Evidence showed that Kranhold acted as a consultant to Intrastate, worked both in and out of Intrastate's offices, had no set hours of work, often attended meetings at Intrastate's offices, and went to Intrastate's offices to pick up things or drop off things. Largey sued Intrastate for damages.

ISSUE

Is Intrastate liable?

Huddleston v. Roger Dean Chevrolet, Inc.

845 F.2d 900 (11th Cir. 1988)

14.3 FACTS

Shirley Huddleston became the first female sales representative of Roger Dean Chevrolet, Inc. (RDC) in West Palm Beach, Florida. Shortly after she began working at RDC, Philip Geraci, a fellow sales representative, and other male employees began making derogatory comments to and about her, expelled gas in her presence, called her a bitch and a whore, and such. Many of these remarks were made in front of customers. The sales manager of RDC participated in the harassment. On several occasions, Huddleston complained about this conduct to RDC's general manager.

ISSUE

Was Title VII violated?

Dothard, Director, Department of Public Safety of Alabama v. Rawlinson

433 U.S. 321, 97 S.Ct. 2720 (1977)

14.4 FACTS

Dianne Rawlinson, 22 years old, is a college graduate whose major course of study was correctional psychology. After graduation, she applied for a position as a correctional counselor (prison guard) with the Alabama Board of Corrections. Her application was rejected because she failed to meet the minimum 120-pound weight requirement of an Alabama statute that also established a height minimum of 5 feet 2 inches. In addition, the Alabama Board of Corrections adopted Administrative Regulation 204, which established gender criteria for assigning correctional counselors to maximum-security prisons for "contact positions." These are correctional counselor positions that require continual close physical proximity to inmates. Under this rule, Rawlinson did not qualify for contact positions with male prisoners in Alabama maximum-security prisons. Rawlinson brought this class action lawsuit against Dothard, who was the director of the Department of Public Safety of Alabama.

ISSUE

Does either the height-weight requirement or the contact position rule constitute a bona fide occupational qualification that justifies the sexual discrimination in this case? Does society owe a duty of social responsibility to protect women from dangerous job positions? Or is this "romantic paternalism"?

Read the following case, excerpted from the court of appeals opinion. Review and brief the case. In your brief, answer the following questions:

1. Was A. Louis Jagoe hired by the District of Columbia as an employee or as an independent contractor?
2. Describe the accident. Who was injured?

3. Normally, an employer is not liable for the tortious conduct of an independent contractor it has hired. What is the "special risks" exception to this rule?
4. What damages were awarded to the plaintiff?

Farrell, Associate Judge.

The Murch School Summer Discovery Program was designed to provide hands-on education for gifted and talented eight- and nine-year-old children. The program originated in 1985 when Mrs. Gill, the Murch School principal, attended a reception at Mount Vernon College arranged by Greg Butta, a Ph.D. candidate at The American University, to advertise the success of a summer program he had conducted at Mount Vernon. The program interested Mrs. Gill, and after several discussions Butta sent her a formal proposal for conducting a similar program at the Murch School. Gill proposed changes to the proposal, then solicited and received approval for the program from the Assistant Superintendent for the District of Columbia Public Schools.

Butta hired the staff for the summer program, including some of the instructors who had taught in the Mount Vernon program. Mrs. Gill, however, reviewed all of the instructors' resumes, had veto authority over their hiring, and interviewed most of the staff, including A. Louis Jagoe, before the hiring was made final. Jagoe, who was hired to teach chemistry to the eight- and nine-year-olds in the program, held a master's degree in chemistry and was a Ph.D. candidate at The American University. Before the first general staff meeting, he told Butta that as part of the class he would do a luminescence experiment and a "cold-pack" experiment and wanted to make sparklers with the children. Jagoe and Butta discussed the safety of the sparkler experiment only in regard to the location where the children would be allowed to light the sparklers.

On August 1, 1985, a staff meeting was held at which Gill, Butta, and all instructors and counselors were present. Each instructor gave a brief talk about what he or she intended to do in class. Several instructors testified that Jagoe told the group, including Mrs. Gill, that he planned to make sparklers as one of the chemistry experiments. Gill, who was in and out of the meeting, did not remember hearing Jagoe discuss the experiment, although notes she took at the meeting reflect that she heard him discuss the luminescence and cold-pack experiments and asked him questions about these. Gill spoke and emphasized the "hands-on" nature of the program and her hopes for its success.

One child attending the program was nine-year-old Dedrick Howell, whose parents enrolled him after receiving the school brochure in the mail. The accident occurred on August 12, 1985. At the beginning of the chemistry class, Jagoe distributed his "recipe" for sparklers to the children and also wrote it on the blackboard. Along with other chemical ingredients, the recipe called for the use of potassium perchlorate as the oxidizing agent. Potassium perchlorate was described at trial as an extremely unstable and highly volatile chemical often used to make rocket fuel. Commercially made sparklers are not made with potassium perchlorate.

The children scooped the chemicals, including the potassium perchlorate, out of jars and, using pestles, ground up the mixture in mortars. While they were combining the chemicals, Jagoe ignited three different chemical mixtures at the front of the room with a butane lighter. Butta was present for one of the ignitions when he entered the room to drop off metal hangers for use in the experiment. Mrs. Gill also entered the room at one point, and saw the children working at tables wearing goggles or glasses. She also saw Jagoe at the front of the room lighting the chemicals with a fire extinguisher on the table next to him.

The children continued to grind the material while a counselor, Rebecca Seashore, distributed pieces of metal hangers to be dipped into the mixture at a later time. Dedrick Howell was specifically told not to dip the hanger into the material until instructed to do so. Moments later the chemicals exploded in front of Dedrick. The chemicals burned at 5000 degrees Fahrenheit, and Dedrick was burned over 25% of his body including his hands, arms, chest, and face.

An employer generally is not liable for injuries to third parties caused by an independent contractor over whom (or over whose work) the employer has reserved no control. There are exceptions to the rule, however, one of which is that one who employs an independent contractor to do work involving a special danger to others which the employer knows or has reason to know to be inherent in or normal to the work, or which he contemplates or has reason to contemplate when making the contract, is subject to liability for physical harm caused to such others by the contractor's failure to take reasonable precautions against such danger.

It is sufficient that work of any kind involves a risk, recognizable in advance, of physical harm to others which is inherent in the work itself, or normally to be expected in the ordinary course of the usual or prescribed way of doing it, or that the employer has special reason to contemplate such a risk under the particular circumstances under which the work is to be done.

The sparkler experiment combined flammable, combustible chemicals, open flames, and children; for that very reason, presumably, the children had been equipped with goggles. Though sparklers are explosives of a lesser order, conducting controlled explosions is a textbook example of an inherently dangerous activity. It was not unreasonable for the jury to conclude that the manufacture of sparklers by nine-year-old children was an inherently dangerous activity.

Therefore, the jury was well within its authority in finding that Jagoe was an independent contractor performing inherently dangerous work of which the District had actual or constructive knowledge.

The judgment is affirmed as to liability and as to the award of $8 million in damages both for pain and suffering and for past medical expenses.

CHAPTER 15

CHAPTER OBJECTIVES

After studying this chapter, you should be able to:

1. Define a *sole proprietorship* and the liability of a sole proprietor.

2. Describe how a business files for a d.b.a.—a fictitious business name.

3. Define *general partnership* and describe how general partnerships are formed.

4. Define *limited partnership* and distinguish between limited and general partners.

5. Define *limited liability partnership (LLP)* and describe the limited liability of partners of an LLP.

6. Define *limited liability company (LLC)* and describe the process of organizing an LLC.

7. Define *corporation* and list the major characteristics of a corporation.

8. Describe the process of forming a corporation.

9. Describe the functions of shareholders, directors, and officers in managing the affairs of a corporation.

10. Describe multinational corporations and their role in international trade.

Business Organizations

The biggest corporation, like the humblest private citizen, must be held to strict compliance with the will of the people.

THEODORE ROOSEVELT

Introduction

A person who wants to start a business must decide whether the business should operate as one of the major forms of business organization—*sole proprietorship, general partnership, limited partnership, limited liability partnership, limited liability company,* and *corporation*—or under some other available legal business form. These are called *business organizations.* The selection depends on many factors, including the ease and cost of formation, capital requirements of the business, flexibility of management decisions, government restrictions, extent of personal liability, tax considerations, and the like. This chapter covers the noncorporate forms of business, including sole proprietorships, general partnerships, limited partnerships, limited liability partnerships, and limited liability companies. The chapter also includes corporations.

Many lawyers' practices involve counseling entrepreneurs who want to start new businesses, preparing the legal documents to start a new business, and advising existing businesses on a variety of legal matters. Paralegals must have knowledge of this field of the law to prepare necessary documents, conduct research, and work with the lawyer in providing legal services to entrepreneurs and business organizations.

SOLE PROPRIETORSHIP

Sole proprietorships are the simplest form of business organization. The owner, called a *sole proprietor*, is the business; there is no separate legal entity. Sole proprietorships are the most common form of business organization in the United States. Many small businesses—and a few large ones—operate this way.

Operating a business as a sole proprietorship has several major advantages:

1. The ease and low cost of formation.
2. The owner's right to make all management decisions concerning the business, including those involving hiring and firing employees.
3. The sole proprietor owns all of the business and has the right to receive all of the business's profits.
4. A sole proprietorship can be easily transferred or sold if and when the owner desires to do so; no other approval (such as from partners or shareholders) is necessary.

This business form has disadvantages, too, among them: (1) the sole proprietor's access to capital is limited to personal funds plus any loans he or she can obtain, and (2) the sole proprietor is legally responsible for the business's contracts and the torts he or she or any of his or her employees commit in the course of employment.

Creation of a Sole Proprietorship

It is easy to create a sole proprietorship. There are no formalities, and no federal or state government approval is required. Some local governments require all businesses, including sole proprietorships, to obtain a license to do business within the city. If no other form of business organization is chosen, the business is a sole proprietorship by default.

Personal Liability of Sole Proprietors

The sole proprietor bears the entire risk of loss of the business; that is, the owner will lose his or her entire capital contribution if the business fails. In addition, the sole proprietor has unlimited personal liability (see Exhibit 15.2). Therefore, creditors may recover claims against the business from the sole proprietor's personal assets (e.g., home, automobile, and bank accounts).

Consider this example: Suppose Ken Smith opens a clothing store called The Rap Shop and operates it as a sole proprietorship. Smith files the proper statement and publishes the necessary notice of the use of the trade name. He contributes $25,000 of his personal funds to the business and borrows $100,000 in the name of the business from a bank. Assume that after several months Smith closes the business because it was unsuccessful. At the time it is closed, the business has no assets, owes the bank $100,000, and owes rent, trade credit, and other debts of $25,000. Here, Smith is personally liable to pay the bank and all of the debts from his personal assets.

SIDEBAR

"Doing Business As"

A sole proprietorship can operate under the name of the sole proprietor or a *trade name*. For example, the author of this book can operate a sole proprietorship under the name "Henry R. Cheeseman" or under a trade name such as "The Big Cheese." Operating under a trade name is commonly designated as a **d.b.a. (doing business as)** (e.g., Henry R. Cheeseman, doing business as "The Big Cheese").

Most states require all businesses that operate under a trade name to file a *fictitious business name statement* (or *certificate of trade name*) with the appropriate government agency. The statement must contain the name and address of the applicant, the trade name, and the address of the business. Most states also require that notice of the trade name be published in a newspaper of general circulation serving the area in which the applicant does business.

These requirements are intended to disclose the real owner's name to the public. Noncompliance can result in a fine. Some states prohibit violators from maintaining lawsuits in the state's courts. A sample fictitious business name statement is shown in Exhibit 15.1.

Sample fictitious business name statement.   *exhibit* **15.1**

Return To:

Name: Richard S. Roe
Address: 9000 Wilshire Boulevard
City: Beverly Hills, CA 90210
Telephone # (213) 273-5000
Cust. Ref. # 53247

☒ First Filing   ☐ Renewal Filing
Current Registration No.

PUBLISH IN:

COUNTY CLERK'S FILING STAMP

FICTITIOUS BUSINESS NAME STATEMENT

THE FOLLOWING PERSON(S) IS (ARE) DOING BUSINESS AS:

1 Fictitious Business Name(s)
Mountain and Shore Mortgage Company

2 Street Address & City of Principal place of Business in California   Zip Code
9000 Wilshire Boulevard   Beverly Hills   California   90210

(if corporation - incorporated in what state)

3 Full name of Registrant
Richard S. Roe

Residence Address   City   State   Zip Code
100 Palm Drive   Beverly Hills   California   90212
(if corporation - incorporated in what state)

Full Name of Registrant

Residence Address   City   State   Zip Code
(if corporation - incorporated in what state)

Full name of Registrant

Residence Address   City   State   Zip Code
(if corporation - incorporated in what state)

Full name of Registrant

Residence Address   City   State   Zip Code

4 This Business is   (X) an individual   ( ) a general partnership   ( ) joint venture   ( ) a business trust
conducted by: ( ) co-partners   ( ) husband and wife   ( ) a corporation   ( ) a limited partnership
(check one only)   ( ) an unincorporated association other than a partnership   ( ) other—please specify___

5 The registrant commenced to transact business under the fictitious business name or names listed above on___

6
a. Signed:

_____   Richard S. Roe
SIGNATURE   TYPE OR PRINT NAME

_____   _____
SIGNATURE   TYPE OR PRINT NAME

_____   _____
SIGNATURE   TYPE OR PRINT NAME

b. If Registrant a corporation sign below:

_____
CORPORATION NAME

_____
SIGNATURE & TITLE

_____
TYPE OR PRINT NAME

This statement was filed with the County Clerk of___Los Angeles___County on date indicated by file stamp above.

NOTICE THIS FICTITIOUS NAME STATEMENT EXPIRES FIVE YEARS FROM THE DATE IT WAS FILED IN THE OFFICE OF THE COUNTY CLERK. A NEW FICTITIOUS BUSINESS NAME STATEMENT MUST BE FILED BEFORE THAT TIME. THE FILING OF THIS STATEMENT DOES NOT OF ITSELF AUTHORIZE THE USE IN THIS STATE OF A FICTITIOUS BUSINESS NAME IN VIOLATION OF THE RIGHTS OF ANOTHER UNDER FEDERAL, STATE, OR COMMON LAW (SEE SECTION 14400 ET SEQ., BUSINESS AND PROFESSIONS CODE).

I HEREBY CERTIFY THAT THIS COPY IS A CORRECT COPY OF THE ORIGINAL STATEMENT ON FILE IN MY OFFICE.

_____
COUNTY CLERK   DEPUTY

BY _____
File No.___

exhibit 15.2   *Sole proprietorship.*

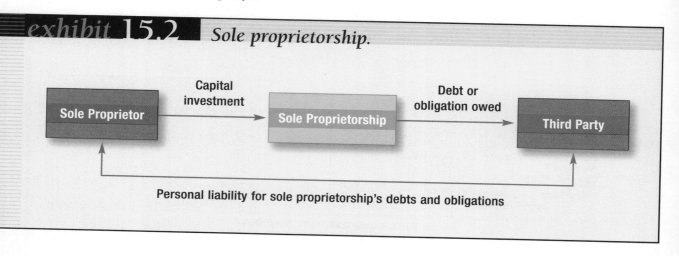

Personal liability for sole proprietorship's debts and obligations

GENERAL PARTNERSHIP

General, or *ordinary, partnerships* have been recognized since ancient times. The English common law of partnerships governed early U.S. partnerships. The individual states expanded the body of partnership law.

A **general partnership,** or partnership, is a voluntary association of two or more persons for carrying on a business as co-owners for profit. The formation of a partnership creates certain rights and duties among partners and with third parties. These rights and duties are established in the partnership agreement and by law. **General partners,** or *partners,* are personally liable for the debts and obligations of the partnership (see Exhibit 15.3).

Formation of a Partnership

A business must meet four criteria to qualify as a partnership under the Uniform Partnership Act [UPA § 6(1)]. It must be

exhibit 15.3   *General partnership.*

Personal liability for partnership's debts and obligations

1. an association of two or more persons
2. carrying on a business
3. as co-owners
4. for profit.

Partnerships are voluntary associations of two or more persons. All partners must agree to the participation of each co-partner. A person cannot be forced to be a partner or to accept another person as a partner. The UPA definition of "person" includes natural persons, partnerships (including limited partnerships), corporations, and other associations. A business—trade, occupation, or profession—must be carried on. The organization or venture must have a profit motive to qualify as a partnership, even though the business does not actually have to make a profit.

A general partnership may be formed with little or no formality. Co-ownership of a business is essential to create a partnership. The most important factor in determining co-ownership is whether the parties share the business's profits and management responsibility.

Receipt of a share of business profits is prima facie evidence of a partnership because nonpartners usually are not given the right to share in the business's profits. No inference of the existence of a partnership is drawn if profits are received in payment of (1) a debt owed to a creditor in installments or otherwise, (2) wages owed to an employee, (3) rent owed to a landlord, (4) an annuity owed to a widow, widower, or representative of a deceased partner, (5) interest owed on a loan, or (6) consideration for the sale of goodwill of a business [UPA § 7]. An agreement to share losses of a business is strong evidence of a partnership.

The right to participate in the management of a business is important evidence for determining the existence of a partnership, but it is not conclusive evidence because the right to participate in management is sometimes given to employees, creditors, and others. If a person is given the right to share in profits, losses, and management of a business, it is compelling evidence of the existence of a partnership.

The Partnership Agreement

The agreement to form a partnership may be oral, written, or implied from the conduct of the parties. It may even be created inadvertently. No formalities are necessary, although a few states require general partnerships to file certificates of partnership with an appropriate government agency. Partnerships that exist for more than one year or are authorized to deal in real estate must be in writing under the Statute of Frauds.

It is good practice for partners to put their partnership agreement in writing. A written document is important evidence of the terms of the agreement, particularly if a dispute arises among the partners.

A written partnership agreement is called a **partnership agreement** or **articles of partnership.** The partners can agree to almost any terms in their partnership agreement, except terms that are illegal. The articles of partner-

Uniform Partnership Act

In 1914, the National Conference of Commissioners on Uniform State Laws (a group of lawyers, judges, and legal scholars) promulgated the **Uniform Partnership Act (UPA),** which codifies partnership law. Its goal was to establish consistent partnership law that would be uniform throughout the United States. The UPA has been adopted in whole or in part by 48 states, the District of Columbia, Guam, and the Virgin Islands.

The UPA covers most problems that arise in the formation, operation, and dissolution of ordinary partnerships. Other rules of law or equity govern if there is no applicable provision of the UPA [UPA § 5].

The UPA adopted the **entity theory** of partnership, which considers partnerships as separate legal entities. As such, partnerships can hold title to personal and real property, transact business in the partnership name, and the like.

Checklist

PARTNERSHIP AGREEMENT

The partnership agreement should contain the following information:

○ The firm name

○ Names and addresses of the partners

○ Principal office of the partnership

○ Nature and scope of the partnership business

○ Duration of the partnership

○ Capital contributions of each partner

○ The division of profits and losses among the partners

○ The salaries, if any, to be paid to partners

○ Duties of the partners regarding management of the partnership

○ Limitations, if any, on the authority of partners to bind the partnership

○ Provisions for the admission and withdrawal of partners from the firm and the terms, conditions, and notices required for withdrawal

○ Provisions for continuing the partnership upon withdrawal of a partner, death of a partner, or other dissolution of the partnership

○ Any other provisions deemed relevant by the partners

ship can be short and simple or long and complex. If the agreement fails to provide for an essential term or contingency, the provisions of the UPA control. Thus, the UPA acts as a gap-filling device to the partners' agreement.

Contract Liability

As a legal entity, a partnership must act through its agents, that is, its partners. Contracts entered into with suppliers, customers, lenders, or others on the partnership's behalf are binding on the partnership.

Under the UPA, partners have **joint liability** for the contracts and debts of the partnership [UPA § 15(b)]. This means that a third party who sues to recover on a partnership contract or debt must name all of the partners in the lawsuit. If the lawsuit is successful, the plaintiff can collect the entire amount of the judgment against any or all of the partners. If the third party's suit does not name all of the partners, the judgment cannot be collected against any of the partners or the partnership assets. Similarly, releasing any partner from the lawsuit releases them all. A partner who is made to pay more than his or her proportionate share of contract liability may seek **indemnification** from the partnership and from those partners who have not paid their share of the loss.

Tort Liability

While acting on partnership business, a partner or an employee of the partnership may commit a tort that causes injury to a third person. This tort could be caused by a negligent act, a breach of trust (such as embezzlement from a customer's account), a breach of fiduciary duty, defamation, fraud, or other intentional tort. The partnership is liable if the act is committed while the person is acting within the ordinary course of partnership business or with the authority of his or her co-partners.

Under the UPA, partners have **joint and several liability** for torts and breaches of trust [UPA § 15(a)]. This is so even if a partner did not participate in the commission of the act. This type of liability permits a third party to sue one or more of the partners separately. Judgment can be collected only against the partners who are sued. The partnership and partners who are made to pay tort liability may seek indemnification from the partner who committed the wrongful act. A release of one partner does not discharge the liability of other partners.

Consider this example: Suppose Nicole, Jim, and Maureen form a partnership. Assume that Jim, while on partnership business, causes an automobile accident that injures Kurt, a pedestrian. Kurt suffers $100,000 in injuries. Kurt, at his option, can sue Nicole, Jim, or Maureen separately, or any two of them, or all of them.

Dissolution of Partnerships

The duration of a partnership can be for a fixed term (e.g., five years) or until a particular undertaking is accomplished (e.g., until a real estate development is completed), or it can be for an unspecified term. A partnership with a fixed duration is called a **partnership for a term.** A partnership with no fixed duration is called a **partnership at will.**

Although a partner has the *power* to withdraw and dissolve the partnership at any time, he or she may not have the *right* to do so. For example, a partner who withdraws from a partnership before expiration of the term stated in the partnership agreement does not have the right to do so. The partner's action causes a **wrongful dissolution** of the partnership. The partner is liable for damages caused by the wrongful dissolution of the partnership.

LIMITED PARTNERSHIP

Limited partnerships are statutory creations that have been used since the Middle Ages. They include both general (manager) and limited (investor) partners. Today, all states have enacted statutes that provide for the creation of limited part-

Liability of General Partners

The court applied the doctrine of joint and several liability in the following situation. Jose Pena and Joseph Antenucci were both medical doctors who were partners in a medical practice. Both doctors treated Elaine Zuckerman during her pregnancy. Her son, Daniel Zuckerman, was born with severe physical problems. Elaine, as Daniel's mother and natural guardian, brought this medical malpractice suit against both doctors. The jury found that Pena was guilty of medical malpractice but that Antenucci was not. The amount of the verdict totaled $4 million. The trial court entered judgment against Pena but not against Antenucci. The plaintiffs have made a posttrial motion for judgment against both defendants.

Is Antenucci jointly and severally liable for the medical malpractice of his partner, Pena? The court said yes.

The court noted that a partnership is liable for the tortious act of a partner, and a partner is jointly and severally liable for tortious acts chargeable to the partnership. When a tort is committed by the partnership, the wrong is imputable to all of the partners jointly and severally, and an action may be brought against all or any of them in their individual capacities or against the partnership as an entity. Therefore, even though the jury found that defendant Antenucci was not guilty of malpractice in his treatment of the patient, but that defendant Pena, his partner, *was* guilty of malpractice in his treatment of the patient, they were then both jointly and severally liable for the malpractice committed by defendant Pena by operation of law. [*Zuckerman v. Antenucci*, 478 N.Y.S.2d 578 (N.Y. 1984)]

nerships. In most states these partnerships are called **limited partnerships** or *special partnerships*. Limited partnerships are used for business ventures such as investing in real estate, drilling oil and gas wells, investing in movie productions, and the like.

General and Limited Partners

Limited partnerships have two types of partners: (1) general partners, who invest capital, manage the business, and are personally liable for partnership debts and (2) **limited partners,** who invest capital but do not participate in management and are not personally liable for partnership debts beyond their capital contribution (see Exhibit 15.4).

A limited partnership must have at least one or more general partners and one or more limited partners [RULPA § 101(7)]. There are no restrictions on the number of general or limited partners allowed in a limited partnership. Any person may be a general or limited partner. This includes natural persons, partnerships, limited partnerships, trusts, estates, associations, and corporations. A person may be both a general and a limited partner in the same limited partnership.

Formation of Limited Partnerships

The creation of a limited partnership is formal and requires public disclosure. The entity must comply with the statutory requirements of the Revised Uniform Limited Partnership Act or other state statutes.

Revised Uniform Limited Partnership Act

In 1916 the National Conference of Commissioners on Uniform State Laws, a group composed of lawyers, judges, and legal scholars, promulgated the **Uniform Limited Partnership Act (ULPA).** The ULPA contains a set of provisions for the formation, operation, and dissolution of limited partnerships. Most states originally enacted this law.

In 1976, the National Conference on Uniform State Laws promulgated the **Revised Uniform Limited Partnership Act (RULPA),** which provides a more modern comprehensive law for the formation, operation, and dissolution of limited partnerships. This law supersedes the ULPA in the states that have adopted it. The RULPA provides the basic foundation for our discussion of limited partnership law.

Limited partnership. **exhibit 15.4**

Under the RULPA, two or more persons must execute and sign a *certificate of limited partnership* [RULPA §§ 201 and 206]. The certificate must contain the following information:

1. Name of the limited partnership
2. General character of the business
3. Address of the principal place of business, and the name and address of the agent to receive service of legal process
4. Name and business address of each general and limited partner
5. The latest date upon which the limited partnership is to dissolve
6. Amount of cash, property, or services (and description of property or services) contributed by each partner, and any contributions of cash, property, or services promised to be made in the future
7. Any other matters that the general partners determine to include

The certificate of limited partnership must be filed with the secretary of state of the appropriate state and, if required by state law, with the county recorder in the county or counties in which the limited partnership carries on business. The limited partnership is formed when the certificates of limited partnership is filed.

Limited Partnership Agreement

Although not required by law, the partners of a limited partnership often draft and execute a **limited partnership agreement** (also called the **articles of limited partnership**) that sets forth the rights and duties of the general

SIDEBAR

Written Agreements

It is good practice to have a written partnership agreement that sets forth in detail the rights and duties of the partners. This will reduce later disputes and lawsuits.

and limited partner(s), terms and conditions regarding the operation, termination, and dissolution of the partnership, and so on. Where there is no such agreement, the certificate of limited partnership serves as the articles of limited partnership.

The limited partnership agreement may specify how profits and losses from the limited partnership are to be allocated among the general and limited partners. If there is no such agreement, the RULPA provides that profits and losses from a limited partnership are shared on the basis of the value of the partner's capital contribution [RULPA § 503]. A limited partner is not liable for losses beyond his or her capital contribution.

In addition, it is good practice to establish voting rights in the limited partnership agreement or certificate of limited partnership. The limited partnership agreement can provide which transactions must be approved by which partners (i.e., general, limited, or both). General and limited partners may be given unequal voting rights. A sample limited partnership agreement is set forth in Exhibit 15.5.

Liability of General and Limited Partners

The general partners of a limited partnership have *unlimited liability* for the debts and obligations of the limited partnership. This liability extends to debts that cannot be satisfied with the existing capital of the limited partnership. Generally limited partners are liable only for the debts and obligations of the limited partnership up to their capital contributions.

As a trade-off for *limited liability*, limited partners give up their right to participate in the control and management of the limited partnership. This means, in part, that limited partners have no right to bind the partnership to contracts or other obligations. Under the RULPA, a limited partner is liable as a general partner if his or her participation in the control of the business is substantially the same as that of a general partner, but the limited partner is liable only to persons who reasonably believed him or her to be a general partner [RULPA § 303(a)].

Family Court building on the Benjamin Franklin Parkway, Philadelphia, Pennsylvania.

LIMITED LIABILITY PARTNERSHIP (LLP)

Many states have enacted legislation to permit the creation of **limited liability partnerships (LLPs).** An LLP does not have to have a general partner who is personally liable for the debts and obligations of the partnership. Instead, *all* partners are limited partners who stand to lose only their capital contribution if the partnership fails. None of the partners is personally liable for the debts and obligations of the partnership beyond his or her capital contribution (see Exhibit 15.6).

Sample limited partnership agreement.   **exhibit 15.5**

LIMITED PARTNERSHIP AGREEMENT

1. Introduction. This agreement of Limited Partnership dated January 2, 2002 by and between John Weston, Wai Chan, and Susan Martinez (General Partners) and Shari Berkowitz, Raymond Wong, and Harold Johnson (Limited Partners).

The General Partners and Limited Partners agree to form a Limited Partnership (Partnership) pursuant to the provisions of the California Revised Limited Partnership Act on the terms and conditions hereinafter set forth.

2. Name of Partnership. The name of the Partnership shall be "The Wilshire Investment Company, a California Limited Partnership." The business of the Partnership shall be conducted in that name.

3. Principal Place of Business. The principal office of the Partnership shall be at 4000 Wilshire Boulevard, Los Angeles, California 90010 or at such other place within California as may be determined from time to time by the General Partners.

4. Purpose of the Partnership. The Partnership shall be engaged in the business of buying, selling, and developing commercial and industrial real estate and such activities as are related or incidental thereto.

5. Agent for Service of Process. The name of the agent for service of process is Frederick Friendly, whose address is 2500 Century Park East, Suite 600, Los Angeles, California 90067.

6. Term of Partnership. The term of the Partnership shall commence on the date on which the Partnership's Certificate of Limited Partnership is filed by the Secretary of State of California and shall continue until it terminates in accordance with the provisions of this Agreement.

7. Certificate of Limited Partnership. The General Partners shall immediately execute a Certificate of Limited Partnership and cause that Certificate to be filed in the office of the secretary of state of California. The General Partners shall also record a certified copy of the Certificate in the office of the county recorder of every county in which the Partnership owns real property.

8. Members of the Partnership.
    (a) The names and addresses of each original General Partner are as follows:

NAME	John Weston	ADDRESS	500 Ocean Boulevard, Los Angeles, California
	Wai Chan		700 Apple Road, Seattle, Washington
	Susan Martinez		800 Palm Drive, Miami, Florida

   (b) The names and addresses of each original Limited Partner are as follows:

NAME	Shari Berkowitz	ADDRESS	700 Apple Street, New York, New York
	Raymond Wong		900 Flower Avenue, San Francisco, California
	Harold Johnson		300 Oil Field Road, Houston, Texas

9. General Partners' Capital Contributions. The General Partners shall make the following contributions to the Partnership's capital no later than January 2, 2002.

CASH	John Weston	$60,000
PROPERTY	Wai Chan	$30,000
	Susan Martinez	$30,000

No interest will be paid on any balances in the General Partners' capital accounts.

10. Limited Partners' Capital Contributions. The Limited Partners shall make the following contributions to the Partnership's capital no later than January 2, 2002.

CASH	Shari Berkowitz	$100,000
	Raymond Wong	$ 50,000
	Harold Johnson	$ 50,000

No interest will be paid on any balances in the Limited Partners' capital accounts.

11. Additional Capital Contributions from Limited Partners. The General Partners may call for additional cash contributions to the Partnership's capital from the Limited Partners. The aggregate of all additional capital contributions made by the Limited Partners pursuant to this Paragraph shall not exceed 100 percent of the original capital contributions made by them pursuant to Paragraph 10 of this Agreement. Notice of the call shall be made by registered mail, return receipt requested, and shall be deemed made when posted. The Limited Partners' additional capital contribution must be made no later than 60 days following the call.

12. Division of Profits. Each Partner shall receive the following share of the net profits of the Partnership:

exhibit **15.5**   *Sample limited partnership agreement, continued.*

	PARTNER	PERCENT
General Partners:	John Weston	30%
	Wai Chan	15%
	Susan Martinez	15%
Limited Partners:	Shari Berkowitz	20%
	Raymond Wong	10%
	Harold Johnson	10%

13. Sharing of Losses. Each Partner shall bear a share of the losses of the Partnership equal to the share of the profits to which he or she is entitled. The share of the losses of each Partner shall be charged against his contribution to the capital of the Partnership.

The Limited Partners will not be liable for any Partnership debts or losses beyond the amounts to be contributed to them pursuant to Paragraphs 10 and 11 of this Agreement.

After giving effect to the share of losses chargeable against the capital contributions of Limited Partners, the remaining Partnership losses shall be borne by the General Partners in the same proportions in which, between themselves, they are to share profits.

14. Management of Partnership. The General Partners shall have the sole and exclusive control of the Limited Partnership.

The General Partners shall have an equal voice in the management of the Partnership, and each shall devote his or her full time to the conduct of the Partnership's business.

The General Partners shall have the power and authority to take such action from time to time as they may deem to be necessary, appropriate, or convenient in connection with the management and conduct of the business and affairs of the Partnership, including, without limitation, the power to

(a) Acquire property, including real and personal property.

(b) Dispose of Partnership property.

(c) Borrow or lend money.

(d) Make, deliver, or accept commercial paper.

(e) Pledge, mortgage, encumber, or grant a security interest in the Partnership properties as security for repayment of loans.

(f) Take any and all other action permitted by law that is customary in or reasonably related to the conduct of the Partnership business or affairs.

15. Limited Partners Not to Manage Business. The Limited Partners will not manage the business of the Partnership or assist in its management.

16. Partnership Books and Records. The Partnership books of account will be kept in accordance with generally accepted accounting principles. The books and supporting records will be maintained at the Partnership's principal office and will be examined by the Partnership's certified public accountants at least annually. The Partnership's fiscal year shall start on January 1 and close on December 31.

17. General Partners' Salaries. The General Partners shall each receive a salary of $60,000 per annum, payable in monthly installments, as compensation for managing the Partnership. No increases shall be made in the General Partners' salaries without the written consent of a majority of the Limited Partners.

18. Admission of New General Partners. No new General Partners will be admitted to the Partnership without the written consent of all the General Partners and Limited Partners as to both his or her admission and the terms on which the new General Partner is admitted.

19. Admission of New Limited Partners. No new Limited Partners will be admitted to the Partnership without the written consent of all the General Partners and Limited Partners as to both his or her admission and the terms on which the new Limited Partner is admitted.

20. No Sale or Assignment of, or Granting Lien on Partnership Interest by General Partner. Without the written consent of all the General Partners and Limited Partners, no General Partner shall assign, mortgage, or give a security interest in his or her Partnership interest.

21. Right of Limited Partner to Assign Partnership Interest or Substitute New Limited Partner. Upon 30 days' written notice to the General Partners, a Limited Partner can assign his or her interest in the Partnership's profits to a third party. Such assignment shall not constitute a substitution of the third party as a new Limited Partner in the place of the assignor. A Limited Partner may substitute a third party in his or her place as a new Limited Partner only with the consent in writing of all the General Partners and Limited Partners.

22. Effect of Death, Disability, or Retirement of a General Partner. The death, retirement, or permanent disability of a General Partner (the withdrawing General Partner) that makes it impossible for him or her to carry out his or her duties under this Agreement shall terminate the Partnership.

Sample limited partnership agreement, continued.   *exhibit* **15.5**

If a General Partner survives, the remaining General Partners may continue the Partnership business and may purchase the interest of the withdrawing General Partner in the assets and goodwill of the Partnership. The remaining General Partners have the option, exercisable by them at any time within 30 days after the date on which the withdrawing General Partner ceases to be a General Partner, to purchase the withdrawing General Partner's interest by paying to the person legally entitled thereto the value of that interest as shown on the last regular accounting of the Partnership preceding the date on which the General Partner ceased to be a General Partner, together with the full unwithdrawn portion of the withdrawing General Partner's distributive share of any net profits earned by the Partnership between the date of that accounting and the date on which the withdrawing General Partner ceased to be a General Partner of the Partnership.

23. Duties of Remaining Purchasing General Partners. Upon the purchase of a withdrawing General Partner's interest, the remaining General Partners shall assume all obligations of the Partnership and shall hold the withdrawing General Partner, the personal representative and estate of the withdrawing General Partner, and the property of the withdrawing General Partner free and harmless from all liability for those obligations.

The remaining General Partners shall immediately amend the Certificate of Limited Partnership and shall file such amendment with the office of the Secretary of State, and shall cause to be prepared, filed, served, and published all other notices required by law to protect the withdrawing General Partner or the personal representative and estate of the withdrawing General Partner from all liability for the future obligations of the Partnership business.

24. Effect of Death of Limited Partner or Substitution of Limited Partner. The death of a Limited Partner or the substitution of a new Limited Partner for a Limited Partner shall not affect the continuity of the Partnership or the conduct of its business.

25. Voluntary Dissolution. A General Partner may terminate the Partnership at any time upon 120 days written notice to each Limited Partner. Upon termination of the Partnership, it shall be liquidated in accordance with Paragraph 26 of this Agreement.

26. Liquidation of Partnership. If the Partnership is liquidated, its assets, including its goodwill and name, shall be sold in the manner designed to produce the greatest return. The proceeds of the liquidation shall be distributed in the following order:

  (a) To creditors of the Partnership including Partners who are creditors to the extent permitted by law, in satisfaction of liabilities of the Partnership
  (b) To Partners in payment of the balances in their income accounts
  (c) To Partners in payment of the balances in their capital accounts
  (d) To Partners in payment of the remainder of the proceeds

27. Certificate of Dissolution. Upon dissolution of the Partnership, the General Partners shall execute and file in the office of the Secretary of State a Certificate of Dissolution. If dissolution occurs after a sole General Partner ceases to be a General Partner, the Limited Partners conducting the winding up of the Partnership's affairs shall file the Certificate of Dissolution.

28. Entire Agreement. This Agreement contains the entire understanding among the Partners and supersedes any prior written or oral agreements between them respecting the subject matter contained herein. There are no representations, agreements, arrangements, or understandings, oral or written, between and among the Partners relating to the subject matter of this Agreement that are not fully expressed herein.

29. Controlling Law. This Agreement shall be interpreted under the law of the State of California. Further, each Partner consents to the jurisdiction of the courts of the State of California.

30. Service of Notices. Service of notice upon the Partnership will be made by registered or certified mail, return receipt requested, addressed to the Partnership's principal place of business.

Service of notice upon any or all Partners will be made by certified mail, return receipt requested, addressed to the addresses given in this Agreement or such other addresses as a Partner may from time to time give to the Partnership.

31. Severability. If any provisions of this Agreement shall be declared by a court of competent jurisdiction to be invalid, void, or unenforceable, the remaining provisions shall continue in full force and effect.

32. Arbitration of Disputes. Any controversy concerning this Agreement will be settled by arbitration according to the rules of the American Arbitration Association, and judgment upon the award may be entered and enforced in any court.

_____   _____
GENERAL PARTNER   LIMITED PARTNER

_____   _____
GENERAL PARTNER   LIMITED PARTNER

exhibit 15.6 Limited liability partnership (LLP).

LLPs enjoy the "flow-through" tax benefit of other types of partnerships, that is, no tax is paid at the partnership level and all profits and losses are reported on the individual partners' income tax returns.

LLPs must be created formally by filing **articles of limited liability partnership** with the secretary of state of the state in which the LLP is organized. This is a public document. The LLP is a domestic LLP in the state in which it is organized. The limited liability partnership law of the state governs the operation of the LLP. An LLP may do business in other states, however. To do so, the LLP must register as a foreign LLP in any state in which it wants to conduct business.

LIMITED LIABILITY COMPANY (LLC)

A majority of states have approved a new form of business entity called a **limited liability company (LLC).** An LLC is an unincorporated business entity that combines the most favorable attributes of general partnerships, limited partnerships, and corporations. An LLC may elect to be taxed as a partnership, the owners can manage the business, and the owners have limited liability. Many entrepreneurs who begin new businesses chose the LLC as their legal form for conducting business.

Formation of an LLC

Forming an LLC is similar to organizing a corporation. Two or more persons (which include individuals, partnerships, corporations, and associations) may form an LLC for any lawful purpose. To form an LLC, articles of organization must be filed with the appropriate state office, usually the Secretary of State's office (see Exhibit 15.7). The articles of organization must state the LLC's name, duration, and other information required by statute or that the

Accounting Firms Operating as LLPs

Prior to the advent of the limited liability partnership (LLP) form of doing business, accounting firms operated as general partnerships. As such, the general partners were personally liable for the debt and obligations of the general partnership. In large accounting firms, this personal liability was rarely imposed because the general partnership usually carried sufficient liability insurance to cover most awards to third-party plaintiffs in negligence tort actions. Creditors usually extended credit to the large accounting firms based on the reputation of the firms and the fact that these large accounting firms had sufficient capital in the partnership to meet most loan obligations.

Beginning in the early 1980s, large accounting firms were hit with many large court judgments. These cases were brought in conjunction with the failure of large savings banks and commercial banks and the failure of other large firms that accountants had audited. Many of these firms failed because of fraud by their major owners and officers. The shareholders and creditors of these failed companies sued the auditors, alleging that the auditors had been negligent in not catching the fraud. Many juries agreed and awarded large sums against the accounting firms.

Sometimes the accounting firm's liability insurance was not enough to cover the judgment, thus imposing personal liability on the partners. General partners in accounting firms became worried that the inability of the profession to shield itself from such liability jeopardized the profession.

In response, in the 1990s state legislatures created a new form of business, the limited liability partnership (LLP). This entity was particularly created for accountants, lawyers, and other professionals to offer their services under an umbrella of limited liability. The partners of an LLP have limited liability up to their capital contribution; the partners do not have personal liability for the debts and liabilities of the LLP, however.

Once LLPs were permitted by law, all of the Big Four accounting firms changed their status from general partnerships to LLPs. The signs and letterhead of the Big Four accounting firms prominently announce that the accounting firm is an "LLP." Many accounting firms other than the Big Four also have changed to LLP status, as have many law firms. The LLP form of business has transformed how accountants, lawyers, and other professionals offer their services.

---

organizers deem important to include. The name of an LLC must contain the words *Limited Liability Company* or the abbreviation *L.L.C.* or *L.C.*

Members of an LLC may enter into an **operating agreement** that regulates the affairs of the company and the conduct of its business and governs relations among the members, managers, and company [ULLCA § 103(a)]. The operating agreement may be amended by the approval of all members unless otherwise provided in the agreement. The operating agreement and amendments may be oral but usually are written.

The Check-the-Box Regulations have default rules that provide that eligible entities, such as an LLC, are treated as partnerships with flow-through taxation unless an election is made to be taxed as a corporation. This election is made by filing Form 8832 with the IRS and must be signed by all owners or a manager who is given authority to sign such an election. The Check-the-Box Regulations make it easier for LLCs to obtain partnership taxation status for federal income tax purposes. Most states automatically apply the federal classification rules for state income tax purposes, although a few do not.

exhibit **15.7**   *Sample LLC articles of organization.*

ARTICLES OF ORGANIZATION
FOR FLORIDA LIMITED LIABILITY COMPANY

ARTICLE I – NAME

The name of the Limited Liability Company is

iCitrusSystems.com

ARTICLE II – ADDRESS

The mailing address and street address of the principal office of the Limited Liability Company is

3000 Dade Boulevard

Suite 200

Miami Beach, Florida 33139

ARTICLE III – DURATION

The period of duration for the Limited Liability Company shall be

50 years

ARTICLE IV – MANAGEMENT

The Limited Liability Company is to be managed by a manager and the name and address of such manager is

Susan Escobar

1000 Collins Avenue

Miami Beach, Florida 33141

Thomas Blandford

Pam Rosales

Partnership Taxation for LLCs

Effective January 1, 1997, the IRS adopted "Check-the-Box" Regulations, making it easier for LLCs to be taxed as partnerships. These regulations provide that a business entity falls into one of the following categories:

1. *Per se corporations:* corporations incorporated under state law and taxed as corporations for federal income tax purposes.

2. *Eligible entities:* entities other than *per se* corporations. Eligible entities include unincorporated businesses with two or more owners, such as LLCs, LLPs, limited partnerships, and general partnerships. An eligible entity is taxed as a partnership unless it elects to be taxed as a corporation.

3. *Single-owner entities:* entities that are taxed as sole proprietorships unless the owner elects to be taxed as a corporation.

The Check-the-Box Regulations have default rules that provide that eligible entities, such as an LLC, are treated as partnerships with flow-through taxation unless an election is made to be taxed as a corporation. This election is made by filing Form 8832 with the IRS and must be signed by all owners or a manager who is given authority to sign such an election. The Check-the-Box Regulations make it easier for LLCs to obtain partnership taxation status for federal income tax purposes. Most states automatically apply the federal classification rules for state income tax purposes, although a few do not.

Members' Limited Liability

The owners of LLCs are usually called *members.* The general rule is that members are not personally liable to third parties for the debts, obligations, and liabilities of an LLC beyond their capital contribution. Members are said to have **limited liability** (see Exhibit 15.8). The debts, obligations, and liabilities of an LLC, whether arising from contracts, torts, or otherwise, are solely those of the LLC [ULLCA § 303(a)].

Consider this example: Jasmin, Shan-Yi, and Vanessa form an LLC and each contributes $25,000 in capital. The LLC operates for a period of time during which it borrows money from banks and purchases goods on credit from suppliers. After some time, the LLC experiences financial difficulty and goes out of business. If the LLC fails with $500,000 in debts, each of the members will lose her capital contribution of $25,000 but will not be personally liable for the rest of the unpaid debts of the LLC.

CORPORATION

Corporations are the dominant form of business organization in the United States, generating more than 85 percent of the country's gross business receipts. Corporations range in size from one owner to thousands of owners. Owners of corporations are called **shareholders.** Exhibit 15.9 depicts the hierarchy of a corporation.

Uniform Limited Liability Company Act

In 1995, the National Conference of Commissioners on Uniform State Laws (a group of lawyers, judges, and legal scholars) issued the **Uniform Limited Liability Company Act (ULLCA).** The ULLCA codifies limited liability company law. Its goal is to establish comprehensive LLC law that is uniform throughout the United States. The ULLCA covers most problems that arise in the formation, operation, and termination of LLCs. The ULLCA is not law unless a state adopts it as its LLC statute. Many states have adopted all or part of the ULLCA as their limited liability company law.

Limited liability companies are creatures of state law, not federal law. Limited liability companies can be created only pursuant to the laws of the state in which the LLC is being organized. These statutes, commonly referred to as limited liability company codes, regulate the formation, operation, and dissolution of LLCs. The state legislature may amend its LLC statute at any time. The courts interpret state LLC statutes to decide LLC and member disputes.

SIDEBAR

exhibit **15.8** *Limited liability company (LLC).*

DreamWorks SKG, LLC

In 1995, Steven Spielberg, Jeffrey Katzenberg, and David Geffen formed DreamWorks SKG, a major movie and recording production company. Spielberg's fame and money came from directing films such as *E. T.,* Katzenberg was a leading executive at Disney, and Geffen built and sold Geffen Records. These multimillionaire multimedia giants combined their talents to form a formidable entertainment company.

Interestingly, DreamWorks was hatched as a Delaware limited liability company, or LLC. The organizers chose an LLC because it is taxed as a partnership and the profits (or losses) flow directly to the owners, but like a corporation, the owners are protected from personal liability beyond their capital contributions.

DreamWorks issued several classes of stock, or interests. The three principals put up $100 million ($33.3 million each) for "SKG" stock, which grants the principals 100 percent voting control and 67 percent of the firm's profits. In addition, each principal has a seven-year employment contract that pays him $1 million annually,

plus other fringe benefits and perquisites on terms that are customary for similarly situated executives in the entertainment industry.

DreamWorks raised the other $900 million of its $1 billion capital from other investors, who received a third of future profits. The other investors were issued the following classes of stock:

CLASS	INVESTMENT
A	*Outside investors.* Class A stock was sold to big investors with more than $20 million to invest. Microsoft's cofounder, Paul Allen, purchased $500 million of Class A stock. Class A investors got seats on the board of directors.
S	*Outside investors.* Class S stock was issued for smallish, "strategic" investments with other companies for cross-marketing purposes.
E	*Employees.* Employees were granted the right to participate in an employee stock purchase plan.

A corporation is a separate *legal entity* (or *legal person*) for most purposes. Corporations are treated, in effect, as artificial persons created by the state who can sue or be sued in their own names, enter into and enforce contracts, hold title to and transfer property, and be found civilly and criminally liable for violations of law. Corporations cannot be put in prison, so the normal criminal penalty is the assessment of a fine, loss of a license, or other sanction.

Corporations have the following unique characteristics:

- *Limited liability of shareholders.* As separate legal entities, corporations are liable for their own contracts and debts. Generally, the shareholders have only limited liability. They are liable only to the extent of their capital contributions.

- *Free transferability of shares.* Corporate shares are freely transferable by the shareholder, by sale, assignment, pledge, or gift, unless they are issued pursuant to certain exemptions from securities registration. Shareholders may agree among themselves on restrictions on the transfer of shares. National securities markets, such as the New York Stock Exchange, the American Stock Exchange, and NASDAQ, have been developed for the organized sale of securities.

- *Perpetual existence.* Corporations exist in perpetuity unless a specific duration is stated in the corporation's articles of incorporation. The existence of a corporation can be voluntarily terminated by the shareholders. Corporations may be involuntarily terminated by the corporation's creditors if an involuntary petition for bankruptcy against the corporation is granted. The death, insanity, or bankruptcy of a shareholder, a director, or an officer of the corporation does not affect its existence.

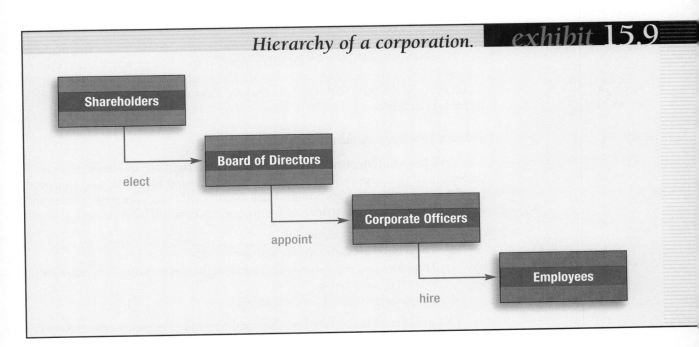

Hierarchy of a corporation.   *exhibit* 15.9

- *Centralized management.* The **board of directors** makes policy decisions concerning the operation of the corporation. Members of the board of directors are elected by the shareholders. The directors, in turn, appoint corporate *officers* to run the corporation's day-to-day operations. Together, the directors and the officers form the corporate "management."

Revised Model Business Corporation Act

The Committee on Corporate Laws of the American Bar Association drafted the Model Business Corporation Act (MBCA) in 1950. The model act was intended to provide a uniform law regulating the formation, operation, and termination of corporations.

In 1984, the committee completely revised the MBCA and issued the **Revised Model Business Corporation Act (RMBCA).** Certain provisions of the RMBCA have been amended since 1984. The RMBCA arranged the provisions of the Act more logically, revised the language of the Act to be more consistent, and made substantial changes in the provisions of the model act. Many states have adopted all or part of the RMBCA as their corporations codes. The RMBCA serves as the basis for our discussion of corporations law in this book.

Classifications of Corporations

A private, for-profit corporation is a **domestic corporation** in the state in which it is incorporated. It is a **foreign corporation** in all other states and jurisdictions. Suppose a corporation is incorporated in Texas and does business in Montana. The corporation is a domestic corporation in Texas and a foreign corporation in Montana. An **alien corporation** is a corporation that is incorporated in another country.

Incorporation Procedure

Corporations are creatures of statute. Thus, the organizers of the corporation must comply with the state's incorporation statute to form a corporation. Although relatively similar, the procedure for **incorporating** a corporation varies somewhat from state to state.

Selecting a State for Incorporation

A corporation can be incorporated in only one state even though it can do business in all other states in which it qualifies to do business. In choosing a state for incorporation, the incorporators, directors, and/or shareholders must consider the corporations law of the states under consideration.

For the sake of convenience, most corporations (particularly small ones) choose as the state for incorporation the state in which the corporation will be doing most of its business. Large corporations generally opt to incorporate in the state with the laws that are most favorable to the corporation's internal operations.

Articles of Incorporation

The **articles of incorporation** (or **corporate charter**) are the basic governing document of the corporation. They must be drafted and filed with, and approved by, the state before the corporation can be officially incorporated. Under the RMBCA [§ 2.02(a)], the articles of incorporation must include:

1. The name of the corporation
2. The number of shares the corporation is authorized to issue
3. The address of the corporation's initial registered office and the name of the initial registered agent
4. The name and address of each incorporator

The articles of incorporation also may include provisions concerning (1) the period of duration, which may be perpetual, (2) the purpose or purposes for which the corporation is organized, (3) limitation or regulation of the powers of the corporation, (4) regulation of the affairs of the corporation, and (5) any provision that otherwise would be contained in the corporation's bylaws.

The RMBCA provides that corporate existence begins when the articles of incorporation are filed. The secretary of state's filing of the articles of incorporation is *conclusive proof* that the incorporators satisfied all conditions to incorporations. The corollary to this rule is that failure to file articles of incorporation is conclusive proof of the nonexistence of the corporation.

The articles of incorporation can be amended to contain any provision that could have been lawfully included in the original document. After the amendment is approved by the shareholders, the corporation must file articles of amendment with the secretary of state [RMBCA § 10.06]. Exhibit 15.10 shows sample articles of incorporation.

Corporate Bylaws

In addition to the articles of incorporation, corporations are governed by their *corporate bylaws.* Either the incorporators or the initial directors can adopt the bylaws of the corporation. The bylaws are much more detailed than are the articles of incorporation. Bylaws may contain any provision for managing the business and affairs of the corporation that are not inconsistent with law or the articles of incorporation [RMBCA § 2.06]. They do not have to be filed with any government official. The bylaws are binding on the directors, officers, and shareholders of the corporation.

The bylaws govern the internal management structure of the corporation. Typically, they specify the time and place of the annual shareholder's meeting, how special meetings of shareholders are called, the time and place of annual and monthly board of directors' meetings, how special meetings of the board of directors are called, the notice required for meetings, the quorum necessary to hold a shareholders' or board of directors' meeting, the required vote necessary to enact a corporate matter, the corporate officers and their duties, the committees of the board of directors and their duties, where the records of the corporation are to be kept, directors' and shareholders' inspection rights of corporate records, the procedure for transferring shares of the corporation, and such.

The board of directors has the authority to amend the bylaws unless the articles of incorporation reserve that right for the shareholders. The shareholders of the corporation have the absolute right to amend the bylaws even though the bylaws also may be amended by the board of directors. Sample provisions of corporate bylaws are set forth in Exhibit 15.11.

Organizational Meeting

An **organizational meeting** of the initial directors of the corporation must be held after the articles of incorporation are filed. At this meeting the directors must adopt the bylaws, elect corporate officers, and transact other business that may come before the meeting [RMBCA § 2.05]. The latter category includes matters such as accepting share subscriptions, approving the form of the stock certificate, authorizing the issuance of the shares, ratifying or adopting promoters' contracts, selecting a bank, choosing an auditor, forming committees of the board of directors, fixing the salaries of officers, hiring *exhibit* **15.10** *Sample articles of incorporation.*

ARTICLES OF INCORPORATION
OF
THE BIG CHEESE CORPORATION

ONE: The name of this corporation is:

THE BIG CHEESE CORPORATION

TWO: The purpose of this corporation is to engage in any lawful act or activity for which a corporation may be organized under the General Corporation Law of California other than the banking business, the trust company business, or the practice of a profession permitted to be incorporated by the California Corporations Code.

THREE: The name and address in this state of the corporation's initial agent for service of process is:

Nikki Nguyen, Esq.   1000 Main Street, Suite 800
Los Angeles, California 90010

FOUR: This corporation is authorized to issue only one class of shares which shall be designated common stock. The total number of shares it is authorized to issue is 1,000,000 shares.

FIVE: The names and addresses of the persons who are appointed to act as the initial directors of this corporation are:

Shou-Yi Kang	100 Maple Street	Los Angeles, California 90005
Frederick Richards	200 Spruce Road	Los Angeles, California 90006
Jessie Qilan	300 Palm Drive	Los Angeles, California 90007
Richard Eastin	400 Willow Lane	Los Angeles, California 90008

SIX: The liability of the directors of the corporation from monetary damages shall be eliminated to the fullest extent possible under California law.

SEVEN: The corporation is authorized to provide indemnification of agents (as defined in Section 317 of the Corporations Code) for breach of duty to the corporation and its stockholders through bylaw provisions or through agreements with the agents, or both, in excess of the indemnification otherwise permitted by Section 317 of the Corporations Code, subject to the limits on such excess indemnification set forth in Section 204 of the Corporations Code.

IN WITNESS WHEREOF, the undersigned, being all the persons named above as the initial directors, have executed these Articles of Incorporation.

_____   _____

_____   _____

_____   _____

Dated: January 1, 2003

Sample provisions from corporate bylaws.   *exhibit* **15.11**

BYLAWS OF
THE BIG CHEESE CORPORATION

ARTICLE I   Offices

Section 1. Principal Executive Office. The corporation's principal executive office shall be fixed and located at such place as the Board of Directors (herein called the "Board") shall determine. The Board is granted full power and authority to change said principal executive office from one location to another.

Section 2. Other Offices. Branch or subordinate offices may be established at any time by the Board at any place or places.

ARTICLE II   Shareholders

Section 1. Annual Meetings. The annual meetings of shareholders shall be held on such date and at such time as may be fixed by the Board. At such meetings, directors shall be elected and any other proper business may be transacted.

Section 2. Special Meetings. Special meetings of the shareholders may be called at any time by the Board, the Chairman of the Board, the President, or by the holders of shares entitled to cast not less than ten percent of the votes at such meeting. Upon request in writing to the Chairman of the Board, the President, any Vice President or the Secretary by any person (other than the Board) entitled to call a special meeting of shareholders, the officer forthwith shall cause notice to be given to the shareholders entitled to vote that a meeting will be held at a time requested by the person or persons calling the meeting, not less than thirty-five nor more than sixty days after the receipt of the request. If the notice is not given within twenty days after receipt of the request, the persons entitled to call the meeting may give the notice.

Section 3. Quorum. A majority of the shares entitled to vote, represented in person or by proxy, shall constitute a quorum at any meeting of shareholders. If a quorum is present, the affirmative vote of a majority of the shares represented and voting at the meeting (which shares voting affirmatively also constitute at least a majority of the required quorum) shall be the act of the shareholders, unless the vote of a greater number or voting by classes is required by law or by the Articles, except as provided in the following sentence. The shareholders present at a duly called or held meeting at which a quorum is present may continue to do business until adjournment, notwithstanding the withdrawal of enough shareholders to leave less than a quorum, if any action taken (other than adjournment) is approved by at least a majority of the shares required to constitute a quorum.

ARTICLE III   Directors

Section 1. Election and Term of Office. The directors shall be elected at each annual meeting of the shareholders, but if any such annual meeting is not held or the directors are not elected thereat, the directors may be elected at any special meeting of shareholders held for that purpose. Each director shall hold office until the next annual meeting and until a successor has been elected and qualified.

Section 2. Quorum. A majority of the authorized number of directors constitutes a quorum of the Board for the transaction of business. Every act or decision done or made by a majority of the directors present at a meeting duly held at which a quorum is present shall be regarded as the act of the Board, unless a greater number be required by law or by the Articles. A meeting at which a quorum is initially present may continue to transact business notwithstanding the withdrawal of directors, if any action taken is approved by at least a majority of the required quorum for such meeting.

Section 3. Participation in Meetings by Conference Telephone. Members of the Board may participate in a meeting through use of conference telephone or similar communications equipment, so long as all members participating in such meeting can hear one another.

Section 4. Action Without Meeting. Any action required or permitted to be taken by the Board may be taken without a meeting if all members of the Board shall individually or collectively consent in writing to such action. Such consent or consents shall have the same effect as a unanimous vote of the Board and shall be filed with the minutes of the proceedings of the Board.

employees, authorizing the filing of applications for government licenses to transact the business of the corporation, and empowering corporate officers to enter into contracts on behalf of the corporation.

S Corporations

In 1982, Congress enacted the Subchapter S Revision Act. The act divided all corporations into two groups: **S Corporations,** which are those that elect to be taxed under Subchapter S, and C Corporations, which are all other corporations [26 U.S.C. §§ 6242 et seq.].

If a corporation elects to be taxed as an S Corporation, it pays no federal income tax at the corporate level. As in a partnership, the corporation's income or loss flows to the shareholders' individual income tax returns. Thus, this election is particularly advantageous if (1) the corporation is expected to have losses that can be offset against other income of the shareholders, or (2) the corporation is expected to make profits and the shareholders' income tax brackets are lower than the corporation's. Profits are taxed to the shareholders even if the income is not distributed. The shares retain other attributes of the corporate form, including limited liability.

Corporations that meet the following criteria can elect to be taxed as S Corporations:

1. The corporation must be a domestic corporation.
2. The corporation cannot be a member of an affiliated group.
3. The corporation can have no more than 75 shareholders.
4. Shareholders must be individuals, estates, or certain trusts. Corporations and partnerships cannot be shareholders.
5. Shareholders must be citizens or residents of the United States. Nonresident aliens cannot be shareholders.
6. The corporation cannot have more than one class of stock. Shareholders do not have to have equal voting rights.
7. No more than 20 percent of the corporation's income can be from passive investment income.

Shareholders of an S Corporation must be individuals, estates, or certain trusts.

An S Corporation election is made by filing a Form 2553 with the Internal Revenue Service (IRS). The election can be rescinded by shareholders who collectively own at least a majority of the shares of the corporation. However, if the election is rescinded, another S Corporation election cannot be made for five years.

Shareholders

Common stock is an equity security that represents the residual value of the corporation. Common stock has no preferences. That is, creditors and preferred shareholders must receive their required interest and dividend payments before common shareholders receive anything. Common stock does not have a fixed maturity date. If the corporation is liquidated, the creditors and preferred shareholders are paid the value of their interests first, and the common shareholders are paid the value of their interest (if any) last. Corporations may issue different classes of common stock [RMBCA § 6.01 (a) and (b)].

Rights and Duties of Common Stockholders

Persons who own common stock are called common stockholders. A common stockholder's investment in the corporation is represented by a common stock certificate. Common shareholders have the right to elect directors and to vote on mergers and other important matters. In return for their investment, common shareholders receive dividends declared by the board of directors.

A corporation's shareholders *own* the corporation. Nevertheless, they are not agents of the corporation (i.e., they cannot bind the corporation to any contracts), and the only management duties they have are the right to vote on matters such as the election of directors and the approval of fundamental changes in the corporation.

Disregard of the Corporate Entity

Shareholders of a corporation generally have limited liability (i.e., they are liable for the debts and obligations of the corporation only to the extent of their capital contribution). But if a shareholder or shareholders dominate a corporation and misuse it for improper purposes, a court of equity can *disregard the corporate entity* and hold the shareholders of a corporation personally liable for the corporation's debts and obligations. This doctrine is commonly referred to as piercing the corporate veil. It is often resorted to by unpaid creditors who are trying to collect from shareholders a debt owed by the corporation. The piercing the corporate veil doctrine is also called the *alter-ego doctrine* because the corporation has become the alter ego of the shareholder.

Courts will pierce the corporate veil if (1) the corporation has been formed without sufficient capital—called *thin capitalization*—or (2) the corporation and its shareholders have not maintained separateness (e.g., commingling of personal and corporate assets, failure to hold required shareholders' meetings, failure to maintain corporate records and books). The courts examine this doctrine on a case-by-case basis.

Board of Directors

Typically, boards of directors are composed of inside directors and outside directors. An **inside director** is a person who is also an officer of the corporation. For example, the president of a corporation often sits as a director of the corporation. An **outside director** is a person who sits on the board of directors of a corporation but is not an officer of that corporation. Outside directors often are officers and directors of other corporations, bankers, lawyers, professors, and others. Outside directors usually are selected for their business knowledge and expertise.

The board of directors of a corporation is responsible for formulating the policy decisions affecting the management, supervision, and control of the operation of the corporation [RMBCA § 8.01]. Such policy decisions include deciding the business or businesses in which the corporation should be engaged, selecting and removing the top officers of the corporation, determining the capital structure of the corporation, declaring dividends, and the like.

Kinney Shoe Corp. v. Polan

939 F.2d 209 (1991)

United States Court of Appeals, Fourth Circuit

FACTS

In 1984, Lincoln M. Polan formed Industrial Realty Company (Industrial), a West Virginia corporation. Polan was the sole shareholder of Industrial. Although a certificate of incorporation was issued, no organizational meeting was held and no officers were elected. Industrial issued no stock certificates because nothing was ever paid in to the corporation. Other corporate formalities were not observed. Polan, on behalf of Industrial, signed a lease to sublease commercial space in a building controlled by Kinney Shoe Corporation (Kinney). The first rental payment to Kinney was made out of Polan's personal funds, and no further payments were made on the lease. Kinney filed suit against Industrial and obtained a judgment of $66,400 for unpaid rent. When the amount was unpaid by Industrial, Kinney sued Polan individually and sought to pierce the corporate veil to collect from Polan. The district court held for Polan. Kinney appealed.

ISSUE

Is Polan personally liable for Industrial's debts?

IN THE LANGUAGE OF THE COURT

Chapman, Senior Circuit Judge.

Kinney seeks to pierce the corporate veil of Industrial so as to hold Polan personally liable on the sublease debt. The Supreme Court of Appeals of West Virginia has set forth a two-prong test to be used in determining whether to pierce a corporate veil in a breach of contract case. This test raises two issues: first, is the unity of interest and ownership such that the separate personalities of the corporation and the individual shareholder no longer exist; and second, would an equitable result occur if the acts are treated as those of the corporation alone.

The district court found that the two-prong test had been satisfied. The court concluded that Polan's failure to carry out the corporate formalities with respect to Industrial, coupled with Industrial's gross undercapitalization, resulted in damage to Kinney. We agree. It is undisputed that Industrial was not adequately capitalized. Actually, it had not paid in capital. Polan had put nothing into this corporation, and it did not observe any corporate formalities. Polan was obviously trying to limit his liability by setting up a paper curtain constructed of nothing more than Industrial's certificate of incorporation. These facts present the classic scenario for an action to pierce the corporate veil so as to reach the responsible party and produce an equitable result.

DECISION AND REMEDY

The court of appeals pierced the corporate veil and held Polan personally liable on Industrial's debt to Kinney. Reversed.

Questions

1. Is the doctrine of piercing the corporate veil needed? Should parties like Kinney bear the risk of dealing with corporations like Industrial?

2. Is it ethical for persons to form corporations to avoid personal liability? Should this be allowed?

3. What is the risk if corporate formalities are not observed? Explain.

INFORMATION TECHNOLOGY

DELAWARE AMENDS CORPORATION CODE TO RECOGNIZE ELECTRONIC COMMUNICATIONS

The state of Delaware leads the nation as the site for incorporation of the United States' largest corporations. This is the result of the Delaware corporation code itself, as well as the expertise of the Delaware courts in resolving corporate disputes. To keep this leadership position, in 2000 the state legislature amended the Delaware General Corporation law to recognize evolving electronic technology. The major changes to the law are:

- Delivery of notices to stockholders may be made electronically if the stockholder consents to the delivery of notice in this form.
- Proxy solicitation for shareholder votes may be made by electronic transmission.
- The shareholder list of a corporation that must be made available during the 10 days prior to a stockholder meeting may be made available either at the principal place of business of the corporation or by posting the list on an electronic network.
- Stockholders who are not physically present at a meeting may be deemed present, participate in, and vote at the meeting by electronic communication; a meeting may be held solely by electronic communication without a physical location.
- The election of directors of the corporation may be held by electronic transmission.
- Directors' actions by unanimous consent may be taken by electronic transmission.

The use of electronic transmissions, electronic networks, and communication by email will make the operation and administration of corporate affairs more efficient in Delaware. Other states are expected to amend their corporation codes to recognize the importance of electronic communications.

The directors can act only as a board. They cannot act individually on the corporation's behalf. Every director has the right to participate in any meeting of the board of directors. Each director has one vote. Directors cannot vote by proxy.

Regular meetings of the board of directors are held at the times and places established in the bylaws. Such meetings can be held without notice. The board can call special meetings as provided in the bylaws [RMBCA § 8.20(a)]. They usually are convened for reasons such as issuing new shares, considering proposals to merge with other corporations, adopting maneuvers to defend against hostile takeover attempts, and the like.

The board of directors may act without a meeting if all of the directors sign written consents that set forth the actions taken. Such consent has the effect of a unanimous vote. The RMBCA permits meetings of the board to be held via conference calls.

Corporate Officers

The board of directors has the authority to appoint the **officers** of the corporation. The officers are elected by the board of directors at such time and by such manner as prescribed in the corporation's bylaws. The directors can delegate certain management authority to the officers of the corporation.

At minimum, most corporations have the following officers: (1) a president, (2) one or more vice presidents, (3) a secretary, and (4) a treasurer. The

Ethical PERSPECTIVE *Directors' and Officers' Duty of Loyalty*

The **duty of loyalty** requires directors and officers to subordinate their personal interests to those of the corporation and its shareholders. Justice Benjamin Cardozo defined this duty of loyalty as follows:

> [A corporate director or officer] owes loyalty and allegiance to the corporation—a loyalty that is undivided and an allegiance that is influenced by no consideration other than the welfare of the corporation. Any adverse interest of a director [or officer] will be subjected to scrutiny rigid and uncompromising. He may not profit at the expense of his corporation and in conflict with its rights; he may not for personal gain divert unto himself the opportunities that in equity and fairness belong to the corporation.
>
> Many forms of conduct permissible in a workaday world for those acting at arm's length are forbidden to those bound by fiduciary ties. Not honesty alone, but the punctilio of an honor the most sensitive, is then the standard of behavior. As to this there has developed a tradition that is unbending and inveterate. [*Meinhard v. Salmon,* 164 N.E.2d 545, 546 (N.Y.App. 1928)]

If a director or officer breaches his or her duty of loyalty and makes a secret profit on a transaction, the corporation can sue the director or officer to recover the secret profit.

bylaws or the board of directors can authorize duly appointed officers the power to appoint assistant officers. The same individual may simultaneously hold more than one office in the corporation [RMBCA § 8.40]. The duties of each officer are specified in the bylaws of the corporation.

Officers of the corporation have such authority as may be provided in the bylaws of the corporation or as determined by resolution of the board of directors.

Duty of Care

The **duty of care** requires corporate directors and officers to use *care and diligence* when acting on behalf of the corporation. To meet this duty, the directors and officers must discharge their duties (1) in good faith, (2) with the care that an *ordinary prudent person* in a like position would use under similar circumstances, and (3) in a manner he or she reasonably believes to be in the best interests of the corporation [RMBCA §§ 8.30(a) and 8.42(a)].

A director or officer who breaches this duty of care is personally liable to the corporation and its shareholders for any damages caused by the breach. Such breaches, which are normally caused by **negligence,** often involve a director's or officer's failure to (1) make a reasonable investigation of a corporate matter, (2) attend board meetings on a regular basis, (3) properly supervise a subordinate who causes a loss to the corporation through embezzlement and such, or (4) keep adequately informed about corporate affairs. Breaches are examined by the courts on a case-by-case basis.

The determination of whether a corporate director or officer has met his or her duty of care is measured as of the time the decision is made. The benefit of hindsight is not a factor. Therefore, the directors and officers are not liable to the corporation or its shareholders for honest mistakes of judgment. This is called the **business judgment rule.**

In the past, the size, power, and range of activities of corporations were limited. This changed at the beginning of the twentieth century, when corporations won the right to own stock in each other. National corporate networks soon followed. Eventually, parent corporations, mostly American, expanded these networks overseas by setting up subsidiary corporations under the laws of other countries. These international networks (or **multinational corporations**) are made up of companies of different nationalities that constitute a single economic unit connected by shareholding, managerial control, or contractual agreement.

The simplest international operating structure is one that subcontracts with independent firms in the host country to carry out sales or purchases. "National multinational" firms that establish wholly owned branches and subsidiaries overseas are somewhat more complex. "International multinational" firms are even more complicated. They are made up of two or more parents from different countries that co-own operating businesses in two or more countries.

The Ford Motor Company is an example of a national multinational firm. Organized in the United States at the beginning of the twentieth century, Ford has always viewed the entire world as its market. The company's policy is for the American parent to own and control all of its overseas subsidiaries. Ford's ten European subsidiaries are all owned entirely by the American parent. The Mitsubishi Group is another example of this organizational format. It is actually made up of several Japanese companies that use joint directors' meetings to coordinate their activities in Japan and overseas.

The Royal Dutch/Shell Group is an example of an international multinational corporation. In 1907, the Dutch and British parents each formed a wholly owned holding company in their respective countries. Each then transferred the ownership of the operating subsidiary to the holding company and exchanged shares in the holding companies. The Dutch parent held 60 percent of each holding company, and the British parent held 40 percent. In addition, the management and operation of the two companies were organized to function as a single economic unit. Unilever, Dunlop Pirelli, and VFW/Fokker also operate under an international multinational umbrella.

A special type of international multinational is a *publicly owned transnational enterprise*. One example is Air Afrique, which was created by several West African countries through the use of a treaty granting each government a voice in the company's operation.

Consider this example: Suppose, after conducting considerable research and investigation, the directors of a major automobile company decide to produce a large and expensive automobile. When the car is introduced to the public for sale, few of the automobiles are sold because of the public's interest in buying smaller, less expensive automobiles. Because this was an honest mistake of judgment on the part of corporate management, their judgment is shielded by the business judgment rule.

Franchise

A **franchise** is established when one party (the *franchisor* or *licensor*) licenses another party (the *franchisee* or *licensee*) to use the franchisor's trade name, trademarks, commercial symbols, patents, copyrights, and other property in the

exhibit 15.12 Parties to a typical franchise arrangement.

| Franchisor (Licensor) | → Grant of franchise and license to use trademarks, service marks, and trade secrets. | Franchisee (licensee) |

distribution and selling of goods and services. Generally, the franchisor and the franchisee are established as separate corporations. The term *franchise* refers to both the agreement between the parties and the franchise outlet.

There are several advantages to franchising, including

1. The franchisor can reach lucrative new markets.
2. The franchisee has access to the franchisor's knowledge and resources while running an independent business.
3. Consumers are assured of uniform product quality.

A typical franchise arrangement is illustrated in Exhibit 15.12.

A prospective franchisee must apply to the franchisor for a franchise. The application often includes detailed information about the applicant's previous employment, financial and educational history, credit status, and so on. If an applicant is approved, the parties enter into a franchise agreement that sets forth the terms and conditions of the franchise.

Franchisors and franchisees are liable for their own *contracts*. The same is true of *tort liability*. For example, if a person is injured by a franchisee's negligence, the franchisee is liable.

LEGAL TERMINOLOGY

Alien corporation

Articles of incorporation (corporate charter)

Articles of limited liability partnership

Board of directors

Business judgment rule

Common stock certificate

Common stockholder

Corporation

"Doing business as" (d.b.a.)

Domestic corporation

Duty of care

Duty of loyalty

Entity theory

Foreign corporation

Franchise

General partner

General partnership

Indemnification

Inside director

Joint and several liability

Joint liability

Limited liability

Limited liability company (LLC)

Limited liability partnership (LLP)

Limited partner

Limited partnership

Limited partnership agreement
    (articles of limited partnership)

Multinational corporation

Negligence

Officers (of corporation)

Operating agreement

Organizational meeting

Outside director

Partnership agreement (articles of
    partnership)

Partnership at will

Partnership for a term

Piercing the corporate veil

Revised Model Business Corporation
    Act (RMBCA)

Revised Uniform Limited
    Partnership Act (RULPA)

S Corporations

Shareholders

Sole proprietorship/sole proprietor

Uniform Limited Liability Company
    Act (ULLCA)

Uniform Partnership Act (UPA)

Wrongful dissolution

Summary

CHAPTER 15 BUSINESS ORGANIZATIONS

Sole Proprietorship	
Definition	A form of business in which the owner and the business are one; the business is not a separate legal entity.
Business Name	A sole proprietorship can operate under the name of the sole proprietor or a *trade name*. Operating under a trade name is commonly designated as a *d.b.a. (doing business as)*. If a trade name is used, a *fictitious business name statement* must be filed with the appropriate state government office.
Liability	The sole proprietor is personally liable for the debts and obligations of the sole proprietorship.
General Partnership	
Definition	An association of two or more persons to carry on as co-owners of a business for profit [UPA § 6(1)].
Uniform Partnership Act (UPA)	Model act that codifies partnership law; most states have adopted all or part of the UPA. *(continued)*

Entity Theory of Partnerships	A theory that holds that partnerships are *separate legal entities* that can hold title to personal and real property, transact business in the partnership name, and the like.
Taxation of Partnerships	Partnerships do not pay federal income taxes; the income and losses of partnerships flow onto individual partners' federal income tax returns.
Partnership Agreement	Agreement establishing a general partnership; sets forth terms of the partnership. It is good practice to have a written partnership agreement that the partners sign.
Partners' Contract Authority	A contract entered into by a partner with a third party on behalf of a partnership is binding on the partnership.
Tort Liability	1. *Tort:* Occurs when a partner causes injury to a third party by his or her negligent act, breach of trust, breach of fiduciary duty, or intentional tort. 2. *Partnership liability:* The partnership is liable to third persons who are injured by torts committed by a partner while he or she is acting within the ordinary course of partnership business. 3. *Joint and several liability of partners:* Partners are *personally liable* for torts committed by partners acting on partnership business. This liability is *joint and several*, which means that the plaintiff can sue *one or more* of the partners separately. If successful, the plaintiff can recover the entire amount of the judgment from any or all of the defendant-partners.
Dissolution of Partnerships	Change in the relation of the partners caused by any partner ceasing to be associated in carrying on the business [UPA § 29].
Wrongful Dissolution	Occurs when a partner withdraws from a partnership without having the *right* to do so at the time. The partner is liable for damages caused by the wrongful dissolution of the partnership.

Limited Partnership

Uniform Limited Partnership Act (ULPA)	A 1916 model act that contains a uniform set of provisions for the formation, operation, and dissolution of limited partnerships.
Revised Uniform Limited Partnership Act (RULPA)	A 1976 revision of the ULPA that provides a more modern comprehensive law for the formation, operation, and dissolution of limited partnerships.
Limited Partnership	A special form of partnership that has both limited and general partners. 1. *General partners:* Partners in a limited partnership who invest capital, manage the business, and are personally liable for partnership debts.

Limited Partnership, *continued*	2. *Limited partners:* Partners in a limited partnership who invest capital but do not participate in management and are not personally liable for partnership debts beyond their capital contributions.
Formation of Limited Partnerships	1. *Certificate of limited partnership:* A document that two or more persons must execute and sign that establishes a limited partnership. The certificate of limited partnership must be filed with the secretary of state of the appropriate state. 2. *Limited partnership agreement:* A document that sets forth the rights and duties of general and limited partners, the terms and conditions regarding the operation, termination, and dissolution of the partnership and so on.
Liability of General and Limited Partners	1. *General partners:* General partners of a limited partnership have *unlimited personal liability* for the debts and obligations of the limited partnership. 2. *Limited partners:* Limited partners of a limited partnership are liable only for the debts and obligations of the limited partnership up to their capital contributions. 3. *Limited partners and management:* Limited partners have no right to participate in the management of the partnership. A limited partner is *liable as a general partner* if his or her participation in the control of the business is substantially the same as that of a general partner, but the limited partner is liable only to persons who reasonably believed him or her to be a general partner.

Limited Liability Partnership (LLP)

Definition	A form of business in which there does not have to be a general partner who is personally liable for debts and obligations of the partnership. All partners are limited partners and stand to lose only their capital contribution should the partnership fail. LLPs are formed by accountants and other professionals as allowed by LLP law.
Partners	Owners of an LLP.
Articles of Partnership	A document that the partners of an LLP must execute, sign, and file with the secretary of state of the appropriate state to form an LLP.
Taxation	An LLP does not pay federal income taxes unless it elects to do so. If an LLP is taxed as a partnership, the income and losses of the LLP flow onto individual partners' federal income tax returns.

Limited Liability Company (LLC)

Definition	A special form of unincorporated business entity that combines the tax benefits of a partnership with the limited personal liability attribute of a corporation. *(continued)*

Members	Owners of an LLC.
Articles of Organization	A document that owners of an LLC must execute, sign, and file with the secretary of state of the appropriate state to form an LLC.
Operating Agreement	An agreement entered into among members that governs the affairs and business of the LLC and the relations among partners, managers, and the LLC.
Taxation	An LLC does not pay federal income taxes unless it elects to do so. If an LLC is taxed as a partnership, the income and losses of the LLP flow onto individual members' federal income tax returns.

Nature of the Corporation

Definition	A legal entity created pursuant to the laws of the state of incorporation. A corporation is a separate legal entity—an *artificial person*—that can own property, sue and be sued, enter into contracts, and such.
Characteristics of Corporations	1. *Limited liability of shareholders:* Shareholders are liable for the debts and obligations of the corporation only to the extent of their capital contributions. 2. *Free transferability of shares:* Shares of a corporation are freely transferable by the shareholders unless they are expressly restricted. 3. *Perpetual existence:* Corporations exist in perpetuity unless a specific duration is stated in the corporation's articles of incorporation. 4. *Centralized management: Board of directors* of the corporation makes policy decisions of the corporation. Corporate *officers* appointed by the board of directors run the corporation's day-to-day operations. Together, the directors and officers form the corporation's management.
Business Corporation Acts	1. *Model Business Corporation Act (MBCA):* A model act drafted in 1950 that was intended to provide a uniform law for the regulation of corporations. 2. *Revised Model Business Corporation Act (RMBCA):* A revision of the MBCA promulgated in 1984 that arranged the provisions of the model act more logically, revised the language to be more consistent, and made substantial changes that modernized the provisions of the act.
Classifications of Corporations	1. *Domestic corporation:* A corporation in the state in which it is incorporated. 2. *Foreign corporation:* A corporation in any state other than the one in which it is incorporated. A domestic corporation often transacts business in states other than its state of incorporation; hence it is a foreign corporation in these other states. A foreign corporation must obtain a *certificate of authority* from these other states in order to transact intrastate business in those states.

(continued)

Classifications of Corporations, *continued*	3. *Alien corporation:* A corporation that is incorporated in another country. Alien corporations are treated as foreign corporations for most purposes.
Procedure	*Incorporation:* The process of incorporating (forming) a new corporation.
Selecting a State of Incorporation	A corporation can be incorporated in only one state, although it can conduct business in other states.
Articles of Incorporation	1. The basic governing document of a corporation; must be filed with the secretary of state of the state of incorporation. It is a public document, also called the *corporate charter*. 2. The corporation code of each state sets out the information that must be included in the articles of incorporation. Additional information may be included in the articles of incorporation as deemed necessary or desirable by the incorporators.
Corporate Bylaws	A detailed set of rules adopted by the board of directors after the corporation is formed, containing provisions for managing the business and affairs of the corporation. This document does not have to be filed with the secretary of state.
Organizational Meeting	A meeting that must be held by the initial directors of the corporation after the articles of incorporation are filed. At this meeting, the directors adopt the bylaws, elect corporate officers, ratify promoters' contracts, adopt a corporate seal, and transact such other business as may come before the meeting.
Common Stock	A type of equity security that represents the *residual value* of the corporation. Common stock has no preferences, and its shareholders are paid dividends and assets upon liquidation only after creditors and preferred shareholders have been paid. 1. *Common stockholder:* A person who owns common stock. 2. *Common stock certificate:* A document that represents the common shareholders' investment in the corporation.
Liability of Shareholders	Shareholders of corporations generally have *limited liability*; that is, they are liable for the debts and obligations of the corporation only to the *extent of their capital contribution* to the corporation.
Liability	Shareholders may be found *personally liable* for the debts and obligations of the corporation under the doctrine called *piercing the corporate veil*. Courts can *disregard the corporate entity* and hold shareholders personally liable for the debts and obligations of the corporation if (a) the corporation has been formed without sufficient capital (*thin capitalization*) or (b) separateness has not been maintained between the corporation and its shareholders (e.g., commingling of personal and corporate assets, failure to hold required shareholders' meetings, and such). Also called the *alter-ego doctrine*. *(continued)*

Board of Directors	A panel of decision makers for the corporation, the members of which are elected by the shareholders. 1. The directors of a corporation are responsible for formulating the *policy* decisions affecting the corporation, such as deciding what businesses to engage in, determining the capital structure of the corporation, selecting and removing top officers of the corporation, and the like. 2. *Inside director:* A member of the board of directors who is also an officer of the corporation. 3. *Outside director:* A member of the board of directors who is not an officer of the corporation.
Meetings of the Board of Directors	1. *Regular meeting:* A meeting of the board of directors held at the time and place scheduled in the bylaws. 2. *Special meeting:* A meeting of the board of directors convened to discuss an important or emergency matter, such as a proposed merger, a hostile takeover attempt, and such. 3. *Written consents:* The board of directors may act without a meeting if all of the directors sign written consents that set forth the action taken.
Officers	Employees of the corporation who are appointed by the board of directors to manage the *day-to-day operations* of the corporation.
Duty of Loyalty	A duty that directors and officers have not to act adversely to the interests of the corporation and to subordinate their personal interests to those of the corporation and its shareholders.
Duty of Care	A duty that corporate directors and officers have to use care and diligence when acting on behalf of the corporation. This duty is discharged if they perform their duties (a) in good faith, (b) with the care that an *ordinary prudent person* in a like position would use under similar circumstances, and (c) in a manner they reasonably believe to be in the best interests of the corporation. 1. *Negligence:* Failure of a corporate director or officer to exercise this duty of care when conducting the corporation's business. 2. *Business judgment rule:* A rule that says directors and officers are not liable to the corporation or its shareholders for honest mistakes of judgment.
Franchise	
Description	Established when one party licenses another party to use the franchisor's trade name, trademarks, commercial symbols, patents, copyrights, and other property in the distribution and selling of goods and services. 1. *Franchisor:* The party who does the licensing in a franchise arrangement. Also called the *licensor.* 2. *Franchisee:* The party who is licensed by the franchisor in a franchise arrangement. Also called the *licensee.*

Working the Web

1. Check the U.S. Small Business Administration for information about SBA programs and services at www.sbaonline.sba.gov.

2. Find federal agencies and gateways to related business websites at www.business.gov/busadv/onestop.cfm.

3. Find information on individual companies using the Securities and Exchange Commission website at www.sec.gov/edgar/searchedgar/webusers.htm.

4. Check FirstGov—which has more than 47 million federal web pages indexed and organized by topic area—at http://fic.info.gov/.

5. See the Government Printing Office (GPO) for government information in a wide range of formats, including print, microfiche, CD-ROM, and online technology, through GPO Access at www.gpo.gov/gpoaccess.

Questions

CRITICAL LEGAL THINKING AND WRITING

1. Define a *sole proprietorship*. Describe the tort and contract liability of a sole proprietor for the debts and obligations of the sole proprietorship.

2. Define a *general partnership*. Describe the liability of general partners for the debts and obligations of the general partnership.

3. Define a *limited partnership*. Describe the liability of general partners versus limited partners for the debts and obligations of the limited partnership.

4. Define a *limited liability partnership* (LLP). What is the liability exposure of partners of an LLP?

5. Define a *limited liability company* (LLC). What is the liability exposure of the member-owners of an LLC?

6. Define a *corporation*. What are the major attributes of a corporation? What is the liability exposure of shareholders for the debts and obligations of the corporation?

7. Describe the articles of incorporation, bylaws, and minutes of a corporation.

8. Define an S Corporation. What requirements must be met for a corporation to qualifty as an S Corporation?

9. Explain an officer's and director's duty of care to the corporation. Explain how the business judgment rule protects officers and directors from liability.

10. Define a *franchise*. Describe the tort and contract liability of the franchisor and franchisee.

Questions

ETHICS: ANALYSIS AND DISCUSSION

1. May a paralegal be a partner with a client of the law firm?
2. May a paralegal be a partner in a law firm?
3. May a paralegal take advantage of inside information learned about a public corporate client to trade in stock of the client?

Use of Confidential Information

There are few certainties in the area of ethics, for paralegals or in any profession. What qualifies as ethical conduct is in most cases based on state law and court interpretation applied to a set of facts. For the following:

- *Prepare a written statement based on your state law.*
- *Use your state bar association website as a starting point.*

Because of the volume of work and an impending deadline, you are hired as a temporary paralegal in a large Wall Street law firm to work on a case involving a major corporate client. One of the lawyers tells you that the client will soon announce a major breakthrough that will lead to a highly profitable business opportunity. Can you act on the information and purchase the stock?

CASES *for Discussion*

National Lumber Co. v. Advance Development Corp.

732 S.W.2d 840 (Ark. 1987)

15.1 FACTS

Pat McGowan, Val Somers, and Brent Robertson were general partners of Vermont Place, a limited partnership formed on January 20, 1984, for the purpose of constructing duplexes on an undeveloped tract of land in Fort Smith, Arkansas. The general partners appointed McGowan and his company, Advance Development Corporation, to develop the project, including contracting with material men, mechanics, and other suppliers. None of the limited partners took part in the management or control of the partnership.

On September 3, 1984, Somers and Robertson discovered that McGowan had not been paying the suppliers. They removed McGowan from the partnership and took over the project. The suppliers sued the partnership to recover the money owed them. The partnership assets were not sufficient to pay all of their claims.

ISSUE

Who is liable to the suppliers?

Singer v. Microhard.com, LLC et al.

Hypothetical

15.2 FACTS

Harold, Jasmine, Caesar, and Yuan form "Microhard.com, LLC," a limited liability company, to sell computer hardware and software over the Internet. Microhard.com, LLC hires Heather, a recent graduate of the University of Chicago and a brilliant software designer, as an employee. Heather's job is to design and develop software that will execute a computer command when the computer user thinks of the next command he or she wants to execute on the computer.

Using Heather's research, Microhard.com, LLC, develops the "Third Eye" software program that does this. Microhard.com, LLC, sends Heather to the annual Comdex Computer Show in Las Vegas, Nevada, to unveil this revolutionary software. Heather goes to Las Vegas and while there rents an automobile to get from the hotel to the computer show and to meet interested buyers at different locations in Las Vegas. While Heather is driving from her hotel to the site of the Comdex Computer Show, she negligently causes an accident and runs over Harold Singer, a pedestrian. Singer, who suffers severe personal injuries, sues Microhard.com, LLC as well as Heather, Harold, Jasmine, Caesar, and Yuan to recover monetary damages for his injuries.

ISSUE

Who is liable?

Billy v. Consolidated Mach. Tool Corp.

412 N.E.2d 934, 51 N.Y.2d 152 (N.Y.App. 1980)

15.3 FACTS

Joseph M. Billy was an employee of the USM Corporation. USM is a publicly held corporation. On October 21, 1976, Billy was at work when a 4,600-pound ram from a vertical boring mill broke loose and crushed him to death. Billy's widow brought suit against USM alleging that the accident was caused by certain defects in the manufacture and design of the vertical boring mill and in the two moving parts directly involved in the accident, a metal lifting arm and the 4,600-pound ram.

ISSUE

If Mrs. Billy's suit is successful, can the shareholders of USM Corporation be held personally liable for any judgment against USM?

Chelsea Industries, Inc. v. Gaffney

449 N.E.2d 320 (Mass. Sup. 1983)

15.4 FACTS

Lawrence Gaffney was the president and general manager of Ideal Tape Co. Ideal, a subsidiary of Chelsea Industries, Inc., was engaged in the business of manufacturing pressure-sensitive tape. In 1975, Gaffney recruited three other Ideal executives to join him in starting a tape-manufacturing business. The four men remained at Ideal for the two years it took them to plan the new enterprise. During this time they used their positions at Ideal to travel around the country to gather business ideas, recruit potential customers, and purchase equipment for their business. At no time did they reveal to Chelsea their intention to open a competing business. In November 1977, the new business was incorporated as Action Manufacturing Co. When executives at Chelsea discovered the existence of the new venture, Gaffney and the others resigned from Chelsea. Chelsea sued them for damages.

ISSUE

Who wins?

United States v. WRW Corporation

986 F.2d 138 (1993)   United States Court of Appeals, Sixth Circuit

Read the following case, excerpted from the court of appeals opinion. Review and brief the case. In your brief, answer the following questions.

1. Who was the plaintiff? What was it suing for?
2. Who were the defendants?

3. What is the doctrine of piercing the corporate veil?
4. Did the court find the defendants personally liable?

Peck, Judge.

In 1985, civil penalties totaling $90,350 were assessed against WRW Corporation (WRW), a Kentucky corporation, for serious violations of safety standards under the Federal Mine Safety and Health Act (the Act) which resulted in the deaths of two miners. Following the imposition of civil penalties, WRW liquidated its assets and went out of business.

Three individual defendants, who were the sole shareholders, officers, and directors of WRW, were later indicted and convicted for willful violations of mandatory health and safety standards under the Act. Roger Richardson, Noah Woolum, and William Woolum each served prison sentences and paid criminal fines. After his release from prison, Roger Richardson filed for bankruptcy under Chapter 7 of the Bankruptcy Code.

The United States (the Government) brought this action in May of 1988 against WRW and Roger Richardson, Noah Woolum, and William Woolum to recover the civil penalties previously imposed against WRW. The district court denied the individual defendants' motion to dismiss and granted summary judgment to the Government, piercing the corporate veil under state law and holding the individual defendants liable for the civil penalties assessed against WRW. For the reasons discussed herein, we affirm.

Having determined that the imposition of a $90,350 sanction upon the defendants does not violate principles of double jeopardy, we turn to the defendants' argument that the district court erred in holding the individual defendants liable for the penalty by piercing the corporate veil of WRW under Kentucky law.

The district court held that it was appropriate to pierce WRW's corporate veil under either an equity theory or an alter-ego theory, both of which are recognized under Kentucky law. Under either theory, the following factors must be considered when determining whether to pierce the corporate veil: (1) undercapitalization; (2) a failure to observe the formalities of corporate existence; (3) nonpayment or overpayment of dividends; (4) a siphoning off of funds by dominant shareholders; and (5) the majority shareholders having guaranteed corporate liabilities in their individual capacities.

The court first found that WRW was undercapitalized because it was incorporated with only $3,000 of capital, which the record indicates was insufficient to pay normal expenses associated with the operation of a coal mine. The district court next found that WRW failed to observe corporate formalities, noting that no bylaws were produced by the defendants, and all corporate actions taken by the individual defendants were without corporation authorization. Finally, although WRW never distributed any dividends to the individual defendants, and there was no evidence that the individual defendants siphoned off corporate funds, these factors alone do not mitigate against piercing the corporate veil in this case because WRW was never sufficiently capitalized and operated at a loss during its two years of active existence.

In addition to holding that the equities of this case support piercing the corporate veil, the district court held that the corporate veil should be pierced under the "alter ego" theory, because WRW and the defendants did not have separate personalities. In light of the lack of observance of corporate formalities or distinction between the individual defendants and the corporation, we agree with the district court's conclusion that "there was a complete merger of ownership and control of WRW with the individual Defendants."

The specific factual findings made by the district court amply support piercing the corporate veil of WRW and holding the individual defendants liable for the penalty assessed against the corporate entity. For all of the foregoing reasons, the judgment of the district court is AFFIRMED.

CHAPTER 16

CHAPTER OBJECTIVES

After studying this chapter, you should be able to:

1. Describe the business tort of misappropriating a trade secret.

2. Describe the criminal conduct that violates the Economic Espionage Act.

3. Describe how an invention can be patented under patent laws and the penalties for patent infringement.

4. List the writings that can be copyrighted and describe the penalties for copyright infringement.

5. Describe the legal rights that computer and software designers have in their works.

6. Describe the changes made in copyright law by the Digital Millennium Copyright Act.

7. Define *trademarks* and *service marks,* and describe the penalties for trademark infringement.

8. Describe the process for obtaining Internet domain names.

9. Describe the Uniform Computer Information Transactions Act (UCITA).

10. Describe the protections provided by the federal Anticybersquatting Act.

Intellectual Property and Internet Law

The Congress shall have the power . . . to promote the Progress of Science and useful Arts, by securing for limited Times to Authors and Inventors the exclusive Right to their respective Writings and Discoveries.

ARTICLE I, SECTION 8, CLAUSE 8, U.S. CONSTITUTION

Introduction

The American economy is based on the freedom of ownership of property. In addition to real estate and personal property, intellectual property rights have value to both businesses and individuals. This is particularly the case in the modern era of the Information Age, computers, and the Internet.

Trade secrets from the basis of many successful businesses, which are protected from misappropriation. Federal law provides protections for intellectual property rights, such as patents, copyrights, and trademarks. In addition, businesses and individuals may register domain names to use on the Internet. Anyone who infringes on these rights may be stopped from doing so and is liable for damages. Computers and computer software are accorded special protection from infringement.

Intellectual property rights and Internet law are two of the most important developing areas of the law. United States inventors and companies own valuable intellectual property rights—patents, trademarks, and copyrights—that are licensed worldwide. In addition, the area of Internet law, e-commerce, and domain names is exploding in use. Therefore, a paralegal needs to acquire knowledge of these important areas of the law to conduct patent searches, do research in the areas of intellectual property rights and Internet law, and help prepare documents for the creation and transfer of intellectual property and the use of e-commerce contracts. The topics of this chapter are trade secrets, patents, copyrights, trademarks, domain names, and computer law.

TRADE SECRETS

Many businesses are successful because their **trade secrets** set them apart from their competitors. Trade secrets may be product formulas, patterns, designs, compilations of data, customer lists, or other business secrets. Many trade secrets either do not qualify to be—or simply are not—patented, copyrighted, or trademarked. Many states have adopted the Uniform Trade Secrets Act to give statutory protection to trade secrets.

State unfair competition laws allow the owner of a trade secret to bring a lawsuit for *misappropriation* against anyone who steals a trade secret. To be actionable, the defendant (often an employee of the owner or a competitor) must have obtained the trade secret through unlawful means such as theft, bribery, or industrial espionage. No tort has occurred if there is no misappropriation. For example, a competitor can lawfully discover a trade secret by performing reverse engineering (i.e., taking apart and examining a rival's product).

The owner of a trade secret is obliged to take all reasonable precautions to prevent that secret from being discovered by others. These precautions include fencing in buildings, placing locks on doors, hiring security guards, and the like. If the owner fails to take such actions, the secret is no longer subject to protection under state unfair competition laws.

Generally, a successful plaintiff in a trade secret action can:

1. recover the profits made by the offender from the use of the trade secret
2. recover for damages, and
3. obtain an injunction prohibiting the offender from divulging or using the trade secret.

"'How I Spent My Summer Vacation,' by Lilia Anya, all rights reserved, which includes the right to reproduce this essay or portions thereof in any form whatsoever, including, but not limited to, novel, screenplay, musical, television miniseries, home video, and interactive CD-ROM."

Until recently—although stealing trade secrets exposes the offender to a civil lawsuit by the injured party to recover economic damages—the offender seldom faced criminal charges except under a few state laws. All that changed with enactment of the federal **Economic Espionage Act** of 1996 [18 U.S.C. 1831–1839], which makes it a federal crime to steal another's trade secrets. Previously, no federal statute directly addressed economic espionage and the stealing of trade secrets.

Under the Espionage Act, it is a federal crime for any person to convert a trade secret to his or her benefit or for the benefit of others, knowing or intending that the act would cause injury to the owner of the trade secret. Under the Espionage Act, the definition of *trade secret* is broad and parallels the definition used under the civil laws of misappropriating a trade secret. A trade secret under this Act covers any economic, business, financial, technical, scientific, or engineering information, including processes, software programs, and codes.

One of the major reasons for passing the Espionage Act was to address the ease of stealing trade secrets through espionage and using the Internet. For example, hundreds of pages of confidential information can be downloaded onto a small computer diskette, placed in someone's pocket, and taken from the legal owner. In addition, computer hackers can crack into a company's computers and steal customer lists, databases, formulas, and other trade secrets. The Espionage Act adds an important weapon to address and penalize computer and Internet espionage.

The Espionage Act provides for severe criminal penalties. An organization can be fined up to $5 million per criminal act and $10 million if the criminal act was committed to benefit a foreign government. The Act imposes prison terms on individuals of up to 15 years per criminal violation, which can be increased to 25 years per violation if the criminal act was done with the intent to benefit a foreign government. By adding criminal penalties, the Espionage Act adds another weapon to safeguard trade secrets and intellectual property in the United States.

PATENTS

Pursuant to the express authority granted in the U.S. Constitution [Article I, Section 8, clause 8], Congress enacted the Federal Patent Statute of 1952 [35 U.S.C. § 10 et seq.]. This law is intended to provide an incentive for inventors to invent and make their inventions public and to protect patented inventions from infringement. Federal patent law is exclusive; there are no state patent laws. The United States Court of Appeals for the Federal Circuit in Washington, D.C., was created in 1982 to hear patent appeals. The court was established to promote uniformity in patent law.

Patenting an Invention

To be patented, the invention must be *novel, useful,* and *nonobvious.* In addition, only certain subject matters can be patented. Patentable subject matter includes (1) machines, (2) processes, (3) compositions of matter, (4) improvements to existing machines, processes, or compositions of matter, (5) designs for an article of manufacture, (6) asexually reproduced plants, and (7) living material invented by a person. Abstractions and scientific principles cannot be patented

In 1994, the General Agreement on Tariffs and Trade (GATT) established the World Trade Organization (WTO), an international organization of which the United States is a member. GATT's intellectual property provisions, and implementing legislation passed by Congress, made the following important changes in U.S. patent law:

1. Patents are valid for *20 years,* instead of the previous term of 17 years.

2. The patent term begins to run from the date the patent application is *filed* instead of when the patent is issued, as was the case previously.

These changes, which became effective June 8, 1995, brought the U.S. patent system in harmony with the majority of other developed nations. The United States still follows the first-to-invent rule rather than the first-to-file rule that some other countries follow.

U.S. Patent and Trademark
Office: www.uspto.gov

unless they are part of the tangible environment. For example, Einstein's theory of relativity ($E = MC^2$) cannot be patented.

Patent applicants must file a *patent application* containing a written description of the invention with the United States Patent and Trademark Office in Washington, D.C. If a patent is granted, the invention is assigned a patent number. Patent holders usually affix the word *Patent* or *Pat.* and the patent number to the patented article. If a patent application is filed but a patent has

American Inventors Protection Act

In 1999, Congress enacted the **American Inventors Protection Act.** This statute, which was a watered-down version of the initial bill that was introduced, still made significant changes in federal patent law. The Act reorganized the U.S. Patent and Trademark Office (PTO) and granted the PTO new regulatory powers. The Act:

- Establishes "inventors' rights" by giving the PTO power to regulate "invention promoters." This part of the statute addresses problems created by unscrupulous invention registration services that took advantage of individual inventors by charging substantial fees for marketing services that generally were unsuccessful. The Act provides for penalties and fines for violations of inventors' rights.

- Permits an inventor to file a provisional application with the PTO pending the preparation and filing of a

final and complete patent application. This part of the law grants "provisional rights" to an inventor for three months pending the filing of a final application.

- Requires the PTO to issue a patent within three years after the filing of a patent application unless the applicant engages in dilatory activities.

- Provides that non-patent holders may challenge a patent as overly broad by requesting a contested reexamination of the patent application by the PTO. This provides that the reexamination will be within the confines of the PTO; the decision of the PTO can be appealed to the U.S. Court of Appeals for the Federal Circuit in Washington, D.C.

The Act also upgrades the PTO Commissioner to an Assistant Secretary of Commerce with authority to advise the U.S. government on intellectual policy.

Inventor Wipes Ford's and Chrysler's Windshields Clean

In 1967, Robert Kearns, a professor at Wayne State University in Detroit, Michigan, patented his design for the electronic intermittent windshield wiper for automobiles and other vehicles. He peddled his invention to many automobile manufacturers but never reached a licensing deal with any of them. In 1969, automobile manufacturers began producing cars with Kearns's invention. Virtually all cars sold in the United States today now have these wipers as standard equipment.

Kearns filed patent infringement lawsuits against Ford in 1978 and Chrysler in 1982. He later filed patent infringement cases against virtually all automobile manufacturers. The Ford case went to trial first. Kearns sought $325 million in damages from Ford. Ford alleged that Kearns's patents were not valid because of obviousness and prior art. The jury disagreed with Ford and decided that Kearns's patents were valid. The jury ordered Ford to pay $5.2 million, plus interest. In 1990, Ford settled by paying Kearns $10.2 million and agreeing to drop all appeals. This represented 50¢ per Ford vehicle that used the wiper system.

Kearns sought $468 million in damages from Chrysler. In that case, Kearns fired his lawyers and represented himself. This was at least the fourth law firm hired and fired in the course of Kearns's patent infringement lawsuits. Kearns won a second victory: In 1991, the jury found that Chrysler had infringed Kearns's patents and awarded him $11.3 million. The court denied Kearns injunctive relief because his 17-year patents had expired years ago. The court of appeals affirmed the judgment and the Supreme Court refused to hear Kearns's appeal. Kearns received more than $21 million from Chrysler, which amounted to 90¢ for every vehicle sold by Chrysler with the wiper system.

In 1993 and 1994, courts dismissed Kearns's lawsuits against 23 automobile manufacturers, including General Motors, Porsche, Nissan, Toyota, Honda, and Rolls Royce, among others, because Kearns failed to comply with court orders to disclose documents relevant to the cases. The district court then ordered Kearns to pay his fired lawyers $6.4 million in contingency fees. Thus ended Kearns's 30-plus-year saga and legal battle with the automobile industry. In an interview Kearns stated, "The patent system is a fraud pure and simple."

1. Did the automobile manufacturers act unethically in these cases? Other than Ford and Chrysler, did the other auto manufacturers get off too easily?

2. Do you think Kearns could have won more money by using attorneys to represent him? Explain.

not yet been issued, the applicant usually places the words *patent pending* on the article. Any party can challenge either the issuance of a patent or the validity of an existing patent.

Patent Infringement

Patent holders own exclusive rights to use and exploit their patent. **Patent infringement** occurs when someone makes unauthorized use of another's patent. In a suit for patent infringement, a successful plaintiff can recover:

1. Money damages equal to a reasonable royalty rate on the sale of the infringed articles
2. Other damages caused by the infringement (such as loss of customers)
3. An order requiring the destruction of the infringing article
4. An injunction preventing the infringer from such action in the future.

Protecting a Patent

Inventors spend years dreaming up new products and inventions, then file an application with the Patent and Trademark Office and wait to see if their patent is granted. The day the patent is issued is a cause for celebration—or is it? Ask Donald BonAsia. The young entrepreneur invented "forkchops"—two eating utensils with chopsticks on one end and a knife and fork on the other end. He spent two years and $7,500 to receive a patent on his invention.

But his worst fear became reality. Other manufacturers began copying his invention and selling them without seeking BonAsia's permission or paying him a royalty fee. BonAsia contacted a patent lawyer and found out the following: The normal cost to pursue a patent infringement case through trial is $1.5 million, and $1 million if it settles

near trial. Attorneys typically want more than $100,000 in retainer fees before filing a patent infringement case. BonAsia discovered he had a patent but not enough money to protect it.

BonAsia's plight is typical for small-time inventors who are under the misconception that a patent gives the holder an exclusive right to make the item. Wrong: What a patent gives the holder is the right to defend the patent and try to stop others from making the patented article. BonAsia learned a valuable lesson: Patent law is usually the playing field of big corporations that have deep pockets to protect their patents. Small entrepreneurs have the same legal rights but, as in many areas of the law, justice can be obtained only at a price.

The court has the discretion to award up to treble damages if the infringement was intentional.

Public-Use Doctrine

Under the **public-use doctrine,** a patent may not be granted if the invention was used by the public for more than one year prior to the filing of the patent application. This doctrine forces inventors to file their patent applications at the proper time. For example, suppose Cindy Parsons invents a new invention on January 1. She allows the public to use this invention and does not file a patent application until February of the following year. She has lost the right to patent her invention.

COPYRIGHTS

A **copyright** is the exclusive legal right to reproduce, publish, and sell a literary, musical, or artistic work. Congress enacted a federal copyright law pursuant to an express grant of authority in the U.S. Constitution [Article I, Section 8, clause 8]. This law protects the work of authors and other creative persons from the unauthorized use of their copyrighted materials and provides a financial incentive for authors to write, thereby increasing the number of creative works available in society. The Copyright Revision Act of 1976 governs copyright law [17 U.S.C. §§ 101 et seq.]. Effective March 1, 1989, the United States became a member of the **Berne Convention,** an international copyright treaty. Federal copyright law is exclusive; there are no state copyright laws.

BERNE CONVENTION ON COPYRIGHT NOTICE

In 1989, the United States signed the Berne Convention. This international convention provides the copyright law that is now followed by most countries of the world. The convention made a major change in U.S. copyright law. Prior to 1989, to protect a copyright in a published work in the United States, the copyright holder had to place a copyright notice on the work, containing the following information:

1. Copyright holder's name

2. A "(c)" or "©" or "Copyright," or "copr."

3. The year the material was copyrighted

Under the Berne Convention, however, notice is not required on works entering the public domain on or after March 1, 1989. Although notice is now permissive, it is recommended that notice be placed on copyrighted works to defeat a defendant's claim of innocent infringement.

Registration of Copyrights

Only **tangible writings**—writings that can be physically seen—are subject to copyright registration and protection. The term *writing* has been broadly defined to include books, periodicals, and newspapers; lectures, sermons, and addresses; musical compositions; plays, motion pictures, radio and television productions; maps; works of art, including paintings, drawings, sculpture, jewelry, glassware, tapestry, and lithographs; architectural drawings and models; photographs, including prints, slides, and filmstrips; greeting cards and picture postcards; photoplays, including feature films, cartoons, newsreels, travelogues, and training films; and sound recordings published in the form of tapes, cassettes, compact discs, and phonograph albums.

To be protected under federal copyright law, the work must be the original work of the author. Published and unpublished works may be copyrighted and registered with the United States Copyright Office in Washington, D.C. Registration is permissive and voluntary and can be effected at any time during the term of the copyright. Registration itself does not create the copyright.

Opponents of the new copyright law argue that it was passed to fill the pockets of large publishers and entertainment companies and the heirs of famous writers. They also argue that the Act is unconstitutional because life of the writer plus 70 years and corporate copyrights of 95 or 120 years exceed the constitutional mandate of "limited time" copyrights.

The U.S. Patent and Trademark Office, Washington, D.C.

U.S. Copyright Office:
www.loc.gov/copyright

Proponents of the new copyright act argue that corporations such as the Walt Disney Company should be rewarded for spending millions of dollars in

The advent of new technology challenges the ability of laws to protect it. For example, the invention of computers and the writing of software programs caused problems for existing copyright laws. These laws had to be changed to afford protection to software.

In 1980, Congress enacted the Computer Software Copyright Act, which amended the Copyright Act of 1976. The 1980 amendments include computer programs in the list of tangible items protected by copyright law. The amendments define *computer program* broadly as "a set of statements or instructions to be used directly or indirectly in a computer in order to bring about a certain result" [17 U.S.C. § 101].

A computer program is written first in programming language, which is called a "source code." It then is translated into another language, called an "object code," which is understood by the computer. In an important decision, *Apple Computer, Inc. v. Franklin Computer Corp.,* 714 F.2d 1240 (3d Cir. 1983), the court held that object codes could be copyrighted.

As with other works, the creator of a copyrightable software program obtains automatic copyright protection. The Judicial Improvement Act of 1990 authorizes the Register of Copyright to accept and record any document pertaining to computer software, and to issue a certificate of recordation to the recorder [P.L. 101–650].

Congress passed the Semiconductor Chip Protection Act of 1984 to provide greater protection of the hardware components of a computer. This law protects masks that are used to create computer chips. A *mask* is an original layout of software programs that is used to create a semiconductor chip. This act is sometimes referred to as the "Mask Work Act." Notice on the work is optional but when used must contain (1) the words *Mask Work* or the symbol *M* or (M), and (2) the name of the owner [17 U.S.C. §§ 901–914].

The Red Bluff Tehama County Courthouse, Sacramento Valley, California.

creating cartoon icons such as Mickey Mouse. Proponents also assert that the law is good for the country because the United States is the world's leading exporter of intellectual property.

Copyright Infringement

Copyright infringement occurs when a party copies a substantial and material part of the plaintiff's copyrighted work without permission. The copying does not have to be either word-for-word or the entire work. A successful plaintiff can recover (1) the profit made by the infringer from the copyright infringement, (2) damages suffered by the plaintiff, (3) an order requiring the impoundment and destruction of the infringing works, and (4) an injunction preventing the infringer from doing so in the future. The court, at its discretion, can award statutory damages ranging from $200 for innocent infringement up to $100,000 for willful infringement in lieu of actual damages.

A Mickey Mouse Copyright Law

The Founding Fathers decided to provide copyright protection in the U.S. Constitution when they granted Congress authority to secure for "limited times" to authors the exclusive right to their writings. In 1970, copyright law guaranteed 14 years of protection with a 14-year renewal. The period of protection has been extended several times since, and in 1998 stood at the life of the author plus 50 years. A corporation-owned copyright was good for 75 years from the date of publication, or 100 years from the date of creation, whichever was shorter.

After the copyright period runs out, the work enters the public domain, which means that anyone can publish the work without paying the prior copyright holder. Many small publishers and Internet sites were dedicated to publishing great works—and not-so-great works—once they entered the public domain. These publishers and Internet content providers waited anxiously as popular works such as A. A. Milne's *Winnie the Pooh,* Ernest Hemingway's *Three Stories and Ten Poems,* and the Walt Disney Company's first Mickey Mouse cartoon were set to enter the public domain. Cartoons starring Disney characters such as Donald Duck and Goofy were to follow shortly thereafter.

The Walt Disney Company was driven goofy at the prospect of its leading cartoon characters joining the likes of Santa Claus and Uncle Sam (both created by nineteenth-century cartoonist Thomas Nast) in the public domain. So the long arm of Disney went into action, lobbying Congress for a new copyright law that would increase the length of copyright protection for its characters. Disney, joined by the American Society of Composers, Authors, and Publishers, and other publishing and entertainment companies, persuaded Congress to pass the Sonny Bono Copyright Term Extension Act of 1998 (CTEA). Although not restoring copyright protection to works already in the public domain, the Act added 20 years to existing copyrighted works and works to be copyrighted in the future. The Act grants the following copyright terms to the following copyright holders:

- *Individual copyright holder:* life of the author plus 70 years.
- *Corporate copyright holder:* 95 years from the year of first publication or 120 years from the year of creation, whichever is shorter.

Fair-Use Doctrine

The copyright holder's rights in the work are not absolute. The law permits certain limited unauthorized use of copyrighted materials under the **fair-use doctrine.** The following uses are protected under this doctrine:

1. Quotation of the copyrighted work for review or criticism or in a scholarly or technical work
2. Use in a parody or satire
3. Brief quotation in a news report
4. Reproduction by a teacher or student of a small part of the work to illustrate a lesson
5. Incidental reproduction of a work in a newsreel or broadcast of an event being reported
6. Reproduction of a work in a legislative or judicial proceeding.

The copyright holder cannot recover for copyright infringement where fair use is found.

Castle Rock Entertainment, Inc. v. Carol Publishing Group, Inc.

150 F.3d 132 (1998)

United States Court of Appeals, Second Circuit

FACTS

Castle Rock Entertainment, Inc., is the producer and copyright owner of the successful "Seinfeld" television series. For years, Seinfeld was the highest-rated show on television. The series revolved around petty tribulations in the lives of four single, adult friends in New York: Jerry Seinfeld, George Costanza, Elaine Benes, and Cosmo Kramer.

To take advantage of the public interest in Seinfeld, Carol Publishing Group, Inc. published a book written by Beth Golub entitled *The Seinfeld Aptitude Test* (SAT). The 132-page book contained 643 questions and answers about events and characters in 84 TV episodes of Seinfeld. These included 211 multiple-choice questions, 93 matching questions, and a number of short-answer questions. The correct answers to these questions have as their source fictional moments in Seinfeld episodes, and 41 questions contain exact dialogue from Seinfeld. The name "Seinfeld" appears prominently on front and back covers of the SAT, and pictures of the principal actors in Seinfeld appear on the cover and throughout the book.

In February 1995, Castle Rock filed this action against Carol Publishing and Golub alleging federal copyright infringement. Castle Rock made a motion for summary judgment, alleging that no facts were in dispute and that the court could make a decision as a matter of law whether copyright infringement occurred. The trial court agreed that no facts were in dispute that required a jury's determination. The court, therefore, considered the undisputed evidence that the defendants had violated Castle Rock's copyrights of Seinfeld, and awarded damages and issued an injunction enjoining the defendants from publishing *The Seinfeld Aptitude Test*. The court granted Castle Rock's motion for summary judgment. The defendants appealed.

ISSUE

Is Castle Rock entitled to a summary judgment on its copyright infringement claim?

IN THE LANGUAGE OF THE COURT

Walker, Circuit Judge.

Summary judgment is appropriate if the moving party can show that there is no genuine issue as to any material fact and that the moving party is entitled to a judgment as a matter of law. In the instant case, no one disputes that Castle Rock owns valid copyrights in the Seinfeld television programs and that defendants actually copied from those programs in creating The SAT. Golub freely admitted that she created The SAT by taking notes from Seinfeld programs at the time they were aired on television and subsequently reviewing videotapes of several of the episodes that she or her friends recorded.

Each SAT trivia question is based directly upon original, protectable expression in Seinfeld. Each "fact" tested by The SAT is in reality fictitious expression created by Seinfeld's authors. The SAT does not quiz such true facts as the identity of the actors in Seinfeld, the number of days it takes to shoot an episode, the biographies of the actors, the location of the Seinfeld set, etc. Rather, The SAT tests whether the reader knows that the character Jerry places a Pez dispenser on Elaine's leg during a piano recital or that Kramer enjoys going to the airport because he's hypnotized by the baggage carousels. Because these characters and events spring from the imagination of Seinfeld's authors, The SAT plainly copies copyrightable, creative expression.

DECISION AND REMEDY

The court of appeals held that the defendants had infringed Castle Rock's copyright and affirmed the district court's grant of summary judgment in Castle Rock's favor.

Questions

1. What purpose does the legal doctrine of summary judgment serve?

2. Do you think Carol Publishing and Golub acted unethically in this case?

3. What purpose is served by copyright law?

NAPSTER UNPLUGGED BY THE COURT

In May 1999, 18-year-old Shawn Fanning cofounded Napster, Inc. and instantly created an Internet phenomenon. Using Napster software, Internet users could access digitally compressed MP3-format music files stored on other users' computers that were connected to the Internet. Although Napster did not actually provide a library of songs itself, it kept a directory available to its users that listed the names and computer locations of songs on its users' computers. The Napster program made possible peer-to-peer swapping of music files, including those that were copyrighted, without charge.

There was one major problem: If copyrighted music was being copied for free, the songwriters, artists, and record companies that wrote, sang, and produced the songs were being cut out by the copiers and not paid anything. In December 1999, most of the world's biggest record labels, such as A&M Records, Sony Music, Universal Music, MCA Records, Warner Music, EMI Group, and others sued Napster for contributory copyright infringement. The heavy metal band Metallica and rapper Dr. Dre joined the lawsuit against Napster.

Napster defended, arguing that it did nothing illegal. For one and one-half years Napster continued to operate while the legal maneuverings wound their way through the federal courts. Napster had more than 50 million users who were sharing more than 3 billion songs each month. In February 2001, however, the federal court of appeals issued an almost total victory for the record companies. Although the court did not hold that Napster was an actual copyright infringer (the individual computer users who used Napster to copy copyrighted songs were), the court did find Napster liable for *contributory copyright infringement* in violation of federal copyright law. The court stated that Napster "knowingly encourages and assists in the infringement of copyrights" by others. When Napster tried to argue it did not know of its users' infringing conduct, the court cited a document written by Napster cofounder Sean Parker that mentioned "the need to remain ignorant of users' real names and IP addresses since they are exchanging pirated music."

The court of appeals ordered the lower court to fashion an injunction that required Napster to block its users from swapping copyrighted songs, when music companies notify Napster that the songs are copyrighted and should be blocked. The court's decision permits Napster to be used for authorized song swapping—either of nonprotected songs or of songs that artists are willing to share.

Although the record companies won a victory over Napster, the real victor was the new music-swapping technology. Faced with even more potent free music-swapping programs such as the Gnutella system, record companies began negotiating with record-sharing program owners to provide fee-based subscription services whereby users pay a monthly fee to swap copyrighted music and the fees then are split with the record companies, songwriters, and artists. But even now, record companies face new free music-swapping technologies, including those originating in countries where U.S. copyright laws do not reach. [*A&M Records v. Napster, Inc.,* No. 00-16401 (9th Cir. 2001)]

NET Act: Criminal Copyright Infringement

A copyright holder owns a valuable right and may sue an infringer in a civil lawsuit to recover damages and obtain injunctions and other remedies for copyright infringement. In 1997, Congress enacted the **No Electronic Theft Act (NET Act),** which criminalizes certain copyright infringement as well. The impetus for passage of this act was the failure of the U.S. government to obtain criminal convictions against copyright infringers under existing, non-Internet specific criminal statutes.

In one notable case, David LaMacchia, a 21-year-old student at the Massachusetts Institute of Technology (MIT), encouraged Internet users to upload computer games and software to a bulletin board, which he then transferred to another bulletin board. LaMacchia then made this software available free to Internet users without compensating the copyright holders. The worldwide traffic generated by the availability of free software attracted the notice of university and federal authorities.

The U.S. government sued LaMacchia, asserting a violation of the federal wire fraud statute, but the federal court judge dismissed the case, holding that this statute's language did not prohibit LaMacchia's conduct because he did not recognize financial gain [*United States v. LaMacchia*, 871 F.Supp. 535 (D.Mass. 1994)].

Congress passed the NET Act to directly criminalize such copyright infringement. The NET Act prohibits any person from willfully infringing a copyright for the purpose of commercial advantage or financial gain, or by reproduction or distribution even without commercial advantage or financial gain, including by electronic means, where the retail value of the copyrighted work exceeds $1,000. Criminal penalties for violating the Act include imprisonment for up to one year and fines of up to $100,000.

The NET Act has closed the "LaMacchia loophole." For example, Jeffrey Gerald Levy, a 22-year-old University of Oregon senior, pleaded guilty to criminal copyright infringement in violation of the NET Act because he was caught maintaining a website on the university's server where the public could make copies of thousands of software programs, movies, and musical recordings [*United States v. Levy* (D. Or. 1999)]. The NET Act adds a new law for the federal government to combat copyright infringement and curb digital piracy.

International Trademark Association: www.inta.org

TRADEMARKS

Trademark law is intended to (1) protect the owner's investment and goodwill in a **mark,** and (2) prevent consumers from being confused as to the origin of goods and services. In 1946, Congress enacted the Lanham Trademark Act to provide federal protection to trademarks, service marks, and other marks [15 U.S.C. §§ 1114 et seq.]. Congress passed the Trademark Law Revision Act of 1988, which amended trademark law in several respects. The amendments made it easier to register a trademark but harder to maintain it. States also may enact trademark laws.

Registration of Trademarks

Trademarks are registered with the United States Patent and Trademark Office in Washington, D.C. The original registration of a mark is valid for 10 years and can be renewed for an unlimited number of 10-year periods. The registration of a trademark, which is given nationwide effect, serves as constructive notice that the mark is the registrant's personal property. The registrant is entitled to use the registered trademark symbol ® in connection with a registered trademark or service mark. Use of the symbol is not mandatory. Note that the frequently used notations "TM" and "SM" have no legal significance.

An applicant can register a mark if (1) it was in use in commerce (e.g., actually used in the sale of goods or services), or (2) the applicant verifies a bona fide intention to use the mark in commerce and actually does so within six months of its registration. Failure to do so during this period causes loss of the mark to the registrant. A party other than the registrant can submit an opposition to a proposed registration of a mark or to the cancellation of a previously registered mark.

Distinctiveness of a Mark

To qualify for federal protection, a mark must be **distinctive** or have acquired a **"secondary meaning."** For example, marks such as *Acura, Dr. Pepper,* and *Roto Rooter* are *distinctive*. A term such as *English Leather,* which literally means leather processed in England, has taken on a "secondary meaning" as a trademark for an aftershave lotion. Words that are *descriptive* but have no secondary meaning cannot be trademarked. For example, the word *cola* alone could not be trademarked.

Marks That Can Be Trademarked

The following types of marks can be trademarked:

- *Trademarks.* A **trademark** is a distinctive mark, symbol, name, word, motto, or device that identifies the *goods* of a particular business. For example, the words *Xerox, Coca-Cola,* and *IBM* are trademarks.

- *Service marks.* A **service mark** is used to distinguish the *services* of the holder from those of its competitors. The trade names *United Airlines, Marriott Hotels,* and *Weight Watchers* are examples of service marks.

- *Certification marks.* A **certification mark** is a mark used to certify that goods and services are of a certain quality or originate from particular geographical areas—for example, wines from the "Napa Valley" of California or "Florida" oranges. The owner of the mark is usually a non-profit corporation that licenses producers that meet certain standards or conditions to use the mark.

- *Collective marks.* A **collective mark** is a mark used by cooperatives, associations, and fraternal organizations. An example is "Boy Scouts of America."

The following marks cannot be registered: (1) the flag or coat of arms of the United States or any state, municipality, or foreign nation, (2) marks that are immoral or scandalous, (3) geographical names standing alone (e.g., "South"), (4) surnames standing alone (note that a surname can be registered if it is accompanied by a picture or fanciful name, such as "Smith Brothers'

Cough Drops," and (5) any mark that resembles a mark already registered with the federal Patent and Trademark Office.

Trademark Infringement

The owner of a mark can sue a third party for the unauthorized use of a mark. To succeed in a **trademark infringement** case, the owner must prove that (1) the defendant infringed the plaintiff's mark by using it in an unauthorized manner, and (2) such use is likely to cause confusion, mistake, or deception of the public as to the origin of the goods or services. A successful plaintiff can recover:

1. The profits made by the infringer by the unauthorized use of the mark
2. Damages caused to the plaintiff's business and reputation
3. An order requiring the defendant to destroy all goods containing the unauthorized mark
4. An injunction preventing the defendant from such infringement in the future.

The court has discretion to award up to treble damages where intentional infringement is found.

Generic Names

Most companies promote their trademarks and service marks to increase the public's awareness of the availability and quality of their products and services. At some point in time, however, the public may begin to treat the mark as a common name to denote the type of product or service being sold, rather than as the trademark or trade name of an individual seller. A trademark that becomes a common term for a product line or type of service is called a **generic name**. Once that happens, the term loses its protection under federal trademark law because it has become *descriptive* rather than *distinctive* (see Exhibit 16.1).

THE INTERNET

The **Internet,** or Net, is a collection of millions of computers that provide a network of electronic connections between the computers. The Internet was initiated in 1969 by the U.S. Department of Defense to create electronic communications for military and national defense purposes. Building on this start, in the 1980s the National Science Foundation, the federal government's main scientific and technical agency, established the Net to facilitate high-speed communications among research centers at academic and research institutions around the world.

Eventually, individuals and businesses began using the Internet for communicating information and data. In 1980, fewer than 250 computers were hooked to the Internet. Growth was rapid in the late 1990s and into the early 2000s, and today several hundred million computers are connected to the Internet. The Internet's evolution helped usher in the Information Age of

SIDEBAR

Loss of Trademark

Nestlé Company, Inc., lost its trademark on the term "Toll House" for its chocolate chip cookies when a court ruled that the term had become generic because the public had come to associate the name Toll House with chocolate chip cookies in general, not only those sold by Nestlé. [*Nestlé Company, Inc. v. Chester's Market, Inc.* 571 F.Supp. 763 (D.Conn. 1983)]

Wal-Mart Knocks Off Designer's Clothing Design

Fashion designers spend a fortune of money and time creating unique fashion designs for their clothing. They then produce these clothes and sell them at upscale prices. But what is the designer to do if another manufacturer or retailer copies the original design and sells these "knockoffs" at much lower prices? Sue, that's what! Consider the following case.

Samara Brothers, Inc. (Samara) is a designer and manufacturer of children's clothing. The core of Samara's business is its annual new line of spring and summer children's garments. Wal-Mart Stores, Inc. (Wal-Mart) operates a large chain of budget warehouse stores that sells thousands of items at very low prices.

In 1995, Wal-Mart contacted one of its suppliers, Judy–Philippine, Inc. (JPI) about the possibility of making a line of children's clothes just like Samara's successful line. Wal-Mart sent photographs of Samara's children's clothes to JPI (the name "Samara" was readily discernible on the labels of the garments) and directed JPI to produce children's clothes exactly like those in the photographs. JPI produced a line of children's clothes for Wal-Mart that copied the designs, colors, flower patterns, etc. of Samara's clothing. Wal-Mart then sold this line of children's clothing in its stores, making a gross profit of more than $1.15 million on these clothes sales during the 1996 selling season.

In June 1996, one of the retailers that purchased Samara's children's clothing complained to Samara that Wal-Mart was selling the knockoff clothes at less than the retailer was paying Samara for its clothes. Samara investigated and discovered Wal-Mart had copied its designs. After sending unsuccessful cease-and-desist letters to Wal-Mart, Samara sued Wal-Mart, alleging trade dress infringement in violation of the Lanham Act. The U.S. district court held in favor of Samara and awarded damages. Wal-Mart appealed all the way to the U.S. Supreme Court, which granted review.

In a 9–0 decision, the Supreme Court came down on the side of Wal-Mart and held that, in this case, Wal-Mart had not violated the Lanham Act. The Court ruled that Samara's children's clothing had not acquired a "secondary meaning" in the minds of the public— that is, when most people saw Samara's clothing, they did not automatically think "that is a Samara design." The Supreme Court established the following legal rule for product design infringement cases under the Lanham Act: If a product design has not acquired a secondary meaning in the minds of the public, it can be knocked off; if a product design has acquired a secondary meaning, it cannot be knocked off. Thus, designers of nondistinctive goods, such as dresses, shoes, jewelry, golf clubs, and other products that have not acquired a secondary meaning, will find look-alikes being sold at discount stores such as Wal-Mart, Target, and Mervyn's.

There are some limitations to copying, however. Under the Supreme Court's *Wal-Mart* decision, goods that have acquired a secondary meaning—such as Ferrari automobiles or Apple Computer's iMac computer—are protected from being copied. Goods that are patented, such as Nike's "air" technology in its athletic shoes, cannot be copied because it would constitute patent infringement. And counterfeiting—selling knockoff goods with a fake original manufacturer's trademarked name or logo on them—is illegal trademark infringement. [*Wal-Mart Stores, Inc. v. Samara Brothers, Inc.,* 2000 WL 293238, United States Supreme Court (2000)]

1. Under ethical principles, should Wal-Mart sell knockoff goods?

2. What are the economic effects of the U.S. Supreme Court's decision? Who wins? Who loses?

exhibit **16.1** *Xerox Corporation protects its trademark.*

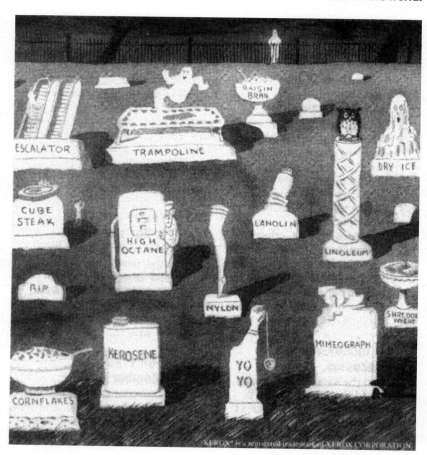

today. Use of the Internet and the World Wide Web has required courts to apply existing laws to new technologies and has spurred the federal Congress and state legislatures to enact new laws to govern modern means of communication and the conduct of electronic business.

World Wide Web

The **World Wide Web** consists of millions of computers that support a standard set of rules for the exchange of information called *hypertext transfer protocol* (HTTP). Web-based documents are formatted using common coding languages such as *hypertext markup language* (HTML) and Java. Businesses and individuals can hook up to the Web by registering with a server such as America Online (AOL).

Individuals and businesses can have their own websites. A website is composed of electronic documents known as web pages. The websites and pages are stored on servers throughout the world. They are viewed by using Web browsing software such as Microsoft Internet Explorer and Netscape Navigator. Each website has a unique online address. Web pages can contain a full range of multimedia content, including text, images, video, sound, and animation. Web pages can include references, called *hyperlinks*, or *links*, to other web pages or sites.

The Web has made it extremely attractive to conduct commercial activities online. Companies such as Amazon.com and eBay are e-commerce powerhouses that sell all sorts of goods and services. Existing companies such as Wal-Mart, Merrill Lynch, and Dell Computers sell their goods and services online as well. E-commerce over the Web will continue to grow dramatically each year.

Electronic Mail

Electronic mail, or **email,** is one of the most widely used applications for communication over the Internet. Using email, individuals can instantaneously communicate in electronic writing with one another around the world. Each person can have his or her own email address, which identifies the user by a unique address. Email will continue to grow in use in the future as it replaces some telephone and paper correspondence and increases new communication between persons.

Internet Domain Names

Each website is identified by a unique Internet **domain name.** For example, the domain name for the publisher of this book is www.prenhall.com. The four top-level suffixes for domain names are:

.com	commercial use
.net	networks
.org	organizations
.edu	educational institutions

Domain names can be registered. The first step in registering a domain name is to determine whether any other party already owns the name. For this

Selling Web Domain Names

What is a name worth? Plenty! It used to be that a person could make money by trademarking a name before a large company wanted to use the name for a product or service or as a new company name. Once in possession of the trademark, the owner could sell it at a profit if some company wanted it desperately enough. But trying to guess what names would be wanted took some work. In addition, trademark law required the name to be used in commerce. Although trademarking and selling trademark names is still a way to make money, the hottest area for name-selling is to register and sell Internet domain names.

Take the case of the domain name *business.com*. This name, which originally was registered as a domain name for $70, was sold to entrepreneur Marc Ostrofsky for $150,000 in 1996. Many people at the time thought this was an outrageous sum to pay for a domain name—that

is, until Mr. Ostrofsky turned around and resold the name to ECompanies in 1999 for $7,500,000. That was the most ever paid for an Internet domain name. ECompanies thought it was a bargain and is now offering a form of Internet Yellow Pages at www.business.com.

Other domain names have been sold at high prices too. *Altavista.com* was purchased by Compaq Computer for its Internet search engine. Other domain names sold for high prices include *wine.com* for $3 million, *bingo.com* for $1.1 million, *wallstreet.com* for $1 million, and *drugs.com* for $800,000. As commerce over the Internet increases, and as unregistered memorable names become harder to find, transactions in the sale of domain names are expected to accelerate, with multimillion dollar price tags being paid for the most desirable names—which originally were registered for $70.

purpose, InterNIC maintains a "Whois" database containing the domain names that have been registered. The InterNIC website is located online at www.internic.net. Domain names also can be registered at Network Solutions, Inc.'s website, located online at www.networksolutions.com, as well as at other online sites. An applicant must complete a registration form, which can be done online. It costs less than $50 to register a domain name for one year, and the fee may be paid by credit card online.

UNIFORM COMPUTER INFORMATION TRANSACTIONS ACT (UCITA)

After years of study and debate, the National Conference of Commissioners on Uniform State Laws (a group of lawyers, judges, and legal scholars) in July 1999 issued the **Uniform Computer Information Transactions Act (UCITA).** This model act establishes a uniform and comprehensive set of rules that governs the creation, performance, and enforcement of computer information transactions. A computer information transaction is an agreement to create, transfer, or license computer information or informational rights [UCITA §102(a)(11)].

The UCITA does not become law until a state's legislature enacts it as a state statute. States are expected to adopt the UCITA or laws similar to the UCITA as their law for computer transactions and the licensing of informational rights.

When the famous actress Julia Roberts went to register her name as the Internet domain name juliaroberts.com, she discovered that someone else had already registered this domain name. So what's a famous person to do? Rely on Congress to pass a law that helps him or her. And that is exactly what the U.S. Congress did.

In November 1999, the U.S. Congress enacted, and the President signed, the **Anticybersquatting Consumer Protection Act** [15 U.S.C. § 1125(d)]. The Act was specifically aimed at cybersquatters who register Internet domain names of famous companies and people and hold them "hostage" by demanding "ransom payments" from the famous company or person.

In the past, trademark law was of little help, either because the famous person's name was not trademarked or because, even if the name was trademarked, trademark law required distribution of goods or services to find infringement and most cybersquatters did not distribute goods or services but merely sat on the Internet domain name.

The new act has two fundamental requirements: (1) The name must be famous, and (2) the domain name must have been registered in bad faith. Thus, the law prohibits the act of cybersquatting itself if it is done *in bad faith*.

The first issue in applying the statute is whether the domain name is someone else's famous name. Trademarked names qualify. Nontrademarked names—such as those of famous actors, actresses, singers, sports figures, political figures, and such—also are protected. In determining bad faith, the law provides that courts may consider the extent that the domain name resembles the holder's name or the famous person's name, whether goods or services are sold under the name, the holder's offer to sell or transfer the name, and whether the holder has acquired multiple Internet domain names of famous companies and persons.

The Act provides for the issuance of cease-and-desist orders and injunctions by the court. In addition, the law adds monetary penalties: A plaintiff has the option of seeking statutory damages of between $1,000 and $300,000 in lieu of proving damages.

The Anticybersquatting Consumer Protection Act gives owners of trademarks and persons with famous names a weapon to attack the kidnapping of Internet domain names by cyberpirates. Julia Roberts immediately sued the holder of juliaroberts.com for violating the Act and won the right to her own domain name. The singer Sting was not so lucky, however, when he found that sting.com was already taken. The court ruled that because the word "sting" is generic and can be found in the dictionary, Sting has no claim under the Anticybersquatting Act to the domain name.

Any provisions of the UCITA that are preempted by federal law are unenforceable to the extent of the preemption [UCITA § 105(a)]. Unless displaced by the UCITA, state law and equity principles, including principal and agent law, fraud, duress, mistake, trade secret law, and other state laws, supplement the UCITA [UCITA § 114].

DIGITAL MILLENNIUM COPYRIGHT ACT

The Internet makes it easier for people to illegally copy and distribute copyrighted works. To combat this, software and entertainment companies developed "wrappers" and encryption technology to protect their copyrighted works from unauthorized access. Not to be outdone, software pirates and other Internet users devised ways to crack these wrappers and protection devices. Seeing that they were losing the battle, software companies and the entertainment industry lobbied Congress to enact legislation that made illegal the cracking of their wrappers and selling of technology to do so. In 1998, Congress responded by enacting the **Digital Millennium Copyright Act (DMCA)** [17 U.S.C. 1201], which does the following:

- Prohibits unauthorized *access* to copyrighted digital works by circumventing the wrapper or encryption technology that protects the intellectual property. This "black-box" protection prohibits simply accessing the protected information and does not require that the accessed information be misused.

- Prohibits the manufacture and distribution of technologies, products, or services designed primarily for the purpose of circumventing wrappers or encryption protection. Multipurpose devices that can be used in ways other than cracking wrappers or encryption technology can be manufactured and sold without violating the DMCA.

The DMCA imposes civil and criminal penalties. A successful plaintiff in a civil action can recover actual damages from first-time offenders and treble damages from repeat offenders, costs and attorney's fees, an order for the destruction of illegal products and devices, and an injunction against future violations by the offender. As an alternative to actual damages, a plaintiff can recover statutory damages of not less than $2,500 and up to $25,000 per act of circumvention.

The following criminal penalties can be accessed for willful violations committed for "commercial advantage" or "private financial gain": First-time violators can be fined up to $500,000 and imprisoned for up to 5 years; subsequent violators can be fined up to $1 million and imprisoned up to 10 years.

LEGAL TERMINOLOGY

American Inventors Protection Act

Anticybersquatting Consumer Protection Act

Berne Convention

Certification mark

Collective mark

Computer Software Copyright Act

Copyright

Copyright infringement

Digital Millennium Copyright Act

Distinctiveness of a mark

Domain name

Economic Espionage Act

Electronic mail (email)

Fair-use doctrine

Generic name

Internet

Mark

No Electronic Theft (NET) Act

Patent

Patent infringement

Public-use doctrine

Secondary meaning

Service mark

Tangible writing

Trademark

Trademark infringement

Trade secret

Uniform Computer Information
    Transactions Act (UCITA)

World Wide Web

Summary

CHAPTER 16 INTELLECTUAL PROPERTY AND INTERNET LAW	
Trade Secrets	
Definition	A *trade secret* is a product formula, pattern, design, compilation of data, customer list, or other business secret that makes a business successful. The owner of a trade secret must take reasonable precautions to prevent its trade secret from being discovered by others.
Misappropriation	Obtaining another's trade secret through unlawful means such as theft, bribery, or espionage is a tort. A successful plaintiff can recover profits, damages, and an injunction against the offender.
Economic Espionage Act	This federal statute makes it a crime for any person to convert a trade secret for his or another's benefit, knowing or intending to cause injury to the owners of the trade secret.
Patents	
Scope	Patent law is exclusively federal law; there are no state patent laws. Patentable subject matter includes inventions such as machines; processes; compositions of matter; improvements to existing machines, processes, or compositions of matter; designs for articles of manufacture; asexually reproduced plants; and living matter invented by man.
Criteria	To be patented, an invention must be: a. Novel b. Useful c. Nonobvious
Patent Application	An application containing a written description of the invention must be filed with the United States Patent and Trademark Office in Washington, D.C.
Term	Patents are valid for 20 years.
Public-use Doctrine	A patent may not be granted if the invention was used by the public for more than one year prior to the filing of the patent application. *(continued)*

Patent Infringement	The patent holder may recover damages and other remedies against a person who makes unauthorized use of another's patent.
American Inventors Protection Act	This federal statute does the following: 1. Permits an inventor to file a *provisional application* with the U.S. Patent and Trademark Office three months pending the filing of a final patent application to gain "provisional rights." 2. Requires the PTO to issue a patent within three years after the filing of a patent application.
Patent Appeal	The United States Court of Appeals for the Federal Circuit in Washington, D.C., hears patent appeals.

Copyrights

Scope	Copyright law is exclusively federal law; there are no state copyright laws. Only tangible writings can be copyrighted. These include books, newspapers, addresses, musical compositions, motion pictures, works of art, architectural plans, greeting cards, photographs, sound recordings, computer programs, and mask works fixed in semiconductor chips.
Requirements for Copyright	The writing must be the original work of the author.
Copyright Registration	Copyright registration is permissive and voluntary. Published and unpublished works may be registered with the United States Copyright Office in Washington, D.C. Registration itself does not create the copyright.
Term	Copyrights are for the following terms: 1. *Individual holder:* Life of the author plus 70 years. 2. *Corporate holder:* Either (1) 120 years from the date of creation, or (2) 95 years from the date of publication, whichever is shorter.
Copyright Infringement	The copyright holder may recover damages and other remedies against a person who copies a substantial and material part of a copyrighted work without the holder's permission.
Fair-use Doctrine	This law permits use of copyrighted material without the consent of the copyright holder for limited uses (e.g., scholarly work, parody or satire, and brief quotation in news reports).
Digital Millennium Copyright Act (DMCA)	This federal statute enacted in 1998 provides civil and criminal penalties that 1. Prohibit the manufacture and distribution of technologies, products, or services primarily designed for the purpose of circumventing wrappers or encryption protection.

(continued)

Digital Millennium Copyright Act, *continued*	2. Prohibit unauthorized *access* to copyrighted digital works by circumventing the wrapper or encryption technology that protects the intellectual property.
No Electronic Theft Act (NET Act)	This federal statute makes it a crime for a person to willfully infringe a copyright work exceeding $1,000 in retail value, even without commercial advantages or financial gain.

Trademarks

Mark	Trade name, symbol, word, logo, design, or device that distinguishes the owner's good or services. Marks are often referred to collectively as *trademarks*.
Types	1. *Trademark:* Identifies goods of a particular business. 2. *Service mark:* Identifies services of a particular business. 3. *Certification mark:* Certifies that goods or services are of a certain quality or origin. 4. *Collective mark:* Used by cooperatives, associations, and fraternal organizations.
Requirements for a Trademark	The mark must either 1. be *distinctive*, or 2. have acquired a *secondary meaning*. The mark must have been used in commerce or the holder must intend to use the mark in commerce and actually do so within six months after registering the mark.
Trademark Registration	Marks are registered with the United States Patent and Trademark Office in Washington, D.C.
Term	The original registration of a mark is valid for 10 years and can be renewed for an unlimited number of 10-year periods.
Trademark Infringement	The mark holder may recover damages and other remedies from a person who makes unauthorized use of another's registered mark.
Generic Name	A mark that becomes a common term for a product line or type of service loses its protection under federal trademark law.

The Internet

Internet	A collection of millions of computers that provide a network of electronic connections between computers.
World Wide Web	An electronic connection of computers that support a standard set of rules for the exchange of information called hypertext transfer protocol (HTTP).

(continued)

Electronic Mail (email)	Electronic written communication between individuals using computers connected to the Internet.
Domain Name	A unique name that identifies an individual's or company's website.
Anticybersquatting Consumer Protection Act	A federal statute that permits a court to issue cease-and-desist orders and injunctions and to award monetary damages against anyone who has registered a domain name (1) of a famous name (2) in bad faith.
Uniform Computer Information Transactions Act (UCITA)	
Model Act	Issued by the National Conference of Commissioners on Uniform State Laws, establishing a uniform and comprehensive set of rules that governs the creation, performance, and enforcement of computer information transactions.
Adoption of UCITA by States	The UCITA does not become law until a state's legislature enacts it as a state statute.

Working the Web

1. Find the Library of Congress website containing a database of copyright records from 1978 to the present at www.loc.gov.
2. Download forms from the U.S. Patent and Trademark Office website at www.uspto.gov.
3. Locate information about copyright law, copyright forms, copyright records, and other copyright materials from the U.S. Copyright Office at www.loc.gov/copyright.
4. See the International Trademark Association (which represents trademark owners to protect and advance the importance of trademarks as essential elements of international commerce) at www.inta.org.
5. Get permission to reproduce copyrighted content such as articles and book chapters in your journals, photocopies, coursepacks, library reserves, websites, email, and more at the Copyright Clearance Center at www.copyright.com.

Questions
CRITICAL LEGAL THINKING AND WRITING

1. What is a trade secret? How long can a trade secret be legally protected?
2. Describe a patent. How is a patent obtained? How long is a patent valid? What is the public policy behind granting patents?

3. Describe patent infringement. What remedies are available for patent infringement?

4. Describe a copyright. How is a copyright obtained? How long is a copyright valid?

5. Describe copyright infringement. What remedies are available for copyright infringement?

6. What is the fairness doctrine? What public policy underlies the fairness doctrine?

7. Describe a trademark. How long is a trademark valid?

8. What is a generic name? What public policy underlies the generic name doctrine?

9. What is a domain name? What protections are provided by the Anticybersquatting Consumer Protection Act?

10. What are the main prohibitions of the Digital Millennium Copyright Act? Why was this act passed?

ETHICS: ANALYSIS AND DISCUSSION

1. Does a paralegal working in the area of intellectual property law have any ethical obligation to obtain specialized training or education?

2. Does the use of electronic mail present any confidentiality issues for the paralegal?

3. Are memoranda of law and other reports prepared by a paralegal protected by copyright law? To whom do the rights belong—the paralegal, the client, or the firm?

Unauthorized Practice of Law—Patent Law

There are few certainties in the area of ethics, for paralegals or in any profession. What qualifies as ethical conduct is in most cases based on state law and court interpretation applied to a set of facts. The citation listed below represents one legal opinion and is provided as a research starting point. Do not assume that the same rule applies in your jurisdiction. For the following:

- *Prepare a written statement based on your state law.*
- *Use your state bar association website as a starting point.*

You are not a lawyer but, under regulations issued by the Commissioner of Patents with the approval of the Secretary of Commerce pursuant to 35 U.S.C. § 31, you are authorized to practice before the United States Patent Office. [*Sperry v. Florida ex rel. Florida Bar*, 373 U.S. 379, 83 S.Ct. 1322, 10 L.Ed.2d 428 (1963).] May you represent patent applicants, prepare and prosecute their applications, and advise them in connection with their applications in Florida?

Acuson Corp. v. Aloka Co., Ltd.

10 U.S.P.Q.2d 1814, 257 Cal.Rptr. 368 (Cal.App. 1989)

16.1 FACTS

Acuson Corporation, a Delaware corporation, and Aloka Co., Ltd., a Japanese company, are competitors who both manufacture ultrasonic imaging equipment, a widely used medical diagnostic tool. The device uses soundwaves to produce moving images of the inside of a patient's body, which a computer processes into an image that is displayed on a video monitor. Acuson's unit provides finer resolution than Aloka's unit. Both companies have sold many units to hospitals and medical centers.

In November 1985, Aloka decided to purchase an Acuson unit. Aloka had another company make the actual purchase because it was concerned that Acuson would not sell the unit to a competitor. After the unit was shipped to Tokyo, Aloka's engineers partially dismantled the Acuson unit. They recorded their observations in notebooks. When Acuson discovered that Aloka had purchased one of its units, it sued Aloka, seeking an injunction and return of the unit.

ISSUE

Is Aloka liable for misappropriation of a trade secret?

AMF Inc. v. Windsurfing International, Inc.

613 F.Supp. (D.C.N.Y. 1985)

16.2 FACTS

In 1967, two friends from California designed a sailing surfboard that combined the sports of sailing and surfing. Originally they called it a "sailboard." They filed for and were granted a patent on the sailboard, which was assigned to the company Windsurfing International, Inc. (WSI). In 1968, WSI's Seattle dealer coined the term *windsurfing*. WSI applied for and was granted trademarks for terms using the word *Windsurfer*. Between 1969 and 1976, WSI produced a particular type of board called the Windsurfer. At that time, WSI controlled more than 95 percent of the market.

In the early years there was no generic word for the sport or craft. To promote sales, WSI and its employees continually referred to the sport as windsurfing and individual sportspeople as windsurfers. WSI also engaged in an extensive advertising campaign using the terms *windsurfing* to describe the sport and *windsurfer* to describe individual sportspersons. People who participated in the sport, trade magazines, and the general public used the word *windsurfing* to describe the sport. In 1977, WSI started to police the use of its trademarked term. However, this effort proved rather futile, as evidence showed that the general public used the terms *windsurfing* and *windsurfer* in a general, common sense to mean the sport and its participants. AMF Incorporated (AMF) seeks cancellation of WSI's trademarks containing the term *Windsurfer*.

ISSUE

Should the trademark be canceled?

Coca Cola Company v. Francis Net

Hypothetical

16.3 FACTS

Francis Net, a freshman in college and computer expert, browses websites for hours each day. One day she thinks to herself, "I can make money registering domain names and selling them for a fortune." She recently has seen an advertisement for Classic Coke, a cola drink produced and marketed by the Coca Cola Company. The Coca Cola Company has a famous trademark on the term *Classic Coke* and has spent millions of dollars advertising this brand and making the term famous throughout the United States and the world. Francis goes to the website www.networksolutions.com, an Internet domain name registration service, to see if the Internet domain name classiccoke.com has been taken. She discovers that it is available, so she immediately registers the Internet domain name classiccoke.com for herself and pays the $70 registration fee with her credit card.

Coca Cola Company decides to register the Internet domain name classiccoke.com, but discovers that Francis Net has already registered the domain name. Coca Cola Company contacts Francis, who demands $500,000 for the name. Coca Cola Company sues Francis to prevent Francis from using the Internet domain name classic coke.com and to recover it from her under the federal Anticybersquatting Consumer Protection Act.

ISSUE

Who wins?

Macy's Department Stores et al. v. BluePeace.org

Hypothetical

16.4 FACTS

BluePeace.org is a new environmentalist group that has decided that expounding its environmental causes over the Internet is the best and most efficient way to spend its time and money to advance its environmental causes. To draw attention to its websites, BluePeace.org comes up with catchy Internet domain names. One is macyswear us.org; another is exxonvaldezesseals.org; and another is generalmotorscrashesdummies.org. The macyswearus.org website first shows beautiful women dressed in mink coats sold by Macy's Department Stores and then goes into graphic photos of minks being slaughtered and skinned and made into the coats. The exxonvaldezes seals.org website first shows a beautiful pristine bay in Alaska with the Exxon Valdez oil tanker quietly sailing through the waters and then shows photos of the ship breaking open and spewing forth oil, and then seals who are gooed with oil suffocating and dying on the shoreline. The website generalmotorscrashesdummies.org shows a General Motors automobile involved in normal crash tests with dummies, followed by photographs of automobile accident scenes where people lie bleeding and dying after accidents involving General Motors automobiles.

Macy's Department Stores, the Exxon Oil Company, and the General Motors Corporation sue Blue Peace.org for violating the federal Anticybersquatting Consumer Protection Act.

ISSUE

Who wins? Has BluePeace.org acted unethically in this case?

CASE FOR BRIEFING

Feist Publications, Inc. v. Rural Telephone Service Co., Inc.

499 U.S. 340, 111 S.Ct. 1282, 113 L.Ed.2d 358 (1991)   Supreme Court of the United States

Read the following case, excerpted from the U.S. Supreme Court's opinion. Review and brief the case. In your brief, answer the following questions.

1. Who was the plaintiff? Who was the defendant?

2. What had the defendant done that caused the plaintiff to sue?

3. What is the issue in this case?

4. What was the decision of the U.S. Supreme Court?

O'Connor, S., delivered the opinion of the Court.

Rural Telephone Service Company is a certified public utility that provides telephone service to several communities in northwest Kansas. It is subject to a state regulation that requires all telephone companies operating in Kansas to issue annually an updated telephone directory. Accordingly, as a condition of its monopoly franchise, Rural publishes a typical telephone directory, consisting of white pages and yellow pages. The white pages list in alphabetical order the names of Rural's subscribers, together with their towns and telephone numbers. The yellow pages list Rural's business subscribers alphabetically by category and feature classified advertisements of various sites. Rural distributes its directory free of charge to its subscribers, but earns revenue by selling yellow pages advertisements.

Feist Publications, Inc. is a publishing company that specializes in areawide telephone directories. Unlike a typical directory, which covers only a particular calling area, Feist's areawide directories cover a much larger geographical range, reducing the need to call directory assistance or consult multiple directories. The Feist directory that is the subject of this litigation covers 11 different telephone service areas in 15 counties and contains 46,878 white pages listings—compared to Rural's approximately 7,700 listings.

Of the 11 telephone companies, only Rural refused to license its listings to Feist. Rural's refusal created a problem for Feist, as omitting these listings would have left a gaping hole in its areawide directory, rendering it less attractive to potential yellow pages advertisers. Unable to license Rural's white pages listings, Feist used them without Rural's consent.

Rural sued for copyright infringement in the District Court for the District of Kansas, taking the position that Feist, in compiling its own directory, could not use the information contained in Rural's white pages. The District Court granted summary judgment to Rural, explaining that "courts have consistently held that telephone directories are copyrightable" and citing a string of lower court decisions. In an unpublished opinion, the Court of Appeals for the Tenth Circuit affirmed "for substantially the reasons given by the district court."

This case concerns the interaction of two well-established propositions. The first is that facts are not copyrightable; the other, that compilations of facts generally are. The key to resolving the tension lies in understanding why facts are not copyrightable. The sine qua non of copyright is originality. To qualify for copyright protection, a work must be original to the author. Original, as the term is used in copyright, means only that the work was independently created by the author (as opposed to copied from other works), and that it possesses at least some minimal degree of creativity.

Originality is a constitutional requirement. The source of Congress' power to enact copyright laws is Article 1, § 8. C. 8, of the Constitution, which authorizes Congress to "secure for limited Times to Authors . . . the exclusive Right to their respective Writings." It is this bedrock principle of copyright that mandates the law's seemingly disparate treatment of facts and factual compilations. No one may claim originality as to facts. This is because facts do not owe their origin to an act of authorship. The distinction is one between creation and discovery: The first person to find and report a particular fact has not created the fact; he or she has merely discovered its existence.

If the selection and arrangement of facts are original, these elements of the work are eligible for copyright protection. No matter how original the format, however, the facts themselves do not become original through association.

There is no doubt that Feist took from the white pages of Rural's directory a substantial amount of factual information. At a minimum, Feist copied the names, towns, and telephone numbers of 1,309 of Rural's subscribers. Not all copying, however, is copyright infringement. Two elements must be proven: (1) ownership of a valid copyright, and (2) copying of constituent elements of the work that are original. The first element is not at issue here: Feist appears to concede that Rural's directory, considered as a whole, is subject to a valid copyright because it contains some foreword text, as well as original material in its yellow pages advertisements.

The question is whether Rural has proven the second element. In other words, did Feist, by taking 1,309 names, towns, and telephone numbers from Rural's white pages, copy anything that was "original" to Rural?

Certainly, the raw data do not satisfy the originality requirement. Rural may have been the first to discover and report the names, towns, and telephone numbers of its subscribers, but these data do not "owe their origin" to Rural. The question that remains is whether Rural selected, coordinated, or arranged these copyrightable facts in an original way. The selection, coordination, and arrangement of Rural's white pages do not satisfy the minimum constitutional standards for copyright protection. Rural's selection of listings could not be more obvious: It publishes the most basic information—name, town, and telephone number—about each person who applies to it for telephone service. This is "selection" of a sort, but it lacks the modicum of creativity necessary to transform mere selection into copyrightable expression. Rural extended sufficient effort to make the white pages directory useful, but insufficient creativity to make it original.

The judgment of the Court of Appeals is Reversed.

CHAPTER 17

CHAPTER OBJECTIVES

After studying this chapter, you should be able to:

1. Describe *family law*.

2. Explain the process of obtaining a legal divorce.

3. List and describe the requirements for making a valid will.

4. Describe how a will can be changed and revoked.

5. Define *ademption* and *abatement*.

6. Explain the effect of entering into a mutual will.

7. Identify how property is distributed under intestacy statutes if a person dies without a will.

8. Describe the process of probate.

9. Explain a living will.

10. Define *trust* and identify the parties to a trust.

498

Family Law, Wills, and Estates

When you have told someone you have left him a legacy, the only decent thing to do is to die at once.

SAMUEL BUTLER

Introduction

Much law has been developed concerning the family unit and its members. Most notable is the law of divorce and its related issues of property distribution, child custody, payment of alimony, and such. Other family law issues include making gifts to minors, custody battles, appointing of conservators, and elder law.

Wills and trusts are a means of transferring property. Wills transfer property upon a person's death. A person who dies without a will is said to have died *intestate.* In this case, the deceased's property is distributed to relatives according to state statute. The property escheats (goes) to the state if there are no relatives. Trusts are used to transfer property that is to be held and managed for the benefit of another person. Trusts are created during one's lifetime, but they may be worded to become effective upon the trustor's death.

Many lawyers' practices consist of representing clients in divorce and family law matters, drafting wills and trust agreements, and handling estates. Many paralegals practice in the family law and estates areas of the law. This chapter covers family law, wills, trusts, and estates.

FAMILY LAW

The term **family law** generally refers to the practice of law concerning marriage, divorce, and child custody and support. Family law practice also frequently includes estate and financial planning because of the impact of finances on the support and care of children in cases of death of one or both parents, as well as providing for the surviving spouse in the event of death or disability.

Marriage

In the tradition of the common law, **marriage** is a voluntary agreement between a man and a woman to become husband and wife. Today, marriage is regulated by the state. Regulations include the following:

1. The state sets minimum ages for marriage; those under certain ages require the consent of a parent or guardian.
2. All of the states today limit marriage to one spouse.
3. A period of residency may be required.
4. A marriage license must be obtained from a state official, valid for a time during which the marriage must be performed or a new license obtained.

Some states still recognize **common-law marriage**—a marriage created without a marriage license. The requirement for a common-law marriage is a present intent to be married expressed by the parties. The problem with common-law marriage is in proving the existence of the words spoken of the present intent to be married. This issue most often arises after the death of one of the parties when survivor benefits or interests in property are sought. In most cases, mere habitation of the parties is not recognized as proof of a common-law marriage.

Divorce

The term used to describe the dissolution of a marriage is **divorce.** Just as the law of marriage is regulated by the state, so is the law on divorce. As with marriage, a residence period frequently is required before a state court will process a request for a divorce action.

Unlike the simple process for obtaining a marriage license, divorce is more involved and is initiated and supervised by the appropriate state court. Potential issues include substantial property interests and child custody, including visitation and support. In the past, most states placed severe limitations on the granting of a divorce, but the modern trend is toward allowing divorce without an allegation of fault, called **no-fault divorce.**

Property Issues in Divorce

One of the biggest areas of controversy in a divorce is that of separation of the property. In addition to division of the real estate and tangible personal property such as furniture and vehicles, a growing area of litigation involves the division of intangibles such as the value of a spouse's professional practice or business interests.

With the increased funding by individuals and employers of unsheltered and tax-sheltered retirement plans has come increased litigation concerning the values for use in property settlements. The spouse with the retirement fund usually looks at it as future security, and the spouse without a fund for future retirement sees the increase in its value during marriage as a contribution from the marital partnership. The rules on property settlement are regulated by the states.

Community property. Eleven states, plus Puerto Rico, have **community-property** laws. These laws generally provide that all property acquired during marriage, except from gift or bequest from a decedent, is owned equally by each spouse. At the time of a divorce, the property is to be shared equally.

Equitable distribution. More and more states are dividing property according to the **equitable distribution** doctrine. Courts divide property after taking into consideration issues such as the amount of time a spouse has been out of the workforce; if this has been to take of care of family, or at the request of the other spouse; age and medical condition of the parties; and the contribution to the education or professional or business success by one spouse to the other, which generally increases the future earning potential of the other spouse.

Child Support

It is generally accepted that children are entitled to be supported by their parents based on the parents' earning ability. This includes the general obligation to educate the child, including higher education when the child has the ability and the parent has the resources. The difficulty in **child support** matters arises from the general unequal earning power of the two parents. In the past, fathers were the ones who worked to support the family and mothers were the ones to stay home and take care of the children. Today it is common for both parents to work and in some cases for the traditional roles to be reversed, with fathers as the primary caregivers.

The increased opportunities for women to work outside the home have sometimes resulted in their earning higher incomes than the fathers and husbands. Courts have struggled with the equities of the situation in providing fair amounts each parent should provide. The courts typically use general guidelines based on income. This eliminates some of the fault concept and provides a more mechanical basis for child support decisions. Difficulties still arise when parents seek to conceal assets and attempt to reduce earnings to obtain a reduced support obligation.

Collecting support payments and enforcing support orders have been a continuing problem—one on which the family law firm spends considerable time. As a further complication, the child often resides with a parent in one state while the other parent resides in another state. Initial support orders may be obtained from a court where the family initially resided, or from one in which the custodial parent has settled with the children after the separation and divorce.

The problem accompanying changes to support orders by other courts and the enforcement of existing support orders has been addressed by the U.S. Congress, which passed the Full Faith and Credit for Child Support Act in 1994. This law provides that a state court may not modify an order of another state court unless the recipient of the child support resides in the state in which the modification is sought [28 U.S.C. 1738B].

Giha v. Giha

609 A.2d 945 (1992)   Supreme Court of Rhode Island

FACTS

On October 7, 1987, Nagib Giha (Husband) filed a complaint for divorce from Nelly Giha (Wife) on the grounds of irreconcilable differences. On May 20, 1988, the parties reached an agreement for the disposition of their property that provided they would divide equally the net proceeds from the sale of their marital assets. They had to wait a statutory waiting period before the divorce was final.

On December 25, 1988, Husband learned that he had won $2.4 million in the Massachusetts Megabucks state lottery. Husband kept this fact secret. After the waiting period was over, the family court entered its final judgment, severing the parties' marriage on April 27, 1989. Husband claimed his lottery prize on October 6, 1989.

In December 1990, after learning of the lottery winnings, Wife sued to recover the lottery prize. She alleged that the lottery prize was a marital asset because her Husband had won it before their divorce was final. The trial court dismissed her complaint. Wife appealed.

ISSUE

Was the $2.4-million lottery prize personal property of the marital estate?

IN THE LANGUAGE OF THE COURT

Fay, Chief Justice.

We have established that the parties to a divorce action remain as husband and wife until the entry of the final decree of divorce. In the present case the husband won the lottery prize four months before the Family Court entered its final judgment. The parties remained as husband and wife until the entry of the final judgment in 1989. Because the parties' marriage remained in effect throughout the waiting period, so did the property rights each spouse had in the property acquired by the other spouse during that period. Therefore, since the husband won the $2.4 million lottery prize during the existence of the parties' marriage, we conclude that the prize is a marital asset and is subject to the equitable-distribution statute. We conclude that the parties to a divorce action have a continuing duty to provide information about changes in their financial condition until the entry of a final judgment of divorce.

DECISION AND REMEDY

The appellate court held that the parties remained husband and wife until the entry of final judgment of divorce in April 1989. Therefore, the lottery prize was a marital asset. Reversed and remanded.

Questions

1. Should a spouse's lottery winnings be considered separate property? Why or why not?

2. Why does the law require a statutory period of time to pass before a divorce is final?

3. Did Husband act ethically in this case?

Child Custody and Parenting Time

Cases of **child custody** and parenting time are the most stressful, emotional, and difficult for all those involved, including legal professionals. Parents and other caregivers often see themselves as the only ones capable of properly caring for the child. Far too often, one parent uses the child as a weapon to secure other concessions in the divorce, property settlement, or support obligation.

The greatest challenge to the legal team comes when one parent decides that the courts and the legal system will not support his or her wishes or what the parent believes is best for the child and removes the child from the jurisdiction of the court, sometimes even disappearing with the child. Recognizing the growing number of cases involving persons shopping for a favorable jurisdiction or evading the state court orders entered, the U.S. Congress passed the Parental Kidnapping Prevention Act of 1980 [28 U.S.C. 1738A].

WILLS

A **will** is a declaration of how a person wants his or her property to be distributed upon his or her death. It is a *testamentary* deposition of property. The person who makes the will is called the *testator* (or *testatrix*). The persons designated in the will to receive the testator's property are called **beneficiaries.**

Requirements for Making a Will

Every state has a Statute of Wills that establishes the requirements for making a valid will in that state. These requirements are:

- *Testamentary capacity.* The testator must have been of legal age and "sound mind" when the will was made. The courts determine **testamentary capacity** on a case-by-case basis. The legal age for executing a will is set by state statute.
- *Writing.* Wills must be in writing to be valid (except for dying declarations, discussed later in this chapter). The writing may be formal or informal. Although most wills are typewritten, they can be handwritten (see the discussion of holographic wills). The writing may be on legal paper, scratch paper, envelopes, napkins, or other paper. A will may incorporate additional documents by reference.
- *Testator's signature.* Wills must be signed.

Most jurisdictions require the testator's signature to appear at the end of the will. This is to prevent fraud that could occur if someone were to add provisions to the will below the testator's signature. Generally, courts have held that initials ("R.K.H."), a nickname ("Buffy"), title ("mother"), or even an "X" is a valid signature on a will if it can be proven that the testator intended it to be his or her signature.

Attestation by Witnesses

Wills must be **attested** to by mentally competent witnesses. Although state law varies, most states require two or three witnesses. The witnesses do not have to reside in the jurisdiction in which the testator is domiciled. Most jurisdictions stipulate that interested parties (e.g., a beneficiary under the will or the testator's attorney) cannot be witnesses. If an interested party has attested to a will, state law either voids any clauses that benefit such person or voids the entire will.

Witnesses usually sign the will following the signature of the testator. This is called the *attestation clause*. Most jurisdictions require that each witness attest to the will in the presence of the other witnesses.

Using Legal Assistants in a Family Law Practice

GP Solo, Jan./Feb. 2002

When I joined my present firm in 1994, I was surprised to learn that, in addition to the four lawyers on staff, the firm employed a legal assistant. I had always believed that only large firms needed legal assistants, and that assistants could be useful only in complex litigation or highly specialized areas of the law. I soon discovered I was wrong.

Today I work closely with my firm's legal assistant, Vicki Voisin, on virtually all types of matters, including family law. Her biggest asset is practical know-how—the ability to track down the resource that holds the key to the answer, whether that resource is a person, book, or website.

Tracking It Down

A matter recently crossed my desk that involved an unusual issue for our firm—division of a military pension. I turned the matter over to Vicki, who tracked down the right people and found out the terms required for governmental approval. Once those terms were received, Vicki got the military advisers to sign off on the language before the order was entered.

I could have spent hours trying to track down these same people, but Vicki is skilled in this type of problem solving—plus her billing rate is significantly lower than mine. Meanwhile, I was able to be working (and billing) for another client.

Vicki performs certain tasks on a routine basis. For cases where government information is involved, she gathers tax statements from the county treasurer, recorded instruments from the county register of deeds, etc. Over the years, Vicki has developed a rapport with these agencies that allows us to get materials "in a pinch"—as long as we don't ask too often, of course!

Client Contact

When I know that a case will be time-consuming or a client might require extra attention, I ask Vicki to sit in on one of the first meetings with the client. I introduce her and explain that she may answer many of their questions as the case moves forward. People like to have a face to go with a voice. Involving the legal assistant early on directly in the case also lets clients know that you are not "dumping" them on a subordinate but, rather, are utilizing an important member of your legal team.

Clients appreciate an explanation of the roles the lawyer, legal assistant, secretary, and other firm lawyers will play in their case. Some clients find it easier to approach Vicki instead of me with questions. When Vicki is able to field the questions, the result is lower costs to the client and continued productivity in the office. (Most clients decrease the number of calls to Vicki once they realize they are billed for them.) If necessary, Vicki turns the question over to me.

Organization and Input

As the case moves forward, Vicki keeps the documents organized. Early on, I try to determine whether a matter will likely resolve easily, go to trial, or require a final settlement conference. I involve Vicki on the cases that are not likely to resolve early on. She organizes and combines all of the file materials. This guarantees that correspondence and documents in these more voluminous files are properly cared for.

A will that meets the requirements of the Statute of Wills is called a *formal will*. A sample will is shown as Exhibit 17.1.

Changing a Will

A will cannot be amended by merely striking out existing provisions and adding new ones. **Codicils** are the legal way to change an existing will. A codicil is a separate document that must be executed with the same formalities as a will. In addition, it must incorporate by reference the will it is amending. The codicil and the will then are read as one instrument. A codicil is shown as Exhibit 17.2.

Allen R. Telgenhof

As the file is organized, Vicki reads or at least reviews every item in the file. There is no substitute for this sort of review. We utilize this information in various ways. Vicki shares her basic impression of the case. I find that as a case moves forward, I sometimes buy into the client's position and am less able to look at things objectively. I make sure to ask Vicki whether my client's testimony seems truthful or how she thinks the judge will rule on a certain issue.

I find these discussions with Vicki more helpful than seeking out the input of my partners who practice family law. Vicki's familiarity with the file gives her greater knowledge of the relevant facts. It is not practical for one of my partners to review file documents because most of our family law files are not large-dollar generators (although a complex litigation situation might benefit from two or more lawyers working a file together).

Trial Support

Even though most of our cases rarely go to trial these days, if the client can afford it, I prefer to be accompanied by Vicki. She has great knowledge of the file as well as a relationship with the client. She assists with witness coordination and, on occasion, witness preparation. While I am questioning one witness, she can be in a conference room interviewing the next or locating witnesses who haven't shown up. She also can run errands, return phone calls, and track down materials. Vicki provides peace of mind; I can focus exclusively on the task at hand while she takes care of the unexpected things that inevitably arise while at trial.

Obviously, many family law matters are small and can't justify such additional expense. I usually tell my clients that if they want the best job my firm can provide on their trial, we should have the help of our experienced legal assistant.

How Far Is Too Far?

Some firms have the legal assistant meet with the client in the initial conference without the lawyer being present. The legal assistant and the client go through a preprinted intake form that covers the basic information needed to prosecute or defend the case. The legal assistant also utilizes form complaints for divorces and motions to reduce child support or for changes of custody. They use the information to prepare rough-draft pleadings, which are reviewed and signed by a lawyer prior to filing.

The primary benefit of this type of system is that large caseloads can be managed with fewer lawyers and more legal assistants, which lowers the firm's overhead. The client still has a contact person for questions; it just isn't the lawyer. But contact between the lawyer and the client is a crucial element to client satisfaction. If anything goes wrong, the client is likely to blame the problem on not having had enough contact with the lawyer. Court appearances can turn into a case of the legal assistant prepping and the lawyer cramming. In an important hearing, this usually isn't the best situation for a client. However, there is no question that such a system maximizes the potential for profits if a large caseload is maintained.

From *GP Solo,* Vol. 19, No. 1, Jan./Feb. 2002. Reprinted with permission of the American Bar Association.

Revoking a Will

A will may be revoked by acts of the testator. A will is revoked if the testator intentionally burns, tears, obliterates, or otherwise destroys it. A properly executed *subsequent will* revokes a prior will if it specifically states that it is the testator's intention to do so. If the second will does not expressly revoke the prior will, the wills are read together. If any will provisions are inconsistent, the provision in the second will controls.

Wills can be revoked by operation of law. For example, divorce or annulment revokes disposition of property to the former spouse under the will. The *exhibit* **17.1** *Sample will.*

Last Will and Testament of Florence Winthorpe Blueblood

I, FLORENCE WINTHORPE BLUEBLOOD, presently residing at Boston, County of Suffolk, Massachusetts, being of sound and disposing mind and memory, hereby make, publish, and declare this to be my Last Will and Testament.

FIRST. I hereby revoke any and all Wills and Codicils previously made by me.

SECOND. I direct that my just debts and funeral expenses be paid out of my Estate as soon as practicable after my death.

THIRD. I am presently married to Theodore Hannah Blueblood III.

FOURTH. I hereby nominate and appoint my husband as the Personal Representative of this my Last Will and Testament. If he is unable to serve as Personal Representative, then I nominate and appoint Mildred Yardly Winthorpe as Personal Representative of this my Last Will and Testament. I direct that no bond or other security be required to be posted by my Personal Representative.

FIFTH. I hereby nominate and appoint my husband as Guardian of the person and property of my minor children. In the event that he is unable to serve as Guardian, then I nominate and appoint Mildred Yardly Winthorpe Guardian of the person and property of my minor children. I direct that no bond or other security be required to be posted by any Guardian herein.

SIXTH. I give my Personal Representative authority to exercise all the powers, rights, duties, and immunities conferred upon fiduciaries under law with full power to sell, mortgage, lease, invest, or reinvest all or any part of my Estate on such terms as he or she deems best.

SEVENTH. I hereby give, devise, and bequeath my entire estate to my husband, except for the following specific bequests:

I give my wedding ring to my daughter, Hillary Smythe Blueblood.

I give my baseball card collection to my son, Theodore Hannah Blueblood IV.

In the event that either my above-named daughter or son predeceases me, then and in that event, I give, devise, and bequeath my deceased daughter's or son's bequest to my husband.

EIGHTH. In the event that my husband shall predecease me, then and in that event, I give, devise and bequeath my entire estate, with the exception of the bequests in paragraph SEVENTH, to my beloved children or grandchildren surviving me, per stirpes.

NINTH. In the event I am not survived by my husband or any children or grandchildren, then and in that event, I give, devise, and bequeath my entire estate to Harvard University.

IN WITNESS WHEREOF, I Florence Winthorpe Blueblood, the Testatrix, sign my name to this Last Will and Testament this 3rd day of January, 2003.

_____
(Signature)

Signed, sealed, published and declared by the above-named Testatrix, as and for her Last Will and Testament, in the presence of us, who at her request, in her presence and in the presence of one another, have hereunto subscribed our names as attesting witnesses, the day and year last written above.

Witness   *Address*

_____   _____

_____   _____

_____   _____

Sample codicil.   exhibit 17.2

SECOND CODICIL TO
THE LAST WILL AND TESTAMENT OF
SARA ELLIOTT

I, SARA ELLIOTT, of Scottsdale, Maricopa County, Arizona, declare this to be a Second Codicil to my Last Will and Testament dated March 13, 1995, and the Codicil to my Last Will and Testament dated June 22, 1999.

ARTICLE FIRST: I hereby revoke Article Third of my Will dated March 13, 1995, as amended by the Codicil of June 22, 1999, and substitute the following:

(a) I devise and bequeath all my jewelry to my daughter, Kaylee E. Sam, presently of Mesa, Arizona.

(b) I devise and bequeath the house and real property located at 1840 Norwood Place, Clearwater, Florida, to my daughter, Kaylee E. Sam, presently of Mesa, Arizona.

ARTICLE SECOND: I do hereby reaffirm all other provisions of my Last Will and Testament dated March 13, 1995, as amended by my First Codicil to my Last Will and Testament dated June 22, 1999.

IN WITNESS WHEREOF, I have hereunto set my hand this _____ day of _____ 2004.

_____
SARA ELLIOTT

The preceding instrument consisting of two typewritten pages, identified by the signature of the testatrix, was on the date thereof, signed, published and declared by SARA ELLIOTT in the presence of us who, in her presence and at her request and in the presence of each other, have subscribed our names as witnesses hereto.

_____   _____
(Name)   (Address)

_____   _____
(Name)   (Address)

_____   _____
(Name)   (Address)

remainder of the will is valid. The birth of a child after a will has been executed does not revoke the will but does entitle the child to receive his or her share of the parents' estate as determined by state statute.

Special Types of Wills

The law recognizes some types of wills that do not meet all of the requirements discussed above. Two special types of wills admitted by the courts are holographic wills and noncupative wills.

Holographic Wills

Holographic wills are entirely handwritten and signed by the testator. The writing may be in ink, pencil, crayon, or some other writing instrument. Many states recognize the validity of such wills even though they are not witnessed.

Noncupative Wills

Noncupative wills are oral wills made before witnesses. These wills are usually valid only if they are made during the testator's last illness. They sometimes are called *deathbed wills* or *dying declarations*.

Types of Testamentary Gifts

In a will, a gift of real estate by will is called a *devise*. A gift of personal property by will is called a **bequest** or **legacy**. Gifts in wills can be *specific*, *general*, or *residuary*:

- **Specific gifts:** specifically named pieces of property, such as a ring, a boat, or a piece of real estate.
- **General gifts:** gifts that do not identify the specific property from which the gift is to be made, such as a cash amount that can come from any source in the decedent's estate.
- **Residuary gifts:** established by a *residuary clause* in the will. The clause might state, for example, "I give my daughter the rest, remainder, and residual of my estate." This means that any portion of the estate left after the debts, taxes, and specific and general gifts have been paid belongs to the decedent's daughter.

Talbot County Courthouse completed 1892, in Talbot, Georgia.

A person who inherits property under a will or an intestacy statute takes the property subject to all of the outstanding claims against it (e.g., liens, mortgages). A person can *renounce* an inheritance—and often does—when the liens or mortgages against the property exceed the value of the property.

Ademption

If a testator leaves a specific gift of property to a beneficiary but the property is no longer in the estate of the testator when he or she dies, the beneficiary receives nothing. This is called the doctrine of **ademption.**

Abatement

If the testator's estate is not large enough to pay all of the devises and bequests, the doctrine of **abatement** applies. The doctrine works as follows:

- If a will provides for both general and residuary gifts, the residuary gifts are abated first (i.e., paid last). Suppose a testator executes a will when he owns $500,000 of property that leaves (1) $100,000 to the Red Cross, (2) $100,000 to a university, and (3) the residue to his niece. When the testator dies, his estate is worth only $225,000. Here the Red Cross and the university receive $100,000 each and the niece receives $25,000.

- If a will provides for only general gifts, the reductions are proportionate. Suppose a testator's will leaves $75,000 to each of two beneficiaries but the estate is only $100,000. Each beneficiary would receive $50,000.

Per-Stirpes and Per-Capita Distribution

A testator's will may state that property is to be left to his or her lineal descendants (children, grandchildren, great-grandchildren, etc.) either *per stirpes* or *per capita*. The difference between these two methods is as follows:

- *Per stirpes:* The lineal descendants inherit by representation of their parent; that is, they split what their deceased parent would have received. If their parent is not deceased, they receive nothing.

- *Per capita:* The lineal descendants equally share the property of the estate without regard to degree of relationship to the testator. That is, children of the testator share equally with grandchildren, great-grandchildren, and so forth.

Consider this example: Suppose Anne dies without a surviving spouse, and she had three children—Bart, Beth, and Bruce. Bart, who survives his mother, has no children. Beth has one child, Carla, and they both survive Anne. Bruce, who predeceased his mother, had two children, Clayton and Cathy; and Cathy, who predeceased Anne, had two children, Deborah and Dominic, both of whom survive Anne.

If Anne leaves her estate to her lineal descendants *per stirpes*, Bart and Beth each get one-third, Carla receives nothing because Beth is alive, Clayton gets one-sixth, and Deborah and Dominic each get one-twelfth. Exhibit 17.3 illustrates this *per-stirpes* example graphically.

But if Anne leaves her estate to her lineal descendants *per capita*, all of the surviving issue—Bart, Beth, Carla, Clayton, Deborah, and Dominic—share equally in the estate. They each get one-sixth of Anne's estate. Exhibit 17.4 illustrates the *per-capita* distribution for this example.

Special Issues Concerning Wills

Some unique issues in wills involve simultaneous deaths, joint and mutual wills, and undue influence.

Simultaneous Deaths

Sometimes people who would inherit property from each other die simultaneously. If it is impossible to determine who died first, the question becomes one of inheritance. The Uniform Simultaneous Death Act provides that each deceased person's property is distributed as if he or she survived.

exhibit 17.3   Per-stirpes *distribution.*

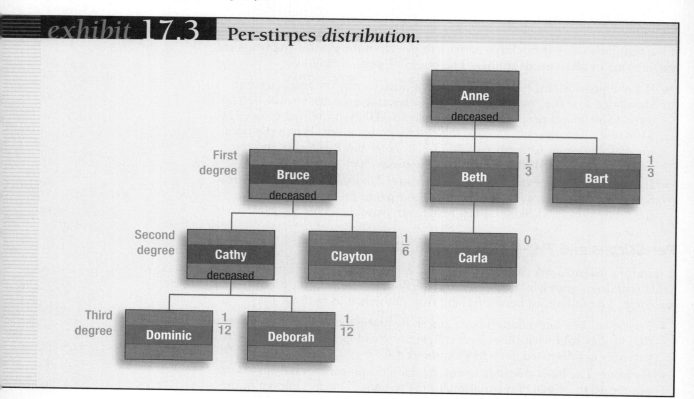

exhibit 17.4   Per-capita *distribution.*

Many acrimonious will contests involve written wills. The contestors allege such things as mental incapacity of the testator at the time the will was made, undue influence, fraud, or duress. Although the written will speaks for itself, the mental capacity of the testator and the voluntariness of his or her actions cannot be determined from the writing alone.

If a challenge to the validity of a will has merit, it, of course, should be resolved. But some will contests are based on unfounded allegations. After all, the testator is not there to defend his or her testamentary wishes.

To prevent unwarranted will contests, a testator can use a videotaped or electronically recorded will to supplement a written will. Videotaping a will that can withstand challenges by disgruntled relatives and alleged heirs involves a certain amount of planning.

A written will should be prepared to comply with the state's Statute of Wills. The video session should not begin until after the testator has become familiar with the document. The video should begin with the testator reciting the will verbatim. Next the lawyer should ask the testator questions to demonstrate the testator's sound mind and understanding of the implications of his or her actions. The last segment on the film should be the execution ceremony—signing of the will by the testator and attestation by the witnesses. The videotape then should be stored in a safe place.

With the testator's actions crystallized on videotape, a judge or jury will be able to determine the testator's mental capacity at the time the will was made and the voluntariness of his or her testamentary gifts. In addition, fraudulent competing wills will crumble in the face of such proof.

In the future, videotaped wills likely will become invaluable evidential tools. Whether such wills alone without a writing will be recognized as testamentary instruments will depend on the development of state laws.

Consider this example: Suppose a husband and wife make wills leaving their entire estate to each other. Assume that the husband and wife are killed simultaneously in an airplane crash. Here, the husband's property would go to his relatives and the wife's property would go to her relatives.

Joint and Mutual Wills

If two or more testators execute the same instrument as their will, the document is called a **joint will.** A joint will may be held invalid as to one testator but not the other(s).

Mutual or **reciprocal wills** are developed when two or more testators execute separate wills that make testamentary dispositions of their property to each other on the condition that the survivor leave the remaining property on his or her death as agreed by the testators. The wills usually are separate instruments with reciprocal terms. Because of their contractual nature, mutual wills cannot be revoked unilaterally after one of the parties has died.

Undue Influence

A will may be found to be invalid if it was made as a result of **undue influence** on the testator. Undue influence can be inferred from the facts and circumstances surrounding the making of the will. For example, if an 85-year-old woman leaves all of her property to the lawyer who drafted her will and ignores her blood relatives, the court is likely to presume undue influence.

Undue influence is difficult to prove by direct evidence, but it may be proved by circumstantial evidence. The elements that courts examine to find the presence of undue influence include the following.

- The benefactor and beneficiary are involved in a relationship of confidence and trust.
- The will contains substantial benefit to the beneficiary.
- The beneficiary caused or assisted in effecting execution of the will.
- There was an opportunity to exert influence.
- The will contains an unnatural disposition of the testator's property.
- The bequests constitute a change from a former will.
- The testator was highly susceptible to the undue influence.

Intestate Succession

Entrepreneurs often accumulate a sizeable estate. Such a person therefore should have a proper will designating who is to receive his or her business and other property when he or she dies. If an entrepreneur or other person dies without a will, or his or her will fails for some legal reason, the property is distributed to his or her relatives pursuant to the state's **intestacy statute.**

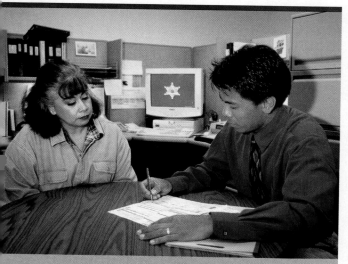

Filling out legal forms in Orange County, California.

Relatives who receive property under these statutes are called **heirs.** Although intestacy statutes differ from state to state, the general rule is that the deceased's real property is distributed according to the intestacy statute of the state where the real property is located and the deceased's personal property is distributed according to the intestacy statute of the state where the deceased had his or her permanent residence.

Intestacy statutes usually leave the deceased's property to his or her heirs in this order: spouse, children, lineal heirs (e.g., grandchildren, parents, brothers and sisters), collateral heirs (e.g., aunts, uncles, nieces, nephews), and other next of kin (e.g., cousins). If the deceased has no surviving relatives, the deceased's property **escheats** (goes) to the state. In-laws do not inherit under most intestacy statutes. If a child dies before his or her parents, the child's spouse does not receive the inheritance.

To avoid the distribution of an estate as provided in an intestacy statute, a person should have a properly written, signed, and witnessed will that distributes the estate property as the testator wishes.

PROBATE

When a person dies, his or her property must be collected, debts and taxes paid, and the remainder of the estate distributed to the beneficiaries of the will or the heirs under the state intestacy statute. This process is called **settlement**

Murder, She Wrote

Most states, by statute or court decision, provide that a person who murders another person cannot inherit the victim's property. This rule, often called the murder disqualification doctrine, is based on the public policy that a person should not benefit from his or her wrongdoing.

Walter A. Gibbs resided with his mother until 1963, when he hired Delores Christenson to help care for her. He married Delores in 1964. The couple were divorced in 1973. Gibbs married Delores's twin sister, Darlene Wahl. That marriage ended in divorce in 1980.

During the winter of 1988–1989, Delores, Darlene, and Darlene's new husband, Jerry Phillips, who were all living together, experienced difficult times due to lack of money. Delores contacted Gibbs, who was older than 80 years at the time, at the nursing home where he resided and offered to move back into his house and care for him. In February 1989, Delores, Darlene, and Jerry moved Gibbs to his house and moved in with him. The group lived together as a "family" for about one year.

Gibbs had a will that named his first cousin, Bernice Boettner, as sole beneficiary. In January 1990, Delores located an attorney who drafted a new will for Gibbs, and she procured two witnesses for the will's execution. The will disinherited Gibbs's relations and left his entire estate, worth about $175,000, to Delores. Gibbs executed the will on January 5, 1990.

On January 8, 1990, Darlene and Jerry discussed killing Gibbs to "activate the will." A few weeks later, Darlene suggested in the presence of Jerry and Delores that they hasten Gibbs's death by mixing sleeping pills and nitroglycerin in his tea. At one time, when Darlene suggested smothering Gibbs with a pillow, Delores went to the bedroom, returned with a pillow, and handed it to Jerry, who held it over Darlene's face to see if she could breathe. On the morning of April 1, 1990, Darlene got a pillow from her bedroom and gave it to Jerry. Delores sat at the kitchen table approximately 17 feet from Gibbs's bed. Darlene held Gibbs's arms while Jerry smothered him. After Jerry removed the pillow, Delores went over and embraced Jerry.

In January 1991, Delores, Darlene, and Jerry were indicted on charges of murder, conspiracy to commit murder, and aiding and abetting murder. Jerry pleaded guilty to conspiracy to commit second-degree murder. Darlene was convicted of murder and sentenced to life in prison. Delores was acquitted of all charges.

Delores offered Gibbs's will for probate. Boettner filed a petition to revoke the probate of Gibbs's will and an application to disqualify Delores as the beneficiary as a willful slayer of Gibbs. Delores argued in defense that she should be allowed to inherit Gibbs's estate because she had not been criminally convicted.

The trial court held that Delores qualified as a willful slayer under the murder disqualification statute even though she had not been convicted at her criminal trial. The state supreme court affirmed.

We are not dealing with criminal responsibility, but with a civil statute which disqualifies a person who procures the death of a testator from reaping the benefits of that death. Moreover, the evidence indicated Delores interjected herself into the conspiracy by voluntarily procuring a pillow to assist Jerry and Darlene in practicing to smother Gibbs. In summation, Delores's claim she was just an innocent bystander and not an accomplice is without merit.

Gibbs's prior will, which left his estate to Boettner, is subject to probate. [*In the Matter of the Estate of Walter A. Gibbs,* 490 N.W.2d 504 (S.D. 1992)]

of the estate or **probate.** The process and procedures for settling an estate are governed by state statute. A specialized state court, called the probate court, usually supervises the administration and settlement of an estate.

A *personal representative* must be appointed to administer the estate during its settlement phase. If the testator's will names the personal representative, that person is called an **executor** or **executrix.** If no one is named or if the decedent

THE COURTHOUSE TEAM — *Registrar of Wills*

Initiation of the proceedings involving wills and the administration of estates may be delegated to the Registrar of Wills, who may be an elected official or one appointed to oversee the authentication of wills. The process, usually referred to as probate, starts with filing of the will and any codicils to the will with the court. Typically this involves presenting the will together with a death certificate to the court-designated officers. The named executor or executrix—or administrator where no executor is available or named in the will—usually must appear at the same time and acknowledge his or her willingness to act as the executor or administrator. Depending upon the requirements of the local jurisdiction, the subscribing witnesses to the will also may be required to appear to authenticate their signatures and the will and the signature of the deceased.

Filing fees are part of the process, and appropriate checks for payment are generally required. Fees may vary depending upon the size of the probate estate. Additional forms may be required with regard to the assets and their values. In some jurisdictions, the Registrar of Wills or his or her agents may come to the attorney's office or to other locations as a convenience to the parties or where the parties, by virtue of age or disability, are unable to go to the courthouse.

dies intestate, the court will appoint an **administrator** or **administratrix.** Usually, this party is a relative or the deceased or a bank. An attorney is usually appointed to help administer the estate and to complete the probate.

The **Uniform Probate Code (UPC)** was promulgated to establish uniform rules for creating wills, administering estates, and resolving conflicts in estate settlements. These rules provide a speedy, efficient, and less expensive method than many existing state laws for settling estates. Only about one-third of the states have adopted all or part of the UPC.

THE COURTHOUSE TEAM

Orphans Court/ Probate Court Clerk

In some jurisdictions, functions related to the administration of wills, including probate and matters related to the protection of children in the form of guardianship and adoption, are handled by a specialized court sometimes referred to as the orphans court and other times as the probate court.

TRUSTS

A **trust** is a legal arrangement under which one person—the **settlor, trustor,** or **transferor**—delivers and transfers legal title to property to another person, the **trustee,** to be held and used for the benefit of a third person, the beneficiary. The property held in trust is called the **trust corpus** or **trust res.** The trustee has *legal title* to the trust corpus, and the beneficiary has *equitable title.* Unlike wills, trusts are not public documents, so property can be transferred in privacy.

Trusts often provide that any trust income is to be paid to a person called the *income beneficiary.* The person to receive the trust corpus upon the termination of the trust is called the **remainderman.** The income beneficiary and the remainderman can be the same person or different persons. The designated beneficiary can be any identifiable person, animal (such as a pet), charitable organization, or other institution or cause that the settlor chooses. An entire class of persons—for example, "my grandchildren"—can be named.

The Right to Die and Living Wills

Technological breakthroughs have greatly increased the lifespan of human beings. This same technology, however, permits life to be sustained long after a person is "brain dead." Some people say they have a right to refuse such treatment. Others argue that human life must be preserved at all costs. The U.S. Supreme Court was called upon to decide the right-to-die issue in the case of Nancy Cruzan.

In 1983, an automobile accident left Cruzan, a 25-year-old Missouri woman, in an irreversible coma. Four years later, Cruzan's parents petitioned a state court judge to permit the hospital to withdraw the artificial feeding tube that had been keeping Cruzan alive. The judge agreed.

But Missouri's attorney general intervened and asked an appellate court to reverse the lower court's decision. The appellate court sided with the attorney general. The appellate court held that the family had not proven with certainty that Cruzan herself would have wanted the treatment stopped.

In reviewing the Missouri court's decision, eight of the nine justices of the U.S. Supreme Court acknowledged that the right to refuse medical treatment is a personal liberty protected by the U.S. Constitution. But the Court also recognized that the states have an interest in preserving life. This interest can be expressed through a requirement for clear and convincing proof that the patient did not want to be sustained by artificial means. The Missouri attorney general then withdrew from the case, and a Missouri judge finally permitted the family to have Cruzan's tubes withdrawn. She died shortly afterward.

The clear message of the Supreme Court's opinion is that people who do not want their lives prolonged indefinitely by artificial means should sign a **living will** that stipulates their wishes before catastrophe strikes and they become unable to express these wishes themselves because of an illness or an accident. Exhibit 17.5 is an example of a living will and health care proxy.

Those who have a living will could state which lifesaving measures they do and do not want. Alternatively, they could state that they want any such treatments withdrawn if doctors determine that there is no hope of a meaningful recovery. The living will provides clear and convincing proof of a patient's wishes with respect to medical treatment.

Although the Supreme Court's opinion seems to sanction the general use of living wills, there is widespread disparity among states on this issue. Several states have yet to enact legislation authorizing the use of living wills. Also, there is no consistency among the states that have passed living will laws. Some states permit living wills to be activated only when death is at hand. Other state statutes complicate the issue by specifying types of treatment, such as artificial feeding tubes, that cannot be withdrawn no matter what the patient's living will states.

People realize that what happened to the Cruzans could happen to them—at any age, in any place, without warning. For the more than 80 percent of the American adult population who support the right to die, the *Cruzan* case gives the ability, through the use of a living will, to control such decisions. [*Cruzan v. Director, Missouri Department of Health*, 497 U.S. 261, 110 S.Ct. 2841 (1990)]

A trust can allow the trustee to invade (use) the trust corpus for certain purposes that can be specifically named (e.g., "for the beneficiary's college education"). The trust agreement usually specifies how the receipts and expenses of the trust are to be divided between the income beneficiary and the remainderman. Exhibit 17.6 shows the parties to a trust.

Generally, the trustee has broad management powers over the trust property. This means that the trustee can invest the trust property to preserve its capital and make it productive. The trustee must follow any restrictions on investments contained in the trust agreement or state statute.

exhibit 17.5 *Sample living will and health care proxy.*

Living Will and Health Care Proxy

I. Living Will Including Statement Concerning Right to Die

Death is as much a reality as birth, growth, maturity and old age—it is the one certainty of life. If the time comes when I, John Doe, can no longer take part in decisions for my own future, let this statement stand as an expression of my wishes and directions to my Health Care Agent and others while I am still of sound mind. I intend, without otherwise limiting the absolute authority granted to my Health Care Agent in this instrument, that this instrument be binding upon my Health Care Agent.

If the situation should arise in which there is no reasonable expectation of my recovery from extreme physical or mental disability, including, but not limited to, a circumstance where there is no reasonable expectation that I will recover consciousness, commonly referred to as "brain dead," I direct that I be allowed to die and not be kept alive by medications, artificial means, including but not limited to artificial nutrition and hydration, or "heroic measures." Without limiting the generality of the foregoing, I hereby consent in such situation to an order not to attempt cardiopulmonary resuscitation. I do, however, ask that medication be mercifully administered to me to alleviate suffering even though this may shorten my remaining life and retard my consciousness.

II. Health Care Proxy

I hereby appoint my spouse, Jane Doe, to be my health care agent to make any and all health care decisions in accordance with my wishes and instructions as stated above and as otherwise known to her. In the event the person I appoint above is unable, unwilling or unavailable to act as my Health Care Agent, I hereby appoint my twin brother, Jack Doe, as my health care agent.

This health care proxy shall take effect in the event that I become unable to make my own health care decisions. I hereby revoke any prior health care proxy given by me to the extent it purports to confer the authority herein granted. I understand that, unless I revoke it, this health care proxy will remain in effect indefinitely.

Although I do not know today the exact circumstances that will exist when my Health Care Agent is called upon to make a decision or decisions on my behalf, I have selected my Health Care Agent with the confidence that such person understands my feelings in these matters and will make the decision I will want made considering the circumstances as they exist at the time. It is my intention, therefore, that the decision of my Health Care Agent be taken as a final and binding decision of mine, and will be the conclusive interpretation of the wishes I have made known in this document.

III. Waiver and Indemnity

To the extent permitted by law, I, for myself and for my heirs, executors, legal representatives and assigns, hereby release and discharge and agree to indemnify and hold harmless my Health Care Agent from and against any claim or liability whatsoever resulting from or arising out of my Health Care Agent's reliance on my wishes and directions as expressed herein. To induce any third party to act hereunder, I hereby agree that any third party receiving a duly executed copy or facsimile of this instrument may act hereunder, and that revocation or termination by me hereof shall be ineffective as to such third party unless and until actual notice or knowledge of such revocation shall have been received by such third party, and, to the extent permitted by law, I, for myself and for my heirs, executors, legal representatives and assigns, hereby release and discharge and agree to indemnify and hold harmless any such third party from and against any claims or liability whatsoever that may arise against such third party by reason of such third party having relied on the provisions of this instrument.

I understand the full import of this directive and I am emotionally and mentally competent to make this directive.

Signed _____

The declarant has been personally known to me and I believe him or her to be of sound mind.

Witness _____

Witness _____

Parties to a trust. exhibit 17.6

Types of Trusts

Trusts may be either *express* or *implied*. There are also several special types of trusts.

Express Trusts

Express trusts are created voluntarily by the settlor. These usually are written and the agreement is called a *trust instrument* or *trust agreement*.

Express trusts fall into two categories.

1. *Inter vivos trusts* or *living trusts:* created while the settlor is alive. The settlor transfers legal title of property to a named trustee to hold, administer, and manage for the benefit of named beneficiaries.

2. *Testamentary trusts:* created by will. The trust comes into existence when the settlor dies. If the will that establishes the trust is found to be invalid, the trust is also invalid.

Implied Trusts

Implied trusts are those imposed by law or by conduct of the parties. These trusts are divided into two categories: *constructive trusts* and *resulting trusts*.

A **constructive trust** is an equitable trust imposed by law to avoid fraud, unjust enrichment, and injustice. In constructive trust arrangements, the holder of the actual title to property (the trustee) holds the property in trust for its rightful owner.

Consider this example: Suppose Thad and Kaye are partners. Assume Kaye embezzles partnership funds and uses the stolen funds to purchase a piece of real estate. In this case, the court can impose a constructive trust under which Kaye (who holds actual title to the land) is considered a trustee who is holding the property in trust for Thad, its rightful owner.

A **resulting trust** is created by the conduct of the parties. Consider this example: Henry is purchasing a piece of real estate but cannot attend the closing. He asks his brother, Gregory, to attend the closing and take title to the property until he can return. In this case, Gregory holds the title to the property as trustee for Henry until he returns.

Special Types of Trusts

Trusts may be created for special purposes. Three types of special trusts that are fairly common are:

1. **Charitable trusts:** created for the benefit of a segment of society or society in general. An example is a trust created for the construction and maintenance of a public park.

2. **Spendthrift trusts:** designed to prevent a beneficiary's personal creditors from reaching his or her trust interest. All control over the trust is removed from the beneficiary. Personal creditors still can go after trust income that is paid to the beneficiary, however.

3. **Totten trusts:** created when a person deposits money in a bank account in his or her own name and holds it as a trustee for the benefit of another person. A totten trust is a tentative trust because (1) the trustee can add to or withdraw funds from the account, and (2) the trust can be revoked at any time prior to the trustee's death or prior to completing delivery of the funds to the beneficiary.

Termination of a Trust

A trust is irrevocable unless the settlor reserves the right to revoke it. Most trusts fall into the first category.

Usually, a trust either contains a specific termination date or provides that it will terminate upon the happening of an event (e.g., when the remainderman reaches a certain age). Upon termination, the trust corpus is distributed as provided in the trust agreement.

LEGAL TERMINOLOGY

Abatement	Constructive trust
Ademption	Divorce
Administrator/administratrix	Equitable distribution
Attestation	Escheat
Beneficiary	Executor/executrix
Bequest (legacy)	Express trust
Charitable trust	Family law
Child custody	General gift
Child support	Heir
Codicil	Holographic will
Common-law marriage	Implied trust
Community property	Intestacy statute

Intestate succession
Joint will
Living will
Marriage
Mutual (reciprocal) will
No-fault divorce
Noncupative will
Per-capita distribution
Per-stirpes distribution
Probate (settlement of the estate)
Remainderman
Residuary gift
Resulting trust

Settlor (trustor, or transferor)
Simultaneous deaths
Specific gift
Spendthrift trust
Testamentary capacity
Totten trust
Trust
Trust corpus (trust res)
Trustee
Undue influence
Uniform Probate Code (UPC)
Will

Summary

CHAPTER 17 FAMILY LAW, WILLS, AND ESTATES

Family Law

Definition	Practice of law concerning marriages, divorce, distribution of property upon divorce, and child support, and custody and parenting time.
Marriage	1. A legal agreement between a man and a woman to become husband and wife; a marriage license is issued. 2. Some states recognize common-law marriage, in which a marriage license between the two parties is not required.
Divorce	1. *Definition:* A legal proceeding whereby a married couple legally undo their marriage. 2. *Property distribution:* Upon divorce, the property of the divorcing couple is distributed to the parties based on legal principles set by the state. 3. *Child custody and parenting time:* The Court will order child custody and parenting time based on the law of the state and facts of the case.

Wills

Definition	A declaration of how a person wants his or her property to be distributed upon his or her death.
Parties to a Will	1. *Testator or testatrix:* Person who makes a will. 2. *Beneficiary:* Person designated in the will to receive the testator's property. There may be multiple beneficiaries.

(continued)

Parties to a Will, *continued*	3. *Executor or executrix:* Person named in a will to administer the testator's estate during settlement of the estate.

Requirements for Making a Will	1. *Statute of Wills:* A state statute that establishes the requirements for making a valid will.
	2. The normal requirements for making a will are:
	    a. *Testamentary capacity* (legal age and "sound mind").
	    b. *In writing.*
	    c. *Testator's signature.*
	    d. *Attestation by witnesses* (mentally competent and uninterested).

Changing a Will	1. *Codicil:* A legal way to change an existing will. 2. Must be executed with the same formalities as a will.

Special Types of Wills

Holographic Will	A will that is entirely handwritten and signed by the testator. Most states recognize the validity of these wills even though they are not witnessed.
Noncupative Will	Oral will made by dying persons before witnesses. Many states recognize these oral wills. Also called a *deathbed will* or a *dying declaration.*

Types of Testamentary Gifts

Specific Gift	Gift of a specifically mentioned piece of property (e.g., a ring).
General Gift	Gift that does not identify the specific property from which the gift is to be made (e.g., gift of cash).
Residuary Gift	Gift of the remainder of the testator's estate after the debts, taxes, and specific and general gifts have been paid.
Ademption	If a testator leaves a specific gift but the property is no longer in the estate when the testator dies, the beneficiary of that gift receives nothing.
Abatement	If the testator's estate is insufficient to pay the stated gifts, the gifts are abated (reduced) in the following order: (1) residuary gifts, then (2) general gifts proportionately.

Per-Stirpes and Per-Capita Distribution

Per-stirpes Distribution	Lineal descendants inherit by representation of their parent; they split what their deceased parent would have received.
Per-capita Distribution	Lineal descendants equally share the property of the estate without regard to degree.

(continued)

Special Issues Concerning Wills

Simultaneous Deaths	Uniform Simultaneous Death Act provides that if people who would inherit property from each other die simultaneously, each deceased person's property is distributed as if he or she had survived.
Joint Will	Two or more testators execute the same instrument as their will.
Mutual or Reciprocal Will	Two or more testators execute separate wills that leave property in favor of the other on condition that the survivor leave the remaining property upon his or her death as agreed by the testators.
Undue Influence	A will may be found to be invalid if it was made under undue influence, in which one person takes advantage of another person's mental, emotional, or physical weakness and unduly persuades that person to make a will.
Murder Disqualification	A person who murders another person cannot inherit the victim's property.
Intestate Succession	1. *Intestacy statute:* State statute that stipulates how a deceased's property will be distributed if he or she dies without leaving a will or if the will fails for some legal reason. 2. *Heirs:* Relatives who receive property under an intestacy statute. 3. *Escheat:* If no heirs, deceased's property goes to the state, under intestacy statutes.

Probate

Definition	Legal process of settling a deceased person's estate.
Administrator or Administratrix	Person named to administer the estate of a deceased person who dies intestate. An administrator also is named if an executor is not named in a will or the executor cannot or does not serve.

Trusts

Definition	A legal arrangement whereby one person delivers and transfers legal title to property to another person to be held and used for the benefit of a third person.
Trust Corpus	The property that is held in trust; also called *trust res.*
Parties	1. *Settlor:* Person who establishes a trust; also called a *trustor* or *transferor.* 2. *Trustee:* Person to whom *legal title* of the trust assets is transferred; responsible for managing the trust assets as established by the trust and law.

(continued)

Parties, *continued*	3. *Beneficiary:* Person for whose benefit a trust is created; holds *equitable title* to the trust assets. There can be multiple beneficiaries, including:
	  a. *Income beneficiary:* person to whom trust income is to be paid.
	  b. *Remainderman:* person who is entitled to receive the trust corpus upon termination of the trust.

Express Trusts	Voluntarily created by the settlor. Two types: 1. Inter vivos *trust:* Created while the settlor is alive; also called a *living trust.* 2. *Testamentary trust:* Created by will and comes into existence when the settlor dies.
Implied Trusts	Imposed by law or from the conduct of the parties. Two types: 1. *Constructive trust:* Equitable trust imposed by law to avoid fraud, unjust enrichment, and injustice. 2. *Resulting trust:* Trust created from the conduct of the parties.
Special Types of Trusts	1. *Charitable trust:* Created for the benefit of a segment of society or society in general. 2. *Spendthrift trust:* A trust whereby the creditors of the beneficiary cannot recover the trust's assets to satisfy debts owed to them by the beneficiary. 3. *Totten trust:* Created when a person deposits money in a bank account in his or her own name and holds it as a trust for the benefit of another person.

Working the Web

1. Check the Cornell University uniform probate code website at www.law.cornell.edu/uniform/probate.html.
2. Consult the Social Security Administration website for information about retirement and other social security benefits at www.ssa.gov.
3. See the ABA Division for Public Education for available books on practical law and download the ABA Guide to Wills and Estates at www.abanet.org/publiced/practical/books/wills/home.html.
4. Download the ABA Guide to Family Law at www.abanet.org/publiced/practical/books/family/home.html.
5. For Social Security information in Spanish, see http://ssa-spanish.custhelp.com/cgi-bin/ssa_spanish.

Questions
CRITICAL LEGAL THINKING AND WRITING

1. Define a marriage. Define a common law marriage.
2. Describe a divorce. What is a no-fault divorce? What does the doctrine of equitable distribution provide?
3. Describe the requirements for making a valid will. Why are the requirements so stringent?
4. Describe the following types of testamentary gifts: (1) specific gifts, (2) general gifts, and (3) residuary gifts.
5. Describe the difference between the doctrines of ademption and abatement.
6. Describe how a testator's property is left pursuant to per-stirpes distribution and pursuant to per-capita distribution.
7. Describe the doctrine of undue influence. Is it difficult to prove?
8. Define intestate succession. What is an intestate statute?
9. Define a trust. Who are the parties to a trust?
10. What is a living will? A health care proxy? Is it a good idea for people to have these?

Questions
ETHICS: ANALYSIS AND DISCUSSION

1. Is there a conflict of interest regarding representing both husband and wife in a divorce?
2. Can the firm represent a parent in a custody or support case if they have previously represented a minor child of the couple in any type of legal matter?
3. Is the preparation of divorce papers by a paralegal in an uncontested divorce the unauthorized practice of law in your jurisdiction?

Unauthorized Practice of Law

There are few certainties in the area of ethics, for paralegals or in any profession. What qualifies as ethical conduct is in most cases based on state law and court interpretation applied to a set of facts. The citation listed below represents one legal opinion and is provided as a research starting point. Do not assume that the same rule applies in your jurisdiction. For the following:

- *Prepare a written statement based on your state law.*
- *Use your state bar association website as a starting point.*

As a paralegal, you have gained substantial expertise in the education of children with disabilies. [*Arons v. New Jersey State Bd. of Educ.*, 842 F.2d 58 (3d Cir. 1988).] May you act as a lay advocate on behalf of parents of children with disabilities in administrative hearings to determine the children's appropriate educational placement? May you receive fees for representation in those proceedings?

In the Matter of the Estate of Jansa

670 S.W.2d 767 (Tex.App. 1984)

17.1 FACTS

On or about June 10, 1959, Martha Jansa executed a will naming her two sons as executors of her will and leaving all of her property to them. The will was properly signed and attested to by witnesses. Thereafter, Martha died. When Martha's safe deposit box at a bank was opened, the original of this will was discovered along with two other instruments that were dated after the will. One was a handwritten document that left her home to her grandson, with the remainder of her estate to her two sons; this document was not signed. The second document was a typed version of the handwritten one; this document was signed by Martha but was not attested to by witnesses.

ISSUE

Which of the three documents should be admitted to probate?

Woods v. Woods

379 S.E.2d 291 (GA 1990)

17.2 FACTS

Martha L. Woods and Henry R. Woods, who lived in Georgia, were married on February 21, 1987. Both of them had been previously married, and their respective spouses had died. They had each accumulated separate estates. Prior to departing on an automobile trip to Wichita, Kansas, they executed an instrument entitled "Agreement," dated March 27, 1987. It stated, "It is agreed that in the event of an accident or disaster which would result in the death of one of us, the surviving party is to retain ownership in the other's real and personal property until the time of his or her death." On April 5, 1987, they returned safely from their trip and did not subsequently execute another will. Henry died on June 11, 1988, as a result of a disease.

ISSUE

Should the March 27, 1987, agreement be admitted into probate?

In re Estate of Potter

469 So.2d 957 (Fla.App. 1985)

17.3 FACTS

Mrs. Mildred D. Potter executed a will providing that her residence in Pompano Beach, Florida, was to go to her daughter and an equivalent amount of cash to her son upon her death. Evidence showed that Mrs. Potter's intent was to treat the daughter and son equally in the distribution of her estate. When she died, her will was admitted into probate. At the time, she still possessed her home in Pompano Beach. Unfortunately, assets were insufficient to pay Mrs. Potter's son the equivalent amount of cash.

ISSUE

Can the son share in the value of the house so that his inheritance is equal to his sister's?

Jones v. Jones

718 S.W.2d 416 (Tex.App. 1986)

17.4 FACTS

In 1967, Homer and Edna Jones, husband and wife, executed a joint will that provided, "We will and give to our survivor, whether it be Homer Jones or Edna Jones, all property and estate of which the first of us that dies may be seized and possessed. If we should both die in a common catastrophe, or upon the death of our survivor, we will and give all property and estate then remaining to our children, Leonida Jones Eschman, daughter, Sylvia Marie Jones, daughter, and Grady V. Jones, son, share and share alike."

Homer died in 1975, and Edna Jones received his entire estate under the 1967 will. In 1977, Edna executed a new will that left a substantially larger portion of the estate to her daughter, Sylvia Marie Jones, than to the other two children. Edna Jones died in 1982. Edna's daughter Sylvia introduced the 1977 will for probate. The other two children introduced the 1967 will for probate.

ISSUE

Did Edna act ethically in this case? Who wins?

In re Estate of Vallerius

629 N.E.2d 1185 (1994)

Read the following case, excerpted from the court of appeals opinion. Review and brief the case. In your brief, answer the following questions.

1. Who was to inherit Adella Vallerius's property when she died?

2. What criminal acts did Douglas and Craig White commit?

3. Who is Renie White? Whose property did she inherit and why?

4. Who was to inherit Renie White's property when she died?

5. Were Douglas or Craig White permitted to inherit either Adella's or Renie's property when they died?

Lewis, Presiding Justice.

On December 22, 1987, Douglas White murdered his grandmother, Adella G. Vallerius. On the same day, at the same time, and in the same house, Douglas' brother, Craig White, murdered his grandmother's friend, Carroll Pieper. Douglas was convicted of Mrs. Vallerius' murder. Craig entered a negotiated plea of guilty to, and was convicted of, the murder of Carroll Pieper. Craig testified for the State in Douglas' murder trial as part of his negotiated guilty plea.

Mrs. Vallerius died testate, naming Douglas and Craig as her sole beneficiaries. Mrs. Vallerius' only heir was her daughter, Renie White, Douglas and Craig's mother. On January 11, 1988, Mrs. Vallerius' will was admitted to probate. In compliance with the terms of the will, Douglas White and Dennis Johnson were appointed legal representatives of Mrs. Vallerius' estate. About 2 1/2 months after Mrs. Vallerius was murdered, on March 7, 1988, Renie White died, intestate, of natural causes. She left as her only heirs her two sons, Douglas and Craig.

On March 12, 1990, the appellees, Peter M. Vallerius, Glenna F. Giacoletto, Lawrence Joe Davis, Helen L. Vallerius, Gail Kadavi, Iione V. Henry, Janis Murray, Terrie L. Illies, and Duffy Joe Vallerius, filed a petition to intervene and to consolidate the estates of Mrs. Vallerius and Renie White and an "Objection to Distribution" in the estate of Mrs. Vallerius, wherein they alleged that "Douglas Keith White and Craig Steven White, having intentionally and unjustifiably caused the death of Adella G. Vallerius, cannot lawfully receive any property, benefit or other interest" by reason of her death, through the estate of Mrs. Vallerius or through the estate of Renie White.

After an evidentiary hearing on the appellees' objection to distribution, the court entered an order granting the appellees' request. The trial court found that the issue in the case was whether Douglas and Craig could receive any property or interest by reason of the death of Mrs. Vallerius, whether through her estate or the estate of Renie White. The court determined that, under both statute and common law, the public policy of Illinois has long been to prevent wrongdoers from profiting from intentionally committed wrongful acts. The court further found that the petitioner-objectors (appellees herein) had sustained their burden of proof, by clear and convincing evidence, that Douglas and Craig intentionally caused the death of their grandmother, Mrs. Vallerius.

Appellants argue that the law does not preclude a murderer from inheriting property from a person other than the victim. The obvious intent of the law is that persons like Douglas and Craig White must not profit from their brutal murder of their grandmother. The fact that there is an intervening estate should not expurgate the wrong of the murderer.

The appellants argue that Craig cannot be held accountable for Douglas' murder of Mrs. Vallerius, since Craig did not actually swing the sledgehammer that killed Mrs. Vallerius but only killed Carroll Pieper after Douglas killed Mrs. Vallerius. Appellants argue that even though Craig "may have borne criminal responsibility for the actions of Douglas White under the criminal accountability statute," Craig cannot be denied his right of inheritance from his mother.

Craig White cannot be permitted to receive any benefit by reason of the death of Mrs. Vallerius, whether through her estate directly or indirectly through the estate of her daughter, Renie White. If we were to allow Craig White to receive any property, benefit, or interest from the estate of Renie White, our decision would directly contravene the state's unambiguous mandate that he not receive any property by reason of his grandmother's death in any capacity or by any circumstance.

PART IV

PARALEGAL SKILLS

Professional paralegals must develop a number of personal and professional skills. Verbal and written communication skills are crucial for paralegals, who will be interviewing clients and witnesses and developing professional relationships with the public. Paralegals should develop their ability to think and write critically while conducting legal research and preparing written reports. With the growth of electronic libraries and online resources, today's paralegals must be as comfortable with the computer and the Internet as with traditional research tools. All of these topics are covered in Part IV of this book.

CHAPTER 18

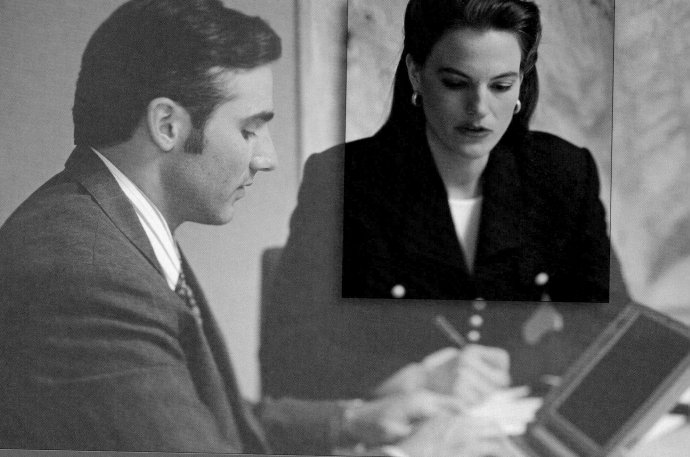

CHAPTER OBJECTIVES

After studying this chapter, you should be able to:

1. Explain the paralegal's need for good communication skills.
2. State the purpose of investigating a claim.
3. Set forth the reasons for visiting the scene of the cause of action.
4. Use an example to illustrate the importance of a timeline in a case.
5. List some different types of questioning.
6. Differentiate between a moral and an ethical consideration.
7. Explain the concept of privileged communications.
8. Be able to conduct an effective interview and obtain information commonly kept by governmental agencies.
9. Explain the purpose of, and the limitation in, obtaining information under the federal Freedom of Information Act (FOIA).
10. Describe how to locate potential witnesses as part of the investigation of a case.

Interviewing and Investigation Skills

It is the spirit and not the form of law that keeps justice alive.

EARL WARREN

Introduction

Communication skills are at the heart of paralegals' ability to successfully conduct interviews and investigations. The paralegal must be prepared to be the first point of contact with the client. In some practices, clients are interviewed first by the supervising attorney and then referred to the paralegal for a detailed factual interview. In other practices, though, the paralegal is the first one to meet with the client and conduct the initial interview before referring the client to the supervising attorney.

The paralegal must be able to successfully interview clients, fact witnesses, expert witnesses, investigators, and others such as public records custodians who may have access to information necessary for the preparation of a case. The skill of the interviewer or investigator can determine the accuracy and completeness of the information obtained, and ultimately the outcome of the case. The impressions created and the relationship developed with a new client may be the deciding factor in whether the client stays with the firm or seeks other counsel. Professional relationships developed with public officials, public custodians of records, hospital records librarians, police investigators, and similar independent investigators can make the job of the paralegal much easier and ultimately benefit the client.

INVESTIGATING CLAIMS

The legal team must gather all of the relevant information about a cause of action before making a recommendation to a client to file a lawsuit or respond to a claim of wrongdoing. In most cases, before the first interview with the client is conducted, the paralegal has some indication of the area of law or the nature of the claim. It may be from a telephone interview when the client calls for an appointment, or from the referral from the supervising attorney to the paralegal to conduct the interview and investigation. If paralegals specialize in certain areas of law, they are likely to understand the underlying elements of the claims or rights the client wishes to assert. Those in general practice and those entering a new area have to understand the rules of law as they apply to that issue.

For example, in a products liability case, understanding the traditional, or common-law, law of negligence is not enough. One also must understand the law of **strict liability** for product defect cases as found in the **Restatement (Second) of Torts,** section 402A. Where negligence requires a breach of duty, strict liability is without fault in cases where the doctrine applies. An interview conducted strictly considering negligence as the basis for a legal action could improperly result in the client's being advised that he or she does not have a claim when, under the no-fault strict liability concept for defective products, an action might exist.

The first step is to determine the legal basis of a client's claim. With an understanding of the legal basis of the claim and the applicable law, an investigative plan can be prepared to obtain the necessary witness statements, locate physical evidence, and obtain photographs, reports, and other evidence for use in preparation for and at trial. Where a claim of negligence is to be made, photographic evidence may be essential in demonstrating the nature of the hazard.

For example, when a client has injured himself or herself as result of a fall in a store, photographs showing the hazardous condition should be obtained as quickly as possible. In the case of strict liability involving a product defect that caused injury or loss, preservation of the defective product or photographic documentation of the defect becomes essential as a matter of proof. Knowing what elements of the action must be proven dictates what evidence must be located in the form of witnesses, photographs, and physical evidence. Knowing the elements of the claim will ensure that the proper questions are asked in the interview, which then will dictate the necessary investigation steps.

A paralegal interviews a client.

A Defense Perspective

Most people quite naturally think of a lawsuit from the plaintiff's perspective. Most people think in terms of the violation of rights and resulting injury. In a perfect world, only legitimate actions would be filed and the law would provide a perfect remedy for all wrongs. But not every plaintiff is in the right, and some have been known to file frivolous or even fraudulent lawsuits.

The balance in the American legal system is achieved by a vigorous defense on behalf of the defendant. A plaintiff may claim, for example, that she slipped and was injured as a result of the negligence of a storeowner. The defendant storeowner might be innocent of any wrongdoing or breach of any duty. It is well to remember that for every plaintiff there is a defendant, and for each party there is a law firm, an attorney, and a paralegal.

Obtaining Official Reports

Most incidents giving rise to litigation have associated official reports. In the negligence action, it may be a police accident or incident report, emergency medical services report, fire department call report, or incident reports of safety violations by federal, state, or local authorities. These reports are filed in a central depository as public records. A useful starting point is to obtain any official reports associated with the case. These reports frequently indicate time, place, and the names of fact witnesses. In some cases, detailed diagrams or photographs may accompany the reports. Exhibit 18.1 is an example of a police accident report form.

Fact Analysis

Analyzing the facts starts with interviewing the clients and their recitation of the time, place, circumstances, and other people involved as participants or witnesses. Exhibit 18.2 is a sample client interview form. A complete analysis usually requires further field investigation of the location, the object involved, such as an automobile, and interviews of the parties and witnesses. One person's perception may not be reality. A client's recollection and description of the physical surroundings may not be proven by the investigator's visit to the location. What one person describes as a narrow, congested walkway may actually be a standard-width open sidewalk.

The ultimate trier of fact will be the jury, a panel of arbitrators, or a judge acting as the trier of fact. Therefore, analysis of the facts must be sufficient to justify the position taken and the presentation made in pursuing a client's claim or its defense in **arbitration** or in trial.

Locations

Careful analysis of a claim includes verification of the physical aspects of the actual location where the cause of action occurred. Ask any group of people to describe a location, and you're likely to get as many different descriptions as there are people in the group. How the person viewed the location, from the south, from the north, east, or west, may influence their description. Or the driver's view from behind the wheel of a large tractor–trailer might be different from the view from behind the wheel of a small sports car.

Investigation of a case should involve a trip to the location where the incident occurred. The trier of fact will be relying upon the plaintiff's and defendant's counsels to describe in their presentation the characteristics of the physical location. They also will be looking at the location from an impartial, *exhibit* **18.1** *Sample police accident report form.*

POLICE ACCIDENT REPORT

⊗ REFER TO OVERLAY SHEETS   REPORTABLE ☐ NON - REPORTABLE ☐   PENNDOT USE ONLY

POLICE INFORMATION	ACCIDENT LOCATION
1. INCIDENT NUMBER	20. COUNTY ⸻ CODE
2. AGENCY NAME	21. MUNICIPALITY ⸻ CODE
3. STATION/ PRECINCT — 4. PATROL ZONE	PRINCIPAL ROADWAY INFORMATION
5. INVESTIGATOR — BADGE NUMBER	22. ROUTE NO. OR STREET NAME
6. APPROVED BY — BADGE NUMBER	23. SPEED LIMIT — 24. TYPE HIGHWAY — 25. ACCESS CONTROL
7. INVESTIGATION DATE — 8. ARRIVAL TIME	INTERSECTING ROAD:

ACCIDENT INFORMATION

26. ROUTE NO. OR STREET NAME

| 9. ACCIDENT DATE | 10. DAY OF WEEK | 27. SPEED LIMIT — 28. TYPE HIGHWAY — 29. ACCESS CONTROL |

11. TIME OF DAY — 12. NUMBER OF UNITS

IF NOT AT INTERSECTION:

13. # KILLED — 14.# INJURED — 15. PRIV. PROP. ACCIDENT   Y ☐   N ☐

30. CROSS STREET OR SEGMENT MARKER

16. DID VEHICLE HAVE TO BE REMOVED FROM THE SCENE?
UNIT 1 — UNIT 2
Y ☐ N ☐   Y ☐ N ☐

17. VEHICLE DAMAGE
0 - NONE   UNIT 1 ☐
1 - LIGHT
2 - MODERATE
3 - SEVERE   UNIT 2 ☐

31. DIRECTION FROM SITE   N S E W   32. DISTANCE FROM SITE   FT.   MI.

33. DISTANCE WAS   MEASURED ☐   ESTIMATED ☐

18. HAZARDOUS MATERIALS   Y ☐ N ☐
19. PENNDOT PROPERTY   Y ☐ N ☐

34. CONSTRUCTION ZONE ☐
35. TRAFFIC CONTROL DEVICE   PRINCIPAL ☐   INTERSECTING ☐

UNIT # 1

36. LEGALLY PARKED? Y ☐ N ☐   37. REG. PLATE   38. STATE
39. PA TITLE OR OUT-OF-STATE VIN
40. OWNER
41. OWNER ADDRESS
42. CITY, STATE & ZIPCODE
43. YEAR — 44. MAKE
45. MODEL - (NOT BODY TYPE)   46. INS. Y ☐ N ☐ UNK ☐
47. BODY TYPE — 48. SPECIAL USAGE — 49. VEHICLE OWNERSHIP
50. INITIAL IMPACT POINT — 51. VEHICLE STATUS — 52. TRAVEL SPEED
53. VEHICLE GRADIENT — 54. DRIVER PRESENCE — 55. DRIVER CONDITION
56. DRIVER NUMBER   57. STATE
58. DRIVER NAME
59. DRIVER ADDRESS
60. CITY, STATE & ZIPCODE
61. SEX — 62. DATE OF BIRTH — 63. PHONE
64. COMM. VEH. Y ☐ N ☐ — 65. DRIVER CLASS — 66. DRIVER S S #
67. CARRIER
68. CARRIER ADDRESS
69. CITY, STATE & ZIPCODE
70. USDOT # — ICC # — PUC #
72. VEH. CONFIG. — 73. CARGO BODY TYPE — 74. GVWR
75. NO. OF AXLES — 76. HAZARDOUS MATERIALS — 77. RELEASE OF HAZ MAT Y ☐ N ☐ UNK ☐

AA-45 (1/92)

UNIT # 2

36. LEGALLY PARKED? Y ☐ N ☐   37. REG. PLATE   38. STATE
39. PA TITLE OR OUT-OF-STATE VIN
40. OWNER
41. OWNER ADDRESS
42. CITY, STATE & ZIPCODE
43. YEAR — 44. MAKE
45. MODEL - (NOT BODY TYPE)   46. INS. Y ☐ N ☐ UNK ☐
47. BODY TYPE — 48. SPECIAL USAGE — 49. VEHICLE OWNERSHIP
50. INITIAL IMPACT POINT — 51. VEHICLE STATUS — 52. TRAVEL SPEED
53. VEHICLE GRADIENT — 54. DRIVER PRESENCE — 55. DRIVER CONDITION
56. DRIVER NUMBER   57. STATE
58. DRIVER NAME
59. DRIVER ADDRESS
60. CITY, STATE & ZIPCODE
61. SEX — 62. DATE OF BIRTH — 63. PHONE
64. COMM. VEH. Y ☐ N ☐ — 65. DRIVER CLASS — 66. DRIVER S S #
67. CARRIER
68. CARRIER ADDRESS
69. CITY, STATE & ZIPCODE
70. USDOT # — ICC # — PUC #
72. VEH. CONFIG. — 73. CARGO BODY TYPE — 74. GVWR
75. NO. OF AXLES — 76. HAZARDOUS MATERIALS — 77. RELEASE OF HAZ MAT Y ☐ N ☐ UNK ☐

PAGE: ⸻   CENTER FOR HIGHWAY SAFETY

Sample police accident report form, continued.   exhibit 18.1

78. RESPONDING EMS AGENCY	INCIDENT #:
79. MEDICAL FACILITY	ACCIDENT DATE:

80. PEOPLE INFORMATION

A	B	C	D	E	F	G	NAME	ADDRESS	H	I	J	K	L	M

81. ILLUMINATION   82. WEATHER

83. ROAD SURFACE

84. SCHOOL DISTRICT (IF APPLICABLE)

85. DESCRIPTION OF DAMAGED PROPERTY

OWNER

ADDRESS

PHONE

86. DIAGRAM

o

87. NARRATIVE - IDENTIFY PRECIPITATING EVENTS, CAUSATION FACTORS, SEQUENCE OF EVENTS, WITNESS STATEMENTS, AND PROVIDE ADDITIONAL DETAILS. LIKE INSURANCE INFORMATION AND LOCATION OF TOWED VEHILCES, IF KNOWN.

INSURANCE INFORMATION UNIT 1	COMPANY		INSURANCE INFORMATION UNIT 2	COMPANY	
	POLICY NO			POLICY NO	
88. WINTESSES	NAME	ADDRESS			PHONE
	NAME	ADDRESS			PHONE

	89. VIOLATIONS INDICATED	90. SECTION NUMBERS (ONLY IF CHARGED)	TC NTC
UNIT 1			☐ ☐
UNIT 2			☐ ☐

	91. PROBABLE USE	92. TYPE TEST	93. RESULTS		91. PROBABLE USE	92. TYPE TEST	93. RESULTS		94. INVESTIGATION COMPLETE ?
UNIT 1			0.__ __%	☐ NO TEST ☐ REFUSE ☐ UNK UNIT 2			0.__ __%	☐ NO TEST ☐ REFUSE ☐ UNK	YES ☐ NO ☐

AA-45 (1/92)   PAGE: _____   **CENTER FOR HIGHWAY SAFETY** *exhibit* 18.2   *Initial client interview form.*

CLIENT INTERVIEW CHECKLIST

CLIENT PERSONAL INFORMATION

Name

Address

City   State   Zip

Phone (hm)   (wk)   (cell)

How long at this address

Date of birth   Place of birth

Social Security No.

Prior address

City   State   Zip

Dates at this address

Employer:

Job description

Marital status   Maiden name

Spouse's name   Date of birth

Child's name   Date of birth

Child's name   Date of birth

Child's name   Date of birth

CASE INFORMATION

Case referred by

Case type: ☐ Appeal   ☐ Business   ☐ Corporate   ☐ Estate   ☐ Litigation
                    ☐ Municipal   ☐ Real Estate   ☐ Tax   ☐ Trust   ☐ Other

Opposing party(ies)

Opposing party

Address

Opposing attorney

Address

Date of incident   Statute of limitation date

Summary of facts

neutral point of view, usually without prior familiarity with the location. The diagrams usually presented at trial are those of an aerial view with its sterile, one-dimensional presentation. Photographs from the points of view of all the participants can make the difference in understanding the duties and responsibilities of the litigants. Unlike diagrams of the location, these photographs more typically will be from the point of view of the plaintiff, defendant, or witness at ground level, or from behind the wheel of a vehicle, or looking out of a building window.

Tangible Evidence

Tangible evidence consists of the physical objects that may have caused the injury. These may include items as small as a giveaway toy from a fast-food restaurant swallowed by a 2-year-old, to a bottle that exploded, to a large automobile whose brakes failed or whose seat belts snapped. In some cases, the tangible evidence is essential to proving negligence or an element of strict liability in tort.

Much has been written of late about the effects of the plaintiffs' and defendants' failure to preserve critical evidence of this type. In some cases, failure to preserve the evidence has resulted in loss of the case by the plaintiff, and in other cases by the defendant.

It is important to understand the local rules with regard to **spoliation of evidence** and its effect on a cause of action. In determining the proper penalty for spoliation of evidence, courts are most likely to consider [*Schroeder v. Department of Transportation*, 551 Pa. 243, 710 A.2d 23, 26 (1998)]:

1. The degree of fault of the party who altered or destroyed the evidence.
2. The degree of prejudice suffered by the opposing party.
3. The availability of a lesser sanction that will protect the opposing party's rights and deter future similar conduct.

Following a Timeline

Causes of action should be viewed from the events leading up to the incident to the events and occurrences following the incident. (See Exhibit 18.3 for a sample timeline.) Few things in life that give rise to a potential claim occur in a vacuum. Usually some facts lead up to the incident and others follow the incident. The question may be, "Given the time in which the parties allege this happened, could this really have happened?" For example, could the parties have driven the 30 miles in 20 minutes through crowded rush-hour traffic on city streets? In a food-poisoning case, could ingestion of the food at noon have caused the reaction claimed by 1:00 P.M.? The claimant might have been negligent, or the first perceived wrongdoer perhaps was not the correct person, as most food-poisoning cases require 6 to 12 hours from ingestion of the tainted food until onset of symptoms of the illness.

The starting point is the time of the alleged injury. Also important, from a fault standpoint or defense standpoint, is what happened that led up to the incident. From the damages standpoint, what happened after the incident, including treatment and subsequent changes in the person's life or lifestyle, is important.

New Practices in Store for Future Law Office

PR Newswire   New York, July 2, 2001

In the next decade the legal field could feature paperless work environments, redefined roles and responsibilities for partners and associates, and mergers between law firms and financial consulting businesses. These are just a few of the major findings from the Future Law Office research project conducted by The Affiliates, a leading staffing service specializing in attorneys, paralegals, and legal support professionals.

The Affiliates embarked on the national research project to gain a broader perspective on workplace trends impacting the legal field. The firm commissioned surveys of attorneys and legal administrators, consulted leading experts, and conducted extensive research to ascertain how the future law office would look and feel. The results of the project have been chronicled in a comprehensive white paper and are featured online at www.futurelawoffice.com.

"Changes are already taking place in the legal field that are defining how the future law office will take shape," said Kathleen Call, executive director of The Affiliates. "Our research identifies key areas that could significantly influence law firms and corporate legal departments as the decade unfolds."

Redefining the Legal Workforce

Legal professionals will have to adapt to offices that will look and operate differently than those they work in today, according to The Affiliates' research. Call said, "Everyone from lawyers to support specialists will need advanced computer and technical skills, expertise in specific practice areas, and an entrepreneurial business approach." Call noted that growth in responsibility will be the common theme for legal professionals. "Our research indicates that associates, including first- and second-year lawyers, will have increased interaction with clients and more accountability for their firm's profit growth," she said. "In addition, paralegals will assume heightened responsibilities, including some that currently are handled by new associates."

According to a recent poll by The Affiliates, more paralegals already are taking on expanded roles. Seventy-five percent of attorneys surveyed said they believe paralegals have more career-growth opportunities today than five years ago. For every legal professional, technology training will be essential to advancement. Eighty-three percent of attorneys polled said greater proficiency with the Internet will help their own careers in the coming years. In a companion survey, legal administrators chose Internet-related skills as the area of technical proficiency most likely to advance their careers in the future.

Among other workforce trends identified in the research:

- Many firms will offer staff members flextime, expanded retirement packages, more casual work environments, mentoring and career counseling, and child and elder care benefits. These options reflect a changing attitude by employers toward work–life balance for employees. Attorneys surveyed by The Affiliates cited showing appreciation for staff and maintaining high workplace morale among the most effective strategies for boosting employee satisfaction.

- The use of project professionals will grow throughout the legal field. Sixty-two percent of legal administrators surveyed expect their firm's use of project attorneys to increase over the next eight years; 59 percent of respondents predict their office's use of project teams will rise in this same period.

The Technology Revolution

The Affiliates' research shows that as the practice of law becomes a 24-hour, seven-day-a-week operation, law firms increasingly view technology as the key difference between themselves and their competitors. Technological advances will also reinforce relationships between client and attorney. Attorneys polled said that 75 percent of business communication will be conducted via email in the future. According to experts consulted by The Affiliates, security concerns will ease.

"Advanced encryption technology is already being developed that will enable the most sensitive information to be transmitted over the Internet," Call said. She added that attorneys will soon be able to file documents electronically with courts nationwide. E-filing, currently being tested in several jurisdictions, will automate the filing process and alleviate the need for sending physical copies of documents to courts or serving papers to parties involved in litigation.

Other technology trends identified in the research include:

- Application service providers (ASPs)—web portals offering case and document management systems—will allow firms to manage time and billing services, litigation support, and other key software through high-speed Internet connections.

- New technology will continue to increase the viability of telecommuting. Firms will issue laptop computers to most attorneys, enabling them to work from satellite locations. Ninety-eight percent of attorneys surveyed by The Affiliates believe that telecommuting will increase in the next decade.

The Right Look

The Affiliates' research suggests law office design will undergo dramatic changes in the coming years, including a move toward more egalitarian arrangements such as glass walls and similar-sized workspaces for all employees. In addition, noted Call, remote workers increasingly will influence office design decisions. To accommodate visiting attorneys and project professionals, offices will have hotelling areas with desks, telephones, and online access. In another of The Affiliates' surveys, legal administrators identified common offices used by telecommuters and common areas with moveable furniture as typical characteristics of future floor plans.

The traditional law library will also undergo changes. "While hard copies of books will always be part of a law practice, future libraries will be smaller, electronic and more user-friendly," Call said. Sixty-seven percent of attorneys polled by The Affiliates said that law libraries will decrease in size over the next 10 years.

Practice Area Specialization

"Increasingly the concept of the general practice attorney will become obsolete," said Call. The Affiliates'

research indicates there will be regional clusters of legal expertise nationwide—niche markets like Silicon Valley for intellectual property law or New York City for corporate law. Demographics, specialized education, and emerging economic trends will influence what is practiced in a particular region.

Other practice area trends identified in the Future Law Office research include:

- *Intellectual property, e-commerce, patent, and Internet issues.* Technology will continue to fuel growth in the number of firms specializing in these practice areas. Forty-eight percent of lawyers surveyed cited intellectual property as the hottest practice area for the coming decade.

- *Estate planning, medical technology (including privacy issues), elder law, and health care.* The aging baby boom generation will generate demand for these specializations.

- *Alternative dispute resolution (ADR).* With clients seeking ways to avoid lawsuits, issues that would normally find their way to court will be handled with greater frequency through ADR. Ninety-three percent of attorneys surveyed by The Affiliates said they would suggest ADR to their litigation clients as a viable option.

MDPs and Beyond

The Affiliates' findings suggest the legal field will see a shift toward multidisciplinary practices (MDPs). While current American Bar Association guidelines prohibit lawyers from sharing fees or forming partnerships with nonlawyers when activities involve law practice, by the close of the decade, more law firms will form alliances with accounting, management consulting, and real estate professionals to provide clients with a wide range of business services, research shows.

"We'll also see a renewed emphasis on marketing," Call said. "In response to increased competition from legal Web services and emerging MDPs, firms will focus on developing brand awareness." This finding is underscored by the results of The Affiliates' survey in which 94 percent of attorneys said law firm marketing would be important to their firms in the next 10 years.

Among other common business practices in the future law office:

- *Diverse billing procedures.* Increased emphasis on client service will lead to solutions such as value billing, in which fees are based on uniform standards—projecting the time required to complete

a task, for example, and establishing a fee based on that time.

- *Online business opportunities.* Licensed lawyers, as well as nonattorneys, will capitalize on this trend. For example, websites managed by legal information brokers will enable individuals to download advice-oriented columns and materials as well as basic legal forms. Law firms will compete by offering legal services via their external websites.

The Affiliates provides law firms and corporate legal departments with project and full-time professionals including attorneys, paralegals, and legal support personnel. The Affiliates offers online job search services at www.affiliates.com. For more information on the Future Law Office project, including a listing of experts and research sources, please visit www.futurelawoffice.com.

exhibit **18.3**   *Timeline.*

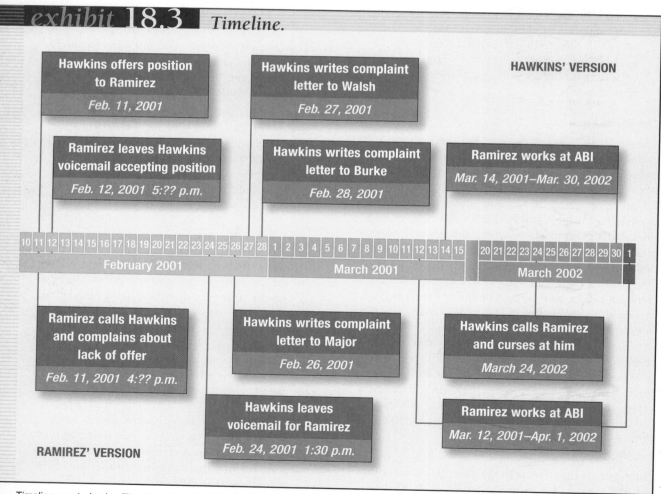

Investigation Checklists

The investigation checklist (Exhibit 18.4) should not be viewed as a static document. The checklist should start with a listing all of the parties involved who should be interviewed, including initial fact witnesses. As additional parties and witnesses are interviewed, more people may have to be added to the list. Exhibit 18.5 is a witness information form. Investigation of locations and physical evidence may result in the need to examine other locations and evidence. Initial interviews also may result in the need to add one or more expert witnesses to the investigati1on checklist.

PREPARING FOR THE INTERVIEW

The first step in preparing for an interview or conducting an investigation is to understand the outcome desired. One of the desired outcomes in an initial interview with a new client is to instill confidence in the firm and its personnel. The fundamentally desired outcome of any interview is to obtain all of the needed relevant facts for the case that has been assigned. Understanding the goals of the interview or investigation, the background or cultural issues of the individual, or the nature of the situation will help in structuring a successful interview. Occasionally an interview has to be conducted without time for preparation, such as when the paralegal is asked to fill in for someone else at the last moment.

A checklist can be a valuable tool to be certain that all the information required for a certain type of case or other legal matter is obtained during the initial interview. The same checklist offers a good foundation for developing a more detailed interview plan when there is time for preparation.

Physical Surroundings

The physical surroundings of the interview location can set the tone for the interview. Depending upon the purpose of the interview and the person being interviewed, the paralegal may wish to create a formal or informal environment. You probably can remember a situation in which someone interviewed you from across a desk. Didn't you feel a certain formality and possibly subservience to the interviewer? Contrast that situation with sitting in an informal setting with a low coffee table and living room-style chairs. This type of setting gives the meeting a more personal tone.

Setting a client at ease may be easier in the informal setting, whereas dealing with opposing counsel might be better handled in the formal "across the desk" type of meeting. In most cases the paralegal will want to create the impression of a competent professional, but in some situations, creating a more casual and less professional impression may be beneficial. Some witnesses are more cooperative and helpful when they feel as if they are in charge and are helping the paraprofessional because of their superiority.

Dress and Appearance

Remember the old saying, "first impressions count"? The impression a paralegal makes when walking into the room for the initial interview may set the stage for the entire relationship with the client or witness. Clothing, posture, and manner of greeting create the first impression.

exhibit 18.4   *Investigation checklist.*

INVESTIGATION CHECKLIST

Client name

Phone (hm)   (wk)   (cell)

Current address

Prior address(es)

Date of birth   Place of birth

Social Security No.

VEHICLE CLIENT OPERATING/PASSENGER

Owner and type of motor vehicle

Insurance Co.   Policy number

Insurance company contact   Phone

Date of incident   Time of day   Weather conditions

Location of incident

City, State   County   Municipality

Opposing party

Address

Phone (hm)   (wk)   (cell)

Owner and type of motor vehicle

Insurance Co.   Policy number

FACT WITNESSES

Name   Address

Name   Address

Name   Address

Name of ambulance

Name of hospital

Police report issued   Copy ordered

Photographs of scene taken

Name of treating physicians

EXPERT WITNESSES

Name   Address

Name   Address

Summary of cause of action

Attach detailed accident/incident description, accident reports and diagrams.

Witness information form.   **exhibit 18.5**

Witness Information

CLIENT PERSONAL DATA

Client Name

	Case No.	File No.

Address

City, State, Zip   Phone

CASE DATA

File Label

Case issue   Date

Responsible Attorney(s)

WITNESS DATA

Witness Name

Aliases, if any

US Citizen
☐ Yes   ☐ No

Current Address   City, State, Zip   Phone

Past Address(es)

Date & Place of Birth	Sex	Race	Age	Current Marital Status
				☐ Single ☐ Divorced
Name of Spouse	Number/Former Marriages	Number/Children		☐ Married ☐ Widowed
				☐ Separated

Name of Children (natural & adopted)   Age   Name   Age

Current Employer

Address   City, State, Zip   Phone

Job Title   Supervisor   From   To

Previous Employer

Address   City, State, Zip   Phone

Job Title   Supervisor   From   To

Education/Name of School	City/State	From	To	Degree
High School				
College				
Technical/Other				

Witness for
☐ Plaintiff   ☐ Defendant

Type of Witness
☐ Expert   ☐ Character   ☐ Eye Witness

Have you ever been a party or witness in a court suit?
☐ No   ☐ Yes

If yes, where & when

OTHER PERTINENT DATA

Form 8567 • 9/86 **SYCOM** Madison, WI Printed in U.S.A.

Clothing sends a nonverbal message about the person and the firm or business. The impression a person makes upon walking into the room can enhance or destroy credibility. In the practice of law, or in a corporate law department, the unexpected can become the norm. Many attorneys, male and female alike, keep a "going-to-court suit" in the office just in case they need to have a more professional appearance at a moment's notice. When the new client comes in, they can change quickly while the receptionist or secretary buys them time to change to the "power" outfit.

A client may be offended by a paralegal's "casual Friday" appearance, believing the paralegal is not taking the matter seriously. However, the working paralegal usually doesn't have time to change when the unexpected arises, often being the one to "buy time" for the attorney. Therefore, paralegals must always be prepared to make a good impression and tailor their appearance appropriately as the situation warrants.

Cultural Sensitivity

Interviewers and investigators must be aware of cultural differences that can influence the results of interviews with clients, witnesses, personnel from the opposing law firm, and others. Of utmost importance is to pronounce correctly the names of the people with whom the paralegal has contact. For example, in some Asian cultures last names appear first and first names last. This may not be obvious when the business card is presented by a client of Asian origin and neither the first nor the last name is familiar.

Many non-Americans are uncomfortable with the informality of being called by their first name, even by their own attorney or paralegal. Titles are important in the form of address, including use of the term *doctor* to address those who have an academic doctorate and not just those with medical degrees.

Cultural issues in clothing also require sensitivity. Head coverings and floor-length dress are normal ways of dressing for a large segment of the world's population. Even in the United States, people whose cultural, ethnic, or religious backgrounds dictate more modest forms of dress may be offended by those they perceive as not respecting their traditions. For example, women paralegals may want to dress more conservatively when interviewing Moslem men and women so as not to appear contemptuous and create an impression of disrespect that can negatively affect the interview. And you can see that making an insensitive comment such as, "How can you wear all that clothing?" might be considered rude. Paralegals also should be aware of the religious calendar and religious or holy days when scheduling appointments. This adds to the overall positive impression.

People tend to think that others think, understand, and conduct themselves the same way we do. In a closed society, such as existed in Japan until the late 1940s and 1950s, this may have been true. But in the United States today, with its diverse cultures and assimilation into the American society of many religious and cultural groups, this is not true. We do not all read with the same level of understanding, nor do we all speak the same language or react the same

Religious Calendar:
www.interfaithcalendar.org/

way to verbal and written instructions. When interviewing clients and witnesses, we should try to determine how they perceive what we present and how the information will be perceived within their cultural understanding. For example, a well-meaning, caring, devoted parent who does not read English may understand verbal English but not appreciate the necessity of reading warning labels on over-the-counter medication.

Paralegals conducting interviews must be able to recognize these issues so they can present them well in their narrative reports. The supervising attorney will be using these reports in preparing the prosecution or the defense of the case, which makes accurate interpretation and representation of interviews essential.

CONDUCTING THE INTERVIEW

In the first meeting, the paralegal must make clear that he or she is a paralegal and not an attorney. During the first few minutes of the interview, paralegals must build a relationship with the interview subjects, let them understand the purpose of the interview, and eliminate any barriers that would prevent obtaining the necessary information. Sometimes the interviewees seem to be fully cooperative when in fact they are not cooperating. Or the subject matter may be embarrassing, or they may have a fear of authority figures, or they might be uncomfortable using certain terms necessary to describe the situation.

Effective interviewers learn the verbal and nonverbal cues that help them understand the reasons for interviewees' reluctance to answer questions. In some situations the solution is first to ask easy questions, such as the person's name and address. Once interviewees start speaking, they have less trouble answering well thought-out questions that build logically on the previous information. This is not always the case, though. In times of great stress, clients have been known to read the name from a nameplate in the office and state it as their own name! The interviewer must be careful to avoid embarrassing the interviewee and have prepared questions that can be answered easily and thereby help the person gain composure, such as, "My records show that you live at 123 South Main Street. Is that correct?" Or "How do you spell your name?"

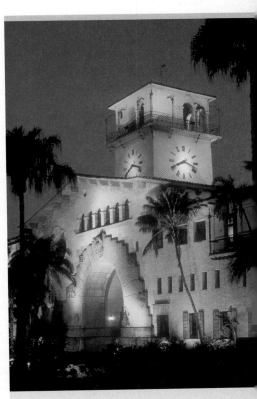

Santa Barbara City Court house, California.

Leading Questions

Leading questions are those that suggest the desired answer. In conducting a cross-examination, lawyers in trial frequently use leading questions to force the witness to answer in a desired manner. An obvious example is, "Have you stopped kicking your dog?"

On direct examination, an attorney might ask a more direct and neutral question: "Have you ever kicked your dog?"

Leading questions do not lead to open-ended answers but are directed toward a desired answer: "You ran the red light, didn't you?"

Open-Ended Questions

Open-ended questions are designed to give interviewees an opportunity to tell their story without the limitation of yes-or-no answers. Open-ended questions create a **narrative opportunity** for the witness. For example: "Tell me about your life"; "Tell me about your life since the accident."

In fact interviews, the witness should receive the opportunity for open-ended narrative answers. Asking a question to solicit an answer that you desire may cut off information essential to your case. For example, you may want to know whether your client was at the scene of an accident and therefore ask the witness, "Did you see my client at the scene of the accident?" The answer to this question may be "yes" or "no." A better question would be, "Who was present at the scene of the accident?" This kind of question may lead to additional information on additional witnesses you may want to interview.

Similarly, the question, "How fast were the cars going prior to the impact?" is much better than, "Were the cars speeding before the impact?" In this context, the term "speeding" may be interpreted as exceeding the speed limit instead of going too fast for the conditions.

With the witness's statements from the interview in hand at the time of trial, the trial attorney might appropriately ask a leading question such as, "My client wasn't present at the scene of the accident, was she?" Or, "Isn't it true that the defendant was speeding before the impact?" With knowledge of the prior statement, there should be no surprise in the answer at trial. If there is, the prior statement can be used to impeach the credibility of the witness, if desired, as part of the trial strategy.

At times the interviewer may want to focus clients or witnesses by asking questions that give them a perspective of time or place, such as, "What did you observe at noon on Saturday?" or, "Tell me what happened on September 11, 2001." The tragedy of that day will haunt the memories of Americans and most of the rest of the world, so little stimulus will be needed to elicit where they were and what they observed. This is true of most traumatic events in people's lives—the loss of a loved one, the birth of a child, or a serious accident in which they were injured. Other days and times tend to blur and have to be brought to the consciousness of the witness by questions such as, "Let's think back to August 19, 2001" and, "What happened to you that day?"

ETHICAL VERSUS MORAL CONSIDERATIONS

At times in the investigation of a case, it is necessary to consider the difference between a moral consideration and an ethical consideration. A **moral obligation** is one based on one's own conscience or a person's perceived rules of correct conduct, generally in the person's own community. Some communities, for instance, may consider it to be morally improper to ask someone to give information about another person. An **ethical obligation,** for members of the legal team including those acting on behalf of a supervising attorney, are the responsibilities of the legal profession under the ABA Model Rules of Professional Conduct, including thoroughness in representing a client.

Is it ethically improper to ask someone to tell the truth surrounding the facts of a case that may lead to a neighbor, relative, or friend being subjected to liability for his or her actions? For the paralegal and the legal team, the primary ethical obligation is the duty to the client. It may offend some members of the legal team, for example, to ask a mother to testify against a child. This is a moral issue for the mother, in which the results may cause financial hardship or ruin upon awarding a verdict for causing injury as the result of negligent conduct, but ethics may require this course of conduct for the paralegal.

ABA Model Rules:
www.abanet.org/cpr/mrpc/mr
pc_toc.html

PRIVILEGED COMMUNICATION

Certain forms of communication are considered privileged and not usable at trial unless the privilege is waived. Forms of **privileged communication** are:

1. Attorney–client communications
2. Doctor–patient communications
3. Priest–penitent communications
4. Spousal communications during marriage.

Each of these privileges can be waived. But the waiver must come from the client, the patient, the penitent, or the spouse making the statement with the belief that it is privileged. Changes in some of the rules of ethics, and by statute, may permit certain otherwise privileged communications to be revealed to prevent harm or injury to another. The spouse, the priest, or the doctor may have a moral issue in revealing what was communicated.

When the paralegal is acting on behalf of the attorney, communications between a client and the paralegal have the same privilege as those between the client and the attorney. Information gathered from the client as part of representation of the client and necessary for rendering competent legal advice is privileged. The paralegal, therefore, is in the same position as the attorney, the doctor, the priest, or the spouse to whom the confidential information has been communicated. Each must carefully guard the confidential information and not inadvertently or intentionally reveal the information. In some cases, such as when another person's life may be in danger, these people may be compelled by a court to testify even when they believe it is a violation of their moral duty to another person from whom they have received information

> ### Expert Witness
>
> (A) A party may depose any person who has been identified as an expert whose opinion may be presented at trial. If a report from the expert is required under (a)(2)(B) [Disclosure of Expert Testimony], the deposition shall not be conducted until after the report is provided. [F.R.C.P. 26(b)(4) Trial Preparation: Witness]
>
> *SIDEBAR*

EXPERT WITNESSES

Expert witnesses are individuals whose background, education, and experience are such that courts recognize them as qualified to give opinions based on a set of facts. The expert witness may be a doctor certified by a board of medical experts or a scientist or engineer specializing in an area of science such as flammability of fabrics. The report of these experts may be advice based on the facts of a potential case to determine whether there is sufficient evidence to believe that a wrong has occurred or malpractice committed. Without this report the lawyers may be obligated to advise clients that they have no actionable cause of action.

There is no clear rule on whether what is revealed to an expert in the preparation of a case is protected as part of the attorney–client privilege in the same manner as that revealed to a member of the trial team, including other attorneys, paralegals, and secretarial staff working on the case with the primary trial attorney. Almost certainly, anything revealed to an expert who is listed as an expert witness on the list of witnesses to be called at trial is discoverable.

Some law firms retain an expert to advise them but do not use that expert to testify. The advice and information provided by these experts to help in the preparation for trial may come under the privilege. Although the privilege is the client's, the paralegal and others on the legal team must be careful not to divulge privileged or confidential material without authorization.

The expert retained for background trial advice must have as much confidence in the legal team as the legal team has in the expert's advice and integrity. Some experts fear that the legal team will give them only selected information. With the limited information provided, they might give an expert opinion that is not what they would have given if they had received the complete set of facts.

Exhibit 18.6 indicates factors to be considered in arranging for an expert witness.

Checklist

DEPOSING EXPERT WITNESSES

Ask an expert witness these ten questions at deposition, even if you don't have time to ask anything else:

○ What opinions have you formed in this matter?

○ What did you do to reach those opinions?

○ How did you do that?

○ Why did you do that?

○ What results did you get?

○ How did the results affect your opinion?

○ Are there reliable authorities in this field?

○ What assumptions did you make in your work?

○ What tasks didn't you do?

○ Is this your current and accurate resume?

Source: Expert Rules: 100 (and More) Points You Need to Know About Expert Witnesses, 2d ed., by David M. Malone & Paul J. Zweir, National Institute for Trial Advocacy, 2000.

Expert witness form.   *exhibit* 18.6

EXPERT WITNESS CHECKLIST

BACKGROUND

Full name _____   Date of birth _____

Business address _____

Business telephone number _____   Business fax number _____

Business email address _____   Business web site _____

Locations of prior offices _____

Home address _____

Home telephone number _____

EDUCATION

Schools attended _____   Dates of attendance _____

Degrees or honors awarded _____

Continuing education courses _____

WORK HISTORY

Place of employment _____   Dates of employment _____

Job description _____

Reasons for leaving _____

Specific area of expertise _____

Published articles and books _____

Professional affiliations _____

Professional magazines subscribed to _____

Licenses and jurisdictions _____

Investigations or disciplinary action _____

PRIOR LEGAL EXPERIENCE

Ratio of plaintiff/defense cases _____

Prior clients including date (plaintiff or defendant) _____

Types of investigations with dates _____

Deposition testimony given with dates _____

Court testimony with dates _____

Legal references _____

AVAILABILITY

Vacation plans and dates _____   Potential meeting dates _____

FREEDOM OF INFORMATION ACT (FOIA)

The **Freedom of Information Act** is a federal statute designed to open to the public the information possessed by the federal government and its agencies. The federal government is a good source of information. Many of the documents required to be filed are available through the government, and frequently online, such as corporate filings with the Securities and Exchange Commission. Other information may be available by request, under the provisions of the Freedom of Information Act (FOIA), 5 U.S.C. § 552. Some limitations apply to the information available. The general exceptions, as found in the statute, are:

1. Classified documents concerning national defense and foreign policy.
2. Internal personnel rules and practices.
3. Exemptions under other laws that require information to be withheld, such as patent applications and income-tax returns.
4. Confidential business information and trade secrets.
5. Intra-agency and inter-agency internal communications not available by law to a party in litigation.
6. Protection of privacy of personnel and medical files and private lives of individuals.
7. Law-enforcement investigatory files.
8. Examination, operation, or condition reports of agencies responsible for the regulation and supervision of financial institutions.
9. Geological and geophysical information and data including maps concerning wells.

Exhibit 18.7 is the Freedom of Information/Privacy Act Request form.

SIDEBAR

Discovery

Always check the rules and consider the effect of taking discovery in an international dispute. Some countries, such as Japan, limit or prohibit the use in trial of material obtained during discovery.

LOCATING WITNESSES

Most witnesses can be located by use of directories. The Web has also become a valuable tool for locating witnesses.

Directories

Investigators usually keep a collection of telephone books of the areas in which they work. Rarely today does a person not have a telephone, even if it is an unlisted number. In addition to the standard-issue telephone directories, the cross-reference directory (also known as a "criss-cross directory") is a standard tool; these list phone numbers by address or by phone number instead of by name. Therefore, an address may be checked for a corresponding phone number—for example, determining the phone number located at 123 Main Street, or using the phone numbers listed at an address to determine the physical location or billing address of the phone.

Telephone directories are not limited to just the United States but typically are published in most parts of the world in one form or another. Companies and businesses also can be located by use of commercial or industrial telephone directories, both domestically and internationally.

In addition to telephone directories, directories are published by trade organizations, professional groups, and educational institutions. These direc-

FOIA/Privacy Act Request form.   *exhibit* 18.7

Page 2 (right form):

7. Verification of Subject's Identity: *(See Instructions for Explanation)(Check One Box)*
   □ In-Person with ID   □ Notarized Affidavit of Identity   □ Other *(Specify)* _____

Signature of Subject of Record: _____   Date: _____
   Telephone No.: (___) ___ - ___   in the Year _____

NOTARY *(Normally needed from individuals who are the subject of the records sought) (See below)*
or a sworn declaration under penalty of perjury.
Subscribed and sworn to before me this _____ day of _____

Signature of Notary _____   My Commission Expires _____

OR

If a declaration is provided in lieu of a notarized signature, it must state, at a minimum, the following: (Include Notary Seal or Stamp in this Space)

If executed outside the United States, its territories, possessions, or commonwealths: "I declare (certify, verify, or state) under penalty of perjury under the laws of the United States of America that the foregoing is true and correct.

Signature: _____

If executed within the United States, its territories, possessions, or commonwealths: "I declare (certify, verify, or state) under penalty of perjury that the foregoing is true and correct.

Signature: _____

Form G-639 (Rev. 7-25-00)N Page 2

Page 1 (left form):

U.S. Department of Justice
Immigration and Naturalization Service

OMB NO. 1115-0087

Freedom of Information/Privacy Act Request

The completion of this form is optional.
Any written format for Freedom of Information or Privacy Act requests is acceptable.

START HERE – Please type or print and read instructions on the reverse before completing this form.

1. Type of Request: *(Check appropriate box)*
   □ Freedom of Information Act (FOIA) *(Complete all items except 7)*
   □ Privacy Act (PA) *(Item 7 must be completed in addition to all other applicable items)*
   □ Amendment *(PA only. Item 7 must be completed in addition to all other applicable items)*

2. Requester Information:

Name of Requester:		Daytime Telephone:
Address *(Street Number and Name)*:		Apt. No
City:	State:	Zip Code:

   By my signature, I consent to the following:
   Pay all costs incurred for search, duplication, and review of materials up to $25.00, when applicable. *(See Instructions)*

   Signature of requester: _____

   □ Deceased Subject - **Proof of death must be attached.** *(Obituary, Death Certificate or other proof of death required)*

3. Consent to Release Information. *(Complete if name is different from Requester)(Item 7 must be completed)*

   Print Name of Person Giving Consent: _____   Signature of Person Giving Consent: _____

   By my signature, I consent to the following: *(check applicable boxes)*
   □ Allow the Requester named in item 2 to see □ all of my records or □ a portion of my record. If a portion, specify
   what part *(i.e. copy of application)*

   (Consent is required for records for United States Citizens (USC) and Lawful Permanent Residents (LPR)

4. Action Requested *(Check One)*:   □ Copy   □ In-Person Review

5. Information needed to search for records:
   Specific information, document(s), or record(s) desired: *(Identify by name, date, subject matter, and location of information)*

   Purpose: *(Optional: you are not required to state the purpose for your request; however, doing so may assist the INS in locating the records needed to respond to your request.)*

6. Data NEEDED on SUBJECT of Record: *(If data marked with asterisk (*) is not provided records may not be located)*

* Family Name	Given Name:	Middle Initial:
*Other names used, if any:	* Name at time of entry into the U.S.:	I-94 Admissions #:
* Alien Registration #:	* Petition or Claim Receipt #:	* Country of Birth:	*Date of Birth or Apps. Year
Names of other family members that may appear on requested record(s) *(i.e., Spouse, Daughter, Son)*:
Country of Origin *(Place of Departure)*:	Port-of-Entry into the U.S.	Date of Entry:
Manner of Entry: *(Air, Sea, Land)*	Mode of Travel: *(Name of Carrier)*	SSN:
Name of Naturalization Certifications:	Certificate #:	Naturalization Date:
Address at the time of Naturalization:	Court and Location:

   Form G-639 (Rev. 7-25-00)N

Checklist

INVESTIGATION INFORMATION SOURCES			
Information Source	Web Address	Physical Location	Comments
Police Records–Local	www.		
Police Records–State	www.		
Birth Records	www.		
Death Records	www.		
Drivers License	www.		
Vehicle Registration	www.		
Corporate Records	www.		
Real Estate–Recorder	www.		
Real Estate–Tax	www.		
Real Estate–Land Mapping	www.		
Register of Wills	www.		
Trial Court	www.		
Federal District Court–Clerk's Office	www.	Room Federal Court House	
Federal Bankruptcy Court	www.		
Occupational License	www.		
Weather Reports	www.		

Personalize this list by adding the local or regional office Web addresses, mailing addresses, and room numbers for personal visits, and comments, with any applicable contact people, costs, or hours of operation.

tories may be limited to membership but can be useful in cases where the name and the association are known, but not the city, state, or country where the person can be found.

Martindale-Hubbell Legal Directory: http://lawyers. martindale.com/xp/Martindale/ home.xml

The Web

As paper is replaced by electronic media, directories are being placed online. Search engines can help locate individuals, businesses, and organizations on the Internet. Communications companies and other private firms offer a number of online white pages for individuals, and yellow pages for businesses. Many organizations and publishers of professional directories now offer their print directories online, such as the Web version of Martindale-Hubbell for attorneys (see Exhibit 18.8). These services may change or cancel their Web address and others may be added, so it is necessary to keep your list of websites up to date.

Online search window from Martindale-Hubbell.   *exhibit* 18.8

Reprinted with the permission of LexisNexis.

LEGAL TERMINOLOGY

Arbitration	Narrative opportunity
Ethical obligation	Open-ended questions
Expert witness	Privileged communication
Freedom of Information Act (FOIA)	Restatement (Second) of Torts
Leading question	Spoliation of evidence
Moral obligation	Strict liability

Summary

CHAPTER 18 INTERVIEWING AND INVESTIGATION SKILLS

Investigating Claims

Obtaining Official Reports	Most incidents giving rise to litigation have associated official reports. In the negligence action it may be a police accident or incident report, emergency medical services report, fire department call report, or incident reports of safety violations by federal, state, or local authorities. These reports are generally filed in a central depository as public records. It is a useful starting point to obtain any official reports associated with the case.
Fact Analysis	Starts with the interview of the client and recitation of the time, place, circumstances, and others involved as participants or as witnesses. A complete analysis usually requires further field investigation of location, object involved, and interviews of parties and witnesses.
Locations	Verification of physical aspects of actual location where the cause of action occurred.
Tangible Evidence	Includes physical objects that may have caused the injury. Requires understanding local rules with regard to "spoliation of evidence" and its effect on a cause of action. In determining proper penalty for spoliation of evidence, courts are most likely to consider (1) degree of fault of the party who altered or destroyed the evidence; (2) degree of prejudice suffered by opposing party, and (3) availability of a lesser sanction that will protect the opposing party's rights and deter future similar conduct.

(continued)

Following a Timeline	Causes of action viewed from events leading up to the incident to events and occurrences following the incident.
Investigation Checklist	Starts with listing all parties involved who should be interviewed; as additional parties and witnesses are interviewed, additional people may be added to the list.

Preparing for the Interview

Outcome	1. First step is to understand the outcomes desired, one of which is to instill confidence in the firm and its personnel. 2. Desired outcome of any interview is to obtain all needed, relevant facts for the case.
Physical Surroundings	Depending upon purpose of interview and the person being interviewed, a formal or an informal environment may be desired.
Dress and Appearance	Clothing worn in an interview sends a nonverbal message about the paralegal and the firm or business, and the initial impression can enhance or destroy credibility.
Cultural Sensitivity	Interviewers and investigators must be aware of cultural differences and issues of clients and witnesses to avoid creating a negative impression.

Conducting the Interview

First Meeting	1. The paralegal must be careful to make clear that he or she is a paralegal and not an attorney. 2. Paralegal must build a relationship with the individual, let him or her understand the purpose of the interview, and eliminate any barriers that would prevent obtaining the necessary information.
Leading Questions	Questions that suggest the desired answer. Lawyers in conducting a cross-examination in trial frequently use leading questions to force the witness to answer in a desired manner.
Open-Ended Questions	Questions designed to create a narrative opportunity for the witness.

Ethical Versus Moral Considerations

Moral Obligations	Based on one's own conscience or perceived rules of correct conduct, generally in the person's own community.

(continued)

Ethical Obligations	Obligations of legal profession under ABA Model Rules of Professional Conduct, including thoroughness in representing a client.
Privileged Communications	
Forms	1. Attorney–client communications 2. Doctor–patient communications 3. Priest–penitent communications 4. Spousal communications during marriage
Waivers	These privileges can be waived, but the waiver must come from the client, the patient, the penitent, or the spouse making the statement with the belief that it is privileged.
Expert Witnesses	
Definition	Individuals whose background, education, and experience are such that courts will recognize them as qualified to give opinions based on a set of facts.
Freedom of Information Act (FOIA)	
Definition	A federal statute designed to open the information in the possession of the federal government and its agencies to the public.
Locating Witnesses	
Directories	1. Phone books 2. Cross-reference directories 3. Membership directories
The Web	Search engines can help locate individuals, businesses, and organizations on the Internet.

Working the Web

1. Using different Web search engines, locate information about yourself. For example, use a website that provides maps, such as MapQuest at www.mapquest.com, to locate the intersection nearest your home.

2. Use a search engine such as Findlaw to find an expert witness with a specialty of automobile tires, airplane accidents, and fire equipment, at http://marketcenter.findlaw.com/experts_consultants.html.

3. Check the listing for attornies in your city or town online in the Martindale Hubbell directory at http://lawyers.martindale.com/xp/ Martindale/Lawyer_Locator/Search_Lawyer_Locator/lawyer_search.xml.

4. Use the Martindale Hubbell site to locate an expert witness at http://lawyers.martindale.com/xp/Martindale/Experts_and_Services/ Search_Experts_and_Services/leg_search.xml.

Questions
CRITICAL LEGAL THINKING AND WRITING

1. Using the Facts in the *Palsgraf* case in Appendix A, prepare a list of witnesses who might be called in that case. Prepare an interview checklist for each of the witnesses.

2. Using the Facts in the *Palsgraf* case in Appendix A, prepare an investigative checklist including a list of the evidence that should be gathered in the case, including a list and description of any photographs needed.

3. In conducting an interview, when would it be appropriate to dress in "Friday casual" attire?

4. Why is it important to visit the site of the accident in a motor-vehicle case being prepared for trial?

5. Under what circumstances might it be advisable for someone else in the firm to handle an interview with a client or witness?

6. Why would someone feel a moral obligation not to answer questions in an interview?

7. Why would a law firm hire an expert witness and not call that person as a witness at trial?

8. How useful is the Freedom of Information Act in obtaining state or local government documents? Explain.

9. Complete the Investigation Information Source Checklist for your area.

10. Can a client restrict the use of information obtained as part of the investigation in preparation for trial even if doing so will have adverse consequences in the opinion of the attorney? Why or why not?

ETHICS: ANALYSIS AND DISCUSSION

1. Is it morally acceptable or ethically permissible to ask someone—such as a doctor, priest, spouse, or parent—who has information that has been communicated in confidence to breach that confidence as part of the interview or investigation in preparation for trial?

2. Under what circumstances should a paralegal decline to accept an assignment to conduct an interview or investigation? Why?

3. What steps should a paralegal take when she has determined that the case she is investigating is at the least frivolous or at worst fraudulent?

Practice Issue—Advising Status

There are few certainties in the area of ethics, for paralegals or in any profession. What qualifies as ethical conduct is in most cases based on state law and court interpretation applied to a set of facts. The citation listed below represents one legal opinion and is provided as a research starting point. Do not assume that the same rule applies in your jurisdiction. For the following:

- *Prepare a written statement based on your state law.*
- *Use your state bar association website as a starting point.*

You are assigned to interview a new client of the firm. You meet the client in the waiting room and say "Hello Mrs. Hannah, I'm Miss Ariel. I will be taking some information from you about your case. Please join me in the conference room." You then proceed to take all the information you need, thank the client, and say "We will be in touch with you. Can you find the way out?" The client leaves. [Canon 6 NFPA Ethics.] What obligation do you have to advise the client of your status as a paralegal?

FOR DISCUSSION

Limitations on Obtaining Information in Criminal Cases Under the FOIA

The FOIA can be a good source of information in criminal cases as well as civil litigation. As with discovery-limitation exemptions in civil cases, additional exemptions exist under the Act in criminal cases. Landano was convicted in New Jersey state court for murdering a police officer during what may have been a gang-related robbery. In an effort to support his claim in subsequent state court proceedings that his rights were violated by withholding material exculpatory evidence, he filed Freedom of Information Act requests with the Federal Bureau of Investigation (FBI) for information it had compiled in connection with the murder investigation.

When the FBI redacted some documents and withheld others, Landano filed an action, seeking disclosure of the contents of the requested files. The court held that the government is not entitled to a presumption that all sources supplying information to the FBI in the course of a criminal investigation are confidential sources within the meaning of Exemption 7(D). Further, a source should be deemed "confidential" if the source furnished information with the understanding that the FBI would not divulge the communication except to the extent it thought necessary for law-enforcement purposes.

Questions

1. Does this unfairly subject an informant to potential harassment?
2. Does limiting information unfairly prevent the defendant from receiving a fair trial?
3. Does the limitation effectively limit any usefulness in making a request under the FOIA?

Dep't of the Interior v. Klamath Water Users Protective Ass'n

Read, and if assigned, brief this case. In your brief, answer the following questions.

1. What are the two conditions under which a document qualifies for exemption under the Freedom of Information Act, Exemption 5?

2. How is "agency" defined under the FOIA?

3. What is the "deliberative process" privilege? Does non-governmental litigation have an equivalent privilege?

4. What is the purpose of the deliberative process privilege?

5. What is the "general philosophy" behind the FOIA?

Justice Souter delivered the opinion of the Court. Documents in issue here, passing between Indian Tribes and the Department of the Interior, addressed tribal interests subject to state and federal proceedings to determine water allocations. The question is whether the documents are exempt from the disclosure requirements of the Freedom of Information Act, as "intra-agency memorandums or letters" that would normally be privileged in civil discovery [5 U.S.C. § 552(b)(5)]. We hold they are not.

I

. . . [T]he Department's Bureau of Indian Affairs (Bureau) filed claims on behalf of the Klamath Tribe alone in an Oregon state-court adjudication intended to allocate water rights. Since the Bureau is responsible for administering land and water held in trust for Indian tribes . . . it consulted with the Klamath Tribe, and the two exchanged written memorandums on the appropriate scope of the claims ultimately submitted. . . . The Bureau does not, however, act as counsel for the Tribe, which has its own lawyers and has independently submitted claims on its own behalf.[1]

. . . [T]he Klamath Water Users Protective Association is a nonprofit association of water users in the Klamath River Basin, most of whom receive water from the Klamath Project, and whose interests are adverse to the tribal interests owing to scarcity of water. The Association filed a series of requests with the Bureau under the Freedom of Information Act (FOIA) [5 U.S.C. § 552] seeking access to communications between the Bureau and the Basin Tribes during the rel-

evant time period. The Bureau turned over several documents but withheld others as exempt under the attorney work-product and deliberative process privileges. These privileges are said to be incorporated in FOIA Exemption 5, which exempts from disclosure "inter-agency or intra-agency memorandums or letters which would not be available by law to a party other than an agency in litigation with the agency" [§ 552(b)(5)]. The Association then sued the Bureau under FOIA to compel release of the documents. . . .

Upon request, FOIA mandates disclosure of records held by a federal agency, see 5 U.S.C. § 552, unless the documents fall within enumerated exemptions. . . .

A

Exemption 5 protects from disclosure "inter-agency or intra-agency memorandums or letters which would not be available by law to a party other than an agency in litigation with the agency" [5 U.S.C. § 552(b)(5)]. To qualify, a document must thus satisfy two conditions: Its source must be a Government agency, and it must fall within the ambit of a privilege against discovery under judicial standards that would govern litigation against the agency that holds it.

Our prior cases on Exemption 5 have addressed the second condition, incorporating civil discovery privileges. . . . So far as they might matter here, those privileges include the privilege for attorney work-product and what is sometimes called the "deliberative process" privilege. Work-product protects "mental processes of the attorney" while deliberative process covers "docu-

---

[1] The Government is "not technically acting as [the Tribes'] attorney. That is, the Tribes have their own attorneys, but the United States acts as trustee" [Tr. of Oral Arg. 5]. "The United States has also filed claims on behalf of the Project and on behalf of other Federal interests" in the Oregon adjudication [Id. at 6]. The Hoopa Valley, Karuk, and Yurok Tribes are not parties to the adjudication. [Brief for Respondent 7]

ments reflecting advisory opinions, recommendations and deliberations comprising part of a process by which governmental decisions and policies are formulated." The deliberative process privilege rests on the obvious realization that officials will not communicate candidly among themselves if each remark is a potential item of discovery and front-page news, and its object is to enhance "the quality of agency decisions," . . . by protecting open and frank discussion among those who make them within the Government. . . .

The point is not to protect Government secrecy pure and simple, however, and the first condition of Exemption 5 is no less important than the second; the communication must be "inter-agency or intra-agency" [5 U.S.C. § 552(b)(5)] . . . . With exceptions not relevant here, "agency" means "each authority of the Government of the United States," . . . and "includes any executive department, military department, Government corporation, Government-controlled corporation, or other establishment in the executive branch of the Government . . . , or any independent regulatory agency." . . .

Although neither the terms of the exemption nor the statutory definitions say anything about communications with outsiders, some Courts of Appeals have held that in some circumstances a document prepared outside the Government may . . . qualify . . . under Exemption 5. . . .

> It is . . . possible . . . to regard as an intra-agency memorandum one that has been received by an agency, to assist it in the performance of its own functions, from a person acting in a governmentally conferred capacity other than on behalf of another agency—e.g., in a capacity as . . . consultant to the agency.

Typically, courts taking the latter view have held that the exemption extends to communications between Government agencies and outside consultants hired by them. . . . In such cases, the records submitted by outside consultants played essentially the same part in an agency's process of deliberation as documents prepared by agency personnel might have done. . . . [T]he fact about the consultant that is constant . . . is that the consultant does not represent an interest of its own, or the interest of any other client, when it advises the agency that hires it. Its only obligations are to truth and its sense of what good judgment calls for, and in those respects the consultant functions just as an employee would be expected to do.

B

. . . The Tribes, on the contrary, necessarily communicate with the Bureau with their own, albeit entirely legitimate, interests in mind. While this fact alone distinguishes tribal communications from the consultants' examples recognized by several Courts of Appeals, the distinction is even sharper, in that the Tribes are self-advocates at the expense of others seeking benefits inadequate to satisfy everyone.

. . . All of this boils down to requesting that we read an "Indian trust" exemption into the statute, a reading that is out of the question for reasons already explored. There is simply no support for the exemption in the statutory text, which we have elsewhere insisted be read strictly in order to serve FOIA's mandate of broad disclosure, which was obviously expected and intended to affect Government operations. In FOIA, after all, a new conception of Government conduct was enacted into law, "a general philosophy of full agency disclosure." Congress had to realize that not every secret under the old law would be secret under the new.

The judgment of the Court of Appeals is affirmed. *It is so ordered.*

CHAPTER 19

CHAPTER OBJECTIVES

After studying this chapter, you should be able to:

1. Explain the basic features of computer-assisted legal research programs.
2. Describe how to use the traditional law library resources to locate applicable statutes and court cases.
3. Explain the difference between primary and secondary sources.
4. Explain the need for parallel citation format.
5. Describe the function of connectors in computer research.
6. Outline the basic features of Lexis, Westlaw, Loislaw, and Versuslaw.
7. Explain the need to update prior legal research.
8. Name the online tools available for updating legal research.
9. Describe how *Shepard's* is compiled and used.
10. Demonstrate how to read traditional citations and use parallel citations.

Traditional and Computer Legal Research

This trial is a travesty; it's a travesty of a mockery of a sham of a mockery of a travesty of two mockeries of a sham. I move for a mistrial.

WOODY ALLEN, *BANANAS*

Introduction

One of the most important skills a paralegal can develop is the ability to find current relevant information in a timely manner. Knowing where to look is just as important as knowing what to look for. Clients expect their legal counsel to use the latest law in advising them. The paralegal is expected to be able to understand the relevant facts and find the current statutory law and case law. The frequent changes in court decisions and statutory enactments present a challenge to the legal profession. Traditional law libraries consisting of printed text may not provide the latest case, statute, or regulation for days or weeks because of the time required to assemble, print, and send out updates. Modern computer technology allows for more rapid distribution. Many courts now issue the electronic version of court opinions at the same time as the printed version. Instant availability is certainly a benefit if you are working on a similar case.

Although the ability to obtain current case law is important, in many cases an older common law case may still be precedent. The problem is that some electronic or online services, such as Versuslaw, may not have included the older cases in their database of available cases. When that happens, being able to find the case the old-fashioned way by checking through the books is a valuable skill. When using an electronic case service such as Versuslaw, the dates of the available cases should be checked to be certain that they cover the time period needed for the search.

RESEARCH STARTING POINT

Legal research is like a puzzle to be solved. Understanding the question is essential. A lot of time may be wasted if the paralegal takes the wrong research path, because the framer of the question has not been clear or the researcher is not clear on the information needed. At times the question is framed with some specificity:

Find the statute . . .
Get me the case of . . .

More often, however, the question is:

What is the law about . . . ?

Researchers first must understand the facts that apply to the case they are asked to research. Unlike the cases in textbooks and court opinions, the relevant facts and the specific area of substantive or procedural law in real life are usually not so clear. The initial interview information may have focused on what the client or the interviewer thought was the applicable law. Further research may indicate other areas of law that must be considered.

For example, what may seem to be a simple rear-end automobile accident caused by negligent driving may in actuality be a case of product liability caused by a manufacturing defect by the automobile manufacturer or the supplier of a defectively manufactured part, such as the tires. To analyze a case properly, the researcher must know the factual elements of a negligence case and of a product liability case. The researcher must understand the facts of the case at hand. Some facts are crucial to the case; others may or may not be important or have no legal significance.

TRADITIONAL VERSUS COMPUTER-BASED LAW LIBRARIES

The traditional law library consisted of books in paper form, case reporters, legal encyclopedias, legal dictionaries, and a host of finding tools including paper card indexes and digests. (See Exhibits 19.1 and 19.2 for samples of traditional text reference materials.) Some modern law libraries are completely electronic, in the form of online computer services such as Westlaw,

Lexis, and Loislaw. Others combine traditional paper-based materials and electronic materials.

Paralegal students who grew up in the era of the ever-available online research sources provided by some high schools and colleges, frequently ask why they need to learn how to use a traditional "paper" law library. In the working world, not every office has access to all the latest computer resources, or the same ones. Ask anyone who has tried a case out of town or in a different courthouse and had to check an unexpected case or resource, about the availability of resources or lack of them.

At times paralegals accompany the lawyer to court. During the trial, they may be asked to slip out of the courtroom and conduct a quick bit of legal research. They may not be able to use a computer for legal research. In some courthouses, computers cannot be connected to outgoing phone lines for security reasons, and even cell phones are retained at the security desk. Other courthouses may not have a public computer terminal available in the law library. In these situations the paralegal must conduct the research quickly and accurately using traditional book methods. In short, the legal assistant must be able to find the information needed when the familiar resources are not available.

Computer research requires the use of appropriate search words to complete a successful search. As with any profession, the legal profession has its own vocabulary. These include words defined by the courts over the years to have specific meaning when used in a legal sense. For example, the legal definition of the term "holder" means a person to whom a negotiable instrument has been properly negotiated. To the layman, it may mean people holding something in their hands—not necessarily a negotiable instrument, or with any legal formality. Other words have a different meaning for a number of different groups. For example, to the medical community the word "head" means the top of a person's body; to the sailor it means a bathroom; and to a bartender it means the top of a beer.

People in all areas of life develop words and phrases that help them understand their fields of interest. In creating laws, legislatures use language in special ways that may not be clear to laypersons or even legal researchers who are not accustomed to the terminology of the lawmakers. The people who create indexes to legal references, such as the professional indexers from the Library of Congress and the indexers of the numerous private legal publications, each have their own vocabulary and method of indexing material.

Elmore County, Alabama, courthouse and jail complex.

For example, West Publishing Company editors index material using the 450 West Digest Topics. Unless the legal assistant understands what items are included under each index classification, it is difficult to find the items even with a fast computer search engine. The word "holder," for example, is listed in the *West Digest Index* as being under "Statutes," but as the word "holder" is defined above, it actually is found under the West Digest Topic "Bills and Notes." *Black's Law Dictionary* defines the same word in the language of the negotiable instrument law. Using the West Topic heading "Bills and Notes" and "holder" in a computer search will not return cases of negotiable *exhibit* **19.1**   *Sample of traditional Supreme Court reporter.*

98   OCTOBER TERM, 2000

                                    Syllabus

               BUSH ET AL. *v.* GORE ET AL.

         CERTIORARI TO THE SUPREME COURT OF FLORIDA

      No. 00–949. Argued December 11, 2000—Decided December 12, 2000

On December 8, 2000, the Florida Supreme Court ordered, *inter alia*, that
   manual recounts of ballots for the recent Presidential election were
   required in all Florida counties where so-called "undervotes" had not
   been subject to manual tabulation, and that the manual recounts should
   begin at once. Noting the closeness of the election, the court explained
   that, on the record before it, there could be no question that there were
   uncounted "legal votes"—*i. e.*, those in which there was a clear indication of the voter's intent—sufficient to place the results of the election
   in doubt. Petitioners, the Republican candidates for President and Vice
   President who had been certified as the winners in Florida, filed an
   emergency application for a stay of this mandate. On December 9, this
   Court granted the stay application, treated it as a petition for a writ of
   certiorari, and granted certiorari.

Held: Because it is evident that any recount seeking to meet 3 U. S. C.
   § 5's December 12 "safe-harbor" date would be unconstitutional under
   the Equal Protection Clause, the Florida Supreme Court's judgment
   ordering manual recounts is reversed. The Clause's requirements
   apply to the manner in which the voting franchise is exercised. Having
   once granted the right to vote on equal terms, Florida may not, by
   later arbitrary and disparate treatment, value one person's vote over
   that of another. See, *e. g., Harper* v. *Virginia Bd. of Elections,* 383
   U. S. 663, 665. The recount mechanisms implemented in response to
   the state court's decision do not satisfy the minimum requirement for
   nonarbitrary treatment of voters. The record shows that the standards
   for accepting or rejecting contested ballots might vary not only from
   county to county but indeed within a single county from one recount
   team to another. In addition, the recounts in three counties were
   not limited to so-called undervotes but extended to all of the ballots.
   Furthermore, the actual process by which the votes were to be counted
   raises further concerns because the court's order did not specify who
   would recount the ballots. Where, as here, a court orders a statewide
   remedy, there must be at least some assurance that the rudimentary
   requirements of equal treatment and fundamental fairness are satisfied.
   The State has not shown that its procedures include the necessary safeguards. Upon due consideration of the difficulties identified to this
   point, it is obvious that the recount cannot be conducted in compliance

Sample of traditional Supreme Court reporter, continued.   exhibit **19.1**

Cite as: 531 U. S. 98 (2000)   99

Syllabus

with the requirements of equal protection and due process without substantial additional work.   The court below has said that the legislature intended the State's electors to participate fully in the federal electoral process, as provided in 3 U. S. C. §5, which requires that any controversy or contest that is designed to lead to a conclusive selection of electors be completed by December 12.   That date is here, but there is no recount procedure in place under the state court's order that comports with minimal constitutional standards.

772 So. 2d 1243, reversed and remanded.

Theodore B. Olson argued the cause for petitioners.   With him on the brief were *Douglas R. Cox, Thomas G. Hungar, Benjamin L. Ginsberg, Michael A. Carvin, Barry Richard, Miguel A. Estrada, George J. Terwilliger III, Timothy E. Flanigan, William K. Kelley, John F. Manning,* and *Bradford R. Clark.   Joseph P. Klock, Jr.,* argued the cause for Katherine Harris et al., respondents under this Court's Rule 12.6 in support of petitioners.   With him on the brief were *John W. Little III, Alvin F. Lindsay III, Ricardo M. Martinez-Cid,* and *Bill L. Bryant, Jr.*   Briefs in support of petitioners were filed by *William Kemper Jennings* for Glenda Carr et al.; by *Robert A. Destro* for Stephen Cruce et al.; and by *George S. LeMieux* and *Frederick J. Springer* for John E. Thrasher, all respondents under this Court's Rule 12.6.

David Boies argued the cause for respondents Gore et al. With him on the brief were *Laurence H. Tribe, Andrew J. Pincus, Thomas C. Goldstein, Jonathan S. Massey, Kendall Coffey,* and *Peter J. Rubin.**

---

*Briefs of *amici curiae* urging reversal were filed for the State of Alabama by *Bill Pryor,* Attorney General, and *Charles B. Campbell, Scott L. Rouse,* and *A. Vernon Barnett IV,* Assistant Attorneys General; for the Florida House of Representatives et al. by *Charles Fried, Einer Elhauge,* and *Roger J. Magnuson;* for William H. Haynes et al. by *Jay Alan Sekulow, Thomas P. Monaghan, Stuart J. Roth, Colby M. May, James M. Henderson, Sr., David A. Cortman, Griffin B. Bell, Paul D. Clement,* and *Jeffrey S. Bucholtz.*

Briefs of *amici curiae* urging affirmance were filed for the Brennan Center for Justice at New York University School of Law by *Burt Neuborne;* and for Robert A. Butterworth, Attorney General of Florida, by *exhibit* **19.2**   *Page from Corpis Juris Secundum—a legal encyclopedia.*

§§ 58–59   SOCIAL SECURITY

81 C.J.S.

individual who died fully insured,[65] and have physical or mental impairments which, under regulations promulgated for the purpose, are deemed to be of such severity as to preclude engaging in any gainful activity.[66]   The requirements for obtaining disability benefits by such persons are more restrictive than requirements for the insured individual himself.[67]   The physical impairment necessary to a finding of disability is placed on a level of severity to be determined administratively,[68] and the regulations adopted to carry out the statutory provisions have been upheld.[69]

A claim for disability is judged solely by medical criteria,[70] without regard to non-medical factors[71] such as age, education, and work experience,[72] in contrast to the considerations given to an insured individual's age, education, and work experience, in determining his ability to engage in substantial gainful activity, as discussed supra § 56.   An individual cannot qualify for disability insurance benefits unless suffering from an impairment listed in the appendix to the regulations applicable to disabilities, or from one or more unlisted impairments that singly or in combination are the medical equivalent of a listed impairment.[73]   The benefits are to be paid only for a disabling medical impairment,[74] and not simply for the inability to obtain employment.[75]

§ 59.   Benefits of Disabled Child

A disabled child of an insured individual who is, or would have been, eligible for social security benefits, may be entitled to disability insurance benefits.

Research Note

Status as child eligible for benefits under statute generally is discussed supra § 41.

Library References

Social Security and Public Welfare ⬳123, 140.5.

Under the provisions of the Social Security Act,[76] disabled children of retired or disabled insured individuals, and of insured individuals who have died, may be paid benefits if they have been disabled since before they reached twenty-two years of age, and if they meet the other conditions of eligibility.[77]   The purpose of the provision is to provide a measure of income and security to those who have lost a wage-earner on whom they depended,[78] or to provide support for the dependents of a disabled wage earner,[79] and not to replace only that support enjoyed by the child prior to the onset of disability.[80]   The liberal perspective of the Act applies to the award of children's disability benefits.[81]

In order to be entitled to recover benefits under this provision, the child must have been disabled,[82] as defined elsewhere in the Act,[83] prior to attaining a specified age,[84] and must be un-

65. U.S.—Sullivan v. Weinberger, C.A. Ga., 493 F.2d 855, certiorari denied 95 S.Ct. 1958, 421 U.S. 967, 44 L.Ed.2d 455.

66. U.S.—Wokojance v. Weinberger, C. A.Ohio, 513 F.2d 210, certiorari denied 96 S.Ct. 106, 423 U.S. 856, 46 L.Ed.2d 82.

Hendrix v. Finch, D.C.S.C., 310 F. Supp. 513.

Baby sitting; domestic work
U.S.—Dixon v. Weinberger, C.A.Ga., 495 F.2d 202.

Time impairment manifest
U.S.—Sullivan v. Weinberger, C.A.Ga., 493 F.2d 855, certiorari denied 95 S.Ct. 1958, 421 U.S. 967, 44 L.Ed.2d 455.

67. U.S.—Wokojance v. Weinberger, C. A.Ohio, 513 F.2d 210, certiorari denied 96 S.Ct. 106, 423 U.S. 856, 46 L.Ed.2d 82.

Solis v. U. S. Secretary of Health, Ed. and Welfare, D.C.Puerto Rico, 372 F.Supp. 1223—Truss v. Richardson, D. C.Mich., 338 F.Supp. 741—Nickles v. Richardson, D.C.S.C., 326 F.Supp. 777.

68. U.S.—Gillock v. Richardson, D.C. Kan., 322 F.Supp. 354.

69. U.S.—Sullivan v. Weinberger, C.A. Ga., 493 F.2d 855, certiorari denied 95 S.Ct. 1958, 421 U.S. 967, 44 L.Ed.2d 455.

Gunter v. Richardson, D.C.Ark., 335 F.Supp. 907—Zanoviak v. Finch, D.C. Pa., 314 F.Supp. 1152—Frasier v. Finch, D.C.Ala., 313 F.Supp. 160, affirmed, C. A., 434 F.2d 597.

70. U.S.—Wokojance v. Weinberger, C. A.Ohio, 513 F.2d 210, certiorari denied 96 S.Ct. 106, 423 U.S. 856, 46 L.Ed.2d 82.

71. U.S.—Sullivan v. Weinberger, C.A. Ga., 493 F.2d 855, certiorari denied 95 S.Ct. 1958, 421 U.S. 967, 44 L.Ed.2d 455.

72. U.S.—Gillock v. Richardson, D.C. Kan., 322 F.Supp. 354.

73. U.S.—Wokojance v. Weinberger, C. A.Ohio, 513 F.2d 210, certiorari denied 96 S.Ct. 106, 423 U.S. 856, 46 L.Ed.2d 82.

Gillock v. Richardson, D.C.Kan., 322 F.Supp. 354—Hendrix v. Finch, D.C.S. C., 310 F.Supp. 513.

74. U.S.—Sullivan v. Weinberger, C.A. Ga., 493 F.2d 855, certiorari denied 95 S.Ct. 1958, 421 U.S. 967, 44 L.Ed.2d 455.

75. U.S.—Sullivan v. Weinberger, C.A. Ga., 493 F.2d 855, certiorari denied 95 S.Ct. 1958, 421 U.S. 967, 44 L.Ed.2d 455.

76. 42 U.S.C.A. § 402(d).

77. U.S.—Lowe v. Finch, D.C.Va., 297 F.Supp. 667—Blevins v. Fleming, D.C. Ark., 180 F.Supp. 287.

78. U.S.—Ziskin v. Weinberger, D.C. Ohio, 379 F.Supp. 124.

79. U.S.—Jimenez v. Weinberger, Ill., 94 S.Ct. 2496, 417 U.S. 628, 41 L.Ed.2d 363, appeal after remand, C.A., 523 F.2d 689, certiorari denied 96 S.Ct. 3200.

80. U.S.—Jimenez v. Weinberger, Ill., 94 S.Ct. 2496, 417 U.S. 628, 41 L.Ed.2d 363, appeal after remand, C.A., 523 F.2d 689, certiorari denied 96 S.Ct. 3200.

81. U.S.—Ziskin v. Weinberger, D.C. Ohio, 379 F.Supp. 124.

82. U.S.—Ziskin v. Weinberger, D.C. Ohio, 379 F.Supp. 124.

83. 42 U.S.C.A. § 423.

84. U.S.—Ziskin v. Weinberger, D.C. Ohio, 379 F.Supp. 124—Moon v. Richardson, D.C.Va., 345 F.Supp. 1182.

110

instrument holder. Using the terms "negotiable instrument" and "holder" as the search words in a computer search will yield the desired result. Because paralegals can never be sure whether the research will be done using a traditional paper library or a computer search, they must understand how each resource files the information.

Knowing how to use both traditional and computer methods, and recognizing the strengths and weaknesses of each system, is important in conducting searches. Traditional research may be better when general background research is needed and the paralegal isn't particularly familiar with an area of law. Indexing systems are grouped by concept, and once the legal assistants get into the right concept of law area, they can browse easily. The ability to flip pages back and forth when they are generally in the right area is particularly helpful in statutory research, as many of the computer-based systems perform that task slowly, if at all—and assuming the paralegal can figure out how the index has been developed to create the computer search term. In contrast, for a narrow, fact-based question, or if the research already has a citation or case name to work from, computer-based research is usually the best approach. Success in research depends on recognizing the best tools for a specific problem and using them efficiently.

TRADITIONAL LEGAL RESOURCES

The traditional law library usually consists of print copies of primary and secondary sources of the law. A **primary source** is the actual law itself; this includes the statutes and the case law. The cases you have been briefing in this text are primary sources. **Secondary sources** are not the laws themselves but instead are writings about the law, such as legal encyclopedias and digests. This textbook is a secondary source. A third set of resources is referred to as **finding tools**—publications, such as digests or the *Index to Legal Periodicals*, used to find primary and secondary sources. Frequently, sources contain both secondary sources and finding tools in one publication, such as the *American Law Reports*. Some services combine all three into one service or publication. Table 19.1 delineates primary and secondary sources and finding tools.

Research materials.   *table* 19.1

PRIMARY SOURCES	SECONDARY SOURCES	FINDING TOOLS
Constitutions	Legal dictionaries	Digests
Statutes	Legal encyclopedias	Citators
Court decisions	Treatises	Indexes
Common-law cases	Law reviews	
Administrative regulations	Textbooks	
Ordinances	Legal periodicals	
Court rules		

Over time, each paralegal develops a personal search strategy based on the nature of the problem or issue to be researched and the resources available. When a legal issue is well-defined and a specific case or statute is in question, it may be possible to start with the original primary source. More likely, though, the research assignment will be less defined and may be just a set of facts describing a situation. A possible area of relevance of law may be suggested. This could be a specific area of law such as "driving too fast for conditions" or a general area of law such as "personal injury from an automobile accident."

The facts will determine the area of law. If the paralegal is unfamiliar with the area of law, the *relevant facts* may not be obvious. Secondary sources provide a good reference source to acquire a general understanding about an area of law. As you learn more about the specifics of the area of law and the essential elements of causes of actions, the relevant facts should become clearer. One of the advantages of using the traditional book form of research is the ability to flip pages back and forth and scan many items that can lead to a specific point of law. This is some times referred to as "the serendipity of research."

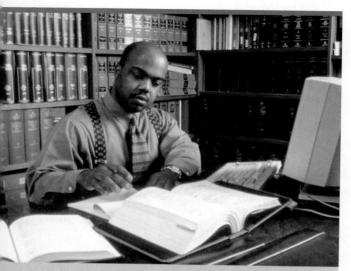

Often a combination of traditional and online research is needed for a case.

Computer search engines can lead to specific case law and statutes. The problem is in how to construct the search question. If you do not know the relevant facts to include, the resulting report may not be accurate. Computers, for the most part, are limited to finding only the things the search question specifically asks for. Learning the relevant facts to create the proper question may involve using the print resources first to determine the relevant facts or the proper terminology. For example, in a fair-use doctrine case of alleged copyright violation, is the status of the alleged violator as a nonprofit organization relevant?

Using Legal Reference Works

Most legal references have a set of common features. They generally have a section, usually in the introduction, that explains the coverage and how to use the specific book or service.

This usually includes the abbreviations used throughout the work (Exhibit 19.3), and the method of pagination—for example, standard page numbering or use of section numbers. A table of contents at the beginning of the work (Exhibit 19.4) provides a general list of major topics. The index at the end of the work provides the detailed coverage. Multivolume sets might have a separate set of volumes containing the index. Each volume also might contain an index for the specific volume.

Most legal works also contain a table of cases that are mentioned in the text. This is a useful feature when a case seems to be on point or relevant and the paralegal wants to research the area of law and other cases on the same issue. A table of statutes also may be included, to help the researcher find cases or discussions of a statute.

Sample list of abbreviations.   *exhibit* 19.3

ABBREVIATIONS

A.   *Atlantic Reporter*

A.2d   *Atlantic Reporter, Second Series*

Abb.   *Abbott's Circuit Court Reports, U.S.*

Abb.Adm.   *Abbott's Admiralty Reports, U.S.*

Adams L.J.   *Adams County Legal Journal*

Add.   *Addison's Reports*

Am.Dec.   *American Decisions*

Am.L.J.,N.S.   *American Law Journal, New Series*

Am.L.J.,O.S.   *American Law Journal, Hall's*

Am.L.Reg.,N.S.   *American Law Register, New Series*

Am.L.Reg.,O.S.   *American Law Register, Old Series*

Am.Rep.   *American Reports*

Am.St.Rep.   *American State Reports*

Ann.Cas.   *American & English Annotated Cases*

Ashm.   *Ashmead's Reports*

Baldw.   *Baldwin's Reports, U.S.*

Beaver   *Beaver County Legal Journal*

Ben.   *Benedict's Reports, U.S.*

Berks   *Berks County Legal Journal*

Binn.   *Binney's Reports*

Binns' Just.   *Binns' Justice*

Biss.   *Bissell's Reports, U.S.*

Black   *Black's United States Supreme Court Reports*

Blair   *Blair County Law Reports*

Blatchf.C.C.   *Blatchford's Reports, U.S.*

Bond   *Bond's Reports, U.S.*

B.R.   *Bankruptcy reports*

Bright.E.C.   *Brightly's Election Cases*

Bright.N.P.   *Brightly's Nisi Prius Reports*

Browne   *P. A. Browne's reports*

Brock.   *Brockenbrough's Reports, U.S.*

Bucks   *Bucks County Law Reporter*

C.A.   *United States Court of Appeals*

C.C.A.   *United States Circuit Court of Appeals*

Cambria   *Cambria County Legal Journal*

Cambria C.R.   *Cambria County Reports*

Camp.   *Campbell's Legal Gazette Reports*

Cent.   *Central Reporter*

C.C. (see Pa.C.C.)   *County Court Reports*

Chest.   *Chester County Reports*

From Purdon's *Pennsylvania Statutes Annotated,* © 1994 by West Group, a Thomson Company. Reproduced with permission.

Updates

Print material is updated in a number of ways. One of the most frequent is the use of **pocket parts,** so called because they are slipped into a pocket in the back of the print volume. Usually these are annual updates, but they may be produced more or less frequently depending on the publisher and the need for updates. Also used are supplemental pamphlets, usually paperbacks, to supplement the annual updates. Some are issued monthly, and others quarterly or semiannually. It is essential that the pocket part or supplement be consulted. In statutory research, the main volumes may be many years old and sections of the law repealed. The pocket parts or other supplements, not the main volume, contain the latest information. For this reason, some researchers look at the pocket part first, before consulting the main volume. More and more frequently, additional updates are provided online. The paralegal must learn how each resource is updated and the frequency of the updates. Exhibit 19.5 is a sample pocket part supplement.

Research Strategy

Before starting your research, prepare a list of words and phrases from a general index or descriptive words index. Use them to create online searches and conduct hard-copy book research.

SIDEBAR

exhibit **19.4**   *Sample table of contents.*

Checklist

PRIMARY SOURCES	SECONDARY SOURCES
Case	**Encyclopedia—National**
○ Name	○ Name
○ Citation	○ Key or descriptive word
Federal statute	**Encyclopedia—State**
○ Federal citation	○ Name
○ Popular name	○ Key or descriptive word
State (name)	**Treatises**
○ State citation	○ Name
○ Popular name	○ Citation
Local jurisdiction name	**Restatement of law**
○ Local citation	○ Name
○ Popular name	○ Citation
Administrative regulations	**Periodicals**
○ Federal agency name	○ Citation
○ Citation	
State agency name	**Practice Books**
○ Citation	○ Name
	○ Citation
Local agency name	**Dictionary**
○ Citation	○ Name
Constitution	**Digest**
○ Federal citation	○ Name
○ State citation	○ Citation

exhibit **19.5**   *Sample pocket part supplement.*

13 Pa.C.S.A. § 1105   COMMERCIAL CODE

DIVISION 1
GENERAL PROVISIONS
CHAPTER 11
SHORT TITLE, CONSTRUCTION, APPLICATION
AND SUBJECT MATTER OF TITLE

§ 1105.   **Territorial application of title; power of parties to choose applicable law**

Notes of Decisions

Bankruptcy   6

1. In general

In re Eagle Enterprises, Inc., Bkrtcy.E.D.Pa. 1998, 223 B.R. 290, [main volume] affirmed 237 B.R. 269.

2. Law governing

When parties agree to apply foreign law, pursuant to which their contract to "lease" goods kept in Pennsylvania will be deemed a true "lease," despite fact that contract does not permit lessor to terminate agreement but affords him an option to purchase goods for nominal consideration, Pennsylvania law will not give effect to that choice. In re Eagle Enterprises, Inc., E.D.Pa.1999, 237 B.R. 269.

4. Third parties

In re Eagle Enterprises, Inc., Bkrtcy.E.D.Pa. 1998, 223 B.R. 290, [main volume] affirmed 237 B.R. 269.

6. Bankruptcy

While Chapter 7 debtor and equipment lessor were generally free, under Pennsylvania statute, to agree what law would govern their rights and duties, debtor and equipment lessor could not impose their choice of law on Chapter 7 trustee, as party who never agreed to choice-of-law provision, in order to prevent trustee from challenging parties' characterization, as equipment "lease," of agreement which required debtor to pay alleged rent throughout full term of lease, and which then allowed debtor to acquire equipment at end of lease for nominal consideration of one dollar, merely because lease would allegedly have been recognized as true lease under law of foreign country that parties chose to govern their agreement. In re Eagle Enterprises, Inc., E.D.Pa.1999, 237 B.R. 269.

CHAPTER 12
GENERAL DEFINITIONS AND PRINCIPLES OF INTERPRETATION

§ 1201.   **General definitions**

Notes of Decisions

11. Lease or lease intended as security

Under Pennsylvania law, "lease" transaction in which "lessee" cannot terminate "lease" during its term, but may thereafter become owner of "leased" goods for no additional or nominal additional consideration, does not create lease, but rather a security interest. In re Eagle Enterprises, Inc., E.D.Pa.1999, 237 B.R. 269.

When parties agree to apply foreign law, pursuant to which their contract to "lease" goods kept in Pennsylvania will be deemed a true "lease," despite fact that contract does not permit lessor to terminate agreement but affords him an option to purchase goods for nominal consideration, Pennsylvania law will not give effect to that choice. In re Eagle Enterprises, Inc., E.D.Pa.1999, 237 B.R. 269.

13. Security interest

Revised Pennsylvania statute defining term "security interest" seeks to correct shortcomings

of its predecessor by focusing inquiry of lease/security interest analysis on economics of the transaction, rather than on intent of the parties. In re Kim, Bkrtcy.E.D.Pa.1999, 232 B.R. 324.

Whether, under Pennsylvania law, lease or security interest is created by a particular transaction is no longer within exclusive control of the parties and subject to possible manipulation through artful document drafting; rather, issue is to be determined by reference to uniform criteria set forth in revised statute defining term "security interest." In re Kim, Bkrtcy.E.D.Pa.1999, 232 B.R. 324.

In determining whether debtor's lease was a disguised security interest or a true lease under Pennsylvania law, bankruptcy court was required to consider entire "transaction" and was not constrained to look solely to documents signed by the parties which were designated "lease" or which made use of terms commonly found in leases, but could examine both parol and extrin-

4

Electronic Searching Strategy

"Searching is a process, not an event. . . . Searching a library is not about spending time and mental energy formulating the 'golden query' that retrieves your desired information in a single stroke. In practice, good online searching involves formulating a succession of queries until you are satisfied with the results. As you view results from one search, you'll come across additional leads that you did not identify in your original search. You can incorporate these new terms into your existing query or create a new one. After each query, evaluate its success by asking:

- Did I find what I was looking for?
- What better information could still be out there?
- How can I refine my query to find better information?

Issuing multiple queries can be frustrating or rewarding, depending on how long it takes you to identify the key material you need to answer your research problem."

Source: VersusLaw Research Manual, Part 1

CONSTRUCTING A SEARCH QUERY

Constructing a search query requires one to select a computer search index, then to create the query.

Creating a Computer Search

The three primary full-service online providers of computer research services—Lexis, Loislaw, and Westlaw—provide a broad range of legal materials including cases, statutes, and regulations. In addition, a limited-service search provider, VersusLaw, specializes in providing cases and limited access to additional items, such as the *Code of Federal Regulations*.

Search Method and Query

Each of the online providers uses words to find and retrieve documents. As part of the publication process, indexes are prepared of every word in the document, the words are tabulated for frequency, and a word index is prepared. The search you create searches this index. VersusLaw uses a full-text retrieval method that searches every word except "stop words"—words that are used too commonly in documents to be used in a search, such as "the," "not," "of," and "and." Exhibit 19.6 is the VersusLaw home page.

Creating the Query

When you conduct a search, you are asking the search engine to find the indexed words you have chosen. These may be legal specialty words or common English words. Single words may be in any of the Internet or legal search engines. Frequently you will be looking for more detailed information. Using combinations of words in the search can narrow the search results. In most cases, the most productive search contains a combination of words. This combination of words may consist of terms such as "strict liability," "legal malpractice," "automobile accident," or "reckless indifference," for example.

VersusLaw Research Manual: www.versuslaw.com/Support/ R_Manual_Preface.asp

Lexis: www.lexisnexis.com/

Westlaw: www.westlaw.com/ about/

VersusLaw: www.versuslaw.com

Loislaw: www.loislaw.com

exhibit 19.6   *VersusLaw home page.*

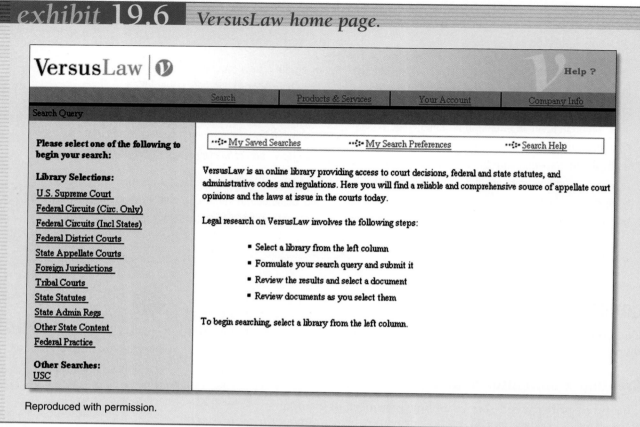

Reproduced with permission.

Using Connectors

Connectors are instructions to the search engine to look for documents containing combinations of words. Connectors may be thought of as instructions to the search engine: Find me documents in which the words "strict" AND "liability" appear. The word AND is a connector that instructs the search not to return the documents in which only one of the words is found. Exhibit 19.7 shows a Loislaw search with the AND connector.

The connector OR instructs the search engine to find either term—the word "strict" OR the word "liability"—and retrieve the documents. Exhibit 19.8 depicts a Lexis search with the OR connector. The NOT connector instructs the search to eliminate certain words. For example, you may wish to review documents in which the word "malpractice" is found but *not* those with the word "medical."

In some cases it might be assumed that there will be other words between the desired terms, such as in the phrase "Paralegals are bound by the ethics of their profession." The NEAR connector helps you locate documents where the terms are near each other; for example: find "paralegal" NEAR "ethics." The NEAR connector allows you to search for words near each other by specifying the number of words apart that is acceptable. Exhibit 19.9 shows a Westlaw search using the NEAR connector.

Loislaw search with AND connector.   *exhibit* 19.7

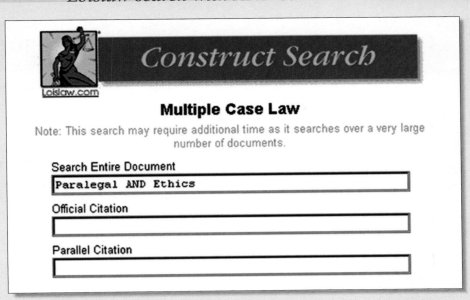

Construct Search

Multiple Case Law

Note: This search may require additional time as it searches over a very large number of documents.

Search Entire Document

Paralegal AND Ethics

Official Citation

Parallel Citation

Lexis search with OR connector.   *exhibit* 19.8

▸ News
▸ Business
▾ Legal Research
▸ Legal News
▸ Law Reviews
▸ Get a Case
  Shepard's® for U.S.
  Supreme Court
▸ Federal Case Law
▸ State Case Law
▸ Area of Law by Topic
▸ Federal Code
▸ Federal Regulations
▸ State Code
▸ Tax Law
  Canadian Legislative
▸ Materials
  Canadian Statutes &
  Regulations
▸ EU Law (CELEX)
  International Case

| Basic | Guided Search |

Federal Case Law   ◐ *Tips*

Keyword and Additional Terms search the full text of cases. Only cases that match all the criteria you enter will be found.

Keyword: Paralegal OR Ethics
Entry Required *e.g.* speech OR expression

**Narrow search
with additional terms:** *e.g.* picketing OR demonstration

Court: Supreme Court Cases   ◐ *Source List*

Date: ◉ Previous two years

○ From: ____ To: ____   ◐ *Examples*

[Search]   [Clear Form]

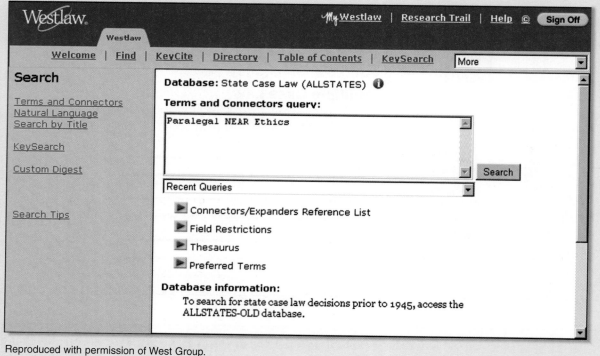

Exhibit 19.10 gives a comparison of these concepts, by VersusLaw, and Exhibit 19.11 gives a guide to connectors from Westlaw.

UPDATING LEGAL RESEARCH

The legal team always must use the most current statutory and case law in advising clients and arguing cases to the court. One of the features of the American legal system is its constant change. Courts attempt to meet the needs of a changing society by reviewing prior case law and, when appropriate, overruling or modifying it as the contemporary American view of justice dictates. The American legal system concept of ***stare decisis*** provides that we use prior case law as precedent but change the law as American society changes. Occasionally, existing case law may be held unconstitutional, such as happened with the landmark case of *Roe v. Wade*.

Knowing if the case law being used in a legal argument is the current case law is a vital part of the lawyer's obligation to the client and to the court. Up to the moment before the arguments are made to the court or the brief is submitted, a case that the attorney or the opponent is using as a basis for a legal argument may be overturned. The ethical obligation of candor to the court and of professional competency requires the use of current case law.

Comparison grid from VersusLaw. *exhibit* 19.10

VersusLaw	LEXIS	Westlaw
Connectors		
and	and	and, &
or	or	or, *space*
not	and not	but not, %
Proximity operators		
w/n	w/n	w/n, /n
w/n	pre/n	pre/n, +n
Exact phrase match		
unlawful entry	unlawful entry	"unlawful entry"
Wild Cards - end of root words		
*	!	!
Wild Cards - single character		
?	*	*
Order of operators		
proximity operators, not, and, or	or, *proximity operators*, and, and not	or, *proximity operators*, and, but not

Reproduced with permission.

Westlaw guide to connectors. *exhibit* 19.11

Using Connectors

Connector	You type	Westlaw retrieves documents
AND	&	containing both search terms: **work-place & safety**
OR	a space	containing either search term or both search terms: **landlord lessor**
Grammatical Connectors	/p	containing search terms in the same paragraph: **warrant! /p habitat!**
	/s	containing search terms in the same sentence: **danger! /s defect!**
	+s	in which the first term precedes the second within the same sentence: **capital +s gain**
Numerical Connectors	/n (where *n* is a number)	containing search terms within *n* terms of each other: **issues /5 fact**
	+n (where *n* is a number)	in which the first term precedes the second by *n* terms: **20 + 5 1080**
BUT NOT	%	not containing the term or terms following the percent symbol (%): **tax taxation % tax taxation /3 income**

Reproduced with permission from West Group.

Thus, an essential part of legal research for paralegals is to verify that they have the latest case or statute. The process is complicated by the method by which changes in statutes or case law are released to the public. Ultimately, new statutes and new case law are reported in a published form, both in paper and electronically, but not all publications are able to disseminate the information daily. Paper versions take time to print and distribute. Not all electronic versions are posted immediately. Therefore, it becomes important to know how quickly the reporting or electronic services of the law firm or practice distribute post-statutory changes and new cases. More and more courts have their own websites and release case opinions electronically along with the print versions to the public and publishing companies. For example, you can check decisions of the U. S. Supreme Court daily.

What is difficult is knowing if the new cases or new statutes affect the case being researched. When the court specially mentions a case being cited in a memo of law or court brief, the paralegal needs to know if the new case follows the older case law, reverses it, or in some way differs from the older case.

As soon as a case is entered into an electronic case law database, such as Westlaw, Lexis, Loislaw, or Versuslaw, a general search can be made for references to the case name or citation. Before it is entered, the same search will not show the newest reference. Even a reference to the case will not tell whether the case law has changed, only that another case has referred to it. Someone must actually read the case to see how the court has used it or referred to it in the opinion.

Shepard's

Long a standard tool of legal research in law libraries has been *Shepard's Citations*, a multivolume set of books listing cases and statutes by their respective citations and giving the citation of every other case in which the listed case was mentioned. The listings originally were compiled by editors who physically read through every case reported to find citations. These then were reported by case citation, with every other mention of the case reported by its citation in chronological fashion, with notations indicating if the opinion was reversed, affirmed, followed, overruled, and so on. The process of using *Shepard's* to check legal citations came to be called "Shepardizing," a term that many legal assistants still use, even when using other citation-checking services such as Westlaw's KeyCite. An advantage to the *Shepard's Citator* is the editorial symbol system used to indicate how the new case affects the case being checked, as shown in Exhibit 19.12.

The problem with the traditional paper form of Shepard's is the lag in time for the print version to be prepared and sent out to subscribers. *Shepard's* now provides the same service online through the Lexis service—subscribers can obtain the latest case information, to the day, by calling a toll-free number. One of the difficulties in using the print version of *Shepard's* is the number of hardbound volumes and paperback updates required to be consulted, and finding the latest update pamphlet if someone has misfiled it in the law library.

Shepard's symbols showing effects of new cases.   *exhibit* 19.12

Shepard's Signal

⬢ Warning	Strong negative treatment indicated. Includes:
	• Overruled by
	• Questioned by
	• Superceded by
	• Revoked
	• Obsolete
	• Rescinded

▲ Caution	Possible negative treatment indicated. Includes:
	• Limited
	• Criticized by
	• Clarified
	• Modified
	• Corrected

✚ Positive	Positive treatment indicated. Includes:
	• Followed
	• Affirmed
	• Approved

Ⓐ Citing References with Analysis	Other cases cited the case and assigned some analysis that is not considered positive or negative. Includes:
	• Appeal denied by
	• Writ of certiorari denied

Ⓘ Citation Information	References have not applied any analysis to the citation. For example the case was cited by law reviews, ALR® Annotations, or in other case law not warranting an analysis. Example: Cited By

Many educational institutions and public libraries subscribe to the web-based LexisNexis Academic Universe. *Shepard's* citation service (Exhibit 9.13) usually is available for the U. S. Supreme Court as part of the service, but other federal and state *Shepard* citation services may not be included because of the cost of the additional license fees involved.

Westlaw provides the same function, calling its service KeyCite. Loislaw offers a case reference search called GlobalCite.

GlobalCite™

Loislaw **GlobalCite** provides a reverse chronological list of the case law, statutes in the order of the highest number of citation occurrences, the regulations listed in relevancy order, and reference to other databases in the Loislaw library. Exhibit 19.14 shows a GlobalCite screen.

KeyCite™

KeyCite is the Westlaw online citation update service. The Westlaw KeyCite is a combination citator and case finder (see Exhibit 19.15). Unlike other similar services, KeyCite uses the West Key number system and West Headnotes.

exhibit 19.13   *Shepard's citation service.*

Edit Search | FOCUS | Print/Save Options | E-Mail

KWIC™ | Full

Shepard's® - 240 Citing References

All Neg | All Pos | Any | Custom Restrictions | Unrestricted

▲ 365 U.S. 127

Signal: ▲ Caution - Possible negative treatment
Citation: 365 U.S. 127
Restrictions: Analysis: Followed, Criticized, Dissenting Op.

Eastern R. Presidents Conference v. Noerr Motor Freight, Inc., 365 U.S. 127, 5 L. Ed. 2d 464, 81 S. Ct. 523, 1961 U.S. LEXIS 2128, 1961 Trade Cas. (CCH) P69927

PRIOR HISTORY (4 citing references) ◆ Hide Prior History

☐ Noerr Motor Freight, Inc. v. Eastern R. Presidents Conference, 155 F.Supp. 768, 1957 U.S. Dist. LEXIS 3019, 1957 Trade Cas. (CCH) P68827 (D. Pa. 1957)

Affirmed by:

☐ Noerr Motor Freight, Inc. v. Eastern R. Presidents Conference, 273 F.2d 218, 1959 U.S. App. LEXIS 5485, 1959 Trade Cas. (CCH) P69546 (3d Cir. Pa. 1959)

▶   Reversed by (CITATION YOU ENTERED):

☐ Eastern R. Presidents Conference v. Noerr Motor Freight, Inc., 365 U.S. 127, 5 L. Ed. 2d 464, 81 S. Ct. 523, 1961 U.S. LEXIS 2128, 1961 Trade Cas. (CCH) P69927 (1961)

Reprinted with the permission of LexisNexis.

exhibit 19.14   *Loislaw GlobalCite screen.*

GlobalCite Results

U.S. 7th Circuit Court of Appeals Reports
LAWLINE v. AMERICAN BAR ASS'N. , 956 F.2d 1378 (7th Cir. 1992)
20 Found. (1 - 20 shown)

Click the case name to view the document.

Arkansas Cases
CAMBIANO v. NEAL, 342 Ark. 691 (2000)
00-283.
Opinion delivered November 16, 2000. [Substituted Opinion on Denial of
Petition for Rehearing delivered December 15, 2000]

interests of consumer protection and the integrity of the legal system.
Further we hold that it is no more restrictive than necessary and is thus
constitutional. In Lawline v. American Bar Association, 956 F.2d 1378 (7th
Cir. 1992), the United States Court of Appeals for the Eleventh Circuit held
that Illinois had the right to regulate the practice of law

LOIS Federal District Court Opinions: Non-Referenced
TSAU v. NATIONAL SCIENCE FOUNDATION, (N.D. III. 2000)

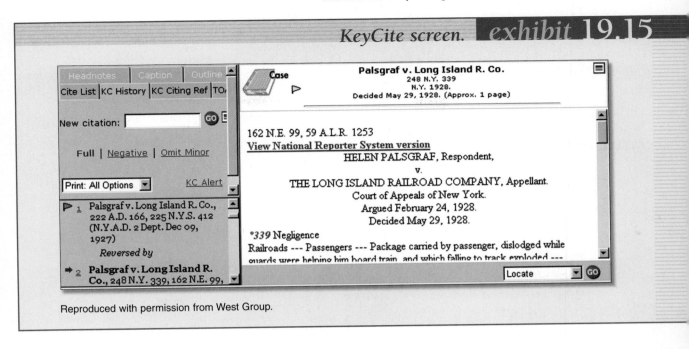

KeyCite screen. *exhibit* 19.15

Reproduced with permission from West Group.

PARALLEL CITATIONS

Most cases are reported in more than one service or set of books. A **parallel cita-tion** is a cite to the same material, usually a case, in another source. Frequently a state has an official publication, such as the court's own publication, and a private publication, such as the *West Reporter*. In some cases, West was and is the official reporter, and there may not be a parallel print source. One of the many uses of *Shepard's* is to find the parallel citation to other locations for the same case.

Shepard's also provides update information on statutory citations. Amend-ments and repeals of statutory information are listed in *Shepard's*. Citations to any cases in which the statute has been cited also are listed, with information on how the case law considered the statute.

Checklist

RESEARCH SEARCH ITEMS

○ Client:	○ Date:

○ Issue:

○ Search terms and phrases:

○ Search combinations used:

Checklist

			RESEARCH SOURCES CHECKED	
CHECKED	SOURCE	CITATION	POCKET PART CHECKED ▼	WEB LOCATION
PRIMARY SOURCES				
	State statute			www.
	USC			www.
	USCA			www.
	CFR			www.
	Local ordinance			www. www.
SECONDARY SOURCES				
	State digest			www.
	Federal digest			www.
	ALR			www. www.
	Encyclopedia			www.
	State			www.
	C.J.S.			www.
	Periodicals			www.
	Treatises			www.

lēʹgəl tur'mə nälʹə jē
LEGAL TERMINOLOGY

Connector
Finding tool
GlobalCite
KeyCite
Parallel citation
Pocket part
Primary source
Relevant fact
Secondary source
Stare decisis

Summary

CHAPTER 19 TRADITIONAL AND COMPUTER LEGAL RESEARCH

Traditional and Computer Research

Online Law Libraries	1. Westlaw 3. Loislaw 2. Lexis 4. VersusLaw
Research Services	1. *Shepard's* 2. KeyCite 3. GlobalCite
Research Starting Point	1. The question typically is framed with some specificity. 2. Researchers must understand the facts that apply to the case they are asked to research.
Traditional Versus Computer-Based Law Libraries	1. *Traditional law library:* Books in paper form, case reporters, legal encyclopedias, legal dictionaries, and finding tools including paper card indexes and digests. 2. *Modern law library:* Electronic, with online computer services such as Westlaw, Lexis, and Loislaw. 3. Not every office will have access to all the latest computer resources, or the same ones.
Traditional Legal Resources	1. *Primary source:* The actual law itself, including statutes and case law. 2. *Secondary sources:* Not the laws themselves, but writings about the law, such as legal encyclopedias and digests. 3. *Finding tools.* *(continued)*

Computer Research

Constructing a Search Query	Each online provider uses words to find and retrieve documents. As part of the publication process, indexes are prepared of every word in the document, the words are tabulated for frequency, and a word index is prepared. The search you create searches this index.
Creating a Computer Search	Search engine is used to find the indexed words you have chosen; may be legal specialty words or common English words. Using combinations of words in the search can narrow the search results.

Search Method and Query

Connectors in Legal Research	1. AND—instructs the search not to return documents in which only one of the words is found. 2. OR—instructs search engine to find either term. 3. NEAR—may be used to find occurrence of desired words within a set number of words of each other.
Updating Legal Research	1. *Shepard's:* A multivolume set of books listing cases and statutes by their respective citations and giving the citation of every other case in which the listed case was mentioned; checking citations is often called "Shepardizing." 2. *GlobalCite* (Loislaw): Provides a reverse chronological list of the case law, a list of statutes in the order of the highest number of citation occurrences, regulations in relevancy order, and reference to other databases in Loislaw library. 3. *KeyCite* (Westlaw): Online citation update service.
Parallel Citation	A citation to the same material, usually a case, in another source.
Statutory Law Updates	*Shepard's* provides update information on amendments and repeals of statutory information. Citations to any cases in which the statute has been cited are also listed, with information on how the case law considered the statute.

Working the Web

1. Search the term "paralegal ethics" using at least two different general search engines such as:
    a. www.google.com
    b. www.yahoo.com
    c. www.altavista.com
2. Search the term "paralegal ethics" using two or more legal research sites (if available to you), such as Westlaw, Lexis, Loislaw, or VersusLaw. Are the results the same?
3. Find the features that Westlaw offers for research and writing at its website at www.westlaw.com.
4. Find the features, including those without charge, that Lexis offers for research and writing at its websites at www.lexisnexis.com and www.lexisone.com.
5. Find the features that Loislaw offers for research and writing at its website at www.loislaw.com.
6. Find the features that VersusLaw offers for research and writing at its website at www.versuslaw.com.

Questions
CRITICAL LEGAL THINKING AND WRITING

1. Using the facts in the *Palsgraf* case in Appendix A, prepare a search query using connectors to locate the law or a similar case in your jurisdiction. Run the search using an online legal research service, if available.
2. Why does a paralegal have to be familiar with both traditional and electronic research tools and methods?
3. Why does the paralegal have to know how quickly changes in statutory and case law are updated by online and traditional primary and secondary sources?
4. Why is knowledge of the underlying law in an area important in constructing a question for online research?
5. How can a researcher be certain that a case that seems to be on point is still the current case law?
6. Why should secondary sources not be relied upon in citing binding authority?
7. Why would a researcher use a traditional paper resource before using an online research tool?
8. How does the use of connectors help in conducting online research? Give an example.

9. Why might an identical search query return different results?

10. Why must researchers clearly understand the question they are being asked to research? How can they be certain they do?

Questions
ETHICS: ANALYSIS AND DISCUSSION

1. Is there an ethical obligation under the Model Rules to perform legal research competently? Explain.

2. What is the ethical obligation under the Model Rules to provide the court with legal authority that is not favorable to your client's legal position?

3. What is the ethical obligation to "Shepardize" cases and statutes before submitting a brief or memo of law to the court?

For answers, look at American Bar Association Rule 3.3, Candor Toward the Tribunal, and Rule 1.1, Competence (ABA *Model Rules of Professional Conduct,* 2002).

Confidentiality

There are few certainties in the area of ethics, for paralegals or in any profession. What qualifies as ethical conduct is in most cases based on state law and court interpretation applied to a set of facts. The citation listed below represents one legal opinion and is provided as a research starting point. Do not assume that the same rule applies in your jurisdiction. For the following:

- *Prepare a written statement based on your state law.*
- *Use your state bar association website as a starting point.*

You are waiting for a fax needed for a case on which you are working. While you are standing by the fax machine, a fax comes in from an attorney at an opposing firm containing a letter about settlement that was clearly intended for the attorney's client and not for opposing counsel. Your best friend in the office is the paralegal who is working on that case at the other law office. She is stressed out by the case and made the mistake of dialing your fax number. From your reading of the letter it appears the information will be of major help in your law office winning the case. [*ABA Formal Ethics Opinion, State Compensation Insurance Fund v. The WPS, Inc.,* 70 CA 4644; 82 C.R.2 799 (1999)] Do you quietly return the fax to your friend and say nothing to anyone? Do you read it carefully to be sure of the contents? Do you return it to opposing counsel? Do you tell your supervising attorney about the letter? The contents?

Case
FOR DISCUSSION

American Geophysical Union v. Texaco Inc.   37 F.3d 881 (2d Cir. 1994)

Copying of Material for Future Research and Law Library Archives from Copyrighted Magazines and Journals

Most researchers understand that misuse of copyright material may subject them to liability under the copyright laws. The case of *American Geophysical Union v. Texaco* illustrates the potential liability in regularly copying copyrighted articles for personal archives. Researchers of Texaco regularly made copies of articles for future reference from the works of the plaintiff and 82 other publishers of scientific and technical journals. Texaco raised the defense of "fair use" as permitted under the copyright law.

Fair use as a defense depends on four tests: (1) the purpose and character of the use—including whether for nonprofit educational purposes or commercial use; (2) the nature of copyright work—the law generally recognizes a greater need to disseminate factual works than works of fiction or fantasy; (3) amount and substantiality of portion used—was the quantity used reasonable in relation to the purpose of the copying? (4) effect on potential market or value—will the copying have an impact on the sale of the works, and is there an efficient mechanism for the licensing of the works?

Questions

1. How does copyright law apply to a student copying copyrighted materials while doing research for a class project?
2. Would the answer be the same if the student were doing the research as part of an assignment while working in a law office?
3. Does it matter if the work copied is a court case or an article by an expert in automobile airbags liability? Why?

Hart v. Massanari

266 F.3d 1155 (2001)   United States Court of Appeals, Ninth Circuit

Read, and if assigned, brief this case. In your brief, answer the following questions.

1. Why are unpublished dispositions (opinion) of courts not valid as precedent in future cases?

2. What is the difference between controlling authority and persuasive authority?

3. How does a court decide if it is bound by an earlier decision?

4. Why does this court believe it is important, in writing an opinion of the court, to recite all the relevant facts?

5. What is the effect of binding precedent on other courts?

Kozinski, Circuit Judge.

Appellant's . . . brief cites . . . an unpublished disposition, not reported in the *Federal Reporter*. . . . The full text . . . is marked with the following notice: "This disposition is not appropriate for publication and may not be cited to or by the courts of this circuit. . . ." Unpublished dispositions and orders of this Court are not binding precedent . . . [and generally] may not be cited to or by the courts of this circuit." . . . [9th Cir.R.36-3.]

We ordered counsel to show cause as to why he should not be disciplined for violating Ninth Circuit Rule 36-3. Counsel responds by arguing that Rule 36-3 may be unconstitutional . . . [relying] . . . on the Eighth Circuit's opinion in *Anastasoff v. United States*, [which] while vacated, continues to have persuasive force. . . .

A. Anastasoff held that Eighth Circuit Rule 28A(i), . . . that unpublished dispositions are not precedential* . . . violates Article III of the Constitution. . . . We believe that Anastasoff overstates the case. . . .

Anastasoff focused on one aspect of the way federal courts do business—the way they issue opinions—and held that they are subject to a constitutional limitation derived from the [constitutional] framers' conception of what it means to exercise the judicial power. . . . We question whether the "judicial power" clause contains any limitation at all, separate from the specific limitations of Article III and other parts of the Constitution. . . . The term "judicial power" in Article III is more likely descriptive than prescriptive. . . .

B. Modern federal courts are the successors of the English courts that developed the common law. . . . Common law judges did not make law as we understand that concept; rather, they "found" the law with the help of earlier cases that had considered similar matters. An opinion was evidence of what the law is, but it was not an independent source of law. . . . The idea that judges declared rather than made the law remained firmly entrenched in English jurisprudence until the early nineteenth century. . . . For centuries, the most important sources of law were not judicial opinions themselves, but treatises that restated the law. . . .

The modern concept of binding precedent . . . came about only gradually over the nineteenth and early twentieth centuries. Lawyers began to believe that judges made, not found, the law. This coincided with monumental improvements in the collection and reporting of case authorities . . . and [as] a more comprehensive reporting system began to take hold, it became possible for judicial decisions to serve as binding authority. . . .

II

Federal courts today do follow some common law traditions. When ruling on a novel issue of law, they will generally consider how other courts have ruled on the same issue. . . . Law on point is the law. If a court must decide an issue governed by a prior opinion that constitutes binding authority, the later court is bound to reach the same result, even if it considers the rule unwise or incorrect. Binding authority must be followed unless and until overruled by a body competent to do so.

In determining whether it is bound by an earlier decision, a court considers not merely the "reason and spirit of cases" but also "the letter of particular precedents." . . . This includes not only the rule announced, but also the facts giving rise to the dispute, other rules considered and rejected, and the views expressed in response to any dissent or concurrence. Thus, when crafting binding authority, the precise language employed is often crucial to the contours and scope of the rule announced.

. . . A decision of the Supreme Court will control that corner of the law unless and until the Supreme Court itself overrules or modifies it. . . . Thus, the first panel to consider an issue sets the law not only for all the inferior courts in the circuit, but also future panels of the court of appeals. Once a panel resolves an issue in a precedential opinion, the matter is deemed resolved, unless overruled by the court itself sitting en banc, or by the Supreme Court. . . .

Controlling authority has much in common with persuasive authority. Using the techniques developed at common law, a court confronted with apparently controlling authority must parse the precedent in light of the facts presented and the rule announced. Insofar as there may be factual differences between the current case and the earlier one, the court must determine whether those differences are material to the application of the rule or allow the precedent to be distinguished on a principled basis. . . . But there are also very important differences between controlling and persuasive authority. . . . [I]f a controlling precedent is determined to be on point, it must be followed. . . . Thus, an opinion of our court is binding within our circuit, not elsewhere. . . .

III

While we agree with Anastasoff that the principle of precedent was well established in the common law courts by the time Article III of the Constitution was written, we do not agree that it was known and applied in the strict sense in which we apply binding authority today. . . .

In writing an opinion, the court must be careful to recite all facts that are relevant to its ruling, while omitting facts that it considers irrelevant. Omitting relevant facts will make the ruling unintelligible to those not already familiar with the case; including inconsequential facts can provide a spurious basis for distinguishing the case in the future. . . .

While federal courts of appeals generally lack discretionary review authority, they use their authority to decide cases by unpublished—and nonprecedential—dispositions to achieve the same end. . . . That a case is decided without a precedential opinion does not mean it is not fully considered. . . . The disposition is not written in a way that makes it suitable for governing future cases. . . . An unpublished disposition is, more or less, a letter from the court to parties familiar with the facts, announcing the result and the essential rationale of the court's decision. . . .

IV

We conclude that Rule 36-3 is constitutional. We also find that counsel violated the rule. Nevertheless, we are aware that Anastasoff may have cast doubt on our rule's constitutional validity. Our rules are obviously not meant to punish attorneys who, in good faith, seek to test a rule's constitutionality. We therefore conclude that the violation was not willful and exercise our discretion not to impose sanctions.

The order to show cause is DISCHARGED.

* Our rule operates . . . differently from . . . the Eighth Circuit . . . Rule 28A(i) [that] says that "[u]npublished decisions are not precedent." [W]e say that unpublished dispositions are "not binding precedent." . . . Our rule . . . prohibits citation of an unpublished disposition to any of the courts of our circuit. The Eighth Circuit's rule allows citation . . . , but provides that the authority is persuasive rather than binding.

CHAPTER 20

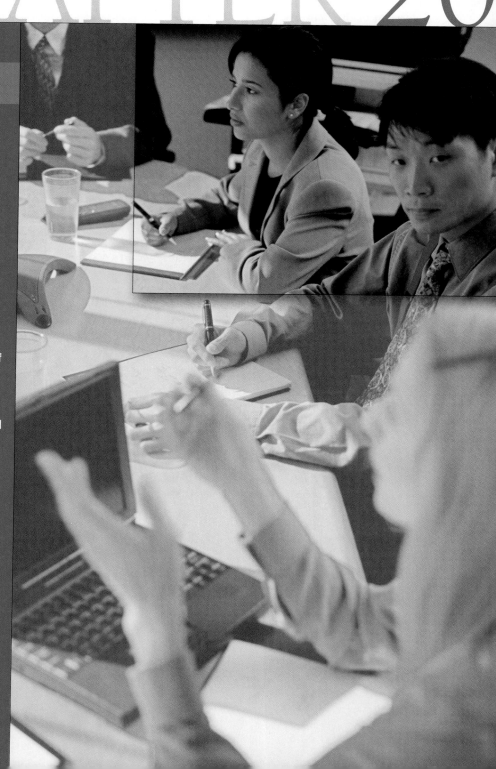

CHAPTER OBJECTIVES

After studying this chapter, you should be able to:

1. Explain the need for proper citation format.

2. Describe how to use appropriate traditional citation format.

3. Explain the Universal Citation Format.

4. Describe the *Bluebook* citation format.

5. Describe the AWLD Citation Format.

6. Define the ethical duty of candor to the court.

7. Differentiate the writing style in preparing an internal memo of law and the style for writing a court memo of law.

8. Explain the need for a clear definition of the facts and assignment before preparing a memorandum.

9. Explain the need to write for the intended audience.

10. Describe the impact of Federal Rule of Civil Procedure 11 on submitting briefs to the court.

Critical Legal Thinking and Writing

Justice is the end of government. It is the end of civil society. It ever has been, and ever will be pursued, until it be obtained, or until liberty be lost in the pursuit.

JAMES MADISON

Introduction

Critical legal thinking is the process of identifying legal issues, determining the relevant facts, and applying the applicable law to come to a conclusion that answers the legal question the issues present. A written opinion by a court is an example of critical legal thinking combined with writing. In the law office this is frequently seen in the office memorandum of law and the legal case brief submitted to a court.

COURT BRIEF AND OFFICE MEMORANDUM WRITING STYLES

Both the brief and the memorandum may be on the exact same set of facts, legal issue, and applicable law, but the writing style is totally different. The **memorandum** is a working document for the legal team to be used in the preparation and presentation of a case. As a result, it has to be an objective analysis of the case, including factual subtleties and analysis of the applicable law with any alternate interpretations. The brief written for the court is designed to provide written advocacy of the client's position and must be written to convince the court to adopt a position favorable to the client.

Candor to the Court

Comment to *Model Rules of Professional Conduct* Rule 3.3. The comment states in relevant part:

> The advocate's task is to present the client's case with persuasive force. Performance of that duty while maintaining confidences of the client is qualified by the advocate's duty of candor to the tribunal. . . . Legal argument based on a knowingly false representation of law constitutes dishonesty toward the tribunal.

A lawyer is not required to make a disinterested exposition of the law, but must recognize the existence of pertinent legal authorities. . . . (a)(3), an advocate has a duty to disclose directly adverse authority in the controlling jurisdiction which has not been disclosed by the opposing party. The underlying concept is that legal argument is a discussion seeking to determine the legal premises properly applicable to the case.

Checklist

MEMORANDUM OF LAW TEMPLATE

- ○ To:
- ○ From:
- ○ Date:
- ○ Subject:
- ○ Facts
- ○ Issue(s)
- ○ Discussion
- ○ Conclusion

HONESTY

Above all is an obligation to be honest with the court, called the **duty of candor.** The legal team has an ethical obligation not to mislead the court. Just one brief that intentionally distorts or hides the truth or intentionally misleads the court can destroy a legal career. Even if it doesn't result in sanctions, suspension, or disbarment, judges talk with their colleagues, and a bad reputation for integrity to the court is hard to correct. At the least, the court always will remember that the attorney did shoddy work and may give more credibility to the opposing side in the future, even if later cases by the offending attorney are better prepared and more accurately on point.

OFFICE MEMORANDUM

In doing research and preparing the memorandum of law, the legal assistant must be careful to include all the relevant applicable statutes and case law. Some paralegals are intimidated by the gruff and sometime downright nasty attitude of lawyers, particularly trial counsel in the middle of a stressful case. They are afraid that the lawyer will "shoot the messenger." The reality is that the attorney *must* know the weaknesses in the case along with the strengths. Nothing is more upsetting to the attorney, whether in court or in a meeting with a client or opposing counsel, than to be surprised by a case, facts, or law that has not been covered in the office memorandum of law.

Office memoranda are frequently indexed by subject and filed in the office for future reference. If the same or a similar fact pattern requires research, these provide a good starting point and can be a major time-saver. So that a memorandum may be indexed properly, the facts upon which the conclusion is based must be clearly stated. All statutes, regulations, and cases must be cited properly so anyone reading the memorandum in the future can look them up. Listing relevant websites used in the preparation is also helpful.

Ethical PERSPECTIVE

Email

When sending confidential information through electronic mail (whether direct link, commercial service, or Internet), there is a reasonable expectation of privacy. Use of electronic mail will not affect the confidentiality of client communications under South Carolina Rule of Professional Conduct 1.6.

Starting Point

The starting point for the legal researcher is to understand the specific assignment. What is it that you have been asked to research? For the memorandum of law, it usually is to answer a question:

What is the current law on . . . ?
What happens if . . . ?
What is the procedure for . . . ?

Before starting an assignment, the paralegal must be certain what is really being asked. Any questions should be resolved by asking the person for whom the memorandum is being prepared: "What does the attorney expect?" Where the paralegal's knowledge of the subject area is sufficient, he or she may know that certain facts may change the outcome—such as the requirement in some states that a subscribing witness to a decedent's will cannot be a beneficiary. Before starting, paralegals must be sure to have all the relevant facts, then restate what they believe they are being asked to research in the form of a statement of the question. For example: "You have asked for the law on the rights of individuals to . . . ."

Facts

Paralegals, of course, must have a clear statement of the facts from which to work. The facts relied upon in writing the memo must be part of the ultimate final memorandum. Other people may read the memorandum. They need to understand the specific facts upon which the analysis is based, particularly if

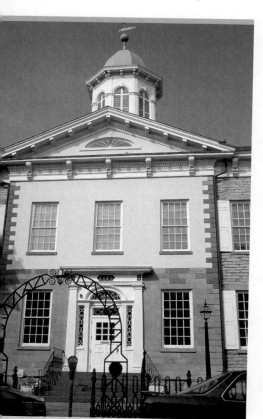

County courthouse, Kingston, New York.

they read it at a time when the paralegal is not available to answer questions, such as the middle of a case, out ill, on vacation, or after the paralegal has left the firm. It also is frequently necessary to recite other facts not relied upon and the reason for not considering them—that the result would be different. An example is a notation that this fact pattern is based upon the participants all being over the age of majority for contracting, or over the age to purchase and consume alcoholic beverages.

Analysis

A memorandum must present both sides of the issue and, in that respect, be a neutral, unbiased, objective presentation of applicable laws as they apply to the facts of the case. Issues that the opposing attorney or the judge may raise should be considered and presented. A good analysis will include a discussion of how the fact pattern may differ in cases that are not on point but may be used by opposing counsel.

The memorandum the paralegal prepares may be the basis for the court brief that the attorney or someone else will prepare. To be able to meet the ethical obligation to the court, the person who presents a persuasive argument favoring the client must know all the relevant statutory and case law.

Editing and Rewriting

The written word is a reflection of the writer. Everyone who reads the memorandum will measure the researcher's reputation and skill level. Each person who reads the memorandum will measure the writer's communication skills. The paralegal, however, may be writing for a certain audience, and someone other than that might read the memorandum, unaware of the intended reader.

Certain elements of writing style transcend the audience. For example:

Is it clear?

Are the words used properly?

Is the spelling correct?

Is it written using proper English grammar?

If it is being written for an audience for whom English is a second language, is that made clear?

Where there are variations in translation of foreign language terms, have these been clarified? For example, were the facts translated from words spoken by someone from Spain or someone from Puerto Rico, from someone who speaks Northern High German or Bavarian Southern German or Swiss German?

CITATIONS

A legal **citation** is a reference to the source of the information that allows someone else to find the case or other material mentioned in a document. The form of the citation must allow others to find the material. The format must be one that others in the legal community generally accept and use. If a person in California submits a brief to a court, a person in New York or in Florida must be able to use the citation to locate the items referred to in the document in a traditional legal library or electronic law source such as Loislaw, VersusLaw, Lexis, or Westlaw.

All legal authorities can be divided into two groups—primary authority and secondary authority. **Primary authority** includes constitutions, statutes, cases, and administrative regulations. Everything else is a **secondary authority** explaining the primary authority or a finding tool providing a method of locating primary authority. With a consistent citation format, the reader can determine the source of the authority mentioned and find the applicable primary source (constitution, statute, regulation, or case) or secondary source or finding tool (treatise, encyclopedia, digest, or dictionary).

Traditional Sources (Print)

The traditional method for publishing primary and secondary authority is the paper form, including books, collections of books, and series of books. Where a case, statute, or regulation is available in more than one series of books, such as the official reporter of the state and a private publication such as those published by West Publishing, the citation to both locations—known as parallel citations—is required. The citation form is basically the same:

Volume	Book or Series	Page
232	Atlantic 2d	44

In this example, written as 232 A.2d 44, 232 refers to the volume in the Atlantic 2d series reporter service of West Publishing Company, and 44 refers to the page on which the authority may be found.

Bluebook

The most commonly used guide to citation form is the publication *The Bluebook: A Uniform System of Citation.* This is the generally accepted authority for proper citation form unless the rules of a particular court dictate a different citation format. For example, the executive administrator of the Superior Court of Pennsylvania issued this notice:

> Pennsylvania Superior Court will be issuing opinions containing a Universal Citation. This citation will be as follows:
>
> Jones v. Smith, 1999 PA Super, 1.
>
> The second number is a Court-issued number on the opinion. Each opinion will also have numbered paragraphs, to be used for pinpoint citation, e.g., Jones v. Smith, 1999 PA Super, 1,15. Citation to opinions that have not yet been issued an Atlantic 2d citation are to be in the Universal Citation number. After the official citation has been issued, citation is to be only the official citation, and not the Universal Citation.

Effectively the old citation format, citing to the book, is still to be used.

Legal Citations Are on Trial in Innovation v. Tradition

The New York Times   July 8, 2001

For a couple of centuries, judges and lawyers have been including arcane numbers smack in the middle of their writing. They call them sentence citations—see, e.g., *Bush v. Gore*, 531 U.S. 98, 121 S. Ct. 525, 148 L. Ed. 2d 388 (2000).

Lots of people call them annoying. Now, at the prompting of one of the country's leading authorities on legal writing, lawyers and judges are joining the ranks of the complainers. In court opinions and legal briefs, they are flouting convention by tucking those numbers into footnotes. In the process, they are irritating some of their colleagues and changing the look of legal documents from coast to coast. They say they are also taking an important step toward making the law slightly more comprehensible to people who have not spent three years in law school.

But the defenders of legal tradition say the rebels are ruining a superior system of legal citation with unorthodox ideas. "It's a nuisance" and "aggravating" and "an obstacle to proper opinion writing," said Ned E. Doucet Jr., chief judge of a Louisiana appeals court that divided over the issue this spring. He exchanged tartly conflicting decisions with another judge over whether the new approach was a violation of all they held dear.

Still, some lawyers and judges in Texas, Michigan, Delaware, California, Alaska, and many other states are trying the new, cleaner look in legal documents by putting their citations at the bottom of the page. Legal citations can include references to the date, volume, and page number of legal publications where precedents can be found. Some converts say they are making the switch to democratize the law because the public is put off by strings of numbers that can make legal prose seem even more impenetrable than it is.

"We hear that all the time: 'Your opinions are oatmeal; they're not readable,'" said a Michigan Court of Appeals judge, William C. Whitbeck. "Judges see this as one way to respond."

Most of the judges did not think of the idea themselves. They have an authority to cite on the question: Bryan A. Garner, a silver-penned legal writing special-ist who is, among other things, the editor of *Black's Law Dictionary*, a volume that has ruled the world of legal language since 1891. Mr. Garner, 42, has 12 books in print on language and legal writing. He revels in his role as the persnickety stylist for a linguistically challenged profession. Based in Dallas, he travels the country lecturing to lawyers and judges about how to avoid being "a workaday hack," as he put it to 150 New York lawyers the other day.

Mr. Garner's standing is such that a new book of his on American language was the subject of an occasionally playful critique by the novelist David Foster Wallace in *Harper's* magazine in April. Mr. Wallace suggested that sticklers like Mr. Garner may very likely have been "savagely and repeatedly Wedgied" in their grammatical adolescences. It is a charge Mr. Garner smilingly denies to audiences of chortling lawyers. Mr. Garner was recently named "the E. B. White of legal prose" by a San Francisco legal newspaper, *The Recorder*, and he has wide influence in the legal profession. The power of Mr. Garner's name has lent credibility to the movement for "citational footnotes." But the battle against entrenched tradition would not be possible, he said, were it not for the sheer logic of the idea of denuding legal prose of numbers.

In the legal profession, Mr. Garner said, "we have certain conventions—mind-numbing conventions—that keep us from writing coherently, and one of those is that we have these constant hiccups." Nobody really likes hearing that his writing is full of hiccups like this.* So Mr. Garner has made points.

Christopher W. Madel, a Minneapolis lawyer, changed the citation method he learned in law school after attending a Garner seminar. "You're reading, you're understanding," Mr. Madel said. "Then all of a sudden, there's an obscure 'Deposition, paragraph 48 at 7.' It makes no sense."

Rodney Davis, a California appeals judge in Sacramento, was also persuaded. After hearing Mr. Garner in October, Associate Justice Davis tried taking all the numbers out of the text of his decisions. He was stunned to see his words all by themselves. "Once

William Glaberson

I dropped the citations down to the bottom of the page and looked at what was left, it became apparent that what was left read like legal code," he said. "It would be very difficult to understand what I was saying."

But plenty of judges and lawyers say Mr. Garner is a false prophet. Some say the footnote approach undermines respect for precedent. In a 1999 article in a state bar journal, Mark E. Steiner, an assistant professor at the South Texas College of Law in Houston, warned fellow lawyers that Mr. Garner's ideas about putting citations in footnotes were catching on. Mr. Garner, he wrote, had a "Rasputin-like influence" over Texas judges. Since then, Mr. Steiner said in an interview, his views about Mr. Garner's proposal have grown extreme.

Scott Turow, the best-selling writer and practicing lawyer, said the idea of putting citations in footnotes would only make legal briefs confusing. "By the time your eyes get to the bottom of the page," Mr. Turow said, "you forget whether you're looking for footnote 22 or 23."

In San Francisco, Judge Joanne C. Parrilli, a state appeals judge, agreed. She said she tried the Garner approach, but all the looking up and down at footnotes "produced a certain amount of optical indigestion."

On the Delaware Supreme Court, Justice Joseph T. Walsh is the lone holdout on a bench where the four other justices have been putting their citations in footnotes. Justice Walsh explained his allegiance to the traditional method. Whatever his colleagues in Delaware may be doing, he said, Mr. Garner has yet to win a single convert on the highest court of the land. "If it's good enough for the Supreme Court," Justice Walsh said, "it's good enough for me."

Informed over lunch of Justice Walsh's assertion, Mr. Garner displayed the understated feistiness that makes him a hit on the continuing legal education circuit. "Although I have the highest respect for the justices of the U. S. Supreme Court," he said, "most of their opinions cannot be held up as literary models by any means." The Supreme Court's public information officer, Kathy Arberg, declined to comment.

Mr. Garner's willingness to experiment no matter whose literary feelings are hurt is a characteristic of many of his followers. "I love change," said Judge Billie Colombaro Woodard, the Louisiana judge who irked colleagues by writing opinions in the new style in April.

Chief Judge Doucet, who presides over the 12-judge court that hears appeals from a large area of southern Louisiana, agreed with the ruling Judge Woodard made in a workers' compensation case. But he refused to sign her opinion. He wrote his own, calling the use of footnotes "contrary to this court's officially adopted citation rules." Judge Woodard then filed a response calling Judge Doucet's opinion a "disconcerting" attack on judicial independence.

In an interview, Judge Doucet said a "bunch of judges" had been offended by the citational footnotes because that is not the way writing is done in rulings. Judge Woodard acknowledged that her colleagues' reactions were less than effusive. "I may be tarred and feathered and run out of town," she said. But she added that it was important for judges to experiment with ways of making legal opinions more accessible to ordinary people.

Many lawyers and judges agree that stripping the numbers out of their paragraphs might make them more readable. But it might be wrong to suggest that anything will make people wade through court decisions, said J. Michael Luttig, a judge on the United States Court of Appeals for the Fourth Circuit in Richmond. "It would make it more accessible, but the lay public still won't read legal opinions," Judge Luttig said, sounding a little forlorn. "They're too complex, laborious, and uninteresting to the lay public."

---

* For opinions using the new citational footnotes, see *TXU Elec. Co. v. Public Util. Comm'n of Texas*, 44 Tex. Sup. Ct. J. 854, 2001 WL 618186 Tex. LEXIS 53 (Tex. 2001) (Owen, J., concurring); *Shaw v. State Farm Mut. Auto Ins. Co.*, 19 P.3d 588, 2001 Alas. LEXIS 24 (2001).

ALWD Citation Format

A new citation format, written by the **Association of Legal Writing Directors (ALWD),** is provided in the *ALWD Citation Manual, A Professional System of Citation.* The ALWD is a society for professors who coordinate legal writing instruction in legal education.

One of the attributes of the manual, as set out in the preface, is that it is "a set of rules that reflects a consensus in the legal profession about how citations should function." The ALWD manual includes, in addition to the general citation rules, an appendix containing court citation rules for the individual states.

Universal Citation Format

The *Universal Citation Guide* represents an attempt by the American Association of Law Libraries (AALL), Committee on Citation Formats, to create a set of universal citation rules for American law that are vendor (publisher) neutral and medium (print and electronic) neutral (see Exhibit 20.1).

The various formats of electronic distribution require a system of citation that can be applied consistently to allow researchers to find the referenced authority regardless of the research tool used. Whereas the traditional, paper or book-based, citation uses information based on internal page numbers, the **Universal Citation Format** relies upon the courts to use numbered paragraphs in their opinions. Any publisher of the case law then can preserve the information provided by the court including the citation references to the case and paragraph.

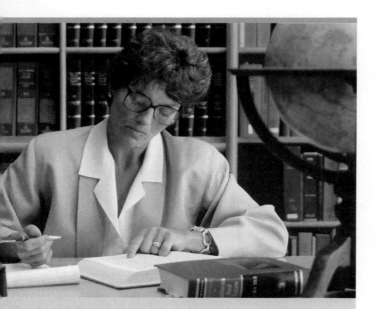

Paralegal preparing memoranda of law in a law library.

Anyone who has read and compared a case in a book with a case online is aware that the page size and the display are different. Unless the online computer display is in a photo-image format, such as Adobe PDF, locating a specific page or reference can be difficult. Librarians and courts are recognizing the need for pinpoint citations for the on-screen user.

The Universal Citation Format represents an attempt to solve this problem. The difficulty with some courts is the requirement that the Universal Citation Format be used only until the hard copy is published, at which time the traditional citation must be used. As a result, you may see the following citation format within documents:

Jones v. Smith, 1999 Pennsylvania Superior 1, ___Pa Super___, ____A2d____(1999)

in which the blank spaces are provided to insert the ultimate volume and page number in the print version when it is available. Exhibit 20.2 lists court name abbreviations.

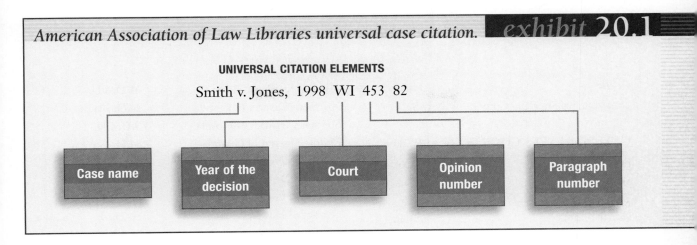

American Association of Law Libraries universal case citation.   *exhibit* 20.1

UNIVERSAL CITATION ELEMENTS

Smith v. Jones, 1998 WI 453 82

| Case name | Year of the decision | Court | Opinion number | Paragraph number |

Other Citation Formats

Many states, including Pennsylvania, have adopted as their official citation format one that originally was created by publishers such as West Publishing Company. These sometimes are referred to as **vendor-specific citation formats.** The West Publishing Company format is based on the West Regional Reporter system and its publications of federal material.

New methods of electronic information technology, in the form of databases, CD-ROMs, and the Internet, have created a number of problems with the traditional citation format. Some of the vendors have claimed copyright protection for their pagination systems.

In 1985, West Publishing Company in a case against Mead Data Central successfully argued that the wholesale use of its *pagination* by a competing online publisher infringed West's copyright interest in the arrangement of cases in its court reports. And in a 1998 case involving Matthew Bender & Company and West Publishing Company, the Second Circuit held that West's pagination was not protected by copyright. Obviously, all claims to a pagination system or citation system that is vendor-specific will result in some action to protect the corporate claim for copyright, trademark, or potential patent for some electronic methodology.

Cite Checking

Cite checking is the process of verifying that the proper citation format has been used in a document. The term also means checking the referenced case or statute to determine that it is valid and that it has not been repealed or overturned. The strictness with which the citation rules must be applied, as well as the method—*Bluebook, ALWD Citation Manual*, or Universal Citation Format—depends on the wishes and demands of the attorney for whom the document is prepared or the court or judge to whom it is submitted. Some courts view the presentation of improper citation format with a jaundiced eye, just as they view improper punctuation, improper spelling, and bad grammar. Others are upset if the citation to the paper references or online legal research service available to them is not used.

exhibit **20.2**   *Federal court name abbreviations.*

Court	Abbrev.
United States Supreme Court	U.S.

UNITED STATES COURTS OF APPEALS

First Circuit	1st Cir.
Second Circuit	2d Cir.
Third Circuit	3d Cir.
Fourth Circuit	4th Cir.
Fifth Circuit	5th Cir.
Sixth Circuit	6th Cir.
Seventh Circuit	7th Cir.
Eighth Circuit	8th Cir.
Ninth Circuit	9th Cir.
Tenth Circuit	10th Cir.
Eleventh Circuit	11th Cir.
D.C. Circuit	D.C. Cir.
Federal Circuit	Fed. Cir.

UNITED STATES DISTRICT COURTS

Middle District of Alabama	M.D. Ala.
Northern District of Alabama	N.D. Ala.
Southern District of Alabama	S.D. Ala.
District of Alaska	D. Alaska
District of Arizona	D. Ariz.
Eastern District of Arkansas	E.D. Ark.
Western District of Arkansas	W.D. Ark.
Central District of California	C.D. Cal.
Eastern District of California	E.D. Cal.
Northern District of California	N.D. Cal.
Southern District of California	S.D. Cal.
District of the Canal Zone	D.C.Z.

(Note: The D.C.Z. ceased to exist on March 31, 1982.)

District of Colorado	D. Colo.
District of Connecticut	D. Conn.
District of Delaware	D. Del.
District of D.C.	D.D.C.

Middle District of Florida	M.D. Fla.
Northern District of Florida	N.D. Fla.
Southern District of Florida	S.D. Fla.
Middle District of Georgia	M.D. Ga.
Northern District of Georgia	N.D. Ga.
Southern District of Georgia	S.D. Ga.
District of Guam	D. Guam
District of Hawaii	D. Haw.
District of Idaho	D. Idaho
Central District of Illinois	C.D. Ill.
Northern District of Illinois	N.D. Ill.
Southern District of Illinois	S.D. Ill.
Northern District of Indiana	N.D. Ind.
Southern District of Indiana	S.D. Ind.
Northern District of Iowa	N.D. Iowa
Southern District of Iowa	S.D. Iowa
District of Kansas	D. Kan.
Eastern District of Kentucky	E.D. Ky.
Western District of Kentucky	W.D. Ky.
Eastern District of Louisiana	E.D. La.
Middle District of Louisiana	M.D. La.
Western District of Louisiana	W.D. La.
District of Maine	D. Me.
District of Maryland	D. Md.
District of Massachusetts	D. Mass.
Eastern District of Michigan	E.D. Mich.
Western District of Michigan	W.D. Mich.
District of Minnesota	D. Minn.
Northern District of Mississippi	N.D. Miss.
Southern District of Mississippi	S.D. Miss.
Eastern District of Missouri	E.D. Mo.
Western District of Missouri	W.D. Mo.
District of Montana	D. Mont.
District of Nebraska	D. Neb.
District of Nevada	D. Nev.
District of New Hampshire	D.N.H.
District of New Jersey	D.N.J.

Federal court name abbreviations, continued.   *exhibit* 20.2

District of New Mexico	**D.N.M.**	Western District of Washington	**W.D. Wash.**
Eastern District of New York	**E.D.N.Y.**	Northern District of West Virginia	**N.D.W. Va.**
Northern District of New York	**N.D.N.Y.**	Southern District of West Virginia	**S.D.W. Va.**
Southern District of New York	**S.D.N.Y.**	Eastern District of Wisconsin	**E.D. Wis.**
Western District of New York	**W.D.N.Y.**	Western District of Wisconsin	**W.D. Wis.**
Eastern District of North Carolina	**E.D.N.C.**	District of Wyoming	**D. Wyo.**
Middle District of North Carolina	**M.D.N.C.**		
Western District of North Carolina	**W.D.N.C.**	**MILITARY COURTS**	
District of North Dakota	**D.N.D.**		
District of the Northern Mariana Islands	**D.N. Mar. I.**	United States Court of Appeals for the Armed Forces	**Armed Forces App.**
Northern District of Ohio	**N.D. Ohio**	United States Court of Veterans Appeals	**Vet. App.**
Southern District of Ohio	**S.D. Ohio**	United States Air Force Court of Criminal Appeals	**A.F. Crim. App.**
Eastern District of Oklahoma	**E.D. Okla.**	United States Army Court of Criminal Appeals	**Army Crim. App.**
Northern District of Oklahoma	**N.D. Okla.**		
Western District of Oklahoma	**W.D. Okla.**	United States Coast Guard Court of Criminal Appeals	**Coast Guard Crim. App.**
District of Oregon	**D. Or.**	United States Navy-Marine Corps Court of Criminal Appeals	**Navy-Marine Crim. App.**
Eastern District of Pennsylvania	**E.D. Pa.**		
Middle District of Pennsylvania	**M.D. Pa.**		
Western District of Pennsylvania	**W.D. Pa.**		
District of Puerto Rico	**D.P.R.**	**BANKRUPTCY COURTS**	
District of Rhode Island	**D.R.I.**	Each United States District Court has a corresponding bankruptcy court. To cite a bankruptcy court, add Bankr. to the district court abbreviation.	
District of South Carolina	**D.S.C.**		
District of South Dakota	**D.S.D.**	*Examples:*	
Eastern District of Tennessee	**E.D. Tenn.**	Bankr. N.D. Ala.	
Middle District of Tennessee	**M.D. Tenn.**	Bankr. D. Mass.	
Western District of Tennessee	**W.D. Tenn.**		
Eastern District of Texas	**E.D. Tex.**		
Northern District of Texas	**N.D. Tex.**	**OTHER FEDERAL COURTS**	
Southern District of Texas	**S.D. Tex.**	Court of Federal Claims	**Fed. Cl.**
Western District of Texas	**W.D. Tex.**	Court of Customs and Patent Appeals	**Cust. & Pat. App.**
District of Utah	**D. Utah**		
District of Vermont	**D. Vt.**	Court of Claims	**Ct. Cl.**
Eastern District of Virginia	**E.D. Va.**	Claims Court	**Cl. Ct.**
Western District of Virginia	**W.D. Va.**	Court of International Trade	**Ct. Intl. Trade**
District of the Virgin Islands	**D.V.I.**	Tax Court	**Tax**
Eastern District of Washington	**E.D. Wash.**		

Reprinted from *ALWD Citation Manual: A Professional System of Citation*, with the permission of Aspen Law and Business.

exhibit **20.3** *Comparison of* Bluebook *and* ALWD Manual *parts.*

BLUEBOOK	ALWD MANUAL
Part 1 General standards of citation and style	Part 1 Introductory material
Part 2 Specific rules for citation to cases, statutes, books, periodicals, foreign materials, international materials, and so forth	Part 2 Citation basics
	Part 3 Citation format for print versions
	Part 4 Citation format for electronic materials
Part 3 Tables to be used in conjunction with the rules, including state and foreign jurisdiction citation formats	Part 5 Incorporating citations into documents
	Part 6 How to quote material
	Part 7 Appendices, including local jurisdictional requirements

Reprinted from *ALWD Citation Manual: A Professional System of Citation,* with the permission of Aspen Law and Business.

Bluebook and ALWD Compared

Which citation format is used depends on the local custom and courts in which the firm or supervising attorney practices (and the wishes of your instructors!). The two forms most commonly used—the *Bluebook* and the *ALWD Manual*—have a number of similarities. Both of these documents are divided into parts and rules, the *Bluebook* into three parts and the *ALWD Manual* into seven parts, as indicated in Exhibit 20.3.

The parts are further divided into rules (see Table 20.1). The *Bluebook* has 20 basic rules, and the *ALWD* 50 rules. Most of the rules have a common pattern, and some are the same, such as *Bluebook* Rule 12–Statutes, and *ALWD* Rule 14 on the method of citing the United State Code: 18 U.S.C. § 1965 (1994). Others are minor variations in presentation, such as *Bluebook* Rule 10.2.2, which provides "Do not abbreviate 'United States'" and *ALWD* Rule 12.2 (g) "United States as party: Cite as U. S. Omit 'America.'"

Sample *Bluebook* citation formats:

Rule 11 Constitutions:	U.S.Const.art.I, § 9, cl.2.
Rule 10 Cases:	United States v Shaffer Equip. Co., 11 F.3d 450 (4th Cir. 1993)
Rule 12 Statutes:	42 U.S. C. § 1983 (1994)

Sample *ALWD* citation formats:

Rule 13 Constitutions:	U.S. Const.art. IV, § 5(b)
Rule 12 Cases:	Brown v. Bd. Of Educ., 349 U.S. 294
	U.S. v. Chairse, 18 F.Supp. 2d 1021 (D. Minn. 1998)
Rule 14 Statutory Codes, Session Laws, SlipLaws:	18 U.S.C. § 1965 (1994)

Comparison of selected ALWD and Bluebook rules.   *table* 20.1

RULE	*ALWD* CITATION	*BLUEBOOK* CITATION	DIFFERENCES
Typeface (Rule 1)	Ordinary type and *italics* (or <u>underlining</u>). No distinctions based on type of document (law review v. court document) or placement of citation within the paper.	Ordinary type, *italics* (or <u>underlining</u>), and small caps. Different fonts required depending on type of document and where source is cited within the paper.	*ALWD* has one set of conventions, not two. *ALWD* eliminates small caps as a typeface.
Spacing (Rule 2)	F. Supp. F.3d	F. Supp. F.3d	No substantial differences.
Capitalization (Rule 3)	*Federal Civil Procedure before Trial*	*Federal Civil Procedure Before Trial*	*ALWD* eliminates the "and prepositions of four or fewer letters" part of the *Bluebook,* which brings legal citation closer to non-legal style.
Ordinal Numbers (Rule 4)	1st, 2d, 3d, 4th	1st, 2d, 3d, 4th	No substantial differences.
Page spans (Rule 5)	125-126 **or** 125-26	125-26	*ALWD* gives a choice on how to present a page span; you may retain all digits or drop repetitive digits and retain two digits on the right hand side of the span, as in *Bluebook* 3.3(d).
Footnotes and endnotes (Rule 7)	n. 7 nn. 12-13	n.7 nn.12-13	*ALWD* requires a space after n. or nn. abbreviation.
Supra and *infra* (Rule 10)	*Supra* n. 45.	*Supra* note 45.	Under *ALWD,* abbreviate note as "n." and place a space after the period.
Id. (Rule 11.3)	*Id.* at 500.	*Id.* at 500.	Basically similar rules. *ALWD* eliminates the "5 *id.* in a row" rule found in *Bluebook* 10.9.
Cases (Rule 12)	*Brown v. Bd. of Educ.,* 349 U.S. 294, 297 (1955). *MBNA Am. Bank, N.A. v. Cardoso,* 707 N.E.2d 189 (Ill. App. 1st Dist. 1998). [required inclusion of district court information]	*Brown v. Board of Educ.,* 349 U.S. 294, 297 (1955). *MBNA Am. Bank, N.A. v. Cardoso,* 707 N.E.2d 189 (Ill. App. Ct. 1st Dist. 1998). [permissive inclusion of district information]	Case names are always italicized. Under *ALWD,* first word of a party's name may be abbreviated. *Bluebook*'s 17th edition will be consistent with this rule. Do not have to abbreviate words in case names. For those who want to abbreviate, Appendix 3 provides a longer list of words. *ALWD* eliminates the "multiple date" rule found in *Bluebook* 10.5. *ALWD* uses S. instead of So. for the regional reporter. *ALWD* requires division and district information for state appellate courts. "Ct." is eliminated from most court abbreviations. *(continued)*

table 20.1   *Comparison of ALWD and Bluebook rules, continued.*

RULE	*ALWD* CITATION	*BLUEBOOK* CITATION	DIFFERENCES
Constitutions (Rule 13)	U.S. Const. amend. V	U.S. Const. amend. V.	No substantial differences.
Statutes (Rule 14)	18 U.S.C. § 1965 (1994).	18 U.S.C. § 1965 (1994).	No substantial differences.
Legislative Materials (Rules 15 and 16)	Sen. Res. 35, 106th Cong. (1999).	S. Res. 35, 106th Cong. (1999).	*ALWD* abbreviates Senate as "Sen." instead of "S." to avoid confusion with other abbreviations. Most forms are relatively consistent.
Court Rules (Rule 17)	Fed. R. Civ. P. 11 (1999).	Fed. R. Civ. P. 11.	*ALWD* requires a date, even for current rules, to help avoid confusion.
Administrative Materials (Rules 19 and 20)	42 C.F.R. § 422.206(a) (1999). 64 Fed. Reg. 12473 (Mar. 12, 1999).	42 C.F.R. § 422.206(a) (1999). 64 Fed. Reg. 12473 (1999).	C.F.R. citation is the same. *ALWD* requires an exact date for Fed. Reg. citations.

Books and Treatises (Rule 22)	Charles Alan Wright, Arthur R. Miller & Mary Kay Kane, *Federal Practice and Procedure* vol. 6A, § 1497, 70-79 (2d ed., West 1990).
	OR
	Charles Alan Wright et al., *Federal Practice and Procedure* vol. 6A, § 1497, 70-79 (2d ed., West 1990).
		6A Charles Alan Wright et al., *Federal Practice and Procedure* § 1497, at 70-79 (2d ed. 1990).	Under *ALWD* you may, but are not required to, use et al. for more than two authors. The *Bluebook*'s 17th edition will be consistent with this rule.
			    ALWD places volume information after the title, just like any other subdivision.
			    ALWD separates subdivisions with a comma, but no "at."
			    ALWD requires that the publisher be included.

Legal Periodicals (Rule 23)	L. Ray Patterson, *Legal Ethics and the Lawyer's Duty of Loyalty,* 29 Emory L.J. 909, 915 (1980).
	    Hope Viner Samborn, *Navigating Murky Waters,* 85 ABA J. 28 (July 1998).
	    Tara Burns Koch, Student Author, *Betting on Brownfields—Does Florida's Brownfields Redevelopment Act Transform Liability into Opportunity?,* 28 Stetson L. Rev. 171 (1998).
		L. Ray Patterson, *Legal Ethics and the Lawyer's Duty of Loyalty,* 29 Emory L.J. 909, 915 (1980).
		    Hope Viner Samborn, *Navigating Murky Waters,* A.B.A. J., July 1998, at 28
		    Tara Burns Koch, Comment, *Betting on Brownfields—Does Florida's Brownfields Redevelopment Act Transform Liability into Opportunity?,* 28 Stetson L. Rev. 171 (1998).
			ALWD eliminates most distinctions between consecutively and nonconsecutively paginated articles; includes longer date for nonconsecutively paginated journals, but does so within the parenthetical.
			    ALWD uses the term "Student Author" to replace Note, Comment, etc.

A.L.R. Annotations (Rule 24)	Marjorie A. Caner, *Validity, Construction, and Application of Stalking Statutes,* 29 A.L.R.5th 487, 489 (1995).	Marjorie A. Caner, Annotation, *Validity, Construction, and Application of Stalking Statutes,* 29 A.L.R.5th 487, 489 (1995).	*ALWD* eliminates the "Annotation" reference.
Legal dictionaries (Rule 25)	*Black's Law Dictionary* 101 (Bryan A. Garner ed., 7th ed., West 1999).	*Black's Law Dictionary* 101 (7th ed. 1999).	*ALWD* treats dictionaries like treatises.
Legal Encyclopedias (Rule 26)	11 C.J.S. *Bonds* § 21 (1995). 76 Am. Jur. 2d *Trusts* §§ 1-4 (1992 & Supp. 1999).	11 C.J.S. *Bonds* § 21 (1995). 76 Am. Jur. 2d *Trusts* §§ 1-4 (1992 & Supp. 1999).	No substantial differences; however, *ALWD* provides expanded coverage and includes a list of many abbreviations for state encyclopedias.

Comparison of ALWD and Bluebook rules, continued.   *table* 20.1

RULE	*ALWD* CITATION	*BLUEBOOK* CITATION	DIFFERENCES
Websites (Rule 40)	Federal Judicial Center, *Federal Judicial Center Publications* <http://www.fjc.gov/pubs.html> (accessed July 10, 1999).	Federal Judicial Center, *Federal Judicial Center Publications* (visited July 10, 1999) <http://www.fjc.gov/pubs.html>.	*ALWD* moved the date to end to be more consistent with other sources. *ALWD* uses "accessed" instead of "visited" to give a more professional tone and be consistent with non-legal citation guides.
Neutral Citation (Rule 43)	*ALWD* indicates that neutral citation may be used (not limited to cases). *ALWD* also indicates that a parallel citation to a print source should also be used. *ALWD* permits use of the citation format used by the state whose case is being cited, the citation used on the source, or the form suggested by the AALL.	The *Bluebook* indicates that a public domain citation for cases should be used when available and allows a parallel citation.	
Signals (Rule 45)	"No signal" is not treated like a signal. No signal is used for direct support and quotations. Signals are *e.g., see, cf., contra, compare . . . with, but see, but cf.,* and *see generally.*	[no signal]: Cited authority (i) identifies the source of a quotation, or (ii) identifies an authority referred to in text. *See:* Cited authority *directly states or clearly supports the proposition.*	*ALWD* returns to long-used definitions. The *Bluebook*'s 17th edition will return to 15th-edition signals. *ALWD* eliminates the *accord* and *see also* signals because they are too close to other signals. Under *ALWD*, all signals may be separated with semicolons. *ALWD* does not have a comma after *e.g.*
Order of Citations (Rule 46)	*ALWD* lists federal and state court cases first by jurisdiction, then in reverse chronological order.	The *Bluebook* lists federal and state court cases in reverse chronological order.	
Quotations (Rule 48)	*ALWD* says to block-indent passages if they contain at least 50 words OR if they exceed four lines of typed text.	The *Bluebook* says to block-indent passages if they contain at least 50 words.	*ALWD* does not require counting the exact number of words in long quotations.

Reprinted from *ALWD Citation Manual: A Professional System of Citation,* with the permission of Aspen Law and Business.

LEGAL TERMINOLOGY

Association of Legal Writing
   Directors (ALWD)
Citation
Cite checking
Critical legal thinking
Duty of candor

Memorandum
Primary authority
Secondary authority
Universal Citation Format
Vendor-specific citation format

Summary

CHAPTER 20 CRITICAL LEGAL THINKING AND WRITING

Critical Legal Thinking

Definition	The process of identifying legal issues, determining the relevant facts, and applying the applicable law to come to a conclusion that answers the legal question the issues present. The paralegal must understand the audience for whom the document is being prepared: the client, the supervising attorney and other members of the legal team, or the court.

Critical Legal Writing

Standards	1. The language used must be clear to the intended reader. 2. The writer must make an honest presentation of the facts and argument. 3. Arguments advocating a new interpretation to the existing law, as well as the current law, must be clearly stated. 4. The ethical obligation to the court must be obeyed, including the presentation of adverse authority in the jurisdiction. 5. Factual variation must be presented, and the sources used clearly identified by proper citation in a format acceptable to the reader.

Court Brief and Office Memorandum Writing Styles

Differences	Both the brief and the memorandum may be on the exact same set of facts, legal issue, and applicable law, but the writing style is totally different. 1. The memorandum is a working document for the legal team to be used in preparation and presentation of a case. 2. The brief written for the court provides written advocacy of the client's position and must be written to convince the court to adopt a position favorable to the client.

(continued)

Duty of Candor	There is an obligation to be honest with the court and not to mislead the court.
Office Memorandum	1. Office memoranda are frequently indexed by subject and filed in the office for future reference; if the same or a similar fact pattern requires research, it is a good starting point and can be a major time-saver. 2. The paralegal must understand the specific assignment. What have you been asked to research? For the memorandum of law, it usually is the answer to a question. 3. The facts relied upon in writing the memo must be a part of the final memorandum; other people who read the memorandum need to understand the specific facts. 4. A memorandum must present both sides of the issue, and in that respect be a neutral, unbiased, objective presentation of applicable laws as they apply to the facts of the case. Issues that the opposing attorney or the judge may raise should be considered and presented. A good analysis includes a discussion of how the fact pattern may differ in cases that are not on point. 5. The written word is a reflection of the writer. Everyone who reads the memorandum will measure the writer's reputation and level of researching skill.

Citations

Purpose	A citation should allow someone else to find the case or other material mentioned in a document, and the form of citation must do this. The format must be generally accepted and used by others in the legal community.
Traditional Sources (Print) Citation Format	Basic paper or traditional citation form: Volume • Book or Series • Page e. g., 232 Atlantic 2d 44 232 refers to the volume in the Atlantic 2d series reporter service of West Publishing Company, and 44 refers to the page on which the authority may be found.
Bluebook Citation Format	*Bluebook* has been the generally accepted authority for proper citation form unless the rules of a particular court dictated a different citation format.
ALWD Manual Citation Format	A citation format authority written by Association of Legal Writing Directors.
Universal Citation Format	Traditional, paper or book-based citation used information based on internal page numbers; Universal Citation Format relies upon the courts to provide numbered paragraphs in their opinions.

(continued)

Cite Checking	Document must be checked to verify that the proper citation format has been used, and that the referenced cases and statutes are valid and the cases have not been repealed or overturned. The strictness with which the citation rules must be applied, as well as the method—*Bluebook, ALWD,* or Universal Citation Format—depends on the wishes and demands of the attorney for whom the document is being prepared, or the court or judge to whom it is submitted.

Working the Web

1. Bookmark for future reference the citation primer based on the 17th edition of the *Bluebook* at the Cornell University LII website, at www.law.cornell.edu/citation.
2. Find and download the comparison between the *Bluebook* rules and the *ALWD* rule at www.alwd.org.
3. Locate and download any updates to the *ALWD* manual from www.alwd.org.
4. Check your local and state courts online for any citation requirements or rules.
5. Take the tour of *Shepard's* at the Lexis website at www.lexis.com.

Questions
CRITICAL LEGAL THINKING AND WRITING

1. Prepare a memo of law based on the following facts, using your state law and ethics rules.

   A client who is traveling in Asia requests a paralegal to immediately forward to him by email a copy of an opinion letter, which was mailed to his home. The opinion letter contains a summary of the facts, including details about opposing parties, strategy, and potential violations of law. Are there any ethical issues? May the paralegal send it as requested?

2. Prepare a memo of law on the question: Is there a continuing duty to advise the court of any changes in the law or facts after the case has been presented? (*Triverton Board of License Commissioners v. Patore,* 469 U.S. 238)

3. How does the general duty to inform the court preserve the integrity of the judicial process? (*Hazel-Atlas Glass Co. v. Hartford-Empire Co.*, 322 U.S. 238)

4. Are sanctions against attorneys for failing to observe a duty of candor to the court an appropriate remedy? [*Beam v. IPCO Corp.*, 838 F.2d 242 (7th Cir. 1998)]

5. What are the relevant facts in the *Palsgraf v. LIRR* case found in Appendix A? What facts are interesting but not relevant facts? Create a search query using the facts in the *Palsgraf* case, and search the case law of your jurisdiction using these relevant facts. Prepare a short brief of the latest case you find, including proper *Bluebook* and *ALWD* citation format.

6. What questions should a paralegal ask before preparing a memo of law or a brief?

7. Why should both sides of a case be presented in an office memo of law?

8. Why would an attorney request that all parallel citations be listed for each case listed in a memo of law?

9. How would knowing the intended audience influence the writing of a memo of law or a legal brief?

10. What level of confidentiality should be attached to the preparation and handling of a memo of law? Why?

ETHICS: ANALYSIS AND DISCUSSION

1. What are the ethical issues in failing to properly cite authorities used in a document?

2. What are the ethical obligations in arguing to the court for a change in the law and not the current law?

3. What are the ethical obligations to the client when analysis of the law indicates there is no valid claim?

Unauthorized Practice of Law—Supervision

There are few certainties in the area of ethics, for paralegals or in any profession. What qualifies as ethical conduct is in most cases based on state law and court interpretation applied to a set of facts. The citation listed below represents one legal opinion and is provided as a research starting point. Do not assume that the same rule applies in your jurisdiction. For the following:

- *Prepare a written statement based on your state law.*
- *Use your state bar association website as a starting point.*

You have been working for a legal specialist in estate law for a number of years and have taken a number of advanced courses in the field. You are highly regarded in the paralegal community as the person to call for help in the field. Your supervising attorney decides to take a three-week bicycle trip through the Swiss Alps and leaves you in charge of the office.

During his absence you give a talk to a local senior citizens group on the advantages of preparing a will. You meet with most of the people in the audience after the talk and tell them a simple will can be prepared for $25 (your office's standard fee) and proceed to take the information from them for a will. You prepare the individual wills and send copies marked DRAFT to each person along with an invoice for the $25 fee with a note to return the fee if they wish to have the will completed. Everyone accepts and sends in the fee.

Upon his return the attorney looks over the wills and tells you they are "letter perfect," and says "It's just what I would have done." [*Cincinnati Bar v. Kathman*, 92 Ohio St. 92 (2001) quoting *People v. Cassidy*, 884 P.2d 309 (Colo. 1994).] What are the legal and ethical issues?

FOR DISCUSSION

United States v. Shaffer Equipt. Co.   11 F.3d 450 (4th Cir. 1993)

Issue: Continuing Duty to Inform Court of Changes in the Law

Government counsel learned that its expert witness had lied about his credentials and that the witness had lied in other litigation. The attorney did not immediately notify the court or opposing counsel. In finding against the government, the court extended the duty of candor to include a continuing duty to inform the court of any development that may conceivably affect the outcome of litigation.

Questions

1. Is preserving the integrity of the judicial process more important than the duty to vigorously pursue a client's case?

2. Is there a duty to inform the court when an attorney suspects that a client may have committed perjury?

3. What additional burden is placed on the paralegal in preparing material for a case in light of this decision?

Read, and if assigned, brief this case. In your brief, answer the following questions.

1. What is the intent of Federal Rules of Civil Procedure Rule 11?

2. What test does the court use to determine if sanctions should be imposed under FRCP Rule 11?

3. What is meant by the "ethical duty of candor"?

4. Is there a conflict between the attorney's ethical obligations under the ABA Model Rules and the requirements of FRCP 11?

5. Do attorneys have any duty to cite cases adverse to their case? Explain.

Schroeder, Circuit Judge.

This is an appeal from the imposition of sanctions under Rule 11 of the Federal Rules of Civil Procedure as amended in 1983. The appellant, a major national law firm, raises significant questions of first impression.

The relevant portions of the amended Rule provide: Every pleading, motion, and other paper of a party represented by an attorney shall be signed by at least one attorney. . . . The signature of an attorney . . . constitutes a certificate by him that he has read the pleading, motion, or other paper; that to the best of his knowledge, information, and belief formed after reasonable inquiry, it is well grounded in fact and is warranted by existing law or a good faith argument for the extension, modification, or reversal of existing law. . . . If a pleading, motion, or other paper is signed in violation of this rule, the court, upon motion or upon its own initiative, shall impose upon the person who signed it, a represented party, or both, an appropriate sanction. . . .

In this appeal, we must decide whether the district court correctly interpreted Rule 11.

. . . Golden Eagle Distributing Corporation filed the underlying action in Minnesota state court for fraud, negligence, and breach of contract against Burroughs, because of an allegedly defective computer system. Burroughs removed the action to the federal district court in Minnesota. Burroughs then moved pursuant to 28 U.S.C. § 1404(a) to transfer the action to the Northern District of California. . . . Burroughs next filed the motion for summary judgment, which gave rise to the sanctions at issue here. It argued that the California, rather than the Minnesota, statute of limitations applied and that all of Golden Eagle's claims were time-barred under California law. It also contended that Golden Eagle's claim for economic loss arising from negligent manufacture lacked merit under California law. Golden Eagle filed a response, arguing that Minnesota law governed the statute of limitations question and that Burroughs had misinterpreted California law regarding economic loss. . . .

After a hearing, the district judge denied Burroughs' motion and directed the Kirkland & Ellis attorney who had been responsible for the summary judgment motion to submit a memorandum explaining why sanctions should not be imposed under Rule 11. . . . Proper understanding of this appeal requires some comprehension of the nature of Burroughs' arguments and the faults which the district court found with them. . . .

Kirkland & Ellis's opening memorandum argued that Golden Eagle's claims were barred by California's three-year statute of limitations. The question was whether the change of venue from Minnesota to California affected which law applied. . . . In imposing sanctions, the district court held that Kirkland & Ellis's argument was "misleading" because it suggested that there already exists a *forum non conveniens* exception to the general rule that the transferor's law applies. . . . [The case cited] raised the issue but did not decide it. . . . Kirkland & Ellis's corollary argument, that a Minnesota court would have dismissed the case on *forum non conveniens* grounds, was found to be "misleading" because it failed to note that one prerequisite to such a dismissal is that an alternative forum be available. . . .

Kirkland & Ellis also argued that Golden Eagle's claim for negligent manufacture lacked merit because Golden Eagle sought damages for economic loss, and such damages are not recoverable under California law [as demonstrated in the *Seely* case]. . . . The district court sanctioned Kirkland & Ellis for not citing three cases whose holdings it concluded were adverse to *Seely*: . . . The district court held that these omissions violated counsel's duty to disclose adverse authority, embodied in Model Rule 3.3, Model Rules of Professional Conduct Rule 3.3 (1983), which the court viewed as a "necessary corollary to Rule 11."

. . . The district court's application of Rule 11 in this case strikes a chord not otherwise heard in discussion of this Rule. The district court did not focus on whether a sound basis in law and in fact existed for the defendant's motion for summary judgment. Indeed it indicated that the motion itself was nonfrivolous. . . . Rather, the district court looked to the manner in which the motion was presented. The district court in this case held that Rule 11 imposes upon counsel an ethical "duty of candor." . . . It said:

The duty of candor is a necessary corollary of the certification required by Rule 11. A court has a right to expect that counsel will state the controlling law fairly and fully; indeed, unless that is done the court cannot perform its task properly. A lawyer must not misstate the law, fail to disclose adverse authority (not disclosed by his opponent), or omit facts critical to the application of the rule of law relied on. . . .

With the district court's salutary admonitions against misstatements of the law, failure to disclose directly adverse authority, or omission of critical facts, we have no quarrel. It is, however, with Rule 11 that we must deal. The district court's interpretation of Rule 11 requires district courts to judge the ethical propriety of lawyers' conduct with respect to every piece of paper filed in federal court. This gives us considerable pause. . . .

The district court's invocation of Rule 11 has two aspects. The first, which we term "argument identification," is the holding that counsel should differentiate between an argument "warranted by existing law" and an argument for the "extension, modification, or reversal of existing law." The second is the conclusion that Rule 11 is violated when counsel fails to cite what the district court views to be directly contrary authority.

. . . The text of the Rule . . . does not require that counsel differentiate between a position which is supported by existing law and one that would extend it. The Rule on its face requires that the motion be either

one or the other. . . . The district court's ruling appears to go even beyond the principle of Rule 3.3 of the ABA Model Rules, which proscribes "knowing" false statements of material fact or law. The district court made no finding of a knowing misstatement, and, given the well-established objective nature of the Rule 11 standard, such a requirement would be inappropriate. Both the earnest advocate exaggerating the state of the current law without knowingly misrepresenting it, and the unscrupulous lawyer knowingly deceiving the court, are within the scope of the district court's interpretation.

This gives rise to serious concerns about the effect of such a rule on advocacy. It is not always easy to decide whether an argument is based on established law or is an argument for the extension of existing law. Whether the case being litigated is . . . materially the same as earlier precedent is frequently the very issue which prompted the litigation in the first place. Such questions can be close.

Sanctions under Rule 11 are mandatory. . . . In even a close case, we think it extremely unlikely that a judge, who has already decided that the law is not as a lawyer argued it, will also decide that the loser's position was warranted by existing law. Attorneys who adopt an aggressive posture risk more than the loss of the motion if the district court decides that their argument is for an extension of the law which it declines to make. What is at stake is often not merely the monetary sanction but the lawyer's reputation.

The "argument identification" requirement adopted by the district court therefore tends to create a conflict between the lawyer's duty zealously to represent his client, Model Code of Professional Responsibility Canon 7, and the lawyer's own interest in avoiding rebuke. The concern on the part of the bar that this type of requirement will chill advocacy is understandable. . . .

. . . Were the scope of the rule to be expanded as the district court suggests, mandatory sanctions would ride on close decisions concerning whether or not one case is or is not the same as another. We think Rule 11 should not impose the risk of sanctions in the event that the court later decides that the lawyer was wrong. The burdens of research and briefing by a diligent lawyer anxious to avoid any possible rebuke would be great. And the burdens would not be merely on the lawyer. If the mandatory provisions of the Rule are to be interpreted literally, the court would have a duty to research authority beyond that provided by the parties to make sure that they have not omitted something.

The burden is illustrated in this case, where the district court based its imposition of sanctions in part upon Kirkland & Ellis's failure to cite authorities which the court concluded were directly adverse to a case it did cite. The district court charged the appellant with constructive notice of these authorities because they were identified in Shepard's as "distinguishing" the case Kirkland & Ellis relied on.

. . . Amended Rule 11 of the Federal Rules of Civil Procedure does not impose upon the district courts the burden of evaluating under ethical standards the accuracy of all lawyers' arguments. Rather, Rule 11 is intended to reduce the burden on district courts by sanctioning, and hence deterring, attorneys who submit motions or pleadings which cannot reasonably be supported in law or in fact. We therefore reverse the district court's imposition of sanctions for conduct which it felt fell short of the ethical responsibilities of the attorney. Reversed.

CHAPTER 21

CHAPTER OBJECTIVES

After studying this chapter, you should be able to:

1. Give an overall view of how a paralegal can use the computer and the Internet.

2. Explain in general how the Internet works.

3. Describe the function of Internet browsers and LAN browsers.

4. Explain what a URL is and its use in searching the Web.

5. Describe the types of image formats available on the Web.

6. Explain how to find and download documents and forms.

7. Give the steps in sending documents as attachments to email.

8. Explain how the computer can be used to file documents with the court.

9. Discuss computer viruses and how to prevent damage from them.

10. Broach some ethical issues for paralegals in the use of the Web.

The Internet, the Computer, and the Paralegal

Laws too gentle are seldom obeyed; too severe, seldom executed.

BENJAMIN FRANKLIN, *POOR RICHARD'S ALMANACK* (1756)

Introduction

Use of the computer in the law office has been increasing, not just in its traditional use for document preparation but also for maintaining databases, keeping accounting records, and engaging in electronic communications. Computers also are being used increasingly to share information in digital form between remote offices, courthouses, government agencies, and clients. Computer files are easily shared today in the form of CDs, floppy disks, and tape cartridges, and by dial-up or Internet connection and as attachments to emails. In the past, paper had to be copied and sent, frequently by messenger or express mail service. Today large files can be quickly exchanged electronically almost instantly to any point in the world, without any paper (hard copy). Where there are concerns about the safety of the contents of regular mail, electronic transfer of information avoids this danger.

The paralegal is the member of the legal team who is most likely to spend time in the office using the Web and the Internet for more than just pure legal research. Access to most government information is obtained online through Internet websites. Private service providers, such as the yellow pages and white pages for finding businesses and individuals, is handled most efficiently through Web search engines. This involvement puts the paralegal in potentially the best position to have meaningful input to development of the firm's website, as seeing and using many websites gives one a sense of the best and the worst features of a website. With the increasing development and use of legal firm websites, only the best retain clients and attract new clients.

THE INTERNET

In its most basic form, the Internet or the World Wide Web may be thought of as nothing more than a group of computers linked together with the added ability to search all the connections for information. If you work in an office that has all of its computers networked together, you have a small version of the Internet. Each person's computer is connected to other people's computers, generally with a main computer on which resides the frequently shared data files and the software (network operating system) that controls the connections and how the requests from each computer are handled and directed. This main control computer usually is referred to as the **file server** (see Exhibit 21.1).

The local area, or office, network (**LAN**) search tool is usually a program such as Microsoft Windows Explorer—not to be confused with the Internet browser Internet Explorer—which permits files to be found on the local computer or the other computers with shared access, by location or other characteristics. Exhibit 21.2 shows the Explorer screen, and Exhibit 21.3 shows the Find screen.

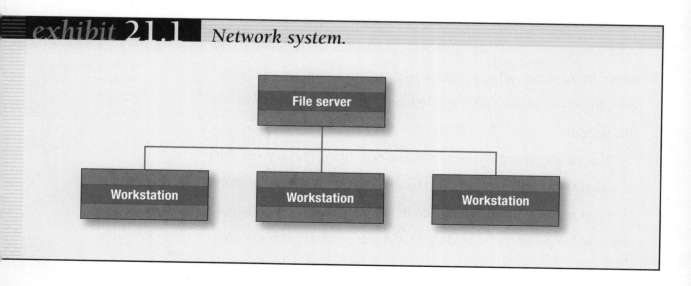

exhibit **21.1** *Network system.*

Through its website the Library of Congress provides a series of Country Studies information. The information contained in Country Studies Online is not copyrighted and therefore is available for free, unrestricted use by researchers.

www Library of Congress: www.loc.gov

If you think of your office network as being connected to other similar office networks, and all these other offices together with many other companies and government agencies around the world on some connecting line (a backbone), you have the World Wide Web. The connection is by some form of telephone line or wireless connection using radio signals. The connection is usually to an **Internet service provider (ISP)**. There are literally thousands of these ISP companies, from very small to international in scope,

Explorer screen. *exhibit 21.2*

exhibit **21.3**   *Find screen.*

Find: All Files

File   Edit   View   Options   Help

| Name & Location | Date | Advanced |

Named:

Containing text: Paralegal

Look in: Disk1part01 (C:)

☑ Include subfolders   Browse...

Find Now

Stop

New Search

such as AOL and CompuServe. ISPs provide local or toll-free access numbers that most people use to connect to their service. Larger offices and companies may have a direct connection (hard-wired or by dedicated telephone line) that eliminates the need to dial up the ISP. A device called a **modem** is used to translate the electrical signals for transmission over these connections so the computers can "talk" to each other. The modem converts (modulates) the information from the keyboard and computer into a form that can be transferred electronically over telephone lines, cable connections, and radio waves.

| MO | DEM |
| Modulate | Demodulate |

At the receiving end of the signal is another modem that reconverts (demodulates) the signal into a form usable by the computer. Depending on the modem and the ISP service, speeds of transmission vary widely. The slower the connection provided by the modem and the service, the longer it takes to transmit and receive information. As with most services, the greater the speed, the higher is the cost. It is easy to see that a multipage document will take longer to transmit or receive than a single-page document. The reasonableness of the cost of a high-speed connection depends upon the volume of pages regularly sent or received.

Perhaps less obvious is the size of the files and those that are in graphic format. Most government forms are available in a graphic form rather than a text form. A single one-page form in graphic format may be the equivalent of a 10-page text document. Again depending upon the frequency of downloads of forms, it might be advisable to upgrade to a high-speed line.

ONLINE COMPUTER RESOURCES

Online resources include Internet browsers and search engines.

Internet Browsers

An Internet or **Web browser** is a software program that allows a person to use a computer to access the Internet. Unless you have a direct connection to a computer database, you will be working with a software program known as a Web browser. The two most popular Web browsers are Microsoft Internet Explorer and Netscape, both of which provide content. These browsers typically are used with Internet service providers that do not themselves provide any content but, rather, act as an intermediary between the user and the World Wide Web. Some services, such as America OnLine (AOL) and CompuServe, provide content, such as news and weather and specialty sections for sharing information, along with providing the traditional Internet connections and email.

All of the browsers basically provide two main screens—one to display email (see Exhibit 21.4) and one to display content and Internet search results (see Exhibit 21.5).

AOL: www.aol.com

CompuServe: www.compuserve.com

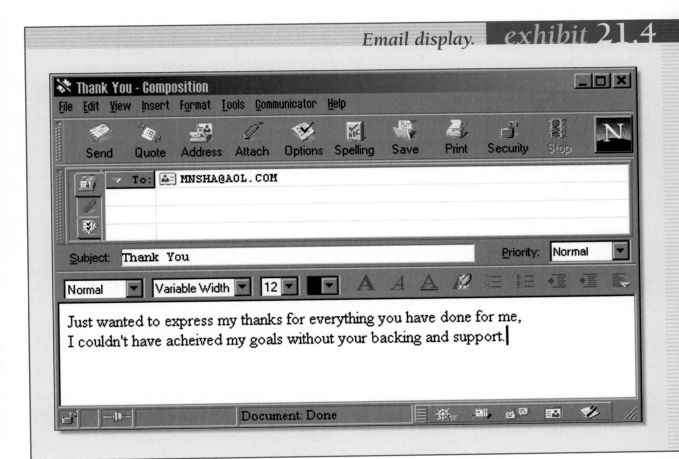

Email display.   *exhibit 21.4*

exhibit 21.5   *Netscape window.*

Search Engines

An **Internet search engine** is a program designed to take a word or set of words and search websites on the Internet. Of the available Internet search engines, each searches in a different fashion. The same search request may generate totally different results on different search engines. The number of search engines is expanding constantly. Some search engines are more suitable than others for legal searches. Many search engines are designed for use by children and families, so they may not return the results needed in the professional areas.

It is useful to create a search query and run the query through a number of different search engines, then compare the results. For example, you may wish to search the topic "regulation of paralegals." Each of the search engines shown below may be accessed by entering its **URL** (uniform resource locator) in your Web browser:

AltaVista	www.altavista.com
Ask Jeeves	www.askjeeves.com

Dogpile	www.dogpile.com
Excite	www.excite.com
Google	www.google.com
MetaCrawler	www.metacrawler.com
Netscape	www.netscape.com
Yahoo!	www.yahoo.com

Some of the information is shown on the screen and will not require any more searching. The data—such as a phone number, address, or other limited information—will appear and may be copied manually or printed out to capture the displayed page. Other information may be in the form of large text or graphic files. These may be many pages long or involve use of graphic display programs such as the popular Adobe series. Typical of the graphic images are the tax forms available from the Internal Revenue Service.

Addresses and Locations

Obviously, finding something requires knowing where it resides. We find people by looking for their home or business address or by their telephone number. The modern equivalent of a telephone number is the email address. Web pages also have addresses, known as uniform resource locators, or URLs.

The URL is made up of three parts:

Protocol :// Computer / Path

The **protocol** is usually http (hypertext transfer protocol). The computer is the Internet computer name, such as www.bucks.edu. And the path is the directory or subdirectory on the computer where the information can be found.

The URL may be thought of as a file cabinet, in which the protocol is the name of the file cabinet, the computer is the drawer in the file cabinet, and the path is the file folder in the drawer. Not all URLs have a path as part of the address.

Part of the naming protocol is a domain nomenclature, with extensions such as the "edu" in www.bucks.edu. Common extensions are:

.org	organizations
.edu	educational institutions
.com	commercial operations
.gov	government agencies
.bus	business
.mil	military

In addition, there are extensions such as

.jp	Japan
.fr	France
.uk	United Kingdom

These designations refer to the country where the computer is located.

Internal Revenue Service:
www.irs.gov

Checklist

	WEBSITE PROFILE
○ Address (URL):	
○ Name of organization or site:	
○ Key subject:	
○ Secondary subject:	
○ Cost:	
○ Comments:	

Potentially one of the biggest time-savers for the paralegal is the ready availability of information, forms, and files on the Internet or World Wide Web. Public information that would have required a trip to the courthouse or other government office is instantly available without leaving the office. This information may come from public or private sources. Government information typically is available without cost or at minimum cost. Private information may be free to all, such as that found on the IBM patent website, or at a cost per use, per page, or per time period (such as a month).

FORMATS OF AVAILABLE INFORMATION

Most of the items that are displayed can be printed to a printer attached to a computer. At the top of most Web browsers is a printer icon or a Print command in the FILE icon at the top of the page. Clicking on the icon or word PRINT in the FILE pull-down menu will initiate the print process. Patience may be necessary, as this may require the computer to access the original source of the information; clicking several times will not speed up the process and actually may result in several copies being printed.

File Attachments

A popular method for transmitting text files and graphic images is by *attachment* of the file to an email. This is much easier than it sounds. Today almost everyone has an email address, whether at home or at work or both. To send or receive email requires the use of an Internet service provider and a browser such as Internet Explorer, Netscape Communicator, or one of the other specialty email programs. In the traditional email, text is entered by the keyboard, transmitted to the email account of a recipient, and read online.

Virtually any file can be attached (linked) and sent with an email. The receiver needs only to click the mouse on the attachment, which may appear as an icon. In most cases the file will open using the same program from which it was created, such as Microsoft Word or Corel WordPerfect. Occasionally a file may be transmitted in a format that the receiver does not have the software to open. This is particularly true with regard to graphic images, pictures, and drawings.

Receiving and Downloading Files and Attachments

The method for downloading files and attachments is the same. You should first determine the directory (folder) into which you will be downloading these files. In Windows this is usually a folder called My Download Files or My Files. If there is no existing folder, you can use your Windows Explorer to create a file with a name such as Download. Windows Explorer is a program in your Start Directory under Programs. This is not the same as Windows Internet Explorer, which is an Internet browser.

Most of the files attached as part of email will be document files created and saved as either Microsoft Word documents or WordPerfect documents. You may want to save these files directly into your Word or WordPerfect directory. Saving them in your computer download is one option, as is opening the file on the screen immediately instead of saving it for later use.

Normally, text files and graphic images are static files; that is, by themselves they do not perform any function but are merely data usable within another program such as a word processor or graphic image viewer. It has become common, however, to send as attachments files that have within them miniprograms such as macros that perform functions when activated, such as those used to calculate sums in spreadsheets. Others are self-contained software programs such as screensavers containing animation and animated cartoons.

Most of these program files will have an extension of either .exe or .zip. Files with the .exe extension can be run immediately after downloading and saving. Files with the .zip extension are in a compressed form. Very large files, such as spreadsheets, photographs, diagrams, and some program files can take a long time to transmit over the Internet. This ties up the line, may increase the cost if the service is on a charge-per-minute basis, and can result in bad transmission if the line accidentally disconnects or suffers from electrical interference.

To minimize these problems, and out of courtesy, large files are run through a program that will compress them. After the compressed file is downloaded, it has to be decompressed. A number of programs are available to decompress files. Some of these require multiple steps to open the files, and others perform the task automatically. For occasional use, the manual method is acceptable, but, with the increase in the number of compressed files, it may be more time-efficient to purchase one of the automatic programs.

Sample Dial-up PACER District Court Docket Information

PUBLIC ACCESS TO COURT ELECTRONIC RECORDS
Docket Report Output Menu
Docket for case 3:99cv00001 consists of 2 pages.
Case was last updated on: 05/10/19 . Report was generated on: 5/11/99.

OPTIONS
    View report
    view Recent entries (last twenty lines of report)
    view First twenty lines of report
    view Both first and last twenty lines
    List report non-stop
    Download directly to disk file
    Mark for later download to disk file
    Escape to select another (previous screen)
    Exit to Main Menu
    Enter your choice (v/r/f/b/l/d/m/Esc/e):
    Ready to display docket information non-stop.

To halt during a very long docket report, press ESCape one time. This escape may take several seconds to catch and stop the listing. Press ESCape to return to previous menu, any other key to continue.
[CAPTURE POINT]

X————————————————————————————————X

PACER session date: Tuesday May 25, 1999 02:32:15 PM PDT
Case docket was last updated on: 05/10/1999.

Docket as of May 11, 1999 0:21 am   Page 1
Proceedings include all events.   TERMED
3:99cv1 Peterson v. Bowden   IFP
                                                     2241
                                                     TERMED IFP
                                                     2241

U.S. District Court
U.S. District Court for the District of State (Division)
CIVIL DOCKET FOR CASE #: 99-CV-1
Peterson v. Bowden   Filed: 01/04/99
Assigned to: Judge Dennis S. Houston
Demand: $0,000   Nature of Suit: 540

Sample Dial-up PACER District Court Docket, continued

Lead Docket: None

Dkt# in other court: None

Cause: 28:2241 Petition for Writ of Habeas Corpus

ROBIN LEE PETERSON

Petitioner

Jurisdiction: US Defendant

Robin Lee Peterson

FRN #62554123

[COR LD NTC] [PRO SE]

FCI-SHERIDAN

FDC J-2

PO Box 4500

Anytown, US 12345

v.

J BOWDEN, Warden FCI

Anytown

Respondent

Docket as of May 11, 1999 0:21 am

Proceedings include all events.

3:99cv1 Peterson v. Bowden

Page 2

TERMED

IFP

2241

1/4/99	1	APPLICATION TO PROCEED IN FORMA PAUPERIS by Petitioner Robin Lee Peterson Pursuant to LR3.6(b), Petitioner's application to proceed in forma pauperis is conditionally granted subject to further review and order of the court. Petitioner's complaint may be filed without prepayment of fees and costs or security therefor. (peg)
1/4/99	2	PETITION FOR WRIT OF HABEAS CORPUS PURSUANT TO 28 USC: 2241 (peg)
3/19/99	3	ORDER DENYING APPLICATION TO PROCEED IN FORMA PAUPERIS by Judge Dennis S. Houston DENYING MOTION [1-1]; Plaintiff given 30 days to file amended application; Amended application Deadline set for 4/19/99; Signed 3/18/99 (counsel notified) (wri) [Entry date 03/22/99]
4/13/99	4	AMENDED APPLICATION TO PROCEED IN FORMA PAUPERIS by Petitioner Robin Lee Peterson (ecp)
5/6/99	5	MOTION by Petitioner Robin Lee Peterson FOR VOLUNTARY WITHDRAW PETITION (ecp) [Edit date 05/06/99]
5/10/99	6	ORDER by Honorable Gary L. Silas: GRANTING Plaintiff's MOTION FOR VOLUNTARY WITHDRAW OF PETITION [5-1]; This action is DISMISSED without prejudice; Signed 5/10/99 (counsel notified) (ecp)
5/10/99	7	JUDGMENT: IT IS ORDERED AND ADJUDGED that this action is dismissed without prejudice; Signed 5/10/99; microfilmed; Honorable Gary L. Silas (counsel notified) (ecp)

[END OF DOCKET: 3:99cv1]

X————————————————————————————————X

Press any key to continue.

TYPES OF IMAGE FORMATS

PACER:
www.pacer.psc.uscourts.gov/

With increasing frequency, the Internet is being used to obtain needed forms. These may be government agency forms, tax forms, or court forms. Even the best-equipped office will require one form or another that is not in the office supply room for completing a case. This may be an unusual federal tax form or a form from your state or another state.

The most popular format for the federal government forms is PDF form, and many state agencies also use the PDF format for document delivery. Other options may be presented for selection. Knowing which option will work on your computer and with your printer will save time.

PDF

Adobe Systems:
www.adobe.com

Portable Document Format (PDF) is one of the most popular file formats. Most of the forms available for downloading are in this format. To retrieve these files, your computer must have a program called Adobe Acrobat Reader. Acrobat Reader is readily available as a free download from Adobe Systems Inc. If it is not on your computer, you will receive an onscreen message alerting you and giving you instructions to obtain this program. After you have downloaded it, the file will open automatically on your computer screen and be available either for download or printing. Acrobat Reader is updated regularly.

PCL

Printer Control Language (PCL) is the computer language used with Hewlett Packard and compatible HP printers. It is not widely used because of the size of the files and the general need to un-compress them before use. The required reader for this format is available from Page Technology Marketing, Inc.

PS

Postscript Language Format (PS) is a programming language that contains all of the page characteristics that tell the printer that has this programming language how to print the document. This format requires large files that usually must be un-compressed before use.

SGML

Standard Generalized Markup Language (SGML) is a federal and international standard that requires a commercially available software program to view and print.

Ohio Rule on Commercial Law-Related Websites

Ohio lawyers may not participate in a commercial law-related website that provides them with clients if the arrangement entails prohibited payment for referrals or if the business is engaged in the unauthorized practice of law. (Ohio Supreme Court Board of Commissioners on Grievances and Discipline opinion 2001–2)

COMPUTER VIRUSES

Unfortunately, some computer-knowledgeable people take sadistic pleasure in developing and disseminating programs that attack and destroy computer programs, internal computer-operating systems, and occasionally even the hard disk drives of computers. These programs are known as *computer viruses*. Viruses range from those that create minor inconvenience to those that can destroy data and cause computer shutdowns.

Some simple precautions can prevent disaster. A virus-protection program, such as those sold by Norton, McAfee, and others, is as important to have on your computer as the computer operating system itself. This should be the first program loaded on a new computer.

Anti-virus programs scan the computer to identify the presence of viruses, and the better programs eliminate the virus. Every disk should be scanned with a virus program before being used. Files that are downloaded from other computers or over the Internet also should be checked. As good as these programs are, they quickly go out of date as new viruses are created and unleashed. Therefore, these virus checking programs should be updated regularly.

PERSPECTIVE

Interception of Electronic Communications

Interception or monitoring of email communications for purposes other than assuring quality of service or maintenance is illegal under the Electronic Communications Privacy Act of 1986, as amended in 1994. [18 U. S. C. ß2511(2)(a)(i)]

ELECTRONIC FILING

A number of courts have established procedures for the electronic filing of pleadings. Each court is free to set up its own rules and procedures and must be consulted before attempting to use this service. The Internal Revenue Service and some states have combined in a joint effort to allow electronic filing of both the federal and state individual income tax returns in one step. The local or state tax authority retrieves the information from the Internal Revenue Service. A feature of this service, known as IRS e-file, is the return receipt when the federal and state governments receive the form.

Checklist

TO RETRIEVE AND DOWNLOAD A FORM

○ Select a file format.

○ Select the file(s) you wish to receive. To select multiple items, hold the Control button down while selecting.

○ Click the Review Selected Files button. A Results page will be displayed with links to the file(s) you requested.

○ Select the file title to retrieve.

Be a Legal Eagle Techie

First Things First

Law office technology is an expanding field with lots of varied opportunities. If you're interested in computers, computer networks, software, computer support, and the like, it's a specialty arena you may want to consider. Likewise, if you are currently a legal secretary or paralegal, you may be interested in learning more about technology and specializing in law office automation.

One of the simplest ways to get into this specialty arena is to become network- or hardware-certified in a high-demand skill and go to work for an existing network installation and maintenance company that specializes in law firms. This work and knowledge base isn't too much different than doing the same sort of technical job within most any industry or business office setting.

There's much broader opportunity, however, in software (application development, installation, configuration, or *training*) and/or in law office automation consulting. Additionally, you could work on-staff for a law firm (or the court system) as a technical support person, software trainer, programmer, etc.

But if you plan to pursue software, training, or a tech-support role within the legal field, it will be vital to learn a bit about law office applications first. LegalTech (law office automation tradeshow) is a pretty good place to do that. It's a huge show with hundreds of displays and demonstrations.

Like all companies, law offices use email, word-processing, and spreadsheets, of course. They also use databases, although often in a different way than does the business world (so there are a wide variety of specialty database applications, and tools for law offices). In fact, the difference in the way law offices use databases is a good starting point for demonstrating the unique slant to law office technology.

What's So Special About Legal Technology?

Word processing (Word or WordPerfect, usually) is the core automation product of a law office because the product in a law office is documents—and the knowledge or research contained within those documents. Huge numbers of documents quickly pile up and can become hard to find and track. Therefore, many law offices use document-management software.

Because many documents produced in a law office contain research or legal opinion, these documents can themselves become a valuable source of research to the firm. (If a similar problem or case should arise in the near future, it may not be necessary to repeat all the research, providing the previous documents can be found.) Enter full-text indexing of documents in the computer to allow phrase and keyword searching, enabling the use of previous documents as research sources (often referred to as a "Brief Bank").

Taking all this a step further, many legal documents have repetitive portions of text that must be included with custom portions (like wills, trusts, real estate contracts, for instance). Utilizing the appropriate software, one can enter the repetitive portions only once, store them, and speed the construction of each similar document into the future.

Plus, there is always much original research and fact-searching to be done. One traditional source for this, of course, is books. But books use up a lot of room and cost quite a good deal. They can also be slower to investigate than some of the newer tools—publications on CD, or Internet research. Once again, however, it's text that is being searched, analyzed, manipulated, and excerpted. And, as always, time is of the essence. To help out, there are big, specialized legal research databases (pay-per-view) such as Lexis. And now there are some software tools cropping up to ease Net legal research on the Web's free areas.

Because so much of what a law firm does relies on documents and text or phrases within those documents, even databases in a law firm are often "full-text indexed and searchable." This is particularly necessary in the area of litigation. Usually there will be many, many (into the hundreds or thousands even) of documents to sort through and categorize for court proceedings. And there will be depositions to take from key personnel, trial transcripts to organize, etc. All this information is text and must somehow be categorized so that it's easy to find—by various word or phrase searches.

Donna Fell

Where Do I Learn All This?

"OK," you say, "Sounds good. Where do I find training in law office automation?" Well, that can be tough. Legal technology has only begun, in recent years, to define itself as a complex niche specialty. Undoubtedly, there will someday be specific educational programs for this tech specialty, but there are few comprehensive curriculums now. Certainly, some automation training is included in legal secretarial, legal assistant, and paralegal courses, but on its own it is often not enough if you want to be an information systems professional with a law firm or a consulting company that specializes in law firm technology.

At the moment, you can garner information from several sources, the American Bar Association being one of them, and your state or city's local Bar being another. There are also legal news specific sites and newsgroups that may prove interesting and helpful.

As for formal education toward pursuing a career in law office automation (or court system automation, another area in this niche), I think the best way to proceed at this point is to first get strong, general, information technology training in either hardware or software. Once you have that under your belt, you could attend legal technology training classes offered by law firm technology consultants. And/or you could pursue a paralegal certification, to learn about the law itself. Alternatively, you could get a technical job in a law firm and learn the specialty niche as you go.

My route into law office automation combined these things. I'd been involved with technology, technology training, and tech management for a number of years in both the business and education communities. At one point I was technology manager for a professional services company (consulting) that, like law firms, sold services for an hourly rate. Once in the legal tech arena, however, I noted the significant differences between the ways business uses technology and law offices use technology. In an effort to better acquaint myself with the requirements of law office automation, I pursued a paralegal course of study that included law office automation training, in my own time. That helped immensely to indoctrinate my thinking and orientation into the legal technology specialty.

Whichever route you choose, though, the important thing is to learn the key procedures and processes of a law office and then learn about software that has been developed to address these functions. You'll find there is some difference in need from firm to firm, depending upon the firm's practice specialty areas. If a small firm environment is your aim, you might want to decide whether you would like to focus on "business"-oriented legal technology (i.e., trusts and estates, real estate dealings, etc.), or if you are more interested in pursuing a "litigation"-oriented legal technology specialty (personal injury, trial law of various types). In larger firms, there are often several departments focusing on various practice areas and offering great diversity for the law office automation expert.

Here are a couple of books that can help:

Fundamentals of Law Office Management
By: Pamela Everett
From Delmar Publishers, 1/2000

This book familiarizes the reader with the procedures, systems, and ethics that make the law office different from other industries.

Using Computers in the Law Office
By: Brent Roper
From Thomson Learning, 12/1999

Book and CD-ROM package that educates the reader about computer applications within legal organizations.

Once you have learned a bit about these basics, if you look hard for the right position, you'll discover that considerable opportunity awaits. Remember, law offices, big and small, are everywhere. As a result, legal technology is a high-demand, very portable, specialty focus.

From the late 1980s through the mid 1990s, Diana Fell was Head of Technology for a large USA law firm with several offices nationwide.

CONTEMPORARY PERSPECTIVE CONTEMPORARY PERSPECTIVE

Software companies in the United States led the development of encryption technology. For years, the U. S. government permitted American software companies to sell its encryption software domestically but prohibited export of the most powerful encryption technology to foreigners. The U. S. government worried that powerful encryption and data-scrambling technology would fall into the hands of criminals and terrorists who would use it to protect their illegal and clandestine activities.

Based on this fear, President Bill Clinton issued an executive order prohibiting the export of much of the most powerful encryption technology developed in the United States. These export restrictions remained in effect during most of the 1990s. In September 1999, after much lobbying by software companies located in the United States, the Administration changed its export policy to allow the export of the most powerful American-made encryption technology.

The export rule was changed because criminals and terrorists could obtain similar data-scrambling technology from software producers in other countries. Therefore, the American policy prohibiting the export of encryption technology to foreigners was no longer effective. The Clinton Administration's export controls on encryption technology were lifted for all countries except Iran, Iraq, Syria, Sudan, North Korea, and Cuba—countries with a history of terrorist activities.

WWW Database

Create a computerized database, using Microsoft Excel™ or a similar database program, with a template of useful websites, by name, URL, and topic. You will then be able to sort it by any of the database items and print it in hardcopy.

ENCRYPTION TECHNOLOGY

Encryption technology permits a computer user to basically put a lock around its computer information to protect it from being discovered by others. Encryption technology is like a lock on a house. Without the lock in place, unwanted persons can easily enter the house and steal its contents; with the lock in place, it is more difficult to enter and take the house's contents. Encryption software serves a similar function in that it lets computer users scramble information so only those who have the encryption code can enter the database and discover the information.

LEGAL TERMINOLOGY

File server

Internet search engine

Internet service provider (ISP)

LAN

Modem

Protocol

Uniform resource locator (URL)

Web browser

Summary

CHAPTER 21 THE INTERNET, THE COMPUTER, AND THE PARALEGAL

The Internet

What Is It?	The Internet or the World Wide Web is a group of computers linked together with the added ability to search all the connections for information.

Online Computer Resources

Internet Browsers	An Internet or Web browser is a software program that allows a person to use a computer to access the Internet. The two most popular Web browsers are Microsoft Internet Explorer and Netscape.
Search Engines	An Internet search engine is a program designed to take a word or set of words and locate websites on the Internet.
Addresses and Locations	The modern equivalent of a person's telephone number is the email address. Pages on the Internet also have addresses known as the Uniform Resource Locator (URL). The URL is made up of three parts: protocol, computer, and path.

Formats of Available Information

File Attachments	A popular method for transmitting text files, and occasionally graphic images, is to attach the file to an email.
Receiving and Downloading Files and Attachments	The method for downloading files and attachments is the same. They are downloaded into a directory (a folder), which in Windows, usually is called My Download Files or My Files. If there is no existing folder, Windows Explorer can be used to create a file with a name such as Download.

Types of Image Formats

Portable Document Format (PDF)	One of the most popular file formats; must have Acrobat Reader program to view documents.
Printer Control Language (PCL)	Computer language used with Hewlett Packard and compatible HP printers.
Postscript Language Format (PS)	A programming language that contains all of the page characteristics that tell printers that have this programming language how to print out the document.
Standard Generalized Markup Language (SGML)	A federal and international standard that requires a commercially available software program to view and print.

(continued)

Computer Viruses	
Definition	Programs that attack and destroy computer programs, internal computer operating systems, and occasionally the hard disk drives of computers.
Precautions	Virus-protection programs such as Norton or McAfee; should be updated regularly.

Electronic Filing of Pleadings	
Courts	Many courts have established procedures for the electronic filing of pleadings. Each court is free to set up its own rules and procedures and must be consulted before attempting to use this service.
IRS	The Internal Revenue Service and some states have combined in a joint effort to allow the filing of both the federal and state individual income tax returns.

Encryption	
Definition	Technology that allows computer user to put a "lock" around information to prevent discovery by others.

Working the Web

1. Download the latest 1040 tax form and instructions from the Internal Revenue Service website at www.irs.gov.
2. Check the information available on the Library of Congress website at www.loc.gov.
3. Use the Government Printing Office website to access other government agencies and resources at www.gpo.gov/.
4. Access the Code of Federal Regulations online at www.access.gpo.gov/nara/cfr/index.html.
5. Use one of the search engines listed below to find information on your school or local government:
   a. AltaVista: www.altavista.com
   b. Ask Jeeves: www.askjeeves.com
   c. Dogpile: www.dogpile.com
   d. Excite: www.excite.com
   e. Google: www.google.com
   f. MetaCrawler: www.metacrawler.com
   g. Netscape: www.netscape.com
   h. Yahoo!: www.yahoo.com

Questions
CRITICAL LEGAL THINKING AND WRITING

1. What is a computer virus, and what should a paralegal do to protect the firm against computer viruses?
2. How reliable are forms and documents obtained over the Internet?
3. What copyright issues must a paralegal consider in using the Internet in preparing written documents and reports?
4. How can the computer and the Internet increase a paralegal's productivity?
5. What are the limitations of using a website to attract new clients in your state?
6. Do cross-jurisdictional boundary websites present any problems for the law firm in using the Internet?
7. Would an email intended for a client but accidentally sent to an opposing attorney be usable by the opposing attorney? Is this an interception of email under federal law?
8. Can information heard or monitored over a baby monitor be used in trial or in the prosecution of a civil case? Why or why not?
9. What advantages does knowing how to use the Internet provide the paralegal in the law office?
10. Should encryption software be used regularly in transmitting files electronically? Why?

Questions
ETHICS: ANALYSIS AND DISCUSSION

1. What are the ethical issues related to a law firm website that is available around the world when the firm is licensed to practice only in one jurisdiction?
2. Explain the ethical implication of the following: "In today's society, with the advent of the information superhighway, federal and state legislation and regulations, as well as information regarding industry trends, are easily accessed."
3. What are the ethical issues of erroneously sending or receiving by email or fax a confidential trial strategy memorandum?

Confidentiality

There are few certainties in the area of ethics, for paralegals or in any profession. What qualifies as ethical conduct is in most cases based on state law and court interpretation applied to a set of facts. The citation listed below represents one legal opinion and is provided as a research starting point. Do not assume that the same rule applies in your jurisdiction. For the following:

- *Prepare a written statement based on your state law.*
- *Use your state bar association website as a starting point.*

You are working in a sophisticated law firm that has the latest computers and software. You have not been trained in the use of the firm's computer encryption software for transmitting email and other electronic documents to clients and other offices of the firm. You live a few blocks from the office and consent to stay late on Friday night before a major holiday weekend when everyone has left early to avoid the rush hour traffic.

A client calls and asks for a copy of the trial strategy memorandum for a major case to take with him for review over the weekend. He advises that he is getting ready to get on a plane but has a computer with him that has reverse encryption software the firm gave him and tells you he wants to read the memo while he is on the plane for the next 14 hours on his way to Tokyo. He hangs up and you do not have his cell phone number. You send the email without using the encryption software. [*U.S. v. Thomas*, 74 F.3d. 701 (1996), ABA Ethics Opinion, Utah ethics Opinion 00-01.] Have you breached any rules on client confidentiality by sending unencrypted email containing confidential client information?

Case FOR DISCUSSION

Issue: Are Images Displayed on the Internet as a Result of a Search Protected by Copyright?

Defendant operates a "visual search engine" on the Internet that allows a user to obtain a list of related Web content in response to a search query entered by the user. Unlike other Internet search engines, defendant's search engine, the "Ditto" crawler retrieves images instead of descriptive text. It produces a list of reduced, "thumbnail" pictures related to the user's query. By clicking on the desired thumbnail, a user could view the "image attributes" window displaying the full-size version of the image, a description of its dimensions, and an address for the website where it originated. By clicking on the address, the user could link to the originating website for the image. The search engine works by maintaining an indexed database of approximately two million thumbnail images obtained through a "crawler"—a computer program that travels the Web in search of images to be converted into thumbnails and added to the index.

Plaintiff Kelly is a photographer specializing in photographs of California Gold Rush country and photographs related to the works of Laura Ingalls Wilder. He does not sell the photographs independently, but his photographs have appeared in several books. Plaintiff also maintains two websites, one of which (www.goldrush1849.com) provides a "virtual tour" of California's Gold Rush country and promotes plaintiff's book on the subject. The other (www.showmethegold.com) markets corporate retreats in California's Gold Rush country. Thirty-five of plaintiff's images were indexed by the Ditto crawler and put in defendant's image database. As a result, these images were made available in thumbnail form to users of defendant's visual search engine. After being notified of plaintiff's objections, Ditto removed the images from its database.

Plaintiff filed a copyright-infringement action. One of the questions of first impression is whether the display of copyrighted images by a "visual search engine" on the Internet constitutes fair use under the Copyright Act. The court found that defendant never held out plaintiff's work as its own, or even engaged in conduct specifically directed at plaintiff's work. Plaintiff's images were swept up along with two million others available on the Internet, as part of defendant's efforts to provide its users with a better way to find images on the Internet. Defendant's purposes were and are inherently transformative, even if its realization of those purposes was at times imperfect. Where, as here, a new use and new technology are evolving, the broad transformative purpose of the use weighs more heavily than the inevitable flaws in its early stages of development.

Questions

1. As the use of the Internet matures, will courts view use of information from the Web differently?
2. What are the implications in taking material off the Internet and including it in reports, memos, and briefs?
3. Would the decision have been different if the items were copyrighted legal forms also located by a "crawler" and displayed as a visual image such as a PDF file?

CoStar Group, Inc. v. LoopNet, Inc.

164 F. Supp. 2d 688 (D.C. Md. 2001)   **United States District Court, Maryland**

Read, and if assigned, brief this case. In your brief, include answers to the following questions.

1. What is a "contributory infringer" under the Digital Millennium Copyright Act?

2. Who is an online service provider as defined by the Digital Millennium Copyright Act (DMCA)?

3. When does a service provider lose its immunity under the DMCA?

4. What is a "safe harbor" under the DMCA?

5. What conduct takes a service provider out of the safe harbor?

Deborah K. Chasanow.

I. Background

Plaintiffs CoStar Group, Inc. and CoStar Realty Information, Inc. (collectively CoStar) filed suit against LoopNet, Inc. (LoopNet) alleging copyright infringement. CoStar is a national provider of commercial real estate information services . . . which includes photographs. . . .

LoopNet is an Internet-based company offering a service through which a user . . . may post a listing of commercial real estate available for lease. . . . To include a photograph, . . . it is uploaded into a separate "folder," . . . where it is reviewed by a LoopNet employee to determine that it is . . . a photograph of commercial property and that there is no obvious . . . violation of LoopNet's terms and conditions. If the photograph meets LoopNet's criteria . . . it is automatically posted. . . . CoStar claims that over 300 of its copyrighted photographs have appeared on LoopNet's site (the number has increased over time). . . .

Application of copyright law in cyberspace is elusive and perplexing. The World Wide Web has progressed far faster than the law and, as a result, courts are struggling to catch up. Legislatures and courts endeavor in this growing area to maintain the free flow of information over the Internet while still protecting intellectual property rights. . . .

CONTRIBUTORY COPYRIGHT INFRINGEMENT

1. Overview

It is, today, a given that: one who, with knowledge of the infringing activity, induces, causes, or materially contributes to the infringing conduct of another, may be held liable as a "contributory" infringer. . . . Put differently, liability exists if the defendant engages in "personal conduct that encourages or assists the infringement." . . .

CoStar does not claim that LoopNet had knowledge of its users' infringements prior to its giving notice. . . . Given the nature of the infringements in this case, it was impossible for LoopNet to have knowledge of the alleged infringement before receiving notice from CoStar. CoStar does not attach a copyright notice to its photos and even CoStar's own expert could not identify a CoStar photo simply by reviewing it. . . . Thus, LoopNet cannot be charged with . . . knowledge before receiving claims of infringement from CoStar. . . . CoStar does not claim that LoopNet had knowledge of infringement prior to receiving notice from CoStar. [T]here remain . . . disputes about [its] knowledge . . . after receiving the claims of infringement. CoStar alleges that once it gave LoopNet notice that its photographs were being infringed, LoopNet can be charged with knowledge of continuing infringements. . . .

The DMCA was enacted both to preserve copyright enforcement in the Internet and to provide immunity to service providers from copyright infringement liability for "passive," "automatic" actions in which a service provider's system engages through a technological process initiated by another without the knowledge of the service provider. . . . The DMCA's protection of an innocent service provider disappears at the moment the service provider loses its innocence, i.e., at the moment it becomes aware that a third party is using its system to infringe. At that point, the Act shifts responsibility to the service provider to disable the infringing matter, "preserving the strong incentives for service providers and copyright owners to cooperate to detect and deal with copyright infringements that take place in the digital networked environment."

The DMCA seeks to strike a balance by shielding online service providers from liability in damages as long as they remove or prevent access to infringing material. . . . The initial inquiry is whether LoopNet can be considered a service provider for the purposes of the DMCA.

a. Service Provider

In order to qualify for the safe harbor in the DMCA, LoopNet must meet the definition of "online service provider." Under § 512 (k)(1)(A), a service provider is "an entity offering the transmission, routing, or providing of connections for digital online communications, between or among points specified by a user, of material of the user's choosing, without modification to the content of the material as sent or received." 17 U.S.C. § 512(k)(1)(A) (1998). . . . For the other safe harbor provisions, including (c), which is at issue here, the definition is broader: "a provider of online services or network access, or the operator of facilities therefor." . . .

"Online services" is surely broad enough to encompass the type of service provided by LoopNet that is at issue here. The term is, of course, only a threshold to the protections of the Act. Even if LoopNet qualifies as a service provider, it must meet the other criteria.

b. Stored at the Instance of the User

A service provider is only protected from liability by the DMCA, "for infringement of copyright by reason of its storage at the direction of a user of material." 17 U.S.C. § 512(c)(1). . . . [The photographs at issue] are uploaded at the volition of the user and are subject . . . to a mere screening to assess whether they are commercial property and to catch any obvious infringements. . . . Although humans are involved rather than mere technology, they serve only as a gateway and are not involved in a selection process. . . . Therefore, this threshold requirement is met and LoopNet is not disqualified from the safe harbor on these grounds.

c. Knowledge

The safe harbor protects service providers from liability unless they have knowledge of copyright infringement. There are three types of knowledge of infringement that can take a service provider out of the safe harbor: (1) the service provider can have actual knowledge of infringement; (2) it can be aware of facts which raise a "red flag" that its users are infringing; or (3) the copyright owner

can notify the service provider in a manner "substantially" conforming with § 512 (c)(3) that its works are being infringed. . . . The service provider does not automatically lose its liability shield upon receiving notice, but "the Act shifts responsibility to the service provider to disable the infringing matter. . . ."

. . . LoopNet received notification of claimed infringement . . . so the adequacy of LoopNet's removal policy must be assessed to determine whether LoopNet is protected by the safe harbor.

d. Adequacy of Termination and "Take Down" Policy

Once a service provider has received notification of a claimed infringement as described in [the Act] . . . the service provider can remain in the safe harbor if it "responds expeditiously to remove, or disable access to, the material that is claimed to be infringing or to be the subject of infringing activity." 17 U.S.C. § 512(c)(1)(C) (1998). . . .

There are several material factual disputes remaining as to whether the removal of allegedly infringing photographs was satisfactorily expeditious and whether LoopNet's termination policy was reasonable and effective. CoStar's infringement claims are based on the posting of specific photographs. Additionally, LoopNet's knowledge of the alleged infringements and its "take down" and termination policies have changed over time in fairly significant ways. In order to resolve this issue, the factfinder will have to focus on each photo and the policy in effect prior to the posting of each photo. Hence, neither party is entitled to summary judgment on this issue. . . .

3. Liability for Contributory Infringement

With regard to the photographs that were infringed before the safe harbor applied . . . and in case LoopNet's termination policy and take down of infringing photographs is found to be inadequate so as to remove it from the safe harbor, the analysis shifts from the DMCA back to contributory infringement. The determination of contributory infringement liability turns on a different issue of knowledge than the standard used to determine LoopNet's eligibility for the safe harbor. Here, the question is whether CoStar's notice of claimed infringement was sufficient to satisfy the knowledge prong of the test for contributory infringement either by providing actual knowledge, a "red flag" that infringement was occurring, or constructive knowledge.

. . . [T]he fact finder must determine along a continuum the adequacy of the policy in place prior to the posting of each specific photograph. Therefore, neither party is entitled to summary judgment on this issue.

e. Preemption of Non-Copyright Claims

. . . The Copyright Act preempts state law that is "equivalent to any of the exclusive rights within the general scope of copyright as specified by section 106." 17 U.S.C. § 301(a) (1996) . . . "To determine whether a state claim is preempted by the Act, courts must make a two-part inquiry: (1) the work must be within the scope of the subject matter of copyright, and (2) the state law rights must be equivalent to any exclusive rights within the scope of federal copyright." *Fischer v. Viacom Intern. Corp.*, 115 F. Supp. 2d 535, 540 (D.Md. 2000). . . . The critical question, then, is whether CoStar's unfair competition claim contains an additional element or whether it is based solely on the alleged copying.

. . . Essentially, CoStar's claim is that LoopNet is exhibiting as its own photographs on its website that CoStar has an exclusive right to exhibit or license for exhibition. This type of reverse passing off is, in effect, a "disguised copyright infringement claim." . . . Therefore, this claim does not satisfy the "extra-element" test and so is equivalent to CoStar's claim under the Copyright Act. Accordingly, it is preempted. . . .

V. Conclusion

For the foregoing reasons, by separate order, both motions concerning the safe harbor defense of the DMCA will be denied, . . . both motions concerning contributory infringement will be denied, . . . summary judgment will be granted in favor of LoopNet on the . . . preemption of the state law claims.

How to Brief a Case

Critical Legal Thinking

Judges apply *legal reasoning* in reaching a decision in a case. That is, the judge must specify the issue presented by the case, identify the key facts in the case and the applicable law, and then apply the law to the facts to come to a conclusion that answers the issue presented. This process is called **critical legal thinking.** Skills of analysis and interpretation are important in deciding legal cases.

Key Terms

Before you embark upon the study of law, you should know the following key legal terms.

Plaintiff   The party who originally brought the lawsuit.

Defendant   The party against whom the lawsuit has been brought.

Petitioner or Appellant   The party who has appealed the decision of the trial court or lower court. The petitioner may be either the plaintiff or defendant, depending on who lost the case at the trial court or lower court level.

Respondent or Appellee   The party who must answer the petitioner's appeal. The respondent may be either the plaintiff or defendant, depending upon which party is the petitioner. In some cases, both the plaintiff *and* the defendant may disagree with the trial court's or lower court's decision, and both parties may appeal the decision.

Briefing a Case

It is often helpful for a student to "brief" a case in order to clarify the legal issues involved and to gain a better understanding of the case.

The procedure for briefing a case is as follows. The student must summarize, or brief, the court's decision in no more than 400 words (some professors may shorten or lengthen this limit). The assignment's format is highly structured, consisting of five parts, each of which is numbered and labeled:

Part	Maximum Words
1. Case name and citation	25
2. A summary of the key facts in the case	125
3. The issue presented by the case, stated as a one-sentence question answerable only by *yes* or *no*	25
4. The court's resolution of the issue (the "holding")	25
5. A summary of the court's reasoning justifying the holding	<u>200</u>
Total words	*400*

Briefing a case consists of making a summary of each of the following items of the case.

1. Case Name and Citation

The name of the case should be placed at the beginning of each briefed case. The case name usually contains the names of the parties to the lawsuit. Where there are multiple plaintiffs or defendants, however, some of the names of the parties may be omitted from the case name. Abbreviations are also often used in case names.

The case citation, which consists of a number plus the year in which the case was decided, such as "126 L.Ed.2d 295 (1993)," is set forth below the case name. The case citation identifies the book in the law library in which the case may be found. For example, the case in the above citation may be found in volume 126 of the *Supreme Court Reporter Lawyer's Edition (Second)*, page 295. The name of the court that decided the case should be set forth below the case name.

2. Summary of the Key Facts in the Case

The important facts of a case should be stated briefly. Extraneous facts and facts of minor importance should be omitted from the brief. The facts of the case can usually be found at the beginning of the case, but not necessarily. Important facts may be found throughout the case.

3. Issue Presented by the Case

It is crucial in the briefing of a case to identify the issue presented to the court to decide. The issue on appeal is most often a legal question, although questions of fact are sometimes the subject of an appeal. The issue presented in each case is usually quite specific and should be asked in a one-sentence question that is answerable only by a *yes* or *no*. For example, the issue statement, "Is Mary liable?" is too broad. A more proper statement of the issue would be, "Is Mary liable to Joe for breach of the contract made between them based on her refusal to make the payment due on September 30?"

4. Holding

The "holding" is the decision reached by the present court. It should be *yes* or *no*. The holding should also state which party won.

5. Summary of the Court's Reasoning

When an appellate court or supreme court issues a decision, which is often called an *opinion*, the court will normally state the reasoning it used in reaching its decision. The rationale for the decision may be based on the specific facts of the case, public policy, prior law, or other matters. In stating the reasoning of the court, the student should reword the court's language into the student's own language. This summary of the court's reasoning should pick out the meat of the opinions and weed out the nonessentials.

Following are two U.S. Supreme Court opinions for briefing. The case is presented in the language of the U.S. Supreme Court. A "Brief of the Case" follows each of the two cases. A third case, from the New York State Court of Appeals, is also included for briefing.

FOR BRIEFING

Harris v. Forklift Systems, Inc.
510 U.S. 17, 114 S.Ct. 367, 126 L.Ed.2d 295

CASE NAME
CITATION   1993 U.S. LEXIS 7155 (1993)
COURT   Supreme Court of the United States

OPINION OF THE COURT. O'CONNOR, JUSTICE

FACTS. Teresa Harris worked as a manager at Forklift Systems, Inc., an equipment rental company, from April 1985 until October 1987. Charles Hardy was Forklift's president. Throughout Harris's time at Forklift, Hardy often insulted her because of her gender and often made her the target of unwanted sexual innuendos. Hardy told Harris on several occasions, in the presence of other employees, "You're a woman, what do you know" and "We need a man as the rental manager"; at least once, he told her she was "a dumb-ass woman." Again in front of others, he suggested that the two of them "go to the Holiday Inn to negotiate Harris' raise." Hardy occasionally asked Harris and other female employees to get coins from his front pants pocket. He threw objects on the ground in front of Harris and other women, and asked them to pick the objects up. He made sexual innuendos about Harris' and other women's clothing.

In mid-August 1987, Harris complained to Hardy about his conduct. Hardy said he was surprised that Harris was offended, claimed he was only joking, and apologized. He also promised he would stop and based on his assurance Harris stayed on the job. But in early September, Hardy began anew: While Harris was arranging a deal with one of Forklift's customers, he asked her, again in front of other employees, "What did you do, promise the guy some sex Saturday night?" On October 1, Harris collected her paycheck and quit.

LOWER COURTS' OPINIONS. Harris then sued Forklift, claiming that Hardy's conduct had created an abusive work environment for her because of her gender. The United States District Court for the Middle District of Tennessee found this to be "a close case," but held that Hardy's conduct did not create an abusive environment. The court found that some of Hardy's comments offended Harris, and would offend the reasonable woman," but that they were not "so severe as to be expected to seriously affect Harris' psychological well-being." A reasonable woman manager under like circumstances would have been offended by Hardy, but his conduct would not have risen to the level of interfering with that person's work performance. The United States Court of Appeals for the Sixth Circuit affirmed in a brief unpublished decision.

ISSUE. We granted certiorari to resolve a conflict among the Circuits on whether conduct, to be actionable as "abusive work environment" harassment, must "seriously affect an employee's psychological well-being" or lead the plaintiff to "suffer injury."

STATUTE BEING INTERPRETED. Title VII of the Civil Rights Act of 1964 makes it "an unlawful employment practice for an employer . . . to discriminate against any individual with respect to his compensation, terms, conditions, or privileges of employment, because of such individual's race, color, religion, sex, or national origin." 42 U.S.C. §2000e-2(a)(1).

U.S. SUPREME COURT'S REASONING. When the workplace is permeated with discriminatory intimidation, ridicule, and insult that is sufficiently severe or pervasive to alter the conditions of the victim's employment and create an abusive working environment, Title VII is violated. This standard takes a middle path between making actionable any conduct that is merely offensive and requiring the conduct to cause a tangible psychological injury. Mere utterance of an epithet which engenders offensive feelings in an employee does not sufficiently affect the conditions of employment to implicate Title VII. Conduct that is not severe or pervasive enough to create an objectively hostile or abusive work environment—an environment that a reasonable person would find hostile or abusive—is beyond Title VII's purview. Likewise, if the victim does not subjectively perceive the environment to be abusive, the conduct has not actually altered the conditions of the victim's employment, and there is no Title VII violation.

But Title VII comes into play before the harassing conduct leads to a nervous breakdown. A discriminatorily abusive work environment, even one that does not seriously affect employees' psychological well-being, can and often will detract from employees' job performance, discourage employees from remaining on the job, or keep them from advancing in their careers. Moreover, even without regard to these tangible effects, the very fact that the discriminatory conduct was so severe or pervasive that it created a work environment abusive to employees because of their race, gender, religion, or national origin offends Title VII's broad rule of workplace equality.

HOLDING. We therefore believe the district court erred in relying on whether the conduct "seriously affected plaintiff's psychological well-being" or led her to "suffer injury." Such an inquiry may needlessly focus the factfinder's attention on concrete psychological harm, an element Title VII does not require. So long as the environment would reasonably be perceived, and is perceived, as hostile or abusive, there is no need for it also to be psychologically injurious. This is not, and by its nature cannot be, a mathematically precise test. But we can say that whether an environment is "hostile" or "abusive" can be determined only by looking at all the circumstances.

We therefore reverse the judgment of the Court of Appeals, and remand the case for further proceedings consistent with this opinion.

CONCURRING OPINION. GINSBURG, JUSTICE

The critical issue, Title VII's text indicates, is whether members of one sex are exposed to disadvantageous terms or conditions of employment to which members of the other sex are not exposed. The adjudicator's inquiry should center, dominantly, on whether the discriminatory conduct has reasonably interfered with the plaintiff's work performance. To show such interference, the plaintiff need not prove that his or her tangible productivity has declined as a result of the harassment.

Brief of the Case: *Harris v. Forklift Systems, Inc.*

1. Case Name, Citation, and Court

Harris v. Forklift Systems, Inc.
126 L.Ed.2d. 295 (1993)
United States Supreme Court

2. Summary of the Key Facts

A. While Harris worked at Forklift, Hardy continually insulted her because of her gender and made her the target of unwanted sexual innuendos.

B. This conduct created an abusive and hostile work environment, causing Harris to terminate her employment.

C. Harris sued Forklift, alleging sexual harassment in violation of Title VII of the Civil Rights Act of 1964, which makes it an unlawful employment practice for an employer to discriminate in employment because of an individual's sex.

3. The Issue

Must an employee prove that she suffered psychological injury before she can prove a Title VII claim for sexual harassment against her employer?

4. The Holding

No. The Supreme Court remanded the case for further proceedings consistent with its opinion.

5. Summary of the Court's Reasoning

The Supreme Court held that a workplace that is permeated with discrimin*-* tory intimidation, ridicule, and insult so severe that it alters the conditions of the victim's employment creates an abusive and hostile work environment that violates Title VII. The Court held that the victim is not required to prove that she suffered tangible psychological injury to prove her Title VII claim. The Court noted that Title VII comes into play before the harassing conduct leads the victim to have a nervous breakdown.

FOR BRIEFING

PGA TOUR, Inc. v. Martin
121 S.Ct. 1879, 149 L.Ed.2d 904 (2001)

CASE NAME	
CITATION	2001 U.S. LEXIS 4115
COURT	Supreme Court of the United States

OPINION OF THE COURT. STEVEN, JUSTICE

ISSUE. This case raises two questions concerning the application of the Americans with Disabilities Act of 1990 [42 U.S.C. § 12101 *et seq.*] to a gifted athlete: first, whether the Act protects access to professional golf tournaments by a qualified entrant with a disability; and second, whether a disabled contestant may be denied the use of a golf cart because it would "fundamentally alter the nature" of the tournaments to allow him to ride when all other contestants must walk.

FACTS. Petitioner PGA TOUR, Inc., a nonprofit entity formed in 1968, sponsors and cosponsors professional golf tournaments conducted on three annual tours. About 200 golfers participate in the PGA TOUR; about 170 in the NIKE TOUR; and about 100 in the SENIOR PGA TOUR. PGA TOUR and NIKE TOUR tournaments typically are 4-day events, played on courses leased and operated by petitioner. The revenues generated by television, admissions, concessions, and contributions from cosponsors amount to about $300 million a year, much of which is distributed in prize money. The "Conditions of Competition and Local Rules," often described as the "hard card," apply specifically to petitioner's professional tours. The hard cards for the PGA TOUR and NIKE TOUR require players to walk the golf course during tournaments, but not during open qualifying rounds. On the SENIOR PGA TOUR, which is limited to golfers age 50 and older, the contestants may use golf carts. Most seniors, however, prefer to walk.

RESPONDENT. Casey Martin is a talented golfer. As an amateur, he won 17 Oregon Golf Association junior events before he was 15, and won the state championship as a high school senior. He played on the Stanford University golf team that won the 1994 National Collegiate Athletic Association (NCAA) championship. As a professional, Martin qualified for the NIKE TOUR in 1998 and 1999, and based on his 1999 performance, qualified for the PGA TOUR in 2000. In the 1999 season, he entered 24 events, made the cut 13 times, and had 6 top-10 finishes, coming in second twice and third once.

Martin is also an individual with a disability as defined in the Americans with Disabilities Act of 1990 (ADA or Act). Since birth he has been afflicted with Klippel-Trenaunay-Weber Syndrome, a degenerative circulatory disorder that obstructs the flow of blood from his right leg back to his heart. The disease is progressive; it causes severe pain and has atrophied his right leg. During the latter part of his college career, because of the progress of the disease, Martin could no longer walk an 18-hole golf course. Walking not only caused him pain, fatigue, and anxiety, but also created a significant risk of hemorrhaging, developing blood clots, and fracturing his tibia so badly that an amputation might be required.

When Martin turned pro and entered the petitioner's Qualifying-School, the hard card permitted him to use a cart during his successful progress through the first two stages. He supported by detailed medical records, for ... a golf cart during the third stage. Petitioner ... view those records, or to waive its walking rule ... stage. Martin therefore filed this action.

COURT'S DECISION

SUPP. 1242 [DISTRICT: OREGON (1998)] At trial, petitioner PGA TOUR did not contest the conclusion that Martin has a disability covered by the ADA, or the fact that his disability prevents him from walking the course during a round of golf. Rather, petitioner asserted that the condition of walking is a substantive rule of competition, and that waiving it as to any individual for any reason would fundamentally alter the nature of the competition. Petitioner's evidence included the testimony of a number of experts, among them some of the greatest golfers in history. Arnold Palmer, Jack Nicklaus, and Ken Venturi explained that fatigue can be a critical factor in a tournament, particularly on the last day when psychological pressure is at a maximum. Their testimony makes it clear that, in their view, permission to use a cart might well give some players a competitive advantage over other players who must walk.

The judge found that the purpose of the rule was to inject fatigue into the skill of shot-making, but that the fatigue injected "by walking the course cannot be deemed significant under normal circumstances." Furthermore, Martin presented evidence, and the judge found, that even with the use of a cart, Martin must walk over a mile during an 18-hole round, and that the fatigue he suffers from coping with his disability is "undeniably greater" than the fatigue his able-bodied competitors endure from walking the course. As a result, the judge concluded that it would "not fundamentally alter the nature of the PGA Tour's game to accommodate him with a cart." The judge accordingly entered a permanent injunction requiring petitioner to permit Martin to use a cart in tour and qualifying events.

COURT OF APPEALS DECISION

204 F.3D 994 [9TH CIRCUIT (2000)] The Court of Appeals concluded that golf courses remain places of public accommodation during PGA tournaments. On the merits, because there was no serious dispute about the fact that permitting Martin to use a golf cart was both a reasonable and a necessary solution to the problem of providing him access to the tournaments, the Court of Appeals regarded the central dispute as whether such permission would "fundamentally alter" the nature of the PGA TOUR or NIKE TOUR. Like the District Court, the Court of Appeals viewed the issue not as "whether use of carts generally would fundamentally alter the competition, but whether the use of a cart by Martin would do so." That issue turned on "an intensively fact-based inquiry," and, the court concluded, had been correctly resolved by the trial judge. In its words, "all that the cart does is permit Martin access to a type of competition in which he otherwise could not engage because of his disability."

FEDERAL STATUTE BEING INTERPRETED. Congress enacted the ADA in 1990 to remedy widespread discrimination against disabled individuals. To effectuate its sweeping purpose, the ADA forbids discrimination against disabled individuals in major areas of public life, among them employment (Title I of the Act), public services (Title II), and public accommodations (Title III). At issue now is the applicability of Title III to petitioner's golf tours and qualifying rounds, in particular to petitioner's treatment of a qualified disabled golfer wishing to compete in those events.

U.S. SUPREME COURT'S REASONING. It seems apparent, from both the general rule and the comprehensive definition of "public accommodation," that petitioner's golf tours and their qualifying rounds fit comfortably within the coverage of Title III, and Martin within its protection. The events occur on "golf courses," a type of place specifically identified by the Act as a public accommodation. Section 12181(7)(L). In this case, the narrow dispute is whether allowing Martin to use a golf cart, despite the walking requirement that applies to the PGA TOUR, the NIKE TOUR, and the third stage of the Qualifying-School, is a modification that would "fundamentally alter the nature" of those events.

As an initial matter, we observe that the use of carts is not itself inconsistent with the fundamental character of the game of golf. From early on, the essence of the game has been shot-making—using clubs to cause a ball to progress from the teeing ground to a hole some distance away with as few strokes as possible. Golf carts started appearing with increasing regularity on American golf courses in the 1950's. Today they are everywhere. And they are encouraged. For one thing, they often speed up play, and for another, they are great revenue producers. There is nothing in the Rules of Golf that either forbids the use of carts, or penalizes a player for using a cart.

Petitioner, however, distinguishes the game of golf as it is generally played from the game that it sponsors in the PGA TOUR, NIKE TOUR, and the last stage of the Qualifying-School—golf at the "highest level." According to petitioner, "the goal of the highest-level competitive athletics is to assess and compare the performance of different competitors, a task that is meaningful only if the competitors are subject to identical substantive rules." The waiver of any possibly "outcome-affecting" rule for a contestant would violate this principle and therefore, in petitioner's view, fundamentally alter the nature of the highest level athletic event. The walking rule is one such rule, petitioner submits, because its purpose is "to inject the element of fatigue into the skill of shot-making," and thus its effect may be the critical loss of a stroke. As a consequence, the reasonable modification Martin seeks would fundamentally alter the nature of petitioner's highest level tournaments.

The force of petitioner's argument is, first of all, mitigated by the fact that golf is a game in which it is impossible to guarantee that all competitors will play under exactly the same conditions or that an individual's ability will be the sole determinant of the outcome. For example, changes in the weather may produce harder greens and more head winds for the tournament leader than for his closest pursuers. A lucky bounce may save a shot or two. Whether such happenstance events are more or less probable than the likelihood that a golfer afflicted with Klippel-Trenaunay-Weber Syndrome would one day qualify for the NIKE TOUR and PGA TOUR, they at least demonstrate that pure chance may have a greater impact on the outcome of elite golf tournaments than the fatigue resulting from the enforcement of the walking rule.

Further, the factual basis of petitioner's argument is undermined by the District Court's finding that the fatigue from walking during one of petitioner's 4-day tournaments cannot be deemed significant. The District Court credited the testimony of a professor in physiology and expert on fatigue, who calculated the calories expended in walking a golf course (about five miles) to be approximately 500 calories—"nutritionally less than a Big Mac." What is more, that energy is expended over a 5-hour period, during which golfers have numerous intervals for rest and refreshment. In fact, the expert concluded, because golf is a low intensity activity, fatigue from the game is primarily a psychological phenomenon in which stress and motivation are the key ingredients. And even under conditions of severe heat and humidity, the critical factor in fatigue is fluid loss rather than exercise from walking. Moreover, when given the option of using a cart, the majority of golfers in petitioner's tournaments have chosen to walk, often to relieve stress or for other strategic reasons. As NIKE TOUR member Eric Johnson testified, walking allows him to keep in rhythm, stay warmer when it is chilly, and develop a better sense of the elements and the course than riding in a cart. As we have demonstrated, the walking rule is at best peripheral to the nature of petitioner's athletic events, and thus it might be waived in individual cases without working a fundamental alteration.

HOLDING AND REMEDY. Under the ADA's basic requirement that the need of a disabled person be evaluated on an individual basis, we have no doubt that allowing Martin to use a golf cart would not fundamentally alter the nature of petitioner's tournaments. As we have discussed, the purpose of the walking rule is to subject players to fatigue, which in turn may influence the outcome of tournaments. Even if the rule does serve that purpose, it is an uncontested finding of the District Court that Martin "easily endures greater fatigue even with a cart than his able-bodied competitors do by walking." The purpose of the walking rule is therefore not compromised in the slightest by allowing Martin to use a cart. A modification that provides an exception to a peripheral tournament rule without impairing its purpose cannot be said to "fundamentally alter" the tournament. What it can be said to do, on the other hand, is to allow Martin the chance to qualify for and compete in the athletic events petitioner

offers to those members of the public who have the skill and desire to enter. That is exactly what the ADA requires. As a result, Martin's request for a waiver of the walking rule should have been granted.

The judgment of the Court of Appeals is affirmed. It is so ordered.

DISSENTING OPINION. SCALIA, JUSTICE

In my view today's opinion exercises a benevolent compassion that the law does not place it within our power to impose. The judgment distorts the text of Title III, the structure of the ADA, and common sense. I respectfully dissent.

The Court, for its part, assumes that conclusion for the sake of argument, but pronounces respondent to be a "customer" of the PGA TOUR or of the golf courses on which it is played. That seems to me quite incredible. The PGA TOUR is a professional sporting event, staged for the entertainment of a live and TV audience. The professional golfers on the tour are no more "enjoying" (the statutory term) the entertainment that the tour provides, or the facilities of the golf courses on which it is held, than professional baseball players "enjoy" the baseball games in which they play or the facilities of Yankee Stadium. To be sure, professional baseball players *participate* in the games, and *use* the ballfields, but no one in his right mind would think that they are *customers* of the American League or of Yankee Stadium. They are themselves the entertainment that the customers pay to watch. And professional golfers are no different. A professional golfer's practicing his profession is not comparable to John Q. Public's frequenting "a 232-acre amusement area with swimming, boating, sun bathing, picnicking, miniature golf, dancing facilities, and a snack bar."

Having erroneously held that Title III applies to the "customers" of professional golf who consist of its practitioners, the Court then erroneously answers—or to be accurate simply ignores—a second question. The ADA requires covered businesses to make such reasonable modifications of "policies, practices, or procedures" as are necessary to "afford" goods, services, and privileges to individuals with disabilities; but it explicitly does not require "modifications that would fundamentally alter the nature" of the goods, services, and privileges. Section 12182(b)(2)(A)(ii). In other words, disabled individuals must be given *access* to the same goods, services, and privileges that others enjoy.

A camera store may not refuse to sell cameras to a disabled person, but it is not required to stock cameras specially designed for such persons. It is hardly a feasible judicial function to decide whether shoe stores should sell single shoes to one-legged persons and if so at what price, or how many Braille books the Borders or Barnes and Noble bookstore chains should stock in each of their stores. Eighteen-hole golf courses, 10-foot-high basketball hoops, 90-foot baselines, 100-yard football fields—all are arbitrary and none is essential. The only support for any of them is tradition and (in more modern times) insistence by what has come to be regarded as the ruling body of the sport—both of which factors support the PGA TOUR's position in the present case. One can envision the parents of a Little League player with attention deficit disorder trying to convince a judge that their son's disability makes it at least 25% more difficult to hit a pitched ball. (If they are successful, the only thing that could prevent a court order giving a kid four strikes would be a judicial determination that, in baseball, three strikes are metaphysically necessary, which is quite absurd.)

Agility, strength, speed, balance, quickness of mind, steadiness of nerves, intensity of concentration—these talents are not evenly distributed. No wild-eyed dreamer has ever suggested that the managing bodies of the competitive sports that test precisely these qualities should try to take account of the uneven distribution of God-given gifts when writing and enforcing the rules of competition. And I have no doubt Congress did not authorize misty-eyed judicial supervision of such revolution. The year was 2001, and "everybody was finally equal." K. Vonnegut, Harrison Bergeron, in *Animal Farm and Related Readings* 129 (1997).

Brief of Case: *PGA TOUR, Inc. v. Martin*

1. Case Name, Citation, and Court

PGA TOUR, Inc. v. Martin
121 S.Ct. 1879, 2001 LEXIS 415 (2001)
Supreme Court of the United States

2. Summary of the Key Facts

A. PGA TOUR, Inc. is a nonprofit organization that sponsors professional golf tournaments.

B. The PGA establishes rules for its golf tournaments. A PGA rule requires golfers to walk the golf course, and not use golf carts.

C. Casey Martin is a professional golfer who suffers from Klippel-Trenaunay-Weber Syndrome, a degenerative circulatory disorder that atrophied Martin's right leg and causes him pain, fatigue, and anxiety when walking.

D. When Martin petitioned the PGA to use a golf cart during golf tournaments, the PGA refused.

E. Martin sued the PGA, alleging discrimination against a disabled individual in violation of the American with Disabilities Act of 1990, a federal statute.

3. Issue

Does the Americans with Disabilities Act require the PGA to accommodate Martin by permitting him to use a golf cart while playing in PGA golf tournaments?

4. Holding

Yes. The Supreme Court held that the PGA must allow Martin to use a golf cart when competing in PGA golf tournaments. Affirmed.

5. Court's Reasoning

The Supreme Court held that:

A. Martin was disabled and covered by the Act.

B. Golf courses are "public accommodations" covered by the Act.

C. The use of golf carts is not a fundamental characteristic of the game of golf.

D. Other than the PGA rule, there is no Rule of Golf that forbids the use of golf carts.

E. It is impossible to guarantee all players in golf will play under the exact same conditions, so allowing Martin to use a golf cart gives him no advantage over other golfers.

F. Martin, because of his disease, will probably suffer more fatigue playing golf using a golf cart than other golfers will suffer without using a cart.

G. The PGA's "walking rule" is only peripheral to the game of golf and not a fundamental part of golf.

H. Allowing Martin to use a golf cart will not fundamentally alter the PGA's highest-level professional golf tournaments.

FOR BRIEFING

Palsgraf v. Long Island R.R. Co.	**CASE NAME**
248 N.Y. 339 (1928)	**CITATION** 162 N.E. 99
	COURT Court of Appeals of the State of New York

OPINION OF THE COURT. CARDOZO, Ch. J.

FACTS. Plaintiff was standing on a platform of defendant's railroad after buying a ticket to go to Rockaway Beach. A train stopped at the station, bound for another place. Two men ran forward to catch it. One of the men reached the platform of the car without mishap, though the train was already moving. The other man, carrying a package, jumped aboard the car, but seemed unsteady as if about to fall. A guard on the car, who had held the door open, reached forward to help him in, and another guard on the platform pushed him from behind. In this act, the package was dislodged, and fell upon the rails. It was a package of small size, about fifteen inches long, and was covered by a newspaper. In fact it contained fireworks, but there was nothing in its appearance to give notice of its contents. The fireworks when they fell exploded. The shock of the explosion threw down some scales at the other end of the platform, many feet away. The scales struck the plaintiff, causing injuries for which she sues.

The conduct of the defendant's guard, if a wrong in its relation to the holder of the package, was not a wrong in its relation to the plaintiff, standing far away. Relatively to her it was not negligence at all. Nothing in the situation gave notice that the falling package had in it the potency of peril to persons thus removed. Negligence is not actionable unless it involves the invasion of a legally protected interest, the violation of a right. "Proof of negligence in the air, so to speak, will not do" (Pollock, *Torts* [11th ed.], p. 455; *Martin v. Herzog*, 228 N.Y. 164, 170; cf. Salmond, *Torts* [6th ed.], p.24). "Negligence is the absence of care, according to the circumstances" (WILLES, J., in *Vaughan v. Taff Vale Ry. Co.*, 5 H. & N. 679, 688; 1 Beven, Negligence [4th ed.], 7; *Paul v. Consol. Fireworks Co.*, 212 N.Y. 117; *Adams v. Bullock*, 227 N.Y. 208, 211; *Parrott v. Wells-Fargo Co.*, 15 Wall. [U.S.] 524). The plaintiff as she stood upon the platform of the station might claim to be protected against intentional invasion of her bodily security. Such invasion is not charged. She might claim to be protected against unintentional invasion by conduct involving in the thought of reasonable men an unreasonable hazard that such invasion would ensue. These, from the point of view of the law, were the bounds of her immunity, with perhaps some rare exceptions, survivals for the most part of ancient forms of liability, where conduct is held to be at the peril of the actor (*Sullivan v. Dunham*, 161 N.Y. 290 Page 342). If no hazard was apparent to the eye of ordinary vigilance, an act innocent and harmless, at least to outward seeming, with reference to her, did not take to itself the quality of a tort because it happened to be a wrong, though apparently not one involving the risk of bodily insecurity, with reference to some one else. "In every instance, before negligence can be predicated of a given act, back of the act must be sought and found a duty to the individual complaining, the observance of which would have averted or avoided the injury" (McSHERRY, C.J., in *W. Va. Central R. Co. v. State*, 96 Md. 652, 666; cf. *Norfolk & Western Ry. Co. v. Wood*, 99 Va. 156, 158, 159; *Hughes v. Boston & Maine R.R. Co.*, 71 N.H. 279, 284; *U.S. Express Co. v. Everest*, 72 Kan. 517; *Emry v. Roanoke Nav. Co.*, 111 N.C. 94, 95; *Vaughan v. Transit Dev. Co.*, 222 N.Y. 79; *Losee v. Clute*, 51 N.Y. 494; *DiCaprio v. N.Y.C.R.R. Co.*, 231 N.Y. 94; 1 Shearman & Redfield on Negligence, § 8, and cases cited; Cooley on Torts [3d ed.], p. 1411; Jaggard on Torts, vol. 2, p.826; Wharton, *Negligence*, § 24; Bohlen, *Studies in the Law of Torts*, p. 601). "The ideas of negligence and duty are strictly correlative" (BOWEN, L.J., in *Thomas v. Quartermaine*, 18 Q.B.D. 685, 694). The plaintiff sues in her own right for a wrong personal to her, and not as the vicarious beneficiary of a breach of duty to another.

A different conclusion will involve us, and swiftly too, in a maze of contradictions. A guard stumbles over a package which has been left upon a platform. It seems to be a bundle of newspapers. It turns out to be a can of dynamite. To the eye of ordinary vigilance, the bundle is abandoned waste, which may be kicked or trod on with impunity. Is a passenger at the other end of the platform protected by the law against the unsuspected hazard concealed beneath the waste? If not, is the result to be any different, so far as the distant passenger is concerned, when the guard stumbles over a valise which a truckman or a porter has left upon the walk? The passenger far away, if the victim of a wrong at all, has a cause of action, not derivative, but original and primary. His claim to be protected against invasion of his bodily security is neither greater nor less because the act resulting in the invasion is a wrong to another far removed. In this case, the rights that are said to have been violated, the interests said to have been invaded, are not even of the same order. The man was not injured in his person nor even put in danger. The purpose of the act, as well as its effect, was to make his person safe. If there was a wrong to him at all, which may very well be doubted, it was a wrong to a property interest only, the safety of his package. Out of this wrong to property, which threatened injury to nothing else, there has passed, we are told, to the plaintiff by derivation or succession a right of action for the invasion of an interest of another order, the right to bodily security. The diversity of interests emphasizes the futility of the effort to build the plaintiff's right upon the basis of a wrong to some one else. The gain is one of emphasis, for a like result would follow if the interests were the same. Even then, the orbit of the danger as disclosed to the eye of reasonable vigilance would be the orbit of the duty. One who jostles one's neighbor in a crowd does not invade the rights of others standing at the outer fringe when the unintended contact casts a bomb upon the ground. The wrongdoer as to them is the man who carries the bomb, not the one who explodes it without suspicion of the danger. Life will have to be made over, and human nature transformed, before prevision so extravagant can be accepted as the norm of conduct, the customary standard to which behavior must conform. The argument for the plaintiff is built upon the shifting meanings of such words as "wrong" and "wrongful," and shares their instability. What the plaintiff must show is "a wrong" to herself, i.e., a violation of her own right, and not merely a wrong to some one else, nor conduct "wrongful" because unsocial, but not "a wrong" to any one. We are told that one who drives at reckless speed through a crowded city street is guilty of a negligent act and, therefore, of a wrongful one irrespective of the consequences. Negligent the act is, and wrongful in the sense that it is unsocial, but wrongful and unsocial in relation to other travelers, only because the eye of vigilance perceives the risk of damage. If the same act were to be committed on a speedway or a race course, it would lose its wrongful quality. The risk reasonably to be perceived defines the duty to be obeyed, and risk imports relation; it is risk to another or to others within the range of apprehension (Seavey, Negligence, Subjective or Objective, 41 H.L. Rv. 6; *Boronkay v. Robinson & Carpenter*, 247 N.Y. 365). This does not mean, of course, that one who launches a destructive force is always relieved of liability if the force, though known to be destructive, pursues an unexpected path. "It was not necessary that the defendant should have had notice of the particular method in which an accident would occur, if the possibility of an accident was clear to the ordinarily prudent eye" (*Munsey v. Webb*, 231 U.S. 150, 156; *Condran v. Park & Tilford*, 213 N.Y. 341, 345; *Robert v. U.S.E.F. Corp.*, 240 N.Y. 474, 477). Some acts, such as shooting, are so imminently dangerous to any one who may come within reach of the missile, however unexpectedly, as to impose a duty of prevision not far from that of an insurer. Even today, and much oftener in earlier stages of the law, one acts sometimes at one's peril (Jeremiah Smith, Tort and Absolute Liability, 30 H.L. Rv. 328; Street, *Foundations of Legal Liability*, vol. 1, pp. 77, 78). Under this head, it may be, fall certain cases of what is known as transferred intent, an act willfully dangerous to A resulting by misadventure in injury to B (*Talmage v. Smith*, 101 Mich. 370, 374) These cases aside, wrong is defined in terms of the natural or probable, at least when unintentional (*Parrot v. Wells-Fargo Co.* [The Nitro-Glycerine Case], 15 Wall. [U.S.] 524). The range of reasonable apprehension is at times a question for the court, and at times, if varying inferences are possible, a question for the jury. Here, by concession, there was nothing in the situation to suggest to the most cautious mind that the parcel wrapped in newspaper would spread wreckage through the station. If the guard had thrown it down knowingly and willfully, he would not have threatened the plaintiff's safety, so far as appearances could warn him. His conduct would not have involved, even then, an unreasonable probability of invasion of her bodily security. Liability can be no greater where the act is inadvertent.

Negligence, like risk, is thus a term of relation. Negligence in the abstract, apart from things related, is surely not a tort, if indeed it is understandable at all (BOWEN, L.J., in *Thomas v. Quartermaine*, 18 Q.B.D. 685, 694). Negligence is not a tort unless it results in the commission of a wrong, and the commission of a wrong imports the violation of a right, in this case, we are told, the right to be protected against interference with one's bodily security. But bodily security is protected, not against all forms of interference or aggression, but only against some. One who seeks redress at law does not make out a cause of action by showing without more that there has been damage to his person. If the harm was not willful, he must show that the act as to him had possibilities of danger so many and apparent as to entitle him to be protected against the doing of it though the harm was unintended. Affront to personality is still the keynote of the wrong. Confirmation of this view will be found in the history and development of the action on the case. Negligence as a basis of civil liability was unknown to mediaeval law (8 Holdsworth, *History of English Law*, p. 449; Street, *Foundations of Legal Liability*, vol. 1, pp. 189, 190). For damage to the person, the sole remedy was trespass, and trespass did not lie in the absence of aggression, and that direct and personal (Holdsworth, op. cit. p. 453; Street, op. cit. vol. 3, pp. 258, 260, vol. 1, pp. 71, 74.) Liability for other damage, as where a servant without orders from the master does or omits something to the damage of another, is a plant of later growth (Holdsworth, op. cit. 450, 457;Wigmore, *Responsibility or Tortious Acts*, vol. 3, *Essays in Anglo-American Legal History*, 520, 523, 526, 533). When it emerged out of the legal soil, it was thought of as a variant of trespass, an offshoot of the parent stock. This appears in the form of action, which was known as trespass on the case (Holdsworth, op. cit. p. 449; cf. *Scott v. Shepard*, 2 Wm. Black. 892; Green, *Rationale of Proximate Cause*, p. 19). The victim does not sue derivatively, or by right of subrogation, to vindicate an interest invaded in the person of another. Thus to view his cause of action is to ignore the fundamental difference between tort and crime (Holland, *Jurisprudence* [12th ed.], p.328). He sues for breach of a duty owing to himself.

The law of causation, remote or proximate, is thus foreign to the case before us. The question of liability is always anterior to the question of the measure of the consequences that go with liability. If there is no tort to be redressed, there is no occasion to consider what damage might be recovered if there were a finding of a tort. We may assume, without deciding, that negligence, not at large or in the abstract, but in relation to the plaintiff, would entail liability for any and all consequences, however novel or extraordinary (*Bird v. St. Paul F. & M. Ins. Co.*, 224 N.Y. 47, 54; *Ehrgott v. Mayor, etc., of N.Y*, 96 N.Y. 264; *Smith v. London & S.W. Ry. Co.*, L.R. 6 C.P. 14; 1 Beven, Negligence, 106; Street, op. cit. vol. 1, p.

90; Green, *Rationale of Proximate Cause*, pp. 88, 118; cf. *Matter of Polemis*, L.R. 1921, 3 K.B. 560; 44 *Law Quarterly Review*, 142). There is room for argument that a distinction is to be drawn according to the diversity of interests invaded by the act, as where conduct negligent in that it threatens an insignificant invasion of an interest in property results in an unforeseeable invasion of an interest of another order, as, e.g., one of bodily security. Perhaps other distinctions may be necessary. We do not go into the question now. The consequences to be followed must first be rooted in a wrong.

HOLDING. The judgment of the Appellate Division and that of the Trial Term should be reversed, and the complaint dismissed, with costs in all courts.

DISSENTING OPINION. ANDREWS, J.

Assisting a passenger to board a train, the defendant's servant negligently knocked a package from his arms. It fell between the platform and the cars. Of its contents the servant knew and could know nothing. A violent explosion followed. The concussion broke some scales standing a considerable distance away. In falling they injured the plaintiff, an intending passenger.

Upon these facts may she recover the damages she has suffered in an action brought against the master? The result we shall reach depends upon our theory as to the nature of negligence. Is it a relative concept—the breach of some duty owing to a particular person or to particular persons? Or where there is an act which unreasonably threatens the safety of others, is the doer liable for all its proximate consequences, even where they result in injury to one who would generally be thought to be outside the radius of danger? This is not a mere dispute as to words. We might not believe that to the average mind the dropping of the bundle would seem to involve the probability of harm to the plaintiff standing many feet away whatever might be the case as to the owner or to one so near as to be likely to be struck by its fall. If, however, we adopt the second hypothesis we have to inquire only as to the relation between cause and effect. We deal in terms of proximate cause, not of negligence.

Negligence may be defined roughly as an act or omission which unreasonably does or may affect the rights of others, or which unreasonably fails to protect oneself from the dangers resulting from such acts. Here I confine myself to the first branch of the definition. Nor do I comment on the word "unreasonable." For present purposes it sufficiently describes that average of conduct that society requires of its members.

There must be both the act or the omission, and the right. It is the act itself, not the intent of the actor, that is important. (*Hover v. Barkhoof*, 44 N.Y. 113; *Mertz v. Connecticut Co.*, 217 N.Y. 475.) In criminal law both the intent and the result are to be considered. Intent again is material in tort actions, where punitive damages are sought, dependent on actual malice—not on merely reckless conduct. But here neither insanity nor infancy lessens responsibility. (*Williams v. Hays*, 143 N.Y. 442.)

As has been said, except in cases of contributory negligence, there must be rights which are or may be affected. Often though injury has occurred, no rights of him who suffers have been touched. A licensee or trespasser upon my land has no claim to affirmative care on my part that the land be made safe. (*Meiers v. Koch Brewery*, 229 N.Y. 10.) Where a railroad is required to fence its tracks against cattle, no man's rights are injured should he wander upon the road because such fence is absent. (*DiCaprio v. N.Y.C.R.R.*, 231 N.Y. 94.) An unborn child may not demand immunity from personal harm. (Drobner v. Peters, 232 N.Y. 220.)

But we are told that "there is no negligence unless there is in the particular case a legal duty to take care, and this duty must be one which is owed to the plaintiff himself and not merely to others." (Salmond Torts [6th ed.], 24.) This, I think too narrow a conception. Where there is the unreasonable act, and some right that may be affected there is negligence whether damage does or does not result. That is immaterial. Should we drive down Broadway at a reckless speed, we are negligent whether we strike an approaching car or miss it by an inch. The act itself is wrongful. It is a wrong not only to those who happen to be within the radius of danger but to all who might have been there—a wrong to the public at large. Such is the language of the street. Such the language of the courts when speaking of contributory negligence. Such again and again their language in speaking of the duty of some defendant and discussing proximate cause in cases where such a discussion is wholly irrelevant on any other theory. (*Perry v. Rochester Line Co.*, 219 N.Y. 60.) As was said by Mr. Justice HOLMES many years ago, "the measure of the defendant's duty in determining whether a wrong has been committed is one thing, the measure of liability when a wrong has been committed is another." (*Spade v. Lynn & Boston R.R. Co.*, 172 Mass. 488.) Due care is a duty imposed on each one of us to protect society from unnecessary danger, not to protect A, B or C alone.

It may well be that there is no such thing as negligence in the abstract. "Proof of negligence in the air, so to speak, will not do." In an empty world negligence would not exist. It does involve a relationship between man and his fellows. But not merely a relationship between man and those whom he might reasonably expect his act would injure. Rather, a relationship between him and those whom he does in fact injure. If his act has a tendency to harm some one, it harms him a mile away as surely as it does those on the scene. We now permit children to recover for the negligent killing of the father. It was never prevented on the theory that no duty was owing to them. A husband may be compensated for the loss of his wife's services. To say that the wrongdoer was negligent as to the husband as well as to the wife is merely an attempt to fit facts to theory. An insurance company paying a fire loss recovers its payment of the negligent incendiary. We speak of subrogation—of suing in the right of the insured.

Behind the cloud of words is the fact they hide, that the act, wrongful as to the insured, has also injured the company. Even if it be true that the fault of father, wife or insured will prevent recovery, it is because we consider the original negligence not the proximate cause of the injury. (Pollock, *Torts* [12th ed.], 463.)

In the well-known *Polemis* case (1921, 3 K.B. 560), SCRUTTON, L.J., said that the dropping of a plank was negligent for it might injure "workman or cargo or ship." Because of either possibility the owner of the vessel was to be made good for his loss. The act being wrongful the doer was liable for its proximate results. Criticized and explained as this statement may have been, I think it states the law as it should be and as it is. (*Smith v. London & Southwestern Ry. Co.*, [1870-71] 6 C.P. 14; *Anthony v. Slaid*, 52 Mass. 290; *Wood v. Penn. R.R.Co.*, 177 Penn. St. 306; *Trashansky v. Hershkovitz*, 239 N.Y. 452.)

The proposition is this. Every one owes to the world at large the duty of refraining from those acts that may unreasonably threaten the safety of others. Such an act occurs. Not only is he wronged to whom harm might reasonably be expected to result, but he also who is in fact injured, even if he be outside what would generally be thought the danger zone. There needs be duty due the one complaining but this is not a duty to a particular individual because as to him harm might be expected. Harm to some one being the natural result of the act, not only that one alone, but all those in fact injured may complain. We have never, I think, held otherwise. Indeed in the Di Caprio case we said that a breach of a general ordinance defining the degree of care to be exercised in one's calling is evidence of negligence as to every one. We did not limit this statement to those who might be expected to be exposed to danger. Unreasonable risk being taken, its consequences are not confined to those who might probably be hurt.

If this be so, we do not have a plaintiff suing by "derivation or succession." Her action is original and primary. Her claim is for a breach of duty to herself—not that she is subrogated to any right of action of the owner of the parcel or of a passenger standing at the scene of the explosion.

The right to recover damages rests on additional considerations. The plaintiff's rights must be injured, and this injury must be caused by the negligence. We build a dam, but are negligent as to its foundations. Breaking, it injures property down stream. We are not liable if all this happened because of some reason other than the insecure foundation. But when injuries do result from our unlawful act we are liable for the consequences. It does not matter that they are unusual, unexpected, unforeseen and unforeseeable. But there is one limitation. The damages must be so connected with the negligence that the latter may be said to be the proximate cause of the former.

These two words have never been given an inclusive definition. What is a cause in a legal sense, still more what is a proximate cause, depend in each case upon many considerations, as does the existence of negligence itself. Any philosophical doctrine of causation does not help us. A boy throws a stone into a pond. The ripples spread. The water level rises. The history of that pond is altered to all eternity. It will be altered by other causes also. Yet it will be forever the resultant of all causes combined. Each one will have an influence. How great only omniscience can say. You may speak of a chain, or if you please, a net. An analogy is of little aid. Each cause brings about future events. Without each the future would not be the same. Each is proximate in the sense it is essential. But that is not what we mean by the word. Nor on the other hand do we mean sole cause. There is no such thing.

Should analogy be thought helpful, however, I prefer that of a stream. The spring, starting on its journey, is joined by tributary after tributary. The river, reaching the ocean, comes from a hundred sources. No man may say whence any drop of water is derived. Yet for a time distinction may be possible. Into the clear creek, brown swamp water flows from the left. Later, from the right comes water stained by its clay bed. The three may remain for a space, sharply divided. But at last, inevitably no trace of separation remains. They are so commingled that all distinction is lost.

As we have said, we cannot trace the effect of an act to the end, if end there is. Again, however, we may trace it part of the way. A murder at Sarajevo may be the necessary antecedent to an assassination in London twenty years hence. An overturned lantern may burn all Chicago. We may follow the fire from the shed to the last building. We rightly say the fire started by the lantern caused its destruction.

A cause, but not the proximate cause. What we do mean by the word proximate" is, that because of convenience, of public policy, of a rough sense of justice, the law arbitrarily declines to trace a series of events beyond a certain point. This is not logic. It is practical politics. Take our rule as to fires. Sparks from my burning haystack set on fire my house and my neighbor's. I may recover from a negligent railroad. He may not. Yet the wrongful act as directly harmed the one as the other. We may regret that the line was drawn just where it was, but drawn somewhere it had to be. We said the act of the railroad was not the proximate cause of our neighbor's fire. Cause it surely was. The words we used were simply indicative of our notions of public policy. Other courts think differently. But somewhere they reach the point where they cannot say the stream comes from any one source.

Take the illustration given in an unpublished manuscript by a distinguished and helpful writer on the law of torts. A chauffeur negligently collides with another car which is filled with dynamite, although he could not know it. An explosion follows. A, walking on the sidewalk nearby, is killed. B, sitting in a window of a building opposite, is cut by flying glass. C, likewise sitting in a window a block away, is similarly injured. And a further illustration. A nursemaid, ten blocks away, startled by the noise, involuntarily drops a baby from her arms to the walk. We are told that C may not

recover while A may. As to B it is a question for court or jury. We will all agree that the baby might not. Because, we are again told, the chauffeur had no reason to believe his conduct involved any risk of injuring either C or the baby. As to them he was not negligent.

But the chauffeur, being negligent in risking the collision, his belief that the scope of the harm he might do would be limited is immaterial. His act unreasonably jeopardized the safety of any one who might be affected by it. C's injury and that of the baby were directly traceable to the collision. Without that, the injury would not have happened. C had the right to sit in his office, secure from such dangers. The baby was entitled to use the sidewalk with reasonable safety.

The true theory is, it seems to me, that the injury to C, if in truth he is to be denied recovery, and the injury to the baby is that their several injuries were not the proximate result of the negligence. And here not what the chauffeur had reason to believe would be the result of his conduct, but what the prudent would foresee, may have a bearing. May have some bearing, for the problem of proximate cause is not to be solved by any one consideration.

It is all a question of expediency. There are no fixed rules to govern our judgment. There are simply matters of which we may take account. We have in a somewhat different connection spoken of "the stream of events." We have asked whether that stream was deflected—whether it was forced into new and unexpected channels. (*Donnelly v. Piercy Contracting Co.*, 222 N.Y. 210). This is rather rhetoric than law. There is in truth little to guide us other than common sense.

There are some hints that may help us. The proximate cause, involved as it may be with many other causes, must be, at the least, something without which the event would not happen. The court must ask itself whether there was a natural and continuous sequence between cause and effect. Was the one a substantial factor in producing the other? Was there a direct connection between them, without too many intervening causes? Is the effect of cause on result not too attenuated? Is the cause likely, in the usual judgment of mankind, to produce the result? Or by the exercise of prudent foresight could the result be foreseen? Is the result too remote from the cause, and here we consider remoteness in time and space. (*Bird v. St. Paul F. & M. Ins. Co.*, 224 N.Y. 47, where we passed upon the construction of a contract—but something was also said on this subject.) Clearly we must so consider, for the greater the distance either in time or space, the more surely do other causes intervene to affect the result. When a lantern is overturned the firing of a shed is a fairly direct consequence. Many things contribute to the spread of the conflagration—the force of the wind, the direction and width of streets, the character of intervening structures, other factors. We draw an uncertain and wavering line, but draw it we must as best we can.

Once again, it is all a question of fair judgment, always keeping in mind the fact that we endeavor to make a rule in each case that will be practical and in keeping with the general understanding of mankind.

Here another question must be answered. In the case supposed it is said, and said correctly, that the chauffeur is liable for the direct effect of the explosion although he had no reason to suppose it would follow a collision. "The fact that the injury occurred in a different manner than that which might have been expected does not prevent the chauffeur's negligence from being in law the cause of the injury." But the natural results of a negligent act—the results which a prudent man would or should foresee—do have a bearing upon the decision as to proximate cause. We have said so repeatedly. What should be foreseen? No human foresight would suggest that a collision itself might injure one a block away. On the contrary, given an explosion, such a possibility might be reasonably expected. I think the direct connection, the foresight of which the courts peak, assumes prevision of the explosion, for the immediate results of which, at least, the chauffeur is responsible.

It may be said this is unjust. Why? In fairness he should make good every injury flowing from his negligence. Not because of tenderness toward him we say he need not answer for all that follows his wrong. We look back to the catastrophe, the fire kindled by the spark, or the explosion. We trace the consequences—not indefinitely, but to a certain point. And to aid us in fixing that point we ask what might ordinarily be expected to follow the fire or the explosion.

This last suggestion is the factor which must determine the case before us. The act upon which defendant's liability rests is knocking an apparently harmless package onto the platform. The act was negligent. For its proximate consequences the defendant is liable. If its contents were broken, to the owner; if it fell upon and crushed a passenger's foot, then to him. If it exploded and injured one in the immediate vicinity, to him also as to A in the illustration. Mrs. Palsgraf was standing some distance away. How far cannot be told from the record—apparently twenty-five or thirty feet. Perhaps less. Except for the explosion, she would not have been injured. We are told by the appellant in his brief "it cannot be denied that the explosion was the direct cause of the plaintiff's injuries." So it was a substantial factor in producing the result—there was here a natural and continuous sequence—direct connection. The only intervening cause was that instead of blowing her to the ground the concussion smashed the weighing machine which in turn fell upon her. There was no remoteness in time, little in space. And surely, given such an explosion as here it needed no great foresight to predict that the natural result would be to injure one on the platform at no greater distance from its scene than was the plaintiff. Just how no one might be able to predict. Whether by flying fragments, by broken glass, by wreckage of machines or structures no one could say. But injury in some form was most probable.

Under these circumstances I cannot say as a matter of law that the plaintiff's injuries were not the proximate result of the negligence. That is all we have before us. The court refused to so charge. No request was made to submit the matter to the jury as a question of fact, even would that have been proper upon the record before us.

The judgment appealed from should be affirmed, with costs.

Professional Rules of Conduct

NATIONAL FEDERATION OF PARALEGAL ASSOCIATIONS, INC.

Model Code of Ethics and Professional Rsponsibility and Guidelines for Enforcement*

PREAMBLE

The National Federation of Paralegal Associations, Inc. ("NFPA") is a professional organization comprised of paralegal associations and individual paralegals throughout the United States and Canada. Members of NFPA have varying backgrounds, experiences, education and job responsibilities that reflect the diversity of the paralegal profession. NFPA promotes the growth, development and recognition of the paralegal profession as an integral partner in the delivery of legal services.

In May 1993 NFPA adopted its Model Code of Ethics and Professional Responsibility ("Model Code") to delineate the principles for ethics and conduct to which every paralegal should aspire.

Many paralegal associations throughout the United States have endorsed the concept and content of NFPA's Model Code through the adoption of their own ethical codes. In doing so, paralegals have confirmed the profession's commitment to increase the quality and efficiency of legal services, as well as recognized its responsibilities to the public, the legal community, and colleagues.

Paralegals have recognized, and will continue to recognize, that the profession must continue to evolve to enhance their roles in the delivery of legal services. With increased levels of responsibility comes the need to define and enforce mandatory rules of professional conduct. Enforcement of codes of paralegal conduct is a logical and necessary step to enhance and ensure the confidence of the legal community and the public in the integrity and professional responsibility of paralegals.

In April 1997 NFPA adopted the Model Disciplinary Rules ("Model Rules") to make possible the enforcement of the Canons and Ethical Considerations contained in the NFPA Model Code. A con-

current determination was made that the Model Code of Ethics and Professional Responsibility, formerly aspirational in nature, should be recognized as setting forth the enforceable obligations of all paralegals.

The Model Code and Model Rules offer a framework for professional discipline, either voluntarily or through formal regulatory programs.

§1.
NFPA MODEL DISCIPLINARY RULES AND ETHICAL CONSIDERATION

1.1 A Paralegal Shall Achieve and Maintain a High Level of Competence.

ETHICAL CONSIDERATIONS

EC-1.1(a) A paralegal shall achieve competency through education, training, and work experience.

EC-1.1(b) A paralegal shall aspire to participate in a minimum of twelve (12) hours of continuing legal education, to include at least one (1) hour of ethics education, every two (2) years in order to remain current on developments in the law.

EC-1.1(c) A paralegal shall perform all assignments promptly and efficiently.

1.2 A Paralegal Shall Maintain a High Level of Personal and Professional Integrity.

ETHICAL CONSIDERATIONS

EC-1.2(a) A paralegal shall not engage in any ex parte communications involving the courts or any other adjudicatory body in an attempt to exert undue influence or to obtain advantage or the benefit of only one party.

EC-1.2(b) A paralegal shall not communicate, or cause another to communicate, with a party the paralegal knows to be represented by a lawyer in a pending matter without the prior consent of the lawyer representing such other party.

EC-1.2(c) A paralegal shall ensure that all timekeeping and billing records prepared by the paralegal are thorough, accurate, honest, and complete.

EC-1.2(d) A paralegal shall not knowingly engage in fraudulent billing practices. Such practices may include, but are not limited to: inflation of hours billed to a client or employer; misrepresentation of the nature of tasks performed; and/or submission of fraudulent expense and disbursement documentation.

EC-1.2(e) A paralegal shall be scrupulous, thorough and honest in the identification and maintenance of all funds, securities, and other assets of a client and shall provide accurate accounting as appropriate.

EC-1.2(f) A paralegal shall advise the proper authority of non-confidential knowledge of any dishonest or fraudulent acts by any person pertaining to the handling of the funds, securities or other assets of a client. The authority to whom the report is made shall depend on the nature and circumstances of the possible misconduct, (e.g., ethics committees of law firms, corporations and/or paralegal associations, local or state bar associations, local prosecutors, administrative agencies, etc.). Failure to report such knowledge is in itself misconduct and shall be treated as such under these rules.

1.3 A Paralegal Shall Maintain a High Standard of Professional Conduct.

ETHICAL CONSIDERATIONS

EC-1.3(a) A paralegal shall refrain from engaging in any conduct that offends the dignity and decorum of proceedings before a court or other adjudicatory body and shall be respectful of all rules and procedures.

EC-1.3(b) A paralegal shall avoid impropriety and the appearance of impropriety and shall not engage in any conduct that would adversely affect his/her fitness to practice. Such conduct may include, but is not limited to: violence, dishonesty, interference with the administration of justice, and/or abuse of a professional position or public office.

EC-1.3(c) Should a paralegal's fitness to practice be compromised by physical or mental illness, causing that paralegal to commit an act that is in direct violation of the Model Code/Model Rules and/or the rules and/or laws governing the jurisdiction in which the paralegal practices, that paralegal may be protected from sanction upon review of the nature and circumstances of that illness.

EC-1.3(d) A paralegal shall advise the proper authority of non-confidential knowledge of any action of another legal professional that clearly demonstrates fraud, deceit, dishonesty, or misrepresentation. The authority to whom the report is made shall depend on the nature and circumstances of the possible misconduct, (e.g., ethics committees of law firms, corporations and/or paralegal associations, local or state bar associations, local prosecutors, administrative agencies, etc.). Failure to report such knowledge is in itself misconduct and shall be treated as such under these rules.

EC-1.3(e) A paralegal shall not knowingly assist any individual with the commission of an act that is in direct violation of the Model Code/Model Rules and/or the rules and/or laws governing the jurisdiction in which the paralegal practices.

EC-1.3(f) If a paralegal possesses knowledge of future criminal activity, that knowledge must be reported to the appropriate authority immediately.

1.4 A Paralegal Shall Serve the Public Interest by Contributing to the Improvement of the Legal System and Delivery of Quality Legal Services, Including Pro Bono Publico Services.

ETHICAL CONSIDERATIONS

EC-1.4(a) A paralegal shall be sensitive to the legal needs of the public and shall promote the development and implementation of programs that address those needs.

EC-1.4(b) A paralegal shall support efforts to improve the legal system and access thereto and shall assist in making changes.

EC-1.4(c) A paralegal shall support and participate in the delivery of Pro Bono Publico services directed toward implementing and improving access to justice, the law, the legal system or the paralegal and legal professions.

EC-1.4(d) A paralegal should aspire annually to contribute twenty-four (24) hours of Pro Bono Publico services under the supervision of an attorney or as authorized by administrative, statutory or court authority to:

1. persons of limited means; or
2. charitable, religious, civic, community, governmental and educational organizations in matters that are designed primarily to address the legal needs of persons with limited means; or
3. individuals, groups or organizations seeking to secure or protect civil rights, civil liberties or public rights.

1.5 A Paralegal Shall Preserve All Confidential Information Provided by the Client or Acquired from Other Sources Before, During, and After the Course of the Professional Relationship.

ETHICAL CONSIDERATIONS

EC-1.5(a) A paralegal shall be aware of and abide by all legal authority governing confidential information in the jurisdiction in which the paralegal practices.

EC-1.5(b) A paralegal shall not use confidential information to the disadvantage of the client.

EC-1.5(c) A paralegal shall not use confidential information to the advantage of the paralegal or of a third person.

EC-1.5(d) A paralegal may reveal confidential information only after full disclosure and with the client's written consent; or, when required by law or court order; or, when necessary to prevent the client from committing an act that could result in death or serious bodily harm.

EC-1.5(e) A paralegal shall keep those individuals responsible for the legal representation of a client fully informed of any confidential information the paralegal may have pertaining to that client.

EC-1.5(f) A paralegal shall not engage in any indiscreet communications concerning clients.

1.6 A Paralegal Shall Avoid Conflicts of Interest and Shall Disclose Any Possible Conflict to the Employer or Client, as Well as to the Prospective Employers or Clients.

ETHICAL CONSIDERATIONS

EC-1.6(a) A paralegal shall act within the bounds of the law, solely for the benefit of the client, and shall be free of compromising influences and loyalties. Neither the paralegal's personal or business interest, nor those of other clients or third persons, should compromise the paralegal's professional judgment and loyalty to the client.

EC-1.6(b) A paralegal shall avoid conflicts of interest that may arise from previous assignments, whether for a present or past employer or client.

EC-1.6(c) A paralegal shall avoid conflicts of interest that may arise from family relationships and from personal and business interests.

EC-1.6(d) In order to be able to determine whether an actual or potential conflict of interest exists a paralegal shall create and maintain an effective recordkeeping system that identifies clients, matters, and parties with which the paralegal has worked.

EC-1.6(e) A paralegal shall reveal sufficient non-confidential information about a client or former client to reasonably ascertain if an actual or potential conflict of interest exists.

EC-1.6(f) A paralegal shall not participate in or conduct work on any matter where a conflict of interest has been identified.

EC-1.6(g) In matters where a conflict of interest has been identified and the client consents to continued representation, a paralegal shall comply fully with the implementation and maintenance of an Ethical Wall.

1.7 A Paralegal's Title Shall be Fully Disclosed.

ETHICAL CONSIDERATIONS

EC-1.7(a) A paralegal's title shall clearly indicate the individual's status and shall be disclosed in all business and professional communications to avoid misunderstandings and misconceptions about the paralegal's role and responsibilities.

EC-1.7(b) A paralegal's title shall be included if the paralegal's name appears on business cards, letterhead, brochures, directories, and advertisements.

EC-1.7(c) A paralegal shall not use letterhead, business cards or other promotional materials to create a fraudulent impression of his/her status or ability to practice in the jurisdiction in which the paralegal practices.

EC-1.7(d) A paralegal shall not practice under color of any record, diploma, or certificate that has been illegally or fraudulently obtained or issued or which is misrepresentative in any way.

EC-1.7(e) A paralegal shall not participate in the creation, issuance, or dissemination of fraudulent records, diplomas, or certificates.

1.8 A Paralegal Shall Not Engage in the Unauthorized Practice of Law.

ETHICAL CONSIDERATIONS

EC-1.8(a) A paralegal shall comply with the applicable legal authority governing the unauthorized practice of law in the jurisdiction in which the paralegal practices.

§2.
NFPA GUIDELINES FOR THE ENFORCEMENT OF THE MODEL CODE OF ETHICS AND PROFESSIONAL RESPONSIBILITY

2.1 Basis for Discipline

2.1(a) Disciplinary investigations and proceedings brought under authority of the Rules shall be conducted in accord with obligations imposed on the paralegal professional by the Model Code of Ethics and Professional Responsibility.

2.2 Structure of Disciplinary Committee

2.2(a) The Disciplinary Committee ("Committee") shall be made up of nine (9) members including the Chair.

2.2(b) Each member of the Committee, including any temporary replacement members, shall have demonstrated working knowledge of ethics/professional responsibility-related issues and activities.

2.2(c) The Committee shall represent a cross-section of practice areas and work experience. The following recommendations are made regarding the members of the Committee.

1) At least one paralegal with one to three years of law-related work experience.

2) At least one paralegal with five to seven years of law related work experience.

3) At least one paralegal with over ten years of law related work experience.

4) One paralegal educator with five to seven years of work experience; preferably in the area of ethics/ professional responsibility.

5) One paralegal manager.

6) One lawyer with five to seven years of law-related work experience.

7) One lay member.

2.2(d) The Chair of the Committee shall be appointed within thirty (30) days of its members' induction. The Chair shall have no fewer than ten (10) years of law-related work experience.

2.2(e) The terms of all members of the Committee shall be staggered. Of those members initially appointed, a simple majority plus one shall be appointed to a term of one year, and the remaining members shall be appointed to a term of two years. Thereafter, all members of the Committee shall be appointed to terms of two years.

2.2(f) If for any reason the terms of a majority of the Committee will expire at the same time, members may be appointed to terms of one year to maintain continuity of the Committee.

2.2(g) The Committee shall organize from its members a three-tiered structure to investigate, prosecute and/or adjudicate charges of misconduct. The members shall be rotated among the tiers.

2.3 Operation of Committee

2.3(a) The Committee shall meet on an as-needed basis to discuss, investigate, and/or adjudicate alleged violations of the Model Code/Model Rules.

2.3(b) A majority of the members of the Committee present at a meeting shall constitute a quorum.

2.3(c) A Recording Secretary shall be designated to maintain complete and accurate minutes of all Committee meetings. All such minutes shall be kept confi- dential until a decision has been made that the matter will be set for hearing as set forth in Section 6.1 below.

2.3(d) If any member of the Committee has a conflict of interest with the Charging Party, the Responding Party, or the allegations of misconduct, that member shall not take part in any hearing or deliberations concerning those allegations. If the absence of that member creates a lack of a quorum for the Committee, then a temporary replacement for the member shall be appointed.

2.3(e) Either the Charging Party or the Responding Party may request that, for good cause shown, any member of the Committee not participate in a hearing or deliberation. All such requests shall be honored. If the absence of a Committee member under those circumstances creates a lack of a quorum for the Committee, then a temporary replacement for that member shall be appointed.

2.3(f) All discussions and correspondence of the Committee shall be kept confidential until a decision has been made that the matter will be set for hearing as set forth in Section 6.1 below.

2.3(g) All correspondence from the Committee to the Responding Party regarding any charge of misconduct and any decisions made regarding the charge shall be mailed certified mail, return receipt requested, to the Responding Party's last known address and shall be clearly marked with a "Confidential" designation.

2.4 Procedure for the Reporting of Alleged Violations of the Model Code/Disciplinary Rules

2.4(a) An individual or entity in possession of non-confidential knowledge or information concerning possible instances of misconduct shall make a confidential written report to the Committee within thirty (30) days of obtaining same. This report shall include all details of the alleged misconduct.

2.4(b) The Committee so notified shall inform the Responding Party of the allegation(s) of misconduct no later than ten (10) business days after receiving the confidential written report from the Charging Party.

2.4(c) Notification to the Responding Party shall include the identity of the Charging Party, unless, for good cause shown, the Charging Party requests anonymity.

2.4(d) The Responding Party shall reply to the allegations within ten (10) business days of notification.

2.5 Procedure for the Investigation of a Charge of Misconduct

2.5(a) Upon receipt of a Charge of Misconduct ("Charge"), or on its own initiative, the Committee shall initiate an investigation.

2.5(b) If, upon initial or preliminary review, the Committee makes a determination that the charges are either without basis in fact or, if proven, would not constitute professional misconduct, the Committee shall dismiss the allegations of misconduct. If such determination of dismissal cannot be made, a formal investigation shall be initiated.

2.5(c) Upon the decision to conduct a formal investigation, the Committee shall:

1) mail to the Charging and Responding Parties within three (3) business days of that decision notice of the commencement of a formal investigation. That notification shall be in writing and shall contain a complete explanation of all Charge(s), as well as the reasons for a formal investigation and shall cite the applicable codes and rules;

2) allow the Responding Party thirty (30) days to prepare and submit a confidential response to the Committee, which response shall address each charge specifically and shall be in writing; and

3) upon receipt of the response to the notification, have thirty (30) days to investigate the Charge(s). If an extension of time is deemed necessary, that extension shall not exceed ninety (90) days.

2.5(d) Upon conclusion of the investigation, the Committee may:

1) dismiss the Charge upon the finding that it has no basis in fact;

2) dismiss the Charge upon the finding that, if proven, the Charge would not constitute Misconduct;

3) refer the matter for hearing by the Tribunal; or

4) in the case of criminal activity, refer the Charge(s) and all investigation results to the appropriate authority.

2.6 Procedure for a Misconduct Hearing Before a Tribunal

2.6(a) Upon the decision by the Committee that a matter should be heard, all parties shall be notified and a hearing date shall be set. The hearing shall take place no more than thirty (30) days from the conclusion of the formal investigation.

2.6(b) The Responding Party shall have the right to counsel. The parties and the Tribunal shall have the right to call any witnesses and introduce any documentation that they believe will lead to the fair and reasonable resolution of the matter.

2.6(c) Upon completion of the hearing, the Tribunal shall deliberate and present a written decision to the parties in accordance with procedures as set forth by the Tribunal.

2.6(d) Notice of the decision of the Tribunal shall be appropriately published.

2.7 Sanctions

2.7(a) Upon a finding of the Tribunal that misconduct has occurred, any of the following sanctions, or others as may be deemed appropriate, may be imposed upon the Responding Party, either singularly or in combination:

1) letter of reprimand to the Responding Party; counseling;

2) attendance at an ethics course approved by the Tribunal; probation;

3) suspension of license/authority to practice; revocation of license/authority to practice;

4) imposition of a fine; assessment of costs; or

5) in the instance of criminal activity, referral to the appropriate authority.

2.7(b) Upon the expiration of any period of probation, suspension, or revocation, the Responding Party may make application for reinstatement. With the application for reinstatement, the Responding Party must show proof of having complied with all aspects of the sanctions imposed by the Tribunal.

2.8 Appellate Procedures 2.8(a) The parties shall have the right to appeal the decision of the Tribunal in accordance with the procedure as set forth by the Tribunal.

DEFINITIONS

"Appellate Body" means a body established to adjudicate an appeal to any decision made by a Tribunal or other decision-making body with respect to formally-heard Charges of Misconduct.

"Charge of Misconduct" means a written submission by any individual or entity to an ethics committee, paralegal association, bar association, law enforcement agency, judicial body, government agency, or other appropriate body or entity, that sets forth non-confidential information regarding any instance of alleged misconduct by an individual paralegal or paralegal entity.

"Charging Party" means any individual or entity who submits a Charge of Misconduct against an individual paralegal or paralegal entity.

"Competency" means the demonstration of: diligence, education, skill, and mental, emotional, and physical fitness reasonably necessary for the performance of paralegal services.

"Confidential Information" means information relating to a client, whatever its source, that is not public knowledge nor available to the public. ("Non-Confidential Information" would generally include the name of the client and the identity of the matter for which the paralegal provided services.)

"Disciplinary Hearing" means the confidential proceeding conducted by a committee or other designated body or entity concerning any instance of alleged misconduct by an individual paralegal or paralegal entity.

"Disciplinary Committee" means any committee that has been established by an entity such as a paralegal association, bar association, judicial body, or government agency to: (a) identify, define and investigate general Ethical Considerations and concerns with respect to paralegal practice; (b) administer and enforce the Model Code and Model Rules and; (c) discipline any individual paralegal or paralegal entity found to be in violation of same.

"Disclose" means communication of information reasonably sufficient to permit identification of the significance of the matter in question.

"Ethical Wall" means the screening method implemented in order to protect a client from a conflict of interest. An Ethical Wall generally includes, but is not limited to, the following elements: (1) prohibit the paralegal from having any connection with the matter; (2) ban discussions with or the transfer of documents to or from the paralegal; (3) restrict access to files; and (4) educate all members of the firm, corporation, or entity as to the separation of the paralegal (both organizationally and physically) from the pending matter. For more information regarding the Ethical Wall, see the NFPA publication entitled "The Ethical Wall—Its Application to Paralegals."

"Ex parte" means actions or communications conducted at the instance and for the benefit of one party only, and without notice to, or contestation by, any person adversely interested.

"Investigation" means the investigation of any charge(s) of misconduct filed against an individual paralegal or paralegal entity by a Committee.

"Letter of Reprimand" means a written notice of formal censure or severe reproof administered to an individual paralegal or paralegal entity for unethical or improper conduct.

"Misconduct" means the knowing or unknowing commission of an act that is in direct violation of those Canons and Ethical Considerations of any and all applicable codes and/or rules of conduct.

"Paralegal" is synonymous with "Legal Assistant" and is defined as a person qualified through education, training, or work experience to perform substantive legal work that requires knowledge of legal concepts and is customarily, but not exclusively performed by a lawyer. This person may be retained or employed by a lawyer, law office, governmental agency, or other entity or may be authorized by administrative, statutory, or court authority to perform this work.

"Pro Bono Publico" means providing or assisting to provide quality legal services in order to enhance access to justice for persons of limited means; charitable, religious, civic, community, governmental and educational organizations in matters that are designed primarily to address the legal needs of persons with limited means; or individuals, groups or organizations seeking to secure or protect civil rights, civil liberties or public rights.

"Proper Authority" means the local paralegal association, the local or state bar association, Committee(s) of the local paralegal or bar association(s), local prosecutor, administrative agency, or other tribunal empowered to investigate or act upon an instance of alleged misconduct.

"Responding Party" means an individual paralegal or paralegal entity against whom a Charge of Misconduct has been submitted.

"Revocation" means the recision of the license, certificate or other authority to practice of an individual paralegal or paralegal entity found in violation of those Canons and Ethical Considerations of any and all applicable codes and/or rules of conduct.

"Suspension" means the suspension of the license, certificate or other authority to practice of an individual paralegal or paralegal entity found in violation of those Canons and Ethical Considerations of any and all applicable codes and/or rules of conduct.

"Tribunal" means the body designated to adjudicate allegations of misconduct.

OUTLINE OF AND EXCERPTS FROM THE
ABA MODEL RULES OF PROFESSIONAL CONDUCT, 2002 *

American Bar Association: www.abanet.org
The full text of the rules may be viewed on the ABA website.

Rule 1.0 Terminology

CLIENT–LAWYER RELATIONSHIP

Rule 1.1 **Competence**

Rule 1.2 **Scope of Representation and Allocation of Authority Between Client and Lawyer**

Rule 1.3 **Diligence**

Rule 1.4 **Communications**

Rule 1.5 **Fees**

Rule 1.6 **Confidentiality of Information**

(a) A lawyer shall not reveal information relating to the representation of a client unless the client gives informed consent, the disclosure is impliedly authorized in order to carry out the representation or the disclosure is permitted by paragraph

(b) A lawyer may reveal information relating to the representation of a client to the extent the lawyer reasonably believes necessary:

(1) to prevent reasonably certain death or substantial bodily harm;

(2) to secure legal advice about the lawyer's compliance with these Rules;

(3) to establish a claim or defense on behalf of the lawyer in a controversy between the lawyer and the client, to establish a defense to a criminal charge or civil claim against the lawyer based upon conduct in which the client was involved, or to respond to allegations in any proceeding concerning the lawyer's representation of the client; or

(4) to comply with other law or a court order.

Comment:

[1] This Rule governs the disclosure by a lawyer of information relating to the representation of a client during the lawyer's representation of the client. See Rule 1.18 for the lawyer's duties with respect to information provided to the lawyer by a prospective client, Rule 1.9(c)(2) for the lawyer's duty not to reveal information relating to the lawyer's prior representation of a former client and Rules 1.8(b) and 1.9(c)(1) for the lawyer's duties with respect to the use of such information to the disadvantage of clients and former clients.

[2] A fundamental principle in the client-lawyer relationship is that, in the absence of the client's informed consent, the lawyer must not reveal information relating to the representation. See Rule 1.0(e) for the definition of informed consent. This contributes to the trust that is the hallmark of the client-lawyer relationship. The client is thereby encouraged to seek legal assistance and to communicate fully and frankly with the lawyer even as to embarrassing or legally damaging subject matter. The lawyer needs this information to represent the client effectively and, if necessary, to advise the client to refrain from wrongful conduct. Almost without exception, clients come to lawyers in order to determine their rights and what is, in the complex of laws and regulations, deemed to be legal and correct. Based upon experience, lawyers know that almost all clients follow the advice given, and the law is upheld.

[3] The principle of client-lawyer confidentiality is given effect by related bodies of law: the attorney-client privilege, the work product doctrine and the rule of confidentiality established in professional ethics. The attorney-client privilege and work-product doctrine apply in judicial and other proceedings in which a lawyer may be called as a witness or otherwise required to produce evidence concerning a client. The rule of client-lawyer confidentiality applies in situations other than those where evidence is sought from the lawyer through compulsion of law. The confidentiality rule, for example, applies not only to matters communicated in confidence by the client but also to all information relating to the representation, whatever its source. A lawyer may not disclose such information except as authorized or required by the Rules of Professional Conduct or other law. See also Scope.

[4] Paragraph (a) prohibits a lawyer from revealing information relating to the representation of a client. This prohibition also applies to disclosures by a lawyer that do not in themselves reveal protected information but could reasonably lead to the discovery of such information by a third person. A lawyer's use of a hypothetical to discuss

issues relating to the representation is permissible so long as there is no reasonable likelihood that the listener will be able to ascertain the identity of the client or the situation involved.

Authorized Disclosure

[5] Except to the extent that the client's instructions or special circumstances limit that authority, a lawyer is impliedly authorized to make disclosures about a client when appropriate in carrying out the representation. In some situations, for example, a lawyer may be impliedly authorized to admit a fact that cannot properly be disputed or to make a disclosure that facilitates a satisfactory conclusion to a matter. Lawyers in a firm may, in the course of the firm's practice, disclose to each other information relating to a client of the firm, unless the client has instructed that particular information be confined to specified lawyers.

Disclosure Adverse to Client

[6] Although the public interest is usually best served by a strict rule requiring lawyers to preserve the confidentiality of information relating to the representation of their clients, the confidentiality rule is subject to limited exceptions. Paragraph (b)(1) recognizes the overriding value of life and physical integrity and permits disclosure reasonably necessary to prevent reasonably certain death or substantial bodily harm. Such harm is reasonably certain to occur if it will be suffered imminently or if there is a present and substantial threat that a person will suffer such harm at a later date if the lawyer fails to take action necessary to eliminate the threat. Thus, a lawyer who knows that a client has accidentally discharged toxic waste into a town's water supply may reveal this information to the authorities if there is a present and substantial risk that a person who drinks the water will contract a life-threatening or debilitating disease and the lawyer's disclosure is necessary to eliminate the threat or reduce the number of victims.

[7] A lawyer's confidentiality obligations do not preclude a lawyer from securing confidential legal advice about the lawyer's personal responsibility to comply with these Rules. In most situations, disclosing information to secure such advice will be impliedly authorized for the lawyer to carry out the representation. Even when the disclosure is not impliedly authorized, paragraph (b)(2) permits such disclosure because of the importance of a lawyer's compliance with the Rules of Professional Conduct.

[8] Where a legal claim or disciplinary charge alleges complicity of the lawyer in a client's conduct or other misconduct of the lawyer involving representation of the client, the lawyer may respond to the extent the lawyer reasonably believes necessary to establish a defense. The same is true with respect to a claim involving the conduct or representation of a former client. Such a charge can arise in a civil, criminal, disciplinary or other proceeding and can be based on a wrong allegedly committed by the lawyer against the client or on a wrong alleged by a third person, for example, a person claiming to have been defrauded by the lawyer and client acting together. The lawyer's right to respond arises when an assertion of such complicity has been made. Paragraph (b)(3) does not require the lawyer to await the commencement of an action or proceeding that charges such complicity, so that the defense may be established by responding directly to a third party who has made such an assertion. The right to defend also applies, of course, where a proceeding has been commenced.

[9] A lawyer entitled to a fee is permitted by paragraph (b)(3) to prove the services rendered in an action to collect it. This aspect of the rule expresses the principle that the beneficiary of a fiduciary relationship may not exploit it to the detriment of the fiduciary.

[10] Other law may require that a lawyer disclose information about a client. Whether such a law supersedes Rule 1.6 is a question of law beyond the scope of these Rules. When disclosure of information relating to the representation appears to be required by other law, the lawyer must discuss the matter with the client to the extent required by Rule 1.4. If, however, the other law supersedes this Rule and requires disclosure, paragraph (b)(4) permits the lawyer to make such disclosures as are necessary to comply with the law.

[11] A lawyer may be ordered to reveal information relating to the representation of a client by a court or by another tribunal or governmental entity claiming authority pursuant to other law to compel the disclosure. Absent informed consent of the client to do otherwise, the lawyer should assert on behalf of the client all nonfrivolous claims that the order is not authorized by other law or that the information sought is protected against disclosure by the attorney-client privilege or other applicable law. In the event of an adverse ruling, the lawyer must consult with the client about the possibility of appeal to the extent required by Rule 1.4. Unless review is sought, however, paragraph (b)(4) permits the lawyer to comply with the court's order.

[12] Paragraph (b) permits disclosure only to the extent the lawyer reasonably believes the disclosure is necessary to accomplish one of the purposes specified. Where practicable, the lawyer should first seek to persuade the client to take suitable action to obviate the need for disclosure. In any case, a disclosure adverse to the client's interest should be no greater than the lawyer reasonably believes necessary to accomplish the purpose. If the disclosure will be made in connection with a judicial proceeding, the disclosure should be made in a manner that limits access to

the information to the tribunal or other persons having a need to know it and appropriate protective orders or other arrangements should be sought by the lawyer to the fullest extent practicable.

[13] Paragraph (b) permits but does not require the disclosure of information relating to a client's representation to accomplish the purposes specified in paragraphs (b)(1) through (b)(4). In exercising the discretion conferred by this Rule, the lawyer may consider such factors as the nature of the lawyer's relationship with the client and with those who might be injured by the client, the lawyer's own involvement in the transaction and factors that may extenuate the conduct in question. A lawyer's decision not to disclose as permitted by paragraph (b) does not violate this Rule. Disclosure may be required, however, by other Rules. Some Rules require disclosure only if such disclosure would be permitted by paragraph (b). See Rules 1.2(d), 4.1(b), 8.1 and 8.3. Rule 3.3, on the other hand, requires disclosure in some circumstances regardless of whether such disclosure is permitted by this Rule. See Rule 3.3(c).

Withdrawal

[14] If the lawyer's services will be used by the client in materially furthering a course of criminal or fraudulent conduct, the lawyer must withdraw, as stated in Rule 1.16(a)(1). After withdrawal the lawyer is required to refrain from making disclosure of the client's confidences, except as otherwise permitted by Rule 1.6. Neither this Rule nor Rule 1.8(b) nor Rule 1.16(d) prevents the lawyer from giving notice of the fact of withdrawal, and the lawyer may also withdraw or disaffirm any opinion, document, affirmation, or the like. Where the client is an organization, the lawyer may be in doubt whether contemplated conduct will actually be carried out by the organization. Where necessary to guide conduct in connection with this Rule, the lawyer may make inquiry within the organization as indicated in Rule 1.13(b).

Acting Competently to Preserve Confidentiality

[15] A lawyer must act competently to safeguard information relating to the representation of a client against inadvertent or unauthorized disclosure by the lawyer or other persons who are participating in the representation of the client or who are subject to the lawyer's supervision. See Rules 1.1, 5.1 and 5.3.

[16] When transmitting a communication that includes information relating to the representation of a client, the lawyer must take reasonable precautions to prevent the information from coming into the hands of unintended recipients. This duty, however, does not require that the lawyer use special security measures if the method of communication affords a reasonable expectation of privacy.

Special circumstances, however, may warrant special precautions. Factors to be considered in determining the reasonableness of the lawyer's expectation of confidentiality include the sensitivity of the information and the extent to which the privacy of the communication is protected by law or by a confidentiality agreement. A client may require the lawyer to implement special security measures not required by this Rule or may give informed consent to the use of a means of communication that would otherwise be prohibited by this Rule.

Former Client

[17] The duty of confidentiality continues after the client-lawyer relationship has terminated. See Rule 1.9(c)(2). See Rule 1.9(c)(1) for the prohibition against using such information to the disadvantage of the former client.

Rule 1.7 Conflict of Interest: Current Clients

(a) Except as provided in paragraph (b), a lawyer shall not represent a client if the representation involves a concurrent conflict of interest. A concurrent conflict of interest exists if:

(1) the representation of one client will be directly adverse to another client; or

(2) there is a significant risk that the representation of one or more clients will be materially limited by the lawyer's responsibilities to another client, a former client or a third person or by a personal interest of the lawyer.

(b) Notwithstanding the existence of a concurrent conflict of i\nterest under paragraph (a), a lawyer may represent a client if:

(1) the lawyer reasonably believes that the lawyer will be able to provide competent and diligent representation to each affected client;

(2) the representation is not prohibited by law;

(3) the representation does not involve the assertion of a claim by one client against another client represented by the lawyer in the same litigation or other proceeding before a tribunal; and

(4) each affected client gives informed consent, confirmed in writing.

Comment:

General Principles

[1] Loyalty and independent judgment are essential elements in the lawyer's relationship to a client. Concurrent conflicts of interest can arise from the lawyer's responsibilities to another client, a former client or a third person or from the lawyer's own interests. For specific Rules regarding certain concurrent conflicts of interest, see Rule 1.8. For former client conflicts of interest, see Rule 1.9.

For conflicts of interest involving prospective clients, see Rule 1.18. For definitions of "informed consent" and "confirmed in writing," see Rule 1.0(e) and (b).

[2] Resolution of a conflict of interest problem under this Rule requires the lawyer to: 1) clearly identify the client or clients; 2) determine whether a conflict of interest exists; 3) decide whether the representation may be undertaken despite the existence of a conflict, i.e., whether the conflict is consentable; and 4) if so, consult with the clients affected under paragraph (a) and obtain their informed consent, confirmed in writing. The clients affected under paragraph (a) include both of the clients referred to in paragraph (a)(1) and the one or more clients whose representation might be materially limited under paragraph (a)(2).

[3] A conflict of interest may exist before representation is undertaken, in which event the representation must be declined, unless the lawyer obtains the informed consent of each client under the conditions of paragraph (b). To determine whether a conflict of interest exists, a lawyer should adopt reasonable procedures, appropriate for the size and type of firm and practice, to determine in both litigation and non-litigation matters the persons and issues involved. See also Comment to Rule 5.1. Ignorance caused by a failure to institute such procedures will not excuse a lawyer's violation of this Rule. As to whether a client-lawyer relationship exists or, having once been established, is continuing, see Comment to Rule 1.3 and Scope.

[4] If a conflict arises after representation has been undertaken, the lawyer ordinarily must withdraw from the representation, unless the lawyer has obtained the informed consent of the client under the conditions of paragraph (b). See Rule 1.16. Where more than one client is involved, whether the lawyer may continue to represent any of the clients is determined both by the lawyer's ability to comply with duties owed to the former client and by the lawyer's ability to represent adequately the remaining client or clients, given the lawyer's duties to the former client. See Rule 1.9. See also Comments [5] and [29].

[5] Unforeseeable developments, such as changes in corporate and other organizational affiliations or the addition or realignment of parties in litigation, might create conflicts in the midst of a representation, as when a company sued by the lawyer on behalf of one client is bought by another client represented by the lawyer in an unrelated matter. Depending on the circumstances, the lawyer may have the option to withdraw from one of the representations in order to avoid the conflict. The lawyer must seek court approval where necessary and take steps to minimize harm to the clients. See Rule 1.16. The lawyer must continue to protect the confidences of the client from whose representation the lawyer has withdrawn. See Rule 1.9(c).

Identifying Conflicts of Interest: Directly Adverse

[6] Loyalty to a current client prohibits undertaking representation directly adverse to that client without that client's informed consent. Thus, absent consent, a lawyer may not act as an advocate in one matter against a person the lawyer represents in some other matter, even when the matters are wholly unrelated. The client as to whom the representation is directly adverse is likely to feel betrayed, and the resulting damage to the client-lawyer relationship is likely to impair the lawyer's ability to represent the client effectively. In addition, the client on whose behalf the adverse representation is undertaken reasonably may fear that the lawyer will pursue that client's case less effectively out of deference to the other client, i.e., that the representation may be materially limited by the lawyer's interest in retaining the current client. Similarly, a directly adverse conflict may arise when a lawyer is required to cross-examine a client who appears as a witness in a lawsuit involving another client, as when the testimony will be damaging to the client who is represented in the lawsuit. On the other hand, simultaneous representation in unrelated matters of clients whose interests are only economically adverse, such as representation of competing economic enterprises in unrelated litigation, does not ordinarily constitute a conflict of interest and thus may not require consent of the respective clients.

[7] Directly adverse conflicts can also arise in transactional matters. For example, if a lawyer is asked to represent the seller of a business in negotiations with a buyer represented by the lawyer, not in the same transaction but in another, unrelated matter, the lawyer could not undertake the representation without the informed consent of each client.

Identifying Conflicts of Interest: Material Limitation

[8] Even where there is no direct adverseness, a conflict of interest exists if there is a significant risk that a lawyer's ability to consider, recommend or carry out an appropriate course of action for the client will be materially limited as a result of the lawyer's other responsi- bilities or interests. For example, a lawyer asked to represent several individuals seeking to form a joint venture is likely to be materially limited in the lawyer's ability to recommend or advocate all possible positions that each might take because of the lawyer's duty of loyalty to the others. The conflict in effect forecloses alternatives that would otherwise be available to the client. The mere possibility of subsequent harm does not itself require disclosure and consent. The critical questions are the likelihood that a difference in interests will eventuate and, if it does, whether it will materially interfere with the lawyer's independent professional judgment in considering alternatives

or foreclose courses of action that reasonably should be pursued on behalf of the client.

Lawyer's Responsibilities to Former Clients and Other Third Persons

[9] In addition to conflicts with other current clients, a lawyer's duties of loyalty and independence may be materially limited by responsibilities to former clients under Rule 1.9 or by the lawyer's responsibilities to other persons, such as fiduciary duties arising from a lawyer's service as a trustee, executor or corporate director.

Personal Interest Conflicts

[10] The lawyer's own interests should not be permitted to have an adverse effect on representation of a client. For example, if the probity of a lawyer's own conduct in a transaction is in serious question, it may be difficult or impossible for the lawyer to give a client detached advice. Similarly, when a lawyer has discussions concerning possible employment with an opponent of the lawyer's client, or with a law firm representing the opponent, such discussions could materially limit the lawyer's representation of the client. In addition, a lawyer may not allow related business interests to affect representation, for example, by referring clients to an enterprise in which the lawyer has an undisclosed financial interest. See Rule 1.8 for specific Rules pertaining to a number of personal interest conflicts, including business transactions with clients. See also Rule 1.10 (personal interest conflicts under Rule 1.7 ordinarily are not imputed to other lawyers in a law firm).

[11] When lawyers representing different clients in the same matter or in substantially related matters are closely related by blood or marriage, there may be a significant risk that client confidences will be revealed and that the lawyer's family relationship will interfere with both loyalty and independent professional judgment. As a result, each client is entitled to know of the existence and implications of the relationship between the lawyers before the lawyer agrees to undertake the representation. Thus, a lawyer related to another lawyer, e.g., as parent, child, sibling or spouse, ordinarily may not represent a client in a matter where that lawyer is representing another party, unless each client gives informed consent. The disqualification arising from a close family relationship is personal and ordinarily is not imputed to members of firms with whom the lawyers are associated. See Rule 1.10.

[12] A lawyer is prohibited from engaging in sexual relationships with a client unless the sexual relationship predates the formation of the client-lawyer relationship. See Rule 1.8(j).

Interest of Person Paying for a Lawyer's Service

[13] A lawyer may be paid from a source other than the client, including a co-client, if the client is informed of that fact and consents and the arrangement does not compromise the lawyer's duty of loyalty or independent judgment to the client. See Rule 1.8(f). If acceptance of the payment from any other source presents a significant risk that the lawyer's representation of the client will be materially limited by the lawyer's own interest in accommodating the person paying the lawyer's fee or by the lawyer's responsibilities to a payer who is also a co-client, then the lawyer must comply with the requirements of paragraph (b) before accepting the representation, including determining whether the conflict is consentable and, if so, that the client has adequate information about the material risks of the representation.

Prohibited Representations

[14] Ordinarily, clients may consent to representation notwithstanding a conflict. However, as indicated in paragraph (b), some conflicts are nonconsentable, meaning that the lawyer involved cannot properly ask for such agreement or provide representation on the basis of the client's consent. When the lawyer is representing more than one client, the question of consentability must be resolved as to each client.

[15] Consentability is typically determined by considering whether the interests of the clients will be adequately protected if the clients are permitted to give their informed consent to representation burdened by a conflict of interest. Thus, under paragraph (b)(1), representation is prohibited if in the circumstances the lawyer cannot reasonably conclude that the lawyer will be able to provide competent and diligent representation. See Rule 1.1 (competence) and Rule 1.3 (diligence).

[16] Paragraph (b)(2) describes conflicts that are nonconsentable because the representation is prohibited by applicable law. For example, in some states substantive law provides that the same lawyer may not represent more than one defendant in a capital case, even with the consent of the clients, and under federal criminal statutes certain representations by a former government lawyer are prohibited, despite the informed consent of the former client. In addition, decisional law in some states limits the ability of a governmental client, such as a municipality, to consent to a conflict of interest.

[17] Paragraph (b)(3) describes conflicts that are nonconsentable because of the institutional interest in vigorous development of each client's position when the clients are aligned directly against each other in the same litigation or other proceeding before a tribunal. Whether clients are

aligned directly against each other within the meaning of this paragraph requires examination of the context of the proceeding. Although this paragraph does not preclude a lawyer's multiple representation of adverse parties to a mediation (because mediation is not a proceeding before a "tribunal" under Rule 1.0(m)), such representation may be precluded by paragraph (b)(1).

Informed Consent

[18] Informed consent requires that each affected client be aware of the relevant circumstances and of the material and reasonably foreseeable ways that the conflict could have adverse effects on the interests of that client. See Rule 1.0(e) (informed consent). The information required depends on the nature of the conflict and the nature of the risks involved. When representation of multiple clients in a single matter is undertaken, the information must include the implications of the common representation, including possible effects on loyalty, confidentiality and the attorney-client privilege and the advantages and risks involved. See Comments [30] and [31] (effect of common representation on confidentiality).

[19] Under some circumstances it may be impossible to make the disclosure necessary to obtain consent. For example, when the lawyer represents different clients in related matters and one of the clients refuses to consent to the disclosure necessary to permit the other client to make an informed decision, the lawyer cannot properly ask the latter to consent. In some cases the alternative to common representation can be that each party may have to obtain separate representation with the possibility of incurring additional costs. These costs, along with the benefits of securing separate representation, are factors that may be considered by the affected client in determining whether common representation is in the client's interests.

Consent Confirmed in Writing

[20] Paragraph (b) requires the lawyer to obtain the informed consent of the client, confirmed in writing. Such a writing may consist of a document executed by the client or one that the lawyer promptly records and transmits to the client following an oral consent. See Rule 1.0(b). See also Rule 1.0(n) (writing includes electronic transmission). If it is not feasible to obtain or transmit the writing at the time the client gives informed consent, then the lawyer must obtain or transmit it within a reasonable time thereafter. See Rule 1.0(b). The requirement of a writing does not supplant the need in most cases for the lawyer to talk with the client, to explain the risks and advantages, if any, of representation burdened with a conflict of interest, as well as reasonably available alternatives, and to afford the client a reasonable opportunity to consider the risks and alterna-

tives and to raise questions and concerns. Rather, the writing is required in order to impress upon clients the seriousness of the decision the client is being asked to make and to avoid disputes or ambiguities that might later occur in the absence of a writing.

Revoking Consent

[21] A client who has given consent to a conflict may revoke the consent and, like any other client, may terminate the lawyer's representation at any time. Whether revoking consent to the client's own representation precludes the lawyer from continuing to represent other clients depends on the circumstances, including the nature of the conflict, whether the client revoked consent because of a material change in circumstances, the reasonable expectations of the other client and whether material detriment to the other clients or the lawyer would result.

Consent to Future Conflict

[22] Whether a lawyer may properly request a client to waive conflicts that might arise in the future is subject to the test of paragraph (b). The effectiveness of such waivers is generally determined by the extent to which the client reasonably understands the material risks that the waiver entails. The more comprehensive the explanation of the types of future representations that might arise and the actual and reasonably foreseeable adverse consequences of those representations, the greater the likelihood that the client will have the requisite understanding. Thus, if the client agrees to consent to a particular type of conflict with which the client is already familiar, then the consent ordinarily will be effective with regard to that type of conflict. If the consent is general and open-ended, then the consent ordinarily will be ineffective, because it is not reasonably likely that the client will have understood the material risks involved. On the other hand, if the client is an experienced user of the legal services involved and is reasonably informed regarding the risk that a conflict may arise, such consent is more likely to be effective, particularly if, e.g., the client is independently represented by other counsel in giving consent and the consent is limited to future conflicts unrelated to the subject of the representation. In any case, advance consent cannot be effective if the circumstances that materialize in the future are such as would make the conflict nonconsentable under paragraph (b).

Conflicts in Litigation

[23] Paragraph (b)(3) prohibits representation of opposing parties in the same litigation, regardless of the clients' consent. On the other hand, simultaneous representation of parties whose interests in litigation may conflict, such as coplaintiffs or codefendants, is governed by paragraph (a)(2). A conflict may exist by reason of substantial dis-

crepancy in the parties' testimony, incompatibility in positions in relation to an opposing party or the fact that there are substantially different possibilities of settlement of the claims or liabilities in question. Such conflicts can arise in criminal cases as well as civil. The potential for conflict of interest in representing multiple defendants in a criminal case is so grave that ordinarily a lawyer should decline to represent more than one codefendant. On the other hand, common representation of persons having similar interests in civil litigation is proper if the requirements of paragraph (b) are met.

[24] Ordinarily a lawyer may take inconsistent legal positions in different tribunals at different times on behalf of different clients. The mere fact that advocating a legal position on behalf of one client might create precedent adverse to the interests of a client represented by the lawyer in an unrelated matter does not create a conflict of interest. A conflict of interest exists, however, if there is a significant risk that a lawyer's action on behalf of one client will materially limit the lawyer's effectiveness in representing another client in a different case; for example, when a decision favoring one client will create a precedent likely to seriously weaken the position taken on behalf of the other client. Factors relevant in determining whether the clients need to be advised of the risk include: where the cases are pending, whether the issue is substantive or procedural, the temporal relationship between the matters, the significance of the issue to the immediate and long-term interests of the clients involved and the clients' reasonable expectations in retaining the lawyer. If there is significant risk of material limitation, then absent informed consent of the affected clients, the lawyer must refuse one of the representations or withdraw from one or both matters.

[25] When a lawyer represents or seeks to represent a class of plaintiffs or defendants in a class-action lawsuit, unnamed members of the class are ordinarily not considered to be clients of the lawyer for purposes of applying paragraph (a)(1) of this Rule. Thus, the lawyer does not typically need to get the consent of such a person before representing a client suing the person in an unrelated matter. Similarly, a lawyer seeking to represent an opponent in a class action does not typically need the consent of an unnamed member of the class whom the lawyer represents in an unrelated matter.

Nonlitigation Conflicts

[26] Conflicts of interest under paragraphs (a)(1) and (a)(2) arise in contexts other than litigation. For a discussion of directly adverse conflicts in transactional matters, see Comment [7]. Relevant factors in determining whether there is significant potential for material limita-

tion include the duration and intimacy of the lawyer's relationship with the client or clients involved, the functions being performed by the lawyer, the likelihood that disagreements will arise and the likely prejudice to the client from the conflict. The question is often one of proximity and degree. See Comment [8].

[27] For example, conflict questions may arise in estate planning and estate administration. A lawyer may be called upon to prepare wills for several family members, such as husband and wife, and, depending upon the circumstances, a conflict of interest may be present. In estate administration the identity of the client may be unclear under the law of a particular jurisdiction. Under one view, the client is the fiduciary; under another view the client is the estate or trust, including its beneficiaries. In order to comply with conflict of interest rules, the lawyer should make clear the lawyer's relationship to the parties involved.

[28] Whether a conflict is consentable depends on the circumstances. For example, a lawyer may not represent multiple parties to a negotiation whose interests are fundamentally antagonistic to each other, but common representation is permissible where the clients are generally aligned in interest even though there is some difference in interest among them. Thus, a lawyer may seek to establish or adjust a relationship between clients on an amicable and mutually advantageous basis; for example, in helping to organize a business in which two or more clients are entrepreneurs, working out the financial reorganization of an enterprise in which two or more clients have an interest or arranging a property distribution in settlement of an estate. The lawyer seeks to resolve potentially adverse interests by developing the parties' mutual interests. Otherwise, each party might have to obtain separate representation, with the possibility of incurring additional cost, complication or even litigation. Given these and other relevant factors, the clients may prefer that the lawyer act for all of them.

Special Considerations in Common Representation

[29] In considering whether to represent multiple clients in the same matter, a lawyer should be mindful that if the common representation fails because the potentially adverse interests cannot be reconciled, the result can be additional cost, embarrassment and recrimination. Ordinarily, the lawyer will be forced to withdraw from representing all of the clients if the common representation fails. In some situations, the risk of failure is so great that multiple representation is plainly impossible. For example, a lawyer cannot undertake common representation of clients where contentious litigation or negotiations between them are imminent or contemplated. Moreover,

because the lawyer is required to be impartial between commonly represented clients, representation of multiple clients is improper when it is unlikely that impartiality can be maintained. Generally, if the relationship between the parties has already assumed antagonism, the possibility that the clients' interests can be adequately served by common representation is not very good. Other relevant factors are whether the lawyer subsequently will represent both parties on a continuing basis and whether the situation involves creating or terminating a relationship between the parties.

[30] A particularly important factor in determining the appropriateness of common representation is the effect on client-lawyer confidentiality and the attorney-client privilege. With regard to the attorney-client privilege, the prevailing rule is that, as between commonly represented clients, the privilege does not attach. Hence, it must be assumed that if litigation eventuates between the clients, the privilege will not protect any such communications, and the clients should be so advised.

[31] As to the duty of confidentiality, continued common representation will almost certainly be inadequate if one client asks the lawyer not to disclose to the other client information relevant to the common representation. This is so because the lawyer has an equal duty of loyalty to each client, and each client has the right to be informed of anything bearing on the representation that might affect that client's interests and the right to expect that the lawyer will use that information to that client's benefit. See Rule 1.4. The lawyer should, at the outset of the common representation and as part of the process of obtaining each client's informed consent, advise each client that information will be shared and that the lawyer will have to withdraw if one client decides that some matter material to the representation should be kept from the other. In limited circumstances, it may be appropriate for the lawyer to proceed with the representation when the clients have agreed, after being properly informed, that the lawyer will keep certain information confidential. For example, the lawyer may reasonably conclude that failure to disclose one client's trade secrets to another client will not adversely affect representation involving a joint venture between the clients and agree to keep that information confidential with the informed consent of both clients.

[32] When seeking to establish or adjust a relationship between clients, the lawyer should make clear that the lawyer's role is not that of partisanship normally expected in other circumstances and, thus, that the clients may be required to assume greater responsibility for decisions than when each client is separately represented. Any limitations on the scope of the representation made necessary as a result of the common representation should be fully explained to the clients at the outset of the representation. See Rule 1.2(c).

[33] Subject to the above limitations, each client in the common representation has the right to loyal and diligent representation and the protection of Rule 1.9 concerning the obligations to a former client. The client also has the right to discharge the lawyer as stated in Rule 1.16.

Organizational Clients

[34] A lawyer who represents a corporation or other organization does not, by virtue of that representation, necessarily represent any constituent or affiliated organization, such as a parent or subsidiary. See Rule 1.13(a). Thus, the lawyer for an organization is not barred from accepting representation adverse to an affiliate in an unrelated matter, unless the circumstances are such that the affiliate should also be considered a client of the lawyer, there is an understanding between the lawyer and the organizational client that the lawyer will avoid representation adverse to the client's affiliates, or the lawyer's obligations to either the organizational client or the new client are likely to limit materially the lawyer's representation of the other client.

[35] A lawyer for a corporation or other organization who is also a member of its board of directors should determine whether the responsibilities of the two roles may conflict. The lawyer may be called on to advise the corporation in matters involving actions of the directors. Consideration should be given to the frequency with which such situations may arise, the potential intensity of the conflict, the effect of the lawyer's resignation from the board and the possibility of the corporation's obtaining legal advice from another lawyer in such situations. If there is material risk that the dual role will compromise the lawyer's independence of professional judgment, the lawyer should not serve as a director or should cease to act as the corporation's lawyer when conflicts of interest arise. The lawyer should advise the other members of the board that in some circumstances matters discussed at board meetings while the lawyer is present in the capacity of director might not be protected by the attorney-client privilege and that conflict of interest considerations might require the lawyer's recusal as a director or might require the lawyer and the lawyer's firm to decline representation of the corporation in a matter.

Rule 1.8 Conflict of Interest: Current Clients: Specific Rules

Rule 1.9 Duties to Former Clients

Rule 1.10 Imputation of Conflicts of Interest: General Rule

Rule 3.3 Candor Toward the Tribunal

(a) A lawyer shall not knowingly:

(1) make a false statement of fact or law to a tribunal or fail to correct a false statement of material fact or law previously made to the tribunal by the lawyer;

(2) fail to disclose to the tribunal legal authority in the controlling jurisdiction known to the lawyer to be directly adverse to the position of the client and not disclosed by opposing counsel; or

(3) offer evidence that the lawyer knows to be false. If a lawyer, the lawyer's client, or a witness called by the lawyer, has offered material evidence and the lawyer comes to know of its falsity, the lawyer shall take reasonable remedial measures, including, if necessary, is closure to the tribunal. A lawyer may refuse to offer evidence, other than the testimony of a defendant in a criminal matter, that the lawyer reasonably believes is false.

(b) A lawyer who represents a client in an adjudicative proceeding and who knows that a person intends to engage, is engaging or has engaged in criminal or fraudulent conduct related to the proceeding shall take reasonable remedial measures, including, if necessary, disclosure to the tribunal.

(c) The duties stated in paragraphs (a) and (b) continue to the conclusion of the proceeding, and apply even if compliance requires disclosure of information otherwise protected by Rule 1.6.

(d) In an ex parte proceeding, a lawyer shall inform the tribunal of all material facts known to the lawyer that will enable the tribunal to make an informed decision, whether or not the facts are adverse.

Comment:

[1] This Rule governs the conduct of a lawyer who is representing a client in the proceedings of a tribunal. See Rule 1.0(m) for the definition of "tribunal." It also applies when the lawyer is representing a client in an ancillary proceeding conducted pursuant to the tribunal's adjudicative authority, such as a deposition. Thus, for example, paragraph (a)(3) requires a lawyer to take reasonable remedial measures if the lawyer comes to know that a client who is testifying in a deposition has offered evidence that is false.

[2] This Rule sets forth the special duties of lawyers as officers of the court to avoid conduct that undermines the integrity of the adjudicative process. A lawyer acting as an advocate in an adjudicative proceeding has an obligation to present the client's case with persuasive force. Performance of that duty while maintaining confidences of the client, however, is qualified by the advocate's duty of candor to the tribunal. Consequently, although a lawyer in an adversary proceeding is not required to present an impartial exposition of the law or to vouch for the evidence submitted in a cause, the lawyer must not allow the tribunal to be misled by false statements of law or fact or evidence that the lawyer knows to be false.

Representations by a Lawyer

[3] An advocate is responsible for pleadings and other documents prepared for litigation, but is usually not required to have personal knowledge of matters asserted therein, for litigation documents ordinarily present assertions by the client, or by someone on the client's behalf, and not assertions by the lawyer. Compare Rule 3.1. However, an assertion purporting to be on the lawyer's own knowledge, as in an affidavit by the lawyer or in a statement in open court, may properly be made only when the lawyer knows the assertion is true or believes it to be true on the basis of a reasonably diligent inquiry. There are circumstances where failure to make a disclosure is the equivalent of an affirmative misrepresentation. The obligation prescribed in Rule 1.2(d) not to counsel a client to commit or assist the client in committing a fraud applies in litigation. Regarding compliance with Rule 1.2(d), see the Comment to that Rule. See also the Comment to Rule 8.4(b).

Legal Argument

[4] Legal argument based on a knowingly false representation of law constitutes dishonesty toward the tribunal. A lawyer is not required to make a disinterested exposition of the law, but must recognize the existence of pertinent legal authorities. Furthermore, as stated in paragraph (a)(2), an advocate has a duty to disclose directly adverse authority in the controlling jurisdiction that has not been disclosed by the opposing party. The underlying concept is that legal argument is a discussion seeking to determine the legal premises properly applicable to the case.

Offering Evidence

[5] Paragraph (a)(3) requires that the lawyer refuse to offer evidence that the lawyer knows to be false, regardless of the client's wishes. This duty is premised on the lawyer's obligation as an officer of the court to prevent the trier of fact from being misled by false evidence. A lawyer does not violate this Rule if the lawyer offers the evidence for the purpose of establishing its falsity.

[6] If a lawyer knows that the client intends to testify falsely or wants the lawyer to introduce false evidence, the lawyer should seek to persuade the client that the evidence should not be offered. If the persuasion is ineffective and the lawyer continues to represent the client, the lawyer must refuse to offer the false evidence. If only a portion of a witness's testimony will be false, the lawyer may call the witness to testify but may not elicit or otherwise permit the witness to present the testimony that the lawyer knows is false.

[7] The duties stated in paragraphs (a) and (b) apply to all lawyers, including defense counsel in criminal cases. In some jurisdictions, however, courts have required counsel to present the accused as a witness or to give a narrative statement if the accused so desires, even if counsel knows that the testimony or statement will be false. The obligation of the advocate under the Rules of Professional Conduct is subordinate to such requirements. See also Comment [9].

[8] The prohibition against offering false evidence only applies if the lawyer knows that the evidence is false. A lawyer's reasonable belief that evidence is false does not preclude its presentation to the trier of fact. A lawyer's knowledge that evidence is false, however, can be inferred from the circumstances. See Rule 1.0(f). Thus, although a lawyer should resolve doubts about the veracity of testimony or other evidence in favor of the client, the lawyer cannot ignore an obvious falsehood.

[9] Although paragraph (a)(3) only prohibits a lawyer from offering evidence the lawyer knows to be false, it permits the lawyer to refuse to offer testimony or other proof that the lawyer reasonably believes is false. Offering such proof may reflect adversely on the lawyer's ability to discriminate in the quality of evidence and thus impair the lawyer's effectiveness as an advocate. Because of the special protections historically provided criminal defendants, however, this Rule does not permit a lawyer to refuse to offer the testimony of such a client where the lawyer reasonably believes but does not know that the testimony will be false. Unless the lawyer knows the testimony will be false, the lawyer must honor the client's decision to testify. See also Comment [7].

Remedial Measures

[10] Having offered material evidence in the belief that it was true, a lawyer may subsequently come to know that the evidence is false. Or, a lawyer may be surprised when the lawyer's client, or another witness called by the lawyer, offers testimony the lawyer knows to be false, either during the lawyer's direct examination or in response to cross-examination by the opposing lawyer. In such situations or if the lawyer knows of the falsity of testimony elicited from the client during a deposition, the lawyer must take reasonable remedial measures. In such situations, the advocate's proper course is to remonstrate with the client confidentially, advise the client of the lawyer's duty of candor to the tribunal and seek the client's cooperation with respect to the withdrawal or correction of the false statements or evidence. If that fails, the advocate must take further remedial action. If withdrawal from the representation is not permitted or will not undo the effect of the false evidence, the advocate must make such disclosure to the tribunal as is reasonably necessary to remedy the situation, even if doing so requires the lawyer to reveal information that otherwise would be protected by Rule 1.6. It is for the tribunal then to determine what should be done - making a statement about the matter to the trier of fact, ordering a mistrial or perhaps nothing.

[11] The disclosure of a client's false testimony can result in grave consequences to the client, including not only a sense of betrayal but also loss of the case and perhaps a prosecution for perjury. But the alternative is that the lawyer cooperate in deceiving the court, thereby subverting the truth-finding process which the adversary system is designed to implement. See Rule 1.2(d). Furthermore, unless it is clearly understood that the lawyer will act upon the duty to disclose the existence of false evidence, the client can simply reject the lawyer's advice to reveal the false evidence and insist that the lawyer keep silent. Thus the client could in effect coerce the lawyer into being a party to fraud on the court.

Preserving Integrity of Adjudicative Process

[12] Lawyers have a special obligation to protect a tribunal against criminal or fraudulent conduct that

undermines the integrity of the adjudicative process, such as bribing, intimidating or otherwise unlawfully communicating with a witness, juror, court official or other participant in the proceeding, unlawfully destroying or concealing documents or other evidence or failing to disclose information to the tribunal when required by law to do so. Thus, paragraph (b) requires a lawyer to take reasonable remedial measures, including disclosure if necessary, whenever the lawyer knows that a person, including the lawyer's client, intends to engage, is engaging or has engaged in criminal or fraudulent conduct related to the proceeding.

Duration of Obligation

[13] A practical time limit on the obligation to rectify false evidence or false statements of law and fact has to be established. The conclusion of the proceeding is a reasonably definite point for the termination of the obligation. A proceeding has concluded within the meaning of this Rule when a final judgment in the proceeding has been affirmed on appeal or the time for review has passed.

Ex Parte Proceedings

[14] Ordinarily, an advocate has the limited responsibility of presenting one side of the matters that a tribunal should consider in reaching a decision; the conflicting position is expected to be presented by the opposing party. However, in any ex parte proceeding, such as an application for a temporary restraining order, there is no balance of presentation by opposing advocates. The object of an ex parte proceeding is nevertheless to yield a substantially just result. The judge has an affirmative responsibility to accord the absent party just consideration. The lawyer for the represented party has the correlative duty to make disclosures of material facts known to the lawyer and that the lawyer reasonably believes are necessary to an informed decision.

Withdrawal

[15] Normally, a lawyer's compliance with the duty of candor imposed by this Rule does not require that the lawyer withdraw from the representation of a client whose interests will be or have been adversely affected by the lawyer's disclosure. The lawyer may, however, be required by Rule 1.16(a) to seek permission of the tribunal to withdraw if the lawyer's compliance with this Rule's duty of candor results in such an extreme deterioration of the client-lawyer relationship that the lawyer can no longer competently represent the client. Also see Rule 1.16(b) for the circumstances in which a lawyer will be permitted to seek a tribunal's permission to withdraw. In connection with a request for permission to withdraw that is premised on a client's misconduct, a lawyer may reveal information relating to the representation only to the extent reason- ably necessary to comply with this Rule or as otherwise permitted by Rule 1.6.

Rule 3.4 Fairness to Opposing Party and Counsel

Rule 3.5 Impartiality and Decorum of the Tribunal

Rule 3.6 Trial Publicity

Rule 3.7 Lawyer as Witness

Rule 3.8 Special Responsibilities of a Prosecutor

Rule 3.9 Advocate in Nonadjudicative Proceedings

TRANSACTIONS WITH PERSONS OTHER THAN CLIENTS

Rule 4.1 Truthfulness in Statements to Others

Rule 4.2 Communication with Person Represented by Counsel

Rule 4.3 Dealing with Unrepresented Person

Rule 4.4 Respect for Rights of Third Persons

LAW FIRMS AND ASSOCIATIONS

Rule 5.1 Responsibilities of a Partner or Supervisory Lawyer

Rule 5.2 Responsibilities of a Subordinate Lawyer

Rule 5.3 Responsibilities Regarding Nonlawyer Assistants

With respect to a nonlawyer employed or retained by or associated with a lawyer:

(a) a partner, and a lawyer who individually or together with other lawyers possesses comparable managerial authority in a law firm shall make reasonable efforts to ensure that the firm has in effect measures giving reasonable assurance that the person's conduct is compatible with the professional obligations of the lawyer;

(b) a lawyer having direct supervisory authority over the nonlawyer shall make reasonable efforts to ensure that the person's conduct is compatible with the professional obligations of the lawyer; and

(c) a lawyer shall be responsible for conduct of such a person that would be a violation of the Rules of Professional Conduct if engaged in by a lawyer if:

(1) the lawyer orders or, with the knowledge of the specific conduct, ratifies the conduct involved; or

(2) the lawyer is a partner or has comparable managerial authority in the law firm in which the person is

employed, or has direct supervisory authority over the person, and knows of the conduct at a time when its consequences can be avoided or mitigated but fails to take reasonable remedial action.

Comment:

[1] Lawyers generally employ assistants in their practice, including secretaries, investigators, law student interns, and paraprofessionals. Such assistants, whether employees or independent contractors, act for the lawyer in rendition of the lawyer's professional services. A lawyer must give such assistants appropriate instruction and supervision concerning the ethical aspects of their employment, particularly regarding the obligation not to disclose information relating to representation of the client, and should be responsible for their work product. The measures employed in supervising nonlawyers should take account of the fact that they do not have legal training and are not subject to professional discipline.

[2] Paragraph (a) requires lawyers with managerial authority within a law firm to make reasonable efforts to establish internal policies and procedures designed to provide reasonable assurance that nonlawyers in the firm will act in a way compatible with the Rules of Professional Conduct. See Comment [1] to Rule 5.1. Paragraph (b) applies to lawyers who have supervisory authority over the work of a nonlawyer. Paragraph (c) specifies the circumstances in which a lawyer is responsible for conduct of a nonlawyer that would be a violation of the Rules of Professional Conduct if engaged in by a lawyer.

Rule 5.4 Professional Independence of a Lawyer

Rule 5.5 Unauthorized Practice of Law

A lawyer shall not:

(a) practice law in a jurisdiction where doing so violates the regulation of the legal profession in that jurisdiction; or

(b) assist a person who is not a member of the bar in the performance of activity that constitutes the unauthorized practice of law.

Comment:

[1] A lawyer may practice law only in a jurisdiction in which the lawyer is authorized to practice. A lawyer may be admitted to practice law in a jurisdiction on a regular basis or may be authorized by court rule or order or by law to practice for a limited purpose or on a restricted basis. Paragraph (a) applies to unauthorized practice of law by a lawyer, whether through the lawyer's direct action or by the lawyer assisting another person.

[2] The definition of the practice of law is established by law and varies from one jurisdiction to another. Whatever the definition, limiting the practice of law to members of the bar protects the public against rendition of legal services by unqualified persons. This Rule does not prohibit a lawyer from employing the services of paraprofessionals and delegating functions to them, so long as the lawyer supervises the delegated work and retains responsibility for their work. See Rule 5.3.

[3] A lawyer may provide professional advice and instruction to nonlawyers whose employment requires knowledge of the law; for example, claims adjusters, employees of financial or commercial institutions, social workers, accountants and persons employed in government agencies. Lawyers also may assist independent nonlawyers, such as paraprofessionals, who are authorized by the law of a jurisdiction to provide particular law-related services. In addition, a lawyer may counsel nonlawyers who wish to proceed pro se.

[4] Other than as authorized by law or this Rule, a lawyer who is not admitted to practice generally in this jurisdiction violates paragraph (b) if the lawyer establishes an office or other systematic and continuous presence in this jurisdiction for the practice of law. Presence may be systematic and continuous even if the lawyer is not physically present here. Such a lawyer must not hold out to the public or otherwise represent that the lawyer is admitted to practice law in this jurisdiction. See also Rules 7.1(a) and 7.5(b).

[5] There are occasions in which a lawyer admitted to practice in another United States jurisdiction, and not disbarred or suspended from practice in any jurisdiction, may provide legal services on a temporary basis in this jurisdiction under circumstances that do not create an unreasonable risk to the interests of their clients, the public or the courts. Paragraph (c) identifies four such circumstances. The fact that conduct is not so identified does not imply that the conduct is or is not authorized. With the exception of paragraphs (d)(1) and (d)(2), this Rule does not authorize a lawyer to establish an office or other systematic and continuous presence in this jurisdiction without being admitted to practice generally here.

[6] There is no single test to determine whether a lawyer's services are provided on a "temporary basis" in this jurisdiction, and may therefore be permissible under paragraph (c). Services may be "temporary" even though the lawyer provides services in this jurisdiction on a recurring basis, or for an extended period of time, as when the lawyer is representing a client in a single lengthy negotiation or litigation.

[7] Paragraphs (c) and (d) apply to lawyers who are admitted to practice law in any United States jurisdiction, which includes the District of Columbia and any state, territory or commonwealth of the United States. The word

"admitted" in paragraph (c) contemplates that the lawyer is authorized to practice in the jurisdiction in which the lawyer is admitted and excludes a lawyer who while technically admitted is not authorized to practice, because, for example, the lawyer is on inactive status.

[8] Paragraph (c)(1) recognizes that the interests of clients and the public are protected if a lawyer admitted only in another jurisdiction associates with a lawyer licensed to practice in this jurisdiction. For this paragraph to apply, however, the lawyer admitted to practice in this jurisdiction must actively participate in and share responsibility for the representation of the client.

[9] Lawyers not admitted to practice generally in a jurisdiction may be authorized by law or order of a tribunal or an administrative agency to appear before the tribunal or agency. This authority may be granted pursuant to formal rules governing admission pro hac vice or pursuant to informal practice of the tribunal or agency. Under paragraph (c)(2), a lawyer does not violate this Rule when the lawyer appears before a tribunal or agency pursuant to such authority. To the extent that a court rule or other law of this jurisdiction requires a lawyer who is not admitted to practice in this jurisdiction to obtain admission pro hac vice before appearing before a tribunal or administrative agency, this Rule requires the lawyer to obtain that authority.

[10] Paragraph (c)(2) also provides that a lawyer rendering services in this jurisdiction on a temporary basis does not violate this Rule when the lawyer engages in conduct in anticipation of a proceeding or hearing in a jurisdiction in which the lawyer is authorized to practice law or in which the lawyer reasonably expects to be admitted pro hac vice. Examples of such conduct include meetings with the client, interviews of potential witnesses, and the review of documents. Similarly, a lawyer admitted only in another jurisdiction may engage in conduct temporarily in this jurisdiction in connection with pending litigation in another jurisdiction in which the lawyer is or reasonably expects to be authorized to appear, including taking depositions in this jurisdiction.

[11] When a lawyer has been or reasonably expects to be admitted to appear before a court or administrative agency, paragraph (c)(2) also permits conduct by lawyers who are associated with that lawyer in the matter, but who do not expect to appear before the court or administrative agency. For example, subordinate lawyers may conduct research, review documents, and attend meetings with witnesses in support of the lawyer responsible for the litigation.

[12] Paragraph (c)(3) permits a lawyer admitted to practice law in another jurisdiction to perform services on a temporary basis in this jurisdiction if those services are in or reasonably related to a pending or potential arbitration, mediation, or other alternative dispute resolution proceeding in this or another jurisdiction, if the services arise out of or are reasonably related to the lawyer's practice in a jurisdiction in which the lawyer is admitted to practice. The lawyer, however, must obtain admission pro hac vice in the case of a court-annexed arbitration or mediation or otherwise if court rules or law so require.

[13] Paragraph (c)(4) permits a lawyer admitted in another jurisdiction to provide certain legal services on a temporary basis in this jurisdiction that arise out of or are reasonably related to the lawyer's practice in a jurisdiction in which the lawyer is admitted but are not within paragraphs (c)(2) or (c)(3). These services include both legal services and services that nonlawyers may perform but that are considered the practice of law when performed by lawyers.

[14] Paragraphs (c)(3) and (c)(4) require that the services arise out of or be reasonably related to the lawyer's practice in a jurisdiction in which the lawyer is admitted. A variety of factors evidence such a relationship. The lawyer's client may have been previously represented by the lawyer, or may be resident in or have substantial contacts with the jurisdiction in which the lawyer is admitted. The matter, although involving other jurisdictions, may have a significant connection with that jurisdiction. In other cases, significant aspects of the lawyer's work might be conducted in that jurisdiction or a significant aspect of the matter may involve the law of that jurisdiction. The necessary relationship might arise when the client's activities or the legal issues involve multiple jurisdictions, such as when the officers of a multinational corporation survey potential business sites and seek the services of their lawyer in assessing the relative merits of each. In addition, the services may draw on the lawyer's recognized expertise developed through the regular practice of law on behalf of clients in matters involving a particular body of federal, nationally-uniform, foreign, or international law.

[15] Paragraph (d) identifies two circumstances in which a lawyer who is admitted to practice in another United States jurisdiction, and is not disbarred or suspended from practice in any jurisdiction, may establish an office or other systematic and continuous presence in this jurisdiction for the practice of law as well as provide legal services on a temporary basis. Except as provided in paragraphs (d)(1) and (d)(2), a lawyer who is admitted to practice law in another jurisdiction and who establishes an office or other systematic or continuous presence in this jurisdiction must become admitted to practice law generally in this jurisdiction.

[16] Paragraph (d)(1) applies to a lawyer who is employed by a client to provide legal services to the client

or its organizational affiliates, i.e., entities that control, are controlled by, or are under common control with the employer. This paragraph does not authorize the provision of personal legal services to the employer's officers or employees. The paragraph applies to in-house corporate lawyers, government lawyers and others who are employed to render legal services to the employer. The lawyer's ability to represent the employer outside the jurisdiction in which the lawyer is licensed generally serves the interests of the employer and does not create an unreasonable risk to the client and others because the employer is well situated to assess the lawyer's qualifications and the quality of the lawyer's work.

[17] If an employed lawyer establishes an office or other systematic presence in this jurisdiction for the purpose of rendering legal services to the employer, the lawyer may be subject to registration or other requirements, including assessments for client protection funds and mandatory continuing legal education.

[18] Paragraph (d)(2) recognizes that a lawyer may provide legal services in a jurisdiction in which the lawyer is not licensed when authorized to do so by federal or other law, which includes statute, court rule, executive regulation or judicial precedent.

[19] A lawyer who practices law in this jurisdiction pursuant to paragraphs (c) or (d) or otherwise is subject to the disciplinary authority of this jurisdiction. See Rule 8.5(a).

[20] In some circumstances, a lawyer who practices law in this jurisdiction pursuant to paragraphs (c) or (d) may have to inform the client that the lawyer is not licensed to practice law in this jurisdiction. For example, that may be required when the representation occurs primarily in this jurisdiction and requires knowledge of the law of this jurisdiction. See Rule 1.4(b).

[21] Paragraphs (c) and (d) do not authorize communications advertising legal services to prospective clients in this jurisdiction by lawyers who are admitted to practice in other jurisdictions. Whether and how lawyers may communicate the availability of their services to prospective clients in this jurisdiction is governed by Rules 7.1 to 7.5.

Rule 5.6 Restrictions on Rights to Practice

Rule 5.7 Responsibilities Regarding Law-Related Services

PUBLIC SERVICE

Rule 6.1 Voluntary Pro Bono Publico Service

Rule 6.2 Accepting Appointments

Rule 6.3 Membership in Legal Services Organization

Rule 6.4 Law Reform Activities Affecting Client Interests

Rule 6.5 Nonprofit and Court Annexed Limited Legal Services Programs

INFORMATION ABOUT LEGAL SERVICES

Rule 7.1 Communications Concerning a Lawyer's Services

Rule 7.2 Advertising

Rule 7.3 Direct Contact with Prospective Clients

Rule 7.4 Communication of Fields of Practice

Rule 7.5 Firm Names and Letterheads

Rule 7.6 Political Contributions to Obtain Legal Engagements or Appointments by Judges

MAINTAINING THE INTEGRITY OF THE PROFESSION

Rule 8.1 Bar Admission and Disciplinary Matters

Rule 8.2 Judicial and Legal Officials

Rule 8.3 Reporting Professional Misconduct

Rule 8.4 Misconduct

Rule 8.5 Disciplinary Authority; Choice of Law

Effective Learning: How To Study

Everyone learns differently. Some people seem to absorb information like a sponge while others must work hard to soak up any information. Although it is true that some people have photographic memories, they are few and far between. Most likely the people who seem to absorb information "like a sponge" have learned how to maximize their learning experiences. Most of us do not take the time to figure out how we learn best and as a result probably spend more time than necessary to achieve the same level of results as more proficient learners. Have you ever wondered how some people, who are just average students, seem to always get A's? If you were to ask them, they would probably tell you that they spend more time than most people studying and preparing, or that they have learned how to study more effectively and efficiently in the time they have available. A good starting point is to determine how you learn best and work out methods to maximize the time and effort you have available.

LEARNING STYLES

A learning style is the way you learn most effectively. Everyone has his or her own learning style; there are no "better" or "correct" ways to learn. Somewhere in your school career you may have been given tests to determine your personal learning styles, such as the Hogan/Champagne Personal Style Indicator or the Kolb Learning Style Inventory. These and similar assessments are available through most school advisors and guidance counselors. If you want help in determining your learning styles, take the initiative for your own success and immediately make an appointment with someone who can administer an assessment.

Learning styles fall into these categories:

- independent (competitive) versus collaborative
- structured versus unstructured
- auditory versus visual
- spatial versus verbal
- practical versus creative
- applied versus conceptual
- factual versus analytical
- emotional versus logical

It sounds like a lot to consider, but taking a few minutes to determine which learning style best suits you can save you countless hours of frustration—hours that could be better devoted to studying or other activities.

Independent vs. Collaborative

Do you prefer working with a group or independently? Some people find it easier to avoid all distractions by working alone; others prefer working in a study group and sharing information as part of the learning process.

If you prefer working independently, you may want to obtain additional course information from study guides and computer assisted instruction. You may prefer lecture-format classes to small discussion courses. If you prefer working collaboratively, you may wish to form study groups early in the semester or find a tutor to work with, and you should choose courses that include small discussion groups or group projects.

Structured vs. Unstructured

Structured learners feel more comfortable when they formalize their study habits, for example, by selecting a definite time and place in which to study every day. If you are a structured learner, you may find it useful to create to-do lists and keep a written schedule of classes, study times, and activities.

Unstructured learners tend to resist formalizing their study plan and try to avoid feeling "locked-in." The unstructured learner tends to procrastinate. Procrastinators need to find ways to give more structure to their learning activities. One method is to join a study group of students who are more organized.

Auditory vs. Visual

Auditory learners learn best by listening. Visual learners learn best from what they see. For visual learners, it is not always possible to learn everything by listening to lectures or by reading and watching video presentations. Auditory learners may find it more efficient to listen to lectures and then read related material. Visual learners may do better reading the book first and then attending lectures. Auditory learners may also find group discussion and study group activities beneficial.

Spatial vs. Verbal

Spatial learners are better at reading and interpreting maps, charts, and other graphics. Verbal learners prefer to read words rather than interpret graphics. Spatial learners need to create and incorporate their own diagrams, maps, timelines, and other such graphics into their notes. Verbal learners need to translate or obtain translations of graphics into words. A useful technique for verbal learners is to take notes that describe the material, including the graphics, in such a way that a visually impaired student could understand the graphic representation from the verbal description. Teaming up with a visually impaired student may be mutually beneficial.

Practical vs. Creative

Practical learners tend to be methodical and systematic. They prefer specific instruction that is directed and focused. Creative learners prefer experimentation and creative activities. Practical learners may benefit from creating an organized study plan for each course, including detailed to-do lists and a calendar. For the creative learner, courses that allow writing and other creative approaches may be more satisfying.

Applied vs. Conceptual

Applied learners want to know how information can be applied to given situations. The conceptual learner is not so much concerned with the application as with the underlying concepts. Applied learners need to focus on ways in which the ideas presented in courses and lectures can be applied. Taking of notes that include examples for applying the concepts helps them recall the concepts later. Conceptual learners may find it useful to consider the concepts in a broader context than that of the narrow lecture presentation.

Factual vs. Analytical

Factual learners are good with details and enjoy learning interesting and unusual facts. They prefer objective tests. Analytical learners like to break a topic down into its component parts in order to understand how the parts relate to each other. Analytical learners prefer essay exams that allow them to demonstrate how their knowledge relates to the question. Factual learners may want to make lists of facts, which they can associate with prior knowledge. Analytical learners may want to analyze the organization as they read a textbook, looking for trends and patterns.

Emotional vs. Logical

Emotional learners tend to prefer human-interest stories to material that presents just facts and logic. Logical learners prefer to understand the factual basis, including statistics, of an argument. Emotional learners may find that reading biographical sketches helps them understand factual subjects.

PUTTING IT ALL TOGETHER

1. Understand yourself. From the previous list of types of learners, select the descriptions in each category that best fit your style of learning. Look back at courses and classes you have taken in which you have done well or that you enjoyed the most. You may see a pattern that will help you understand your learning style.

2. Set goals. Determine your personal and occupational goals. Do you want a career working with people or with things? Do you want a professional career working directly with people or behind the scenes supporting others? What courses will help you acquire the skills and knowledge you need to achieve these goals?

3. Make a plan. At the end of your educational path should be a goal. It may be a personal goal to be an outstanding parent or partner, or it may be a goal to be a generalist or a specialist in an occupation or profession. To achieve these goals you will need to focus on courses that give you the necessary skills and knowledge. Within the courses may be options that accommodate your learning style, such as large lecture classes versus small group discussion classes, face-to-face courses versus distance learning courses, and so on. Create a personal plan that allows for flexibility as your goals or interests change—a good foundation will allow you more flexibility in courses and curriculum. Don't be afraid to admit that you did not enjoy some courses you expected to enjoy or

that you enjoyed some classes you never thought would give you pleasure. Such insights may help you fine-tune your personal and professional goals.

4. Check your progress. Periodically assess how well you are doing in individual classes as well as in your overall program of study. Use the opportunity to assess why you are doing better than you expected in some classes and not as well in others. You may need to adjust your overall plan or merely your learning methods. Or, outside influences such as work, family, or personal issues may be interfering with your learning. Periodic self-assessment is the first step to modifying your goals.

5. Make adjustments. As your goals change, so will your plan. Don't be afraid to make the adjustments necessary to achieve your goals or to change your goals as your interests change. Life rarely follows a straight path. Be adaptable and make adjustments when necessary.

SCHEDULING TIME

Most people use a calendar to keep track of information such as birthdays, appointments, or upcoming events. They may include vacations, concerts, or other special events or activities. Depending on your personal style, you might include to-do lists or an hour-by-hour schedule of classes and other activities. Scheduling school and study time is helpful to most students.

Whichever method works best for you, use it to track the amount of time you spend in all of your activities so that you can budget your time more accurately. When scheduling, keep in mind that there is a limit to everyone's power of concentration. Don't schedule so many activities that they exceed your mental or physical abilities.

SUPPLEMENTAL LEARNING AIDS

1. Study guides. Most textbooks have a study guide that will give you additional information; they frequently include sample tests and quizzes. Your instructor may or may not require the use of a study guide. If you need additional reinforcement, you may want to purchase a study guide even if it is not a required part of the course.

2. Flash cards. Flash cards are available for many courses in college bookstores. However, you will learn more by preparing your own and customizing them to the course you are taking. On the front side of an index card write a word, phrase, or concept, and write the definition or explanation on the reverse side. With a properly prepared set of flash cards, you may not need to refer to the text or your notes when studying for a test.

3. Companion websites. Many publishers offer companion websites for their textbooks. Many of these websites are available on the publisher's website without cost or for a nominal fee. Often these websites are the equivalent of an online study guide. Others offer self-tests. The publisher may post information that has become available since the publication of the textbook.

4. Outlining. Few people have a photographic memory or the ability to absorb material on one reading. The following approach can help you use your textbook effectively.

a. *How long is the chapter?* Check the length of the chapter and your reading assignment before you start. Most textbooks are filled with graphics and illustrations that reduce the amount of actual reading time to a manageable level.

b. *Scan the chapter.* Scan the material to get a feel for what will be covered.

c. *Chapter objectives.* At the beginnings of chapters, most textbooks list what you should learn from reading the chapter. These chapter objectives help you focus on important topics, information, and themes.

d. *Read the chapter.* Quickly read through the chapter to get an overall sense of the material and how the sections relate to each other.

e. *Underline the important items.* After you have read quickly through the chapter, go back over the material and underline the items you believe are important in pencil.

f. *Go to class.* From the instructor's lecture and class discussion you may find that what you think is important changes.

g. *Highlight the important material.* After class, use a highlighter to highlight what you now believe to be the important information in the

text. You will probably find that it is substantially less than what you underlined in pencil.

h. *Make your flash cards.* From the highlighted information, create a set of flash cards for each chapter.

5. Tutors. Not everyone can afford the luxury of a personal tutor. However, most colleges and universities have a tutoring center or some form of tutoring assistance. If you are having difficulty, don't be afraid to ask for help before it is too late. At the beginning of the semester determine what personalized help is available for each course. You may not need to use this information, but having it will reduce your anxiety and panic if you realize that you need some help. Don't be afraid to ask your instructor for help. Your instructor wants you to succeed. If you are doing everything you can to be successful in a class, the instructor should be more than happy to help you or direct you for help.

6. Study groups. If you are the type of learner who benefits from working with others, form a study group at the beginning of each semester in each course. After the first class ask if there are others who wish to form a study group, or post a notice on the course bulletin board website. One advantage of study groups is the opportunity to share class notes as well as ideas. Verbal learners can benefit from having visual learners in the study group who can interpret and explain charts, graphs, and maps. Study groups can motivate procrastinators to complete tasks on time.

7. Tests. Most students suffer from some form of test anxiety. At the beginning of each course, ask the instructor the exam schedule and the type of tests he or she will be giving. Some schools maintain copies of all tests that students can use for practice. If your school does not maintain these, ask your instructors if they will make available sample tests and quizzes. Practice tests may be available in the study guide for the text or on a companion website. If you are in a study group, members can prepare practice tests as part of test preparation.

For more detailed information about study skills, see Judy M. Roberts, *Effective Study Skills: Maximizing Your Academic Potential* (Prentice Hall, 1998).

PREAMBLE

We the People of the United States, in Order to form a more perfect Union, establish Justice, insure domestic Tranquility, provide for the common defense, promote the general Welfare, and secure the Blessings of Liberty to ourselves and our Posterity, do ordain and establish this Constitution for the United States of America.

ARTICLE I

Section 1. All legislative Powers herein granted shall be vested in a Congress of the United States, which shall consist of a Senate and House of Representatives.

Section 2. The House of Representatives shall be composed of Members chosen every second Year by the People of the several States, and the Electors in each State shall have the Qualifications requisite for Electors of the most numerous Branch of the State Legislature.

No Person shall be a Representative who shall not have attained to the Age of twenty five Years, and been seven Years a Citizen of the United States, and who shall not, when elected, be an Inhabitant of that State in which he shall be chosen.

Representatives and direct Taxes shall be apportioned among the several States which may be included within this Union, according to their respective Numbers, which shall be determined by adding to the whole Number of free Persons, including those bound to Service for a Term of Years, and excluding Indians not taxed, three fifths of all other Persons. The actual Enumeration shall be made within three Years after the first Meeting of the Congress of the United States, and within every subsequent Term of ten Years, in such Manner as they shall by Law direct. The Number of Representatives shall not exceed one for every thirty Thousand, but each State shall have at Least one Representative; and until such enumeration shall be made, the State of New Hampshire shall be entitled to chuse three, Massachusetts eight, Rhode-Island and Providence Plantations one, Connecticut five, New-York six, New Jersey four, Pennsylvania eight, Delaware one, Maryland six, Virginia ten, North Carolina five, South Carolina five, and Georgia three.

When vacancies happen in the Representation from any State, the Executive Authority thereof shall issue Writs of Election to fill such Vacancies.

The House of Representatives shall chuse their Speaker and other Officers; and shall have the sole Power of Impeachment.

Section 3. The Senate of the United States shall be composed of two Senators from each State, chosen by the Legislature thereof for six Years; and each Senator shall have one Vote.

Immediately after they shall be assembled in Consequence of the first Election, they shall be divided as equally as may be into three Classes. The Seats of the Senators of the first Class shall be vacated at the Expiration of the second Year, of the second Class at the Expiration of the fourth Year, and of the third Class at the Expiration of the sixth Year, so that one third may be chosen every second Year; and if Vacancies happen by Resignation, or otherwise, during the Recess of the Legislature of any State, the Executive thereof may make temporary Appointments until the next Meeting of the Legislature, which shall then fill such Vacancies.

No Person shall be a Senator who shall not have attained to the Age of thirty Years, and been nine Years a Citizen of the United States, and who shall not, when elected, be an Inhabitant of that State for which he shall be chosen.

The Vice President of the United States shall be President of the Senate, but shall have no Vote, unless they be equally divided.

The Senate shall chuse their other Officers, and also a President pro tempore, in the Absence of the Vice President, or when he shall exercise the Office of President of the United States.

The Senate shall have the sole Power to try all Impeachments. When sitting for that Purpose, they shall be on Oath or Affirmation. When the President of the United States is tried, the Chief Justice shall preside: And no Person shall be convicted without the Concurrence of two thirds of the Members present.

Judgment in Cases of Impeachment shall not extend further than to removal from Office, and disqualification to hold and enjoy any Office of honor, Trust or Profit under the United States: but the Party convicted shall nevertheless be liable and subject to Indictment, Trial, Judgment and Punishment, according to Law.

Section 4. The Times, Places and Manner of holding Elections for Senators and Representatives, shall be prescribed in each State by the Legislature thereof; but the Congress may at any time by Law make or alter such Regulations, except as to the Places of chusing Senators.

The Congress shall assemble at least once in every Year, and such Meeting shall be on the first Monday in December, unless they shall by Law appoint a different Day.

Section 5. Each House shall be the Judge of the Elections, Returns and Qualifications of its own Members, and a Majority of each shall constitute a Quorum to do Business; but a smaller Number may adjourn from day to day, and may be authorized to compel the Attendance of absent Members, in such Manner, and under such Penalties as each House may provide.

Each House may determine the Rules of its Proceedings, punish its Members for disorderly Behaviour, and, with the Concurrence of two thirds, expel a Member.

Each House shall keep a Journal of its Proceedings, and from time to time publish the same, excepting such Parts as may in their Judgment require Secrecy; and the Yeas and Nays of the Members of either House on any question shall, at the Desire of one fifth of those Present, be entered on the Journal.

Neither House, during the Session of Congress, shall, without the Consent of the other, adjourn for more than three days, nor to any other Place than that in which the two Houses shall be sitting.

Section 6. The Senators and Representatives shall receive a Compensation for their Services, to be ascertained by Law, and paid out of the Treasury of the United States. They shall in all Cases, except Treason, Felony and Breach of the Peace, be privileged from Arrest during their Attendance at the Session of their respective Houses, and in going to and returning from the same; and for any Speech or Debate in either House, they shall not be questioned in any other Place.

No Senator or Representative shall, during the Time for which he was elected, be appointed to any civil Office under the Authority of the United States, which shall have been created, or the Emoluments whereof shall have been encreased during such time; and no Person holding any Office under the United States, shall be a Member of either House during his Continuance in Office.

Section 7. All Bills for raising Revenue shall originate in the House of Representatives; but the Senate may propose or concur with Amendments as on other Bills.

Every Bill which shall have passed the House of Representatives and the Senate, shall, before it become a Law, be presented to the President of the United States: If he approve he shall sign it, but if not he shall return it, with his Objections to that House in which it shall have originated, who shall enter the Objections at large on their Journal, and proceed to reconsider it.If after such Reconsideration two thirds of that House shall agree to pass the Bill, it shall be sent, together with the Objections, to the other House, by which it shall likewise be reconsidered, and if approved by two thirds of that House, it shall become a Law. But in all such Cases the Votes of both Houses shall be determined by yeas and Nays, and the Names of the Persons voting for and against the Bill shall be entered on the Journal of each House respectively. If any Bill shall not be returned by the President within ten Days (Sundays excepted) after it shall have been presented to him, the Same shall be a Law, in like Manner as if he had signed it, unless the Congress by their Adjournment prevent its Return, in which Case it shall not be a Law.

Every Order, Resolution, or Vote to which the Concurrence of the Senate and House of Representatives may be necessary (except on a question of Adjournment) shall be presented to the President of the United States; and before the Same shall take Effect, shall be approved by him, or being disapproved by him, shall be repassed by two thirds of the Senate and House of Representatives, according to the Rules and Limitations prescribed in the Case of a Bill.

Section 8. The Congress shall have Power To lay and collect Taxes, Duties, Imposts and Excises, to pay the Debts and provide for the common Defence and general Welfare of the United States; but all Duties, Imposts and Excises shall be uniform throughout the United States;

To borrow Money on the credit of the United States;

To regulate Commerce with foreign Nations, and among the several States, and with the Indian Tribes;

To establish an uniform Rule of Naturalization, and uniform Laws on the subject of Bankruptcies throughout the United States;

To coin Money, regulate the Value thereof, and of foreign Coin, and fix the Standard of Weights and Measures;

To provide for the Punishment of counterfeiting the Securities and current Coin of the United States;

To establish Post Offices and post Roads;

To promote the Progress of Science and useful Arts, by securing for limited Times to Authors and Inventors the exclusive Right to their respective Writings and Discoveries;

To constitute Tribunals inferior to the supreme Court;

To define and punish Piracies and Felonies committed on the high Seas, and Offences against the Law of Nations;

To declare War, grant Letters of Marque and Reprisal, and make Rules concerning Captures on Land and Water;

To raise and support Armies, but no Appropriation of Money to that Use shall be for a longer Term than two Years;

To provide and maintain a Navy;

To make Rules for the Government and Regulation of the land and naval Forces;

To provide for calling forth the Militia to execute the Laws of the Union, suppress Insurrections and repel Invasions;

To provide for organizing, arming, and disciplining, the Militia, and for governing such Part of them as may be employed in the Service of the United States, reserving to the States respectively, the Appointment of the Officers, and the Authority of training the Militia according to the discipline prescribed by Congress;

To exercise exclusive Legislation in all Cases whatsoever, over such District (not exceeding ten Miles square) as may, by Cession of particular States, and the Acceptance of Congress, become the Seat of the Government of the United States, and to exercise like Authority over all Places purchased by the Consent of the Legislature of the State in which the Same shall be, for the Erection of Forts, Magazines, Arsenals, dock-Yards, and other needful Buildings;—And

To make all Laws which shall be necessary and proper for carrying into Execution the foregoing Powers, and all other Powers vested by this Constitution in the Government of the United States, or in any Department or Officer thereof.

Section 9. The Migration or Importation of such Persons as any of the States now existing shall think proper to admit, shall not be prohibited by the Congress prior to the Year one thousand eight hundred and eight, but a Tax or duty may be imposed on such Importation, not exceeding ten dollars for each Person.

The Privilege of the Writ of Habeas Corpus shall not be suspended, unless when in Cases of Rebellion or Invasion the public Safety may require it.

No Bill of Attainder or ex post facto Law shall be passed.

No Capitation, or other direct, Tax shall be laid, unless in Proportion to the Census or enumeration herein before directed to be taken.

No Tax or Duty shall be laid on Articles exported from any State.

No Preference shall be given by any Regulation of Commerce or Revenue to the Ports of one State over those of another; nor shall Vessels bound to, or from, one State, be obliged to enter, clear, or pay Duties in another.

No Money shall be drawn from the Treasury, but in Consequence of Appropriations made by Law; and a regular Statement and Account of the Receipts and Expenditures of all public Money shall be published from time to time.

No Title of Nobility shall be granted by the United States: And no Person holding any Office of Profit or Trust under them, shall, without the Consent of the Congress, accept of any present, Emolument, Office, or Title, of any kind whatever, from any King, Prince, or foreign State.

Section 10. No State shall enter into any Treaty, Alliance, or Confederation; grant Letters of Marque and Reprisal; coin Money; emit Bills of Credit; make any Thing but gold and silver Coin a Tender in Payment of Debts; pass any Bill of Attainder, ex post facto Law, or Law impairing the Obligation of Contracts, or grant any Title of Nobility.

No State shall, without the Consent of the Congress, lay any Imposts or Duties on Imports or Exports, except what may be absolutely necessary for executing it's inspection Laws: and the net Produce of all Duties and Imposts, laid by any State on Imports or Exports, shall be for the Use of the Treasury of the United States; and all such Laws shall be subject to the Revision and Controul of the Congress.

No State shall, without the Consent of Congress, lay any Duty of Tonnage, keep Troops, or Ships of War in time of Peace, enter into any Agreement or Compact with another State, or with a foreign Power, or engage in War, unless actually invaded, or in such imminent Danger as will not admit of delay.

ARTICLE II

Section 1. The executive Power shall be vested in a President of the United States of America. He shall hold his Office during the Term of four Years, and, together with the Vice President, chosen for the same Term, be elected, as follows:

Each State shall appoint, in such Manner as the Legislature thereof may direct, a Number of Electors, equal to the whole Number of Senators and Representatives to which the State may be entitled in the Congress: but no Senator or Representative, or Person holding an Office of Trust or Profit under the United States, shall be appointed an Elector.

The Electors shall meet in their respective States, and vote by Ballot for two Persons, of whom one at least shall not be an Inhabitant of the same State with themselves. And they shall make a List of all the Persons voted for, and of the Number of Votes for each; which List they shall sign and certify, and transmit sealed to the Seat of the Government of the United States, directed to the President of the Senate. The President of the Senate shall, in the Presence of the Senate and House of Representatives, open all the Certificates, and the Votes shall then be counted. The Person having the greatest Number of Votes shall be the President, if such Number be a Majority of the whole Number of Electors appointed; and if there be more than one who have such Majority, and have an equal Number of Votes, then the House of Representatives shall immediately chuse by Ballot one of them for President; and if no Person have a Majority, then from the five highest on the List the said House shall in like Manner chuse the President. But in chusing the President, the Votes shall be taken by States, the Representation from each State having one Vote; A quorum for this purpose shall consist of a Member or Members from two thirds of the States, and a Majority of all the States shall be necessary to a Choice. In every Case, after the Choice of the President, the Person having the greatest Number of Votes of the Electors shall be the Vice President. But if there should remain two or more who have equal Votes, the Senate shall chuse from them by Ballot the Vice President.

The Congress may determine the Time of chusing the Electors, and the Day on which they shall give their Votes; which Day shall be the same throughout the United States.

No Person except a natural born Citizen, or a Citizen of the United States, at the time of the Adoption of this Constitution, shall be eligible to the Office of President; neither shall any Person be eligible to that Office who shall not have attained to the Age of thirty five Years, and been fourteen Years a Resident within the United States.

In Case of the Removal of the President from Office, or of his Death, Resignation, or Inability to discharge the Powers and Duties of the said Office, the Same shall devolve on the Vice President, and the Congress may by Law provide for the Case of Removal, Death, Resignation or Inability, both of the President and Vice President, declaring what Officer shall then act as President, and such Officer shall act accordingly, until the Disability be removed, or a President shall be elected.

The President shall, at stated Times, receive for his Services, a Compensation, which shall neither be increased nor diminished during the Period for which he shall have been elected, and he shall not receive within that Period any other Emolument from the United States, or any of them.

Before he enter on the Execution of his Office, he shall take the following Oath or Affirmation:—"I do solemnly swear (or affirm) that I will faithfully execute the Office of President of the United States, and will to the best of my Ability, preserve, protect and defend the Constitution of the United States."

Section 2. The President shall be Commander in Chief of the Army and Navy of the United States, and of the Militia of the several States, when called into the actual Service of the United States; he may require the Opinion, in writing, of the principal Officer in each of the executive Departments, upon any Subject relating to the Duties of their respective Offices, and he shall have Power to grant Reprieves and Pardons for Offences against the United States, except in Cases of Impeachment.

He shall have Power, by and with the Advice and Consent of the Senate, to make Treaties, provided two thirds of the Senators present concur; and he shall nominate, and by and with the Advice and Consent of the Senate, shall appoint Ambassadors, other public Ministers and Consuls, Judges of the supreme Court, and all other Officers of the United States, whose Appointments are not herein otherwise provided for, and which shall be established by Law: but the Congress may by Law vest the Appointment of such inferior Officers, as they think proper, in the President alone, in the Courts of Law, or in the Heads of Departments.

The President shall have Power to fill up all Vacancies that may happen during the Recess of the Senate, by granting Commissions which shall expire at the End of their next Session.

Section 3. He shall from time to time give to the Congress Information of the State of the Union, and recommend to their Consideration such Measures as he shall judge necessary and expedient; he may, on extraordinary Occasions, convene both Houses, or either of them, and in Case of Disagreement between them, with Respect to the Time of Adjournment, he may adjourn them to such Time as he shall think proper; he shall receive Ambassadors and other public Ministers; he shall take Care that the Laws be faithfully executed, and shall Commission all the Officers of the United States.

Section 4. The President, Vice President and all civil Officers of the United States, shall be removed from Office on Impeachment for, and Conviction of, Treason, Bribery, or other high Crimes and Misdemeanors.

ARTICLE III

Section 1. The judicial Power of the United States shall be vested in one supreme Court, and in such inferior Courts as the Congress may from time to time ordain and establish. The Judges, both of the supreme and inferior Courts, shall hold their Offices during good Behaviour, and shall, at stated Times, receive for their Services a Compensation, which shall not be diminished during their Continuance in Office.

Section 2. The judicial Power shall extend to all Cases, in Law and Equity, arising under this Constitution, the Laws of the United States, and Treaties made, or which shall be made, under their Authority;—to all Cases affecting Ambassadors, other public Ministers and Consuls;—to all Cases of admiralty and maritime Jurisdiction;—to Controversies to which the United States shall be a Party;—to Controversies between two or more States;— between a State and Citizens of another State;—between Citizens of different States;—between Citizens of the same State claiming Lands under Grants of different States, and between a State, or the Citizens thereof, and foreign States, Citizens or Subjects.

In all Cases affecting Ambassadors, other public Ministers and Consuls, and those in which a State shall be Party, the supreme Court shall have original Jurisdiction. In all the other Cases before mentioned, the supreme Court shall have appellate Jurisdiction, both as to Law and Fact, with such Exceptions, and under such Regulations as the Congress shall make.

The Trial of all Crimes, except in Cases of Impeachment, shall be by Jury; and such Trial shall be held in the State where the said Crimes shall have been committed; but when not committed within any State, the Trial shall be at such Place or Places as the Congress may by Law have directed.

Section 3. Treason against the United States, shall consist only in levying War against them, or in adhering to their Enemies, giving them Aid and Comfort. No Person shall be convicted of Treason unless on the Testimony of two Witnesses to the same overt Act, or on Confession in open Court.

The Congress shall have Power to declare the Punishment of Treason, but no Attainder of Treason shall work Corruption of Blood, or Forfeiture except during the Life of the Person attainted.

ARTICLE IV

Section 1. Full Faith and Credit shall be given in each State to the public Acts, Records, and judicial Proceedings of every other State. And the Congress may by general Laws prescribe the Manner in which such Acts, Records and Proceedings shall be proved, and the Effect thereof.

Section 2. The Citizens of each State shall be entitled to all Privileges and Immunities of Citizens in the several States.

A Person charged in any State with Treason, Felony, or other Crime, who shall flee from Justice, and be found in another State, shall on Demand of the executive Authority of the State from which he fled, be delivered up, to be removed to the State having Jurisdiction of the Crime.

No Person held to Service or Labour in one State, under the Laws thereof, escaping into another, shall, in Consequence of any Law or Regulation therein, be discharged from such Service or Labour, but shall be delivered up on Claim of the Party to whom such Service or Labour may be due.

Section 3. New States may be admitted by the Congress into this Union; but no new State shall be formed or erected within the Jurisdiction of any other State; nor any State be formed by the Junction of two or more States, or Parts of States, without the Consent of the Legislatures of the States concerned as well as of the Congress.

The Congress shall have Power to dispose of and make all needful Rules and Regulations respecting the Territory or other Property belonging to the United States; and nothing in this Constitution shall be so construed as to Prejudice any Claims of the United States, or of any particular State.

Section 4. The United States shall guarantee to every State in this Union a Republican Form of Government, and shall protect each of them against Invasion; and on Application of the Legislature, or of the Executive (when the Legislature cannot be convened), against domestic Violence.

ARTICLE V

The Congress, whenever two thirds of both Houses shall deem it necessary, shall propose Amendments to this Constitution, or, on the Application of the Legislatures of two thirds of the several States, shall call a Convention for proposing Amendments, which, in either Case, shall be valid to all Intents and Purposes, as Part of this Constitution, when ratified by the Legislatures of three fourths of the several States, or by Conventions in three fourths thereof, as the one or the other Mode of Ratification may be proposed by the Congress; Provided that no Amendment which may be made prior to the Year One thousand eight hundred and eight shall in any Manner affect the first and fourth Clauses in the Ninth Section of the first Article; and that no State, without its Consent, shall be deprived of its equal Suffrage in the Senate.

ARTICLE VI

All Debts contracted and Engagements entered into, before the Adoption of this Constitution, shall be as valid against the United States under this Constitution, as under the Confederation.

This Constitution, and the Laws of the United States which shall be made in Pursuance thereof; and all Treaties made, or which shall be made, under the Authority of the United States, shall be the supreme Law of the Land; and the Judges in every State shall be bound thereby, any Thing in the Constitution or Laws of any State to the Contrary notwithstanding.

The Senators and Representatives before mentioned, and the Members of the several State Legislatures, and all executive and judicial Officers, both of the United States and of the several States, shall be bound by Oath or Affirmation, to support this Constitution; but no religious Test shall ever be required as a Qualification to any Office or public Trust under the United States.

ARTICLE VII

The Ratification of the Conventions of nine States, shall be sufficient for the Establishment of this Constitution between the States so ratifying the Same.

AMENDMENTS TO THE CONSTITUTION OF THE UNITED STATES

[Amendments I-X make up the Bill of Rights]

AMENDMENT I

Congress shall make no law respecting an establishment of religion, or prohibiting the free exercise thereof; or abridging the freedom of speech, or of the press; or the right of the people peaceably to assemble, and to petition the Government for a redress of grievances.

AMENDMENT II

A well regulated Militia, being necessary to the security of a free State, the right of the people to keep and bear Arms, shall not be infringed.

AMENDMENT III

No Soldier shall, in time of peace be quartered in any house, without the consent of the Owner, nor in time of war, but in a manner to be prescribed by law.

AMENDMENT IV

The right of the people to be secure in their persons, houses, papers, and effects, against unreasonable searches and seizures, shall not be violated, and no Warrants shall issue, but upon probable cause, supported by Oath or affirmation, and particularly describing the place to be searched, and the persons or things to be seized.

AMENDMENT V

No person shall be held to answer for a capital, or otherwise infamous crime, unless on a presentment or indictment of a Grand Jury, except in cases arising in the land or naval forces, or in the Militia, when in actual service in time of War or public danger; nor shall any person be subject for the same offence to be twice put in jeopardy of life or limb; nor shall be compelled in any criminal case to be a witness against himself, nor be deprived of life, liberty, or property, without due process of law; nor shall private property be taken for public use, without just compensation.

AMENDMENT VI

In all criminal prosecutions, the accused shall enjoy the right to a speedy and public trial, by an impartial jury of the State and district wherein the crime shall have been committed, which district shall have been previously ascertained by law, and to be informed of the nature and cause of the accusation; to be confronted with the witnesses against him; to have compulsory process for obtaining witnesses in his favor, and to have the Assistance of Counsel for his defence.

AMENDMENT VII

In suits at common law, where the value in controversy shall exceed twenty dollars, the right of trial by jury shall be preserved, and no fact tried by a jury, shall be otherwise reexamined in any Court of the United States, than according to the rules of the common law.

AMENDMENT VIII

Excessive bail shall not be required, nor excessive fines imposed, nor cruel and unusual punishments inflicted.

AMENDMENT IX

The enumeration in the Constitution, of certain rights, shall not be construed to deny or disparage others retained by the people.

AMENDMENT X

The powers not delegated to the United States by the Constitution, nor prohibited by it to the States, are reserved to the States respectively, or to the people.

AMENDMENT XI

The Judicial power of the United States shall not be construed to extend to any suit in law or equity, commenced or prosecuted against one of the United States by Citizens of another State, or by Citizens or Subjects of any Foreign State.

AMENDMENT XII

The Electors shall meet in their respective states and vote by ballot for President and Vice-President, one of whom, at least, shall not be an inhabitant of the same state with themselves; they shall name in their ballots the person voted for as President, and in distinct ballots the person voted for as Vice-President, and they shall make distinct lists of all persons voted for as President, and of all persons voted for as Vice-President, and of the number of votes for each, which lists they shall sign and certify, and transmit sealed to the seat of the government of the United States, directed to the President of the Senate; — the President of the Senate shall, in the presence of the Senate and House of Representatives, open all the certificates and the votes shall then be counted; — The person having the greatest number of votes for President, shall be the President, if such number be a majority of the whole number of Electors appointed; and if no person have such majority, then from the persons having the highest numbers not exceeding three on the list of those voted for as President, the House of Representatives shall choose immediately, by ballot, the President. But in choosing the President, the votes shall be taken by states, the representation from each state having one vote; a quorum for this purpose shall consist of a member or members from two-thirds of the states, and a majority of all the states shall be necessary to a choice. [And if the House of Representatives shall not choose a President whenever the right of choice shall devolve upon them, before the fourth day of March next following, then the Vice-President shall act as President, as in case of the death or other constitutional disability of the President. —]* The person having the greatest number of votes as Vice-President, shall be the Vice-President, if such number be a majority of the whole number of Electors appointed, and if no person have a majority, then from the two highest numbers on the list, the Senate shall choose the Vice-President; a quorum for the purpose shall consist of two-thirds of the whole number of

Senators, and a majority of the whole number shall be necessary to a choice. But no person constitutionally ineligible to the office of President shall be eligible to that of Vice-President of the United States.

AMENDMENT XIII

Section 1. Neither slavery nor involuntary servitude, except as a punishment for crime whereof the party shall have been duly convicted, shall exist within the United States, or any place subject to their jurisdiction.

Section 2. Congress shall have power to enforce this article by appropriate legislation.

AMENDMENT XIV

Section 1. All persons born or naturalized in the United States, and subject to the jurisdiction thereof, are citizens of the United States and of the State wherein they reside. No State shall make or enforce any law which shall abridge the privileges or immunities of citizens of the United States; nor shall any State deprive any person of life, liberty, or property, without due process of law; nor deny to any person within its jurisdiction the equal protection of the laws.

Section 2. Representatives shall be apportioned among the several States according to their respective numbers, counting the whole number of persons in each State, excluding Indians not taxed. But when the right to vote at any election for the choice of electors for President and Vice-President of the United States, Representatives in Congress, the Executive and Judicial officers of a State, or the members of the Legislature thereof, is denied to any of the male inhabitants of such State, being twenty-one years of age,* and citizens of the United States, or in any way abridged, except for participation in rebellion, or other crime, the basis of representation therein shall be reduced in the proportion which the number of such male citizens shall bear to the whole number of male citizens twenty-one years of age in such State.

Section 3. No person shall be a Senator or Representative in Congress, or elector of President and Vice-President, or hold any office, civil or military, under the United States, or under any State, who, having previously taken an oath, as a member of Congress, or as an officer of the United States, or as a member of any State legislature, or as an executive or judicial officer of any State, to support the Constitution of the United States, shall have engaged in insurrection or rebellion against the same, or given aid or comfort to the enemies thereof. But Congress may by a vote of two-thirds of each House, remove such disability.

Section 4. The validity of the public debt of the United States, authorized by law, including debts incurred for payment of pensions and bounties for services in suppressing insurrection or rebellion, shall not be questioned. But neither the United States nor any State shall assume or pay any debt or obligation incurred in aid of insurrection or rebellion against the United States, or any claim for the loss or emancipation of any slave; but all such debts, obligations and claims shall be held illegal and void.

Section 5. The Congress shall have the power to enforce, by appropriate legislation, the provisions of this article.

AMENDMENT XV

Section 1. The right of citizens of the United States to vote shall not be denied or abridged by the United States or by any State on account of race, color, or previous condition of servitude—

Section 2. The Congress shall have the power to enforce this article by appropriate legislation.

AMENDMENT XVI

The Congress shall have power to lay and collect taxes on incomes, from whatever source derived, without apportionment among the several States, and without regard to any census or enumeration.

AMENDMENT XVII

The Senate of the United States shall be composed of two Senators from each State, elected by the people thereof, for six years; and each Senator shall have one vote. The electors in each State shall have the qualifications requisite for electors of the most numerous branch of the State legislatures.

When vacancies happen in the representation of any State in the Senate, the executive authority of such State shall issue writs of election to fill such vacancies: Provided, That the legislature of any State may empower the executive thereof to make temporary appointments until the people fill the vacancies by election as the legislature may direct.

This amendment shall not be so construed as to affect the election or term of any Senator chosen before it becomes valid as part of the Constitution.

AMENDMENT XVIII

Section 1. After one year from the ratification of this article the manufacture, sale, or transportation of intoxicating liquors within, the importation thereof into, or the exportation thereof from the United States and all territory subject to the jurisdiction thereof for beverage purposes is hereby prohibited.

Section 2. The Congress and the several States shall have concurrent power to enforce this article by appropriate legislation.

Section 3. This article shall be inoperative unless it shall have been ratified as an amendment to the Constitution by the legislatures of the several States, as provided in the Constitution, within seven years from the date of the submission hereof to the States by the Congress.

AMENDMENT XIX

The right of citizens of the United States to vote shall not be denied or abridged by the United States or by any State on account of sex.

Congress shall have power to enforce this article by appropriate legislation.

AMENDMENT XX

Section 1. The terms of the President and the Vice President shall end at noon on the 20th day of January, and the terms of Senators and Representatives at noon on the 3d day of January, of the years in which such terms would have ended if this article had not been ratified; and the terms of their successors shall then begin.

Section 2. The Congress shall assemble at least once in every year, and such meeting shall begin at noon on the 3d day of January, unless they shall by law appoint a different day.

Section 3. If, at the time fixed for the beginning of the term of the President, the President elect shall have died, the Vice President elect shall become President. If a President shall not have been chosen before the time fixed for the beginning of his term, or if the President elect shall have failed to qualify, then the Vice President elect shall act as President until a President shall have qualified; and the Congress may by law provide for the case wherein neither a President elect nor a Vice President shall have qualified, declaring who shall then act as President, or the manner in which one who is to act shall be selected, and such person shall act accordingly until a President or Vice President shall have qualified.

Section 4. The Congress may by law provide for the case of the death of any of the persons from whom the House of Representatives may choose a President whenever the right of choice shall have devolved upon them, and for the case of the death of any of the persons from whom the Senate may choose a Vice President whenever the right of choice shall have devolved upon them.

Section 5. Sections 1 and 2 shall take effect on the 15th day of October following the ratification of this article.

Section 6. This article shall be inoperative unless it shall have been ratified as an amendment to the Constitution by the legislatures of three-fourths of the several States within seven years from the date of its submission.

AMENDMENT XXI

Section 1. The eighteenth article of amendment to the Constitution of the United States is hereby repealed.

Section 2. The transportation or importation into any State, Territory, or Possession of the United States for delivery or use therein of intoxicating liquors, in violation of the laws thereof, is hereby prohibited.

Section 3. This article shall be inoperative unless it shall have been ratified as an amendment to the Constitution by conventions in the several States, as provided in the Constitution, within seven years from the date of the submission hereof to the States by the Congress.

AMENDMENT XXII

Section 1. No person shall be elected to the office of the President more than twice, and no person who has held the office of President, or acted as President, for more than two years of a term to which some other person was elected President shall be elected to the office of President more than once. But this Article shall not apply to any person holding the office of President when this Article was proposed by Congress, and shall not prevent any person who may be holding the office of President, or acting as President, during the term within which this Article becomes operative from holding the office of President or acting as President during the remainder of such term.

Section 2. This article shall be inoperative unless it shall have been ratified as an amendment to the Constitution by the legislatures of three-fourths of the several States within seven years from the date of its submission to the States by the Congress.

AMENDMENT XXIII

Section 1. The District constituting the seat of Government of the United States shall appoint in such manner as Congress may direct:

A number of electors of President and Vice President equal to the whole number of Senators and Representatives in Congress to which the District would be entitled if it were a State, but in no event more than the least populous State; they shall be in addition to those appointed by the States, but they shall be considered, for the purposes of the election of President and Vice President, to be electors appointed by a State; and they shall meet in the District and perform such duties as provided by the twelfth article of amendment.

Section 2. The Congress shall have power to enforce this article by appropriate legislation.

AMENDMENT XXIV

Section 1. The right of citizens of the United States to vote in any primary or other election for President or Vice President, for electors for President or Vice President, or for Senator or Representative in Congress, shall not be denied or abridged by the United States or any State by reason of failure to pay poll tax or other tax.

Section 2. The Congress shall have power to enforce this article by appropriate legislation.

AMENDMENT XXV

Section 1. In case of the removal of the President from office or of his death or resignation, the Vice President shall become President.

Section 2. Whenever there is a vacancy in the office of the Vice President, the President shall nominate a Vice President who shall take office upon confirmation by a majority vote of both Houses of Congress.

Section 3. Whenever the President transmits to the President pro tempore of the Senate and the Speaker of the House of Representatives his written declaration that he is unable to discharge the powers and duties of his office, and until he transmits to them a written declaration to the contrary, such powers and duties shall be discharged by the Vice President as Acting President.

Section 4. Whenever the Vice President and a majority of either the principal officers of the executive departments or of such other body as Congress may by law provide, transmit to the President pro tempore of the Senate and the Speaker of the House of Representatives their written declaration that the President is unable to discharge the powers and duties of his office, the Vice President shall immediately assume the powers and duties of the office as Acting President.

Thereafter, when the President transmits to the President pro tempore of the Senate and the Speaker of the House of Representatives his written declaration that no inability exists, he shall resume the powers and duties of his office unless the Vice President and a majority of either the principal officers of the executive department or of such other body as Congress may by law provide, transmit within four days to the President pro tempore of the Senate and the Speaker of the House of Representatives their written declaration that the President is unable to discharge the powers and duties of his office. Thereupon Congress shall decide the issue, assembling within forty-eight hours for that purpose if not in session. If the Congress, within twenty-one days after receipt of the latter written declaration, or, if Congress is not in session, within twenty-one days after Congress is required to assemble, determines by two-thirds vote of both Houses that the President is unable to discharge the powers and duties of his office, the Vice President shall continue to discharge the same as Acting President; otherwise, the President shall resume the powers and duties of his office.

AMENDMENT XXVI

Section 1. The right of citizens of the United States, who are eighteen years of age or older, to vote shall not be denied or abridged by the United States or by any State on account of age.

Section 2. The Congress shall have power to enforce this article by appropriate legislation.

AMENDMENT XXVII

No law, varying the compensation for the services of the Senators and Representatives, shall take effect, until an election of representatives shall have intervened.

Courts—Alternative Dispute Resolution—Government

U.S. Courts	www.uscourts.gov
U.S. Tax Court	www.ustaxcourt.gov/ustcweb.htm
U.S. Court of Federal Claims	www.uscfc.uscourts.gov/
U.S. Court of International Trade	www.uscit.gov/
U.S Court for the Federal Circuit	www.fedcir.gov/
U.S. Supreme Court	www.supremecourtus.gov
National Mediation Board	www.nmb.gov
American Arbitration Association	www.adr.org
Pacer System	http://pacer.psc.uscourts.gov/
U.S. Court of Appeals	www.uscourts.gov/courtsofappeals.html
Internal Revenue Service	www.irs.gov
Government Printing Office	www.gpo.gov/
Code of Federal Regulations	www.access.gpo.gov/nara/cfr/index.html

Legal Research

VersusLaw	www.versuslaw.com/
Lexis	www.lexisnexis.com/
Westlaw	www.westlaw.com/
Library of Congress	www.loc.gov
Loislaw	www.loislaw.com
Cornell University LII	www.law.cornell.edu/citation
ALWD Manual	www.alwd.org

Legal Organizations

American Bar Association	www.abanet.org
National Federation of Paralegal Associations, Inc	www.paralegals.org
National Association of Legal Assistants	www.nala.org
American Association of Legal Administrators	www.alanet.org/home.html
American Association for Paralegal Education	www.aafpe.org
ABA Standing Committee on Legal Assistants	www.abanet.org/legalassts
Legal Nurse Consultants	www.aalnc.org

State Bar Associations

Alabama	www.alabar.org	Montana	www.montanabar.org
Alaska	www.alaskabar.org	Nebraska	www.nebar.org
Arizona	www.azbar.org.org	Nevada	www.nvbar.org
Arkansas	www.arkbar.org	New Hampshire	www.nhbar.org
California	www.calbar.org	New Jersey	www.njsba.com
Colorado	www.cobar.org	New Mexico	www.nmbar.org
Connecticut	www.ctbar.org	New York	www.nysba.org
Delaware	www.dsba.org	North Carolina	www.ncbar.com
District of Columbia	www.dcbar.org	North Dakota	www.sband.org
Florida	www.flabar.org	Ohio	www.ohiobar.org
Georgia	www.gabar.org	Oklahoma	www.okbar.org
Hawaii	www.hsba.org	Oregon	www.osbar.org
Idaho	www2.state.id.us/isb/	Pennsylvania	www.pa-bar.org
Illinois	www.isba.org	Rhode Island	www.ribar.com
Indiana	www.inbar.org	South Carolina	www.scbar.org
Iowa	www.iowabar.org	South Dakota	www.sdbar.org
Kansas	www.ksbar.org	Tennessee	www.tba.org
Kentucky	www.kybar.org	Texas	www.texasbar.com
Louisiana	www.lsba.org	Utah	www.utahbar.org
Maine	www.maine.org	Vermont	www.vtbar.org
Maryland	www.msba.org	Virginia	www.vsb.org
Massachusetts	www.massbar.org	Washington	www.wsba.org
Michigan	www.michbar.org	West Virginia	www.wvbar.org
Minnesota	www.mnbar.org	Wisconsin	www.wisbar.org
Mississippi	www.msbar.org	Wyoming	www.wyomingbar.org
Missouri	www.mobar.org		

Other

Religious calendar	www.interfaithcalendar.org/
AOL	www.aol.com
Compuserve	WWW.compuserve.com
The Affiliate	www.futurelawoffice.com/practice.html
Adobe Systems	www.adobe.com
Mapquest	www.mapquest.com

Internet Search Engines

AltaVista	www.altavista.com
Ask Jeeves	www.askjeeves.com
Dogpile	www.dogpile.com
Excite	www.excite.com
Google	www.google.com
Metacrawler	www.metacrawler.com
Netscape	www.netscape.com
Yahoo!	www.yahoo.com
Findlaw	www.findlaw.com

Glossary of Spanish Equivalents for Important Legal Terms

a priori   Desde antes, del pasado.

AAA Siglas para **American Arbitration Association** Asociación de Arbitraje.

ABA Siglas para **American Bar Association** Colegio de Abogados Estadounidenses.

accept   Aceptar, admitir, aprobar, recibir reconocer.

accession   Accesión, admisión, aumento, incremento.

accord   Acuerdo, convenio, arreglo, acordar, conceder.

acquittal   Absolución, descargo, veredicto de no culpable.

act   Acto, estatuto, decreto, actuar, funcionar.

actionable   Justiciable, punible, procesable.

adjourn   Levantar, posponer, suspender la sesión.

adjudicate   Adjudicar, decidir, dar fallo a favor de, sentenciar, declarar.

administrative   Administrativo, ejecutivo.

administrative agency   Agencia administrativa.

administrative hearing   Juicio administrativo.

administrative law   Derecho administrativo.

administrative law judge   Juez de derecho, Administrativo.

administrator   Administrador.

admit   Admitir, conceder, reconocer, permitir entrada, confesar, asentir.

adverse   Adverso, contrario, opuesto.

adverse possession   Posesión adversa.

advice   Consejo, asesoramiento, notificación.

affected class   Clase afectada, grupo iscriminado.

affidavit   Declaración voluntaria, escrita y bajo uramento, afidávit, atestiguación, testificata.

affirmative action   Acción positiva.

affirmative defense   Defensa justificativa.

after acquired property   Propiedad adquirida con garantía adicional.

against   En contra.

agency   Agencia, oficina, intervención.

agent   Agente, representante autorizado.

aggrieved party   Parte dañada, agraviada, perjudicada.

agreement   Acuerdo, arreglo, contrato, convenio, pacto.

alibi   Coartada.

alien   Extranjero, extraño, foráneo.

annul   Anular, cancelar, invalidar, revocar, dejar sin efecto.

answer   Contestación, réplica, respuesta, alegato.

antecedent   Antecedente, previo, preexistente.

appeal   Apelar, apelación.

appear   Aparecer, comparecer.

appellate court   Tribunal de apelaciones.

appellate jurisdiction   Competencia de apelación.

applicable   Aplicable, apropiado, pertinente a, lo que puede ser aplicado.

arraign   Denunciar, acusar, procesar, instruir de cargos hechos.

arrears   Retrasos, pagos atrasados, decursas.

arrest   Arresto, arrestar, aprehensión, aprehender, detener.

arson   Incendio intencional.

articles of incorporation   Carta de organización corporativa.

assault   Agresión, asalto, ataque, violencia carnal, agredir, atacar, acometer.

assault and battery   Amenazas y agresión, asalto.

assign   Asignar, ceder, designar, hacer cesión, traspasar, persona asignada un derecho.

attachment   Secuestro judicial.

attorney   Abogado, consejero, apoderado.

award   Fallo, juicio, laudo, premio.

bail   Caución, fianza.

bail bondsman   Fiador, fiador judicial.

bailee   Depositario de bienes.

bailment   Depósito, encargo, depósito mercantil, depósito comercial.

bailment   For hire, depósito oneroso.

bailor   Fiador.

bankruptcy   Bancarrota, quiebra, insolvencia.

battery   Agravio, agresión.

bearer bond   Título mobiliario.

bearer instrument   Título al portador.

bench   Tribunal, los jueces, la magistratura.

beneficiary   Beneficiario, legatario.

bequeath   Legar.

bilateral contract   Contrato bilateral.

bill of lading   Póliza de embarque, boleto de carga, documento de tránsito.

bill of rights   Las primeras diez enmiendas a la Constitución de los Estados Unidos de América.

binder   Resguardo provisional, recibo para garantizar el precio de un bien inmueble.

birth certificate   Acta de nacimiento, partida de nacimiento, certificado de nacimiento.

blue sky laws   Estatutos para prevenir el fraude en la compraventa de valores.

bond   Bono, título, obligación, deuda inversionista, fianza.

booking   Término dado en el cuartel de policía al registro de arresto y los cargos hechos al arrestado.

breach of contract   Violación, rotura, incumplimiento de contrato.

brief   Alegato, escrito memorial.

burglary   Escalamiento, allanamiento de morada.

buyer   Comprador.

bylaws   Estatutos sociales, reglamentos internos.

capacity to contract   capacidad contractual.

case   Causa, caso, acción legal, proceso, proceso civil, asunto, expediente.

case law   Jurisprudencia.

cashier's check   Cheque bancario.

cease and desist order   Orden judicial de cese.

censure   Censura.

certificate of deposit   Certificado de depósito.

certified check   Cheque certificado.

certify   Certificar, atestiguar.

charge   Cobrar, acusar, imputar.

charitable trust   Fideicomiso caritativo.

chattel   Bienes muebles, bártulos.

cheat   Fraude, engaño, defraudador, trampa, tramposo, estafar.

check   Cheque, talón, comprobación.

cite   Citación, citar, referir, emplazar.

citizenship   Ciudadanía.

civil action   Acción, enjuiciamiento civil, demanda.

civil law   Derecho civil.

Claims Court   Tribunal federal de reclamaciones.

client   Cliente.

closing arguments   Alegatos de clausura.

closing costs   Gastos ocasionados en la venta de bienes raíces.

clue   Pista, indicio.

codicil   Codicilo.

coercion   Coerción, coacción.

collateral   Colateral, auxiliar, subsidiario, seguridad colateral, garantía prendaria.

collect   Cobrar, recobrar, recaudar.

collision   Choque, colisión.

common law   Derecho consuetudinario.

comparative negligence   Negligencia comparativa.

compensatory damages   Indemnización compensatoria por daños y perjuicios, daños compensatorios.

competency   Competencia, capacidad legal.

concurrent conditions   Condiciones concurrentes.

concurrent jurisdiction   Jurisdicción simultanea, conocimiento acumulativo.

concurrent sentences   Sentencias que se cumplen simultáneamente.

concurring opinion   Opinión coincidente.

condemn   Condenar, confiscar, expropiar.

condition precedent   Condición precedente.

condition subsequent   Condición subsecuente.

confession   Confesión, admisión.

confidential   Confidencial, íntimo, secreto.

confiscation   Confiscación, comiso, decomiso.

consent decree   Decreto por acuerdo mutuo.

consequential damages   Daños especiales.

consideration   Contraprestación.

consolidation   Consolidación, unión, concentración.

courts   Cortes o tribunales establecidas por la constitución.

constructive delivery   Presunta entrega.

contempt of court   Desacato, contumacia o menosprecio a la corte.

contract   Contrato, convenio, acuerdo, pacto.

contributory negligence   Negligencia contribuyente.

conversion   Conversión, canje.

conviction   Convicción, fallo de culpabilidad, convencimiento, sentencia condenatoria, condena.

copyright   Derecho de autor, propiedad literaria, propiedad intelectual, derecho de impresión.

corroborate   Corroborar, confirmar.

counterclaim   Contrademanda, excepción de compensación.

counteroffer   Contra oferta.

covenant for quiet enjoyment   Convenio de disfrute y posesión pacífica.

creditor   Acreedor.

crime   Crimen, delito.

criminal act   Acto criminal.

criminal law   Derecho penal.

cross examination   contrainterrogatorio, repregunta.

cure   Curar, corregir.

damages   Daños y perjuicios, indemnización pecuniaria.

DBA   Sigla para **doing business as** En negociación comercial.

deadly force   Fuerza mortífera.

debt   Deuda, débito.

debtor   Deudor.

decision   Decisión judicial, fallo, determinación auto, sentencia.

deed   Escritura, título de propiedad, escritura de traspaso.

defamation   Difamación, infamación.

default   Incumplir, faltar, no comparecer, incumplimiento.

defendant   Demandado, reo, procesado, acusado.

delinquent   Delincuente, atrasado en pagos, delictuoso.

denial   Denegación, negación, denegatoria.

deponent   Deponente, declarante.

deportation   Deportación, destierro.

deposition   Deposición, declaración bajo juramento.

detain   Detener, retardar, retrasar.

devise   Legado de bienes raíces.

direct examination   Interrogatorio directo, interrogatorio a testigo propio.

directed verdict   Veredicto expedido por el juez, veredicto por falta de pruebas.

disaffirm   Negar, rechazar, repudiar, anular.

discharge   Descargo, cumplimiento, liberación,

disclose   Revelar.

discovery   Revelación de prueba, exposición reveladora.

discriminate   Discriminar.

dismiss   Despedir, desechar, desestimar

dissenting opinion   Opinión en desacuerdo.

dissolution   Disolución, liquidación.

diversity of citizenship   Diversidad de ciudadanías, ciudadanías diferentes.

dividend   Acción librada, dividendo.

divorce   Divorcio, divorciar.

docket   Orden del día, lista de casos en la corte.

double jeopardy   Non bis in idem.

driving under the influence   Manejar bajo los efectos de bebidas alcohólicas o drogas.

duress   Coacción.

earnest money   Arras, señal.

easement   Servidumbre.

edict   Edicto, decreto, auto.

embezzlement   Malversación de fondos.

eminent domain   Dominio eminente.

encroachment   Intrusión, usurpación, invasión, uso indebido.

encumbrance   Gravamen, afectación, cargo.

enforce   Hacer cumplir, dar valor, poner en efecto.

entitlement   Derecho, título.

equal protection clause Cláusula de protección de igualdad ante la ley.

equal protection of the law Igualdad ante la ley.

equity Equidad. Derecho equitativo.

escheat Reversión al estado al no haber herederos.

estate Bienes, propiedad, caudal hereditario, cuerpo de la herencia, caudal, derecho, título, interés sobre propiedad.

estop Impedir, detener, prevenir.

ethics Sistema ético.

eviction Evicción, desalojo, desalojamiento, desahucio, lanzamiento.

evidence Testimonio, prueba, pruebas documentales, pieza de prueba.

examination Examen, reconocimiento, interrogatorio.

executed contract Contrato firmado, contrato ejecutado.

execution Ejecución, desempeño, cumplimiento.

executory contract Contrato por cumplirse.

executory interests Intereses futuros.

exempt Franquear, exentar, exencionar, eximir, libre, franco, exento, inmune.

exoneration Exoneración, descargo, liberación.

expert witness Testigo perito.

express contract Contrato explícito.

expropriation Expropiación, confiscación.

eyewitness Testigo ocular o presencial.

fact Hecho falsificado.

failure to appear Incomparecencia.

fault Falta, defecto, culpa, negligencia.

fee Honorarios, retribución, cuota, cargo, derecho, dominio, asesoría, propiedad, bienes raíces.

fee simple estate Propiedad en dominio pleno.

felon Felón, autor de un delito.

felony Delito mayor o grave.

fiduciary Fiduciario.

find against Fallar o decidir en contra.

find for Fallar o decidir a favor.

finding Determinación de los hechos.

fine Multa, castigo.

fixture Accesorio fijo.

foreclose Entablar juicio hipotecario, embargar bienes hipotecados.

forgery Falsificación.

franchise Franquicia, privilegio, patente, concesión social, derecho de votar.

fraud Fraude, engaño, estafa, trampa, embuste, defraudación.

full disclosure Revelación completa.

garnishment Embargo de bienes.

gift Regalo, dádiva, donación.

gift causa mortis Donación de propiedad en expectativa de muerte.

gift inter vivos Donación entre vivos.

gift tax Impuesto sobre donaciones.

good and valid consideration Causa contractual válida.

good faith Buena fe.

goods Mercaderías, bienes, productos.

grace period Período de espera.

grantee Concesionario, cesionario.

grantor Otorgante, cesionista.

grievance Agravio, injuria, ofensa, queja formal.

gross negligence Negligencia temeraria, negligencia grave.

habitation Habitación, lugar donde se vive.

harassment Hostigamiento.

hearing Audiencia, vista, juicio.

hearsay Testimonio de oídas.

holder Tenedor, poseedor.

holding Decisión, opinión, tenencia posesión, asociación, grupo industrial.

holographic will Testamento hológrafo.

homeowner Propietario, dueño de casa.

homestead Casa, solariega, hogar, heredad, excepción de embargo, bien de familia.

hung jury Jurado sin veredicto.

identify Identificar, verificar, autenticar.

illegal Ilegal, ilícito, ilegítimo.

illegal entry Entrada ilegal.

illegal search Registro domiciliario, allanamiento ilegal, cacheo ilegal.

immunity Inmunidad, exención.

implied warranty Garantía implícita.

impossibility of performance Imposibilidad de cumplimiento.

impound Embargar, incautar, confiscar, secuestrar.

inadmissible Inadmisible, inaceptable.

income   Ingreso, ganancia, entrada, renta, rédito.

incriminate   Incriminar, acriminar.

indictment   Procesamiento, acusación por jurado acusatorio, inculpatoria.

indorsement   Endose, endoso, respaldo, garantía.

informant   Informador, denunciante, delator.

information   Información, informe, acusación por el fiscal, denuncia.

informed consent   Conformidad por información.

inherit   Heredar, recibir por herencia.

injunction   Mandato judicial, amparo, prohibición judicial, interdicto.

innocent   Inocente, no culpable.

inquiry   Indagatoria judicial, pesquisa.

insufficient evidence   Prueba insuficiente.

interrogation   Interrogación.

interstate commerce   Comercio interestatal.

intestate   Intestado, intestar, sin testamento.

intestate succession   Sucesión hereditaria.

investigation   Investigación, indagación, encuesta.

issue   Emisión, cuestión, punto, edición, número, tirada, sucesión, descendencia, resultado, decisión.

jail   Cárcel, calabozo, encarcelar.

joint tenancy   Condominio.

judge   Magistrado, juez, juzgar, adjudicar, enjuiciar, fallar.

judgment   Sentencia, fallo, juicio, decisión, dictamen, criterio.

judicial proceeding   Proceso o diligencia judicial.

judicial review   Revisión judicial.

jump bail   Fugarse bajo fianza.

jurisdiction   Jurisdicción, fuero competencia.

jury   Jurado

landlord   Arrendatario, propietario.

larceny   Hurto, latrocinio, ladronicio.

law   Ley, derecho.

lease   Contrato de arrendamiento, arrendamiento, arriendo, contrato de locación, arrendar, alquilar.

leasehold estate   Bienes forales.

legatee   Legatario, asignatario.

lender   Prestamista.

lessee   Arrendatario, locatario, inquilino.

lessor   Arrendatario, arrendador, arrendante, locador.

letter of credit   Letra de crédito.

liability   Responsiva, responsabilidad.

libel   Libelo por difamación por escrito.

license   Licencia, permiso, privilegio, matrícula, patente, título, licenciar, permitir.

lien   Gravamen, derecho prendario o de retención, embargo preventivo.

life estate   Hipoteca legal, dominio vitalicio.

limited liability company   Sociedad de responsabilidad limitada.

limited partnership   Sociedad en comandita, sociedad comanditaria.

litigated   Pleiteado, litigado, sujeto a litigación.

majority opinion   Opinión que refleja la mayoría de los miembros de la corte de apelaciones.

maker   Otorgante, girador.

malice   Malicia, malignidad, maldad.

malpractice   Incompetencia profesional.

manslaughter   Homicidio sin premeditación.

material witness   Testigo esencial.

mechanics lien   Gravamen de construcción.

mediation   Mediación, tercería, intervención, interposición.

medical examiner   Médico examinador.

merger   Fusión, incorporación, unión, consolidación.

minor   Menor, insignificante, pequeño, trivial.

misdemeanor   Delito menor, fechoría.

mitigation of damages   Mitigación de daños, minoración, atenuación.

monetary damages   Daños pecuniarios.

mortgage   Hipoteca, gravamen, hipotecar, gravar.

motion to dismiss   Petición para declaración sin lugar.

motion to suppress   Moción para suprimir, reprimir o suspender.

motive   Motivo.

murder   Asesinato, asesinar, homicidio culposo.

naturalization   Naturalización.

negligence   Negligencia, descuido, imprudencia.

negotiable   Negociable.

negotiate   Negociar, agenciar, hacer efectivo, traspasar, tratar.

net assets   Haberes netos.

notice   Aviso, notificación, advertencia, conocimiento.

novation   Novación, delegación de crédito.

nuisance   Daño, molestia, perjuicio.

nuncupative will   Testamento abierto.

oath   Juramento.

objection   Objeción, oposición, disconformidad, recusación, impugnación, excepción, réplica, reclamación.

obstruction of justice   Encubrimiento activo.

offer   Oferta, ofrecimiento, propuesta, ofrecer, proponer.

omission   Omisión, falla, falta.

opinion   Opinión, dictamen, decisión de la corte.

oral argument   Alegato oral.

order instrument   Instrumento de pago a la orden.

owe   Deber, estar en deuda, adeudo.

owner   Dueño, propietario, poseedor.

pain and suffering   Angustia mental y dolor físico.

pardon   Perdón, indulto, absolución, indultar, perdonar.

parol evidence rule   Principio que prohíbe la modificación de un contrato por prueba verbal.

parole   Libertad vigilada.

partnership   Sociedad, compañía colectiva, aparcería, consorcio, sociedad personal.

patent   Patente, obvio, evidente, aparente, privilegio de invención, patentar.

penalty   Pena, multa, castigo, penalidad, condena.

pending   Pendiente, en trámite, pendiente de, hasta que.

per capita   Por cabeza.

performance   Cumplimiento, desempeño, ejecución, rendimiento.

perjury   Perjurio, testimonio falso, juramento falso.

personal property   Bienes personales, bienes mobiliarios.

plea bargain   Declaración de culpabilidad concertada.

plea of guilty   Alegación de culpabilidad.

pleadings   Alegatos, alegaciones, escritos.

pledge   Prenda, caución, empeño, empeñar, dar en prenda, pignorar.

police power   Poder policial.

policy   Póliza, escritura, práctica política.

possession   Posesión, tenencia, goce, disfrute.

possibility of reverter   Posibilidad de reversión.

power of attorney   Poder de representación, poder notarial, procura.

precedent   Precedente, decisión previa por el mismo tribunal.

preemptive right   Derecho de prioridad.

prejudicial   Dañoso, perjudicial.

preliminary hearing   Audiencia preliminar.

premeditation   Premeditación.

presume   Presumir, asumir como hecho basado en la experiencia, suponer.

prevail   Prevalecer, persuadir, predominar, ganar, triunfar.

price discrimination   Discriminación en el precio.

principal   Principal, jefe, de mayor importancia, valor actual.

privileged communication   Comunicación privilegiada.

privity   Coparticipación, intereses comunes.

procedural   Procesal.

proceeds   Ganancias.

profit   Ganancia, utilidad, lucro, beneficio.

prohibited   Prohibido.

promise   Promesa.

promissory estoppel   Impedimento promisorio.

promissory note   Pagaré, vale, nota de pago.

proof   Prueba, comprobación, demostración.

prosecutor   Fiscal, abogado público acusador.

proximate cause   Causa relacionada.

proxy   Poder, delegación, apoderado, mandatario.

punishment   Pena, castigo.

punitive damages   Indemnización punitiva por daños y perjuicios, daños ejemplares.

qualification   Capacidad, calidad, preparación.

qualified indorsement   Endoso limitado endoso con reservas.

quasi contract   Cuasicontrato.

query   Pregunta, interrogación.

question of fact   Cuestión de hecho.

question of law   Cuestión de derecho.

quiet enjoyment   Uso y disfrute.

quitclaim deed   Escritura de traspaso de finiquito.

race discrimination   Discriminación racial.

rape   Estupro, violación, ultraje, rapto, violar.

ratification   Ratificación, aprobación, confirmación.

ratify   Aprobar, confirmar, ratificar, convalidar, adoptar.

real property   Bienes raíces, bienes inmuebles, arraigo.

reasonable doubt   Duda razonable.

rebut   Rebatir, refutar, negar, contradecir.

recognizance   Obligación impuesta judicialmente.

recordation   Inscripción oficial, grabación.

recover   Recobrar, recuperar, obtener como resultado de decreto.

redress   Reparación, compensación, desagravio, compensar, reparar, satisfacer, remediar.

regulatory agency   Agencia reguladora.

reimburse   Reembolsar, repagar, compensar, reintegrar.

rejoinder   Respuesta, réplica, contrarréplica.

release   Descargo, liberación, librar, relevar, descargar, libertar.

relevance   Relevancia.

remainder   Resto, restante, residuo, derecho expectativo a un bien raíz.

remedy   Remedio, recurso.

remuneration   Remuneración, compensación.

reply   Réplica, contestación, contestar, responder.

reprieve   Suspensión de la sentencia, suspensión, indulto, indultar, suspender.

reprimand   Reprender, regañar, reprimenda, represión.

repudiate   Repudiar, renunciar, rechazar.

rescission   Rescisión, abrogación, cancelación de un contrato.

respondeat superior   Responsabilidad civil al supervisor.

respondent   Apelado, demandado.

restitution   Restitución, devolución.

restraining order   Inhibitoria, interdicto, orden de amparo.

retain   Retener, emplear, guardar.

reversion   Reversión, derecho de sucesión.

revocation   Revocación, derogación, anulación.

reward   Premio.

right of first refusal   Retracto arrendaticio.

right of subrogation   Derecho de sustituir.

right of survivorship   Derecho de supervivencia entre dueños de propiedad mancomunada.

right to work laws   Leyes que prohíben la filiación sindical como requisito para poder desempeñar un puesto, derecho de trabajo.

rights   Derechos.

robbery   Robo, atraco.

ruling   Determinación oficial, auto judicial.

sale   Venta.

sale on approval   Venta por aprobación.

satisfaction   Satisfacción, liquidación, cumplimiento, pago, finiquito.

scope of authority   Autoridad explícitamente otorgada o implícitamente concedida.

search and seizure   Allanamiento, registro e incautación.

search warrant   Orden de registro o de allanamiento.

secured party   Persona con interés asegurado.

secured transaction   Transacción con un interés asegurado.

securities   Valores, títulos, obligaciones.

security agreement   Acuerdo que crea la garantía de un interés.

security deposit   Deposito de seguridad.

seize   Arrestar, confiscar, secuestrar, incautar.

settlement   Arreglo, composición, ajuste, liquidación, componenda, acomodo.

sex discrimination   Discriminación sexual.

sexual harassment   Acoso sexual.

shoplifting   Ratería en tiendas.

signature   Firma.

slander   Calumnia, difamación oral, calumniar.

source of income   Fuente de ingresos.

specific performance   Prestación específica contractual.

split decision   Decisión con opiniones mixtas.

spousal abuse   Abuso conyugal.

stare decisis   Vinculación con decisiones judiciales anteriores.

state of mind   Estado de ánimo, estado mental.

statement   Alegación, declaración, relato, estado de cuentas.

statutory foreclosure   Ejecución hipotecaria estatutaria.

statutory law   Derecho estatutario.

statutory rape   Estupro, violación de un menor de edad.

steal   Robar, hurtar, robo, hurto.

stock   Acciones, capital, existencias, semental.

stock option   Opción de comprar o vender acciones.

stop payment order   Suspensión de pago.

strict liability   Responsabilidad rigurosa.

sublease   Subarriendo, sublocación, subarrendar.

subpoena   Citación, citatorio, comparendo, cédula de citación, citación judicial, subpoena.

sue   Demandar, procesar.

summary judgment   Sentencia sumaria.

summon   Convocar, llamar, citar.

suppress   Suprimir, excluir pruebas ilegalmente obtenidas, reprimir, suspender.

surrender   Rendir, entregar, entrega, rendirse, entregarse.

surviving spouse   Cónyuge sobreviviente.

suspect   Sospecha, sospechar, sospechoso

tangible evidence   Prueba real.

tangible property   Propiedad tangible, bienes tangibles.

tenancy at sufferance   Tenencia o posesión por tolerancia.

tenancy at will   Tenencia o inquilinato sin plazo fijo.

tenancy by the entirety   Tenencia conyugal.

tenancy for life   Tenencia vitalicia.

tenancy for years   Inquilinato por tiempo fijo.

tender   Propuesta, oferta, presentar.

testator   Testador.

testify   Atestar, atestiguar, dar testimonio.

theft   Hurto.

title   Título, derecho de posesión, rango, denominación.

tort   Agravio, torticero, entuerto, daño legal, perjuicio, acto ilícito civil.

Totten trust   Fideicomiso bancario Totten.

trade name   Nombre comercial, marca de fábrica, marca comercial.

trademark   Marca registrada, marca industrial.

transgression   Ofensa, delito, transgresión.

trespass   Transgresión, violación de propiedad ajena, translimitación, traspasar, violar, infringir, transgredir.

trial court   Tribunal de primera instancia.

trust   Fideicomiso, confianza, confidencia, confianza, crédito, combinación, consorcio, grupo industrial.

truth   Verdad, verdadero, veracidad.

try   Probar, juzgar.

ultra vires   Mas allá de la facultad de actuar.

unanimous verdict   Veredicto unánime.

unbiased   Imparcial, neutral.

unconditional pardon   Perdón, amnistía, indulto incondicional.

unconscionable   Reprochable, repugnante, desmedido.

under arrest   Arrestado, bajo arresto.

underwrite   Subscribir, asegurar, firmar.

undisclosed   Escondido, no revelado.

undue influence   Influencia indebida, coacción, abuso de poder.

unenforceable   Inejecutable.

unilateral contract   Contrato unilateral.

unlawful   Ilegal, ilícito, ilegítimo.

unsound mind   Privado de razón, de mente inestable.

usury   Usura, agiotaje, logrería.

vagrancy   Vagancia, vagabundeo.

validity   Validez, vigencia.

valuable consideration   Causa contractual con cierto valor, causa contractual onerosa.

venue   Partido judicial.

verbal contract   Contrato verbal.

verbatim   Al pié de la letra.

verdict   Veredicto, fallo, sentencia, decisión.

victim   Víctima.

voidable   Anulable, cancelable.

wage   Salario, jornal, sueldo.

waive   Renunciar, ceder, suspender, abdicar.

waiver   Renunciar, desistir, ceder, suspender, abdicar, renuncia.

warrant   Autorización, resguardo, comprobante, certificado, justificación, decisión judicial.

warranty   Garantía, seguridad.

warranty of habitability   Garantía de habitabilidad.

welfare   Asistencia pública.

will   Testamento, voluntad.

willful misconduct   Mala conducta intencional.

withhold   Retener, detener.

witness   Testigo, declarante, atestar, testificar, atestiguar.

writ of attachment   Mandamiento de embargo.

writ of certiorari   Pedimento de avocación.

writ of execution   Auto de ejecución, ejecutoria.

GLOSSARY

Abatement A principle stating that if the property the testator leaves is not sufficient to satisfy all the beneficiaries named in a will and there are both general and residuary bequests, the residuary bequest is paid last—(abated first).

Acceptance A manifestation of assent by the offeree to the terms of the offer in a manner invited or required by the offer as measured by the objective theory of contracts.

Actus reus "Guilty act"—actual performance of criminal act.

Ademption A principle stating that if a testator leaves a specific devise of property to a beneficiary but the property is no longer in the estate when the testator dies, the beneficiary receives nothing.

Administrative agencies Agencies that the legislative and executive branches of federal and state governments establish to set rules and regulations.

Administrative law judge (ALJ) A judge presiding over administrative proceedings who decides questions of law and fact concerning the case.

Administrative Procedure Act (APA) A law establishing certain administrative procedures that federal administrative agencies must follow in conducting their affairs.

Administrative subpoena An order that directs the subject of the subpoena to disclose the requested information.

Administrator or administratrix A court-appointed personal representative who administers the estate during its settlement phase when no one is named in the will or if the decedent dies intestate.

Adverse possession the wrongful possession of someone else's property; the adverse possessor may obtain title to that property if certain statutory requirements are met.

Affirm To agree with; to let stand.

Agency The principal–agent relationship; the fiduciary relationship "which results from the manifestation of consent by one person to another that the other shall act in his behalf and subject to his control, and consent by the other so to act" (Restatement [Second] of Agency).

Agency by ratification An agency that occurs when (1) a person misrepresents himself or herself as another's agent when in fact he or she is not, and (2) the purported principal ratifies the unauthorized act.

Agent The party who agrees to act on behalf of another, such as a person who has been authorized to sign a negotiable instrument on behalf of another person.

Agreement The manifestation by two or more persons of the substance of a contract.

Aiding and abetting Rendering support, assistance, or encouragement to the commission of a crime; harboring a criminal after he or she has committed a crime.

Air-space parcel A property right that is a three-dimensional cube of air above the surface of the earth.

Alien corporation A corporation that is incorporated in another country.

Alternative dispute resolution (ADR) Methods of resolving disputes other than litigation.

American Association for Paralegal Education (AAfPE) National organization of paralegal educators and institutions offering paralegal education programs.

American Bar Association (ABA) Largest professional legal organization in the United States.

American Inventors Protection Act A law that reorganized the U.S. Patent and Trademark Office (PTO), granting it new regulatory powers for inventions and patents and upgrading the PTO Commissioner to Assistant Secretary of Commerce with advisory powers.

Americans with Disabilities Act (ADA) A law that imposes obligations on employers and providers of public transportation, telecommunications, and public facilities to accommodate individuals with disabilities.

Analytical skill The ability to follow a step-by-step process to solve a problem.

Answer Defendant's written response to plaintiff's complaint, filed with the court and served on plaintiff.

Anticybersquatting Consumer Protection Act Legislation aimed at preventing "cybersquatters" who register domain names based on names of famous companies and people and hold them "hostage."

Apparent agency (agency by estoppel) (1) Agency that arises when a principal creates the appearance of an agency that in actuality does not exist; (2) agency that arises when a franchisor creates the appearance that a franchisee is its agent when in fact an actual agency does not exist.

Appeal The act of asking an appellate court to overturn a decision after the trial court's final judgment has been entered.

Appellant The appealing party in an appeal; also known as *petitioner*.

Appellee Responding party in an appeal; also known as *respondent*.

Arbitration A form of alternative dispute resolution in which the parties choose an impartial third party to hear and decide the dispute.

Arraignment A hearing during which the accused is brought before a court and is (1) informed of the charges against him or her, and (2) asked to enter a plea.

Arrest warrant A document for a person's detainment based upon a showing of probable cause that the person committed the crime.

Arson Willfully or maliciously burning another's building.

Article 2 (Sales) of Uniform Commercial Code Article of the Uniform Commercial Code that governs sale of goods.

Article 2A (Leases) of Uniform Commercial Code Article of the Uniform Commercial Code that governs lease of goods.

Articles of incorporation (corporate charter) The basic governing document of the corporation; must be filed with the secretary of state of the state of incorporation.

Articles of limited liability partnership A public document that must be filed with the secretary of state to form a limited liability partnership.

Assault Either (1) the threat of immediate harm or offensive contact, or (2) any action that arouses reasonable apprehension of imminent harm; actual physical contact is unnecessary.

Associate's degree A college degree in science (AS) or arts (AA) or applied arts (AAS), generally requiring two years of full-time study.

Association of Legal Writing Directors (ALWD) A society for professors who coordinate legal writing instruction in legal education.

Assumption of the risk A defense a defendant can use against a plaintiff who knowingly and voluntarily enters into or participates in a risky activity that results in injury; defendant must prove that (1) plaintiff knew and appreciated the risk, and (2) plaintiff voluntarily assumed the risk.

Attachment Seizure by creditors of property in debtor's possession to collect on a debt while their lawsuit is pending.

Attempt to commit a crime Trying to commit a crime but not completing it.

Attestation Action of a will being witnessed by two or three objective and competent people.

Attorney–client privilege A rule that says a client can tell his or her lawyer anything about the case without fear that the attorney will be called as a witness against the client.

Attorney-in-fact Agent who has power of attorney; does not actually have to be an attorney.

Bachelor's degree A college degree generally requiring four years of full-time study.

Bailee Holder of goods who is not a seller or a buyer (e.g., a warehouse).

Bailment A transaction whereby an owner transfers his or her personal property to another to be held, stored, delivered, or for some other purpose; title to the property does not transfer.

Bailor Owner of property in a bailment.

Barrister A lawyer in the English legal system who is brought cases by a solicitor and litigates the cases.

Battery Unauthorized and harmful or offensive physical contact with another person; direct physical contact is not necessary.

Bench trial Trial without a jury; also called a *waiver trial*.

Beneficiary (1) A person or organization designated in the will to receive all or a portion of the testator's property at the time of the testator's death. (2) The person for whose benefit a trust is created. (3) The person who is to receive life insurance proceeds when the insured dies. (4) The creditor in a deed of trust and note transaction.

Bequest　A gift of personal property by will; also known as a *legacy*.

Berne Convention　An international copyright treaty to which the United States and many other nations are signatories.

Bill of Rights　Constitutional Amendments I through X.

Biosafety protocol　An agreement sponsored by United Nations in which countries agreed that all genetically engineered foods will be clearly labeled with the phrase "May contain living modified organisms."

Board of directors　A panel of decision makers, the members of which are elected by the shareholders of a corporation.

Bluebook, The　A uniform system of citation published by the *Harvard Law Review*.

Bona fide occupational qualification (BFOQ)　Employment discrimination based on a protected class (other than race or color) that is lawful if it is job-related and a business necessity.

Breach of the duty of care　Failure to exercise care or to act as a reasonable person would act.

Bribery　A person's giving another person money, property, favors, or anything else of value in exchange for a favor; often called a payoff or "kickback."

Briefs　Documents submitted by the parties' attorneys to the judge; contain legal support for their side of the case.

Burden of proof　The weight a plaintiff carries in proving the allegations made in his or her complaint.

Burglary　Taking personal property from another's home, office, or commercial or other type of building.

Business judgment rule　A rule that protects the decisions of board of directors, which acts on an informed basis, in good faith, and in the honest belief that the action taken is in the best interests of the corporation and its shareholders.

Causation　Concept that a person who commits a negligent act is not liable unless his or her act was the cause of the plaintiff's injuries. Two types: (1) causation in fact (actual cause), and (2) proximate cause (legal cause).

Causation in fact　Actual cause of negligence.

Certification mark　A mark certifying that goods and services are of a certain quality or originate from particular geographical areas.

Certified legal assistant (CLA)　Designation by National Association of Legal Assistants for those who take and pass NALA certification program two-day comprehensive examination.

Chain of distribution　All manufacturers, distributors, wholesalers, retailers, lessors, and subcomponent manufacturers involved in a transaction.

Chain-style franchise　License by franchisor to franchisee to make and sell its products or distribute services to the public from a retail outlet serving an exclusive territory.

Charitable trust　A trust created for the benefit of a segment of society or society in general.

Chief justice　The U.S. Supreme Court justice responsible for administration of the Court.

Child custody　A divorce issue concerning who is to be the child's primary caregiver (or joint custodian) and the amount of time the noncustodial parent is to spend with the child (parenting time).

Child support　Entitlement of children to be financially supported by their parents upon divorce, based on the parents' earning ability.

Circuits　The geographical area served by a U.S. court of appeals.

Citation　A reference to the source of the information.

Cite checking　(1) Verifying that the proper citation format has been used in a document and (2) checking the referenced case to determine its validity and that it has not been repealed or overturned.

Civil law system　A major legal system derived from the Roman Empire, in which a civil code and statutes interpreting it are the sole sources of law; thus, case law and court decisions do not have the force of law.

Civil litigation　Involves legal action to resolve disputes between parties (as contrasted with criminal litigation).

Closing arguments　Statements made by plaintiff's and defendant's attorneys to the jury at the end of a trial to try to convince the jury to render a verdict for their client.

Codicil　A separate document that must be executed to amend a will; must be executed with the same formalities as a will.

Codified law　Statutes organized into code books, organized by topic.

Collective mark   A mark used by cooperatives, associations, and fraternal organizations.

Color discrimination   Employment discrimination based upon skin color prohibited under Title VII of Civil Rights Act of 1964.

"Coming and going"   A rule that says a principal is generally not liable for injuries caused by its agents and employees while they are on their way to or from work.

Commerce Clause   A clause of the U.S. Constitution that grants Congress the power "to regulate commerce with foreign nations, and among the several states, and with Indian tribes."

Commitment   The dedication to finish that which one starts out to do or complete.

Common-law marriage   A marriage recognized by some states without a marriage license between the parties.

Common stock certificate   A document that represents a common shareholder's investment in a corporation.

Common stockholder   A person who owns common stock.

Communication   The act of expressing oneself in written or spoken words.

Community property   A form of co-ownership in which husband and wife share equally in the fruits of the marital partnership.

Comparative negligence   A doctrine that applies to strict liability actions that says a plaintiff who is contributorily negligent for his or her injuries is responsible for a proportional share of the damages.

Compensatory damages   (1) An award of money intended to compensate a nonbreaching party for the loss of the bargain; they place the nonbreaching party in the same position as if the contract had been fully performed by restoring the "benefit of the bargain." (2) Damages that are generally equal to the difference between the value of the goods as warranted and the actual value of the goods accepted at the time and place of acceptance.

Complaint   Document the plaintiff files with the court and serves on the defendant to initiate a lawsuit.

Complete performance   Action that occurs when a party to a contract renders performance exactly as required by the contract; discharges that party's obligations under the contract.

Computer Software Copyright Act   Amended the Copyright Act of 1976 to include computer programs in the list of tangible items protected by copyright law.

Conciliation   A form of mediation in which the parties choose an interested third party to act as the mediator.

Concurring opinion   Issued by a justice who agrees with the outcome of a case but not the reason proffered by other justices, to set forth his or her reasons for deciding the case.

Condition precedent   A condition that requires the occurrence (or nonoccurrence) of an event before a party is obligated to perform a duty under a contract.

Condominium   A common form of ownership in a multiple-dwelling building in which the purchaser has title to the individual unit and owns the common areas as a tenant in common with the other condominium owners.

Conflict checking   Comparing current and prior representations of parties and matters handled to verify that the acceptance of a new client or legal matter will not present a conflict of interest for the firm.

Conflict of interest   The representation of one client being directly adverse to the interest of another client.

Connector   Instructions to a search engine to look for combinations of words; include "and," "near," and "or."

Consequential damages   Foreseeable damages that arise from circumstances outside a contract; to be liable for these damages, the breaching party must know or have reason to know that the breach will cause special damages to the other party.

Consideration   Something of legal value given in exchange for a promise.

Consolidation   (1) Act of a court to combine two or more separate lawsuits into one lawsuit. (2) The combining of two or more corporations to form an entirely new corporation.

Constructive trust   An equitable trust imposed by law to avoid fraud, unjust enrichment, and injustice.

Contempt of court   A party to a lawsuit may be held in contempt of court for refusing to comply with the court's orders; punishment may include a fine or jail time.

Contract   An agreement that is enforceable by a court of law or equity.

Contracts contrary to public policy   Contracts that have a negative impact on society or interfere with the public's safety and welfare.

Contractual capacity   One of the requirements of a valid contract is that both parties must have the capacity to contract; those not having capacity include minors, mentally incompetent persons, and intoxicated persons.

Contributory negligence (1) A doctrine that says a plaintiff who is partially at fault for his or her own injury cannot recover against the negligent defendant. (2) A defense that says a person who is injured by a defective product but has been negligent and has contributed to his or her own injuries cannot recover from the defendant.

Conversion of personal property A tort that deprives a true owner of the use and enjoyment of his or her personal property by taking over such property and exercising ownership rights over it.

Cooperative (1) A voluntary joining together of businesses that provides services to its members. (2) A form of co-ownership of a multiple-dwelling building in which a corporation owns the building and the residents own shares in the corporation.

Co-ownership Two or more persons own a piece of real property; forms of co-ownership include joint tenancy, tenancy in common, tenancy by the entirety, community property, condominium, and cooperative.

Copyright The exclusive legal right to reproduce, publish, and sell a literary, musical, or artistic work.

Copyright infringement The copying of a substantial and material part of the plaintiff's copyrighted work without permission; copyright holder may recover damages and other remedies against the infringer.

Corporation A fictitious legal entity that (1) is created according to statutory requirements, and (2) is a separate taxpaying entity for federal income tax purposes.

Counteroffer A response by an offeree that contains terms and conditions different from or in addition to those of the offer; a counteroffer terminates an offer.

Court of Appeals for the Federal Circuit A court of appeals in Washington, D.C. that has special appellate jurisdiction to review the decisions of the claims court, the Patent and Trademark Office, and the Court of International Trade.

Court of record A state's general-jurisdiction trial court, in which testimony and evidence are recorded and stored for future reference.

Covenant An unconditional promise to perform.

Crime Violation of a statute for which the government imposes a punishment.

Criminal conspiracy Two or more persons entering into an agreement to commit a crime and taking an overt act to further the crime.

Criminal fraud Obtaining title to property through deception or trickery; also known as *false pretenses* or *deceit*.

Criminal law Federal, state, and local government laws for the purpose of defining crimes and setting forth punishments for those found guilty of violating criminal laws.

Critical legal thinking The process of specifying the issue presented by a case, identifying the key facts in the case and applicable law, and then applying the law to the facts to come to a conclusion that answers the issue presented.

Cross-complaint Document filed by defendant against plaintiff to seek damages or some other remedy.

Cross-examination Questioning of a witness following direct examination; precedes redirect examination and recross examination.

Cruel and unusual punishment A clause in the Eighth Amendment that protects criminal defendants from torture or other abusive punishment.

Cultural sensitivity Awareness of the differences in the way people behave, based on religious and ethnic backgrounds and belief systems, and reacting appropriately.

"Danger invites rescue" Doctrine that provides that a rescuer who is injured while going to someone's rescue can sue the person who caused the dangerous situation.

Deed Document that describes a person's ownership interest in a piece of real property.

Defamation of character False statement(s) made by one person about another; in court, the plaintiff must prove that (1) the defendant made an untrue statement of fact about the plaintiff, and (2) the statement was intentionally or accidentally published to a third party.

Default judgment If a defendant does not file an answer to a plaintiff's complaint, a default judgment is entered against him or her, establishing the defendant's liability.

Defendant The party against whom a lawsuit is brought.

Defendant's case Process by which the defendant (1) rebuts the plaintiff's evidence, (2) proves affirmative defenses, and (3) proves allegations made in a cross-complaint.

Defense attorney Attorney working on behalf of the defendant.

Deferred posting rule A rule that allows banks to fix an afternoon hour of 2:00 P.M. or later as a cutoff hour for the purpose of processing items.

Delegation doctrine A doctrine that says when an administrative agency is created, it receives certain powers and the agency can use only those legislative, judicial, and executive powers bestowed on it.

De novo appeal   To appeal to a higher court as if there has been no prior decision.

Deponent   Party who gives a deposition.

Deposition   Oral testimony given under oath by a party or witness and transcribed prior to trial.

Digital Millennium Copyright Act   Enacted in 1998 to protect "wrappers" and encryption technology of copyrighted works from infringement; imposes civil and criminal penalties.

Direct examination   The initial questioning of witnesses in a case by an attorney; often followed by cross-examination, redirect examination, and recross examination.

Disaffirm   The act of a minor to rescind a contract under the infancy doctrine; may be done orally, in writing, or by the minor's conduct.

Discovery   A legal process during which both parties engage in various activities to find facts of the case from the other party and witnesses prior to trial.

Dissenting opinion   Issued by a justice who does not agree with the court's decision, setting forth the reasons for his or her dissent.

Distinctiveness of a mark   The quality of a brand name that has acquired a secondary meaning; necessary to be trademarked.

District attorney–prosecutor   The lawyer representing the government in a criminal lawsuit.

Diversity of citizenship   A case between (1) citizens of different states, (2) a citizen of a state and a citizen or subject of a foreign country, and (3) a citizen of a state and a foreign country where a foreign country is the plaintiff.

Divorce   Legal proceeding whereby a married couple legally undo their marriage.

Doctrine of strict liability   A tort doctrine that makes manufacturers, distributors, wholesalers, retailers, and others in the chain of distribution of a defective product liable for damages caused by the defect, irrespective of fault.

"Doing business as" (d.b.a.)   Operating under a trade name.

Domain name   A unique name that identifies an individual's or company's website.

Domestic corporation   A corporation in the state in which it was formed.

Double jeopardy   A clause in the Fifth Amendment that protects persons from being tried twice for the same crime.

Dram shop act   State statutes that make taverns and bartenders liable for injuries caused to or by patrons who are served too much alcohol.

Dual-purpose mission   An errand or other act that a principal requests of an agent while the agent is on his or her own personal business.

Due Process Clause   A clause in the Fourteenth Amendment to the U.S. Constitution that provides that no person shall be deprived of "life, liberty, or property" without due process of the law.

Duty not to willfully or wantonly injure   The obligation an owner owes a trespasser to prevent intentional injury or harm to the trespasser when the trespasser is on the owner's premises.

Duty of candor   The obligation to be honest with the court.

Duty of care   (1) The obligation we all owe each other not to cause any unreasonable harm or risk of harm; a breach is negligence. (2) An obligation owed by a member of a member-managed LLC and a manager of a manager-managed LLC not to engage in (a) a known violation of law, (b) intentional conduct, (c) reckless conduct, or (d) grossly negligent conduct that injures the LLC. (3) An obligation that corporate directors and officers have to use care and diligence when acting on behalf of the corporation.

Duty of loyalty   (1) An obligation of directors and officers not to act adversely to the interests of the corporation and to subordinate their personal interests to those of the corporation and its shareholders. (2) An obligation of a partner not to act adversely to the interests of the partnership.

Duty of ordinary care   The obligation of an owner to an invitee or a licensee to prevent injury or harm when the invitee or licensee steps on the owner's premises.

Duty of reasonable care   The obligation of a reasonable bailee in like circumstances to protect the bailed property.

Duty of utmost care   An obligation of care, going beyond ordinary care, that says common carriers and innkeepers have a responsibility to provide security to their passengers or guests.

Easement   A right to use someone else's land without owning or leasing it.

Economic Espionage Act   A law enacted in 1996 that makes it a federal crime to steal another's trade secret.

Elective course   An educational offering not required as part of a program of study.

Electronic mail (email)   Written communication between individuals and businesses using computers connected to the Internet or an internal network.

Embezzlement   Fraudulent conversion of property by a person to whom that property was entrusted.

Employer–employee relationship   A relationship that results when an employer hires an employee to perform some form of physical service.

Employment-at-will   Employment without an employment contract.

Employment-related injury   Injury arising out of and in the course of employment, under the Workers' Compensation Act.

Entity theory   An approach holding that partnerships are separate legal entities that can have title to personal and real property, transact business in the partnership name, sue in the partnership name, and the like.

Enumerated powers   Certain powers delegated to the federal government by the states.

Environmental Protection Agency (EPA)   An administrative agency created by the U.S. Congress in 1970 to coordinate implementation and enforcement of federal environmental protection laws.

Equal Access to Justice Act   A law enacted to protect persons from harassment by federal administrative agencies.

Equitable distribution   In property division in divorce, the doctrine that takes into account issues of rearing a family rather than being in the workplace, age and medical condition of the parties, and the contribution to the education or professional or business success by one spouse to the other.

Escheat   Goes to; used to describe property that goes to the state when an individual dies intestate (without a will).

Estate   Ownership rights in real property; the bundle of legal rights of the owner to possess, use, and enjoy property.

Estate *pur autre vie*   A life estate measured in the life of a third party.

Estray statutes   Statutes that permit a finder of mislaid or lost property to clear title to the property if (1) the finder reports the found property to the appropriate government agency and turns over possession of the property to this agency, (2) either the finder or the government agency posts notices and publishes advertisements describing the lost property, and (3) a specified amount of time has passed without the rightful owner's reclaiming the property.

Ethical obligation   The obligation to conform to a set of ethics, in general or that of a profession, such as the ABA Model Rules for lawyers.

Ethical wall   An environment in which an attorney or a paralegal is isolated from a particular case or client to avoid a conflict of interest or to protect a client's confidences and secrets.

Exclusionary rule   A rule that says evidence obtained from an unreasonable search and seizure generally can be prohibited from introduction at a trial or administrative proceeding against the person searched.

Exclusive agency contract   A contract between a principal and an agent that says the principal cannot employ any agent other than the exclusive agent.

Exculpatory clause   A contractual provision that relieves one or both parties to the contract from tort liability for ordinary negligence.

Executive branch of government   The part of the federal government that consists of the President and Vice President.

Executive order   An order issued by a member of the executive branch of the government, such as the President.

Executive powers   Authority granted to administrative agencies, such as the investigation and prosecution of possible violations of statutes, administrative rules, and administrative orders.

Executor or executrix   A personal representative named in a will to administer an estate during its settlement phase.

Expert witnesses   Those individuals whose background, education, and experience are such that courts will recognize them as qualified to give opinions based on a set of facts.

Express agency   An agency that occurs when a principal and an agent expressly agree to enter into an agency agreement with each other.

Express contract   An agreement in written or oral words.

Express trust   A trust created voluntarily by the settlor.

Extortion   Threat to expose something about another person unless that other person gives money or property; often called "blackmail."

Fair-use doctrine   A doctrine that permits certain limited use of a copyright by someone other than the copyright holder without the permission of the copyright holder.

False imprisonment The intentional confinement or restraint of another person without authority or justification and without that person's consent.

Family law The practice of law concerning marriage, divorce, and child custody and support.

Federal administrative agencies Administrative agencies that are part of the executive or legislative branch of government.

Federal question A case arising under the U.S. Constitution, treaties, or federal statutes and regulations.

Federal Rules of Appellate Procedure (F.R.A.P.) Rules governing appeals in both civil and criminal cases to the federal appellate court.

Federal Rules of Civil Procedure Rules governing civil trials in the federal system.

Federalism The U.S. form of government, in which the federal government and the 50 state governments share powers.

Fee simple absolute (fee simple) A type of ownership of real property that grants the owner the fullest bundle of legal rights that a person can hold in real property.

Fee simple defeasible (qualified fee) A type of ownership of real property that grants the owner all the incidents of a fee simple absolute except that it may be taken away if a specified condition occurs or does not occur.

Felony The most serious type of crime; most crimes against the person and some business-related crimes are felonies.

File server The central computer in a network computer system that controls the flow of information over the network.

Final order rule A rule that says the decision of an administrative agency must be final before judicial review can be sought.

Finding tools Publications, such as digests or the *Index to Legal Periodicals*, used to find primary and secondary sources.

Fireman's rule A rule stating that a firefighter who is injured while putting out a fire may not sue the party whose negligence caused the fire.

Fixture Personal property that is permanently affixed to the real property, such as built-in cabinets in a house.

***Force majeure* clause** Clause in a contract that excuses nonperformance of the contract if certain events occur.

Foreign corporation A corporation in any state or jurisdiction other than the one in which it was formed.

Forgery Unauthorized signature of a maker, drawer, or indorser.

Forum-selection clause Contract provision that designates a certain court to hear any dispute concerning nonperformance of the contract.

Franchise An arrangement whereby the franchisor (owner) licenses another party to use the franchisor's trade name, trademarks, commercial symbols, patents, copyrights, and other property in the distribution and selling of goods and services.

Franchisee The party who is licensed by the franchisor in a franchise situation.

Fraud Intentional misrepresentation.

Freedom of Information Act (FOIA) A law enacted to give the public access to documents in the possession of federal administrative agencies.

Freehold estate An estate in which the owner has a present possessory interest in the real property.

Frolic and detour A situation in which an agent does something during the course of his or her employment to further his or her own interests rather than the principal's.

Fully disclosed agency An agency that results if the third party entering into a contract knows (1) that the agent is acting as an agent for a principal, and (2) the actual identity of the principal.

Future interest The interest that a grantor retains for himself or herself or a third party.

General gift Testamentary gift that does not identify the specific property from which the gift is to be made.

General-jurisdiction trial court A court that hears cases of a general nature that are not within the jurisdiction of limited-jurisdiction trial courts; testimony and evidence at trial are recorded and stored for future reference.

General partner Partner in a limited partnership who invests capital, manages the business, and is personally liable for partnership debts.

General partnership An association of two or more persons to carry on as co-owners of a business for profit [UPA § 6(1)].

General power of attorney A type of power of attorney that confers broad powers on the agent to act in any matters on the principal's behalf.

General practice A law firm that handles all types of cases.

Generic name   A term for a mark that has become a common term for a product line or type of service and therefore has lost its trademark protection.

Gift promise   An unenforceable promise because it lacks consideration.

GlobalCite   The Loislaw reverse chronological list of case law; statutes in the order of the highest number of citation occurrences; regulations in relevancy order; and references to other databases in the Loislaw library.

Good Samaritan law   Statute that relieves medical professionals from liability for ordinary negligence when they stop and render aid to victims in emergency situations.

Government in the Sunshine Act   A law that opens certain federal administrative agency meetings to the public.

Grantee   The party to whom an interest in real property is transferred.

Grantor   The party who transfers an ownership interest in real property.

Guest statute   Statute providing that if a driver of a vehicle voluntarily and without compensation gives a ride to another person, the driver is not liable to the passenger for injuries caused by driver's ordinary negligence.

Heirs   Relatives who receive property under intestacy statutes when a person dies without a will.

Holographic will   Will that is entirely handwritten and signed by the testator.

Hung jury   A jury that cannot come to a unanimous decision about the defendant's guilt; the government may choose to retry the case.

Illegal contract   A contract to perform an unlawful act; cannot be enforced by either party to the contract.

Immunity from prosecution   The government's agreeing not to use any evidence given by a person granted immunity against that person.

Implied agency   An agency that occurs when a principal and an agent do not expressly create an agency but it is inferred from the conduct of the parties.

Implied-in-fact contract   Contracts that are implied from the action and conduct of the parties rather than stated in oral or written words.

Implied trust   A trust that is imposed by law or from the conduct of the parties.

Implied warranty of habitability   A warranty that provides that the leased premises must be fit, safe, and suitable for ordinary residential use.

Inchoate crimes   Incomplete crimes or crimes committed by nonparticipants, including criminal conspiracy, attempt to commit a crime, and aiding and abetting the commission of a crime.

Incidental beneficiary   A party who unintentionally benefits from another's contract.

Indemnification   Right of a partner to be reimbursed for expenditures incurred on behalf of a partnership.

Independent contractor   "A person who contracts with another to do something for him who is not controlled by the other nor subject to the other's right to control with respect to his physical conduct in the performance of the undertaking" (Restatement [Second] of Agency).

Indictment/information   The charge of having committed a crime, based on the judgment of a grand jury.

Infancy doctrine   A doctrine that allows minors to disaffirm (cancel) most contracts they have entered into with adults.

Injunction   A court order prohibiting a person from doing a certain act.

In personam jurisdiction   A court's authority over the parties to a lawsuit; also called *personal jurisdiction*.

In rem jurisdiction   Authority to hear a case because of jurisdiction over the property of the lawsuit; literally, "jurisdiction over the thing."

Inside director   A member of a board of directors who is also an officer of the corporation.

Intangible property   Rights that cannot be reduced to physical form, including stock certificates, certificates of deposit, bonds, and copyrights.

Intentional infliction of emotional distress   A tort that says a person whose extreme and outrageous conduct intentionally or recklessly causes severe emotional distress to another person is liable for that emotional distress; also known as *tort of outrage*.

Intentional misrepresentation   Fraud or deceit; occurs when an agent makes an untrue statement that he or she knows is not true.

Intentional tort   A category of torts requiring that the defendant intended to do the act that caused the plaintiff's injuries; occurs when a person has intentionally committed a wrong against (1) another person or his or her character, or (2) another person's property.

Intermediate appellate court (court of appeal)   A court that hears appeals from trial courts.

Internet A collection of millions of computers that provide a network of electronic connections between computers.

Internet search engine A program designed to search for a word or set of words on the Internet.

Internet service provider (ISP) Organization providing local or toll-free access to connect to the Internet.

Interpersonal skills The ability to work with others.

Interpretive rules Rules issued by administrative agencies that explain existing statutory language as they understand it.

Interrogatories Written questions submitted by one party to another party; the questions must be answered in writing within a stipulated time.

Interstate commerce Movement of goods between states, or business that affects commerce between states.

Intervention The act of others to join as parties to an existing lawsuit.

Inter vivos A trust created by a grantor (settlor) during his or her lifetime.

Intestacy statute A state statute dictating how property is to be distributed to heirs of an individual who dies without a will.

Intestate succession The application of a state's intestacy statutes to determine how property is to be distributed to heirs when an individual dies without an heir.

Intrastate commerce Movement of goods within states, or business that affects commerce within states.

Invasion of the right to privacy A tort that constitutes the violation of a person's right to live his or her life without being subjected to unwarranted and undesired publicity.

Invitee A person who has been expressly or impliedly invited onto owner's premises for mutual benefit of both parties.

Joint and several liability Condition of a partnership in which the partners are jointly and severally liable for tort liability of the partnership; this means that the plaintiff can sue one or more of the partners separately. If successful, the plaintiff can recover the entire amount of the judgment from any or all of the defendant-partners.

Joint liability An aspect of a partnership in which the partners are both or all liable for contracts and debts of the partnership; this means that a plaintiff must name the partnership and all of the partners as defendants in a lawsuit.

Joint tenancy Form of co-ownership that includes the right of survivorship.

Joint will A will executed by two or more testators.

Judgment Official decision of the court.

Judgment notwithstanding the verdict (j.n.o.v.) In a civil case, the judge's overturning the jury's verdict if he or she finds bias or jury misconduct.

Judicial branch of government The part of the federal government that consists of the Supreme Court and other federal courts.

Judicial decision Written opinion explaining the reasoning in an individual lawsuit; issued by federal and state courts.

Jurisdiction Authority of a court to hear a case.

Jurisprudence Philosophy or science of law.

Jury deliberation Process by which a jury discusses the facts and evidence they have witnessed in a trial.

Jury instructions Directions given by judge to jury informing them of the law to be applied in the case.

Just Compensation Clause Clause in the U.S. Constitution mandating that the government compensate owners and lessees for property taken under the power of eminent domain.

KeyCite The Westlaw on-line citation update service.

LAN Local area network.

Land Real property consisting of land and buildings and other structures permanently attached to the land.

Landlord/lessor Owner who transfers a leasehold.

Land-use control Collective term for the laws that regulate the possession, ownership, and use of real property.

Larceny Taking another's personal property other than from his or her person or building.

Law A body of rules of action or conduct prescribed by controlling authority, and having binding legal force; must be obeyed and followed by citizens subject to sanctions or legal consequences.

Law court A court that developed and administered a uniform set of laws decreed by the kings and queens subsequent to William the Conqueror; emphasized legal procedure over merits.

Leading questions Questions that suggest the desired answer.

Lease A transfer of the right to possession and use of real property for a set term in return for certain consideration; rental agreement between landlord and tenant.

Leasehold estate (leasehold)   A tenant's interest in the property.

Legal assistant   A person qualified by education, training, or work experience who is employed or retained by a lawyer, law office, corporation, governmental agency, or other entity who performs specifically delegated substantive legal work for which a lawyer is responsible; *paralegal* is an equivalent term.

Legislative branch of government   The part of the federal government that consists of Congress (the Senate and the House of Representatives).

Libel   A false statement that appears in a letter, newspaper, magazine, book, photograph, movie, video, and so on.

License   (1) A contract that transfers limited rights in intellectual property and informational rights. (2) A contract that grants a person the right to enter upon another's property for a specified and usually short period of time. (3) A government document conferred on people in certain types of industries or professions.

Licensee   The party who is given limited rights in or access to intellectual property and informational rights owned by the licensor.

Licensing power   Statute that requires a person or business to obtain a license from the government prior to engaging in a specified occupation or activity.

Life estate   An interest in the land for a person's lifetime; upon that person's death, the interest is transferred to another party.

Limited-jurisdiction trial court   A court that hears matters of a specialized or limited nature.

Limited liability   Liability of shareholders or limited partners only to the extent of their capital contribution; they generally are not personally liable for debts and obligations of the corporation or partnership.

Limited liability company (LLC)   An unincorporated business entity that combines the most favorable attributes of general partnerships, limited partnerships, and corporations.

Limited liability partnership (LLP)   A type of partnership in which all (limited) partners have limited liability.

Limited partner   Partner in a limited partnership who invests capital but does not participate in management and is not personally liable for partnership debts beyond capital contributions.

Limited partnership   A type of partnership that has two types of partners: (1) general partners, and (2) limited partners.

Limited partnership agreement (articles of limited partnership)   Terms and conditions regarding operation, termination, and dissolution of a partnership; a document that sets forth the rights and duties of the general and limited partners.

Liquidated damages   Damages specified in a contract rather than determined by the court; paid upon a breach of contract established in advance.

Litigation   The process of bringing, maintaining, and defending a lawsuit.

Living will   A will that a person makes before catastrophe strikes and he or she becomes unable to express it because of illness or accident, stipulating that his or her life is not to be prolonged indefinitely by artificial means.

Long-arm statute   A statute that extends a state's jurisdiction to nonresidents who were not served a summons within the state.

Mail fraud   The use of mail to defraud another person.

Mala in se   Term describing crimes that are inherently evil, such as murder, rape, and other crimes against persons.

Mala prohibita   Term describing crimes that are not inherently evil but are prohibited by society; these include non-felony crimes against property, such as robbery.

Malicious prosecution   A lawsuit in which the original defendant sues the original plaintiff; a civil action for damages.

Mark   Any trademark, service mark, certification mark, or collective mark that can be trademarked.

Marriage   A voluntary agreement between a man and a woman to become husband and wife.

Material breach–inferior performance   A breach of contract that occurs when a party renders inferior performance of his or her contractual duties.

Mediation   A form of alternative dispute resolution in which the parties choose a neutral third party to act as mediator of the dispute.

Memorandum   Working document for the legal team, used in preparing for and presenting the case.

Mens rea   From Latin, "evil intent"—possessing the requisite state of mind to commit a prohibited act.

Merchant court   Separate set of courts established in England to administer "law of merchants."

Merchant protection statutes   Statutes that allow merchants to stop, detain, and investigate suspected shoplifters without being held liable for false imprisonment if (1) there are reasonable grounds for the suspicion, (2) suspects are detained for only a reasonable time, and (3) investigations are conducted in a reasonable manner.

Minor breach–substantial performance A breach of contract that occurs when a party renders substantial performance of his or her contractual duties.

Miranda rights The colloquial name for the warning required to be read to a criminal suspect before he or she is interrogated by the police or other government officials; established by the U.S. Supreme Court in the landmark case *Miranda v. Arizona.*

Misappropriation of the right to publicity An attempt by another person to appropriate a living person's name or identity for commercial purposes.

Misdemeanor A crime that is less serious than a felony and is not inherently evil.

Model Guidelines for the Utilization of Legal Assistant Services A set of guidelines by ABA policy-making body, the House of Delegates, intended to govern conduct of lawyers when utilizing paralegals or legal assistants.

Model Rules of Professional Conduct A recommended set of ethics and professional conduct guidelines for lawyers, prepared by American Bar Association, originally released in 1983; prior release was Model Code of Professional Conduct.

Modem A device for converting computer information into an electronic format that will allow it to be transmitted over telephone lines, cable lines, and radio waves.

Moral obligation An obligation based on one's own conscience or a person's perceived rules of correct conduct.

Motion for judgment on the pleadings Motion alleging that if all the facts presented in the pleadings are taken as true, the party making the motion would win the lawsuit when the proper law is applied to these asserted facts.

Motion for summary judgment Motion asserting that there are no factual disputes to be decided by the jury; if so, the judge can apply the proper law to the undisputed facts and decide the case without a jury.

Motivation test A test to determine the liability of a principal; if the agent's motivation in committing an intentional tort is to promote the principal's business, the principal is liable for any injury caused by the tort.

Multinational corporation A single economic unit composed of companies of different nationalities connected by shareholding, managerial control, or contractual agreement.

Mutual benefit bailment A bailment that benefits both the bailor and the bailee; the bailee owes a duty of reasonable care to protect the bailed property.

Mutual (reciprocal) wills Wills in which two or more testators execute separate wills leaving their property to each other on the condition that the survivor leave the remaining property on his or her death as agreed by the testators; also called reciprocal wills.

Narrative opportunity An opportunity to tell a story or answer a question without a limitation.

National Association of Legal Assistants (NALA) Professional organization for legal assistants that provides continuing education and professional certification for paralegals, incorporated in 1975.

National Federation of Paralegal Associations (NFPA) Professional organization of state and local paralegal associations founded in 1974.

National origin discrimination Employment discrimination based on national heritage, prohibited under Title VII of Civil Rights Act of 1964.

Necessaries of life Food, clothing, shelter, medical care, and other items considered necessary to the maintenance of life.

Negligence (1) Tort related to defective products in which the defendant has breached a duty of due care and caused harm to the plaintiff. (2) Failure of a corporate director or officer to exercise the duty of care while conducting the corporation's business.

Negligence per se Tort in which the violation of a statute or ordinance constitutes breach of the duty of care.

Negligent infliction of emotional distress Tort that permits a person to recover for emotional distress caused by defendant's negligent conduct.

Networking Establishing and maintaining contact with others, asking questions and exchanging information.

No Electronic Theft (NET) Act A 1997 law that criminalizes certain copyright infringement.

No-fault divorce Divorce without an allegation of fault.

Nonconforming uses Uses and buildings that already exist in a zoned area that are permitted to continue even though they do not fit within new zoning ordinances.

Noncupative will Oral will that is made before a witness during the testator's last illness.

Nondisclosure agreement (NDA) An enforceable contract swearing the signatory to secrecy regarding confidential information.

Nurse paralegals Nurses who have medical work experience and combine it with paralegal skills.

Offer Manifestation of willingness to enter into a bargain, to justify another person's understanding that the assent to that bargain is invited and will conclude it.

Offeree The party to whom an offer to enter into a contract is made.

Offeror The party who makes an offer to enter into a contract.

Officers (of corporation) Employees of a corporation appointed by the board of directors to manage day-to-day operations of the corporation.

Older Workers Benefit Protection Act (OWBPA) A law prohibiting age discrimination in employee benefits.

One-year rule An executory contract stating that if it cannot be performed by its own terms within one year of its formation, it must be in writing.

Open-ended questions Questions designed to create a narrative opportunity for the witness.

Opening statements Comments made at the beginning of a trial by the attorneys to the jury summarizing the factual and legal issues of the case.

Operating agreement An agreement entered into among members that governs the affairs and business of a limited liability company and the relations among members, managers, and the LLC.

Order Decision issued by an administrative law judge.

Ordinances Laws enacted by local government bodies such as cities and municipalities, counties, school districts, and water districts.

Organizational meeting A meeting that must be held by the initial directors of a corporation after the articles of incorporation are filed.

Outside director A member of a board of directors who is not an officer of the corporation.

PACER (Public Access to Court Electronic Records) An electronic public-access service allowing users to obtain case and docket information from federal appellate, district, and bankruptcy courts and from the U.S. Party/Case Index.

Paralegal A person qualified by education, training, or work experience who is employed or retained by a lawyer, law office, corporation, governmental agency, or other entity who performs specifically delegated substantive legal work for which a lawyer is responsible; equivalent term is *legal assistant*.

Paralegal Advanced Competency Exam (PACE) National Association of Paralegal Association's certification program that requires the paralegal to have two years of experience and a bachelor's degree and have completed a paralegal course at an accredited school.

Parallel citation A citation to the same material, usually a case, in another source.

Partially disclosed agency An agency that occurs if the agent discloses his or her agency status but does not reveal the principal's identity and the third party does not know the principal's identity from another source.

Partnership Two or more natural or artificial (corporation) persons who have joined together to share ownership and profit or loss.

Partnership agreement A written agreement that the partners sign; also called *articles of partnership*.

Partnership at will A partnership with no fixed duration.

Partnership for a term A partnership with a fixed duration.

Patent Registration of an invention that is novel, useful, and nonobvious, as conferred by the United States Patent and Trademark Office.

Patent infringement Unauthorized use of another's patent.

Penal codes A collection of criminal statutes.

Per capita distribution A distribution of the estate that makes each grandchild and great-grandchild of the deceased inherit equally with the children of the deceased.

Periodic tenancy A tenancy created when a lease specifies intervals at which payments are due but does not specify duration of the lease.

Personal property Property that consists of tangible property such as automobiles, furniture, and jewelry, as well as intangible property such as securities, patents, and copyrights.

Per stirpes distribution A distribution of an estate that makes grandchildren and great-grandchildren of the deceased inherit by representation of their parent.

Petition for certiorari A petition asking U.S. Supreme Court to hear one's case.

Petitioner The party appealing the decision of an administrative agency.

Piercing the corporate veil   A doctrine that says if a shareholder dominates a corporation and uses it for improper purposes, a court of equity can disregard the corporate entity and hold the shareholder personally liable for the corporation's debts and obligations.

Plaintiff   The party who files a complaint; in the case of criminal law, the government.

Plaintiff's case   Process in which the plaintiff introduces evidence to prove the allegations contained in his or her complaint.

Plant life and vegetation   Real property that is growing in or on the surface of the land.

Plea bargain   An agreement by an accused to admit to a lesser crime than charged; in return, the government agrees to impose a lesser sentence than might have been obtained had the case gone to trial.

Pleadings   The paperwork filed with a court to initiate and respond to a lawsuit.

Pocket Part   A method of updating a printed volume by inserting a pamphlet in the back of the bound volume in a pocket cut into the inside back cover for that purpose.

Police powers   The power of states to regulate private and business activity within their borders.

Power of attorney   An express agency agreement used to give an agent the power to sign legal documents on behalf of the principal.

Precedent   A rule of law established in a court decision; lower courts must follow precedent established by higher courts.

Preemption doctrine   The concept that federal law takes precedent over state or local law.

Pretrial hearing   A hearing before a trial to facilitate settlement of a case; also called a *pretrial settlement conference.*

Primary authority   The actual law itself; this includes statutes and case law.

Primary source   The actual law itself; this includes statutes and case law.

Principal   A person who authorizes an agent to sign a negotiable instrument on his or her behalf.

Principal–agent relationship   A relationship in which an employer hires an employee and gives that employee authority to act and enter into contracts on his or her behalf.

Principal–independent contractor relationship   A relationship that results when a person or business that is not an employee is employed by a principal to perform a certain task on his or her behalf.

Privacy Act   A law stipulating that federal administrative agencies can maintain only information about an individual that is relevant and necessary to accomplish a legitimate agency purpose.

Privileged communication   Certain forms of communication not usable at trial unless the privilege is waived; includes attorney–client communications, doctor–patient communications, priest–penitent communications, and spousal communications during marriage.

Pro bono   Work without compensation for individuals and organizations that otherwise could not afford legal assistance.

Probable cause   The substantial likelihood that the person either committed or is about to commit a crime.

Probate (settlement of the estate)   The process of a deceased's property being collected, debts and taxes paid, and the remainder of the estate distributed.

Procedural due process   Type of due process that requires the respondent to be given (1) proper and timely notice of the allegations or charges against him or her, and (2) an opportunity to present evidence on the matter.

Procedural law   Rules defining the ways in which the rights and obligations of individuals will be enforced.

Production of documents   A form of discovery in which one party requests that another party produce all documents relevant to the case prior to trial.

Professional malpractice   Liability of a professional who breaches his or her duty of ordinary care.

Proprietary school   Private, as opposed to public, institution, generally for profit, offering training and education.

Prosecutor   The lawyer representing the government in a criminal lawsuit.

Protocol   The format dictating the arrangement of information.

Proximate cause   A point along a chain of events caused by a negligent party after which this party is no longer legally responsible for the consequences of his or her actions. Also termed *legal cause.*

Public defender   Attorney provided by the government to represent a defendant who cannot afford legal representation.

Public-use doctrine   A doctrine that says a patent may not be granted if the public used the invention for more than one year prior to filing of the patent application.

Punitive damages Damages awarded to punish the defendant, to deter the defendant from similar conduct in the future, and to set an example for others.

***Quasi in rem* jurisdiction** Authority allowed a plaintiff who obtains a judgment in one state to try to collect the judgment by attaching property of the defendant located in another state.

Quasi- or implied-in-law contract An equitable doctrine whereby a court may award monetary damages to a plaintiff for providing work or services to a defendant even though no actual contract existed; this doctrine intends to prevent unjust enrichment and unjust detriment.

Quiet title An action brought by a party seeking an order of the court declaring who has title to disputed property; the court "quiets title" by its decision.

Quitclaim deed A type of deed that provides the least amount of protection because the grantor conveys only whatever interest he or she has in the property.

Racketeer Influenced and Corrupt Organizations Act (RICO) Federal statute that authorizes civil lawsuits against defendants for engaging in a pattern of racketeering activities; provides for both criminal and civil penalties for securities fraud.

Real property The land itself, as well as buildings, trees, soil, minerals, timber, plants, and other things permanently affixed to the land.

Rebuttal Presentation of a case (calling witnesses and putting forth evidence) by the plaintiff's attorney to rebut the defendant's case.

Record The recorded summary of a trial court proceeding, including memorandum, trial transcript, and evidence produced at trial.

Recross examination An attorney asks questions of the witness, following direct examination, cross-examination, and redirect examination.

Redirect examination An attorney asks questions of the witness, following direct examination and cross-examination.

Reformation An equitable doctrine that permits the court to rewrite a contract to express the parties' true intentions.

Regular meeting of board of directors A meeting held by a board of directors at the time and place established in the bylaws.

Relevant facts Those facts that tend to prove or disprove a matter.

Remainder The right of possession returning to a third party upon expiration of a limited or contingent estate.

Remainderman The person to receive the trust corpus upon termination of a trust.

Remand An appellate court finds that the lower court has made an error that can be corrected and sends the case back to the lower court to take further action or conduct further proceedings.

Repealed Abolishment of an existing law by formal action.

Reply Court document filed by original plaintiff to answer defendant's cross-complaint.

Residuary gift Gift of the estate left after the debts, taxes, and specific and general gifts have been paid.

Res ipsa loquitur Tort in which the presumption of negligence arises because (1) the defendant was in exclusive control of the situation, and (2) the plaintiff would not have suffered injury but for someone's negligence.

Resourcefulness The ability to meet and handle situations and find solutions to problems.

Restatement (Second) of Torts A compilation of model tort law principles drafted by legal scholars. The Restatement is not law.

Resulting trust A trust created by the conduct of the parties.

Resume A short description of a person's educational, work experience, and other related and supporting information that is used in evaluating a person's potential qualifications for a position in a firm or an organization.

Reverse An appellate court decision indicating that the lower court has made a substantial error in deciding a case.

Reverse discrimination Discrimination against a group that usually is thought of as a majority.

Reversion A right of possession that returns to the grantor after expiration of a limited or contingent estate.

Revised Model Business Corporation Act (RMBCA) A revision of the MBCA in 1984 that arranged the provisions of the Act more logically, revised the language to be more consistent, and made substantial changes in the provisions.

Revised Uniform Limited Partnership Act (RULPA) A 1976 revision of the ULPA that updates the comprehensive law for the formation, operation, and dissolution of limited partnerships.

Right of survivorship Rule stating that a deceased partner's right in specific partnership property vests with the remaining partners upon his or her death.

Robbery Taking personal property from another person by use of fear or force.

Rules and regulations A legislative function adopted by administrative agencies to interpret the statutes they are authorized to enforce.

S corporations Corporations that elect to be taxed under the Subchapter S Revision Act (as opposed to C corporations, all other corporations).

Search warrant Document authorizing the police to search a designated place for specified contraband, articles, items, or documents; must be based on probable cause.

Secondary authority Writings about the law, such as legal encyclopedias and digests.

Secondary meaning The distinctiveness that results when an ordinary term has become a brand name; necessary for a trademark.

Secondary source Writings about the law, such as legal encyclopedias and digests.

Self-incrimination The Fifth Amendment protection stating that no person shall be compelled in any criminal case to be a witness against himself or herself.

Service mark A mark that distinguishes the services of the holder from those of its competitors.

Service of process Serving a summons on a defendant to obtain personal jurisdiction over him or her.

Settlement conference Parties meet before the trial for the purpose of facilitating settlement of the case.

Settlor Person who creates a trust. Also termed *trustor* or *transferor.*

Sex discrimination Discrimination against a person solely because of his or her gender.

Sexual harassment Lewd remarks, touching, intimidation, posting pinups, and other verbal or physical conduct of a sexual nature that occurs on the job.

Shareholders Owners of corporations.

Simultaneous deaths Under the Uniform Simultaneous Death Act, a provision that each deceased person's property is distributed as if he or she survived.

Slander Oral defamation of character.

Small-claims court A court that hears civil cases involving small dollar amounts.

Social host liability Rule providing that social hosts are liable for injuries caused by guests who become intoxicated at a social function; this rule is not in effect in all states.

Sole proprietorship A form of business in which the owner is actually the business; the business is not a separate legal entity.

Solicitor In the English legal system, a lawyer who deals directly with clients but does not try cases.

Special federal courts Federal courts that hear matters of limited jurisdiction: U.S. tax court, U.S. court of federal claims, U.S. court of international trade; U.S. bankruptcy court.

Special power of attorney A type of power of attorney that limits the agent to acts specifically enumerated in an agreement.

Specialty practice A firm that engages in a specialized area of law.

Specific gift Testamentary gift of a specifically named piece of property.

Specific performance A decree of the court that orders a seller or lessor to perform his or her obligations under the contract; usually occurs when the goods in question are unique, such as art or antiques.

Spendthrift trust A trust that removes all control over the trust from the beneficiary.

Spoliation of evidence Destruction or loss of evidence.

Standing to sue Plaintiff's having some stake in the outcome of the lawsuit.

Stare decisis From Latin, "to stand by the decision"; adherence to precedent.

State administrative agencies Administrative agencies that states create to enforce and interpret state law.

State supreme court Highest court in a state court system; hears appeals from intermediate state courts and certain trial courts.

Statement of policy A written document issued by an administrative agency announcing a proposed course of action that the agency intends to follow in the future.

Statute of Frauds State statute that requires certain types of contracts to be in writing.

Statute of limitations Statute that establishes the time period during which a lawsuit must be brought; if the lawsuit is not brought within this period, the injured party loses the right to sue.

Strict liability   Liability without fault.

Subject-matter jurisdiction   A court's authority to hear only certain types of cases or certain topics.

Subpoena   A court order.

Substantive due process   Type of due process that requires that government statutes, ordinances, regulations, or other laws be clear on their face and not overly broad in scope.

Substantive law   The law of the case, as opposed to procedural law.

Substantive rules   Government regulations that have the force of law and must be adhered to by the persons and businesses covered.

Subsurface rights   Rights to the earth located beneath the surface of the land; also called *mineral rights*.

Summons   A court order directing a defendant to appear in court and answer the complaint.

Supremacy Clause   A clause in the U.S. Constitution that establishes that the federal Constitution, treaties, federal laws, and federal regulations are the supreme law of the land.

Tangible property   All real property and physically defined personal property such as goods, animals, and minerals.

Tangible writing   Writing that can be physically seen.

Tenancy at sufferance   A tenancy created when a tenant retains possession of property after the expiration of another tenancy or a life estate without the owner's consent.

Tenancy at will   A lease that may be terminated at any time by either party.

Tenancy for years   A tenancy created when the landlord and the tenant agree on a specific duration for the lease.

Tenancy in common/tenancy by the entirety   A form of co-ownership in which the interest of a surviving tenant in common passes to the deceased tenant's estate and not to the co-tenants.

Tenant/lessee   The party to whom a leasehold is transferred.

Tender of performance   An unconditional and absolute offer by a contracting party to perform his or her obligations under the contract.

Testamentary capacity   The Statute of Wills requirement that the testator must have been of legal age and "sound mind."

Timekeeping   Keeping track of billable time to ensure that the law firm will be properly compensated for its advice and efforts on behalf of clients.

Title insurance   Insurance that owners of real property purchase to ensure that they have clear title to the property.

Title VII of Civil Rights Act of 1964 (Fair Employment Practices Act)   Law intended to eliminate job discrimination based on five protected classes: race, color, religion, sex, and national origin.

Tort   French for a "wrong."

Totten trust   A trust created when a person deposits money in a bank account in his or her own name and holds it as a trustee for the benefit of another person.

Trademark   A distinctive mark, symbol, name, word, motto, or device that identifies the goods of a particular business.

Trademark infringement   Unauthorized use of another's mark; the holder may recover damages and other remedies from the infringer.

Trade secret   An idea that makes a franchise successful but not qualify for trademark, patent, or copyright protection; a product formula, pattern, design, compilation of data, customer list, or other business secret.

Transferred intent doctrine   A doctrine under which the law transfers the perpetrator's intent from the target to the actual victim of an act.

Treaty   A compact made between two or more nations.

Trespass to land   A tort that interferes with an owner's right to exclusive possession of land.

Trespass to personal property   A tort that occurs whenever one person injures another person's personal property or interferes with that person's enjoyment of his or her personal property.

Trespasser   A person who has no invitation, permission, or right to be on another's property.

Trier of fact   Jury in a jury trial; or the judge if not a jury trial.

Trust   A legal arrangement established when a person (trustor) transfers title to property to another person (trustee) to be managed for the benefit of specifically named persons (beneficiaries).

Trust corpus   The property held in trust. Also termed *trust res.*

Trustee   (1) Holder of legal title of the real property in a deed of trust and note transaction. (2) Person who holds legal title to trust corpus and manages the trust for the benefit of the beneficiary(ies).

UCC Section 201 (Statute of Frauds)   A rule that requires all contracts for the sale of goods costing $500 or more and lease contracts involving payments of $1,000 or more to be in writing.

Unauthorized practice of law (UPL)   Giving legal advice, if legal rights may be affected, by anyone not licensed to practice law.

Unconscionable contract   Also called a *contract of adhesion,* such a contract is found to be unjust if one party possessed severely unequal bargaining power, if the dominant party unreasonably used its bargaining power to obtain oppressive or manifestly unfair contract terms, and if the adhering party had no reasonable alternative.

Undisclosed agency   An agency that occurs when the third party is unaware of either (1) the existence of an agency, or (2) the principal's identity.

Undue influence   One person's taking advantage of another person's mental, emotional, or physical weakness and unduly persuading that person to enter into a contract: the persuasion by the wrongdoer must overcome the free will of the innocent party.

Uniform Commercial Code (UCC)   Comprehensive statutory scheme including laws that cover aspects of commercial transactions.

Uniform Computer Information Transactions Act (UCITA)   A model Act that provides uniform and comprehensive rules for contracts involving computer information transactions and software and information licenses.

Uniform Limited Liability Company Act (ULLCA)   A model law that provides comprehensive and uniform rules for the formation, operation, and dissolution of limited liability companies.

Uniform Partnership Act (UPA)   Model act that codifies partnership law; most states have adopted the UPA in whole or in part.

Uniform Probate Code (UPC)   A model law promulgated to establish consistent rules for the creation of wills, administration of estates, and resolution of conflicts in settling estates.

Uniform resource locator (URL)   Specific address for an Internet site.

Unintentional tort or negligence   A doctrine that says a person is liable for harm that is the foreseeable consequence of his or her actions.

Universal citation format   A system that relies upon the courts to number all paragraphs in every opinion to allow researchers to find the referenced authority regardless of the electronic or other research tool used.

Unreasonable search and seizure   Any search and seizure by the government that violates the Fourth Amendment to the U.S. Constitution.

Unsecured credit   Credit that does not require any security (collateral) to protect payment of the debt.

U.S. Constitution   Fundamental law of the United States of America; ratified by the states in 1788.

U.S. courts of appeals   The federal court system's intermediate appellate courts.

U.S. district courts   The federal court system's trial courts of general jurisdiction.

U.S. Supreme Court   Court created by Article III of the U.S. Constitution; the highest court in the land, located in Washington, D.C.

Variance   An exception that permits a type of building or use in an area that otherwise would not be allowed by a zoning ordinance.

Vendor-specific citation format   A citation format originally created by publishers for their works.

Venue   Location or jurisdiction in which an incident occurred or where the parties to a lawsuit reside; lawsuits must be heard by the court with nearest jurisdiction.

Verdict   Decision reached by a jury.

Violation   A crime that is neither a felony nor a misdemeanor; usually is punishable by a fine.

Warranty deed   A type of deed that contains the greatest number of warranties and provides the most protection to grantees.

Web browser   A software program that allows a person to use a computer to access and search the Internet.

White-collar crimes   Crimes usually involving cunning and deceit rather than physical force; often committed by businesspersons.

Will   A declaration of how a person wants his or her property distributed upon death.

Wire fraud   Use of the telephone or telegraph to defraud another person.

Withholding delivery   The act of seller or lessor purposefully refusing to deliver goods to buyer or lessee upon breach of sales or lease contract by buyer or lessee or insolvency of buyer or lessee.

Witness   An individual asked to testify in court, under oath.

Work product doctrine   A qualified immunity from discovery for "work product of the lawyer" except on a substantial showing of "necessity or justification" of certain written statements and memoranda prepared by counsel in representation of a client, generally in preparation for trial.

Workers' compensation   Protection for workers providing compensation for injuries that occur on the job.

World Wide Web   An electronic connection of millions of computers that support a standard set of rules for the exchange of information.

Writ of certiorari   An official notice that the U.S. Supreme Court will review one's case.

Wrongful dissolution   A member's withdrawing from (1) a term limited liability company prior to expiration of the term, or (2) an at-will limited liability company when the operating agreement eliminates a member's power to withdraw.

Wrongful termination of an agency   (1) Ending a franchise without just cause. (2) Termination of an agency contract in violation of terms of the agency contract; nonbreaching party may recover damages from breaching party.

Zoning ordinances   Local laws adopted by municipalities and local governments to regulate land use within their boundaries; they are adopted and enforced to protect the health, safety, morals, and general welfare of the community.

Case Index

GLOSSARY OF LATIN TERMS AND PHRASES

Pronunciation Key

Stress. The symbol (´), as in **mother** (muth´er), and **red´ wine´**, marks primary stress; any syllable immediately followed by (´) is pronounced with greater emphasis than syllables not marked (´). The symbol (ˈ), as used following the second syllables of **grandmother** (grand´muth´er), and **ice´ wa´ter**, marks secondary stress; a syllable marked for secondary stress is pronounced with less emphasis than one marked (´) but with more than those bearing no stress mark.

a	act, bat, marry	g	give, trigger, beg	l	low, mellow, all, bottle (bot´l)	ōō	ooze, fool, too	û(r)	urge, burn, cur
ā	age, paid, say					ou	out, loud, cow	v	voice, river, live
â(r)	air, dare, Mary	h	hit, behave, hear	m	my, summer, him	p	pot, supper, stop	w	witch, away
ä	ah, part, balm	hw	which, nowhere			r	read, hurry, near	y	yes, onion
b	back, cabin, cab	i	if, big, mirror, furniture	n	now, sinner, on, button (but´n)	s	see, passing, miss	z	zoo, lazy, those
ch	child, teacher, beach	ī	ice, bite, pirate, deny	ng	sing, Washington	sh	shoe, fashion, push	zh	treasure, mirage
d	do, madder, bed					t	ten, matter, bit	ə	occurs in unaccented syllables to indicate the sound of the reduced vowel in alone, system, easily, gallop, circus
e	edge, set, merry	j	just, tragic, fudge	o	ox, bomb, wasp	th	thin, ether, path	
ē	equal, seat, bee, mighty	k	keep, token, make	ō	over, boat, no	th	that, either, smooth	
				ô	order, ball, raw			
ēr	ear, mere			oi	oil, joint, joy	u	up, sun	
f	fit, differ, puff			ōō	book, tour			

ᵊ occurs between **i** and **r** and between **ou** and **r** to show triphthongal quality, as in **fire** (fīᵊr), **hour** (ouᵊr)

Source: *Random House Dictionary of the English Language* (2nd Edition). New York: Random House, 1987.

---

a fortiori with stronger reason; much more — ā fôr shē ôr´ī

a posteriori from the effect to the cause; from what comes after — ā po ster ē or´ī

a prendre to take; to seize — ä pron dûr

a priori from the cause to the effect; from what comes before — ā prī ôr´ī

ab initio from the beginning — äb i nit´ē ō

actio criminalis a criminal action — ak shē ō kri mä nā lis

actio damni injuria an action for damages — ak shē ō dam nī in ju rē ä

actio ex delicto an action arising out of fault — ak shē ō eks da lik tō

ad damnum to the damage; money loss claimed by the plaintiff — ad dam´nəm

ad hoc for one special purpose — ad hok´

ad infinitum indefinitely; forever — ad in fə nī´təm

ad litem for the suit — ad´lī´tem

ad respondendum to make answer — ad re spon den dəm

additur addition by a judge to the amount of damages awarded by a jury — a də tər

amicus curiae friend of the court — əmī´kəs kyōōr´ē

animus furandi intent to steal — an´əmas fu ran dī

animus testandi intent to make a will — an´əmas tes tən dī

anno Domini (A.D.) in the year of our Lord — an´ō dom´ə nī

ante before — an´tē

arguendo in arguing — ar gōō en dō

assumpsit he promised — ə sump´sit

bona fide in good faith — bō´nə fīd´

caveat beware — kav´ēät

caveat emptor let the buyer beware — kav ēät emp´tôr

caveat venditor let the seller beware — kav ēät ven də tər

...to be informed of; to be assured — sûr´shē ə rär ī

...trust beneficiary of a trust — setē kə trəst

...sound of mind — kom pəs men təs

...wship of husband and — kən sôr´shē əm

contra against — kon´trə

coram before; in the presence of — kôr´am

corpus delicti body of the crime — kôr´pəs di lik´tī

corpus juris body of law — kôr´pəs jōōr´is

cum testamento annexo with the will annexed — kum tes tə men tō an nek sō

damnum absque injuria loss without injury in the legal sense — dam nəm abs kwē in jû ri ya

de facto in fact; actually — dē fak´tō

de jure according to law; rightfully — dē jû rē

de minimis of little importance — dē mi nə məs

de novo anew, afresh, a second time — dē nō´vō

dictum unessential statement or remark in a court decision — dik´təm

doli capaz capable of criminal intent; able to distinguish between right and wrong — dō lī kā paks

duces tecum bring with you — dōō´sēz tē´kəm

ergo therefore; hence — ûr´gō

et al abbreviation for et alii; and others — et al´

et seq abbreviation for et sequentia; and the following

et ux abbreviation for et uxor; and wife

et vir and husband — et vēr´

ex contractu out of a contract — eks kən trak tōō

ex delicto out of a tort or wrong — eks´də lik tō

ex officio by virtue of an office — eks´ə fish´ēō´

ex parte apart from; one side only — eks pär´tē

ex post facto after the fact — eks´pōst´fak·tō

forum non conveniens inconvenient court — for´əm non kən vēn(i) yenz

gratis without reward or consideration — grat´is

habeas corpus you have the body — hā bē əs kôr´pəs

habendum to have thus; clause in a deed that defines extent of ownership — hə ben dəm

ibid abbreviation for ibidem; in the same place — ib´id

id abbreviation for idem; the same — id